Quick Steps toward Greening Your H~~ome~~

Here are some super-quick and easy tips to get you started on a green lifes~~tyle~~

- In winter, throw on a sweater and turn down the thermostat on your furnace to approximately 68°F. In summer, take off your sweater and turn up the thermostat on your air conditioning to about 78°F.
- Unplug chargers for cellphones and other small or portable electronic devices when they're not in use.
- Turn off electrical appliances at the wall (or on a power strip) rather than leaving them on standby.
- Turn off the faucet while you brush your teeth and wash your face.
- Take showers instead of baths and keep them to five minutes or less.

- Get the whole family involved in making these changes. Make it fun!
- Switch to energy-efficient compact fluorescent light bulbs.
- Recycle as much household waste as possible.
- Give away things that you no longer need instead of throwing them out.
- Choose plants that are well suited to your growing conditions — they need less watering and are more pest-resistant.

A Green Cleaning Shopping List ~~WITHDRAWN~~

The following ingredients are regulars in homemade cleaning solutions. You can find complete recipes for green cleaners in Chapter 3 of Book III.

- **Baking soda:** Sodium bicarbonate cleans up after acidic stains and messes, works as a mild abrasive, shines up aluminum, chrome, silver, and other metals, and unclogs and cleans drains. It cuts grease and dirt and also deodorizes.
- **Borax:** Another member of the sodium family (sodium borate), this natural mineral is a disinfectant and is sold at drugstores, supermarkets, and hardware and supply stores.
- **Castor oil:** The colorless or sometimes yellowish oil, from the castor plant, is a fine lubricant and a worthy ingredient in wood cleaners or polishes.
- **Cornstarch:** Just as its name implies, this mild and absorbent cleaner is a starch derived from corn.
- **Cornmeal:** Set aside some the next time you're making corn muffins: This mildly abrasive substance makes easy work of grease stains.
- **Club soda:** Have a big bottle of bubbly on hand for cleaning glass or tackling wine spills on carpet.
- **Cream of tartar:** This white crystalline powder sold in the spice section of supermarkets whips up impressive meringue and makes a great paste for scrubbing cookware.
- **Essential oils:** Tea tree, peppermint, grapefruit, and other oils (found in health-food or craft stores) not only smell great, but they have disinfecting properties, as well.

- **Glycerin:** This common ingredient in hand-wash and dish liquid is an oil that provides lubrication and is often used in milder cleaners.
- **Hydrogen peroxide:** An oxygen bleach that doesn't have the harmful properties of chlorine bleach, this mild acid is used as an antiseptic for minor wounds and kills germs when it's used as a cleaning agent, too.
- **Lemon juice:** This citric acid bleaches, disinfects, deodorizes, and cuts grease. Use the real thing — or bottled concentrate.
- **Liquid castile soap:** This vegetable-based soap, found in grocery or health-food stores, is a mild and versatile cleaning agent.
- **Salt:** Another member of the sodium family, sodium chloride — or common table salt — is a natural scrubbing agent.
- **Washing soda:** Also known as sodium carbonate, this stronger iteration of sodium bicarbonate (baking soda) looks similar and is sometimes available in the laundry section of the supermarket or hardware store.
- **White distilled vinegar:** Count on this wonder cleaner for deodorizing, cutting through grease, removing stains, and freshening.

Green Your Home All-in-One For Dummies®

Cheat Sheet

Analyzing Efficiencies Before Buying

When analyzing efficiencies of appliances or home improvements, be sure to consider the life expectancy of a particular investment. Answer these questions for every option you're considering:

- How long will the appliance last?
- How does the pollution output vary over time?
- Will the energy efficiency decrease over time (the answer is almost always yes because parts wear out, friction increases, and so on), and if so, by how much?
- How much maintenance will be required over time, and will you be able to do the labor and maintenance in subsequent years?
- How long is the warranty, and how much will unwarranted repairs cost?
- Who will be doing the service, and where do parts come from?
- How will the future costs of energy affect the financial efficiencies?
- What are the financing costs, and are there tax advantages now? Will there be tax advantages in the future that aren't available now?

Locating Green Materials

Given the popularity of green building, finding green materials has never been easier — and in the future, it'll be even more so. One great place to start is talking to sales reps in product showrooms. You'll be surprised what you can find out after you start up a conversation. Here are several other places to start your research:

- **BuildingGreen:** The publishers of the *Environmental Building News* and *GreenSpec* have put all their unbiased and perfectly presented information together in a wonderfully straightforward site at www. buildinggreen.com.
- **Green Home Guide:** Although targeted at homeowners, Green Home Guide provides reviews and descriptions of green products by the real professionals using them. Its know-how sections provide all the information you need for greening a kitchen, bathroom, nursery, bedroom, and even your lawn. Check it out at www.greenhomeguide.com.
- **American Institute of Architects (AIA):** The AIA provides resources and case studies for homeowners to use to green their homes. Contact your local chapter of the AIA (you can find it in the phone book or at www.aia.org) and ask about its green resources.
- **United States Green Building Council (USGBC):** The USGBC is a valuable source for data on green building, great for making the argument to skeptical developers and city officials. You can point to its combined experience and knowledge to find hundreds of reports and case studies. Visit the USGBC online at www.usgbc.org.

For Dummies: Bestselling Book Series for Beginners

Green Your Home
ALL-IN-ONE
FOR
DUMMIES®

by Yvonne Jeffery, Liz Barclay,
Michael Grosvenor, Elizabeth B. Goldsmith, PhD,
Betsy Sheldon, Eric Corey Freed, Rik DeGunther,
Ann Whitman, The National Gardening
Association, and Owen Dell

WILEY

Wiley Publishing, Inc.

Green Your Home All-In-One For Dummies®

Published by
Wiley Publishing, Inc.
111 River St.
Hoboken, NJ 07030-5774
www.wiley.com

Copyright © 2009 by Wiley Publishing, Inc., Indianapolis, Indiana

Published by Wiley Publishing, Inc., Indianapolis, Indiana

Published simultaneously in Canada

For general information on our other products and services, please contact our Customer Care Department within the U.S. at 877-762-2974, outside the U.S. at 317-572-3993, or fax 317-572-4002.

For technical support, please visit www.wiley.com/techsupport.

Wiley also publishes its books in a variety of electronic formats. Some content that appears in print may not be available in electronic books.

Library of Congress Control Number: 2008941620

ISBN: 978-0-470-40778-3

Manufactured in the United States of America. This book is printed on recycled paper.

10 9 8 7 6 5 4 3 2 1

WILEY

About the Authors

Yvonne Jeffery, coauthor of *Green Living For Dummies,* is an author, editor, and award-winning feature writer with 15 years' experience writing home and lifestyle stories, many of them focused on sustainable living. Yvonne's work has appeared in newspapers, magazines, and books around the world. Her credits include *National Geographic Traveler, American Profile, The Sunday Telegraph* (UK), and CanWest newspapers.

Liz Barclay, coauthor of *Green Living For Dummies,* has worked as an adviser, trainer, and manager with the Citizens Advice Bureau, a nonprofit organization in the United Kingdom that provides free, impartial advice to help individuals resolve legal, financial, consumer, and other problems. Liz has worked on a wide range of business and finance programs for the BBC and has written for *News Of The World, The Express, Moneywise, Family Circle, Save Money,* and the *Mail On Sunday* personal finance magazine. She also has written *UK Law and Your Rights For Dummies* and *Small Business Employment Law For Dummies.*

Michael Grosvenor, coauthor of *Green Living For Dummies,* is a leading urban planning professional and freelance writer on sustainability. Through his work and writing, Michael promotes the benefits of making sustainable lifestyle choices. He is the director of his own consulting firm and holds maters degrees in Urban Affairs and Applied Social Research and a degree in Town Planning. He's also a member of the Planning Institute of Australia and provides advice to the Institute on integrated land use and transportation planning issues.

Elizabeth B. Goldsmith, PhD, author of *Green Cleaning For Dummies,* is a Family Resource Management professor at Florida State University who green cleans her own home. She is a nationally known expert in how households are run, including the most documented home in America — the White House. Liz is the author of several college textbooks, including *Consumer Economics: Issues and Behavior* (Prentice Hall; 2nd edition Pearson) and *Resource Management for Individuals and Families* (Wadsworth Publishing), now in its 4th edition (Pearson). She was a Fulbright Scholar in Trinidad and Tobago, studying family and home-management practices. Liz presents papers on households and consumers at conferences worldwide and has been quoted in various publications.

Betsy Sheldon, contributor to *Green Cleaning For Dummies,* has served as editor in chief for three travel publications, and is the author or co-author of six books on topics from job-hunting for women to Jewish travel. Betsy writes "Green Watch," a regular column for *Indianapolis Monthly Home* magazine, and contributes articles about environmental issues and sustainability to publications including *Indiana Living Green* and *Vacation Industry Review.* She is involved in a number of environmental initiatives, including the greening task force for the American Resort Development Association and the Indiana Sustainability Coalition, and also serves on the board of Earth Charter Indiana. She facilitates "Low Carbon Diet" workshops, which help participants discover the steps to lowering their own carbon footprint and reducing greenhouse gas emissions.

Eric Corey Freed, author of *Green Building and Remodeling For Dummies,* is an architect, lecturer, and writer based in San Francisco. He has 15 years of experience in green building and is a practitioner in the tradition of organic architecture first developed by Frank Lloyd Wright. Eric is founder and principal of organicARCHITECT, part architecture firm, part think tank. Eric teaches in the Sustainable Design program he co-developed at the Academy of Art University and the University of California, Berkeley. His monthly column, Ask the Green Architect, is published by GreenerBuildings and syndicated to dozens of publications.

Rik DeGunther, author of both *Solar Power Your Home For Dummies* and *Energy Efficient Home For Dummies,* is CEO of Efficient Homes, an energy efficiency auditing firm in Northern California. He is actively engaged in designing and developing new solar equipment, including off-grid lighting systems and off-grid swimming pool heaters. He attended the University of Illinois as an undergraduate and Stanford University as a graduate student, studying both applied physics and engineering economics. He holds several United States patents and has designed a wide range of technical equipment, including solar power systems, weather measurement equipment, and explosive devices (strictly by accident).

Ann Whitman, coauthor of *Organic Gardening For Dummies,* was fortunate enough to grow up around parents, grandparents, aunts, and uncles who kept compost piles out back and had keen interest in growing food and flowers. She's been tending her own patches of soil for more than 30 years. Ann earned a bachelor of science degree in Plant and Soil Science at the University of Vermont. She also completed a master of arts degree in Landscape Design from the Conway School of Landscape Design in Massachusetts. Ann is the author of *Trees and Shrubs For Dummies,* as well as *How-To Landscaping Basics* and *Water Gardens: Simple Steps to Adding Beauty of Water to Your Garden,* both published by Time Life.

The National Gardening Association (NGA), coauthor of *Organic Gardening For Dummies,* is committed to sustaining and renewing the fundamental links between people, plants, and the earth. NGA is best known for its garden-based curricula, educational journals, international initiatives, and several youth garden grant programs. Together, these reach more than 300,000 children nationwide each year. To find out more about the NGA, visit www. garden.org/home.

Owen Dell, author of *Sustainable Living For Dummies,* is an internationally recognized expert in sustainable landscaping. He has authored numerous publications for *Sunset Magazine, National Gardening Magazine, Southern California Gardener, Pacific Horticulture,* and many others. An international speaker, he is also the cowriter and cohost of the California television series *Garden Wise Guys* (www.citytv18.com), a sustainable landscaping sitcom. His book *How to Start a Home-Based Landscaping Business* (Globe Pequot Press) has helped budding professionals get a healthy start on their careers. Owen's work has been featured on HGTV, Peak Moment Television, and NBC and in *The Wall Street Journal, Fortune Magazine, Landscape Architecture magazine, the Los Angeles Times,* and in many other publications.

Publisher's Acknowledgments

We're proud of this book; please send us your comments through our Dummies online registration form located at http://dummies.custhelp.com. For other comments, please contact our Customer Care Department within the U.S. at 877-762-2974, outside the U.S. at 317-572-3993, or fax 317-572-4002.

Some of the people who helped bring this book to market include the following:

Acquisitions, Editorial, and Media Development

Compilation Editor: Traci Cumbay

Project Editor: Kelly Ewing

Acquisitions Editor: Mike Baker

Assistant Editor: Erin Calligan Mooney

Editorial Program Coordinator: Joe Niesen

General Reviewer: Lynn Jenkins

Senior Editorial Manager: Jennifer Ehrlich

Editorial Supervisor and Reprint Editor: Carmen Krikorian

Editorial Assistant: Jennette ElNaggar

Art Coordinator: Alicia B. South

Cover Photos: iStock

Cartoons: Rich Tennant (www.the5thwave.com)

Composition Services

Project Coordinator: Katherine Key

Layout and Graphics: Sarah Philippart, Christin Swinford, Christine Williams

Proofreaders: Melissa Bronnenberg, Nancy Rapoport

Indexer: Valerie Haynes Perry

Publishing and Editorial for Consumer Dummies

 Diane Graves Steele, Vice President and Publisher, Consumer Dummies

 Kristin Ferguson-Wagstaffe, Product Development Director, Consumer Dummies

 Ensley Eikenburg, Associate Publisher, Travel

 Kelly Regan, Editorial Director, Travel

Publishing for Technology Dummies

 Andy Cummings, Vice President and Publisher, Dummies Technology/General User

Composition Services

 Gerry Fahey, Vice President of Production Services

 Debbie Stailey, Director of Composition Services

Contents at a Glance

Table of Contents

Introduction

. . . .

*I*n the grand accounting of the planet, every step you take toward a greener lifestyle makes a difference. Toss your banana peel in a compost pile instead of into a plastic trash bag, and you get to pat yourself on the back. *Of course* you're not going to save the planet by taking your own reusable tote bag to the grocery store, but you're reducing your consumption of fossil fuels and contribution to landfills. Not bad, eh? You won't solve water-shortage issues by using native plants in your landscape, but you save gallons and gallons of the precious stuff.

Those examples are just a few of the zillions of tips you find in this guide. Flip through these pages, find the suggestions that sound do-able to you, and consider yourself a valued contributor to the growing green movement.

About This Book

Don't let the impressive heft of this book fool you: Within it are easy-to-digest overviews of the many ways you might approach taking your home to the next level of ecofriendliness. Under one bright yellow cover are highlights from a stack of books on topics environmentally conscious. The information herein gives you practical tips for going greener — all without waxing judgmental about any current practices.

No home is perfect. Taking steps to make yours better is a hugely commendable effort, and this book can be a springboard for your undertakings.

You aren't expected to commit anything within these pages to memory. Instead, use this guide as a reference, opening it whenever you want to answer a question, revisit advice, or follow steps for a project. Where you open it is up to you — this isn't a typical, read from cover to cover kind of book. It's designed to be at the ready whenever you feel the urge to find out more about the topics within it.

Conventions Used in This Book

To help you navigate the text, this book uses the following conventions:

- ✔ *Italicized* terms are immediately followed by definitions.
- ✔ **Boldface** text indicates key words in a bullet list or the action parts of a numbered list.
- ✔ Web addresses appear in `monofont`.
- ✔ When this book was printed, some Web addresses may have needed to break across two lines of text. No hyphens indicate the break. So, when using one of these Web addresses, just type exactly what you see in this book, pretending the line break doesn't exist.

What You're Not to Read

This book keeps nonessential information to an absolute minimum, but wherever its authors felt powerfully compelled to include information that's interesting but not critical to your understand of the topic, that information appears in a sidebar (shaded gray box of text) or next to a Technical Stuff icon. You may well find this information interesting, but you can skip it and still get all the relevant facts you need.

Foolish Assumptions

Writing this book meant making a few assumptions about who you might be. One or more of the following probably apply:

- ✔ You want to find out more about how you can make your home life greener by taking small steps that work for you and working toward greener steps as you can.
- ✔ You don't want to be scolded for the things you're doing but you do want to make positive changes in your habits.
- ✔ You're ready to dig into making your home more energy efficient, healthier, and more comfortable — even more beautiful.
- ✔ You want any changes you make to be easy on your budget as well as the earth.
- ✔ You have an inkling of the environmental issues facing our planet.

✔ You're not necessarily a crusader, but you *are* interested in practical tips for lessening your household's impact on the community and the planet.

How This Book Is Organized

Within this book is a cornucopia of approaches to making your home more ecofriendly. The following sections give you an idea of what information you find where. Flip right over to whichever topic most excites your green impulses.

Book I: Green Living

Maybe your first thought about making your home greener had to do with solar panels or energy-efficient appliances, but the simplest place to start making your household greener is with the way you live within it. This book introduces you to good reasons for going greener and shows you how to make simple changes. You find out how to reuse or recycle the items that may be ending up in your garbage can, as well as how to grow or choose greener groceries, even outside the produce section. You get tips for bringing your kids into the green act and keeping the air in your home healthier.

Book II: Energy Efficiency

Only a rare home has no room for improvement when it comes to energy efficiency. You might be amazed at the simple fixes that reap huge rewards for making your heating and air conditioning, lighting, water use, and appliances more efficient.

Book III: Green Cleaning

So maybe the cleaners you're using now do a magnificent job of making your floors and windows sparkle, but many of them are doing very ugly things to the water supply. Put to rest any worries that you have to sacrifice that sparkle to lessen your environmental impact. This book shows you how very valuable bringing green to your clean is and gives you all kinds of practical information to do just that, including recipes for inexpensive cleaners you can whip up in your kitchen (just before you clean it).

Book IV: Green Remodeling

Abandon your old house for a new one? Hardly a sustainable action, even if you're moving to a super-efficient model. Remodeling is the greener choice, and you score a gazillion extra points for remodeling with green materials and energy-efficient systems. This book takes you through the choices and projects that make a green difference in your home.

Book V: Sustainable Landscaping

In a beautiful confluence of concept and actuality, you can green up the green things growing in your lawn. Hard to wrap the ol' noggin' around, maybe, but even the way you plan your landscape includes environmental concerns that go beyond what plant is going to look good where — which plant is going to grow best with the least use of resources and which location does the best things for increasing your home's efficiency. (No jive: A well-placed tree helps reduce your energy use.)

Book VI: Organic Gardening

Growing your garden with only what nature gave you — and in reasonable portions — is a satisfying way to go green (thumb). And walking into the back yard to pluck your dinner from branches and plants is the ultimate in staying local. With smart choices for getting your soil in to premium shape, controlling weeds and pests, and raising fruits and veggies the organic way, you get what you need to have the greenest yard on the block.

Book VII: Solar Power

Tapping into just a smidge of the power the sun puts out every day could power the planet. As solar power becomes more and more commonly utilized, the once astronomical (pun totally intended) cost of bringing solar energy to your home is coming down. You can dig into solar with projects small and large, and in this book, you find out how solar works and how best to make it work for your home.

Icons Used in This Book

The icons in this book can quickly steer you toward what you need. Here's a primer about what each one indicates:

Practical ecoknowledge or methods for doing your best by the environment are flagged by this icon.

Certain concepts come up again and again. This icon points you to ideas and points worth repeating.

Wherever you find an idea that saves you time, money, or effort, you find this icon cozied up alongside it.

Some information is worth mentioning but not critical to your understanding of the topic. It's highlighted with this icon, and you're welcome to pass it by.

Keep yourself safe. (The green movement needs you.) This icon directs you to information about practices or items that might hurt you.

Where to Go from Here

This book is designed to put you in the (hybrid car's) driver's seat. No need to start at the beginning and read straight through — each chapter stands on its own, directing you to further information when a term or concept might bear some explaining.

If you're a wanton-abandon kind of reader, pick a page at random. You won't be phased by what you find there. If you're hot to find out more about making your own green cleaners, Chapter 3 of Book III is the spot for you. Looking for information about raising your own organic rutabagas? Turn to Chapter 4 of Book VI. Book IV has what you need if you're considering green remodeling.

Buying this book is a wonderful first step to pampering our environment. And the book itself is full of next steps. Enjoy the discovery.

Book I
Green Living

The 5th Wave   By Rich Tennant

"Maybe a shower curtain wasn't the best thing to try to make into an evening dress."

In this book . . .

Who knew that what you do at home — from the way you handle your garbage to the bulbs you put in your lamps — sends ripples out into your community and the whole planet? And now that news of these effects is inescapable, it's hard not to feel overwhelmed as you start to consider making lifestyle changes.

In this part, you find out why going green is worth everybody's while, and then you find ways to ease into greener practices. You get the lowdown on waste, including reducing it in the first place and recycling anything that's fit for a bin; you discover ways to make your diet greener (figuratively, that is); and you get a wealth of ideas for starting your children on a green lifestyle.

Here are the contents of Book I at a glance:

Chapter 1

The World's Gone Green!

*J*ust what does *green living* mean, anyway? Different people use different definitions, but it all comes down to one fundamental concept: The earth's resources shouldn't be depleted faster than they can be replenished. From that concept comes everything else, including caring for the environment, animals and other living things, your health, your local community, and communities around the world.

When you start to look at all the different kinds of resources — from fossil fuels to forests, agricultural land to wildlife, and the ocean's depths to the air that you breathe — you see how everything is interconnected and how the actions that you take today can affect the future. This chapter looks at the impact your lifestyle has on the earth's resources and then summarizes positive steps that you can take to protect and preserve those resources — starting today.

Understanding the Impact of Your Choices

Think about the concept of green living (also called *sustainable living*) as being a lot like your family budget. If you spend more than you make each month and neglect your bills as a result, the bill collectors start calling. If you keep going down the same path, you end up owing so much that you can't possibly pay it back. On the other hand, if you're careful with your monthly expenses (maybe even saving a little), you're able to live within your means and keep everyone happy — especially you.

The planet's no different. Right now, its resources are being depleted far faster than they can be replenished. The call of the bill collectors is getting louder all the time, with the clear implication that bankruptcy's down the road if something doesn't change. Fossil fuels such as oil are becoming more difficult and more expensive to bring out of the ground, and their reserves are dwindling. Burning fossil fuels to provide energy for homes, vehicles, and industries emits carbon dioxide and other greenhouse gases along with pollutants that affect the health of the planet and its people.

Other resources are in trouble too, including water. In some parts of the United States, drought conditions are becoming more common and more widespread. Debates continue about where to find sources of water: to pipe it in from other areas, to drill into underground aquifers, or even to build desalination plants to take the salt out of seawater. One possible effect of global warming is the further reduction of groundwater sources. Decreasing the demand that people place on water sources is essential in order to continue having enough water to go around.

Thankfully, it's not too late to turn the situation around — to make the changes that the planet and its people need for a safe, healthy, prosperous, and compassionate future. Changes need to happen quickly, however: According to the United Nations, some parts of the world are nearing the tipping point, after which the damage will be irreparable.

A useful way to understand your impact on the environment is to measure your *ecological footprint,* which is the land and water needed to support your consumption of goods and resources. Think of it as a way of describing the amount of land and water required to farm your food, mine your energy sources, transport your goods and services, and hold your waste. Your *carbon footprint* is a subsection of your ecological footprint and measures the carbon dioxide created by the things you do and the products you buy.

You make decisions every day that have an impact on the planet: choosing between the car and local rapid transit, for example, or selecting local or organic fresh food instead of packaged, processed food that has been transported long distances. Think about the impact that each individual decision has and weigh the pros and cons of your everyday actions.

The Earth Day Network, a network of environmental organizations and projects, estimates that there are 4.5 biologically productive acres worldwide per person. The average American's ecological footprint, however, is 24 acres, which means that a lot of people are using more resources than the planet can afford.

You can measure your own ecological footprint simply by visiting the Earth Day Network Web site at www.earthday.net and entering some information about your lifestyle. If you're just starting a greener lifestyle, reducing your ecological footprint may seem a little daunting. You can reduce it significantly, though, and it won't take long. Use the questions from the Earth Day Network to think about where you'd like to start reducing your impact.

Climate change: A sign of changing times

Climate change (also known as *global warming*) is a huge issue in the world today, but it accounts for only part of all damage being done to the environment — damage that will dramatically change the way that the earth is able to provide for the needs of its residents in the future. In fact, climate change isn't actually the problem but a symptom, or product, of two far more important problems:

✔ The amount of the earth's natural resources that humans consume in order to live, especially in advancing economies

✔ The waste that spills over into the earth's land and atmosphere as a result of that consumption

When you put those two problems together over an extended period of time, they have a domino effect: They contribute to issues such as the earth's climate change and regional food and water shortages, which in turn have their own environmental impacts.

Fortunately, humanity — and each individual — is capable of moving the earth to a healthier place for all by taking small steps every day.

Mother Nature and the law of supply and demand

Human beings naturally aspire to more technologically advanced, convenient lifestyles — the payoff for lots of hard work. Unfortunately, the laws of Mother Nature say that all things come at a cost; in the case of material goods, that cost is in the form of the earth's resources. These resources include not only those used to produce fossil fuels and, therefore, energy, but also resources such as water and the land that produces food.

The vast majority of the energy that people use to heat and power homes and businesses, fuel vehicles, and manufacture home furnishings and all other material goods comes from nonrenewable sources called *fossil fuels,* which are energy-rich organic substances traced back to the remains of organisms that lived 300 to 400 million years ago. Often found under the sea bed, fossil fuels include oil, coal, and natural gas, and they consist primarily of carbon and hydrogen. Today, these substances are extracted from the earth's crust and are mostly refined into suitable fuel products, such as gas, propane, heating oil, and kerosene.

Uranium, the other nonrenewable energy source, is used in nuclear power plants, which can produce very few emissions — but those plants have their own environmental issues in terms of radioactive waste.

Fossil fuels currently provide 85 percent of the energy needs of the United States. They're also responsible for the lion's share of greenhouse gas emissions, such as carbon dioxide, sulfur dioxide, and nitrogen oxides, and they contribute to particles that can cause acid rain.

Pondering pollution's impact

One of the great examples of how humanity directly impacts the planet (and indirectly affects itself) is waste, whether it comes from a factory smokestack or is consigned to a landfill or incinerator, because of its potential to pollute the atmosphere, the land, and the water. It may be "out of sight, out of mind," but waste and its associated pollution still have an impact on the environment.

The burning of fossil fuels is perhaps the greatest contributor to pollution, yet it's currently the primary means for generating and transporting energy. Electrical energy, for example, is one of the most popular forms of energy supplied around the world. The cheapest and most reliable way of providing electricity to cities and towns involves power generation plants that burn fossil fuels, such as coal. The energy required for transporting the coal to the plant comes from refining oil — also a fossil fuel.

Although many waste materials, products, and packaging can find space in landfill sites or incinerators, their components have to be dealt with to avoid emitting potentially toxic chemicals back into the land and the air. True, new landfills are carefully sealed so that their contents don't leak, and incinerators use much cleaner technology than they once did. But all these improvements require energy, which is exactly what the people of the world should consume less of.

Making the Move toward a Sustainable Lifestyle

As you begin to make your life greener, you'll see benefits well beyond the immediate green ones such as reducing carbon emissions, reducing waste, and supporting the local economy. You'll discover that being green can improve your life in all kinds of areas.

Here are just a few of the major benefits of a sustainable lifestyle:

- ✔ **Saving money:** Consuming less of any commodity — from electricity to water to clothes — means that you pay less, too. You'll discover lower utility bills and a budget with breathing room when you take actions such as buying quality items that last a long time and even growing some of your own food.

✔ **Encouraging profits:** When you support green and ethical businesses such as stores and financial institutions, you help them stay profitable enough to continue acting in environmentally and socially responsible ways. You also send a message to less responsible companies that they need to clean up their acts.

✔ **Boosting health:** Following the tips in this book about walking and cycling instead of driving and about reducing the amount of chemicals in your food, your home, and your garden can leave you with an improved cardio-vascular and immune system, stronger muscles, and cleaner lungs.

✔ **Leaving a legacy:** The opportunity to protect what's vital about the planet for future generations is perhaps the most important benefit of all. If you consume only what you need, reduce your trash, live more naturally, and invest carefully, you do a great deal to leave a planet that will benefit people and wildlife for centuries to come.

Changing what you can as you can

Although you can't change the world and save the planet single-handedly, you can make a difference — and you can start right away with whatever budget and time you have available. Buying a hybrid-electric vehicle in order to reduce fossil-fuel consumption and emissions is an excellent strategy, but few people can afford to go out and buy a new car tomorrow (not to mention the implications of getting rid of your old one before its time). You have tons of options that are both easy and affordable, however.

The best strategy is to take change one step at a time and implement small — and eventually bigger — changes when and as you can. Also assess where you're starting from (calculating your ecological footprint is one way to measure this; see the earlier section "Understanding the Impact of Your Choices") and figure out what you can do to counter your effect if you can't yet make the changes you want to make. *Carbon offsets* are one approach to reducing your impact: You buy back your carbon use by purchasing offsets, which fund projects that reduce greenhouse gases. Clean Air–Cool Planet maintains a directory of carbon offset providers at its Web site, `www.cleanair-coolplanet.org`.

Adopting the four primary green strategies

Here are four green living strategies that you can implement in a variety of ways to contribute to the solutions that the planet needs:

✔ **Reduce consumption.** Anything that you do to decrease the amount of the earth's resources that you use — from choosing goods with less packaging to turning down your home's thermostat a few degrees in the winter — helps you lead a more sustainable life.

✔ **Choose carefully.** Assessing where certain products and services come from by thinking about their entire life cycles from manufacture to disposal helps you make the greenest choices possible. You not only protect the environment but also protect the people involved in the manufacturing process.

✔ **Opt for renewable resources.** Using renewable resources (such as solar or wind energy) instead of nonrenewable resources (such as energy based on fossil fuels) is a very powerful green action — and it may be easier than you think.

✔ **Repair when needed.** You can find plenty of ways that you can help fix the damage that's already been done to the environment, from supporting tree-planting projects to helping out with ecological community programs at home and around the world.

Taking those first small steps

Making small changes as and when you can puts you firmly on the road to living a much greener lifestyle. Trying to jump into it all at once can be counterproductive, in fact, because the subject area is immense and is growing all the time. Instead, decide what your priorities are: Think about where it would be easiest for you to begin. Start there and work up to the bigger or more difficult issues.

Your priorities may not be the same as other people's, but that's okay: They're yours, and you're entitled to them. Be prepared to adjust them as new information becomes available, however. Research is ongoing in most areas of green living, so arguments will change. In the meantime, take one small step every time you're ready to, and keep aspiring to be greener.

Great small starts include replacing your light bulbs as they burn out with compact fluorescent models and replacing your cleaning supplies as they run out with environmentally friendly ones.

Another tip that's super-easy to implement is to buy items with less packaging. Consider, for example, what would happen if you bought toilet paper in double rolls, which contain twice as much toilet paper in a roll than regular-size rolls. That cuts down the number of cardboard tubes inside the rolls by half, and it also decreases the amount of plastic that's used to wrap the packages! If you recycle the cardboard tubes that remain, even better. And if you slit the plastic wrap open only at the top of the package, you can reuse the wrap, perhaps as a trash bag. See how easy that was?

As you read through this book, jot down a list of actions that you can see yourself taking fairly easily. When you have a list, it's easier to prioritize the tasks so that you don't feel you need to tackle them all at once.

Turning green choices into habits around your home

Reducing, reusing, repairing, and recycling are the four most important actions when it comes to adopting a greener lifestyle because they all contribute to conserving the earth's resources.

Your home is one of the best places to start making green living changes because you have the control to make the choices that are best for you.

Along with energy efficiency, water conservation is a major issue, and it's where you can really make a difference. Between the source and your faucet, water has to be pumped at various stages, and that takes energy, as does the process of treating the water. If you conserve water, you do double duty by conserving both water and energy, which helps reduce the amount of carbon emissions pumped into the atmosphere.

Most of the water used in homes — whether it's for flushing, washing, cleaning, or drinking — is processed to the point of being high-quality drinking water. Although systems do exist to divert *graywater* (water that's been used in sinks, for example, for hand- or dishwashing) to toilets for flushing, they're not yet a common feature of home building and renovations. However, you can make a difference by preventing as much good-quality water as possible from running down the drain into the sewers, and then back to the processing plant so that it can be finessed into drinking-quality water. Chapter 5 in Book II gives you great ideas for reducing your water usage.

When it comes to waste, reduce what you buy as much as possible — including choosing the least amount of packaging possible — which will naturally reduce the waste you generate. Then assess your waste to see what can be reused or recycled; what's waste to you may be useful to your friends and neighbors or to a nonprofit group (see Chapter 2 of this book).

Of course, your home extends to your yard, as well. Book V describes what a green yard looks like (Hint: The grass *isn't* always greener.), and Book VI provides tips on taking your yard off chemicals and growing your own organic food with the help of composting.

When you introduce green living at home, everyone can be involved. Children learn from adults and then pass the word on to their friends, who pass it on to their parents. Give everyone an age-appropriate role to play by putting them in charge of some aspect of your greener household. You can find more about raising green children in Chapter 4 of this book.

Shopping greenly and ethically

Shopping is a great opportunity to make your lifestyle more sustainable. Choose the greenest options available to you, such as food produced using as few chemicals as possible, grown locally in season, and transported over as short a distance as possible to reduce the amount of fuel used. (Chapter 3 of this book tells you more about green choices for your diet.) Other green options include buying clothes made from organically produced materials, goods made from recycled materials rather than resources that have to be mined from the earth, secondhand or vintage goods, and those made from biodegradable materials.

Ethical issues, including how the people and animals involved in the production processes were treated, are also important to consider. You can find out a lot about the products you buy and the places you buy them by checking out www.ethicalshopping.com.

Avoiding goods produced using child labor or in sweatshop working conditions also may be a priority for you. Animal welfare is a growing concern as well; consider choosing meat and dairy products that come from animals raised in humane conditions rather than intensively farmed, overcrowded pens and cages. Poor conditions for animals often go hand-in-hand with regrettable effects on the planet and on human health.

Finding Chemicals Where You'd Rather Not

The burning of fossil fuels for a variety of energy, transport, and industrial needs affects not only the global climate but also your health. Many toxic chemicals are emitted into the environment, whether into the air, ground, waterways, and even through the food you eat.

In the air

People living close to industrial sites in countries with little or no environmental regulation for emissions and pollution of air, land, and water are at risk for health problems, including asthma and other respiratory diseases.

Even in countries where environmental regulation is taken more seriously, the sheer volume of traffic in urban areas puts people at risk for diseases caused or made worse by air pollution.

So what is an Ozone Action Day?

A state or city declares an Ozone Action Day when weather conditions make an area particularly vulnerable to ozone-producing pollution. On an Ozone Action Day, make an extra effort to reduce your polluting activities. Don't drive, for example, unless you have to. Put off filling up your car's gas tank, mowing the lawn, or using any other gas-powered lawn equipment.

You may not see it, but some of the pollution floating around in the air is a major health hazard. Some of the dangers include

- **Ozone:** Good ozone is the layer that exists between 6.2 and 31 miles above the earth's surface and protects you from the sun's ultraviolet rays. Bad ozone is formed when pollutants emitted by vehicles, factories, and refineries react chemically in the presence of sunlight. Ozone can bring on respiratory infections and increase the incidence of asthma.

- **Particle pollution:** Most fine-particle pollutants are visible only through a microscope, but together they form the smog you see on windless days. Particle pollutants are emitted directly (from vehicle exhausts and manufacturing plants, for example) or are formed in the atmosphere when other pollutants react with them. They can cause major respiratory difficulties and have even been linked to lung and heart illnesses.

- **Carbon monoxide:** Carbon monoxide (CO) is an odorless, colorless gas that's difficult to detect. It forms when the carbon in fuels doesn't completely burn. Vehicles contribute a high proportion of CO to the atmosphere; industry and brushfires also contribute to CO emissions. Carbon monoxide in the body restricts blood flow, affects those with cardiovascular problems, and can even be fatal when it builds up in enclosed spaces (such as homes and garages due to faulty furnaces or venting).

- **Sulfur dioxide:** Sulfur dioxide is also colorless, but its rotten-egg smell makes identifying it easy. It's a reactive gas that's produced when coal and oil are burned in places like power plants and industrial boilers. The smell is the main reason that people stay away from industrial areas using these fuels. But besides being offensive to the nose, it's offensive to the lungs and heart.

The next time you watch the local news on TV, pay attention to the weather report's *air-quality index*. This index measures the extent of major gases and particles delivered into the air on a given day, and it provides an indication of the potential for health issues for those who are vulnerable to respiratory conditions.

Sniffing out some air-freshener alternatives

Air fresheners, most of which simply cover up smells rather than remove them, contain chemicals. Plug-in air fresheners use energy while they're pumping their chemicals into the air. What's more, some people find that air fresheners make them short of breath and give them headaches. In all, air fresheners aren't particularly eco-friendly.

Fortunately, you can enjoy a nice-smelling home while using an air freshener because natural alternatives abound. Both vinegar and baking soda dissolved in water absorb bad smells. Lemon slices in a pan of boiling water make another good air freshener. If you have smokers in your house, hide a small bowl of vinegar under a piece of furniture to deodorize the room. Burning natural beeswax or vegetable wax candles with pure essential oils also takes the cigarette smoke out of the air and stops fabrics from getting smelly.

Another alternative to the conventional air freshener is to use essential oils to make rooms smell nice. Get an oil burner, some small candles, and your favorite pure essential oils to get a more pleasant smell. For even less work, fill up a bowl with petals from flowers and herbs from your garden!

A recent study at Northwestern University sheds some light on how air pollution can cause not just respiratory ailments but also cardiovascular events, such as heart attacks and strokes. The study found that the pollution particles triggered the formation of blood clots in mice, and blood clots can cause both heart attacks and strokes, depending on whether they form or move within the body to the heart or the brain.

In foods

The need to feed the world's growing population and the demand for inexpensive food has led to mass food production. Intensive farming methods have developed to meet demand and to get food onto plates quickly. These methods include

- ✔ **Chemical additives, antibiotics, and artificial hormones** used to make animals and birds grow more quickly and to prevent disease in herds and flocks
- ✔ **Chemical pesticides and fertilizers** used to raise the quantities of crops that can be produced per acre of land while sending environmentally harmful runoff into waterways

The long-term health effects of these farming methods aren't always clear immediately, but they are cause for concern. For example, antibiotics in the food chain can cause people to become resistant to them, which causes problems when the antibiotics are essential to the treatment of a medical condition. The Bovine Spongiform Encephalopathy (BSE, also called mad cow disease) outbreak, which led to the deaths of more than 150 people in the United Kingdom in the 1990s and 2000s, was a direct result of particular bone meal products added to the food given to beef cattle to keep the costs of beef production down. (Chapter 3 of this book looks at the food you eat and how to buy the greenest food available. If you're feeling ambitious, Chapters 4 and 5 in Book VI tell you how to grow your own food.)

In products

The biggest users of chemicals that are potentially harmful to human health are industries that manufacture medicines, plastics, textiles, detergents, paints, and pesticides. Two problems are inherent with the chemicals found in these products:

✔ The products bring people into daily contact with potentially harmful substances.

✔ The processes used to create the products create waste that's potentially harmful.

When the manufacture of these chemical-containing products (see the list of potentially harmful chemicals later in this section) began decades ago, the toxic mess produced was invariably released into nearby waterways, emitted into the air, or simply dumped on the ground. Environmental regulations in many industrialized countries are now in place to prevent some of these issues, but more and more people are at risk from contaminated air, land, and water in areas where environmental regulations haven't kept up with industry. And even in the United States, regulations allow the emission of certain amounts of chemicals as long as they're kept within specific limits.

Toxic chemical leaks from industrial sites do still happen in the United States as well, despite enforcement of environmental regulations. For example, in October 2007, the leak of 500 gallons of hydrochloric acid at a metal plating plant in Melvindale, Michigan, caused the evacuation of approximately 3,000 local residents. In parts of the world where factories routinely get rid of their waste into the nearest stretch of water and where local people are dependent on that water for everyday use, the dangers are huge. And in many parts of the world, untreated wastewater from septic treatment plants also finds it way into the nearest stretch of water, where it routinely causes disease. This contamination leaves people at risk of disease and toxic poisoning.

Some of the major potentially harmful substances that may be introduced into the environment include

- ✔ **Brominated flame retardants:** These substances are used in plastics for computer casings, white goods, car interiors, carpets, and polyurethane foams in furniture and bedding. They can end up in the dust of homes and offices and are linked with cancer and reproductive problems.

- ✔ **Dioxins:** A byproduct of PVC (polyvinyl chloride, made into anything from window frames to plastic), industrial bleaching, and incineration, dioxins can lead to diseases of the immune system, reproductive and developmental disorders, and cancer.

- ✔ **Lead and mercury:** Toxic heavy metals that don't break down in the environment and aren't destroyed at any temperature include lead and mercury (which is also used in people's dental fillings). Lead is the most prevalent industrial toxin released into the environment and therefore causes the most environmentally related health problems. It's released into the atmosphere through gas and paint. Low levels of lead and mercury can cause mental illness, learning disabilities, and stunted growth in children.

- ✔ **Organochlorine pesticides:** These types of pesticide include DDT, dieldrin, heptachlor, chlordane, and mirex, all of which are used in farming and gardening and can end up in soils, the water table, rivers, and streams. Most have been banned in many countries, including the United States, because they can cause cancer and are toxic to the immune system; however, these substances can linger in the ground. DDT is particularly tenacious, and a 2000 study found that DDT is still detectable in blood streams (although thankfully at ever-decreasing levels) despite its being banned for more than 30 years.

- ✔ **Perfluorochemicals:** These acids are used in the manufacture of everyday items, such as clothing, stain-resistant materials, and cosmetics. They're linked to cancer and liver damage.

- ✔ **Phthalates:** One of the most omnipresent groups of chemicals and used mainly as softeners in polyvinyl chloride (PVC), as well as in cosmetics and perfumes, these chemicals disrupt hormones.

Use fewer of the products that contain these substances, and you reduce the need for them, and eventually manufacturers stop producing them.

Taking Care of the Community Outside Your Door

In the past three decades, the world's population living in urban areas has gone from one-third to just over half. In the United States, 80 percent of the population lives in metropolitan areas. Growing world populations, which are moving toward large urban areas, mean that more and more people are living in close quarters near sources of pollution, such as factories and large concentrations of vehicles and even infection from each other.

Clearly, the earth can take only so much. It can't replenish its resources at the same rate that people are currently consuming them, and its rate of replenishment may well decrease further as climate change continues to affect both the land and the oceans. Add to that a growing urbanization of the world's population as a result of economic growth, and you have a situation in which land, water, and wildlife are all at risk.

Simply throwing more fertilizer, genetic modifications, or chemicals at crops isn't a long-term, green solution. Instead, people need to understand where the problems are coming from — including land clearing, water consumption practices, overconsumption, and breaking links in the food chain — so that they can find solutions.

✔ **Clearing the land:** One major concern in modern-day society is that the amount of land available in the world for growing crops and supporting animal herds for food (such as cattle and sheep) is insufficient to support the food needs of the world's population. The causes are urbanization and land clearing for economic development (added to the fact that large areas of the world aren't suitable for agriculture).

Clearing the land has a number of negative effects on ecosystems, among them the following:

 • When you replace forests or wetlands, for example, with agriculture or development, soil erosion occurs. Clouds of dirt can even be seen blowing in the wind over farmland in drier areas as topsoil disappears, leaving the resulting land with fewer nutrients and less ability to soak up rain, which means increased flooding.

 • Stripping the land removes tracts of forest and other vegetation that would otherwise use and store the carbon dioxide in the atmosphere, thus reducing the earth's ability to deal with greenhouse gases.

 • Food and other essential products have to be transported into towns and cities to support people who no longer produce their own food and clothing. As a result, energy consumption for transportation increases.

 • Mass production farming methods are required to produce the food needed for growing populations. This scenario leads to the breakdown of the family farm, which is being replaced by large corporate farming entities that can afford the technology and research needed for mass production.

 • The amount of waste that has to be disposed of in urban areas grows as the population does, in part because as people become separated from the land that supports them, their concern about reducing waste through such techniques as composting decreases.

✔ **Overconsumption:** Also called *affluenza*, *overconsumption* refers to the unsustainable use of the planet's resources. Overconsumption is fed by population growth and by the "keeping up with the Joneses" mentality that requires buying a constant stream of bigger, newer, better products — both of which are a strain to our natural resources.

✔ **Depleting the founts of H2O:** Water supplies are dwindling because of rapid population growth in the developing world and because of the way people consume water in many developed areas. It's essential for people to reduce the amount of water that they use every day to ensure that enough of this resource remains to support not only the people living on the planet but all its ecosystems, too. After all, those ecosystems are at the heart of the world's agricultural production.

✔ **Removing links in the food chain:** Urban development can reduce wildlife abilities to migrate to seasonal feeding grounds, and pesticide spraying for agricultural crops can run off into waterways, introducing chemicals into the water that kill or harm fish. Even when not directly involved in food production, wildlife — from insects to large mammals such as elephants — plays a role in the health and regeneration of the environment.

Removing even one species can have a negative effect on the entire ecosystem. For example, when predators such as wolves are removed from the ecosystem or deer-hunting is banned, the populations of deer increase well beyond the numbers that the local vegetation can support, which in turn leads to the deer starving, or moving into new areas in search of food.

Looking Forward: Thinking Globally, Acting Locally

Is it possible to stop and then reverse the damage that's being done to the planet?

Considering where the world currently stands in terms of resource depletion and greenhouse gas emissions, it's tempting to think that the situation can't possibly be improved. However, the World Wildlife Fund (WWF) has taken a clear look at where things are and where they're going, and it believes that, in fact, the world has more than enough sustainable energy and technology to supply a projected doubling in global demand for energy between now and 2050 while dropping carbon dioxide emissions by 60 to 80 percent.

The WWF believes that this supply will come from six key solutions:

✔ Improving energy efficiency

✔ Stopping forest loss

✔ Accelerating the development of low-emissions technologies

✔ Developing flexible fuels

✔ Replacing high-carbon coal with low-carbon natural gas

✔ Equipping fossil fuel plants with carbon capture and storage technology

Huge gains in environmental progress have been made before — for example, the protection of threatened wildlife species, such as the peregrine falcon and the bald eagle. However, the citizens of the world need to act quickly according to the WWF — in the next five years, in fact! And bringing about change and repair will take a combined effort from individuals, businesses, and governments. Reversing every effect may not be possible, but people can still make a difference.

And your own household is a mighty fine place to start.

Living a green life at a very local level really does help to change the world on a global level because every positive change that you make has a ripple effect. Reducing your energy consumption, for example, means that less fossil fuels need to be burned, which means that fewer greenhouse gases end up in the atmosphere, which in turn creates less global warming and protects more of the environment. Sure, the effect seems minimal when you consider the grandiosity of the environmental problems, but as history shows, individuals can create great waves of change — you just have to be consistent and persistent.

Going green in Güssing

The town of Güssing, Austria is an excellent example of the impact of environmental change. Güssing has cut its carbon emissions by more than 90 percent in the past 15 or so years!

How did they manage that? The town had no major industry; most of its residents commuted to Vienna to work, and the town was losing its population to migration at a quick clip. Its town council had trouble paying its electrical bill, so it decided that all public buildings in Güssing would run on renewable energy instead of fossil fuels. Today, energy sources in Güssing include the sun, cooking oil, and biofuels, such as sawdust and corn; the town generates enough power to sell some back to the national grid!

Most industrialized countries are now focusing on reducing or eliminating waste by educating residents and businesses about how to decrease the amount of waste they're responsible for, how to reuse as much as possible, how to recycle what can't be reused, and how to turn household and garden waste into compost.

You can make plenty of changes to your own lifestyle right away, thus taking care of your own personal responsibility and making an immediate difference to your home and community. You also can help people around you adopt a similar green approach by participating in community and even international initiatives, such as

- ✔ Volunteering for a community action group that has similar interests to you, such as a cyclists' lobby group or a group representing local conservation efforts
- ✔ Writing letters about topics such as waste reduction, greening the local municipality's vehicle fleet, and alternative energy sources to the editors of newspapers, magazines, and Web sites, and to your local, state, and federal politicians
- ✔ Getting involved with an international lobby, policy, or research organization that supports green living
- ✔ Joining a political party that represents your views and through which you think you can have an influence

Getting more people involved in actively promoting greener living makes it more likely that the politicians responsible for policy-making will take environmental issues more seriously. It's important to make your case tactfully and based on science rather than rhetoric, however; otherwise, you'll do more to turn people off green living than on.

Many of the tips in this book are simple ones that you can start immediately without making huge changes to your lifestyle. When you take action, you help turn the tide and provide hope that the planet can sustain its future generations — your grandchildren and great-grandchildren.

Chapter 2

Reducing, Reusing, and Recycling

· ·

In This Chapter

▶ Generating less waste

▶ Giving your possessions a new lease on life

▶ Helping others while saving the environment

▶ Unloading electronics in an ecofriendly manner

· ·

*F*or many people, trash is "out of sight, out of mind" as soon as it leaves their homes. But that's not the end of trash's journey; it's just the beginning. The scope of the trash problem worldwide involves more than just the volume of trash that's produced. For every item you throw out, there's hidden waste — the raw materials that went into its production and the resources such as water and energy that fueled the process, from raw materials to finished goods to landfill. And much of that energy comes from nonrenewable sources.

The green living ideal is to reduce your trash so much that you produce no waste at all; however, achieving that ideal is quite challenging. It's far more practical to focus on reducing your trash as much as you can. Zero waste will become more achievable as recycling and packaging practices catch up with today's culture.

Quick and easy ways to reduce your trash all start with *what* — and *how much* — you buy. When you reduce the amount that you consume, you declutter and simplify your life, automatically reducing the amount of trash that you generate (and maybe even reducing your stress level as well). For those things you can't reduce, reusing and recycling remain the key to dealing with waste. This chapter discusses ways of incorporating all three Rs into your daily life and adds a couple more, including repairing and regifting, plus a C for composting to help you reach your trash-reduction goals.

Cutting Back Consumption and Aiming for Zero Waste

The best way to reduce waste is to reduce what you buy. Bring into your home only what you really need and know that you'll use — whether it's food, clothes, or electrical appliances. Bringing in less not only reduces the items you eventually have to dispose of but reduces their associated packaging, which is where much of your waste likely originates.

Buy less

Living a simpler lifestyle isn't about doing without or cutting out the things you truly enjoy. It's about knowing the difference between what you "need" and what you "want." It's also about prioritizing — looking at your days and deciding what's really important to you so that you can make better decisions about how you spend your money. In this way, being careful about what you bring into the house has more benefits than just reducing the trash that you produce: It also can help to simplify your life and reduce your stress level.

 Some experts suggest keeping a journal of everything that you buy for a month or even a week. When you review the journal, you may see patterns of spending emerge that you weren't even aware of. Perhaps you bring home convenience or takeout food more often than you realize, or maybe you make up for a tough day at work by buying yourself a "treat," such as a new piece of clothing for your closet. Simply recognizing these patterns may be enough to help you break out of them; the next time you're tempted by the fast food drive-through or the mall, think twice and keep going instead of stopping and shopping.

Another way to scale back your purchases is to opt for good quality items over mediocre quality ones. From the kitchen cupboards to the bedroom closet, buying fewer items of good quality keeps your spending in check and doesn't overwhelm your storage space. It also ensures that you're not throwing out items because they've worn out prematurely.

Be mindful of packaging

Keep in mind that the packaging of items you *do* buy is another important part of reducing excess. In an age where you seem to have less time and you're lucky just to get to the grocery store so that you can prepare your meals at home, you certainly don't have time to think about what happens to the packaging that's left over or whether you can recycle it. The good news, though, is that choosing products with minimal or recyclable packaging is easy to do without much inconvenience; you can incorporate this awareness seamlessly into your shopping habits with just a little assessment work on the front end.

Evaluating your output

Take a look at a week's worth of your trash in order to evaluate your output:

- ✔ **Assess how much is coming from typical sources, such as packaging, food waste, and paper (such as junk mail).** You may want to keep track of your trash in separate garbage bags for the week: food scraps in one bag, paper trash in one, packaging in another, and so on. Sorting makes it easy to see what's generating the biggest volume of trash.

- ✔ **If you're not already recycling or composting, make a list of all the items in your trash that you could recycle or compost.** Imagine how that would reduce your weekly trash. Chapter 2 of Book VI gives you details about composting.

- ✔ **Take a look at what's left — the unrecyclable items.** This category is a great place to start considering measures to reduce this type of trash by not purchasing or producing it in the first place.

Prioritize your strategies so that you tackle the biggest unrecyclable source of your waste first — you don't have to reduce everything all at once. Take small, easy steps to get yourself started on a sustainable path.

Adjusting your purchases accordingly

The general guideline for minimizing your trash (other than buying less) is to buy items with either the least possible packaging or recyclable packaging. You also can shop at stores that sell loose items or use refillable containers. Shopping around for the least wasteful packaging takes some time, but you'll immediately see a difference in the amount of trash you throw away.

Here are some general tips to guide you around the grocery store, where most packaging trash comes from:

- ✔ **Buy fresh food that doesn't come prepackaged.** Place fruits and vegetables directly into your cart — skip the plastic bags hanging in the produce department. Or reuse bags from a previous shopping trip.

- ✔ **Avoid individually packaged items.** For example, buy a larger container of juice and send the kids to school with juice in a thermos instead of those small, individual juice containers.

- ✔ **Opt for items in glass or other recyclable containers instead of plastic containers that can't be recycled.** Basically, try to avoid any plastic that can't be recycled through your local system. (See the "Recycling" section, later in this chapter, for more information on recycling plastics.)

✔ **Avoid aerosol cans altogether if at all possible because you can't reuse or recycle them.** For cleaning and toiletry products, purchase products in pump-action bottles, for example.

✔ **Take your own canvas bags, shopping basket, or reused bags with you when you shop so that you don't load up on more plastic or paper bags.** If you must choose between paper and plastic bags, choose paper, which can be composted, reused, or recycled. But try hard to remember to bring your own bags — paper and plastic bags demand a heckuva lot of energy.

Take your attack on product packaging one step further by sending packaging back to manufacturers with a letter telling them why you won't be buying their products again. Stores and manufacturers will get the message if sales drop for heavily packaged items or products in nonrecyclable packaging. Help them understand by telling them why you're buying the competition's product instead.

All packaging isn't necessarily bad, even if it's not recyclable (although, obviously, it's far better if it can be recycled). It may protect goods so that they can be transported without damage, thus reducing waste. Packaging also may maximize the amount of a particular product that can be packed into a container, such as a large box; if fewer containers need to be used for the same amount of goods, fewer trucks are needed to transport an order, thus decreasing greenhouse gas emissions. Manufacturers may be thinking primarily of how to cut their transport and damage costs, but they're still being greener as a result of minimizing packaging.

Lengthening the Life of Your Possessions

Cutting back on consumption is an important part of waste reduction, and if you're able to hold on longer to the possessions you already have, you reduce even further your need to buy new items and get rid of the old ones. Not only does this practice reduce your waste, but it also saves you money, which is always a good thing! In this section, we take a look at how reusing and repurposing items can give them a new and longer life at very little environmental cost.

If you can't reuse something directly, recycling is your next best option because it turns the item into something that's once again usable. This conversion costs energy, but it's still better than throwing out the item.

Reusing and repurposing

Sometimes you can't reuse items in the same way you've been using them because they're too worn out for that purpose; in these situations, find a new purpose for that item, adapting it however you need to.

Reusing sits above recycling in the hierarchy of the three Rs because it doesn't require any extra energy for reprocessing and because it cuts down on the need to buy new. The aim is to use items for as long as possible, for as many different uses as possible, or by as many people as possible, before they have to be recycled or disposed of in the trash.

Most things have more than one use. Here are some ideas to get you thinking creatively about how to reuse or repurpose things that you own:

✔ **Reuse paper that has been used only on one side.** Put the other side through your printer again for rough drafts, use it for notepaper, or give it to your children to use as drawing paper.

✔ **Wash plastic food storage bags instead of discarding them.** Use hot soapy water to get them clean, but don't reuse bags that have been in contact with raw or cooked meat.

✔ **Use empty glass jars as containers in your workshop or as organizers at your desk or elsewhere.** If you drill holes in the lids and screw them to the underside of a shelf, you can attach the jars to the lids to reduce clutter on your work surface.

✔ **Use wrapping paper and gift bags again and cut down cards to make gift tags.** Fold gift paper and bags carefully so that they store easily and live to wrap again. Make a wonderful joke or legacy card among your family members and friends by reusing the same birthday card over and over and simply encouraging everyone to keep passing it on to the next person who has a birthday — no apologies, just cross out the last giver's name and add on your own best wishes for many happy returns . . . and returns and returns.

✔ **Alter clothes and cultivate your own vintage look by contributing to and shopping at secondhand clothing boutiques.** Want more ideas for what to do with clothing? Check out *Reconstructing Clothes For Dummies* (Wiley), by Miranda Caroligne Burns.

✔ **Repair damaged items.** Try repairing an item rather than throwing it away and buying a new one. If it's not worth repairing the item — especially with electrical items, where safety is an issue — decide whether it really needs replacing. Life may be too short to darn a sock, but a chair with a broken leg or ripped upholstery, a defunct kettle, or a temperamental toaster may have years of life left with a bit of tender loving repair.

If you can't repair things yourself, find someone who can: Furniture restoration businesses, clothing alteration and repair services, shoe repairers, upholsterers, electronic appliances repair firms, and even toy hospitals can give your items a new lease on life.

✓ **Turn small plastic containers into garden pest traps.** Set the plastic container into the ground and fill it with beer to create a baited trap for harmful pests such as slugs.

✓ **Cut old, worn clothing into rags for cleaning, dusting, or washing vehicles.** Chapter 2 of Book III gives you details about what fabrics work best for which cleaning jobs.

✓ **Turn old pantyhose into plant supports for the garden.** Simply cut off the legs, loop them around plant stems or branches, and then tie them off to stakes.

✓ **Use wine corks to create a corkboard.** Check out the CraftersLoveCrafts site, `www.crafterslovecrafts.com/wine-cork-crafts.html`, for instructions as well as many other ideas for using old corks.

✓ **Cut down a king-size sheet that's worn in the middle into a single-size sheet or a few crib sheets.**

Recycling

If all else fails (meaning that you can't reuse or repurpose items), recycle. *Recycling* involves collecting goods that have reached the end of their lives and processing them, their parts, or some of their parts, into the raw materials from which new goods are made.

Ever wonder just how green recycling is compared to producing new goods from scratch? Consider this fact: Recycling steel, aluminum, copper, lead, paper, and plastics can save up to 95 percent of the energy it takes to produce new goods from these materials.

Recycling doesn't just help reduce the amount of trash that heads to landfills and incinerators: It also reduces the amount of greenhouse gases that are released into the atmosphere. Although the recycling process consumes energy and therefore emits some greenhouse gases, those gases are still less than what would be emitted by a combination of machinery at landfills and incinerators and by the manufacturing processes used to create new goods that would be needed if the recycled goods weren't created. According to the EPA, in 2005, recycling prevented the release of 79 million tons of carbon into the air — about the same as would be produced annually by 39 million cars.

Because recycling isn't as green as reusing or reducing (which don't emit greenhouse gases), you should try to reduce and reuse first and foremost. Glass can be recycled into bottles, for example, but it has to go through a manufacturing process to get there, and that process uses energy. In an ideal world, the energy would be generated using renewable sources such as wind, hydro, and solar power so that the recycling process is completely green, but in the real world, that's not usually how it works.

Despite the drawbacks, recycling an item is far better than throwing it in the trash. And as states and cities increasingly develop and encourage waste-reduction strategies, recycling will become an even more important part of daily life.

Identifying what you can recycle

Not everything can be recycled (yet), but you should be able to put out at the curb or find recycling dropoff facilities for these six main categories of household waste:

- ✔ **Paper:** Most paper is recyclable, including newspapers, cardboard, phone books, packaging, magazines, catalogs, and wrapping paper. If you have a garden, you also can turn most paper into compost; turn to Chapter 2 of Book VI for composting instructions.

  Some recycling facilities and pickup services take paper products, such as milk and juice cartons; others don't. These cartons are made of cardboard sandwiched between very thin layers of plastic, so not all the material is recyclable. Check with your local recycling facility or service provider before you haul your waste for drop off.

- ✔ **Plastics:** Most plastics are recyclable, but recycling rates for plastic tend to be low because of a lack of facilities. Each plastic product has a Plastic Identification Code — a triangle with the number 1, 2, 3, 4, 5, 6, or 7 inside it. The code usually appears on the bottom of the plastic product. Most recycling services and dropoff facilities accept plastics with codes 1 or 2, which includes beverage bottles and containers used for milk, juice, and body-care products. Table 2-1 shares details on the Plastic Identification Codes and the products they're associated with.

  Check with your local service provider or dropoff facility about which plastics it takes for recycling, and if you can, buy only products in plastics with those numbers. If the local provider doesn't accept plastics, try to reduce the plastic that you buy and reuse what you already have.

- ✔ **Glass:** Most household glass can be recycled over and over again — you usually just need to rinse or wash out food containers and remove paper labels. In fact, glass is easier to recycle than plastic, so if your local service provider or dropoff facility doesn't recycle plastic, buy the product you need in a glass bottle or jar if one's available. Recycled glass has a whole variety of uses, but mainly it's used to create new glass containers.

Glass items, such as car windshields, cooking dishes, and light bulbs, aren't usually accepted by local recycling systems. These items may not be recyclable in your area, or you may need to take them to a special dropoff point. Check with your service provider or local government's waste office to find out whether a special dropoff point is near you. For example, compact fluorescent light (CFL) bulbs aren't usually accepted in local recycling programs. Because CFLs contain a small amount of mercury, you need to take them to your local household hazardous waste disposal site. Home Depot stores also accept used CFLs for disposal.

✓ **Metals:** Metal food and drink cans made from aluminum or steel are recyclable. With food cans, wash them out first and remove paper labels — it's worth the extra chore. Aluminum cans in particular are very valuable in terms of recycling material. You can recycle used aluminum foil, too.

✓ **Organics:** Some recyclers include organic materials, such as yard and kitchen waste, in their regular services, whereas others offer seasonal organics recycling, such as Christmas tree dropoff locations after the holiday season.

✓ **Textiles:** Many charitable and nonprofit organizations operate dropoff points for textiles like clothes and shoes; you usually find these sites in supermarket parking lots and in the organizations' own business locations. What the groups can't use they generally sell to private firms dealing in textiles.

Table 2-1	Plastic Identification Codes		
Plastic Identification Code	Type of Plastic	Common Products	Possibilities for Recycling
1	PETE (polyethylene terephthalate)	Soft drink, juice, and toiletry bottles	T-shirt material and carpets
2	HDPE (high-density polyethylene)	Milk jugs, detergent or bleach bottles	Detergent bottles, binders, and fencing
3	PVC (polyvinyl chloride)	Shampoo and mineral water bottles, house siding and piping	New house siding, piping, and other building materials
4	LDPE (low-density polyethylene)	Grocery, garbage, and bread bags	New bags

Plastic Identification Code	Type of Plastic	Common Products	Possibilities for Recycling
5	PP (polypropylene)	Margarine and dairy tubs	Car parts and milk crates
6	PS (polystyrene)	Meat trays, coffee cups, packaging	DVD cases and CD trays
7	Other plastics	Ketchup bottles, other plastics	Park and picnic benches

Paint isn't recyclable, but it's worth a mention in this section because some communities offer a central dropoff point for leftover paints. People can come and pick up the unwanted paint for free, latex paints may be mixed together and reprocessed, and components of oil paints can be reprocessed into fuel (or at least disposed of responsibly if this isn't practical in your location). It's also possible that local organizations, such as Habitat for Humanity (www.habitat.org), can use your unwanted paint, so check with your city or town to see whether such a service is available.

Creating your recycling system: Compost piles and recycling stations

Turning your organic kitchen and yard waste — paper, vegetable peelings, eggshells, grass clippings, and leaves, for example — into new, nutrient-rich dirt is the best possible example of recycling success in action. If you have a yard, you can build or install a composter in a sunny spot; if you don't have the space and your local recycling options don't include organic waste, consider setting up a worm farm indoors to handle the compostable materials. For more information about how to compost, check out Chapter 2 of Book VI.

For those items you can't compost, you can create a recycling station in your home no matter how little room you have to devote to it. Essentially, you set aside a space where you can collect and store your recyclables until it's time for pick up or drop off.

A garage is the perfect place for a recycling station. To save space, install shelves on the wall, one above the other, that will each hold one recycling bin. You can buy brackets and wood or ready-made shelves from local building centers or organizing stores; you also can purchase bins to hold your recyclables. If your recyclables need to be separated, label the bins and allow enough space between them to throw in the recyclable items.

For smaller spaces, especially apartments, check under your kitchen sink. You may already have a trash can there, so it's the ideal spot to add another trash can (or even two or three) for your recyclables. You can buy commercial products, such as pull-out trays, to make the bins easily accessible, or you can rig up your own tray that slides out. If you don't have enough room for trash cans under your kitchen sink, use paper bags to collect recyclables instead.

If you're really tight on space, buy a can compactor to crush metal cans, significantly reducing the space they occupy. You mount the compactor on a wall or sturdy, vertical surface, such as a wood shelf frame. You can crush milk and juice cartons without the aid of a compactor.

Finding places to drop off recyclables

Many local governments have well-established recycling programs that provide either curbside pickup at your home or operate neighborhood dropoff points. You may be asked to put all your material for recycling — bottles, food and beverage cans, paper, newspapers and magazines, cardboard, and recyclable plastics — into one box separate from the rest of your household trash. Or you may be asked to separate each type of recyclable material into different boxes for collection.

If your community doesn't offer government-sponsored services, keep an eye out for school recycling drives and look for commercial businesses in your area that offer weekly recycling pickup. There's likely to be a fee involved, but it's worth it to divert waste that would otherwise end up in the trash. Increasingly, stores also are offering recycling services as a response to customer demand. The office-supply store Staples, for example, lets you drop off used rechargeable batteries, empty printer ink cartridges, and even unwanted electronics such as televisions and computers, and most Ikea stores accept batteries and CFLs for disposal.

To find recycling resources in your community, check with your local government. Earth 911 (earth911.org) and the National Recycling Coalition (www.nrc-recycle.org) also can help. Of course, if your state has instituted a refundable deposit on certain containers (such as plastic beverage bottles), there's likely to be plenty of local bottle depots where you can drop off the items and claim your money.

If your municipality or county doesn't already tackle waste reduction, write to local politicians or representatives asking them to put the issue on their agendas. You can find more information about zero waste initiatives at Zero Waste America (www.zerowasteamerica.org) and Eco-Cycle (www.eco cycle.org).

To make recycling as easy as possible — and to prevent it from becoming an overwhelming task — set up a home recycling center that works for your family. If you need to drive somewhere to drop off the recycling, plan to stop by the recycling center on your way to another destination. That way, you're not making a special trip, which costs you extra time, fuel, and greenhouse gas emissions.

Turning Your Garbage into Someone Else's Gold

If you can't reuse something, you don't know anyone who wants it, and you can't recycle it, you may still have alternatives to throwing it out. You can give things away or sell them if you have access to potential customers.

If you can't reuse something, someone else may be able to.

Deciding what others may want

Walk around your home and pick out things that you don't need but that other people could use. If you have room, create a storage system that allows you to add an item to the "find a new home for this" box when you're done with it. When a box is full, offer it to your local secondhand book or music shop; if you don't get a sale, offer it to a local charity or nonprofit.

Some of the most popular secondhand items include

- ✔ **Books, magazines, CDs, and DVDs:** The market for these items is huge, and they can go on and on being reused.

- ✔ **Clothes:** Used and vintage clothes are fashionable, and someone else may be able to make good use of good-quality clothing even though you never want to wear it — or see it — again. Sift through your wardrobe and drawers and sort out things to give away, swap, sell, or turn into rags. If your items are fashionable or desirable, check out the later section "Cashing in on unwanted items."

- ✔ **Furniture:** Whether it's old or relatively new, valuable or not, in good shape or has seen better days, furniture that you want to get rid of will find a home with someone out there. All sorts of home clearance firms buy furniture; auctions sell antiques and less valuable furniture and household items; and charities often want furniture of all sorts to help furnish homes for those less fortunate.

- ✔ **Electronics such as computers, appliances, and cell phones:** Other people may be able to get electronics in running order either for themselves or for charity.

- ✔ **Household items such as dishes, knickknacks, and storage containers:** If these items are in reasonably good shape (not chipped or cracked, for example), there's no reason why they can't be used by someone else who may find their patterns more attractive than you do. Charity stores often accept such household items.

Giving away your goods

Giving things away may appeal to your green nature more than selling your unwanted items. In terms of being green, offering your used goods to another person reduces waste and fits in with the idea of reusing as much as possible. Try charitable and nonprofit organizations, private waste collectors, scrap metal dealers, friends, family, and work colleagues.

Contributing to sweet charity

If you're interested in giving things away to people who have more need for them than you do, you can donate just about anything.

Make sure that anything you give is in good condition, usable, and clean and that won't create a problem for the person receiving it. Too many people dump unwanted, dirty, or broken items on the doorsteps of charitable organizations, thus also dumping the expense of disposing of the items.

Tips for selling online

Selling items online can seem a little intimidating if you've never done it, but if you take the time to read the Web site's instructions and carefully do a little research, it's not at all difficult. Here are a few tips to help you maximize your sale price:

- **Check out similar items on the Internet to compare prices.** Potential buyers are likely to find items similar to yours, so do some research and price your items competitively. You can sell just about anything through the Internet, so if you get little response from would-be buyers, there's either no demand for your used goods or you've priced them too high. Try dropping the price before you give up completely.

- **Be sure that you're dealing with a well-known, established, reputable site.** The credibility and security of the site you choose is absolutely critical to ensure that your transaction goes smoothly and everyone comes out satisfied. With auction sites such as eBay, the more you buy and sell successfully on the site, the better reputation you'll get within that site's community. If you sell on eBay, for example, everyone who buys on the site has access to your past buying and selling history (and vice versa) thanks to eBay's community ranking system. This feedback system has greatly reduced the chances of being sold a dud product or not receiving payment for an item you sell. For more tips on selling on eBay, check out *eBay For Dummies* (Wiley), by Marsha Collier.

- **Be alert to the possibility that all may not be as it appears.** When dealing with Internet sales sites, you generally have very little protection if you send goods and the money doesn't arrive or if you send money and the goods don't arrive. Internet sales are based on trust. You can find consumer protection information pertaining to online sales on the Web site of the Better Business Bureau at www.bbb.org.

Following are a few organizations that accept household or clothing items:

- ✔ **Habitat for Humanity** (www.habitat.org) accepts tools, building materials, furniture, and appliances in good working order, either for use in homes being built or for resale to the public in order to help raise funds. The organization also accepts vehicle donations!

- ✔ **Lion's Clubs International** (www.lionsclubs.org) conducts eyeglass recycling, collecting used eyeglasses at a number of eyewear chain stores and redistributing them in developing countries.

- ✔ **Nike Re-Use a Shoe** (www.letmeplay.com/reuseashoe) collects worn-out athletic shoes of any brand and processes them into material that's used for sports surfaces, such as playgrounds for youth around the world.

- ✔ **The Salvation Army** (www.salvationarmyusa.org) operates local centers that accept household and clothing items for resale.

- ✔ **Goodwill Industries International** (www.goodwill.org) has local stores that welcome donations of clothing and household items for resale.

- ✔ **Hands Across the Water** (www.surplusbooksforcharity.org) collects unwanted books and sends them to schools and libraries that need them around the world.

Facilities such as hospitals, libraries, senior and rehabilitation centers, daycares, homeless shelters, and churches in your area may be able to use various items that you're ready to donate. Search online or check the phone book under "recycling" or "charitable organizations" to find them. Contact each organization to find out what it really wants and to make sure that it can handle the items that you have to offer. Some may even offer to pick up your items.

Trading goods online

The Freecycle Network (www.freecycle.org) was one of the first Web sites to offer members a way of giving unwanted possessions away for free to other members who would make good use of them. This program takes the principles of reducing, reusing, and recycling into cyberspace. Community members who want to find a new home for something, whether it be a chair, a fax machine, or a piano, send an e-mail offering it to local members, who then respond by e-mail. The rule is that everything offered must be free, legal, and appropriate for all ages. Membership in Freecycle is free.

Sharing Is Giving (www.sharingisgiving.org) is a site with a similar purpose, acting as a one-stop source for all free-transfer Web sites.

Regifting

Regifting — giving a gift you've received to someone else as a gift — isn't for everyone; in fact, some consider it quite rude. It's up to you to assess the potential consequences; for example, it may not be the wisest idea to regift the birthday present your parents gave you. And it's definitely not a good idea to regift an item if there's a chance that either the new recipient or the original giver may find out and be offended.

It's not usually acceptable to regift an item that's used rather than new. On the other hand, regifting something that's important to you and thus sharing its value with the recipient is actually quite generous and thoughtful. Perhaps you have a painting or a book that has always given you inspiration or encouragement during a difficult time and you want to regift it to someone you love who's now facing their own difficult time.

In the right circumstances, regifting offers these significant advantages:

- ✔ **You aren't buying new goods.** You're subscribing to the principle of reducing waste and thus reducing the amount of energy used to produce new products.

- ✔ **You're reusing something.** You're giving something to someone who will make use of it, therefore keeping the item out of a landfill site.

- ✔ **You're eliminating the need to recycle the item.** You're saving the energy required to reprocess the item.

Cashing in on unwanted items

Buying and selling secondhand goods is a hobby for some people, a business for others, and an occasional pastime for the rest. If you like to hunt for secondhand treasures, or if you have something to sell, you have plenty of choices. The only limiting factors are how much someone is willing to pay and whether it's economically viable and green to have the item mailed or delivered to that person's home. If something has to be transported by road or air for long distances, you should consider the carbon emissions that the journey can produce. (See Chapter 1 of this book.)

Here are the more common places where you can trade in or sell items for cash:

- ✔ **Pawnbrokers and secondhand dealers** are much more sophisticated than they used to be, and they abound in most areas.

- ✔ **Secondhand book and music shops** are very popular. Trade in your unwanted books and CDs for others in the store, sell them for cash, or leave them on a *consignment basis* (that is, you leave them in the shop for a certain amount of time, and if they don't sell, you get them back).

- ✔ **Antique shops** are an option for some items. You may be quite surprised at how much you can get for that old painting that's been sitting in the attic for years.

- ✔ **Auction houses** generally sell antiques, jewelry, used cars, unwanted office and household furniture, and larger household items. You can set a reserve amount on an item you want to sell and take it home again if it doesn't make that much.

- ✔ **Classified ads** in the local weekly newspaper or the free advertising papers were the places for advertising your goods or picking up a used bargain long before the Internet, and they're still going strong.

- ✔ **Garage sales** are perfect for selling a lot of unwanted stuff, especially if it's too big or you have too much to sell to a secondhand store. Set up a sale in your front yard or garage. Find out whether your neighborhood organizes an annual sale and participate in order to tap into neighborhood sale advertising. If you live in an apartment or condominium, the owner or condo board of directors may support a community sale — check to find out.

  Phone your local city or county government or check its Web site to see whether you need any permits to hold a garage sale. Rules may be in place about the items you sell, especially food, and about permitted signage or hours of operation.

- ✔ **Online,** you're more likely to get a better price for your goods on the Internet than in your local secondhand store or through a garage sale, and you may be able to find buyers online for unusual or hard-to-sell items that other places won't take. In fact, the success of Internet sales sites has shown that selling things that you no longer need can be quite profitable. Of course, if you list an item that doesn't sell, you're out the money that you spent to list it.

  You'll find two types of Internet sales stores:

  - **Auction sites,** such as eBay (www.ebay.com) and uBid (www.ubid.com) where sellers place items for sale and buyers bid on the items up to a closing date and time. The highest bid wins the item.

  - **Classified advertising sites,** such as Craig's List (www.craigslist.com) and Kijiji (www.kijiji.com) where sellers simply advertise items for sale. Buyers contact the sellers directly if they're interested in the items.

The success of eBay has led to services that help you sell items on the popular Web site. I Sold It (www.i-soldit.com), for example, has outlets in many U.S. cities where you can drop off an item you'd like to sell; service people at the I Sold It location take care of listing the item on eBay and managing payment from the eventual auction winner. The service is expensive compared to listing the item online yourself, which costs just a few dollars; I Sold It outlets charge varying commissions on top of eBay's fees — typically in the range of 35 percent of the first $500 of the sale price and 20 percent on the amount above $500.

Disposing of Electronic Goods

As electronic goods, such as televisions, computers, cellphones, and computer-driven toys, as well as automobiles, assume a more prominent position in your home and daily life, they also contribute more to your home's waste. The pace of technology development means that many items that are even a few years old are difficult to reuse, so recycling them has become an essential issue. In 2005, approximately 2 million tons of electronic products were discarded in the United States, and the vast majority of the items went straight into the trash.

Not only does the fast pace of the technology industry represent huge losses of reuse potential for many electronic items, it also creates a toxic waste issue because of the components in many of these products. Electronics such as computer monitors, cellphones, and televisions can contain toxic materials, such as lead, chromium, cadmium, mercury, and brominated flame retardants. The health of the environment depends on the safe disposal of these components. Thankfully, opportunities for reusing and recycling electronic goods are growing significantly.

The related issues of waste reduction and hazardous waste management have prompted several state governments — including those in California, Maine, Maryland, and Washington — to introduce mandatory electronics recycling programs. Most of these mandates place the responsibility on electronics manufacturers to create recycling programs, with some instituting a recycling fee that's passed on to consumers at the time of a new electronics purchase.

Manufacturers and distributors are putting recycling plans into action, thus joining local businesses that offer electronics recycling. Find an electronics recycler near you through the National Center for Electronics Recycling at www.electronicsrecycling.org.

Leveling the cellphone mountain

The EPA estimates that up to 130 million cellphones are retired each year, which means that a lot of dead phones are sitting around unused in drawers or are headed for the trash. Because cellphones contain toxic materials such as mercury, it's important to keep them out of landfills and incinerators. More importantly, however, your old cellphone may just turn out to be someone's lifeline.

Several organizations reprogram retired cellphones so that they can be used free of charge by people, particularly seniors or victims of domestic abuse, to call 911. Other organizations reprogram and sell the phones to raise funds for charity. The following organizations operate such programs:

- **Collective Good** (www.collectivegood.com) allows you to mail your phone, PDA, or pager in to be recycled.

- **Phones 4 Charity** (www.phones4charity.org) donates or recycles your cellphone or similar device.

- **Wirefly** (www.wirefly.org) offers a trade-in incentive to encourage consumers to recycle wireless devices.

You also can check with your cellphone service provider about a recycling program; many providers collect old phones to reuse parts and to donate to charities.

You can do more than recycle cellphones; consider reducing the number of cellphones in circulation by turning your service provider down the next time you're offered a new model of phone as a free upgrade. If you prefer not to do that, give your old model to a friend or relative who can use it with their own SIM card rather than buy a new phone. The same goes for phone chargers and batteries — pass them on!

Getting rid of computers

If you're thinking about upgrading your computer system, either at home or at work, consider what to do about your old one. The EPA estimates that some 250 million computers will become obsolete in the next five years, which has the potential for a lot of waste. You do have options for reuse and recycling, however: Computers can be donated for reuse by facilities such as schools and charities, or if computers are too old to be useful, they can go to a responsible electronics recycler to break down their components for reuse, recycling, and safe disposal.

Computer refurbishers can upgrade or adapt your unwanted computer so that it can be donated to schools, community centers, and even initiatives in developing countries to enable more people to gain access to the benefits of the information age. To find a computer refurbisher or recycling program in your area, check Earth 911 (www.earth911.org; in the Find a Recycling Center box at the top of the home page, enter "Computer" and then your zip code or city and state) or Tech Soup (www.techsoup.org; click Learning

Center, then Hardware, and then Ten Tips for Donating a Computer). Some computer manufacturers have established computer recycling programs, and you can also take computers to Staples stores (www.staples.com/sbd/content/about/soul/recycling.html), which participate in an electronics recycling program.

Whether you donate your computer for reuse or drop it off for recycling, make sure that you protect the personal information that may be on it. Computer-savvy criminals can access files that you've deleted, so use hard drive disk-cleaning software to properly erase your files. Also make sure that you deal with a reputable refurbisher or recycler with its own disk-cleaning procedures in place as well.

Dealing with old televisions

The same places that recycle computer monitors in your area likely recycle televisions, too, because their technology is quite similar. If you can't find a charity or friend who needs your old television, drop it off at your nearest electronics recycling center.

You may have heard about the switch from analog to digital broadcast television; essentially, after February 17, 2009, all full-power television stations will have switched from analog signals to digital. The switch will affect you only if you have a television that's not hooked up to cable or satellite television services. If you have a television that receives free signals over the air with an antenna, you'll still be able to use your set, but you'll need to add a digital-to-analog converter box for $50 to $70.

Disposing of an older vehicle

If your vehicle can be resold at a reasonable value, then figuring out how to get rid of it is easy: Either trade it in when you purchase a new vehicle or sell it yourself (which can often get you a better value for it). But what if it's no longer in good enough condition to be sold — perhaps it's no longer running, requires far more repair than it's worth, or has been in a major accident — and you don't feel right about selling it on to become someone else's problem?

You may think it's time for the scrap heap, but that comes with some obvious issues. Some of the material that goes into a vehicle can be recycled or reused (the list of potential items includes liquids, such as oil and gas, metal, refrigerants from air-conditioning systems, tires, parts, and even windshields), but other material, including foams and plastics, end up shredded and in landfills.

Although programs and research are in progress to improve the situation, you can help out by checking your local resources to find out whether any municipal or state recycling programs will help you get rid of your vehicle. The U.S. EPA (www.epa.gov) Web site has a section dedicated to vehicles in its Product Stewardship area that lists partners and resources for automotive end-of-life issues, including tire recycling and the removal of mercury switches from vehicles before they head to the landfill. You also can lend your voice to organizations, such as Environmental Defense Fund (www.edf.org/home.cfm) that are pushing for better management of vehicle end-of-life issues beginning at the manufacturing stage.

Book I

Green Living

Up to 11 million vehicles reach the end of their useful lives each year in the United States, generating as much as 5 million tons of nonrecyclable waste. The U.S. Council on Automotive Research, a joint effort from DaimlerChrysler, Ford Motor Company, and General Motors Corporation, is working to improve how much can be recycled or reused. Find more information at www.uscar.org.

Consider donating your older vehicle to charity: You get a receipt for a tax deduction, and the charity sells the car either at auction or perhaps to an auto recycler. As with any charity, research your local options and ensure that it's a 501(c)(3) organization that you're donating to in order to obtain the tax deduction. Try to avoid middlemen agencies that accept car donations and then pass the proceeds on to charities; a better proportion of your money actually gets to the charity if it's the charity itself that runs the donation program rather than a middleman. Charity Navigator has excellent information about car donation programs at www.charitynavigator.org.

Chapter 3

Making Great Green Diet Decisions

· ·

· ·

Choosing what to eat is one of the most important and difficult green decisions you have to make because it's not just about the environment; it's also about your health. Luckily, the right thing for the planet may also be the right thing for your body.

Eating green means knowing where your food comes from, and that involves two issues: how the food was produced, and how it got to you (including what happened to it along the way). To be sure that your food is as green as possible, you need the answers to these questions. Some scientists advise that if you were to buy locally produced foodstuff — especially from within 100 miles of your home — you would do more for the environment than if you simply bought organic foods from farther afield. Most significantly, you'd save all the greenhouse gas emissions from the transportation of the foods from those distant places.

The packaging your food comes in is also a green issue. Even if the food is organically produced, if it travels any distance to get to you, it usually needs packaging to protect it. Whether that packaging is recyclable or not, it would be greener if the packaging weren't needed at all (which it often isn't for locally produced food) because it takes energy to produce the packaging and then to either recycle or dispose of it.

Many factors are important when it comes to making decisions about what you buy and eat. This chapter shows you how to make practical, cost-conscious decisions that improve your green eating habits.

The Big Question: Is Vegetarianism Essential for Green Living?

People become *vegetarians,* meaning that they don't eat meat, and even *vegans,* meaning that they eschew meat, dairy, and other animal products, for health reasons, philosophical reasons, or both. When you ask people why they choose to be vegetarians, you often find that they're protesting the meat industry's production methods. Others give up meat in favor of vegetarianism because they're alarmed by the health issues. Still others are concerned about the resources that go into the production of meat. Grain-feeding animals in a factory farm uses up a lot of resources — gasoline for tractors to plant the stuff, power for lighting and machinery, water to flush away effluent — and in many cases relies on fertilizer and pesticides. Even though many farmers keep their cattle and sheep out in the fields, their diets often are supplemented with grain at times when there's not enough grass.

Researchers now use the word *foodprint* to indicate the amount of land that various diets require to sustain them; the idea is linked closely with the idea of a person's ecological footprint (see Chapter 1 of this book). The diet footprint is a handy way to visualize the environmental impact of your diet; the bottom line is that a more sustainable diet requires less land per person. The popular notion is that a meat-free diet uses the least land per person and is thus the greenest, most sustainable way of eating. This reasoning is in part because animals consume feed grown on land that can otherwise be used to grow vegetable or fruit crops for humans.

However, researchers at Cornell University recently added a new twist to this argument when they explained that, depending on the specific type of land that surrounds you, a diet that contains a small amount of meat and dairy actually can be more efficient than a straight vegetarian diet. That's because vegetarian crops require higher quality land than the pasture land that animals need. So if your geographic area and climate offer more pasture land than crop land, eating a small amount of meat can be more efficient. (The Cornell researchers suggested an annual meat and egg intake that averaged approximately 2 cooked ounces per day.)

The argument over the greenest use of land for food, which is particularly applicable given the current emphasis on eating local food in order to reduce greenhouse gas emissions, demonstrates why green issues are rarely black and white and why one solution doesn't necessarily fit all situations. So if you lust for a lamb shank and pine for a pork chop, you can still pursue a green eating strategy. Meat can be, and is, produced in the same organic and sustainable way that many fruits and vegetables are farmed. You can cut down your impact on the planet's resources by reducing the amount of meat you eat and choosing green meat whenever possible.

Choosing Your Food Source Wisely

Despite all the arguments about what food is best in terms of health, there's agreement from an environmental point of view that buying local food is best. At the heart of all the arguments for eating locally grown produce is the need to cut down on what have become known as *food miles*, the distance food travels from where it's produced to your plate. Transportation over what can be thousands of miles results in a lot of carbon emissions. The food Americans eat travels an average of 1,500 miles before it gets to the plate. In addition, food that travels a long distance and spends time in storage has fewer nutrients than locally produced food.

However, sometimes buying locally isn't an option, particularly when you're talking about foods that aren't grown in the United States. Enter *Fairtrade,* a trade program that works to make sure that

- ✔ Producers in the developing world get fair prices for what they produce.
- ✔ Producers have reasonable working conditions.
- ✔ The processes used in the developing world are sustainable.

Buying Fairtrade items raises the issue of how far the food has traveled to get to you. Is it "greener" to buy the Fairtrade item that may have been transported from the other side of the world but that supports the developing world, or the local item that isn't benefiting the developing world's economy but that contributed far fewer greenhouse gases to the atmosphere? A green lifestyle has room for both: Buy local when you can, and buy Fairtrade when you can't buy local.

Your best bet: Buying locally

Food that flies thousands of miles from other countries is just part of the food miles problem. Even American produce can travel many hundreds of miles before it gets to your plate. Retailers buy from producers and often transport the food over the road to big packaging plants, to huge storage facilities, to distribution centers, and finally to the stores from which you drive it home. To cut down on those miles, you have to buy locally.

From locally owned and operated grocery stores

Because of concerns for animal welfare, and because eating food produced using pesticides and other chemicals may cause health problems, the demand for organic food has increased to such an extent that big businesses are interested in its money-making potential. Most people have limited time to shop, so large grocery stores are the convenient option. They enable you to get everything under one roof and do a big shop every once in a while, reducing the miles you travel to get groceries.

Keep in mind, though, that many large grocery stores tend to treat food grown throughout the United States as if it's locally produced. Even if a cow starts its life in a farm just one mile away from you, the meat will travel to storage and distribution centers miles from home and will have traveled a large distance before it gets back to your grocery store. Big businesses have greater buying power than small competitors, but they also transport food farther to storage and distribution facilities, increasing factory and transport emissions and reducing the nutritional value of the stored food. Also take into account the impact that big business has on local business, particularly small, locally owned specialty grocery stores and farmers' markets.

Take a careful look at where you shop. If your nearby chain grocery store brings in as much local and organic produce as possible, then by all means support it. But if it doesn't, then look for other options. The larger stores' buying power may translate into lower food costs on the shelves, but do what you can — within your budget — to purchase more locally and/or organically produced food.

If you're unable to buy food from a farmers' market or directly from a local farmer, head for smaller specialty stores and co-ops, many of which sell organic and/or local products.

Co-ops are exactly what they sound like: cooperative organizations in which people come together as members to take advantage of the buying power that results from being more than just one individual or one family. Members usually pool money in some way and thus become member-owners of the organization, with a say in how it runs and a share in dividends if any money is left over at the end of the year. Co-ops can be informal, such as when several families pool funds in order to buy from a co-op food warehouse, or they can be more formal with hundreds or even thousands of members. When it comes to food, many have a mandate to support local, organic, or natural food producers. You can find co-ops throughout the country through the Coop Directory Service at www.coopdirectory.org.

Some local shops or co-ops may sell only organically produced and labeled food; others combine organic food with health food, vitamin and mineral supplies, and other well-being and fitness-related products. These kinds of stores are popping up everywhere and are increasingly moving into many large shopping centers thanks to the demand for organic food products.

Wherever you shop, check with the store to see how local "local" is. The distance that experts consider local varies — some say 12 miles; some say 100; some say within your own watershed or climatic region. Decide for yourself what's practical given your geographic location. (If a label says "locally grown," it generally indicates something within 250 miles.) If you live in the northern part of the country, of course, buying local agricultural products during the winter is very difficult; in that case, "local" may mean produce grown within the United States in winter but produce grown much closer to home in summer. Local definitely *does not* mean buying strawberries from Chile in December.

At local farmers' markets

Farmers' markets have increased in popularity in the past few years. That's great news for people who love to eat locally grown food and support local food growers and producers. Farmers' markets may be open one or two days a week during the growing season, or they may operate year-round. They cater to people who are interested in buying fresh, local, and sometimes organic produce.

At most farmers' markets, you can talk to the growers about their produce — they're usually passionate about the subject — so that you know exactly what you're buying and eating. You can find details of local farmers' markets at the U.S. Department of Agriculture (USDA) Web site (www.ams.usda.gov/farmersmarkets/map.htm). If you don't find a market in your town or city listed on the U.S. Department of Agriculture (USDA) Web site, inquire with Local Harvest (www.localharvest.org).

Not all the produce at a farmers' market is certified organic. Some growers use conventional growing methods, some may go through the certification process to convert to organic (see the later section "Getting a Grip on Organic"), and others simply may be keen vegetable gardeners with green fingers.

Straight from a local farm

If you don't have a local farmers' market, you may be able to hook up with a farm not too far away from you that sells its produce straight from the farm or has its own farm store. Even if you live right in the middle of a city, you may find that farmers set up shop temporarily and sell produce straight off their own trucks. (Some farmers even deliver to established regular customers.)

Local Harvest (www.localharvest.org) has lists of family farms and other sources of sustainably grown food. In addition, many state government agricultural departments maintain lists of such farms.

Canning bottled water

Americans are drinking an ever-increasing amount of bottled water — some 27 gallons per person last year, in fact. The environmental resources involved in bottled water are staggering: Energy is required to produce the plastic bottles, tap the water source, fill the bottles, possibly add carbonation or flavoring, transport the bottles to the consumer, and finally dispose of or recycle the plastic bottles.

The water inside the bottles isn't necessarily healthier than the water coming out of your tap. You can reduce your water miles significantly by minimizing your purchase of bottled water and instead choosing a refillable and washable container that you can fill from the tap. If you're concerned about the taste or quality of tap water, consider installing a tap-mounted water filter or using a water filtration pitcher.

The produce from a farm store may be somewhat more expensive because the farm doesn't sell the volume of produce that allows it to cut prices. If you have to drive there and back, you also have to think about the fuel you're using and the impact of your transportation on the environment. However, if you can combine a trip to the farm or farm store with other errands, you reduce your environmental impact.

Getting to know local farmers and shopping directly from farms has the added advantage of providing a fun day out for the whole family. Farms near your home may have pick-your-own operations that offer a variety of fruit and vegetables — often strawberries and raspberries, but the selection depends on the area, the climate, and the farmer.

Look for *community supported agriculture (CSAs)* services that enable members (who buy shares or subscriptions in the CSA or even contribute labor) to take part in local farmers' bounty. Pay the fee, and you get a regular delivery of seasonal produce. Head to the Local Harvest Web site, `www.local harvest.org`, to find a directory of CSAs.

From food-delivery services

Many cities are serviced by companies that deliver fresh fruit and vegetables from local growers, with some specializing in organic produce. Depending on the company, you may be able to sign up for weekly or occasional (on-demand) delivery and order exactly what you want so that you know what will arrive on your doorstep.

Door to Door Organics (`www.doortodoororganics.com`) offers organic food home deliveries in various communities in several states.

To find a food-delivery service in your area, run an Internet search for "food delivery service *(your town or city)*." You may want to add "organic" to the search terms.

Finding Fairtrade food

The idea of Fairtrade is that more of the money you pay when you buy an item goes to the producers who then can pay their workers better and invest more in their businesses. It's a trading partnership that aims at sustainable development for excluded and disadvantaged producers.

In the United States, you can find a range of goods (approximately 300 of them, from chocolate to herbs to footballs!) with the Fairtrade logo on them, many of which are available at stores near you or via online shopping. You can even find coffee shops that distinguish themselves by selling only Fairtrade-certified coffee.

The Fairtrade program aims to make sure that

✔ Producers are paid a fair price that covers their production and living costs so that they have some security, they have long-term contracts and therefore can plan ahead, and their businesses are sustainable.

✔ The extra money you pay goes toward other aspects of the producers' welfare, such as education.

✔ Producers and workers are allowed to join unions and other organizations that can protect their rights and ensure that they have fair working conditions.

✔ No child labor is used.

✔ Production methods are environmentally friendly and pesticide-free.

Find more information about Fairtrade on the Web site for Fairtrade Labelling Organizations International, an umbrella group that deals with a number of different certification programs around the world: www.fairtrade.net.

Growing your own — at home or in a community garden

If you have the time, energy, space, and desire, the greenest option is to grow some of your food yourself using organic methods. Food that comes out of your garden isn't only the most local food you can possibly get, but it contributes to sustainability. You can find more information about what to grow and how to grow it in Book VI.

If you don't have access to space of your own but like the idea of gardening and growing some of your own food, consider joining a community gardening project or even setting up one in your area if one doesn't exist. A *community garden* is essentially any plot of land that a group of people garden together. Many are volunteer-run, perhaps located on land that belongs to a housing association, city council, church, school, or healthcare facility.

Each garden runs by its own rules; in some cases, people sign up for specific duties, whereas in others, the team assigns workers weekly to keep the garden healthy. Part of the community garden team may include members who take responsibility for areas such as volunteer management, fundraising, obtaining plants, garden maintenance, and harvesting.

To find a community garden in your area or to find out how to set one up, visit the American Community Gardening Association's Web site at www.communitygarden.org.

Getting a Grip on Organic

Maybe you focus on taste and convenience when you're thinking about getting supper on the table each night, but a lot more goes into your food than meets the eye. If you ask many schoolchildren where bacon comes from, they're likely tell you "the grocery store." The process of breeding, rearing, feeding, and eventually killing pigs and other animals for food is something many of them know nothing about. And why should they? They live in towns and cities where they may never encounter anything related to farming. But if you want to know what you're eating, you need to know what kind of farming methods get the meat you eat from the farmyard to your plate. Even a simple grilled cheese sandwich likely contains a lot more than wheat flour and milk. When eating green, you need to consider chemicals and additives along with factors such as how the chickens were raised and what went into the field of grain aside from the grain itself.

You may think it should be quite easy to explain exactly what is and isn't organic food. But it's not that straightforward. Hundreds of organizations around the world give certificates to say that products are organic, and each has slightly different criteria by which it makes its judgments.

U.S. farmers have to meet the United States Department of Agriculture's definition of organic through the National Organic Program. Basically, the program says that in growing crops and raising animals the organic way, natural substances are allowed, and synthetic substances aren't. More specifically, it means that

- ✔ Crops are grown without the use of most chemically based pesticides or petroleum- or sewage-based fertilizers.
- ✔ Animals are raised without antibiotics or growth hormones.
- ✔ Genetic engineering and ionizing radiation aren't allowed at any stage of the food-creation process.

Although organic food is produced by greener methods and shouldn't contain pesticides and other substances that can potentially be bad for your health, scientists aren't in agreement about whether organic food is safer and more nutritious than its nonorganic equivalents. In fact, the USDA is careful to point out that the National Organic Program lets consumers know what is and isn't organic; it doesn't make any claims that organic produce is better or safer for you than nonorganic produce.

What isn't disputed, however, is that conventional — and especially intensive — farming methods can be much more damaging to the environment than organic methods.

The words *organic* and *natural* aren't interchangeable. Organic products have been created (or grown) using natural methods and ingredients and haven't come into contact with chemicals. *Natural,* however, means simply that a product doesn't contain artificial ingredients — not that the production process has been organic. What's more, the use of the word *natural* isn't regulated by federal guidelines, so you're trusting the manufacturer on that one.

Avoiding chemicals and unnecessary medicines

Organic farming is much friendlier for the earth and the local economy than mass production of products. Instead of using chemical-based fertilizers to create a high-yield soil, organic farming uses traditional methods of plowing the soil to break down soil compaction that can reduce water and air getting to the plants' roots, rotating the crops to prevent crop-specific diseases or pests from building up in the soil, and growing *cover crops* such as peas or clover that naturally add fertility to the soil in rotation with conventional crops.

Organic farming also emphasizes the use of physical, mechanical, or biological controls to handle weeds, insects, and plant diseases. You can pull weeds by hand or machine, for example, or introduce a beneficial insect to eat a harmful one (for example, ladybugs to eat aphids). If you don't use dangerous substances, you eliminate the risk of their running into nearby rivers, streams, and the water table below, affecting water quality. In turn, you're less likely to be eating any chemicals used to keep bugs at bay and the soil fertile.

When it comes to livestock, organic animals are fed only organic feed along with vitamins and minerals. Depending on the animal, there are specific rules about when and for how long the feed needs to be 100 percent organic.

Growth hormones and antibiotics also are specifically banned in organic food products, although vaccines are allowed. Of course, farmers are allowed — in fact, they're required — to give medication, including antibiotics, to animals that are sick to prevent suffering. However, food products that come from the animal involved may not be called organic if the animal has received a medication that's on the organic-prohibited list.

Letting nature govern production: Say no to genetic modification!

Genetically modified organisms — also known as *genetically engineered organisms* — are living things whose genetic makeup (their DNA structure) has been changed by the addition of genes from another living thing. Genetic modification is used to make plants and animals more beneficial to food production, both in terms of quantity and quality. With this kind of intervention come major concerns that, for the green community, outweigh the pros.

Although cloning doesn't fit the definition of genetic modification (the DNA hasn't been added to but rather replicated), the use of cloned animals or their offspring — especially for animal products such as milk (the cloned animals themselves are currently too valuable to be used for meat) — in the food supply is something that the U.S. Food and Drug Administration (FDA) is assessing as this book goes to print. Although the FDA has stated that there's no scientific evidence to show that the meat or milk products, for example, are unsafe, groups opposing the approval cite research that indicates cloned animals may have some genetic abnormalities. It's not yet clear what effect, if any, those abnormalities may have if they enter the food chain.

The potential effects of genetic modification

Genetic modification (GM) may make foods taste better, last longer before spoiling, or contain certain types of nutrients or medicines. The primary benefit, though, is generally to food producers in terms of higher production capacities, increased disease or pest resistance, or increased herbicide resistance (which enables farmers to use more weed-killing herbicides). Crops, for example, can be genetically modified so that they resist insects, herbicides, and disease or so that they contain extra nutrients or even vaccines. Animals can be genetically modified to produce lower-fat meat, resist certain diseases, or create less waste.

One of the most common genetic changes to food products involves a gene that comes from a bacterium known as *Bt*. When this gene is added to plants such as corn or cotton, those plants begin to produce a protein that's toxic to insects that can otherwise prey on the crops — and, unfortunately, to a lot of other nonpests, such as butterflies and moths.

Proponents of GM crops claim that nutritionally enhanced grain or rice crops can be used in developing countries to solve some of the issues of undernourishment or malnutrition. GM crops also can be used to provide vaccines against diseases, which also would most benefit the developing world. Some scientists believe that, by boosting production efficiency, resource conservation, and nutrition, GM crops and animals can offer solutions to both world hunger and environmental degradation.

With all these potential benefits, you're probably wondering where the concern comes in. Scientists' biggest reservations lay in the unknown; genetic engineering is a relatively new concept (modern genetic engineering began with scientific discoveries in the 1950s through 1970s), so long-term consequences have yet to be determined. And given the amount of time generally needed to link cause and effect in the scientific world, you can safely assume that these consequences won't be identified in your lifetime — and perhaps not even that of your children or grandchildren.

Some scientists also are concerned that GM ingredients may cause toxic poisoning, allergic reactions, antibiotic resistance, and even cancer in humans. Research hasn't proven all the concerns, but there's enough evidence to warrant caution.

Some short-term effects include the potential for GM crops to "contaminate" non-GM crops when their seeds migrate over distances. Contamination means that GM seeds can begin growing in non-GM areas, meaning that the non-GM crops would no longer be considered free of GM material, which is a huge issue, especially for organic growers who — through no fault of their own — would suddenly be prevented from calling their crops organic. Other concerns include the potential for organisms, such as insects and viruses, to evolve and become more powerful super pests that overcome the resistant GM animals and plants.

Examining the world food supply

The issue of what's happening with food around the world is part of the larger discussion of eating green. While famines often make news headlines, children in many developing nations face a more constant (and usually unreported) threat: undernourishment and malnutrition. But does this mean that the world isn't producing enough food to feed everyone? Not necessarily.

The Population Reference Bureau (www.prb.org) reported in 2007 that malnutrition plays a role in the deaths of approximately 6 million young children a year, primarily in the developing world. That's 16,000 children a day.

The issue with food isn't that we can't currently produce enough to feed the world: According to the United Nations' World Food Programme (WFP), there's plenty of food to go around. The problem is that the food isn't always grown where it's needed. Natural disasters, war, lack of infrastructure such as irrigation, overfarming practices that rob the land of its fertility, and poverty all can reduce how much food is available in specific areas. The result is an overabundance of food in some areas and a shortage in others.

Improving the green quotient of your food — buying local and organic — can help protect the environment and support producers near to you. To address issues on a global scale, you can support or get involved with nonprofit organizations that work in developing areas to improve the situation, such as the WFP (www.wfp.org).

In addition, the idea of manipulating living organisms at the DNA structural level raises serious ethical questions. This interference goes well beyond the ways in which humans have traditionally interfered (by cross-breeding, for example). Experience should have taught us that interfering with nature can create unforeseen results (such as when high-end predators like wolves were culled from the food chain, causing an overpopulation of deer that were then prone to starvation because there weren't enough food sources to sustain them).

Genetic engineering changes the fundamental building blocks of life: Researchers don't know how changing the genes of crops will affect wildlife that coexists with the crops, or how changing the genes of animals may affect them (possibly causing diseases or deformities and therefore suffering). If farmers introduce GM crops that have been designed to resist herbicides, for example, how will they be able to remove those crops if they later realize that the GM crops have unexpected and undesirable effects? Until we can answer these ethical questions, we need to err very much on the side of caution.

Recognizing when food has been genetically modified

Because of concerns about foods that contain genetically modified ingredients, GM food has become a major consumer concern in Europe, to the point where any foods that contain GM products as ingredients must be labeled as such. For the most part, European consumers avoid GM-labeled foods, so producers simply aren't growing crops or raising animals that have been genetically modified.

In the United States, however, the issue hasn't captured consumers in the same way. GM crops are common in the United States, and no labeling is required; in fact, it's estimated that upwards of 70 percent of foods in U.S. supermarkets contain some element of genetic engineering. You most likely are eating GM ingredients in your food without even realizing it.

The best way to find out whether your food choices contain genetically engineered ingredients is to choose local options so that you can talk to the producers and find out from them exactly what went into the food. If you can't do that, then try talking to the managers or owners of local grocery stores — they may not be able to tell you about production methods, but the fact that you asked them may help to convince them that they should pay more attention to this issue.

If you can't buy the groceries you need from your community, try contacting food manufacturers directly. Their Web sites often contain information about production methods and a consumer telephone or e-mail hotline for questions. If companies aren't able to categorically deny that they use GM ingredients, chances are good that they use these products.

Some of the foods and ingredients currently subject to genetic modification for reasons such as increasing yield or pest resistance include

- ✔ **Soybeans:** Soy is one of the main sources of genetically modified ingredients in food and can be found in everything from chocolate to potato chips, margarine to mayonnaise, and biscuits to bread.

- ✔ **Canola:** Canola oil comes from certain types of canola plants. GM canola may be used for oils in making potato chips and animal feed.

- ✔ **Corn:** GM corn is used as cattle feed but also is used in all sorts of packaged food, such as breakfast cereal, bread, corn chips, and gravy mixes.

- ✔ **Wheat:** GM wheat has been developed, but its implementation in North America so far has been successfully opposed.

- ✔ **Milk:** Cows may be injected with a genetically engineered growth hormone to increase milk production.

The life and times of a factory-farm chicken

You only have to look at how chickens are treated on a factory farm to understand how viruses such as bird flu strains can evolve and spread quickly and why eating meat can introduce chemicals into your diet. That's not to mention the welfare issues related to treating animals with a significant lack of compassion. Here's some insight into how chickens live their lives on factory farms:

- ✔ Many hens born and raised on a factory farm can live their whole lives crammed inside cages next to other chickens, never seeing anything outside the cage in which they're housed.

- ✔ Most hens raised on a factory farm have never walked, never stretched their wings, never made a nest, and never foraged for food.

- ✔ Because of their desire to move around, the hens can become aggressive and peck at the other chickens around them, causing injury and disease. To avoid that, many hens' beaks are cut off when they're born.

- ✔ Chickens raised for meat (called *broilers*) spend relatively short lives in sheds with hundreds or even thousands of other birds. They're fed with growth hormones so that they grow quickly, which makes them predisposed to disease and physical abnormalities. Many of these birds die of heart attacks, dehydration, or starvation because they can't even stand or walk to feeders.

You can find more information about factory farming from the U.S. Animal Welfare Institute (www.awionline.org), which recently launched its Animal Welfare Approved certification program for family farms.

Freedom rules for organic livestock

Organic livestock farming takes into account both the health of the animals as well as their welfare. Factory farming concentrates many animals in a limited space, which can result in an overflow of animal waste on each farm and the need to use extra water and chemicals to assist in removing the waste. Additional chemical use can lead to chemicals leaching into the soil and the water table, and it can mean that the animals are less healthy and may often need to be treated with antibiotics and other medicines. Organically raised animals, however, must be *free-range,* which means they have access to the outdoors, including pasture. They aren't confined within buildings but may be kept in buildings temporarily for health or safety reasons.

The rules on what constitutes free range aren't always what green experts would wish; free range covers a variety of conditions, from the birds being able to wander in a natural environment to the birds having access to a small outdoor enclosure that may not be very natural. It's a good idea to check with the producer if you can in order to find out what free range means in the context of a particular product.

Factory farming methods have evolved to meet the ever-growing demand for meat. The organic approach may be slower and less profitable — animals must have room to move, and so fewer animals can be produced from the same amount of land, for example — but it produces cleaner and healthier animals.

If you find it difficult to locate organic meat, ask your local butcher to stock some organic and sustainable options; increased demand increases supply. The environment will be better off, and your local butcher will have a guaranteed customer. You also can purchase food from animals that have been raised in a sustainable way through the Eat Well Guide at www.eatwell guide.org. The site has searchable listings of producers across the country.

Fishing for sustainable varieties

Buying fish brings with it a whole range of ethical issues. The world's fish stocks are dwindling, which means that fishermen have to go farther afield into deeper waters to bring home their catch. Fishing in deeper waters means greater use of dragnets that catch endangered species as well as fish for the stores. Fish are taken from the sea younger, further depleting stocks because fewer breeding fish are in the sea. Only 3 percent of the world's fish stocks are underexploited. At the same time, demand for fish is growing, doubling in the last 30 years alone.

Book I

Green
Living

One answer to the decrease in fish stocks has been to farm fish such as salmon. Intensive farming methods have resulted in the same sorts of problems faced in livestock farming, however. The use of chemicals, antibiotics, and disinfectants to protect the farmed fish from disease has led to worries about toxins and cancer-causing chemicals in the fish you eat, and there are concerns about escaping fish carrying contamination into wild fish stocks. All this comes at a time when nutritionists advise eating more cold-water fish species for the benefits of the heart-protecting omega-3 oils that they contain.

Various national and international quotas are in place that set the amount of fish that each country can take from the various fishing grounds. These restrictions have done a lot to conserve fish stocks, but some fishermen cross into non-quota-controlled waters in order to meet demand, and many conservationists are concerned that current quotas aren't low enough.

When you go shopping for fish, you need to think about

- ✔ **Whether the fish you're buying is from sustainable stock:** *Sustainable stock* means that the fish are replacing themselves at the same rate as they're being fished. Cod, for example, used to live up to 40 years and grow up to 6 feet long, but now the stocks are so depleted that most of the fish caught are less than 2 years old and haven't bred replacement fish. People usually are advised not to buy cod in order to allow stocks to build up again.

- ✔ **What the fish's body may contain:** There's a major concern that many fish — including swordfish and Chilean sea bass — contain higher than healthy doses of substances such as mercury.

- ✔ **Whether the fish is farmed or wild:** Buying wild fish may contribute to overfishing, but the fish may be a healthier option than farmed. If you choose to buy farmed varieties, opt for farms that use sustainable practices. Wild Alaskan salmon usually are considered healthy and sustainably caught.

- ✔ **How the fish was caught:** Catching fish by line doesn't cause further damage to the marine environment, but net fishing can do a huge amount of environmental damage. For example, fishing for Yellowfin tuna with purse seine nets in the Eastern Tropical Pacific kills hundreds of thousands of dolphins. Fishing for shrimp and other bottom dwellers often is done using drag nets that destroy the ecosystem of the sea floor being fished.

Buy fish from a store where the staff members know how and where the fish were caught, where any farmed fish come from, and how they were farmed. Check out the fish facts from the Marine Conservation Society Web site at www.fishonline.org or from the Marine Stewardship Council Web site at www.msc.org. Also keep on top of changing information about species that are threatened or potentially contaminated: Check Sea Food Watch at www.seafoodwatch.org for the latest news.

Reading Labels to Apply Green Ideals

Buying food can be confusing, particularly if you're trying to make healthy and sustainable choices. Reading the labels is important because in grocery stores, they're often the only source of information about the content of the food you buy. Food labels aren't perfect, but they do provide basic information about where the food comes from, what it contains, and what nutritional value it offers.

Finding food with good nutritional value and ethical production

When buying a food product, find out whether it has arrived on the shelf from a sustainable production process by checking out the following information on the label:

- **Ingredients list:** Understanding the ingredients and their nutrients gives you an excellent feel for the quality of your food. Heavily processed food is likely to have added salt to assist in preservation and taste and several chemicals for flavoring and coloring. Naturally prepared foods are usually low in added salt, sugar, and saturated fats.

- **Animals used:** Some animals and fish are protected because over-farming, culling, or habitat destruction has led to near extinction. From a food point of view, you're most likely to run into threatened species of fish; you can find the latest news plus handy pocket shopping guides from Sea Food Watch (www.seafoodwatch.org). The site tells you the best choices for seafood, good alternatives if you can't find the best choices, and species that you should avoid.

- **Country of origin:** Somewhere on the label should be a note that says "Product of *(a country)*." Technically, this information tells you the country the food comes from, which is helpful if you're not able to buy a product from local sources. The note on the label can tell you, for example, whether the product is from the United States or from Mexico; however, the reality is that this information can be misleading. It may indicate, for example, where the product was processed and packaged rather than where the original produce actually came from or where it traveled to during the processing. The nuances aren't apparent from the packaging, so you may have to check sources such as the manufacturer's Web site to find out where it processes its products.

Looking for organic and more on labels

Organic food is much more plentiful than it used to be; demand for it continues to increase, so retailers are responding with a wider range of organic products at lower prices. Now most of the big food retailers sell organic fruit, vegetables, and meat, as well as processed foods like bread and breakfast cereal and other foods.

The USDA's National Organic Program has strict rules about what food manufacturers can and can't say regarding organic foods on food labels. Specifically, if a food label has the National Organic Program's seal on it (see Figure 3-1), the producer has been certified under the program. The specifics of the wording, however, are where the differences lie.

Figure 3-1: The USDA's seal confirms that a product is organic.

Here are the USDA's labeling terms, with explanations:

- ✔ **100 Percent Organic:** All ingredients in the product are organic.

- ✔ **Organic:** At least 95 percent of the product's ingredients are organic.

- ✔ **Made with Organic Ingredients:** At least 75 percent of the product's ingredients are organic.

- ✔ **Organic ingredients noted on the ingredients statement:** Less than 70 percent of the product's ingredients are organic, so the producer can identify only the actual organic ingredients within the ingredients listing on the product label.

Meat packaging has additional terminology that you should be aware of, although at this point, no third-party inspectors verify these claims, and you're therefore trusting the packager:

✔ **Natural:** Labels may refer to beef and lamb, in particular, as being produced naturally, but this designation means only that the meat may not have any artificial colors, artificial flavors, preservatives, or other artificial ingredients. Natural production doesn't necessarily mean that the animals led the life of Riley outside, gamboling in the fields.

✔ **Grass fed:** Feeding cows primarily on grass or hay rather than on grain is considered greener (and kinder) because they can digest grass and hay more easily.

✔ **Free-range:** This term means that chickens, for example, weren't confined to cages. There are different degrees of free-range, however — from true free-range where the chickens are allowed to wander in a fairly large space outside to more limited conditions where they may have only short periods outside in an area that's quite small. You may not be able to tell exactly what free-range means when you see it on meat packaging, so if you're looking at a specific product, consider contacting its producer directly for clarification.

The next time you're in the produce aisle, check out the little label that's stuck on the fruit: You should see either a four- or a five-digit code on the label. A four-digit code means that the produce was produced conventionally (it's not organic). A five-digit code that starts with "9" indicates that it's organically grown, and a five-digit code that starts with "8" indicates that it's genetically engineered.

You can get more information on the regulations of food labeling from the FDA at www.cfsan.fda.gov.

Any food producer in the United States that wants to use the word "organic" in its labeling has to follow the National Organic Program, and any producer that's selling more than $5,000 worth of organic food a year has to become certified under the program. In order to become certified, the land has to have been treated organically for at least three years, and an organic plan must be in place to explain production practices and substances. (Converting to organic farming takes time — time for all the existing pesticides and fertilizers to disappear from the soil.) The producer then applies for certification, which involves an initial inspection and then annual inspections for as long as the producer wants to be part of the program. The program's inspectors can show up unannounced, and they can test the food for residues if they think that it may have been in contact with nonorganic substances.

Failsafe ways to buy locally when labels are unclear

If you find no labels on particular foods, or if you find labels with little information — which can be the case in smaller stores and in the fruit and vegetable sections of bigger grocery stores — here are a few tips to help you make the greenest food choices:

- ✔ **Eat fruit and vegetables in season.** They're more likely to have been grown locally. Fruits and vegetables on the shelf that you know aren't in season are likely to have been imported or brought by road from the other end of the country.

- ✔ **Avoid exotic foods.** Some foods and ingredients, such as coffee and tea, likely can't be grown locally; the United States simply doesn't have the climate for them. Find out what grows near where you live by checking out local farmers' markets or by visiting the Web site of your state's department of agriculture, and make the most of it. You'll be supporting your local growers.

  Food retailers say that customers want exotic foods from around the world, partly because people are traveling more widely and experiencing foods that they want to continue to enjoy even after they arrive home. Eating green isn't about sacrificing taste or variety or depriving yourself of a taste that you enjoy. If you're making greener choices most of the time, there's more than enough room for an occasional treat from afar.

- ✔ **Look for local businesses.** Check out the companies close to you that produce, package, and transport things like bread, rice, milk, and so on. Buying those brands means that you're likely cutting down on the miles your food travels and supporting your local economy.

If you try to buy local produce in order to cut down on the environmental impact of food traveling around the globe, you're likely to end up eating what's *in season*. And that's how people used to eat: lettuce in the summer and apples in the fall, for example. Quite apart from the environmental and health benefits of eating this way, there's the added pleasure of rediscovering particular foods each year. When the season is over, you can look forward to tasting something again next year instead of becoming used to it all year and taking it for granted.

Buying local produce may not be practical in areas that are especially hot or cold because there are times of the year when pretty much nothing grows. As always, you need to make compromises based on not just the greenest option but the greenest option that's available to you.

It's possible that local producers extend the growing seasons using different kinds of technology: artificial heating and lighting, for example, or growing under poly tunnels. While this setup isn't as perfectly green as in-season, outdoor growing, it can be done in a way that reduces the impact on the environment. Talk to the producers to find out how they manage their growing seasons.

Eating green when out and about

When you go out for a meal, you have to depend on the chef when it comes to green principles. Many chefs, however, make a point of buying only truly local and/or organic produce. If you want to be sure of what you're getting, call the restaurant before you make a reservation and ask about the ingredients used. Good restaurants are more than happy to answer your questions — and if more customers demand greener restaurant meals, chefs and managers will get the message.

Chapter 4

Setting Your Kids on the Path to a Green Lifestyle

In This Chapter

▶ Finding ways to make your nursery and baby's life green

▶ Bringing up children in an ecofriendly home environment

▶ Painting the school year green

*T*he earlier you encourage your children to become interested in green choices and issues, the more likely they are to carry that interest through the rest of their lives. With that kind of head start, imagine how much better off the planet will be when they're done with it!

Setting a great green example for your children is an excellent beginning. Then add fun green activities and get involved to encourage your children's schools to be as green as possible. What you do in your own home to live a greener lifestyle can translate to the school environment, and what your children learn at school can be put to good use at home — everyone benefits. This chapter shows you how to best instill green values in your youngsters as well as how to live greenly with a baby, who likely values only milk, mushy foods, and snuggling.

Greening Your Baby

There's nothing like starting the green lifestyle immediately — even before your children arrive in the world. From the items you surround them with to the items you dress them in, you have plenty of opportunities to keep the materials as natural and organic as possible. You may want to encourage friends and family who buy baby gifts for you to go green as well — providing hints about where they can find greener items can help. The increasing number of stores that carry environmentally friendly goods for babies is making buying green much easier.

Opting for the most organic and/or local food possible (including breastfeed-ing, if possible) for your baby is not only environmentally friendly but also healthy. (You can find general information on eating green in Chapter 3 of this book.)

Equipping the green nursery

When going green in the nursery, you can take a variety of approaches. Using natural and organic materials whenever possible is one way to reduce the amount of potentially harmful substances that your baby comes in contact with. Another way to focus on ecological protection is simply to reduce the number of items that you buy.

The list of baby paraphernalia, from clothing to furniture and everything in between, can appear endless at first, and if you're having your first child, it's difficult to know what you really need. Get recommendations from other parents: Find out what they used a lot and what they hardly used at all. For example, you may be able to forego a changing table in favor of a low dresser with a pad on top. Your child can keep the dresser and get more use out of it over the years than a changing table.

Stay true to your own lifestyle. If you love to jog and find that it's an excellent stress reliever, go ahead and invest in a good quality wheeled baby carrier that you can jog behind in comfort. (Look for one that's secondhand rather than buying new.) You'll be happier and healthier, which helps your baby to be happy and healthy.

Consider obtaining just these essentials before the baby is born, and add to your list gradually as you find out whether you really need other items:

- ✔ **Diapers:** See the later section "Choosing cloth versus disposable diapers."

- ✔ **Clothing:** Look for comfy secondhand clothes in good condition and forget about all the fancy outfits — they're more for you than the baby anyway.

- ✔ **Personal baby care:** Many experts recommend using a small amount of plain old olive oil for use as baby skin lotion.

- ✔ **Car seats:** Because anchoring car seats properly is a major safety issue and can mean the difference between life and death for your child, relax your green rules here and buy an extra car seat if you have more than one vehicle in which the child will be riding (this includes grandparents' cars). Buy new car seats or ensure that secondhand car seats are in excellent condition.

✔ **Crib:** Look for a crib that turns into a child's bed to reduce the amount of furniture you need to buy later on.

✔ **Toys:** Opt for secondhand toys, soft toys made from organic cotton, and wood toys with nontoxic paints. And keep the number of toys in check.

✔ **High chair:** A sturdy high chair really does make feeding so much easier.

✔ **Baby buggy/stroller:** Look for one that does double duty, converting from a buggy for young babies to a stroller for older babies and toddlers.

For a lot more information, Tree Hugger (http://treehugger.com) has a section on greening your baby; also, you can find a lot of ecofriendly baby products at Ecobaby (http://ecobaby.com) and information on a green nursery from National Geographic's Green Guide (www.thegreenguide.com/doc/119/greenroomtogrow).

When choosing materials such as paint, furniture, and flooring for your nursery, be aware that many new materials that have a distinctive smell (like the scent that new cars often have) are actually *off-gassing*, or releasing volatile organic chemicals (VOCs) into the air. These chemicals, include formaldehyde and toluene and have been linked with health effects that range from breathing passage irritation to cancer. Try to avoid items with VOCs, especially plywood, particleboard, and upholstered furniture or mattresses that contain formaldehyde or PBDEs (polybrominated diphenyl ethers) as flame retardants; Ikea (www.ikea.com) and Select Comfort (www.selectcomfort.com) have said they're avoiding these substances in upholstery and mattresses. You also can decorate the nursery well before the baby arrives in order to let new materials off-gas or keep new items outside or in the garage for a few days to let the worst of the gases dissipate (The items release significantly more gases when they're new, and off-gassing in plywood and pressed wood can go on for months or even years — yet another reason to buy secondhand.)

Here are some strategies for choosing the most ecofriendly items for your nursery:

✔ **Decor:** Choose natural materials wherever possible, including flooring of solid wood, linoleum, bamboo, cork, or organic cotton or wool carpets; water-based finishes for hardwood floors; paint that contains low or no VOCs; and soft furnishings made from natural, organic fabrics.

✔ **Furniture:** Select solid wood furniture with nontoxic finishes and ensure that the item is durable. You may have to spend a little more on quality, well-constructed furniture, but the fact that it will hold up much longer than other offerings makes it worthwhile. Further lengthen the life of nursery furniture by selecting multipurpose furniture: a crib that can later become a bed, for example, or a changing table that incorporates a chest of drawers. Look for mattresses made from natural materials such as rubber and organic wool or cotton.

✔ **Clothing:** Natural fibers are great, but organic natural fibers are even better: Wool, cotton, hemp, and even bamboo if it comes from sustainable and chemical-free sources are all green options that are becoming more widely available in stores and online.

✔ **Baby care:** Look for products made from natural, organic, and fragrance-free ingredients. Avoid antibacterial products and minimize chemical-impregnated items such as wipes — look for biodegradable, chlorine-free wipes, for example, from Seventh Generation (`www.seventhgeneration.com`) and other ecofriendly companies or use washcloths instead. (Because the issue of cloth versus disposable diapers is a bigger discussion, we devote the whole next section to it.)

✔ **Cleaners:** Avoid antibacterial and chemical cleaners. Instead use naturally based products, from household cleaners to laundry detergents. Stay away from chemical-based fabric softeners, too. More information about natural versus chemical cleaners appears in Chapter 5 of this book, but you can look for products such as Ecover, Method's Free & Clear line, Restore, and Seventh Generation for greener alternatives to conventional cleaning and laundry products. Chapter 3 of Book III gives you recipes for homemade cleaners.

Choosing cloth versus disposable diapers

It's *the* big question for prospective parents: cloth or disposable diapers? Considering that the little tykes need approximately 6,000 of the absorbent necessities before they graduate to being toilet-trained, it's a big question and an important one. Is it better to go with disposable and add to the nation's waste or go with cloth and add to the energy output required to launder them (as well as the inconvenience of having to deal with the messy post-baby cleanup)?

On the pro side of disposables, they're easy; on the con side, they take upwards of 500 years to decompose in landfills, and the 18 billion that get thrown out in the United States annually consume approximately 100,000 tons of plastic and 800,000 tons of tree pulp every year — not exactly the greenest products. Plus, there's the question of what's hidden within them, namely dioxin, a byproduct of bleaching the pulp, which has been linked to cancer, plus other chemicals and fragrances that can cause allergic reactions.

Enter cloth diapers, which have the major disadvantage that they're not convenient — you generally have to presoak the dirty diapers and then wash them in the washing machine (or at least rinse them and have a laundry service take care of washing them). This all means that you're handling dirty diapers several times instead of once (as with disposables). Odor also may be an issue, and the time involved to deal with the dirty diapers most definitely is something to think about, too. Removable, biodegradable, flushable liners for cloth diapers can make the worst of the waste much easier to dispose of — it gets flushed away with an environmental impact far less than that of a disposable diaper (which, of course, isn't flushable at all). (One option is gDiapers, cloth diapers that use plastic-free, flushable inserts for easier cleanup; visit www.gdiapers.com for details.) However, the mess involved with cloth diapers is an issue for many parents, especially when the child has a tummy bug.

The super absorbent polymers (SAP) that disposables and some flushable diaper liners contain are the same polymers that were removed from tampons because they were linked to toxic shock syndrome. SAP can absorb many times their weight in liquid; sodium polyacrylate, for example, can take on 100 times its weight. This characteristic makes them great for diapers, but they may not be so great for your baby, although no conclusive studies exist at this point.

The advantage is that you can use cloth diapers again and again, and some studies indicate that cloth can help if your baby's prone to diaper rash. Other studies have shown that washing diapers takes about the equivalent amount of water as flushing a toilet five times a day for the same period (which may be less than you imagined it would take) and that even when you throw in the energy that your washing machine uses, cloth diapers have half the ecological footprint of disposables (even less if you use a laundry service). (See Chapter 1 for a discussion about ecological or environmental footprints.)

So . . . the ultimate in ecofriendliness where diaper duty is concerned appears to be cloth. The good news is that cloth diapers are much more parent-friendly than they used to be. Forget about pins: The new versions come with snaps or hook-and-loop tape for easy on and easy off. They also come in organic fabric options, including hemp, bamboo, and cotton, and you can choose organic wool covers that help protect the diaper against leaks, too.

Cloth diapers are starting to take up more space on store shelves, but if the selection in your neighborhood is sparse, try Cotton Babies (www.cotton babies.com). Diaperco (www.diaperco.com) sells diapers and has an informative section for anyone new to cloth diapering.

Washing cloth diapers is one occasion when you shouldn't save energy by using a cold wash cycle. Hot water kills germs, which is especially important because the clean diapers go back on your baby. (It's no good being green if it negatively affects hygiene.) Presoak cloth diapers in hot water and then wash in hot water with a cold rinse using detergent that's free of perfumes or dyes. Don't use fabric softener, which can reduce absorbency and cause allergic reactions or irritation.

When it comes to diapers, you don't have to go all the way in either direction. In fact, some childcare providers don't allow cloth diapers, so you may have to compromise there. Or you can use cloth at home and save disposable for when you're out and about or for when your child has a digestive upset and you could really use the extra convenience. If you choose disposable diapers, opt for chlorine-free, biodegradable versions in order to be friendlier to the environment and your baby. And whether you use cloth or disposable, change diapers regularly to help prevent diaper rash and dump the waste down the toilet before either laundering or throwing out diapers. (This step puts human waste where it should be, which is in the sewer system, not the landfill.)

Instilling Green Values at Home

Most children understand green issues — sometimes even better than adults do. Children's curiosity about the world gives them a natural empathy for the state of the environment, for the plight of the animals within it, and even for the situations faced by children in developing countries. When children feel that they can do something to help or make a difference, they usually go to it with enthusiasm.

The most effective way to teach your children to live a green lifestyle — with care and consideration for the environment, animals, and people with whom they share the world — is to live that lifestyle yourself and become a life-size example. When kids see you picking up trash from the park even though you weren't the one who dropped it, they see value in keeping public places clean. When they see you volunteering your time for a worthy cause, they see that giving back to society is worthwhile and important.

From walking them to school to finding ways to reduce your family's trash, every choice that you make helps your children make green choices, too. Involving them in the decision-making — in an age-appropriate way, of course — also helps them learn how to continue making even bigger green decisions as they get older. After all, if they grow up green, a sustainable lifestyle will come naturally to them, allowing them to pass that way of life along to their friends, colleagues, and eventually their own children — a very positive, long-lasting ripple effect.

Starting kids young with green behaviors and activities

Even young children can gain an appreciation for nature and what it takes to protect it. Head outside with them whenever you can and introduce them to the wonder that's the world, from grass to caterpillars to daisies. Help them understand that the world is theirs to enjoy and protect; their desire to safeguard it will come naturally.

When you do something at home to make your life greener, explain the change and your reasons to your children, but don't force changes on them. Lead by example, and they'll likely adopt your plans far more quickly than if you were to force them into something.

Use these suggestions to introduce your children to green living:

- ✔ **Choose an active lifestyle.** Walk, bike, and play with your children regularly.

- ✔ **Opt for public transportation.** Use the car only when necessary; otherwise, demonstrate a commitment to public transportation by taking trains and buses with your children.

- ✔ **Ask for their help.** Younger children in particular may be proud and happy to contribute to grown-up activities. Have them carry the container of vegetable scraps to the compost bin, for example, and have them help you dig out the resulting soil to put on garden beds.

  Older children may want to get involved with green activities, such as cleaning up their neighborhood and organizing the household recycling, because they've learned about environmental issues at school. If they're not enthusiastic, however, you may need to convince them by making it a family-time activity that you do together or by making their allowance partially conditional on their help with such projects around the house.

- ✔ **Introduce them to growers.** Take kids with you to places such as farmers' markets and farms where you pick items yourself so that they understand that food doesn't just come from supermarket shelves.

- ✔ **Consider introducing them to animal life.** Petting farms for younger kids may help them to understand that there's a whole other world beyond their community and prevent farm animals from becoming something that they see only in books or on television.

  Zoos offer a valuable educational and conservation lesson. (Many zoos are involved in breeding programs to help support the population of threatened or endangered species, for example.) If you feel that going to a zoo will help your children understand the wider global environment, look for a zoo that's actively involved in conservation, is accredited through the American Zoo and Aquarium Association (www.aza.org/FindZooAquarium), and provides its animals with as natural an environment as possible along with plenty of mental stimulation.

✔ **Create a family garden and get the kids involved.** Gardens are places where the whole family can practice being green. If you don't have room for a garden, you can involve your kids in planting window boxes and pots with herbs and salad greens.

✔ **Limit consumption.** Choose well-made, durable, quality toys over quantity. (See the next section for more details about quality green toys.) Talk to family and friends about not overwhelming children with too many gifts and about checking with you first if they're considering a big gift. Encourage kids to donate toys they no longer use to other children.

✔ **Encourage conservation.** Let kids know that resource-conserving habits, such as switching off lights and turning off water when brushing their teeth, are expected — and even rewarded.

You don't have to become a paragon of green overnight, and you shouldn't expect your children to either. Start with the things that are easiest to change and remember that every little bit helps. Add more changes gradually, and your family will soon be living greener without even realizing it!

Finding green toys

Thanks to the growing green movement and the Internet, finding toys that fit the environmentally friendly lifestyle is much easier than it used to be. Although you don't want to cut off your children from tools such as electronics that can help them learn, it's a good idea to aim for a balance between screen-oriented playthings and those that boost their imagination, especially if the latter don't expose them to harmful materials.

When looking for green toys, keep these points in mind:

✔ **Choose natural materials.** Toys made from solid wood and nontoxic finishes are your best bet along with those made from natural, preferably organic, fabrics. Avoid soft plastics that contain PVC, which has been linked to health hazards. For babies and toddlers, you can choose stuffed toys that are made from organic cotton and puzzles and pull-along toys that are made from solid wood and nontoxic paints.

✔ **Free up energy.** Choose well-made, durable toys that will last for a long time. The fewer toys that you have to replace, the more energy you save in the processes that manufacture the toys in the first place, and the fewer toys end up in the landfill. Also look for toys that don't require batteries and toys that are driven by alternative energy, such as solar power. (You can find solar-powered frogs, robots, and cars suitable for children from ages about 5 through 10 at many toy stores and online at fatbraintoys.com.)

✔ **Boost imagination.** Ensure that your children have access to unstructured play opportunities, whether outdoors or in. Science-based kits are great sources of inspiration and cover every subject from gardening to chemistry to arts and crafts, but even a collection of ecofriendly dress-up clothes (made from natural fabrics or secondhand items from friends and family) or a collection of building blocks can provide hours of imaginative fun.

✔ **Go local or Fairtrade.** Find out whether local artisans or manufacturers produce toys near you and support their businesses. Buying locally helps reduce the energy costs associated with transporting toys to your local store. If you're considering toys that were made elsewhere, research the manufacturer to find out who made them; look for toys that are certified under Fairtrade programs to ensure that those involved in the manufacturing process were treated well and paid fairly. Local, independent toy stores may carry Fairtrade toys; if not, check out Ten Thousand Villages (www.tenthousandvillages.com), which offers a selection of toys including rattles, puzzles, mobiles, simple musical instruments, kites, and games, all of which are Fairtrade items.

Involving children in green choices

Children like to be able to teach their parents a thing or two, so give them the chance to take the lead at home. Put them in charge of various aspects of your environmental policy at home, and they'll likely love the role. You can help them take this leadership position by involving them in decision-making around the house.

Depending on their ages, you may ask your children to help you do the following things:

✔ Plan healthy, green family menus and then turn them into a shopping list.

✔ Find items around the house to reuse, such as turning computer paper printed on one side only into notebooks or scrap paper for art projects.

✔ Sort through their toys to find items that they'd like to donate to children in need in their community.

✔ Save money as a family to help a charity either at home or around the world; examples include donating to a local food bank or helping a community in Africa build a well to provide a reliable source of water.

✔ Shop for secondhand clothing to ensure that they're comfortable early on with wearing used items. Wait until they're teenagers, and you're swimming upstream to make secondhand a viable option.

✔ Set up bins and a composter to make organizing recycling efforts easy (see Chapter 2 of this book).

Staying Green through the School Year

Green education starts before children even arrive at school when you choose ecofriendly transportation, such as walking or carpooling, to get to and from the classroom. In some cases, of course, children have to take big yellow school buses to school; that's actually a very green way to go, too, despite the bus color. Another simple way to keep your child green at school is to load them up with green school supplies.

Walking or biking to school

If your children's schools are close enough to walk to, leave the car in the garage. Explain to your kids that when you take short journeys in the car, it doesn't have enough time to warm up to run most efficiently and so those journeys cause the most pollution. Walking is the greenest way to travel and does the least damage to the environment.

Start out easy by walking on mild, dry mornings and driving when the weather's rainy or freezing. Gradually work up to walking even when the weather's not so good.

Children love to hang out with their friends, so consider joining forces with the friends' parents if they travel the same path to school as you and your children. This arrangement can give you adult company to chat with, or you can split the task of walking with the children to school. If enough children in your area head in the same direction to school, consider setting up a *walking bus* in which the children all walk together with a parent at the front as the "driver" and a parent at the back. The Pedestrian and Bicycle Information Center maintains a Web site that gives you the complete scoop on a walking bus. Find it at www.walkingschoolbus.org.

Walking isn't just green. It's good exercise and saves you money. You may even get your kids to school faster than if you were navigating busy streets in the car.

When your children are old enough and competent enough on bicycles, let them cycle to school. Consider enrolling them in a cycling proficiency class so that you both feel confident that they can handle themselves safely in traffic. Check with schools, the local police department, or your town's parks and recreation organization to find out about safety course offerings.

Setting up a carpool

If you have to drive your children to school, you can cut down on the number of cars going in the same direction each morning and afternoon by sharing the school run. Organize a group of parents to pick up the number of children that can safely be transported in the smallest car and then take it in turns.

To set up a carpool effectively, first talk to parents you know, such as the ones you see when you drop off your kids or others in your neighborhood, to find out whether their children's schedules match yours. Find out which days work best (or worst) for them and create a schedule that works for everyone, distributing the driving responsibilities evenly. If the driving can't be shared equally, suggest that a small fee be paid to help out with the drivers' fuel and maintenance bills.

For safety reasons, everyone involved in the carpool must have full contact information for all the children's parents, along with the children's addresses, allergy notes, and any important health information. Parents should introduce their own children to the parents who are driving so that "stranger danger" strategies can be maintained.

 Have a system in place to notify the day's driver if something happens to prevent a child from taking the carpool. For example, a phone tree in which each parent calls and passes along messages to another parent may work best in these situations. Also consider making up a schedule that you e-mail to the group to keep everyone on track. Also agree ahead of time on rules, such as everyone wears their seatbelts, appropriate behavior while in the car, and no stopping while on the carpool run.

Stocking up on green school supplies

When your kids head to school, their bags should be filled with as many green school supplies as possible. Look for solar-powered calculators to save on batteries, for example, and for post-consumer recycled paper content in printed products, such as loose-leaf paper and notebooks. Glue, crayons, and markers should be nontoxic, and lunches should be packed in reusable containers rather than disposable plastic and paper bags. Rather than re-using plastic water bottles, which can leach chemicals into the liquid they contain, consider using stainless steel beverage containers such as a Klean Kanteens (www.klean kanteen.com), which are not only lightweight but also child-friendly. (You can purchase a sippy cup version of the Klean Kanteen for younger children.)

Many office-supply stores now stock green paper products along with Energy Star–certified computers (that is, models that consume the least possible amount of energy; see the Energy Star Web site — www.energystar.gov). An Internet search for specific items will also turn up green suppliers such as the Green Office, www.thegreenoffice.com, and Green Earth Office Supply, www.greenearthofficesupply.com, from whom you can order online.

Chapter 5

Keeping Your Home Healthy

· ·

In This Chapter:

▶ Steering clear of manmade contaminants

▶ Detecting carbon monoxide in your home

▶ Honing in on the hazards of Mother Nature

· ·

*Y*our house may well be the picture of health, but you can't always tell by looking. That fresh coat of paint that has the living room looking dazzling isn't necessarily great for the air you're breathing. And you're so used to seeing some of the things that may be making your home sick that you don't notice them anymore — aerosol oven cleaner, anyone?

In this chapter, you find a number of the most common sources of home problems, discover how to detect them, and then arm yourself so that you know what to do when trouble strikes.

Know your enemy, and it shall be vanquished.

Getting Started with General Guidelines

As the other sections in this chapter explain, maintaining a healthy environment encompasses a lot of details, but some general rules are worth knowing for starters. Fortunately, most of them are easy enough to follow:

✔ **Get wise.** Find out what kinds of things to avoid. Understand where nasty little critters like to live and breed. (Carpets, anyone?) Pay attention to things you can't see with the naked eye. In particular, read the warning labels, which spell out precisely what the dangers are.

✔ **Ensure proper ventilation.** Ventilation is essential to health. Getting it can be tough sometimes, especially in the winter. But you don't necessarily need to open windows to ventilate your home; fans go a long way, and so does leaving doors between rooms open.

✔ **Store toxic materials away from the living quarters in your home.** The best place to keep them is in your garage. Many people store toxins underneath the kitchen sink, but this is asking for trouble. Of course, the best bet is not to store toxic materials at all. Buy small containers and toss out the empties. This approach may be a little more expensive, but it makes sense, especially if you have kids.

✔ **Pay attention to your cleaning products.** A surprising number of household cleaners are unhealthy. When possible, use environmentally friendly cleaning supplies. Check out the following sources of green cleaning information and products:

- **Household Products Database:** www.householdproducts.nlm.nih.gov

- **Eco-Source:** www.eco-source.com

- **Natural Choices, Home Safe Products, LLC:** www.oxyboost.com

- **Seventh Generation:** www.seventhgeneration.com

- **Sun and Earth, Inc.:** www.sunandearth.com

Avoiding Some of the Worst Offenders

We are surrounded by manmade chemicals, and most of them are quite benign. However, the harmful chemicals that have given their ilk a bad name certainly are worth weeding from your household as much as possible. In the upcoming sections, you find out about the chemicals within your house and suggestions for living without them.

Fighting off formaldehyde

Formaldehyde gas evaporates (technically referred to as *outgassing*) from a wide range of common household materials, such as

✔ Particleboard used as subflooring and in shelving, cabinetry, and furniture

✔ Hardwood plywood paneling and decorative wall coverings

✔ Carpets, draperies, furniture fabrics, and permanent press clothes treated to resist mold and fire

✔ Paints, shellacs, waxes, polishes, oils, and other coating materials

✔ Glues and adhesives

✔ Molded plastics

✔ Insecticides, fumigants, disinfectants, deodorants, germicidal soaps, and embalming fluids

✔ Cosmetics, shampoos, nail hardeners, mouthwashes, and antiperspirants

✔ Household cleaning products

✔ Water heaters and gas ranges

✔ Old mobile homes and prefab-style houses

Exposure to formaldehyde results in cold-like symptoms: coughing, runny nose, sore throat, fatigue, vomiting, and nosebleeds. The Environmental Protection Agency classifies it as a carcinogen and can also cause menstrual disorders, chronic headaches, and periodic memory lapses. To test for formaldehyde, obtain a simple testing monitor (they cost between $25 and $50; search for "formaldehyde monitor" on the Internet). You leave a vial open to your home's interior air for a specified period of time and then cap the vial and send it to a lab. The lab makes the appropriate measurements and then mails you the results.

To avoid formaldehyde:

✔ **Paint over old plywood surfaces with a water-based sealant.** Old kitchen cabinets are good candidates for repainting, as are old paneling and particleboard.

✔ **Check before you buy.** You can usually find out how much formaldehyde a produce contains by consulting with the manufacturer, who is required to supply this information.

✔ **Keep the air flowing.** Formaldehyde is an airborne gas, so good ventilation can alleviate the problem to a great extent. Dangers are more acute in the winter months when homes are closed off.

✔ **If you're buying composite wood or agrifiber products, get them with no added urea formaldehyde.** Look on the label, or call the manufacturer.

Vanquishing Volatile Organic Compounds

Volatile Organic Compounds (VOCs) is the name given to a class of carbon-based gaseous contaminants emitted from a wide range of home products:

✔ Solvents used in lacquers, adhesives, waxes, cleaning agents, cosmetics, paints and paint removers, and leather finishes. Common names are benzene, xylene, methyl collosolve, ethyl collosolve, methyl ethyl ketone, and trichloroethylene (TCE).

✔ Phenols found in household disinfectants, antiseptics, perfumes, mouthwashes, polishes, waxes, glues and, ironically, air fresheners. Phenols are also a byproduct of combustion, so they're more prevalent in winter, when the windows are closed.

✔ Aerosol sprays propelled by propane, butane, and nitrous oxide gases.

✔ Permanent press fabrics, polyesters, and most synthetic materials.

✔ Pesticides, disinfectants, pet collars, and plant food. Pesticides are by far the worst source of contaminants in a home, and the chemicals last for years. Particularly noxious are the chemicals used by pest control companies, which spray heavy concentrations all around the outside of a house and often right inside. These companies have an incentive to make sure that insects don't appear, and the best way to obliterate them is to use more than enough chemicals.

✔ Electrical equipment containing PCBs. This material is used because it's particularly fire-resistant. The problem is that when it's exposed to fire, some of it burns off. That's why whenever an electrical fire involves a utility company transformer, a special unit of the fire department is dispatched with high-tech equipment to protect the firemen. The same sort of contamination occurs in your home.

Avoiding VOCs

One of the easiest ways to avoid these chemicals is by not bringing them into your home. To do that, read the labels on the materials you buy. By law, manufacturers must list the contents of their products, particularly if potentially noxious chemicals are in the mix.

Some prime culprits that you may want to include on your do-not-buy or be-careful-if-you-use list include

✔ **Chlorine bleach:** A component of most household cleansers. Many people use chlorine all the time without realizing it's unhealthy. If you must use it, make sure to allow for ventilation.

✔ **Oven cleaners:** Particularly bad news as they outgas for a long time. Buy an oven with a built-in cleaning feature, and when you're using it, make sure the ventilation is adequate. If you do need to clean your oven, use a mixture of baking soda and water and spread it around the dirty spots. Wait until it dries; then wipe it away. Chapter 3 of Book III gives you more ideas for safe, homemade cleaners.

✔ **Air fresheners:** These don't freshen air. They fool your nose into thinking the room is fresher. They don't remove the odor-causing problem; they simply overwhelm it with superior force (in many cases from phthalates, a harmful chemical group that you can find out about in Chapter 1 of this book). So now your room is completely full of swirling chemicals. Use an air-filter instead, or, better yet, find out what's causing the stink and get rid of it. Unless, of course, it's Uncle Albert.

✔ **Carpet:** Particularly risky, especially if it's old and dirty. In fact, carpet in general is a bad idea for people who are sensitive to chemical exposures of any kind. Find tips for living healthfully with carpeting in Chapter 5 of Book III.

✔ **Aerosol sprays:** Avoid them like the plague. Most household products that used to come in aerosol cans now come in misters, which aren't quite as convenient and fun, but are much better for your family.

✔ **Oil-based paints:** Use latex paints with zero VOCs instead. This paint is easier to use and is better for your health.

✔ **Art supplies:** If you love to paint seascapes and gorgeous landscapes, find out what sorts of chemicals you're breathing. You're right over the work for extended periods, so even if the chemicals aren't particularly strong, you're dosing yourself up more than you would with just about any other hobby you can find. Make sure that the area you work in is well ventilated.

✔ **Ceramics:** Especially ripe for airborne abuses. If you insist on making ceramic artwork, do a lot of research before you partake.

✔ **Pesticides:** Come on now, do you really need pesticides? You may find insects ugly — some have thousands of legs and eyes and furry little tentacles. Many of them can sting and cause other problems; plus they fly around and distract you when you're watching television. But the fact is, when you use pesticides, you're exposing yourself to the same chemicals that kill the insects. Do you think you're any more immune to the assault than a bug? In fact, statistical studies have shown that the only difference between you and a bug is that you are bigger, although this size advantage may not be true in Florida.

✔ **Any product that doesn't list its contents on the label:** Manufacturers aren't required to list their inert ingredients, but that doesn't mean they don't contain harmful chemicals.

Minimizing the risk

Despite your best efforts, chances are you won't be able to purge your home of all VOCs. In that case, you need to minimize the risk:

✔ **Ventilation is imperative.** Many noxious chemicals evaporate quickly, so exposure is only temporary. Always use glues and solvents in adequate ventilation. If possible, paint outdoors and leave whatever you're painting there until the paint is very dry.

✔ **Store paint, fuel, and pesticides well away from human habitats.** Or better yet, don't store them at all. Buy what you need and no more. Even containers that are sealed can still leak poisons. And admit it; when you seal a paint can and store it, you rarely, if ever, end up using the remainder. Most likely it just sits on the shelf until you move.

✔ **Wear protective clothing, safety goggles, and masks with appropriate filters when necessary.** If you must use a potentially toxic chemical, dress accordingly. Most of the stores where you purchase chemicals carry the appropriate equipment and can advise you accordingly. Work outside whenever possible.

✔ **Trust your nose; it's smarter than your brain.** In general, your nose will tell you when something is noxious. Trust your senses, and when in doubt, back off, read the label, open some windows, and start up some fans.

✔ **Never eat food while working with chemicals.** This just makes the ingestion ten times worse. Also, never eat chemicals while working with food — this is somewhat intuitive.

✔ **Never use paint stripper indoors without ventilation.** Never. You may just as well drink a gallon of gasoline while playing with matches to accomplish the same end. And you're better off buying nontoxic, biodegradable paint strippers in the first place.

Eschewing asbestos

Asbestos has been used to provide heating and acoustical insulation and fireproofing, strengthen building materials and make them more durable, enhance the aesthetic value of a product, and even to make it easier to clean. Unfortunately, it's very toxic.

Finding asbestos

Around the home, you can find asbestos fibers

✔ In gypsum wallboard, textured paint, joint compounds, and spackling compounds in older homes (pre-1970).

✔ In older homes in insulation used around pipes, as well as in the paper wrapped around the pipe insulation.

✔ In a lot of old appliances, which use asbestos for insulation. In particular, the seals around doors in old wood-burning stoves are almost always made of asbestos. As they get old and crumbly, they're almost guaranteed to release fibers into the air.

✔ In siding shingles and sheet flooring, especially in older homes.

✔ In some kinds of floor tiles, particularly linoleum, which have asbestos backing. The presence of asbestos is not a problem until you decide to remodel and remove the tiles.

✔ Sprayed onto walls and ceilings for both decoration and insulation.

✔ Spun or woven into textiles, blankets, curtains, ropes, and lamp wicks.

How can you tell whether you have an asbestos issue? It's not easy, but if you're suspicious, finding out for sure may be worth the trouble. Consult an expert (look up "asbestos" in the phone book). Or check with the U.S. Consumer Product Safety Commission (www.cpsc.gov) and the Center for Science in the Public Interest (www.cspinet.org).

A smoking gun

Cigarette smoke is full of hostile chemicals. If you smoke, you know exactly what you're doing to yourself and everybody around you, but consider this new angle: From an efficiency standpoint, smoking is about the worst thing you can possibly do because not only are you introducing health hazards into your home and everywhere else you go, you're paying a hefty price for cigarettes at the same time.

At the very least, go outside and hide behind the garage or something.

Solving your asbestos problem

In the 1970s, asbestos was largely banned due to its correlation with certain types of cancer and other diseases. But fortunately, asbestos is only harmful when the fibers become airborne. Here's what to do to make sure that your asbestos stays grounded:

- ✔ **Simply leave asbestos products alone.** In particular, don't gouge them or tear them apart. It's the same as with mountain lions: Leave them alone, and they'll leave you alone.

- ✔ **Cover them.** Covering them is often better than tearing them out and installing new materials. For example, if you have a floor with asbestos, simply install a new floor over that. If you have asbestos siding, install new siding over it or paint it with a sealant type of paint. (Ask at your paint store; a number of options are available.) If you have asbestos insulation on pipes and it's starting to crumble, wrap it with a new coat of insulation and then paint that with latex. You'll have much better insulation, and you'll have squelched the problem.

If you have to remove old asbestos products, the best bet is to hire a pro. Find one from a local environmental protection agency.

Burning Up with Combustion Products

If you have a gas-burning furnace, a wood-burning fireplace or stove, a gas cooking stove, or gas water heaters (in other words, any type of combustion device) in your home, you need to take extra precautions. You also need to be careful if you have an attached garage, where exhaust fumes may enter your home.

Carbon monoxide (CO) is an invisible, odorless gas that's created by combustion (like carbon dioxide [CO_2], its more newsworthy cousin). In a well-designed home, chimneys and vents carry these gases away.

CO alarms are simple, inexpensive insurance policies to warn you if CO gas is building up in your home. They cost between $20 and $45 and work essentially the same as a smoke detector: They emit a high, shrill squeal when they detect high levels of the gas.

Buy an alarm, or alarms, that are UL-approved. You can get a digital type that plugs into your home's electrical outlet system and has a display that tells you what the concentrations are in your home. (Just make sure that it has a battery backup in case the power goes out.) Even though the level in your home may be low enough for safety, you can see how the levels vary, and many times you can use this information to solve problems before they become extreme.

The best locations for CO alarms are near sleeping rooms on each level of your home. Position them away from drafts and solvents, which can inadvertently trigger a response.

If an alarm triggers, get everybody out of the house. Call your fire department and tell it what happened; then do what it tells you. Don't ignore an alarm. Always find out why it went off and solve the problem.

Beating Back Natural Hazards

Unfortunately, manmade chemicals are not the only noxious chemicals you need to contend with in your home. Mother Nature has a few of her own dirty tricks.

Slipping through the cracks: Radon

Radon can penetrate into a home when uranium is present in nearby soil or rock, thereby introducing radioactivity into your home. Granite, shale, and phosphate bedrock under your house are the prime culprits, as well as gravel derived from these materials. The hazards of radon are the same as with exposure to any radioactive materials. Cancer is the worst.

Radon concentrates in your house — especially in basements, where leaks through the foundation are common. The EPA did random tests across the entire country and found that up to 25 percent of all homes with basements are susceptible to radon poisons in potentially dangerous levels. Many states require radon tests to be performed when a home changes ownership.

The only way to know if a home is contaminated is to test, and a number of inexpensive means are available, the two most common being charcoal detectors and alpha-track devices.

- ✔ **Charcoal detectors:** You can find these tests on the Internet by entering "radon testing" into your browser. You place a charcoal detector in a cool, dry spot in your basement for no more than a week. Then you seal the container and send it to a lab. You need to repeat the test twice to get a good result. The cost is around $10 to $25 apiece.

- ✔ **Alpha-track devices:** These tests give better results than charcoal detectors, and are recommended if your home fails the charcoal test. A strip of special plastic material is exposed to the air in your basement; then you send the plastic to a lab for analysis. Alpha-track devices require a minimum of four weeks of exposure but cost little more than the charcoal devices.

The good news is that, most of the time, radon infiltration can be contained rather easily. Two solutions exist: You can stop it from getting into the house, or you can dilute it once it gets in. When fresh air is imposed into a radon-contaminated region, the levels go down immediately. For ways to restrict radon entry, consult a professional or see Chapter 2 of Book II on sealing your home. You can also search the Internet for solutions. Enter "radon contamination" into your search engine. At the very least, if you have a radon-contaminated basement, seal the doorway between the basement and the ground floor of your home — a good idea in general, as you'll also be preventing other airborne biological agents from entering your living area.

Operating in secret: Biological agents

Natural microscopic organisms include bacteria, viruses, fungi, molds, mildews, and mites — most of which are necessary for life. Pollen is a collector of spores from seed-bearing plants. All these can be either tracked in on shoes and clothing from the outdoors, or simply fly in on the wings of chance. And all multiply indoors; only some of them can cause irritations and illnesses.

The greatest source of nutrition for indoor microbes is the three or four grams of skin that flake off the average human body once every day. (Did you know that most of the dust in your home comes from human skin?)

Symptoms of sensitivity include the usual retinue of allergic reactions: runny nose, sneezing, watery eyes, sore throat, coughing, and upper respiratory discomfort. Hives and rashes are also common. Flu-like symptoms can result, including fever, chills, malaise, muscle aches, and chest tightness.

No easy-to-use kits are available to measure for microbe contamination. If your family seems to suffer from any of these ailments more commonly when the house is closed up (and wet or humid), you should do a bit of investigating.

The first place to look? Wherever there's water. Face it, water can be a big problem. Especially when left standing or combined with just enough warmth to create an oozy stew. Microbes *love* damp places. That's why the biggest front in your war on biological agents is in the marshes — wherever there's water. The following list tells you where to look and what to do to fix the problems you may find:

- Wet carpeting is a virtual breeding ground for all kinds of nasty little critters. If you have carpet in your bathroom, replace it with vinyl or tile and make sure to seal the joints and edges extremely well. No carpet in the laundry room or kitchen, either. If you have area rugs, wash them in hot water occasionally or take them to the cleaners for thorough cleaning.

- Clothes dryers are hot and wet, perfect for microbe propagation. Make sure that your dryer is vented well to the outdoors. If you have a leaky washing machine, especially if it's in your basement and it's perpetually wet underneath, you have a microbe farm.

- Clean all drains once a week with hot water or white vinegar. Microbes love the filthy, wet environment down in a drain. If you have a drain in the basement that seldom sees water flushed into it, it's a prime candidate for a science-fiction movie.

- Repair all leaks in the roof or plumbing system. Leaks generally result in rotting wood or sheetrock. Not only do water issues cause contamination, but they also depreciate the value of your home.

- Repair leaky faucets. In addition to being wasteful, every drop splashes and humidifies far more than you'd guess.

- Wet insulation materials are very fertile. If you have a leak in your roof or siding, you probably have wet insulation, which doesn't work very well and encourages rot, mold, and infestations.

- If you have leaks in your grout, you have wet, oozing sheetrock somewhere beneath. You can fix leaks in grout very easily with silicon caulking. The clear stuff matches any decor.

- Never allow water to pool, especially in your basement. Find and fix whatever problem is causing the water to pool.

- Fix leaky toilets. They're just asking for it. Not to mention the fact that you're going to pay a lot more than you need to when you have to fix the rotted subflooring. And fuzzy toilet seat covers are simply nuts, if you value your health.

✔ Install a vent or a window in your bathroom. An enclosed bathroom with no ventilation equals microbe nirvana. You need to let your bathroom dry out thoroughly. Failing a vent or window, use a fan and keep the bathroom door open when not in use. Make sure that the joints and cracks are sealed well.

Book IV gives you a lot of great suggestions for making changes to your home that improve its health.

Finding Easy Decluttering Tips to Improve Your Home's Health

In an efficient, green home, there's a place for everything, and everything is in its place. (That may well mean cutting back on the buying, which is a great sustainable action.) Here are sundry tips to get you going in the right direction:

✔ **Use the sun to clean and sanitize.** Put cushions, sheets, rugs, clothes, and so forth out into the hot sun. To find out just how well this works, try putting a sweaty shirt in direct sunlight for a couple of hours. It'll smell like new.

✔ **Use stove vent fans.** When grease mixes with dust in the air, it wafts around your kitchen and sticks. Over time, it makes a big mess.

✔ **Avoid humidifiers, if possible.** They encourage bugs and mildew.

✔ **Make sure to keep a good-sized, rough mat at each door.** When you come in, shed your shoes; put slippers by the door and change into them.

✔ **Keep your plants healthy.** Healthy plants clean the air. Fake plants are dust magnets, and they launch colonies.

✔ **Seal the garage floor.** This makes for a cleaner garage, with less dust buildup that would eventually make it into your home. Use a nontoxic, zero-VOC sealer.

✔ **Wax wood.** Doing so keeps moisture from permeating into the grain and keeps the dust down.

✔ **Clean curtains without washing.** Curtains don't need to be washed. Instead, put them in a clothes dryer, turn the setting to no-heat, and tumble the dust out of them in a matter of minutes.

Book I

Green Living

Book II
Energy Efficiency

The 5th Wave   By Rich Tennant

In this book . . .

*J*ust a twist of the thermostat or flip of the light switch away, the energy you use in your home is easy to take for granted. And with all that easily accessible energy, maybe the figures on your utility bills may come to seem inevitable. Far from it: Simple fixes can have a major effect on the amount that shows up on your utility bills.

The chapters in this part of the book show you how to find out where your house has room for energy-efficiency improvement and then how to make the changes that impact your energy use, including insulating your walls and sealing up your ducts, lighting without hogging electricity, cutting back on your water use, and ensuring that your appliances are operating well (or replacing them). You also find information about harnessing the sun's power to power your home.

Here are the contents of Book II at a glance:

Chapter 1

Taking Stock of Your Energy Efficiency and Use

. . . .

In This Chapter

▶ Weighing in on what determines your energy usage

▶ Looking into the details of your energy consumption

▶ Running through a sample energy expenditure

▶ Considering your carbon contribution

▶ Performing energy audits in your home

. . . .

*I*f you want to improve the energy efficiency of your home in an, um, *effi-cient* manner, you need to first understand the economics of your overall consumption. When you make investments in time or money, they should be focused and deliberate in order to ensure good payback.

Unfortunately, most people don't have a good handle on the specifics of how and where they're using energy and other resources in their homes. As the saying goes, "The devil is in the details." In this chapter, you find a detailed system for analyzing your resource use.

Getting a Handle on Your Energy Usage

The ultimate goal is to deduce how much you're paying for different sources of energy and then tackle those costs based on what your main objective is. For example, your primary goal may be cost reduction as you strive for efficiencies, or your main objective may be pollution mitigation or energy conservation. In any case, you need to first consider the total resource consumption in your home.

Looking at nationwide statistics gives you a baseline for comparison. Does your own usage make sense, or can you make easy changes? Do you need to simply change your habits, or are you going to have to invest time and money in equipment improvements? Table 1-1 shows how a typical North American home uses energy (averaged over the course of a year). For the purposes of this data, a typical home has 1,600 square feet, two baths, three bedrooms, and 2.3 occupants in a region with moderate weather patterns.

Table 1-1	Yearly Energy Use for a Typical Home
Purpose or Use	*Percentage of Total Energy Used*
Space heating	47
Water heating	21
Lighting	8
Space cooling	6
Refrigeration	5
Cooking	4
Electronics	3
Clothes washing/drying	3
Computers	1
Other	2

These values represent total energy used, not how much that energy costs. The cost of different energy sources varies widely. For example, if you heat your home by chopping wood yourself and burning it in a wood stove, your heating costs may be almost zero, but that obviously doesn't mean you're consuming zero energy to heat your home. If you have a solar water heater on your roof, your water heating cost may be zero, but 21 percent of your energy consumption can still be attributed to heating water. The cost of equipment also factors into the equation. For example, you had to buy that solar heater, and that's not cheap.

Focusing on your own home sweet home

Obviously, if you don't fit the typical profile described in Table 1-1, your energy consumption will be different. To a large degree, personal lifestyle dictates energy consumption. If you're gone all day and the home is empty, for example, you can lower your thermostat and save. If you're diligent about turning off unused lights, your lighting component will be less. If you tolerate heat and cold better than most, you can save on heating and cooling. And so on.

Energy use around the world

To put the energy consumption of the United States in perspective, take a look at how much energy is used (per capita) in different countries around the world:

Country	Btus Per Person Per Year
Canada	418
United States	339
Western Europe	149
Japan	172
China	33

Canada is cold, so its citizens require a lot of heat. But their high consumption also reflects the fact that energy is relatively inexpensive in Canada. When this is the case, regardless of where in the world it may be, there is little incentive to conserve or practice efficiency.

What's more interesting is to compare American consumption with that of Western Europe. It would be very difficult to argue, as one can do when comparing the United States to China, that the large difference reflects quality of lifestyle. Western Europeans, in many ways, enjoy better lifestyles than Americans. So why is their per capita consumption so low? Because they've been inculcated by high energy prices for so long that energy conservation and efficiency are ingrained into the very fabric of their societies.

As you evaluate how your home varies from the typical energy consumption numbers, spend some time going around your house, looking at all the different ways you consume energy and resources. Just by paying more attention, you can learn a lot.

Where you live and the type of house you live in

Where you live has a big impact on how much energy you use. Folks sweating through summers in the sunny Southwest don't have the same heating and cooling needs as those shivering through winters in the Upper Peninsula of Michigan. If you're in a hot climate, you may need very little heat, but your cooling bill is higher. If you're in Alaska, your heating bill is much higher.

Different home styles also make a difference. Apartments and many condos have common walls, and the heat and cooling losses are less. Homes with a lot of windows have poorer insulation, while those that are surrounded by trees and natural windbreaks suffer less heat loss.

The type of HVAC you have

HVAC stands for *heating, ventilation, and air conditioning*. Most homes have *forced air systems,* which means ducts and fans push air through the home. Some homes have radiant heat, and many homes have wood stoves or other combustion appliances.

Heating is the biggest single component of the utility budget in most homes, and it's subject to the most variation in energy consumption. Thus, it pays to know as much as you can about your home's heating resources. Ask yourself these questions:

- ✓ **What kind of heating source(s) do you use?** A wood-burning stove, gas fireplace, electric heat pump, baseboard heater, free-standing heater, radiator, and so on? Figure out how much you spend on each source of heat.

- ✓ **How old is your system, and what's its expected lifetime?** In general, the older the system, the less efficient it is — not because old technology is inferior, but because back in the day, people didn't worry about energy efficiency as much as we do now, and paying more for an efficient system just wasn't worth it.

- ✓ **Do you have a central air conditioner or window units?** Do you use fans, an evaporative cooler, dehumidifiers, and so on? Include them in your assessment of your energy consumption.

As you think about your own energy consumption, look at your neighbors and see how their consumption differs from yours. What is the most popular HVAC system in your area, for example, and what are new homes in your area being equipped with? The answers to these types of questions can give you valuable information about the kind of technologies that work best in your region. Heat pumps, for example, work well in moderate climates but not in extremely cold climates. If nobody in your area uses a heat pump, there's probably a good reason. And if everybody is burning wood in a stove, it's probably because the availability and cost of wood is advantageous.

The people who live in your home

Heating and cooling don't depend on how large your family is, but on the ways that people in your family use energy. You may have to turn the thermostat lower in the summer and higher in the winter because of personal preference and potential health issues. If a member of your family has special needs, such as air filtration for asthma, for example, you should factor that in. If your family is very sensitive to exposure to contaminants, you're probably paying more for filters and cleaning services.

Your water usage

Where do you get your water, and how much do you use? If a well supplies your water, your electric bill is larger, but your water bill is nonexistent. If you take long, hot showers or if your family is large, your water heating component is higher. If you have a solar water heater, this component may be costing you next to nothing on a monthly basis. And if you have kids, as any parent can tell you, you probably wash a lot of clothes.

The type of amenities you have

Be sure not to leave life's little extras off your radar as you scope out things that consume energy around your home. For example, do you have a swimming pool or spa? Pool pumps consume a lot of electricity, especially in the summer. Spas consume a lot of power, especially in the winter. What about a massive home entertainment center? These items can easily consume more energy than an old refrigerator, which is about the most inefficient appliance ever made. And if you're charging a golf cart or powering a motor home in your driveway, keep in mind that they take a lot of power, too. Room full of aquariums? Giant gym? You get the point.

Special situations

If you're running a business in your home, your lighting, heating, and cooling costs will be higher. Your power bill may also be higher if you're running heavy equipment.

Book II

Energy Efficiency

Other things to think about

Many people who want to become more energy efficient do it for two reasons: to save money and to save the planet. If you're one of the many people interested in polluting less, add the following to your list of possible areas for improvement:

- ✔ What kind of garbage service do you have? Are there alternatives? Does your trash collection agency offer recycling, for example, and if so, what kind of recycling? You can call the customer-service number for answers.

- ✔ Do you have sewer service, or are you using a septic tank? If you're using a septic tank, how old is it and how long has it been since it was serviced? If you don't stay on top of your septic system, you may incur extra costs when problems arise.

- ✔ How much carbon and other pollutions are you producing in the process of consuming energy in your home? If you have a cheap wood stove, your cost may be very low (if you cut your own wood), but your carbon footprint astronomical. Is this important to you? (See the section "Calculating Your Own Carbon Footprint," later in this chapter, for details on how to measure your footprint.)

Do you have equipment that you know is going to need replacement? Are you paying a lot of repair bills for a particular piece of equipment? Would you like to invest in improvement? Check to see whether government agencies in your area are offering subsidies for certain types of equipment. Your utility may offer subsidies, too. See Chapter 4 of Book VII for more details.

Big reasons for high energy bills

Do you have a really high bill? One that sticks out like a sore thumb? Here are the most likely reasons:

✔ The addition of occupants in your home

✔ The addition of appliances, like a freezer in the garage

✔ Faulty appliances

✔ High rates of outdoor air infiltration into your home. You may have a faulty weather seal on a door that needs fixing, or you may have a bad attic trap door.

✔ The use of too much electrical resistance heating

✔ Hot water leaks

✔ Use of appliances with large motors (pumps, compressors, air conditioners)

✔ Seasonal appliances — electric blankets, a dehumidifier, lots of shop lighting, power tools

✔ An estimated bill or one that reflects a higher time period

✔ A wedding or a big party

✔ Uncle Bill's motor home parked in the driveway

Figuring Out What You Spend

The best way to figure out what you spend — and where you potentially can cut back — is to dissect your utility bills. By doing this calculation, you get good data on specifically where to look for the most rewarding investments in efficiency.

Figuring out what you spend is basically a three-step process:

1. **Gather all your data.**

2. **Plot it month by month.**

3. **Analyze your results.**

The following sections give you the details.

Collecting the data

The first thing you need to do is collect a stack of utility bills. If you don't already have them, call your utility companies (customer-service numbers are always listed on the bills) and have them send you copies of your bills for the past few years. Most utilities don't charge for this service, and some even do data analysis for you: They graph the data, which is much nicer than a load of raw numbers; ask when you call. They may even offer other services, such as a free home energy audit.

In addition to your utility bills (water, electric, gas, trash, and sewer), you need to compile a list of all the expenses associated with the resources you use. Here's a sampling of what you need, but you may have other items not on this list:

- ✔ **Trash runs to the dump:** If you take trash to the dump yourself, estimate the cost by including everything: gasoline for your truck, other transport expenses, costs at the landfill, and so on.

- ✔ **Manufactured logs:** If you use manufactured logs, you don't need to come up with receipts; just estimate how many you use and how much they cost. Transport and storage may also be significant.

- ✔ **Power generator:** If you bought one, how much did it cost? If you rent one, include the rental cost. Also include the cost of the gasoline you use to run it.

- ✔ **Firewood:** If you use firewood, include costs for the chainsaw, saw blades, transportation for firewood, and rental (or purchase price) of a wood splitter.

- ✔ **Wood pellets and bio-energy products of any kind:** Include all costs associated with these resources.

- ✔ **Propane or natural gas:** If you use either energy source, include not only the cost of the product, but also rental agreements, maintenance, and so on. A lot of people pay a yearly rental for their propane tank.

- ✔ **Barbecue grill:** Calculate how much you spend for charcoal, the propane, and the tanks. How much did the grill itself cost?

- ✔ **Lawn tools:** Include any gasoline you buy for them, as well as the gas canister if you bought one. If you buy gas (and/or a gas canister) for a generator, include those costs, too.

- ✔ **Kerosene:** If you use kerosene for lanterns, cooking, or heating, include those costs.

- ✔ **Space heaters, portable air conditioners, dehumidifiers, swamp coolers, and so on:** If you bought any of this equipment, include how much it cost and estimate how much it costs to run. Check labels for power consumption and then estimate how much time the equipment is on and when.

- ✔ **Candles and light bulbs:** Add them to your list if you use them.

- ✔ **Batteries and chargers:** In some homes, batteries are very expensive, and most people don't consider them a part of their power consumption, but they definitely are.

- ✔ **Maintenance and repair costs:** These costs apply to energy equipment, such as a woodstove, HVAC filters, appliances, and so on.

- ✔ **New equipment:** If you bought a new water heater, new HVAC, or anything else along these lines, add the replacement costs to your list, as well as any delivery and installation charges.

- ✔ **Insulation:** If you insulated your pipes, the cost is directly related to your energy consumption.

- ✔ **Loans to buy energy-creating equipment:** If you took out a loan to buy something like a generator or woodstove, be sure to include the interest on the loan as you calculate your energy costs.

- ✔ **Permits, fees, and taxes:** Some additions require permits; some up your taxes. You may have to obtain a county permit for installing a wood or gas stove, for example. Or you may pay higher property taxes because of a sunroom addition.

- ✔ **Bottled water:** If you drink it, estimate how much and the cost.

As you compile your list, you're likely to find that you're spending a lot more for resources than you thought, and you may be surprised by some of the details. You're already moving forward!

Plotting the details, month by month

Ultimately, you need to do some month-by-month estimations. The power company bill is the easiest, along with water and trash. Here are some rules for allocating other resource costs by month:

- ✔ If you have a propane tank that's filled periodically by the propane company, you'll have a tough time figuring out the monthly usage. Just get the yearly total and divide that by 12. If you use the propane only for heat, allocate the cost to those months when you use heat. If you use some for hot water and some for heat, divvy it up as best you can. Double-check the total.

- ✔ Ditto with firewood and all the associated expenses. Most people buy a big stack once a year. How much did you use each month? Divvy up the costs as best you can and make sure that the total is right.

- ✔ Servicing for equipment should be allocated according to the use of that equipment. If you serviced a heater, allocate the cost only to those months when you use heat.

✔ Even if your water bill is fixed, estimate how much water you used on a monthly basis. If possible, you should try to divide your water usage according to the various functions for which you use it, such as sewer, laundry, dishwasher, and so on. Landscaping may be the biggest water consumer in your household, and this fact is important to know.

For large equipment expenditures, accountants use a term called *depreciation*. You can use the same calculation to determine monthly costs of a piece of equipment. Here's how:

1. **Determine what you paid.**

   Example: A gas fireplace costs $4,000 plus tax, plus another $200 for permits and inspection.

2. **Estimate how much that equipment increased the value of your home.**

   A gas fireplace may increase the value by $2,500.

3. **Subtract how much the equipment increased the value of your home from its total cost to get the net cost.**

4. **Estimate the lifetime of the equipment, in months.**

   The fireplace should be usable for ten years, or 120 months.

5. **Calculate the monthly depreciation by dividing the net value by the number of months in the equipment's lifetime.**

Book II

Energy Efficiency

You may want to plot several years' worth of graphs to get a comprehensive idea of your energy consumption. Individual years may be subject to strange weather patterns or one-time-only events, like a big wedding or a lot of relatives visiting at Christmas. You also want to watch out for isolated events on your bills. If, for example, one of your monthly statements includes a one-time deduction as a result of your electric company settling a lawsuit with energy providers who charged too much, you need to factor this sort of thing out because it has no bearing on your habits.

Keeping Up with the Joneses: A Real-Life Scenario

The best way to illustrate how to put all your data together is to use Bill Toomuch as an example. Bill and his small family live on a five-acre ranch in California in a 2,700-square-foot house. With the exception of a small gas fireplace in their great room, all their energy comes from the electric company. They have an above-ground swimming pool and a hot tub. Water is supplied by a well. Analyzing Bill's energy consumption demonstrates by example how to go about systematically analyzing your own situation.

Looking at Bill's resource costs

Bill lists his resource costs as follows:

- Bill called his energy company, PG&E, and got four years' worth of history, broken down by month.

- Because his house has a well, Bill doesn't have a water bill, but the cost of his water supply shows up on his electric bill because the well is powered by an electric pump.

- The household fills a 64-gallon trash container every week. They also fill a 64-gallon container for recyclables every other week. Paper, cardboard, bottles, cans, and plastics are all placed into a single recycling bin. The cost is $32 per month.

- Bill uses three gallons of gasoline a month in lawn mowers, leaf blowers, and so on. That's around $8 per month.

- Bill spends $15 per month in propane for a barbecue.

- The HVAC system broke down and cost $267 to fix, for a monthly total of $22.25.

- In the colder months, Bill burns liquid propane in the gas fireplace in the great room. His costs by winter month are

Month	Cost
January	$242
February	$180
March	$65
April	$10
October	$142
November	$265
December (Christmas cheer!)	$342

- Bill's wife loves candles; they cost around $28 per month.

- Bill spends $23 per month in batteries for remotes, flashlights, sprinkler controllers, and so on.

- The house is on a septic tank, so it has no sewer. Every three years the tank must be pumped out at a cost of $300, which is $100 per year, or $8 per month. Last year a repair was made at a cost of $480, which is amortized over ten years at $48 per year.

Plotting Bill's energy expenditures

Table 1-2 shows an example of annual energy expenditures plotted by month.

Table 1-2	Monthly Energy Expenditures, Plotted by Month			
Month	kWh Used	Charges ($)	Price ($)/kWh	Total Utility Cost ($)
Jan	2290	380	0.166	$62
Feb	2449	433	.177	753
Mar	2452	456	.186	602
Apr	2266	407	.18	547
May	1715	290	.17	430
June	1676	325	.194	465
July	1948	404	.21	544
Aug	1963	443	.226	583
Sep	1444	267	.185	407
Oct	1460	267	.183	549
Nov	1663	312	.188	717
Dec	2319	406	.175	888
Total:	23,645	$4,390	.186 average	$7,247
Average per month	1,970	$366		$361

Book II

Energy Efficiency

Analyzing Bill's energy costs

If you take a close look at Bill's data, you notice a few interesting — and enlightening — details:

- ✔ The heater is on a lot in the winter, and the air conditioner is on a lot in the summer. The rates are higher in the summer than they are in the winter. Your data should look similar, unless you have unusual climate conditions. If you're in a cold climate, the magnitudes of the data may be different, but the overall shape will be similar.

- ✔ You can establish your baseline usage by looking at the months in which you use no heating or air conditioning at all. April and October are the usual candidates. In the example, Bill's approximate baseline electric usage is around 1,600 kWh. By subtracting each month's total from the baseline, you can determine approximately how much Bill is spending on heating and air conditioning:

Month	Cost
Jan	$368
Feb	345
Mar	183
Apr	148
May	37
June	34
July	94
Aug	105
Sep	0
Oct	142
Nov	295
Dec	485

✔ The average American consumes around 20 kWh per day. Bill uses over three times that amount. His house is bigger, with a lot of extra goodies, but there still seems to be room for a lot of improvement.

✔ You can see how the kWh charge is higher in the summer on the seasonal rate structure.

Value today versus future value

Strictly speaking, when doing payback calculations, changes in the value of money over time must be taken into account, which basically means that you should discount the value today of a dollar you expect to receive in the future.

Suppose you have a choice between two alternatives: $1 today or $1 a year from now. You take the $1 today, of course. But how much would you take today for a dollar in the future? To determine its future worth, you need to factor in the current interest rate or, even more precisely, what the interest rate is going to be over the course of the next year. Say the interest rate is 6 percent. You would then be trading $1.06 a year from now for $1 today.

In calculating payback, it works the other way around. For example, if you're going to save $100 a year from today, at 6 percent interest that $100 is worth only $94 right now. Saving $100 in ten years is worth only $54 today.

A good way to factor in the value of money over time without getting into weird math is simply to be liberally conservative (not conservatively liberal) in your estimates. The net effect will be the same.

Calculating Your Own Carbon Footprint

In addition to auditing your personal costs, taking a look at how much pollution you're generating in your home is worthwhile, particularly if your main goal is pollution efficiency. A very common term these days is *carbon footprint*, which just means how much carbon you're emitting into the atmosphere through your various energy-consuming activities. Carbon (or more precisely, carbon dioxide) is important because it's the main cause of global warming.

Here's a fact of physics: When you consume energy, it doesn't simply go away; rather, it changes into some other form. Burning gasoline creates carbon dioxide and a thousand other pollutants. The chemical and atomic bonds between the molecules and atoms in the gasoline are broken down, and heat is released in the process. To put things into perspective, consider that a gallon of gasoline weighs only 6 pounds, but in the process of burning it in your auto engine, 20 pounds of carbon dioxide is released. This weight is higher than the original fuel because oxygen from the air is combined with the liquid gasoline in the auto's carburetor. So the pollution that comes from burning gasoline weighs more than the original gasoline, and valuable oxygen is taken from the air and replaced with polluting CO_2. The effects are much more robust than your intuition suggests.

Book II

**Energy
Efficiency**

Table 1-3 lists how much carbon pollution is released into the atmosphere due to the consumption of common energy sources.

Table 1-3	Carbon Pollution of Common Energy Sources
Energy Source	**Pounds CO_2/Unit**
Oil	22.4/gallon
Natural gas	12.1/British thermal unit
Liquid propane	12.7/gallon
Kerosene	21.5/gallon
Gasoline	19.6/gallon
Coal	4,166/ton
Electricity	1.75/kilowatt-hour
Wood	3,814/ton

The amount of carbon pollution generated by the production of electricity varies quite a bit depending on the type of generators being used. States with nuclear power can generate as little as 0.03 lb/kWh, while regions with coal plants may produce as much as 2.24. The national average is 1.75.

Greenhouse effect and global warming

The best way to understand the phenomenon of global warming is to consider your own car sitting in the hot sun. Window glass transmits sunlight so that it enters the interior of your car. The sunlight then hits the seats, the floor, and so on and is converted into heat. The heat begins to build up inside the car because the same window glass that let the sunlight into the car resists letting the heat back out. Windows are excellent transmitters of light, but very poor transmitters of heat (good insulators, in other words).

The earth's atmosphere operates like a window. It lets in sunlight very nicely, but it also has insulation properties. When increased carbon dioxide is trapped in the atmosphere, sunlight transmission is basically unaffected, but the insulation properties are increased, so more heat is trapped. Hence, our planet is getting warmer for the same reason that your car gets warmer when it's sitting in the sun. The phenomenon is called the *greenhouse effect;* it explains why greenhouses work so well in the wintertime (and may get too hot in the summer).

Did you know that your home is probably emitting more CO_2 than your car? Just because you can't see it with your naked eye doesn't mean it's not there. Consider these tidbits:

- A typical midsized automobile that travels 12,000 miles annually emits around 13,000 pounds of CO_2 per year.

- A typical home that uses 600 gallons of home heating oil emits around 13,500 pounds of CO_2 per year.

- A typical North American home consumes around 700 kWh per month in electricity, for an emission of 14,700 pounds of CO_2 per year.

- If you burn a cord of firewood for heat, you're emitting around 3,814 pounds of CO_2.

Auditing Your Home to Find Areas for Improvement

Once you've finished crunching the numbers, you're ready for the next phase of your home audit. (If you haven't done the calculations, see the section "Figuring Out What You Spend," earlier in this chapter.) Now you need to go around and carefully inspect both the interior and exterior of your home and identify areas where you can make improvements. Most people find that a majority of improvements are simple and can be done by a do-it-yourselfer for less than a hundred dollars.

An audit helps you accomplish five key objectives, listed here in order of importance:

- ✔ **Ensuring safety:** Safety is the most important aspect of any home. If your home isn't safe and free of contaminants, it doesn't matter how efficient it is in other regards.

- ✔ **Maximizing your house's longevity and durability:** The biggest detriment to a home's lifetime is moisture, which only gets worse when ignored.

- ✔ **Enhancing your home's livability:** Air leaks affect both the livability of a home and the amount of energy it takes to heat and cool a home.

- ✔ **Analyzing the costs and benefits of making improvements:** All improvements are not equal, and the costs and benefits depend on your particular situation.

- ✔ **Creating a game plan that enables you to make your home more efficient:** When you know what your trouble spots are, you can better determine which fixes take priority.

If you have gas-burning equipment and, like most people, are not well versed in the technology, hiring a professional auditor to inspect it is usually best. This book doesn't give you instructions on how to inspect or adjust gas-fired machinery because too many different kinds exist, and they're too dangerous to be messing around with.

Grunting it out: The inspection

Put on your grungiest clothes because you're going to be climbing around in your basement and attic to systematically inspect your home. First just go around your home and carefully look at everything. You've probably glanced around before, but now you're going to sharpen your focus. The following sections take you through the various areas of your home and explain what to look for.

Foundation and structural elements

The place to begin your inspection is outside and beneath your home. While you live inside, what happens outside is of critical importance:

- ✔ **Look up into all your eaves.** Are there vents? Are they dirty? Are there bug nests? Moisture damage (look for spots and mildew)? Is wood rotting anywhere? How's the paint job?

- ✔ **Inspect the foundation.** Are there openings or gaps? Why? Are the gaps sealed where pipes feed through? Are there vents? Are they dirty? Are there cracks in concrete or masonry walls? Are pads secure and dry?

Book II

Energy
Efficiency

✔ **Underneath your house, look for moisture issues.** Where is the water coming from? Why? Does it stink?

✔ **If you have a basement, look for water leaks and air leaks.** Check to see whether the pipes are insulated. Check for signs of pesky little rodents.

✔ **Check out your roof.** (Be very careful; falling off the roof is more common than you may think.) Is it leaking anywhere that you know of? What's the condition? At what point are you going to have to get a new roof?

✔ **On the outside of your house, inspect any spot where two different types of building materials come together.** Are these joints sealed? Is there leakage?

Attic

Checking for water leaks is your first order of business in the attic. Finding evidence of leaks may be difficult. If you do find evidence of a leak, you may have trouble tracing it up to the roof where it's coming in, but it pays to try.

You also want to pay attention to the insulation in your attic. Are there gaps in it? Are there voids around ceiling light fixtures? Is there evidence of rodents or pests? Do you see a lot of spider webs? Are there vents to the outside world? Are they dirty so that air has a difficult time passing through?

Plumbing

If you can, make a sketch of your plumbing system, including both hot and cold water pipes. Where do they go? Where are the feed-throughs? Are there any leaks? Are the hot water pipes covered with insulation? Are the pipes adequately tacked down, or are they flopping around? Is the system old? Rusty?

After you complete this schematic, look at the following things:

✔ Are there any dripping faucets? Check both inside and out. Do the faucets work the way they should?

✔ Check for clogged drains (especially in a basement floor; these are incredible sources of microbes).

✔ Are you aware of any plumbing problems? Toilets that don't work the way they should? Shower drains that are too slow? Stinks in bathrooms, kitchens, laundry rooms, garages?

✔ Check under all your sinks for leaks. They'll usually stink, and the particleboard will be moldering and warped. Where's the leak coming from? Maybe the disposal is leaking. You may have to turn the water on to find out.

Heating and cooling

Because heating and cooling costs are the biggest factor in most homes' energy use, it pays to check out heating and cooling systems on a periodic basis:

✔ Do certain parts of your house always seem too warm or too cold? Find out why; if you poke around, you may be able to unearth the cause. Is there a draft somewhere? If you have a difficult time, consult an HVAC professional.

✔ Is one heater vent always too hot compared to the others? Too cold? Check out the ductwork to find potential problems. Most homes have gaps in the ductwork, and the owners don't know it. These gaps are easy and inexpensive to fix.

To find leaks in your HVAC's ductwork, turn on your HVAC system (assuming that it's forced air) and get access to the ducts. Chapter 2 gives you complete details on finding the leaks in your system.

Book II

Energy Efficiency

Windows and insulation

Can you find out what kind of insulation is in the walls and ceilings? How thick is it? You don't need a numerical measurement, but you want to try to see whether it fills the voids. If you're in an old house, you probably don't have very good insulation. Also find out whether there's insulation beneath your floors, particularly below the area where you spend the greatest amount of time (probably the family room).

Are your windows single-pane or double-pane? Do you have storm windows? Do you use them? Do you have blinds? Do you use them? How about solar screens for the summertime?

If you have a window that gets condensation between the two panes of glass, you have a leak in the seal. It won't affect the window's net insulation very much, but the windows will sooner or later become permanently obscured.

Filters

Check out all the filters in your home. Furnace filters are located at the input vent; you should replace these regularly. If you don't, they become extremely dirty. Exhaust fans sometimes have filters that you may not even know about. Look up inside; take off the cover cowling if you need to. Dryers have lint filters. Faucets have filters that regularly collect crud. If your faucet is squirting around erratically, change the filter.

Other places to investigate

In addition to the obvious places to look, here are some more candidates:

- Check out your fireplace. Is the damper working properly? (It should move so that it opens and closes easily.) Have you been operating it properly? Are any seals old and frayed?

- Check out your fuse box. Do you have problems with blown fuses for which you can't seem to identify a reason? Are wires frayed? Is the box covered well? Trace some wires and try to get the gist of the overall layout of your home's electrical system.

- Check under all appliances and sinks for moisture. Where is it coming from?

- Go through your home and check out the wattage of each light bulb. Note what type of bulb each is. You can probably get by with a lot less wattage, and in most spots you could change to a fluorescent.

- Look for air leaks. See Chapter 2 to find out how to find leaks.

Hiring professional auditors

If you're not up to the challenge of auditing your own home, simply don't want to, or have gas-burning equipment, you may decide to go with a professional. Several sources are available.

You can call your power company, which will probably do an audit for you at no or little cost. It may be a mail-in type of deal, in which case you may as well just struggle through it yourself because by the time you're done compiling enough information to make the mail-in audit worthwhile, you basically will have done the job yourself. The same applies to Internet audits. Plus, online resources that offer energy audits will probably try to sell you something you don't need.

Professional audit companies will impress you with all their cool stuff. They have fancy gizmos that use invisible infrared light to measure the temperature of your interior surfaces, and they use them to pinpoint leaks. They check out your furnace, which is worthwhile. They inspect your ductwork and look for cracks in your foundation. They can tell you in precise mathematical terms just how leaky your house is.

But the fact is, the biggest inefficiencies are usually easy to detect, especially if you've never even tried before. Most houses have glaring problems that can usually be fixed for less than a few hundred dollars. The biggest culprit? Loose joints in the ductwork, which result in untold hundreds of dollars of wasted energy costs per year. And you can fix them up with aluminum or duct tape for less than $10.

If you do decide to hire an auditor, check out these resources:

- ✔ Consult NAESCO (National Association of Energy Service Companies) at 202-822-0950 or www.naesco.org.

- ✔ In the phone book, look under "energy conservation services and products." Locate utility companies under "electric service," "utility providers," or "gas utility companies."

- ✔ Check out hes.lbl.gov for a free home energy audit and carbon footprint estimates.

As you check out different auditors, consider the following:

- ✔ Do you want to make a change or improvement in your home? Ask how this modification would fit in with the results of your audit, and ask for some advice. Auditors have tons of experience, and they're usually proud to expound.

- ✔ Ask about financing programs the company has for improvements the auditor suggests. You may be surprised by your options.

- ✔ Ask about guarantees for their work. If they tell you that you can achieve a certain cost reduction, how accurate do they warrant that claim to be?

Tell the auditors before they come out to your home that you want them to tell you which jobs you can do yourself. If they balk, find somebody else.

Chapter 2

Sealing and Insulating Your Home

. . . .

In This Chapter

▶ Locating and putting a lid on air leaks

▶ Dealing with HVAC ducts

▶ Getting the lowdown on insulation

▶ Making the most of windows

. . . .

You probably spend more energy on heating and cooling than you do on all the other energy-consuming functions combined. This means the greatest potential for energy savings lies in finding ways to make your heating and cooling efforts more efficient. In this chapter, you find out how to seal and insulate your home.

Here is where you can find the biggest energy-efficiency improvements for the least amount of cash and labor on your part. Most homes have problems that can be fixed for $100 or less — in fact, sometimes all you need to invest are a little time and labor.

Finding Leaks

By knowing where to look for heat loss, you can get a pretty good idea of where to find the problem spots in your own home. Table 2-1 lists the energy losses from heating and cooling equipment in a typical North American home. (**Note:** The first table entry refers to heat escaping or coming in through gaps. The other entries refer to heat moving through solid masses, like doors, walls, and so on.)

Table 2-1 gives you a rough idea of where to look for problems and the order in which you should look for them. You can perform a leak test to find the biggest and worst offenders: air leaks through holes in sheetrock and through hatches or trapdoors that lead into your attic or basement. The next logical place to look for leaks is in your doors and windows, and so on down the list. (For information on how to conduct a leak test, see the upcoming section "Performing a pressure test to find air leaks.")

Table 2-1	Energy Loss in a Typical North American Home
Problem Area	*Percentage of Total Energy Loss*
Air leaks through gaps	35%
Through doors and windows	18%
Through floors and into basement	17%
Through walls	13%
Through ceiling	10%

Looking for cracks in your home

You can find most leaks by simply taking a flashlight around your home and looking with a keen eye. Here are some details:

- Look at faucets, pipes, electrical wiring, and electric outlets. Cracks often occur around the junctions where pipes fit through foundations and siding. You can fix these cracks with caulk.

- Check all interfaces between two different building materials. For example, check where brick or siding meets the roof and the foundation. Check where all corners meet and around the molding strips that are commonly used in corners of walls and between walls and floors and so on. Plug all holes and voids with caulk. (See the later section "Caulking your way to Nirvana" for caulking advice.)

   If icicles cluster around a particular location at your house, you have a leak somewhere above that's melting snow. It warms, drips down, and then refreezes into icicles. If you see icicles, you usually have a pretty good-sized leak.

- Look for cracks in mortar, foundations, siding, and so on.

- Check for cracks and voids around exterior doors and windows.

- Check storm windows for seal integrity. The interior window may be well-sealed, but the storm window will work better if it's also sealed just as well. To work properly, storm windows must fit tightly into the brackets. The way to ensure a tight seal is to check the weatherstripping materials that commonly fit into the gaps.

Performing a pressure test to find air leaks

You can perform a pressure test on your home in rudimentary fashion. You can hire a pro to do an audit that includes a detailed leak test, but you can do an easy one that's 80 percent as effective. The best time to do this test is when it's cold outside and warm inside, although it will work under any conditions if you have patience and tenacity.

Contact your utility company or state energy office to find a professional energy auditor. You can also go right to the phone book; look for listings under "energy."

To conduct a leak test, follow these steps:

1. **Completely extinguish any fireplace fires.**

   Close the fireplace damper as much as possible.

2. **Turn off your HVAC system and any furnaces.**

   If you have a gas water heater, turn that off, too.

3. **Close all the windows and doors in your home.**

   Also make sure to close any skylights or vents.

4. **Turn on all the exhaust fans in your home.**

   These fans are normally located in kitchens, bathrooms, and laundry rooms. If you don't have any exhaust fans, aim a portable fan out a single open window and turn it on. With the fans on, your house is depressurized, so any leaks will be readily apparent.

5. **Go around the house with a bowl of water, dip your hand in the water, and move your wet hand around the area you're testing.**

   You'll be able to feel a leak, especially if it's cold outside. Another way to do this test is with a stick of incense — when the smoke fluctuates, you've found a leak. Or you can use a candle — in this case, flickering of the flame indicates a leak.

   Test the following areas and make a list of all the areas where you find leaks:

   - Test your fireplace. If it's leaky, you'll be drawing in some stink. If so, turn the fans off and inspect your fireplace to find out why it's so leaky. If you can, fix it. If not, forge ahead if the smell isn't too bad. If the smell is really bad, call a fireplace specialist.

     Fixing air leaks around your fireplace is vitally important. You don't want to pull in air from your fireplace because it contains a number of pollutants and volatile chemical compounds.

   - Test windows, doors, molding interfaces, attic hatches, basement hatches, and so on.

   - Get a ladder or a chair and check for leaks in overhead lights. These leaks are very common, but they're unfortunately a little more difficult to fix if you don't have good attic access.

   - Check AC outlets and switch plates.

Book II

Energy Efficiency

6. **After you've tested all the areas of your house, turn the fans off; then fix the leaks.**

You get details on how to fix leaks in the section "Fixing the Leaks You Find" later in this chapter, but here's an important safety tip that bears repeating: If you find a leak in an outlet or switch, flip the main circuit breaker off to turn the electricity off in the entire house before you fix it. You'll have to reset your clocks, but you'll be alive to do it, so don't complain.

7. **Once you've finished fixing leaks, turn the exhaust fans back on and repeat the wet-hand routine.**

Your house will be tighter now, and any remaining leaks will be even more obvious.

8. **Repeat the whole process until you're satisfied.**

Finding attic air leaks

Attic air leaks are quite common. Following is a simple pressurization test that will help you locate air leaks in your attic as well as other air leaks through your ceiling:

1. **Completely extinguish any fireplace fires.**

   Close the fireplace damper as much as possible.

2. **Turn off your HVAC system, any furnaces, and, if you have one, your gas water heater.**

3. **Close all the windows, doors, and any skylights or vents in your home.**

4. **Position a portable fan so that it aims into the house through an open window.**

   Now your house is pressurized (as opposed to depressurized).

5. **Go into the attic with a bowl of water, dip your hand in the water, and then move your hand around potential leak sites.**

   With a wet hand, you'll be able to easily feel the air pushing through from the inside of your house. Pay particular attention to these areas:

   • **The hatch you climbed through to get to the attic.** See the later section, "Weatherstripping," for details on how to fix this.

   • **Recessed lights in the rooms below.** Simply turn the lights on and, from up in the attic space, looking to see whether light is visible. If so, you have a leak. You can fix it by buying a kit at your hardware store that fits over the light from the top and seals the space.

   • **Around chimneys.** If your chimney flue isn't sealed, you likely have a leak here.

The good news is that most attic leaks are straightforward, if not easy, to fix. On the down side, most attics are a hassle to move around in, and some are just plain dangerous.

How heat moves

Heat is a form of energy. When a substance gets hotter, the molecules in that substance are moving faster, with more energy. When a substance gets cooler, heat is moving out of it into other nearby substances. The reason a hot substance can burn your skin is that heat moves very quickly in some cases.

Heat moves out of your home in the winter and into it in the summer — exactly what you don't want. That's why sealing your home is a good way to improve your energy efficiency. So how does heat move from one spot to another? Via the mechanisms explained in the following sections.

✔ **Convection:** In *convection,* heat is either transferred between a surface and a moving fluid (be it liquid, gas, or even the air itself), or it's transferred by the movement of molecules from one point to another. As opposed to conduction (see the next item), the hot molecules themselves move. Convection causes hot air to rise while cold air gravitates downward. Most people have heard of convection ovens; these work by using a fan inside the oven cavity to move the air and cook food faster. Cold air passing over a window removes heat from a home through convection. Wind in general causes a lot of convection loss. But all air is moving because the molecules are always moving, so even air that seems to be still is capable of a lot of convection. That's why convection is the most common culprit of heat loss in your home.

✔ **Conduction:** In *conduction,* only the heat moves, not the molecules. The material remains static while the energy moves through it. This is analogous to billiard balls, where kinetic energy is transferred from one ball to another, without moving the balls themselves. Heat can move through window glass via conduction. Window frames are also prone to conduction heat loss (particularly aluminum or metal frames), as are metal doors. And metal pipes are great heat conductors, too.

✔ **Radiation:** A hot object emits infrared *radiation,* any form of light energy, whether visible or not. The sun is a perfect radiator. Fires radiate heat, some of which you can see (a very hot fire glows white, for example, and as it cools down the color changes to orange, and then red) and most of which is invisible. When you can't see the embers anymore but can still feel the heat, the radiation is entirely infrared. In fact, there is far more invisible radiation than visible, but both versions are capable of heating. When you put blinds over your windows, you are keeping radiant heat from entering your home. On the other hand, when you raise the blinds to let in winter sunshine, you're inviting radiant heat.

Radiation is more of a problem in the summer, when you want to keep your home cool by keeping sunshine out than in the winter when you're trying to retain hot air (assuming you live in a climate where the temperature varies with the seasons). In the winter, you generally seek as much radiation heating as you can get.

Fixing the Leaks You Find

When your windows are all open, your home is basically a part of Mother Nature's fantastic domain. When you shut your windows and doors, it's another matter entirely — unless your house isn't well sealed. Some windows, for example, let in a lot of air, even when they're closed. Same with doors. And electrical outlets can leak air as well, as can the light fixtures in your ceiling. Therefore, you can improve energy efficiency just by closing these gaps. This section gives you valuable tips on how best to fix leaks.

When sealing any home, be careful about indoor air pollution and combustion appliance back drafts. *Back drafting* occurs when the various combustion appliances and exhaust fans in a home have to compete for air because there simply isn't enough to go around. An exhaust fan may pull combustion gases back into the living space, for example, in which case you want to make sure that you're ventilating combustion gases into the great outdoors rather than your home's interior. If your home burns fuel, you can avoid back drafts by making sure that the combustion system has an adequate air supply. (One way to tell whether your home is sealed too tightly is to note whether you get condensation on your windows during the winter. If so, you don't have adequate ventilation.)

Weatherstripping

Weatherstripping works great around doors and windows and where seals can't be made permanent (as with caulking). The trick is to get the right stuff, and the best way to do this is to take a sample of the existing seal (if you have one) to your local hardware store, where the salespeople can sell you the appropriate new material. Foam and *wrapped foam* (a layer of vinyl or plastic wrapped around a foam core) are usually best and cheapest.

Whatever weatherstripping you buy, be sure to follow the directions on the label. Here are a few other suggestions to make weatherstripping a breeze:

- ✔ Make sure to measure how much length you need before you buy. If you end up with too little, don't stretch the material: It'll pull back over time and come loose.

- ✔ If you can, buy a kit to seal a door or window straight from the manufacturer of that door or window.

  The biggest culprits for air leaks are double-wide sliding doors, and the seals for these doors usually are best purchased straight from the manufacturers because they're very specific to a particular style of door.

✔ If you can't buy the same type of weatherstripping (because it's no longer available, for example), have no fear. Weatherstripping is pretty versatile stuff. You may need to use your imagination to figure out ways to cut it to fit into strange spaces, in which case you'll find that a good, sharp box-cutting knife is just the thing.

✔ Sometimes shutting a door or window right after weatherstripping has been applied is difficult, but this problem usually tapers off in a week or two. If it doesn't, give it another week or two. If time doesn't do the trick, get out the box-cutter and hack away.

✔ Most garage doors have a rubber seal on the bottom called an *astragal*. They're expensive, but in some cases, astragals can make a big difference in your home's comfort. If your garage is well sealed from the home, you probably don't have to worry about this seal. But if you get drafts, or your garage is perpetually cold, changing the seal may be worth it.

Book II

Energy Efficiency

Expandable foam sealant

Expandable foam sealant is great stuff and horrid stuff, all at once. Via a long, straw-like wand, you squirt a yellowish foamy liquid into tight spots that have air and insulation gaps. The foam expands and fills in the gap; then it dries, hardens, and solidifies. Very effective. The problem is that expandable foam sealant sticks to everything, and nothing works very well to get it off. So a bit of a mess can easily turn into a big mess.

If you're going to use an expandable foam sealant, practice first in your garage, a barn, or an outbuilding before you try to fix anything inside your house. You'll quickly figure out how — and how *not* — to work with it.

Foam sealant works best for

✔ **Leaks between jambs and wood:** Remove the trim molding from around leaking windows and doors, and you'll often find an air gap between the jamb and the frame wood. Squirt foam sealant in the gaps, wait until it dries, cut off the excess with a sharp knife, and then replace the trim molding. Many old houses benefit greatly from this simple, cheap fix.

✔ **Plumbing feed-throughs:** Squirt foam in the gaps around plumbing *feed-throughs* (where the plumbing goes through exterior walls to the outside world).

✔ **Plumbing vent pipes:** Squirt foam around plumbing vent pipes that pass through your attic.

✔ **Small gaps in insulation:** Squirt foam into any small gaps in insulation to stopper air leaks.

In general, if you can, use foam sealant instead of caulking because it provides both a seal *and* insulation.

Caulking your way to Nirvana

Caulking is fun. There's something about squirting beads of thick, sticky goo that just seems to resonate with the human spirit. So get out your caulking gun because you can use caulk in a lot of places:

- ✔ Around all exterior joints that may be in contact with water
- ✔ Around doors, windows, decks, frames, and anywhere wind can push water in
- ✔ On horizontal surfaces where water may pool and seep in over time
- ✔ Wherever you think water can't get in (because it can, and it will)

Buy a good caulking gun. A pro-style gun may cost $20, but it's worth it, especially if you're doing a lot of caulking. Look for larger handles, a smooth ratcheting action, pressure relief, and a hook on the end to hang on ladder rungs or rafters. An attached wire that pokes a hole in the tube's seal is especially convenient.

You also want to use good-quality caulk. Three types are available:

- ✔ **Acrylic (latex):** Water-based and by far the most common. It skins over (dries on the surface) almost immediately, so you can paint it within minutes of applying (with latex paint, not oil-based).
- ✔ **Silicon acrylic:** More flexible (and expensive). Use this type if you're caulking between two surfaces that may expand and contract with weather. Make sure to get the kind that you can paint, if that's what you intend to do.
- ✔ **Polyurethane:** Performs better than latex but is much more difficult to work with and clean up. Use it between concrete, masonry, bricks, or on a surface that's been painted by oil-based paints or varnish. Because it has better adhesion, you may also want to use it on surfaces, such as on roof lines, where a leak can be potentially costly.

All caulk is rated by years, but don't use the amount of time you want it to last as a guide; instead, buy the best stuff you can afford. Fifty-year caulk works better than 20-year over the course of its entire lifetime. If you must use the cheap stuff, use it where nobody will ever see it and where you need to simply build up mass to fill a space or void.

Here are some suggestions for getting a nice, smooth bead when you caulk:

- If you're a first-time caulker, practice in a place where mistakes can be tolerated.

- Cut the caulk tube ends at an angle to get a better beading action. You can also cut the tube ends of several tubes to squirt out different diameters of material and then use the diameter which best suits the particular joint you're working on.

- Don't squirt a bunch of caulk into a wide gap because it simply won't stick in there when it dries. (Caulk inevitably shrinks and cracks when it dries.) Use foam backer rods (ask for them in your hardware store), which you can jam into wide gaps between materials. Then caulk over the backer rods.

- You can use painters' masking tape to block off surfaces you don't want to get any caulk on, as well as to make nice, crisp, even lines.

- To get into hard-to-reach corners and tight spots, tape a flexible drinking straw onto the tip of your caulking gun

Book II

Energy Efficiency

Inspecting and Repairing HVAC Ducts

Most of the HVAC ducts in your home send heated or cooled air into the house; one large duct is the return to the HVAC machine itself. All these ducts need to be tightly sealed. Yet, in almost every home, especially older ones, the HVAC duct system has some big problems: shredded insulation, broken junctions, holes chewed through insulation and ducts by rats and mice, and so on.

Leaks in the ductwork are worse than air leaks in your house because the ducts are pressurized, which magnifies the amount of air escaping through cracks and openings.

Fortunately, duct problems are usually easy to find and fix (although gaining access may be tricky). It's amazing how many problems you can find with just a flashlight and a quick glance. You can also turn the HVAC on so that the ducts are pressurized, and find leaks with a wet hand. (Refer to the earlier section "Performing a pressure test to find leaks" for instructions.) Follow these bits of advice:

- If the ducts aren't well insulated, you can get a number of different kinds of insulation sealing kits at hardware stores to do the job. Tell your hardware clerk what kind of ducts you have (what they're made of, how they're suspended, and so on) to find the right kit.

↙ If the insulation around the ducts has any rips or tears, fix it. Duct tape works well for this chore, but it may be a real hassle. Once again, ask your hardware clerk what will work best.

Duct tape works wonders, but it doesn't stick to dusty surfaces very well. If you've got a dust problem, wrap the duct tape around and around and just cover up the dust. This approach is easier than trying to clean it off.

↙ If the insulation is thin, you may want to build it up. You can add a new layer directly over the old.

↙ Many leaks occur at the junction between the ducts and the registers that feed the air into your home. You can seal these leaks with caulk.

When working with dusty ducts, wearing a good-quality dust mask is highly recommended. You can get one at your hardware store.

Insulating Your Home

The previous sections in this chapter deal with things that are responsible for *convection* where warm (or cool) air escapes from your home through gaps. The other way to experience unwanted heat loss is through *conduction* — transfer through a solid material, like a window — and that's where insulation comes into play. A well-insulated house is comfortable and efficient, with just enough moisture in the air.

Capacity to resist heat flow is called *R-value*. A higher R-value means greater resistance and depends on how thick, dense, and effective your insulation material is. County building codes have minimum R-values for homes, and you can review them to find out what's right for your area. You can also get more information on insulation levels from your local utility, who may come out and do a home energy audit for you and check your insulation so that you don't have to. (They usually do these audits for free, and they know what they're doing.)

Insulation is generally an expensive fix that you should address only after you've taken care of air leaks. So if you haven't tested your house for air leaks, refer to the earlier sections "Finding Air Leaks" and "Fixing the Leaks Your Find"; then come back to this section.

Types of insulation

There are dozens of different types of insulation schemes, but for most homes, only a few are practical. The vast majority of homes use fiberglass insulation, and most people have a good idea of what this stuff looks like (cotton candy). In distant second comes foam board, a type of insulation that is generally used when a home is being constructed. If you're remodeling or improving existing insulation, you'll probably use some form of fiberglass.

The following sections describe the most common types of insulation, along with the pros and cons of each.

Fiberglass

Fiberglass, which is made of glass fibers, comes in at an R-rating of R3 to 3.8 per inch (thickness). Fiberglass is by far the most common type of insulation, and it's what you should use if you can. It's readily available and comes in spun rolls which you can easily cut and lay into place.

- ✔ **Pros:** It's low-cost, easy to install (once you get the hang of cutting and placing it into the gaps), and can be pressed into place without the use of glues or chemicals. It comes in standard widths and is available with kraft paper backing, which also provides a moisture seal.

- ✔ **Cons:** It's very irritating to your skin and lungs and is susceptible to air gaps. When you get big plastic bags full of it and cut the plastic packaging off, it expands to three or four times the size and is difficult to move around and place.

Loose-fill insulation

Loose-fill insulation is chopped fiberglass material that is blown into place, as opposed to cut and fitted. It comes in at an R-rating of R2.2 to 4 per inch.

- ✔ **Pros:** It's low-cost and gives much better coverage in irregular spaces where the one-piece fiberglass format doesn't fit well. It can be poured or blown into walls and odd spaces, which makes working with it much easier than fiberglass.

- ✔ **Cons:** It's messy, and the quality varies even within the same lot. It can shift or settle over time so that gaps may grow rather large. You can't use it for under-floors without a complex web of nets, which aren't worth the hassle. Depending on the size of the job, you may need to rent a special blower.

Extruded foam insulation

Extruded foam insulation is solid, rigid material made of the same type of foam as a drinking cup. It comes in flat sheets, with an R-rating around R5.2 per inch.

- ✔ **Pros:** It's high-strength, easy to tack up, covers well, and works underground and in wet basements. It's good for covering a house and then tacking up siding over it.

- ✔ **Cons:** It's very expensive and needs to be covered up with siding.

Sprayed urethane foam

Sprayed urethane foam is held in a metal container, under pressure, and then force sprayed onto walls where it sticks. It comes in at an R-value between R6 and 7.3 per inch.

- ✔ **Pros:** It forms a tough, seamless barrier that seals well over all types of surfaces, especially irregular ones.

- ✔ **Cons:** It must be professionally installed, and it needs to be covered up.

Checking and fixing your home's insulation

Visually check insulation wherever you can. Most gaps will be readily evident. Also look for spots where water has damaged insulation, or spots where the insulation is very thin. Small problems, such as gaps or voids in your insulation, usually occur around light fixtures and where somebody (like an electrician or plumber) has been working and pushed it aside. You can fix these voids by hand tucking some loose insulation into the gaps.

If you find your insulation wholly inadequate, you've got a big decision on your hands. Putting in new insulation is expensive — the payback time may seem far off. But if you don't, you'll continue to waste money and leave a big carbon footprint.

 If you're on a limited budget and want to make the biggest difference for the least cost, insulate your family room (or the room you spend the most time in) first. In particular, if you don't have any insulation under your family room floor, adding insulation there is usually easy to do and doesn't cost that much. You'll get the biggest bang for your buck.

The following list outlines the different areas to check and explains how to remedy the problems you may find.

- ✔ **Attic:** Insulation makes the most difference in the attic simply because heat rises. If no heat can leak out of your home through the attic, your home is very well sealed. The easiest thing to do is have the insulation in the attic thickened. You can do this task yourself (use a dust mask at all times), or you can find a company to come in and spray loose fill insulation. Unfortunately, when the insulation in your attic is substandard, it's most likely also substandard in the walls.

Completely seal up the attic for air leaks from the home *before* you apply insulation because once the insulation is in place, taking care of attic leaks is much more difficult.

✔ **Walls:** Substandard insulation in your walls isn't as easy to remedy as substandard insulation in your attic. The best bet may be to simply put new siding on the outside of your house. You can get good-looking siding with great insulation properties, and at least when you spend money in this way, you can accomplish a visual remodel as well.

✔ **Basement:** If you have a basement, check to see whether the ceiling is insulated. If not, putting in insulation is a relatively easy job, probably even easier than working in your attic. If you need to insulate a basement, it's usually best to use foam sheets and then cover them with sheetrock. You can either glue the sheets directly onto the concrete basement walls, or build a wall up with 2 x 4s, which will make the room smaller.

✔ **Pipes:** Hot water pipes should be well insulated. You can eyeball them to see where they aren't, or you can feel the pipes (after you've turned the hot water on in the house for a minute or two) to determine which pipes are for hot water and which ones are for cold. A number of easy options work well for insulating pipes, the easiest being a three-foot-long foam section with a longitudinal slit. You simply slide the piece over the pipe, and you're in business. Ask about your options at the hardware store.

Book II

Energy Efficiency

Tips for applying insulation

Putting in insulation isn't particularly difficult, but it can go more easily if you keep a few things in mind:

✔ **With fiberglass insulation, wear a one-piece jumpsuit, along with a face mask and gloves, and make sure that ventilation is adequate before you begin.** You don't want to breath a lot of fiberglass dust, and you don't want to get it on your skin because you'll be scratching up a storm. Also, in old attics, the dust that collects on insulation can be very nasty. Try not to disturb it, if possible.

✔ **Fiberglass insulation is itchy.** Some versions come with plastic covers to reduce the risk of itch – if you're really sensitive, look for them.

✔ **Apply insulation carefully and evenly.** Fill entire cavities, but be careful not to cover up vents or other means for attics and basements to breathe.

✔ **When you come across electrical wires, arrange half of the insulation in front of them, and half behind.** You will have to tear the insulation open, but this technique works much better than leaving big air gaps without any material at all. If you leave a gap unfilled, you're wasting money. Filling only 80 percent of a cavity prevents only 20 percent of the heat loss.

✔ **Always buy the right width and thickness to fill spaces.** You don't want to piece insulation together to fit a space if you don't have to, because you risk creating air gaps. Still, you can press fiberglass insulation tight into narrow gaps and cracks, and it will perform better than nothing at all. (Using expandable foam is best, but it may not always be practical, and it's not worth a lot of extra hassle.)

Compressing insulation reduces its R-value. (Check out the section "Insulating Your Home" to find out more about R-value.) When you squeeze it down to make it fit into gaps, you're accomplishing the opposite of what you intend. You're actually reducing the effectiveness of the insulation. So press it down only when necessary.

You can get one-piece seals for plugs and switch outlets for about $4 a dozen at your hardware store. Simply remove the plastic cover, set a seal into place, and replace the cover.

✔ **If you have moisture problems in your home, you may want vapor barrier facing on the insulation.** (It comes prefaced on some versions, so look for that type when you buy.) It doesn't cost much more, and it makes the insulation easier to work with to boot.

Use hedge shears to cut insulation, not a knife.

Insulating old homes

In some old homes, it pays to blow loose fill insulation into the walls. Normally this works when the existing insulation is so poor that air gaps are more common than insulation. Sound absurd? It's a lot more common than you think. Some homes have no insulation at all, like the old homes back east. Energy was so cheap (ah, the good old days) that insulation was not cost-effective.

Having a pro do an energy audit of your home to get a second opinion is a good idea. If you decide to go ahead, you'll need to rent a blower, which will come with detailed instructions. You'll need to cut a number of two- or three-inch-diameter holes through your exterior siding so that the blower head can get into each individual cavity between the beams.

A better way may be to simply cover your home with insulation sheets, and then cover that with new siding. This way, not only do you get the added insulation, but your home also gets a nice facelift.

Working with Windows

Of all the investments you can make in your home, windows have the potential to make the most impact. Not only do they provide insulation (and sealing), but they also affect the aesthetics like nothing else in your home. But installing new windows is very expensive, maybe one of the most expensive projects you'll ever take on. A typical residential window costs anywhere from $150 to $400, plus another $100 to $300 for professional installation. And you can easily spend a lot more than this amount.

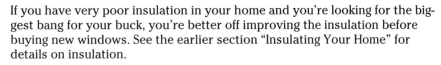

If you have very poor insulation in your home and you're looking for the biggest bang for your buck, you're better off improving the insulation before buying new windows. See the earlier section "Insulating Your Home" for details on insulation.

Single pane windows may be a huge factor in your energy bill. With homes in mild climates, the number of panes doesn't matter much. However, if you're living in extreme climates, single pane windows are almost always worth upgrading to double- or triple-pane options. Besides, single pane windows are always old, and you can buy something better looking.

You don't need to change all the windows in your house to make a significant improvement. One single, large window in a family or living room may make a big difference in both energy efficiency and aesthetic beauty.

You can put up heat-sealing cloth barriers in the summer or storm windows in the winter, and both of these solutions are much cheaper than changing windows.

Before you replace windows, take your time researching all the options. Visit some window stores and check out the different types, like wood, plastic, fiber, and so on (you'll probably be confounded by the variety) and get a number of bids. In particular, pay attention to the following:

- **Glass:** Ask about different types. Some glass selectively filters sunlight for UV; some has low-emittance coating to increase the window's insulative powers.

- **Appearance:** Does the style blend in well with your existing home decor? Do the colors match your home, or are you going to be painting?

  You can get windows that require paint so that they'll match anything, but you don't want to because every five years you'll have a big, tedious job. (Painting windows is very time-consuming. You can't just roller — or even spray — it on.)

✔ **Cleaning:** Are they easy to maneuver so that you can clean them? A lot of new window designs enable you to clean from the inside, which is particularly handy for second-story windows.

✔ **Operation:** Are the windows smooth and easy to open and close? It pays to invest in quality bearings and movements. No one wants to have to remember a complicated schematic just to let in a little summer breeze.

✔ **Maintenance:** Where are you going to get parts when you need them? If you choose wood (and it *is* fairly energy efficient), you have to paint it regularly unless you choose *clad wood,* which is coated with aluminum.

✔ **Warranties:** The seal between double-pane glass inevitably gives out, so make sure that you understand who is going to pay for this expensive repair.

Chapter 3

Maximizing Your Heating and Air-Conditioning System

- -

In This Chapter

▶ Seeing what contributes to your comfort

▶ Reducing your energy requirements the easy, cheap way

▶ Getting the most out of your existing system

▶ Determining when it's time to get new equipment

- -

Most homes have both heating and cooling systems. Together, these items account for a large portion of your total energy use. (To find out just how much of your energy consumption is devoted to heating and cooling your home, do a home energy audit. Refer to Chapter 1 in this book for details.) In this chapter, you find general advice about how to use your equipment more efficiently.

Note: This chapter doesn't present specific details on how to tune up your existing equipment for several reasons:

✔ Far too many different systems are available — so many that this book doesn't have enough room to include even the most common ones.

✔ Many adjustments involve quite a bit of technology and require the expertise of a pro.

✔ Combustion systems are inherently dangerous, and you don't want to mess around with them. Call a pro instead.

Understanding Human Comfort

Human comfort isn't simply determined by room temperature, but by a variety of other factors as well, such as air movement, humidity level, and so on. Yet most people still erroneously think that the best way to make a room more livable is to set the desired room temperature on the thermostat. You can do much better if you're willing to apply some tricks and change a few habits. This section explains the factors that affect how comfortable a room feels and offers a few pointers on how to exploit these factors so that you can use your HVAC less frequently but maintain — or even enhance — the comfort level in your home.

Getting air moving

In summer, people like the feel of air moving over their skin. Just the phrase "summer breeze" generates a cool sensation. Even a warm breeze on a hot day can cool things down. That's because it's not air temperature that's important, but the actual temperature of your skin. Moving air removes heat, so skin temperature goes down.

Fans move air and, in the process, cool you down. They don't change the air temperature (if anything, they make the air hotter), but their effect is still pronounced. Fans, like breezes, cool by convection. You can make a room more comfortable just by installing fans to improve the ventilation.

Don't use fans when no humans are present, because all fans do then is heat up the air. Fans don't cool a room; they just make the people in it *feel* cooler — there's a difference.

The lowdown on portable heaters

Portable heaters are heaters you can move around to wherever you like. You see them underneath people's desks at work when the boss is a miser. If your HVAC system isn't working consistently from room to room, a portable heater may be just the thing.

But here's what's quirky about most of them: They come with fans that move air over a resistance coil. If the fan wasn't moving the air, the coil would get really, truly hot and probably burn up, which is clearly not something you want in your home (unless you want to collect on your fire insurance). The fan also tends to make you feel a lot cooler. So with traditional portable heaters, a conflict exists between their purpose (to generate warmth) and their design (the inclusion of the fan, which cools you down).

The best bet is to use a radiative type of heater, which uses parabolic reflectors with a heating element at the focal point, or something akin to this setup. These heaters spread heat by radiating it rather than by convection, which is the way a portable heater with a fan works. Radiation heaters are also more efficient, and they feel more natural because they're supplying heat the same way the sun does: through radiation.

Remember, though, that either type of heater is dangerous if used incorrectly, and in no case should a portable heater be used around children.

Helping or hindering: Humidity

On humid days, people feel much hotter than they do on less humid days, even if the temperature is the same on both days. Why? Because humid air doesn't carry heat away from your skin nearly as well as dry air does.

For this reason, equipping your home with a dehumidifier that you use in the summer can make the air feel much cooler. As a bonus — and one that's particularly relevant to this book — dehumidifiers are much cheaper to operate than air conditioners, so they save money. Conversely, in the winter you *want* humid air because your skin can draw heat more readily from it than from dry air. In the winter, people don't want to feel moving air from fans because that removes heat.

Sweating is your body's way of eliminating heat and cooling itself down. Many people think the evaporation of sweat is the key, but that's only a small part of it. The truth is, water holds much more heat than air does; sweating is your body's way of expelling this hot water. In other words, the sweat itself cools you down — *if* you can get it off your body. (Otherwise, sweating just moves the hot water from *in* you to *on* you.) That's where evaporation comes in and why humid days feel hotter than dry ones. When it's humid, the air is already full of water and simply can't hold any more, so sweat doesn't evaporate. It just hangs around, making you feel sticky and hot. (Contrary to the way it may feel, you don't actually sweat more on humid days.)

The following sections tell you how to keep humidity levels comfortable throughout the year.

In the summer

Use a dehumidifier in the summer. Keep the filter clean and try placing it in different rooms to get the maximum effect. The best bet is to place it in your family room (or wherever your family congregates the most). Other things to keep in mind include the following points:

- ✔ **Clothes dryers absolutely must be vented to the outside world.** Your dryer is the single biggest source of humidity in a home. If you use a clothesline to dry things (such as delicate garments) and you can't put it outdoors for some reason, put it in the garage, not inside the house.

- ✔ **Install exhaust fans vented to the outside in all bathrooms, the kitchen, and the laundry room.** Use them when you're showering or cooking to get rid of humidity in the summer. You can even install a humidistat to turn the vent fans on when humidity levels exceed a certain threshold.

When you use a vent fan with the whole-house air conditioner on, crack a window near the vent fan. The fan will draw its air from that location instead of the cool air from the house.

- **Don't put carpet in the bathrooms.** It sucks up moisture and then releases it all day long, producing a musty smell through the entire house as well as mold and mildew.

- **Don't allow water to pool in your basement.** Use a sump pump or find another way to get rid of it.

- **Ventilate your attic and basement.** Ventilating these areas lets fresh air in and reduces humidity.

In the winter

Use a humidifier in the winter. Doing so lets you decrease the load on your heating system. (You don't need to turn the heat on nearly as much to maintain comfort levels.) You can make a humidifier by simply hanging clothes to dry in your bathroom — but keep the door open — or by setting up a drying rack in any room.

In the winter, don't use vent fans in the kitchen. You want both the humidity and the heat that you generate when you cook.

Capitalizing on the chimney effect

Heat rises. That's why your house doesn't fill with smoke when you're burning wood in the fireplace. When a fire is burning in your fireplace, cool air from the room is drawn in and the oxygen combines with the biomass in the firewood to create a flame. The heat from the flame moves up into the flue and out the chimney (unless something is preventing it, like a home that is too tightly sealed or a closed damper). Hence, the term *chimney effect.*

In the same way, hot air rises within the confines of a single room. The temperature of the air near the ceiling is always higher than that at the floor. If you live in a two-story house, you may notice that the upstairs gets hotter than the downstairs — that's because of the chimney effect.

Heat rising is a passive effect; you don't need a fan to make this air move. Passive effects are the absolute best when you're looking to maximize efficiency because they're essentially free. To take advantage of them, you just need to exploit physics. So how do you take advantage of the chimney effect? In these ways:

✔ **Install ceiling fans.** Depending on whether the blades push air up or down, ceiling fans can move heat either up into the ceiling, thereby making the ground level cooler, or move heat down (in the winter). With the flip of a switch, you can change the blades' direction.

✔ **Adjust your registers.** During the winter, adjust the registers in your home so that much more heat enters the downstairs than the upstairs. The chimney effect evens out the heat in your home very nicely. During the summer, do just the opposite: Open the upstairs registers and let the majority of cool air enter there. Over the course of the day, the cool air will gravitate down to the lower floors.

Going for the greenhouse effect

Why does a greenhouse get so hot when the sun is shining? The answer is found in the *greenhouse effect*. Essentially, sunlight transmits through the greenhouse's glass walls and is converted into heat on the interior surfaces of the greenhouse. The same glass that transmitted the radiation into the greenhouse serves to insulate that heat from getting back out into the great outdoors. The same effect causes cars to get hot when they're sitting in harsh summertime sunshine.

To take advantage of the greenhouse effect, follow these suggestions:

✔ **Open all your blinds when you want to heat your home and the sun is shining.** Blinds prevent sunlight from entering, so you can't exploit the greenhouse effect when they're drawn.

✔ **Blinds work very well for insulating, so close them whenever you need to retain heat or cool air.** In general, closing your blinds at night is always a good idea. Close them on cold winter days, when the sun is dull, to make your heater work more efficiently (by increasing the insulation of your home).

Making more small changes for even bigger benefits

One of the best ways to reduce your energy costs is with a programmable thermostat. Installing one is a great do-it-yourself project, and it costs less than $100, in most cases.

Find a unit compatible with the equipment you have in your house. Consult your owner's manual to find out what types are compatible, call a heating and air specialist, or ask at your hardware store. Make sure to get one with easy-to-understand instructions. Avoid thermostats that seem complex to operate because that's an indicator that the design just isn't a good one. It doesn't have to be complex.

Available options include the following:

✔ A reminder when it's time to change the filter

✔ The option to automatically change programs between heating and cooling seasons

✔ A low-battery indicator

Most homes don't need every room to be maintained at the same temperature. In general, rooms where you don't spend a lot of time or that tend to warm up or cool down quickly (because of size or design) are good candidates for blocking off. Bathrooms, for example, don't need HVAC very much at all, nor do laundry rooms. The following list shares advice on how to vary the temperature of different rooms:

✔ **To block off rooms, close the registers and the door.** You can further seal the room off from the rest of the house by laying an old towel across the threshold at the bottom of the door. But don't overdo it. Closing more than one out of every five vents may cause your furnace to work too hard.

✔ **Use window air conditioners to cool rooms individually.** A portable air conditioner is much cheaper to run than a big, whole-house unit. Perhaps you need to cool only your family room or a single bedroom upstairs so that your sleep will be more comfortable. (Note, however, that the thermostat that controls your system needs to be in a room that isn't blocked off!)

✔ **Heat a single room using portable heaters.** If you set up a couple of portable heaters in your family room, for example, you may not need to turn on your whole-house system at all. Just don't use them while you sleep.

Here are other ways you can reduce your energy costs while maximizing your comfort:

✔ **Use your grill more.** If possible, do all your summertime cooking outdoors. Gas barbecues are the most efficient and convenient, which may motivate you to cook outdoors more often.

✔ **Adjust the lighting.** The human mind is subliminally sensitive to certain sensory effects, one of which is lighting tone. A harshly lit room makes people feel hotter. A shady, dull room makes people feel cooler. Candlelight makes people feel warmer. You get the idea.

Window air conditioners for a single room

If you're buying a window air conditioner, get one with a Seasonal Energy Efficiency Rating (SEER) between 10 and 17. The higher the rating, the more efficient the air conditioner is. Check with your utility company to see whether it offers rebates for units with high SEER numbers. It may have a list of recommended units you can get at a discount.

You can also buy a stand-alone unit that sits on wheels and move it around your home as you see fit. You can use it in the family room during the evening hours and then push it into your bedroom when you sleep.

When you install your air conditioner, put it in the shade. The cooler it is, the more efficiently it will run.

Fortunately, you can easily do the maintenance yourself:

✔ Clean the fins, evaporator coil, fan, condenser fins, and tubes. Be sure to unplug it first and don't make a big mess. You can use a jet spray to clean out the fins.

✔ Air conditioners also have filters that get clogged. You can replace these inexpensively, or you may be able to vacuum the dust and debris from the filter material.

✔ Buy a cheap fan comb to straighten bent fins. Using the comb to straighten the fins out can make a big difference in the unit's efficiency.

Book II

Energy
Efficiency

Solving Some of the Most Common Inefficiency Problems

In order for any system to be efficient, it needs to be running well and smoothly. Sometimes, though, problems creep up that can decrease the performance of the system, especially HVAC systems. If your existing HVAC equipment isn't working the way you think it should, here are some of the most common problems that you can solve yourself.

If you have a combustion system, have an HVAC pro inspect and tune your equipment every few years. It pays as these systems are prone to carbon buildups and other soot issues that can drastically affect their performance. Heat pumps can work nicely for a decade without being serviced, as can solar water heaters, space heaters, and so on.

Restoring air flow

To work at their peak efficiency, HVACs need adequate air flow. That means that the filters must be clean, and the airflow path must be unobstructed. When air flow is obstructed, the machine basically uses up the same amount of power but does less work for that power, and so it has to be on longer to get the same job done. You waste energy, and your house is noisier to boot. Following are some of the most common problems impeding air flow:

- **Blockage in the air ducts:** Construction debris sometimes falls into the ducts, as do kids' toys, carpet segments or pads, and so on. Small items are easy to remove. Larger items can be more of a problem; you may need to pull the duct from the register either from underneath the floor or from the other side of the wall.

- **Blocked registers:** Something may be sitting over a register, such as curtains, drapes, furniture, toys, or decorations. You may not even realize that the register is closed off. Or maybe the air is flowing freely, but it's headed in the wrong direction. You may be able to add a plastic reflector to aim the air better into the living quarters.

- **Loose joints:** To repair joints, use aluminum tape rather than duct tape. Wear a face mask to protect yourself from the dust, or you'll be sorry about an hour later.

- **Dirty coils, fins, and filters:** You can take the outer cover off of your condenser unit and jet spray the fins to remove debris and crud buildup. If you're still not sure whether enough air is passing through, get your system inspected.

- **A blocked return air path:** A forced-air system can't heat a closed-off room. You must crack the door open or cut an inch or two off the bottom of the door so the air has a gap to move through. Louvers work, but they're difficult to use and neither cheap nor easy to install. If you absolutely need to close off a room, look into a portable heating or air-conditioning unit for that room.

- **Too many bends in the ductwork:** When this is the case, air has a difficult time passing through. Not only are you not getting much air through the maze-like ductwork, but the air you *are* getting is expensive (because the machine has to work harder to push the air through all the turns). If you can't change the ductwork, consider installing a portable heater or air conditioner and simply closing off the inefficient ductwork entirely.

Repositioning the thermostat

Your system's performance is governed by the location of the thermostat. The temperature you set is maintained wherever the thermostat is located. Sometimes systems work poorly because direct sunshine hits the thermostat, resulting in a temperature reading that doesn't accurately reflect the actual temperature of the room. If the thermostat is located directly over a heating duct or in a remote corner of the house, its temperature isn't indicative of the house in general. A well-designed system has the thermostat near the center of the home, usually near the air intake vent.

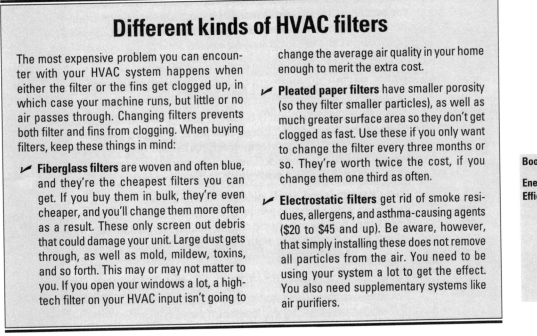

Different kinds of HVAC filters

The most expensive problem you can encounter with your HVAC system happens when either the filter or the fins get clogged up, in which case your machine runs, but little or no air passes through. Changing filters prevents both filter and fins from clogging. When buying filters, keep these things in mind:

✔ **Fiberglass filters** are woven and often blue, and they're the cheapest filters you can get. If you buy them in bulk, they're even cheaper, and you'll change them more often as a result. These only screen out debris that could damage your unit. Large dust gets through, as well as mold, mildew, toxins, and so forth. This may or may not matter to you. If you open your windows a lot, a high-tech filter on your HVAC input isn't going to

change the average air quality in your home enough to merit the extra cost.

✔ **Pleated paper filters** have smaller porosity (so they filter smaller particles), as well as much greater surface area so they don't get clogged as fast. Use these if you only want to change the filter every three months or so. They're worth twice the cost, if you change them one third as often.

✔ **Electrostatic filters** get rid of smoke residues, allergens, and asthma-causing agents ($20 to $45 and up). Be aware, however, that simply installing these does not remove all particles from the air. You need to be using your system a lot to get the effect. You also need supplementary systems like air purifiers.

Book II

Energy
Efficiency

You can have your controller moved, and sometimes doing so is cheap and easy. Or you may be able to find one that uses a remotely located temperature sensor. The latter works well unless your kid takes it to school for show-and-tell.

When Your HVAC's on the Blink

Something's wrong. Your house isn't staying as warm or as cool as it should, even though you've taken steps to maximize your HVAC system's efficiency. What do you do? Well, if you're like many people, you curse the Fates (because these things tend to break down on either the coldest day of the winter or the most searing day of the summer) and then call in the HVAC repair pros. But before you do, make sure that you really need their expertise. While some problems definitely need the attention of an HVAC expert, other problems are relatively easy to fix yourself.

What to check before you call a repairman

You know that your wallet is going to take a hit as soon as you call in a pro. So when your system is down, check out these things first. If you're lucky, you may just solve your own HVAC problem:

✓ **Check the thermostat and make sure that it's on.** Fiddle with it, moving the temperature up and down. Give it a little time — an hour or so — because sometimes fail-safes (timers, clocks, and so on) go off.

✓ **Check breakers at your main panel.** Often when servicemen are called out, it's not the HVAC that's down, but the circuit panel, in which case you've wasted money on a call. Many furnaces also have an on-off switch somewhere on the chassis. Somebody (kids . . .) may have flipped it off, so check to make sure that it's on.

✓ **Change the filter.** HVACs need flowing air to work properly. It's amazing how many times servicemen are called out only to discover that the filter is totally clogged up. They don't mind; they love to charge $80 to change your filter. But you can do it for much less.

✓ **Make sure that the gas is on.** (Or if you have a tank, make sure that it's not empty). Check all the valves by closing them and opening them back up. This check may not seem like it makes any sense, but valves can stick, and by opening and closing them, you may be able to get the fuel flowing again.

✓ **Check to see whether the chimney exhaust flue is clear.** Checking the flue may or may not be an easy thing to ascertain because many chimneys meander back and forth, like an accordion. In other cases, you just plain can't see up into that dirty, black hole. If in doubt, call for service.

✓ **Make sure that the line that drains water isn't clogged.** Many furnaces drain off several gallons of water per day in heating season. If the line becomes clogged and the water can't drain properly, the furnace shuts down due to a fail-safe switch. If the drain hose looks dirty, remove it, fill it with a mixture of bleach and water (30 percent bleach to 70 percent water), wait 15 minutes, and flush it.

✓ **Look for blocked or leaking ducts.** The big ones going into the furnace from the house/filter port are especially problematic. If you can get to the ducts, you can usually fix them yourselves (see Chapter 2 of this book). Or you may need to contact an HVAC pro. (If you do, have them do a complete inspection.)

✓ **Clean the outdoor equipment.** Remove debris like leaves and twigs from fins or intake and exhaust ports.

Symptoms that call for a pro

If your HVAC is exhibiting any of the following symptoms, you need the help of a professional HVAC repairperson:

✔ **Short cycling, or going off and on a lot:** When the thermostat is out of adjustment or the internals are out of balance, a fail-safe shuts the system off. Turn it off and get it repaired.

✔ **Irregular flame from the burners:** An irregular flame indicates a problem with dirty burners or a cracked heat exchanger. The flame should be nice and even over the entire burner surface. Many times you can tell at a glance whether your burners are running optimally.

✔ **Strange sounds like rumbling, clicking, and so on:** Hearing these sounds are okay in hot-water or steam-heating systems, but in a furnace with a forced-air system, they're a sign of trouble.

✔ **Inexplicable illness in your family:** You may have a combustion leak somewhere in the system. Call a pro right away. Get a carbon monoxide alarm right now and use it.

Book II

Energy
Efficiency

✔ **Sooty accumulations:** Deposits usually appear near where the flame is burning. A good clean burn leaves very little residue, and it appears more brown than black. Sooty black grunge, on the other hand, is a sign of incomplete burning — you're not getting all the heat you could be out of your fuel — and you're paying for the inefficiency. Plus, you're going to have to clean the soot out of the system, which can be costly.

Buying a New System or Supplementing the One You Have

If your HVAC system is old, it's probably inefficient compared to newer technology. You're likely to be disappointed with your system's performance. Maybe it doesn't cool the house well enough in the summer, or it's on all the time in the winter and the air isn't hot enough when it comes out. Or perhaps you're getting tired of the twice-a-year service call, in which case you need to add these costs to the payback analysis.

If you're thinking about replacing your current HVAC system, your best bet is to call an HVAC service company and have them come out and analyze your equipment. They can tell you how much better new equipment will perform (although you should keep in mind that their motive is to sell new equipment). Armed with this information, you have a payback decision on your hands. You'll be saving a certain amount of energy per year, which can translate into cost. What you'll probably discover is that, because HVAC equipment is expensive, you're not likely to get a payback in less than 20 years, which is a dubious investment.

Before you spend the big bucks, first try all the little things in this chapter and in Chapter 2 of this book. If you still decide to change, take your time. Do your research and get at least three quotes.

One of the best bets is to install a high-efficiency gas fireplace in your family room or living room. You can use the gas fireplace to heat the room locally, which means you won't be heating your entire home.

Hiring an HVAC Contractor

Whether you decide to replace your existing HVAC system with a brand-new one or supplement the one you have with additional heating and cooling equipment, you need to hire a contractor. Every contractor uses a standard contract and follows approved practices. Contractors can

- ✔ Obtain permits.
- ✔ Manage the schedule and get the parts when they're needed.
- ✔ Deal with all the inspections, and assume responsibility for a failed inspection.
- ✔ Solve problems quickly and efficiently.

To find potential contractors, your best bet is to ask friends who have the same kind of system you want to install for referrals (or warnings to stay away, as the case may be). You can look contractors up with the Better Business Bureau, or you can get information from state regulatory agencies. The Internet contains a lot of referral sites, but beware — these recommendations may be paid for by the contractors themselves. Enter the name of your city or county and the kind of project you want to do.

Never use a family member or friend. You may think they'll give you a better price (they'll probably be thinking they can charge you more since there won't be competitive bids) and better service (they'll be thinking they can work your job when it's convenient because you won't fire them), but the reality is you'll (both) probably regret it if any problems arise or mishaps occur.

Getting and comparing bids

When hiring an HVAC contractor, always, always, always get multiple bids. There's a possibility that you may only be able to find a single contractor who can do the job you have in mind. In this case, try to get some information about how much the job costs in other areas so you'll have something to compare your bids against.

Always let contractors know you're going out for competitive bids. Never make a commitment of any kind when they first visit.

After you get the bids, the problem becomes one of comparing apples to apples. Choosing the contractor comes down to three things:

- **Cost:** This factor may seem very important, but ultimately it may be the least significant. Why? Many things can go wrong, and problems generally add up to more cost. If you get a bid that's much lower than the other ones, beware. Your contractor probably doesn't understand what he's doing, either technically or competitively. Or maybe you're getting a contractor with a much lower overhead rate. Why? Does he not carry insurance? Is he working out of his truck, or off of his bicycle? Will he be around in three months to provide warranty coverage?

- **Craftsmanship:** Get referrals. While referrals may not seem important, it reveals experience and efficiency. How long has the contractor been in the business?

- **Compatibility:** Face it: Some contractors are just dubious characters, and some are living in a different universe. Having a good relationship matters — a lot. Not only does it foster cooperation and increase the likelihood that problems will be ironed out quickly and effectively, but a contractor who doesn't like you is simply not going to go the extra mile for you. (That's right — it can go both ways.) You may get the work done as per spec, but extra time won't be spent to get the pipe joints just right. Or your phone calls won't be returned until it can't be put off any longer. You want a contractor who is happy to answer the phone when he sees your phone number on his Caller ID.

Book II

Energy
Efficiency

Make sure to ask about workmanship warranties. If the contractor offers only the warranty that comes from the manufacturer, beware. Ask about bonding, insurance, licenses, and so on, too. If your contractor doesn't like these questions, beware. Good contractors are glad to hear these questions — it means their shady competitors are being weeded out.

Sealing the deal

A contract should include prices as well as a schedule of events that can be easily established and approved between the two of you. You also need to specify the cash flow: when payment is due and how much it will be.

Get *everything* in writing. Make it clear that throughout the entire project you expect everything to be in writing. Any decisions or changes made will be in writing only. E-mails are okay, but print them and keep them in a file folder. It's not that people are to be distrusted; it's that verbal communication is like that children's game "Telephone," where the message gets garbled each time it's spoken. Writing forces clear articulation.

Working with a contractor after the job begins

When you're on the go, you need to work with your contractor as effectively as possible. Now is not the time to express doubt about your contractor's abilities. Now is the time to follow the Golden Rule: Do unto others as you would have them do unto you.

- ✔ **Always be completely square and decisive.** You may not want to express disappointment about how a job is turning out, but you should do so if that's what you're feeling.

- ✔ **Be friendly no matter what.** Don't get emotional. Problems happen. Be cool when they do, and your contractor will be more honest with you about everything.

- ✔ **Offer cold drinks.** Make a cooler available. Go the extra mile.

- ✔ **Don't forget the need for a restroom.** Make it nice and easy and keep it clean.

Chapter 4

Lighting Your Home
More Efficiently

. . . .

In This Chapter

▶ Noting the differences between various types of light bulbs

▶ Considering the ambience of your lighting schemes

▶ Calculating cost savings that you can achieve

▶ Maximizing your efficiency with special light switches

. . . .

The typical North American home spends between 8 and 10 percent of its energy budget on lighting (excluding the bulbs and equipment). In any given night, the average home uses 32 light bulbs, including not only lighting for rooms, but lighting inside refrigerators, ovens, and microwaves. Most of these light bulbs are the standard, 50-cent, screw-base style using a technology that has been around for more than a hundred years. People have spent the vast majority of their lives with Thomas Edison's original brainstorm. But things are changing. A number of choices are available now that, while more expensive, provide much better economics and performance over the lifetime of the product. They also offer lower pollution, which is very important to many people.

In this chapter, you find out how to review your lighting arrangements and make sensible changes geared toward realizing payback. New lighting technologies can be very expensive, and you may be better off spending the money on other efficiency improvements.

Picking the Right Light: Your Options

When you think of lighting, you may automatically think of Thomas Edison and his incandescent bulb. In fact, you may be reading this very book by the light of a bulb not too different from the one Edison first invented. But lighting options have evolved over time, from natural light to firelight to candles to incandescent bulbs to the energy-efficient products of today. Each has its plusses and minuses when it comes to ambience and energy efficiency.

Visit a good-quality lighting store to see all kinds of lighting options. Stores dedicated to lighting have better displays and a broader range of products than big hardware stores. The sales staff is also able to explain energy-efficient products better.

Natural light

Natural light includes sunlight, firelight, and candlelight. Sunlight has been around a lot longer than humanity, and it provides the overwhelming bulk of our lighting needs. Sunlight has a very broad *spectrum*, or many wavelengths of light — what most people think of as "color." (Think of the colors of the rainbow, and you get the idea.) Sunlight's spectrum goes from ultra-violet, which we can't see, through the visible range (the rainbow colors), and on into the infrared and far infrared, which are also invisible to the human eye. Sunlight gets filtered as it transmits through the atmosphere, and that's why it can look very red in the morning and evenings. But mostly sunlight is white and bright, creating a jaunty mood that people associate with the best of Mother Nature.

Candlelight and firelight preceded all our fancy, electrical light-bulb schemes. Flames cast a rich tone of reddish hues and make people's skin tone appear deep and attractive. Candles are popular because of the benign, tawny tint they cast on a room.

You can increase the lighting efficiency in your home by taking advantage of these natural light sources. Following are some ideas:

- Sunlight is the most efficient way to light your home because it's free and creates zero pollution. Sunlight also creates a specific mood that can't be beat by manmade options.

- Candles don't require any utility power. If you want to use candlelight, use natural beeswax candles with minimal scent and lead-free wicks and try to find the long-burning style, which translates into less crud being released into the air in your home. (Regular candles contain volatile organic compounds and phthalates.) Candles of this type can light your house very nicely and save a lot of money.

Don't blow out your candles when you're finished with them; use a snuffer (a long handle with a cone shape on one end). Blowing out candles causes more pollution than a snuffer because you're blasting the wick with oxygen. (The snuffer is much gentler.) Just notice how much less smoke a snuffer creates.

Old-fashioned incandescent bulbs

Standard-style (incandescent) light bulbs work by using electricity to heat up a narrow, high-resistance filament until it glows very bright. The filament is enclosed in a vacuum-drawn envelope (called the bulb) so that when the filament glows, it doesn't burn up from being combined with oxygen. Incandescent bulbs cast a warm, reddish tint, especially when a dimmer is used. You can get them in a thousand different configurations, and they're inexpensive and widely available but highly inefficient. In fact, the U.S. Congress has acted to phase out incandescent bulbs, removing them from the market starting in 2012.

An important specification for a light bulb is how much light it puts out divided by the amount of energy it consumes (an efficiency standard). Incandescent bulbs are the worst of all lighting options in this regard: Most of the energy an incandescent bulb gobbles up is converted into heat — nearly 90 percent.

REMEMBER

When considering light bulb efficiency, pay attention to the bulb's intensity and spatial focus. A round light bulb emits its spectrum pretty much in all directions at once, while a laser beam, for example, is extremely focused on a specific spot. A 10-watt gooseneck lamp with a highly focused reflector can cast enough light onto the page of a book to make reading easy and comfortable on the eyes. A 100-watt light bulb in a broadly emitting lamp, on the other hand, may be so diffuse that nothing shows up clearly. So when you choose incandescent bulbs, remember that higher wattage doesn't necessarily mean brighter light. Rather than buy the highest wattage you can find, buy the bulb that's labeled a floodlight, which usually means that they're conically shaped and have some reflective material on the inside of the glass envelope.

Book II

Energy Efficiency

Halogen bulbs

Halogen light bulbs operate almost the same as incandescent bulbs, but with a few small differences. Inside a halogen bulb is a peanut-sized glass envelope that contains a tungsten filament and halogen gas. Essentially, it's a light bulb inside of a light bulb. As the tungsten filament burns (the same way an incandescent does), the halogen gas catches the tungsten molecules and redeposits them back onto the filament, yielding a longer lifetime and better lighting uniformity. Halogen bulbs also emit a whiter, brighter, and more easily focused light, comparable to sunshine itself.

Halogen bulbs are good for reading because they're easier on your eyes. They're also good for store displays or for artwork illumination where you want the light to have a color-neutral affect (and let the artwork do its own talking). They work well outdoors because the light is more noticeable. While they may yield the same *lumen output* (a measure of how much light a bulb emits) as an incandescent, the light works better with the human eye, so the spectrum is more efficient.

Halogen bulbs burn hotter than regular incandescent bulbs, so you need to be careful how you handle them, and keep them away from flammable materials. If you use one for a reading light, you may not like having the intense heat source next to your head.

Halogen bulbs can be much more convenient than incandescent bulbs because they last twice as long. However, they aren't nearly as efficient as compact fluorescent bulbs.

Flickering fluorescent bulbs

The best option on the market, compact fluorescent light bulbs (CFLs) use a gas-filled tube and a ballast with electronics. A high-voltage signal excites phosphors on the inside surface of the bulb, which, in turn, emit light. The main difference between CFLs and incandescent or halogen bulbs is that CFLs are far more efficient because they don't put out a lot of heat. A typical 15-watt CFL puts out as much light as a 60-watt incandescent light bulb, meaning CFLs are four times as efficient.

If you plan to replace an incandescent bulb with an equivalent fluorescent bulb, in general, you can divide the wattage of an incandescent by four to get the wattage needed for an equivalent CFL. But the best bet is to compare the lumens, an actual measure of the light output. (*Wattage* is simply the input power the bulb will take.) Almost all light-bulb packages now include lumens in addition to wattages.

CFLs are more expensive, although the gap is closing because so many more fluorescent bulbs are now being manufactured. The typical lifetime of a CFL is around four times that of an incandescent bulb, and herein lies their real benefit: They don't need to be changed nearly as often, so the lifetime costs are actually less than incandescent bulbs, making them cheaper in the long term.

Here are some other things to note about CFLs:

- They're available in the coil form that you probably are used to seeing and in versions that look like incandescents, as well as a host of specialty forms. If you can put a bulb in it, chances are there's a CFL that fits the bill.

- You can use them anywhere you'd use an incandescent bulb. Dimmable and 3-way CFLs are available, and you can even buy CFL bug lights.

✔ You can find CFL bulbs that give off warm, white light that's very much like incandescent bulbs or cool, blue light. A bulb's Kelvin temperature tells you which you're getting: 2,700 K for white light and 5,000 K for bluer light.

✔ CFLs don't like very hot environments, where their lifetimes are drastically reduced. If you use them in enclosed spaces without ventilation, they heat up and grow old quickly, reducing their longevity advantage.

✔ Turning off a lamp that uses a CFL bulb quickly can reduce the bulb's life. Fifteen minutes of on time is enough to avoid cutting into the bulb's life.

✔ CFLs often take a few moments to reach maximum brightness, but waiting a moment is a small price to pay for the impressive energy savings CFLs provide.

Book II

Energy Efficiency

Around 5 milligrams of mercury are contained in each CFL light bulb. (Big bulbs have more, of course.) Mercury is a very poisonous substance, although 5 milligrams isn't much at all (about as much as the tip of a fine-point pencil). The fact that CFLs contain mercury means you have to be particularly careful when disposing of and handling these bulbs:

✔ In most municipalities, you can't simply throw a CFL into the trash. As with rechargeable batteries, paints, and so on, you take used CFL bulbs to your local hazardous materials drop site. Many stores that sell CFLs also take back your used ones. (IKEA stores accept CFLs, and so does Home Depot.) To find further options for dropping off your CFLs, call Earth 911's recycling hotline, 800-CLEANUP, or visit www.earth911.org, where a recycling center locator appears on the home page.

✔ Never send a CFL product to an incinerator, as the mercury becomes airborne when the bulb burns.

✔ Never use a vacuum to clean up a broken bulb; the mercury is aerated into your home environment through the vacuum filter, which is too porous to catch the molecules. Open windows and doors right away and stay clear of the area for about 15 minutes to give the vapors time to dissipate. Use a wet paper towel and stick both the bulb parts and the paper towel in a sealed, plastic bag.

Light-emitting diodes

Light-emitting diodes (LEDs) are extremely efficient — even more so than CFLS — and they have incredibly long lifetimes. However, they're much more expensive than other lighting sources. At present, LEDs are used where ultra-high efficiency or ultra-long lifetime are required — for example, in off-grid homes that run off of batteries or remote cabins that run off of generators. In these applications, LEDs are actually cheaper in the long run, despite their high cost, because they enable owners to use smaller batteries. (In *off-grid homes,* the battery banks are the fundamental power source. Batteries are very expensive, so smaller batteries are economically desirable.) LEDs are also used in stoplights (because of their ultra-high reliability) and in auto taillights.

Portable devices that use batteries also benefit from using LEDs. The availability of LED flashlights and camping lanterns, as well as boat and RV lighting systems, is increasing. You can buy LED-based light modules that interchangeably plug right into existing screw-type light fixtures, but they cost over $25. Furthermore, the light is thin and silvery, which isn't the friendliest hue. Before you buy LEDs, check them out at a lighting store because light bulbs, like kids, aren't returnable items if you're not happy with their performance.

Going for efficiency without sacrificing aesthetics

Lighting does more than illuminate. It creates mood, or ambience. While one type of light produces a warm, cozy glow, another type produces a harsh glare. Either can be just the type of light you want, depending on your lighting needs, the area you want to illuminate, and the mood you want to create.

Most lighting is not for "seeing," but for mood, and for making your home feel homier. By being imaginative — moving your lights around in different setups and trying different light bulbs — you can probably find an optimum configuration that takes less energy than you're using right now without sacrificing a thing.

Here are some ideas for your consideration:

✔ **Find a style of lamp that creates the mood you want.** The lamp is usually more influential than the type of light bulb in creating a mood. Lamps with dimmers are always good, and a lamp that focuses light lets you use a smaller light bulb and attain the same effect.

You can find a lot of interesting lamps at garage sales, often for less than a dollar apiece. Be on the lookout for such a find. It can save you money twice: on the purchase price and on the energy costs. The best finds are gooseneck lamps with dimmers so that you can focus the light on your work and turn the intensity up and down as desired.

✔ **Avoid metal or heavy paper lampshades.** Lampshades are very important in terms of focusing and directing light. Many of them cut off most of the light from a bulb. Look for ones that have the effect you want, but allow most of the light through. Gauzy films are best.

✔ **Vary the intensity of lighting as much as you can.** Vary light bulb intensities to create texture and depth in a room. Disperse the lights around your house to highlight the good and ignore the not-so-good.

✔ **Vary wattage where you can.** The higher the wattage, the colder the light (bluish light "feels" colder than red; it's a human perception thing); the lower the wattage, the redder the light, and the friendlier the tone. The wattage you choose depends on what you're trying to achieve. A number of smaller light bulbs distributed around a room makes for a soft color and even lighting. Plus, lower-wattage bulbs have longer lifetimes simply because they're not being so stressed by heat.

Always use the smallest wattage possible. Experiment instead of just plugging in what you have on hand. You'll probably find that you can use smaller bulbs in most instances. For example, a gooseneck lamp in the bathroom that focuses in on your face gives you the lighting you need *and* keeps wattage down.

✔ **Use lights creatively.** For example, vary the lights on tracks; they don't all have to be the same type or wattage, nor do they all have to be focused on the fireplace. A small spotlight on your favorite picture will bring those colors into play in the room. A small, 10-watt picture light can completely change a room for the better.

✔ **Try candles.** Use them alone or in combination with electric lights. You'll get hooked, and you'll save money if you do it right. (See the earlier section "Natural light" for details on what makes candles energy efficient.)

✔ **Lower the lights before bed.** Too much light right before bed creates a bad sleeping mood. Start to dim the lights or turn them off well before you retire. You'll find yourself gently relaxing into sleep mode.

✔ **Use night lights.** Having strategically placed night lights relieves you of the need to flip every light switch on when you get up in the middle of the night to go to the bathroom or nursery. Besides, blasting yourself with light in the bathroom in the middle of the night wakes you up, and you then need more time to get back to sleep than if you had used a very dim night light.

As your old incandescent lights burn out, replace them with CFLs, which currently are hands-down the most energy-efficient option for your home. And all those energy savings mean reductions in pollution and greenhouse gas production.

Calculating How Much You Can Save

To make a long story short, your potential cost savings (and the payback of installing a more expensive technology) are entirely dependent on how much you use a light (the average number of hours per day). Obviously, the easiest way to save money is to simply use less lighting.

In most homes, some light bulbs are on all the time, particularly outside lights or garage lights. And someone who likes a bright room may have every table lamp on as well as the book light he's reading by. Start thinking greener by asking yourself whether you really need the lights you turn on and making sure that you flip the switch on lights you're done using.

Consider the lights you use. Do you really need all of them? You'd probably answer *no* if you knew how much each one costs. Fortunately, lighting costs are easy to calculate. Here's how to determine how much you're spending on a particular light each month:

1. **Figure out how many watt hours (Whs) the bulb is on per day by multiplying the wattage by the number of hours the light's on daily.**

   You can read the wattage from the light bulb. The value is expressed in watts; 60 watts is very common. Then ask yourself how many hours you typically use that light per day. Two hours? All day (24 hours)?

2. **Multiply the total daily Whs by 30 to get the total Whs per month.**

3. **Divide the total Whs per month by 1,000 to get the total kWhs.**

   Why are kWhs important? Because your utility bill is calculated based on kWhs.

4. **To get your monthly cost, multiply your kWhs by the amount the electric company charges you per kWh.**

   Look at your electric bill to find out how much you're being charged for electricity. Fifteen cents per kWh is typical, but your rate may be a lot higher.

Here are some examples of calculations and the cost savings you may be able to achieve by changing your lighting schemes:

- ✔ A 60-watt bulb left on for an hour consumes 60 Whs, or .06 kWh per day. Ten 60-watt bulbs in recessed lighting in your ceiling turned on for four hours consume 2.4 kWh per day. At a rate of 15 cents per kWh, this amount of usage costs 36 cents a day. For a month, the total comes to $10.80, or $130 per year. Add to that the cost of new bulbs, and you may be spending over $150 a year to leave those overhead lights on every night.

- ✔ A 15-watt CFL costs around $4, while a comparable 60-watt incandescent bulb costs around 75 cents. For a light fixture that is turned on four hours per day, at a cost of 15 cents per kWh, the CFL costs $3.24 per year to operate. The incandescent costs $12.96 per year, for a difference of $9.72. Going with the initially more expensive CFL is actually more cost-efficient, easily paying you back the difference in original equipment cost and saving around 130 pounds of carbon dioxide pollution.

- ✔ Do you have an outside light that burns all night? If it's 600 watts, it's costing you: $0.600 \text{ kW} \times 10 \text{ hours/day} \times 30 \text{ days/month} \times \$.15/\text{kWh} = \$9$ per month, or $108 per year. You could add a motion detector, which turns the light on only when something moves through the viewing area, and save $100 per year while still having light whenever you really need it. (See the next section for more on motion detectors.) Crank up the savings further by putting an outdoor CFL in that motion detector.

✔ A 15-watt CFL bulb costs $3, whereas a 60-watt incandescent bulb costs 50 cents. If a light is on all the time (totally *not* green, by the way), a CFL costs around $20 per year to operate, whereas an incandescent bulb costs $80. However, if the CFL is put into a bathroom light socket that's only used for an hour a day, the annual cost difference is only $2.50, which is the difference in the prices of the bulbs. But keep in mind that money savings are only part of the picture. CFLs cut down on pollution and greenhouse gas production, too.

Using Clever Switches to Reduce Your Bill

You can use different types of light bulbs to increase your energy efficiency, but a better option may be to use clever switching systems that simply and automatically turn off your lights when you don't need them.

Motion detectors

Motion detectors are devices that switch light bulbs off and on when they detect something moving in their *field-of-view,* basically the area where the motion detector is set up to "look." Motion detectors are the exact same technology used in burglar alarms, except that they don't trigger an alarm; they simply turn on the light. Most motion detectors are integrated with a timing switch, so when motion is detected and a light is switched on, it goes off after a set amount of time. (A couple minutes is typical — most devices are adjustable for time delay.)

Motion detectors offer all sorts of benefits, some relating to efficiency and some relating to safety, but all relating to convenience. Burglars, for example, hate being suddenly illuminated while they're sneaking around. When a light is simply left on, a burglar doesn't mind so much; it's when things suddenly change that they get nervous and decide to vamoose. Mount a motion detector light over a porch or on the side of your house where a burglar is most apt to approach (like a dark garage side door).

Motion detectors aren't valuable just for their "gotcha!" effect, though. They turn on when anyone is there, which can be helpful when a neighbor comes up to your porch for a friendly visit, you pull into the driveway at night, and so on.

You get the best return on investment when you combine motion detectors with high-wattage lights, which are usually the kind employed outdoors. Here are some options to consider:

- ✔ **Solar-powered outdoor floodlights with motion detectors:** You can mount them anywhere so that you get light exactly where you want it. Better yet, you don't need an electrical outlet so you avoid the cost of outlet installation. The unit includes a battery that is charged during high intensity solar hours, and so the amount of available energy is limited. At around $65, the solar-powered motion detector can provide huge cost savings if you need light in a remote location. Plus, you can move the lights around at will, which you can't do with a standard hard-wired light fixture.

- ✔ **One-piece outdoor systems:** These systems include one or more motion detectors along with light fixtures in one complete package. These come in flood, decorative, and remote arrangements.

- ✔ **Motion detector switches:** These switches fit right into the standard switch socket you already have in your home. Whenever somebody walks into the field of view, the light goes on for about 30 seconds. Motion detector switches are great for utility rooms where your hands may be full of clothes or groceries, and flipping a switch is inconvenient. They're also good for basements and attics.

- ✔ **Screw-base-style motion detectors.** You install these detectors between a light bulb and the socket that the bulb would normally be screwed into. At around $40, they're not cheap and the payback isn't very good, but they may be just the ticket for a utility room or laundry room or anywhere you often find yourself with your hands full and unable to grapple around for the switch.

Before you buy a motion detector, pay attention to the field of view. With some units, you can adjust the field of view; with others, it's fixed. Getting one with an adjustable sensitivity is best; you don't necessarily want your lights to go on when a cat crosses your yard. (Then again, maybe you do.) When in doubt, save the packing materials and receipt and be prepared to buy something else. And put those marvelous, energy-efficient CFL bulbs in all your shiny, new motion-detecting lights.

Dimmer switches

Light dimmers are used for decreasing and increasing a light's intensity. Although they aren't particularly efficient, the net effect of using them is that you do use less energy (and if you're using dimmable CFLs, you're saving a whole lot of energy and money). There's another benefit as well: The bulbs on dimmer switches last longer because they're operating at lower temperatures. In general, you get a friendlier, richer color, and you can vary the mood in a room like nothing else.

You can change almost any light switch in your house to a dimmer switch, but beware: You need to know a few basic rudiments about electricity before you start poking around inside your electrical junction boxes. You need to understand the difference between the white wire, the black wire, and the green (or bare) wire. The task isn't difficult, but explaining everything you need to know about electrical wiring is beyond the scope of this book. If you're motivated and want to give it a go yourself, keep the following advice in mind:

- ✔ **Before you do anything, the safest bet is to simply turn the main breaker switch off in your house.** You'll have to do your work during daylight hours or with a flashlight, but you won't be able to shock yourself. After you do the work, make sure that you cover the dimmer switch with the faceplate. If you turn the main breaker back on and a circuit breaker trips, you've messed up somewhere, at which point you may want to call in an electrician to do the job right.

- ✔ **Ask for instructions and guidelines at your hardware store.** Someone there can probably tell you how to install a switch and show you the actual hardware to use. When you're getting instructions, make sure that you understand how to maintain the proper grounding scheme, which is very important. You may need to be aware of local electrical codes, so ask your hardware store clerk about those as well.

Another option is to refer to *How To Fix Everything For Dummies* (Wiley) by Gary Hedstrom, Peg Hedstrom, and Judy Ondria Tremore for general information and instructions on common electrical wiring jobs.

If you have aluminum wiring in your house (it's shiny or dull gray, instead of the usual coppery or orange color), don't wire a dimmer yourself because there are technical problems you don't want to deal with. (Specifically, when two dissimilar metals come into contact, the potential for corrosion exists. So when working with aluminum wires, you need to understand what works and what doesn't.)

Whole-house lighting controllers

Whole-house lighting control systems basically switch all your home lights off and on from a central console. For example, you can turn off all your lights from one location when you go to bed. Or when you enter your house, you can turn on a certain preset number of lights so that you don't have to go around and individually activate each light. Some can be turned off and on by a timer. You can even get a system that you can call from a remote location.

If you program one of these contraptions for efficiency, you can achieve some significant cost savings. For example, you could turn off all of your lights at a certain time of night. You could also turn lights on and off according to a clock so that you capture exactly the right mood at different times.

Book II

Energy
Efficiency

Chapter 5

Increasing Your Water Efficiency

The minimal human requirement for water is only around four gallons per day, and that's for both consumption and cleaning. So how much does a typical family (2 adults, 2 kids) use? Between 200 and 350 gallons of water a day. That's 73,000 to 128,000 gallons per year. Landscaping, swimming pools, and spas take even more water. A small, working ranch may use over 270,000 gallons per year. That's a lot of water.

In most homes, water has five main destinations: faucets, toilets, showers (baths), dishwashers, and washing machines. In each case, water heating may be required, which consumes around 20 percent of a typical home's energy costs. Other uses of water include outdoor irrigation, pools, spas, fountains, and so on. This chapter tells you how to save in these areas.

The vast majority of homes get their water from the local utility, some with metered rate structures, some not. If you're not operating off of a water meter, your water utility may give you a better monthly rate if you voluntarily go to a metered rate structure. The utility will come out and install a meter, usually free of charge. If you're frugal, you can save money, and by having a meter, you'll be more conscious of how much water you're using.

Drinking to Your Health

Most of the water used in a home isn't consumed. Instead, it's used for tasks like cleaning, watering, and so on. Yet many people today spend much more money for water they drink than on water they use for these other purposes.

Why? Because our society is fixated on bottled and/or purified drinking water, which is almost always a waste of money and resources and generates far more pollution than is necessary. In fact, evidence increasingly indicates that drinking purified water may lead to health problems. So what's the deal?

The following sections help you sort out what you need to know about your water supply and to give you ideas for reducing the amount of money you spend on drinking water.

Wading through a flood of choices: Tap, well, bottled, and purified

Most homes have a number of choices for their water sources. In this section you find out more about the most common choices. Your best bet is to use the cheapest source for each of your various applications. Most of the time, this choice is very easy; simply use tap water.

Tap water

Most homes get their water from local utilities, which have stringent quality requirements. In fact, federal standards for tap water are actually higher than those for bottled water. In addition, most tap water already contains minerals important to your health — minerals that some purveyors of purifier systems and bottled water deliberately add to their products and charge you more for. Bottom line: The government provides you with safe, healthy water without the hassle and expense of bottled water.

Local utilities are required to make public their testing process and results. If you want to know exactly what's in your water, call the customer-service number on your utility bill and ask to be sent the data. You shouldn't be charged for this information.

Well water

Some homes get their water from wells. Although these sources are generally very good, they may not be the best source for drinking water because contaminants do make their way into wells, and you may have to pay for testing. Well water is especially prone to change over time. If you have a well, you're very likely getting the requisite minerals and other natural components. But you may also be getting pollution and other contaminants like dumped pesticides or other chemicals.

If you have a well, test it at least once a year; if your well fails a test, test more often. Look in the yellow pages under Water Well Drilling.

Bottled water

Bottled water costs 240 to 10,000 times more than tap water — moneywise, that is; the environmental costs are even more enormous. The costs show up in bottling, packaging, shipping, retail, sales, advertising, and so on. If you're paying this price for bottled water simply because you think it's cleaner, you may want to consider these facts:

- **Quality isn't guaranteed.** Unlike the water provided by utilities, the quality of bottled water isn't regulated by the federal government. When you buy bottled water, you have no guarantee that you're even getting water that's as good as your home supply.

- **"Enriched" may not provide enrichment.** Some bottled water is advertised as "oxygen enriched." Absolutely no evidence exists to support the notion that it does anything whatsoever to help you.

- **Transporting water is costly.** Bottled water takes a great deal of energy to transport to your store shelf. Think how far that water from the Italian mountain lake has come and then think of the pollution generated in the process. It doesn't matter that the water is cheap; the cost of pollution isn't reflected in the cost of a product.

  America's appetite for bottled water gobbles up more than 47 million gallons of oil and produces one billion pounds of carbon dioxide per year (that's right — billion!).

- **Plastic bottles stick around for a very long time.** It takes 1,000 years for a plastic bottle to degrade in a landfill. You can recycle the bottles, but if you don't need them in the first place, recycling isn't the best answer. Not using them is.

  If you want to use bottles of water because they're convenient, use reusable bottles. You can fill them up with tap water. Alternatively, buy purified water at a grocery store that lets you bring in and fill up your own bottles and charges you by the gallon.

Book II

Energy Efficiency

Purified water

Many people use water purifiers, systems that in most cases remove impurities but in some instances add minerals and other positive substances.

Humans don't necessarily need perfect water. In fact, evidence suggests that a pristine lifestyle leads to increased immune deficiency. Certain types of minerals and bacteria are required by the human body to enable digestion. And recent studies indicate that children raised on purified water are statistically more likely to suffer from childhood diseases than those brought up on tap water. The reason? The immune system needs to be constantly exercised in order to achieve optimum conditioning (just like muscles). Humans that live in sanitized, pristine environments don't get the necessary exposure.

Having said that, sometimes having a water purifying system is a good idea. The next section explains how to tell when your water supply is problematic and what you can do about it.

Getting the goods on suspicious water

In rare cases, you may actually have good reason to be suspicious of your water source. Potential contaminants include pernicious bacteria, *cysts* (parasites with protective coverings that make them very tenacious), heavy metals, chlorine, sediment, poisons, and many more.

Signs that your water supply may be contaminated include

- **Age of your pipes:** In old plumbing systems, some contaminants reside right in the pipes and are very difficult to get out. If your city water supply is pristine but you have an old home, you may still have a problem because you're running clear water through contaminated pipes.

- **Clarity:** While unclear water isn't a sure indicator of contamination, you should find out what the cause is. Most of the time, it's only minerals, which isn't a problem.

- **Poor taste:** Bad-tasting water may be a sign of a contaminant. But determining whether the bad taste indicates a real problem or just tastes different than you're used to is difficult. (It's very common to go into other cities and find that the water tastes poor, even though it's just fine.) If in doubt, get your water tested.

- **Smell:** The human nose is very sensitive. If your water smells bad, get it tested (although a bad smell isn't necessarily an indicator that it's unhealthy).

If you're suspicious about the quality of your water, the best bet is to get your water tested. Here are your options:

- **Have your water tested by an independent company.** Check the Internet or your phone book for "Water Testing." For around $100, you can get a detailed analysis. (They send you a sterilized container; you fill it and send it back.) You need to do every testing sequence twice, at different times of the year, to get reliable results.

- **Have your water tested by a not-so-objective company.** You can get tests done by water purification companies (probably for free). But beware: Their goal is to sell you water purification equipment or services. They probably won't tell you that humans do better with impurities in their water supply.

✔ **Test your water yourself.** Although you can buy your own equipment and test your water yourself, doing so isn't your best bet. First, it's expensive. Second, and more importantly, you probably don't have the expertise to interpret the results sufficiently. It's best to trust the experts.

Purifying your drinking water

So you've decided to improve your drinking water. Two types of home-based equipment are widely available:

✔ **Distilleries:** Distilled water is boiled, and, in the process, the water separates from the impurities. This type of purification is expensive and energy-intensive, but it's very thorough.

✔ **Filtration systems:** Filtering involves forcing the water through some kind of porous device that removes the impurities. Aerator filters that attach to faucets are the simplest type of filter.

As you consider your water purifying options, look for a system that treats only the water you plan to consume. After all, it makes no sense to filter water for your shower or your dishwasher. In addition, make sure that the system targets the impurities you want to eliminate. Some systems improve only the water's taste and color. Others get rid of contaminants. Make sure that you know what your system does.

Simply buying a filter because it sounds good is a waste of money, although most filters are purchased for this very reason. Purification equipment targets very specific types of contamination. Before you make an investment, make sure that the equipment you're getting is designed to remove the contaminant you're interested in removing. The only way to know is to first have your water tested.

All systems take effort and maintenance. If you don't want to hassle with water purification, consider one of these alternatives:

✔ **Contract with a bottled water company.** They will rent you a dispenser and come out twice a month to refill it with a big jug of distilled or filtered water and do the regular maintenance. The cost is around $8 per month. You can get dispensers that heat the water, which is more efficient than using your water heater but less efficient than using your microwave.

✔ **Get a bottle with a built-in filter.** This method is the cheapest way to go, and you use this system only when you need it. Fill the bottle with water from your tap, screw the filter/lid on, and, when you drink, the water is filtered.

Mechanical filtration occurs when water is forced through a porous medium, like a screen or a chunk of carbon. These strainers use mesh with particular hole sizes. The size of the holes determines the strainer's *porosity,* which is usually specified in terms of microns. (A *micron* is one millionth of a liter.) As you'd expect, strainers with finer porosity remove smaller-sized contaminants than strainers with higher porosity.

To get an idea about what type of porosity you need, you have to determine what type of contaminant you're trying to remove. Sediment filters, for example, remove smaller particles like suspended dirt, sand, rust, and scale (known as *turbidity*). Once again, filters are always very specific to the type of material you're attempting to filter. Look on the filter label (or get on the Internet and research a particular filter's specifications) to see which types of contaminants it's good at filtering.

If you need a filter with a very fine porosity, you're better off removing the biggest impurities by using a higher porosity filter first. Larger porosity filters are generally much cheaper than smaller porosity filters (and easier to clean). Catch the big stuff first, and your overall filter expenses will be less.

Here's a look at how common filter types do their thing:

- **Activated carbon filtration:** Carbon absorption filters are the most widely used because they offer high performance at a low price. They remove many types of contaminants as well as chlorine, but they don't affect water hardness. Few carbon systems work with lead, asbestos, VOCs (dissolved organics), cysts, and coliform, so if these contaminants are your issues, carbon filters aren't recommended.

  In fact, most of the impurities that carbon filters remove aren't the impurities that you're targeting. In addition, carbon filters need to be changed frequently, and this can be very costly.

- **Reverse osmosis (ultrafiltration):** This method uses pressure to force water through a selective, semi-permeable membrane that separates contaminants from the water. Reverse osmosis systems are very good at removing turbidity, asbestos, lead and other heavy metals, radium, and VOCs. But keep these things in mind:

  - **Membranes are costly to replace.** Most are capable of having the membrane washed out (backwashing), but the membranes do eventually need to be replaced, which isn't cheap.

  - **They waste a lot of water.** They use 3 to 9 gallons of water to get one pure gallon. This method is a dubious way to achieve efficiency.

- **Virustat filters:** Virustat filters eliminate viruses from water sources in foreign cities or wild streams. For the most part, these viruses don't affect local folks because they're used to them and have built up a tolerance.

Caring for your filters

As the filter cruds up, its effectiveness diminishes, so when reading specs, always remember that you need to change filters as often as the manufacturer recommends, or you may not achieve the required performance.

Also, as the filter gets older it traps impurities of all kinds, so it may actually become a breeding ground for nasty little critters invisible to the naked eye, making the problem worse, not better.

Directing the Flow of Traffic with Faucets

The typical home has six indoor faucets, and another four or five outdoors. That gives you a lot of opportunities for improved efficiency. Just by making a few changes in your faucets, you can use water more efficiently.

Some relatively easy changes you can make include

- ✔ **Using a two-valve faucet:** A two-valve faucet is more efficient than a single-valve type (where you move the lever around until you get the right temperature). The latter inevitably wastes hot water.
- ✔ **Using aerator filters in the faucets:** These filters add air and keep up the pressure while reducing flow volume. Most of the time, people are looking for greater pressure, not flow volume, from a faucet. In fact, many building codes now require low-flow faucets because they make so much sense. (They save water without being inconvenient.)

Of course, dealing with leaks is a great way to not only increase how efficiently you use water but also to offset some other problems as well.

Leaks: Money and energy down the drain

Leaky faucets waste water. A faucet dripping once per second can waste 2,000 gallons per year. Beyond just the waste factor, leaking faucets can also cause increased health issues because mold and mildew just love damp environments.

In addition, a dripping faucet can humidify your entire house. In the summer, higher humidity means less comfort. Do not underestimate this effect — it's much more pronounced than you may think. So not only are you wasting water, but also your house is uncomfortable and your air conditioner is running more (which means wasted utility costs). Chapter 3 tells you more about the effects of humidity.

The largest cost is the heat being wasted when hot water is drawn from your water heater. If a faucet is dripping, it may be drawing hot water. If it's dripping very slowly, you may not even know it's dripping hot water because by the time that water has come all the way from your water heater through the pipes to your faucet, it has cooled down. But heat is still being wasted.

If your water pressure is high, you probably experience dripping faucets, especially outdoors where leaks are more likely to go unnoticed. High pressure basically means higher force, which can push through questionable seals. You can have a pressure regulator installed on your water system, but it's probably not worth the hassle. If you have high water pressure, you need to be sure to provide adequate maintenance for your seals and gaskets.

Outdoor faucets are more prone to leakage than indoor ones because they're generally cheaper, plus they get beat up by the weather. (Constantly changing temperature is hard on metals.) Replacing outdoor faucets that leak is much easier than replacing indoor faucets; anybody can do it with the right wrench and patience level.

Obviously, the only way to deal with a leaking faucet is to fix it. Before you tackle the job, though, keep these suggestions in mind:

- ✔ **Shut off all the water.** Shut-off valves are generally found below sinks and the like, but shutting off the water in your entire home when doing plumbing jobs is a good idea. You can find a whole house shutoff valve in the utility box either in front of your home or in your basement. (Most of the time it'll be right next to your water meter, if you have one.) Many homes also have an underground container near the roadway (watch out for spiders when you stick your hand in).

- ✔ **Be careful to get it right.** Make sure you understand what you're doing before you start and that you have the right tools (and good ones). To find out how to fix leaky faucets, ask at your local hardware store. They have tons of experience with dripping faucets and usually know the types used in your community. You can also find instructions for fixing dripping faucets in *How to Fix Everything For Dummies* (Wiley) by Gary and Peg Hedstrom and Judy Ondrla Tremore.

    Almost anybody can do plumbing, but if you don't do it exactly right, you have to do it over until you *do* get it exactly right.

- ✔ **Take a picture before you start.** Whenever you take a plumbing system apart for repairs or maintenance, use a digital camera to snap shots once in awhile so that if you forget where things go, you can look back at the pictures.

Don't feel up to the job? Then hire a plumber and watch him fix the leak. Then next time you encounter a leaky tap, you can do the job yourself. Of course, while watching a plumber work, you may decide you never, ever want to do plumbing. Either lesson is worth the money.

A few more tips for using water wisely

Beyond fiddling with the faucets and fixing leaks, you can do a few other things to use water more efficiently:

Book II

Energy
Efficiency

- ✔ **Avoid using your garbage disposal.** It requires a lot of water to run and ends up filling the septic or sewer system far more than is needed. Get a composter and start a little garden — check out Chapter 2 of Book VI to find out more about composting — or toss the waste into your garbage.

- ✔ **Don't waste cold water waiting for the hot.** When you need hot water, you generally run water down the drain until it shows up. Instead, put a pot, bowl, or other container under the faucet while you're waiting for the water to get hot and then use the cold water you collect for cooking, ice cubes, or whatever. Just don't waste it.

- ✔ **Don't leave the tap running while you're doing something else.** Whether you're brushing your teeth or cleaning off the countertop, turn the water off. Leaving the water running is an easy habit to break, and you'd be surprised how much difference it can make.

Savings in Showers and Baths

When you're thinking about water consumption, you need to factor in two things: heat and water. Heating water accounts for around 20 percent of the power bill in a home, and showers and baths use 37 percent of that. That means that around 6 percent of your power bill is dedicated to heating water for your shower and baths. You can save in both areas:

- ✔ **Forget baths.** They'll become a thing of the past when energy rates get high enough. You simply can't take an economical bath.

- ✔ **Double up.** Put the kids (appropriately aged, of course) into the shower together. Or take a shower with your partner.

- ✔ **Use handheld showerheads.** These showerheads focus better, allowing much less water to do the job. (If you think about it, most of the water flowing from a showerhead is wasted.) The downside is you have to hold them.

✔ **Avoid showerheads that "mist" the water.** They humidify your home more than anything, and the mist does no good at all. They're especially inefficient in the summer.

✔ **Take shorter showers.** Lingering in the heat is nice, but it wastes energy because all you get out of it is, well, lingering in the heat. Find something else to linger in. A 5-minute shower is the green ideal.

Avoid things that make your shower a pleasant living quarters, like radios, TVs, nice views, and so on. In order to be truly efficient, a shower should be strictly functional.

✔ **Install a graywater recycle system on your shower and bath drain.** These systems basically recycle your home's water. A tank is connected to certain drains (usually everything but the toilet) and then a chemical-sanitizing process is performed that brings the water up to cleanliness standards suitable for landscaping and even washing. The best systems can clean water well enough to be consumed. Not only does graywater offset the demand for treating water to the highest potable standard, but it also may actually be beneficial to plants as it's likely to contain nitrogen and phosphorous. Installing one of these systems when building a new house is a lot more economical than retrofitting an existing house.

Water-wise, baths take 20 gallons or more of water, but a five-minute shower takes around 10 gallons, making baths about twice as expensive as showers. On the other hand, a shower can consume more water if you have an old-style showerhead, which typically delivers 4 to 5 gallons per minute — quite a rich and wasteful flow of water. To address this issue, the Energy Policy Act of 1992 set maximum water flow rates at 2.5 gallons per minute, so new houses and new showerheads are almost always at or below this number. New showerheads are designed to use less water and create more water pressure, so you aren't aware that you're getting less.

You can easily measure the flow of your showerhead. Simply get a pitcher with gallons marked on the side. While you count one-Mississippi, two-Mississippi, and so on, run your showerhead into the pitcher until you've got one gallon. Divide 60 by your Mississippi count, and you have your flow rate in gallons per minute. The current standard is 2.5 gallons per minute, but you can do better than this number without sacrificing much quality.

Wasting Water in the Toilet

Toilets account for 45 percent of indoor water use, or around 32,000 gallons per year for a family of four. A running toilet (one that makes a constant hissing noise) can waste up to 4,000 gallons of water per year. Fortunately, you can solve these problems, if you're willing to do a little dirty work.

Taking energy efficiency to the limit

One toilet style that's finding widespread use in countries where water is scarce features a little sink on top of the toilet tank. You wash your hands and other sundry items in the sink, and that water then drains down into the toilet tank. When you flush the toilet, it's not clean, pristine water, but it hardly matters. This design makes a lot of sense because it's so simple and effective. Look to see more of these toilets in the future.

If you put a couple of quart bottles filled with water in the tank, each flush will use that much less water. Bricks or rocks also work.

What to do when your toilet runs

If your toilet is running, finding the problem is almost always simple. The most common problem in a running toilet is the *flapper,* which is a rubber disk that covers the hole where the water enters the toilet bowl. Flappers are so ridiculously easy to change that anybody can do it. Go to your hardware store and ask the clerk how to get the job done.

You can completely rebuild the workings of most toilets with new parts (that will probably work better than the old) for less than $60. A plumber will charge a lot more than that, maybe on the order of hundreds of dollars.

If you have to work on the mechanisms in the toilet tank, first drain the tank by turning off the shut-off valve (all toilets have a shut-off valve where the water source comes out of the wall) and flushing. The tank will empty down to an inch or two. Now you can work on the working parts.

Updated toilet designs

Nothing is worse than flushing a toilet and looking back down to find that it wasn't 100 percent effective. (Okay, one thing is worse — when the toilet clogs up and overflows all over the bathroom floor, especially when you're in somebody else's house.)

The old standard technology in toilets simply uses gravity to "rush" the water down into the bowl and carry away the waste. Gravity works well enough most of the time, but it uses a lot of water, so less wasteful designs that accomplished the same thing came into being:

✔ **Pressure-assist toilets:** Pressure-assist toilets use much less water per flush and actually work better. The water is held in the tank under pressure, and when you trigger the flush lever, it "explodes" down into the toilet bowl. These toilets are costly ($250 apiece) and hard to fix, plus they're very loud, so everybody in the house is going to know what you just did.

Most public facilities use pressure-assist toilets. If you're considering a pressure-assist toilet, you can decide firsthand whether you want this loud noise in your own home by going into almost any public facility and sampling the wares.

✔ **Vacuum-assist toilets:** Vacuum-assist toilets suck waste right out of the bowl (which is sort of the opposite of the pressure-assist method of blasting it out). They're cheaper than their pressure-assist counterparts and easier to fix.

✔ **Compost toilets:** Compost toilets don't flush at all. You need to be a hearty soul to consider these devices, but they're very earth-friendly. They basically allow the waste products to decompose in a specially designed chamber. At some point, you take the "materials" out of the "finishing drawer" and to your landscaping.

Watering Your Landscaping

Ah, the great outdoors. Most people have some form of landscaping, and many people have extensive landscaping, including a lawn, which is the most water- and energy-intense form of landscaping you can imagine. In a yard, you can conserve water through your landscaping choices and through your choice of sprinkler. The following sections tell you how to use less water and energy in your yard.

Considering lawn alternatives

The one thing you can do to conserve the most water and energy is to get rid of your lawn. Replace it with drought-resistant plants and don't water them much. (Create a drought of your own!) You can also go *au naturel* by replacing your lawn with native plants that grow and thrive in your climate without need for watering above and beyond what Mother Nature provides. Barring that, you can

✔ Set the height levers on your lawn mower an inch higher. Less heat will hit the dirt beneath the grass, thereby allowing you to water less. And longer grass chokes out the weeds much better than short grass, so you won't have to use herbicides.

✔ Fertilize your lawn less often. When you lighten up on the fertilization, you aren't asking the grass to grow quite so vigorously.

✔ Use a mulching mower, which helps fertilize the grass.

Picking the right sprinkler and watering at the right time

If you need to water your lawn, know that all sprinklers aren't created equal. Some waste more water than they apply to the plants. And you can also control the time of day or night you do your watering to gain better efficiency. Follow these guidelines to water with the least waste:

✔ **If you need to water a large area, use rotary sprinklers.** Avoid misting sprinklers because all they do is mist water into the air where it blows away into the neighbor's yard.

✔ **Use drippers instead of broadcast sprinklers for isolated plants, particularly when they're surrounded by bark or other ground cover that doesn't need any watering at all.** You may have to spend more money up front on hardware, but you'll save a lot of water, and your plants will be much healthier because they're getting water right where they want it — in their root systems.

A drip system needs to be maintained. Check it once in a while by turning it on manually and making sure that all the drippers are working.

✔ **Water at night or early in the morning.** The sunshine will be less likely to evaporate most of the water before it gets to where it's used.

✔ **Use battery-operated valves.** They save water by regulating the amount that's delivered. If you turn your system off and on manually, you'll forget about it. Battery valves can be set to open for a predetermined period of time. These valves generally fit right onto the faucet for a good mechanically rigid mount.

You can get small, cheap valves that you set for a number of gallons instead of time. These work very well for gardens and when your water pressure varies. The Weather TRAK sprinkler controller works according to weather conditions, ensuring that you're not watering unless your lawn really needs it. Check it out at www.weathertrak.com.

✔ **Use barrels under downspouts to catch rainwater.** You can then use the rainwater for other purposes. If you can, position the barrel in an elevated position (for example, set it up on some concrete blocks); then simply use gravity feed when you need water.

Chapter 6

Taking Control of Appliances and Electronics

. . . .

. . . .

*I*ncluding your domestic water heater, around 40 percent of your power bill is consumed by your appliances, big and small. And just because an appliance is small in stature doesn't mean it's small in energy consumption.

Understanding how much power your appliances consume is the first step toward recovering from the rampant disease of appliancism. (Okay, we made up that term.) You can lower your power bills by using your appliances more sensibly — or even better, by not using your appliances at all. For instance, a great way to lower your power bill is to set up a clothesline.

Looking at Typical Appliance Consumption Numbers

Aside from your HVAC system, appliances consume the lion's share of power in your home. The biggest culprits are your washer and dryer, but because your refrigerator is on all the time, it comes in a close second. There are exceptions, of course. Some homes have aquariums that collectively steal the spotlight. Other homes have an old freezer in the garage that cranks kilowatts 24/7. Increasingly common are homes with large entertainment centers, which can gobble kilowatts with the biggest and baddest of energy pigs.

Table 6-1 shows you how many kilowatts per hour (kWh) the average home uses in a year and the annual cost (based on an electric rate of 15 cents per kWh, which is pretty typical). You can determine your own annual usage and cost by gathering your electric bills, which show kWhs used and your rate. (See the next section for details.) If your rate is higher or lower than 15 cents, adjust it accordingly.

Table 6-1	Annual kWh of Usage and Costs for Various Appliances	
Appliance	*kWh Used per Year*	*Annual Cost (Rounded to Nearest Dollar)*
Domestic water heater	5,400	810
Spa (pump and heater)	2,230	335
Pool pump	1,430	215
Refrigerator	1,200	180
Washing machine	900	135
Waterbed heater	850	128
Clothes dryer	845	127
Freezer	750	113
Electric cooking	680	102
Dishwasher	600	90
Aquarium/terrarium	570	86
Well water pump	500	75
Dehumidifier	357	54
Microwave oven	150	23
Television	140	21
Home computer	107	16
Electric blanket	98	15

Note: When calculating how much you can save by cutting back on the usage of your appliances, use your top tiered rate, not your average. Why: Because when you cut back, the top tiered rate applies first.

Analyzing Appliance Consumption in Your Home

To find out how much an appliance costs per month to run, first estimate how much time it's on per day. Then determine how much power it consumes. You can usually find this information on the label, but you may have to consult the instruction manual or go to the manufacturer's Web site.

Use this formula to estimate your monthly cost to run an appliance:

Wattage ÷ 1,000 × hours on per day × cost per kWh × 30 days = total cost per month

Say you want to know how much it costs you to run your washer, dryer, and iron (assume that your rate is 15 cents per kWh):

Washer: You run your 900-watt washing machine for six hours a week. (Figure your daily usage by dividing the number of hours the washer is on by the number of days in a week: 6 ÷ 7 = .86.) Here's what you spend:

900 ÷ 1,000 × .86 × .15 × 30 = $3.48 per month

Dryer: Your clothes dryer uses 5,570 watts (that's a whole lot). If you dry clothes for six hours a week, you spend this much to dry your clothes:

5,570 ÷ 1,000 × .86 × .15 × 30 = $21.56 per month

Iron: If you iron clothes with a 1,200-watt iron each morning for 15 minutes, it's costing you:

1,200 ÷ 1,000 × .25 × .15 × 30 = $1.35 per month

Add up these numbers and you can see that for the appliances you use to keep your clothing clean and pressed, you spend a total of $26.40 per month.

If you put up a clothesline, you would save $21.56 per month (and around 1,748 pounds per year of carbon dioxide emissions). Plus, your clothes would smell better and you could pat yourself on the back for doing your part to save the planet Earth.

You can work this number stuff to death, but what you really want to do is simply make sensible improvements in your efficiency. Start with your biggest appliances and work your way down. Some appliances are easy to use less often; others are harder to do without. It also makes sense to start with the appliances you use the most. Just do your part where you can, and you'll be surprised at the difference it makes.

You can find out how much your old appliances are costing by visiting www.energystar.gov. Click on Home Appliances and enter the year, size, and other data for your old appliance. A calculator tells you how much your current unit is costing, as well as how much you could save if you switched to a new, energy-efficient model.

Making time stand still

Here's an educational project. Try to get your power meter to stand still. Find your meter and note the spinning wheel and the numbers. (These are kWh. When the utility people come to read your meter, they read this number and then subtract the number they read last month to get your monthly consumption.)

First, turn off the main breaker on your circuit panel. If your meter is still spinning, you have a ground fault, and you're paying for electricity that's basically going through the earth beneath your feet. This should not to be misconstrued as generosity; have your utility company come out and fix this right away.

If that checks out, turn the main breaker back on and check to see how fast it's spinning. Now switch off every one of the individual breakers in your box; the spinning should stop, once again.

Now start switching the individual breakers back on, one at a time, and see what happens. The panel should have a well-articulated legend that tells you what each breaker is for:

HVAC, laundry room, upstairs lights, and so on. The biggest switches (those with the biggest numbers, such as 30 or 50) are for your HVAC system and your clothes dryer. You may also have a swimming pool pump or spa that's on a large circuit.

As you switch the individual breakers on, you can see how much power each of the individual circuits consumes. (Make sure each appliance you check is turned on so that it's drawing current.)

Here's where things get interesting. You'll probably find a circuit that draws current even when nothing is turned on in that room. In particular, note that TVs, computers, DVDs, and other digital devices draw current even when they're turned off.

You can take this a step further by plugging in various small appliances like hair dryers, portable fans and heaters, electronic games, and so forth. You can see how fast the meter spins for each of these. Some of these little gadgets can make the meter look like the Tasmanian Devil.

Keeping Water Heaters in Check

The water heater accounts for about 20 percent of the typical home's power budget. Dishwashers and washing machines use up to 80 percent of their energy on heating water, and only 20 percent running the mechanical equipment. The cost of taking showers and baths is almost entirely in the cost of heating water.

Unfortunately, the typical domestic water heater is wasteful. It holds a considerable amount of hot water, and when it's not being used, heat seeps out of the tank, which is sheer inefficiency. The best water heaters have thick insulation, but some heat is still lost. So what can you do to save on water heating costs? Follow the advice in the following sections.

Book II

Energy Efficiency

Paying attention to pipes

When you use hot water, not only do you drain the water you use from the hot water tank, but all the intervening plumbing fills with hot water as well. The amount of hot water trapped in your pipes can be significant, depending on how you're using the water and how far away the faucet or tap is from the tank.

If you're taking a bath, the amount of water in the pipes is small compared to the amount in the tub, so you're not wasting a lot of hot water (aside from the fact that taking a bath is inherently wasteful compared to a shower). But if you're simply filling a cup with hot water, you're leaving a heck of a lot more hot water in the pipes than you're actually using. You're almost always better off heating water in the microwave oven than drawing it from a tap.

Staying on top of maintenance

Regular maintenance goes a long way toward maximizing the efficiency of your hot water heater. As with your HVAC system, you should have your domestic water heater tuned up periodically. (The gas version gets especially gummed up.) The following sections outline areas to pay attention to.

Draining the tank

Every four months or so, drain a quart of water from your tank. There's a valve near the bottom of the unit for this very purpose. Before you begin, consider where the drained water is going to go. If the heater is in your garage, you can broom the water outdoors. Otherwise, you may need a drain bucket. Be sure the bucket is shallow enough to accommodate the valve.

The water you drain from your water heater's tank can be very hot, so be careful.

Draining a quart of water directly from your water heater's tank prevents sediment buildup, which affects efficiency. If you haven't tackled this task in years, you'll be shocked at how much crud comes out.

Changing the heating elements

Change the heating elements in your electric water heater every few years. (Most of them have two elements, one on top and one on bottom.) Use a stainless steel heater element if your old one is corroded. This change makes the unit operate more efficiently and avoids untimely failures.

When you buy the heater element, be sure to purchase a special wrench head that fits the element; ask the hardware store clerk to help you find the right wrench. (You may be able to borrow one from a friend and save some money. And if you don't return it to your friend, you can save even more — although you may lose the friend.) Note that sometimes very old heating elements get stuck in place, in which case you can use WD-40: just spray it on, wait a day, and then give it another try.

Check out Bob Vila's instructions for changing a water heater element on his Web site, www.bobvila.com. Click the "How To" tab for his home improvement library, which gives you the step-by-step rundown.

Finding more ways to save

Beyond regular maintenance, you can do several things to make your water heater more efficient. Temperature, timing, and insulation are all factors that come into play:

> ✔ **Set the water temperature lower.** Most domestic water heaters are set at too high a temperature. Scalding water is too hot. For each 10°F reduction in water heater temperature, you can expect to lower your heating cost by 3 to 5 percent. You may find yourself dialing more hot water in your shower to get to the same comfort level, but so what? The most common problem you may encounter if you lower the temperature is that your dishwasher may not clean as well. You can usually remedy this issues by presoaking your challenging dishes (in cold water, no less) or by changing to a detergent that requires a lower temperature (read the label). See the upcoming section "Lessening the Load on Your Dishwasher" for more information.

✔ **Use timers.** Hot water heaters consume a lot of energy when they're on. Most of them aren't on all that much, but when they are, they gobble up power. Use a timer to turn off your hot water heater at night and during the day when you're gone. Specialty hardware stores sell special units for this purpose. The salespeople can tell you how to install them.

When you're away from home for extended periods, turn the hot water heater off before you go. Either flip off the appropriate circuit breaker in your fuse box or turn off the gas valve (in which case you'll have to re-light the pilot). You may also be able to turn the temperature all the way down to minimum and then turn it back up when you return.

✔ **Add insulation.** Insulate the storage tank with a specially made blanket. Your utility company may give you one free. (Call the customer-service number and ask.) Or you can buy one for $10 to $20 at most hardware stores. A tank that's warm to the touch is a clear sign that you're losing heat and can save money and increase efficiency by adding insulation.

Insulating your hot water pipes is easy, and a number of options are available. The best is a long, cylindrical piece of foam with a slit lengthwise — you just slide it over a pipe, and you're done. Don't worry about corners and inaccessible pipes — whatever you can cover helps increase efficiency. Another option is a fiberglass wrap that you roll around and around the pipe and then cover with a plastic tape material. The wrap covers the pipe more completely than the slit foam, but it's a lot harder to install, especially if the pipe is close to a wall.

Book II

Energy Efficiency

Considering a solar or tankless water heater

Most North Americans (almost 55 percent) heat their water with natural gas. About 38 percent heat water with electricity. (The few others heat with oil and liquid petro gas.) However, two types of water heaters are increasingly being used for their energy efficiency: solar and tankless water heaters.

✔ **Solar water heaters** are the best from an energy-efficiency standpoint, but the economics vary greatly from region to region and depend on your power rates and rate structure. From a pollution perspective, you can't do better than solar.

✔ **Tankless water heaters** have no storage tank; they heat water as it is being used. They're generally gas-powered because of the need for very high, instantaneous power. They're more expensive than conventional water heaters, but if you don't use much hot water, you can save big in the long run.

Smaller units work with a single tap or faucet at one time, so if you have a large family and might need to run two showers simultaneously or you're interested in taking a bath while you're doing laundry, forget it. Large-capacity units cost around $1,000. (A conventional unit costs only $300.) Units can save the typical family $100 per year, so the payback in extra investment cost is around 7 years.

✔ **Hybrid** units combine the attractive features of tankless and traditional tank water heaters: They enable you to get an endless, energy-efficient supply of hot water from more than one faucet at a time. With a system that doles out energy based on how you're using the system (and better utilizes that energy), hybrid units are extremely efficient. And they don't require the maintenance that tankless and traditional water heaters do. Eternal is a gas version, and GE is working on gas and electric versions predicted to hit the market late in 2009.

Washing and Drying without the Crying

The average washing machine wastes more energy than any other appliance in the home. With due diligence, most households can save 50 percent on operating costs and use 50 percent less water (including hot water, which costs a lot more than cold) just by changing the way they do laundry. Following are some practical tips.

Running hot or cold: Changing water temperature

A great way to save energy doing laundry is to use hot water only when you need to. Eighty-five percent of the energy used in washing is consumed by heating the water. A lot of people simply run their machines on hot all the time. You can easily save 25 percent on your washing costs by using cold water most of the time — in particular, for the rinse cycle. Look on the label of your detergent for the best ways to use cold water. You can also effectively *wash* in cold water if you use detergent made for cold water. Check your detergent label to find its temperature requirement.

Another way to save energy is to make every member of the household responsible for cleaning his or her own clothes. You'll see an instant decrease in wash-load quantity, especially if you have kids.

Adjusting load size, water level, and cycle

When you wash clothes, use as little water as necessary to get the job done. To that end, wash only full loads — it's much more efficient, per item of clothing, than partial loads. Always adjust the water level to the lowest possible setting for the load size. For the smallest loads, use a mini-basket insert that fits over the agitator.

You can also take advantage of the cycles your washer offers. If yours has a presoak cycle, use it. Presoaking cycles save energy. They take more time, but so what? Some washers also let you choose the speed of the spin cycle. Faster spin speeds remove more water, resulting in less dryer time. If you're using a clothesline, faster, longer spins make your life much easier because the clothes weigh less and pull the line down less.

Book II

Energy Efficiency

Saving drying costs

Dryers use more power than every appliance save the washing machine and refrigerator. Saving money with your dryer is easy.

Avoiding the dryer altogether

The best way to save money on drying costs is to use a clothesline. Clothes dried outdoors smell much better, particularly if they're in direct sunlight.

The best clothesline style for most users is an *umbrella arrangement.* (True to its name, it folds up like an umbrella.) You mount it into the ground and it rotates, so you can set your laundry basket down and move the line around as you pin up clothes. It features the most length of line for the least amount of space.

To determine the best location for your clothesline, consider the following:

 ✔ **Convenience counts.** If getting to the clothesline is a hassle, you'll be less apt to use it. Garages work well, and they're usually right next to the laundry. Open the garage door if you can. Otherwise, your garage will get humid.

 ✔ **Air movement is helpful.** A breezy spot with direct sunshine is ideal.

Not convinced fresh air can freshen clothes? Try this experiment: Take some sweaty, smelly workout clothes and simply hang them up in direct sunshine. Check them out a couple hours later — they may feel and smell better than clothes you run through the washing machine.

Another way to avoid using the dryer is to hang clothes to dry indoors. A quick, easy way to dry small loads is to simply hang them over your shower curtain rod while you're at work. You need some ventilation in your bathroom or you'll humidify your home, but maybe that's what you want to do — especially in winter. You can also use drying racks anywhere in your house or even use a shower tension rod to hang clothes in hallways.

Putting (drying) time on your side

If you time the use of your dryer just right, you can take the best possible advantage of the heat it puts out. Consider the following tips to decrease your drying costs:

- Overdrying is hard on clothes, and it wastes energy. Take clothes out of the dryer just before they're fully dry and hang them to finish the job.

- Many dryers have moisture sensors, which are much better than timed drying cycles. (Using a timer makes no sense at all, if you think about it.)

- Cool-down cycles are the most efficient because the dryer heater gradually shuts off and the residual heat finishes the cycle.

- Dry two or more loads in a row, thereby taking advantage of the dryer's retained heat.

Taking care of your dryer's ductwork

Dryers have vented pipes (around 4 inches in diameter) that lead outdoors. The purpose of these pipes is to vent the hot air to the outside environment. To work most efficiently, this vent pipe needs to be free of obstruction.

- Clean the removable filter every time you use the dryer. Keep a small waste bin by the machine so that you can toss the coagulated lint into it.

- Check your dryer ductwork. It may be clogged with years' worth of accreted crud, which causes inefficiency. New ductwork is cheap. You can find it at any hardware store; ask the clerk for help.

- Where your ductwork ends outside you'll find a vent, often with a flapping door that opens and closes when the dryer is on and off (to keep birds and rodents out of the line). These vents often get dented and smashed, thereby restricting flow and wasting money. If possible, just get rid of the vent. Or replace the one you have with a better-working model.

- Buy a duct cleaner — a long, snaking wand with a big, bushy brush head that you cram down the duct line — but for the cost, you're probably better off simply rebuilding the ductwork, assuming that you have easy access. Many ducts are built into walls, in which case you're stuck with cleaning.

- Use the straightest, shortest duct possible. Ninety-degree bends cause your dryer to work harder and longer to accomplish the same task. In fact, most ductwork can be rebuilt to good advantage.

Keeping Your Cool with Refrigerators

The No. 1 way to save money with your refrigerator is to keep the coils clean. On either the bottom or the back of your unit is a meandering line of narrow tubing. Air is drawn over this tubing, and, over time, dust accumulates and clogs the flow, decreasing your refrigerator's efficiency. You can get special brushes that enable you to brush the collected dust off the tubes, or you can simply use your vacuum cleaner.

Coils on the bottom of a refrigerator are harder to get to than those on the back, although for the latter, you have to move your refrigerator out. You're likely to be shocked at how much dirt and crud accumulate behind your refrigerator. This stuff causes health problems.

Book II

Energy
Efficiency

If your refrigerator is 15 years old or more, a new one is undoubtedly cost-effective. However, the greenest option is to use your fridge until it dies. Manufacturing a new one still hogs more energy than your old refrigerator. When the time comes to buy, look for a top-bottom model rather than a side-by-side. The top-bottom refrigerator arrangements use around 10 percent less energy than their side-by-side counterparts. The payback on a new energy efficient refrigerator is less than five years.

Wondering what to do with your old fridge? You may be tempted to sell a refrigerator that still works, but you're passing on the energy waste. Depending on where you live, you might be able to recycle it. Check out the Energy Star recycling program for details at www.recyclemyoldfridge. com/findaprogram.aspx. If you aren't near a recycling program, try contacting a scrap metal dealer.

Beyond buying a new refrigerator, you can do other things to make the refrigerator you have run more efficiently. The following sections explain.

It's what's on the inside that counts

How you arrange your food, the temperature settings you select, and how much ice buildup you have in the freezer all contribute to how well or poorly your refrigerator works. Some advice:

- ✔ **Check the temperature.** If your refrigerator allows different temperature settings for different zones, adjust the temperatures accordingly. Recommended temperatures are 37–40°F for the refrigerator, and 5°F for the freezer. Long-term freezer storage (deep freezers) should be set at 0°F.

  Buy a refrigerator thermometer to keep tabs on what's going on inside your fridge. They're inexpensive, and you can easily move them around to different spots inside the refrigerator to get a more accurate reading.

- ✔ **Defrost the freezer.** Ice buildup makes for inefficiency.

- ✔ **Eliminate overcrowding.** When the air inside a refrigerator compartment can't move, the machinery has to work harder.

- ✔ **Cover all foods in the compartments.** Uncovered foods release a lot of moisture and make the compressor work harder. Besides, if you don't cover the food, it'll taste weird.

Close the door!

Keep your refrigerator's doors closed as much as possible — an obvious piece of advice, perhaps, but worth stating anyway.

Tight seals are a must. If they're tattered and leaking, you're wasting up to 25 percent of the refrigerator's energy (even more if your home is hot). If you can't change the seal, use some silicon sealant instead. (The same kind you buy for bathtubs and sinks works just fine.) Follow these steps:

1. **Spray cooking spray over the metal frame surface of the refrigerator where the seal should be located.**

2. **Squirt the silicon over the seal.**

3. **Close the door and let the material dry.**

One refrigerator or two?

Operating one large refrigerator is much more efficient than operating two smaller units. A lot of people have a refrigerator in their garage — usually the one that used to be in the kitchen. You may not want to throw it away, but old reefers cost a lot of money. That unit in your garage is costing you a lot more than the new one. Is it worth it? What do you have in there, anyway? Drinks for the kids? A whole pig? You can surely live without two refrigerators.

Lessening the Load on Your Dishwasher

Dishwashers use as much energy as clothes washers and dryers. Around 80 percent of this energy is consumed by heating the water — which means that one way to maximize your energy efficiency is to reduce the amount of hot water your dishwasher uses. Another way to save energy is to modify the way you rinse your dishes and load the dishwasher. The following sections explain.

Believe it or not, a detailed scientific study was performed to determine whether hand-washing or machine-washing dishes is more efficient. Hand-washing a complete 12-piece setting of dishes in a sink used around 30 gallons of water and 2.5 kWh of electricity for water heating. An automatic dishwasher used only 4 gallons and 1.5kWh of electricity. Not only that, but impartial judges determined the dishes from the machine were much cleaner.

Using less hot water

New dishwashers heat their own water, which is far more efficient than drawing hot water from the water heater the way older models do. Keep this feature in mind if you're in the market for a new dishwasher.

In addition, dishwashers get warm and heat your kitchen. In the winter, this extra warmth is welcomed. In the summer, it makes your air conditioner work harder. During warm months, use the no-heat dry option. If your machine doesn't have a no-heat option, simply stop it after the rinse cycle, open the door, and let the dishes dry that way.

In the summer, the dishwasher humidifies your house quite a bit. Get some ventilation going to get that humidity out of the house, and you'll feel cooler.

Unless your dishwasher heats its own water, the temperature of the water from your domestic heater may affect the quality of your dishwasher's performance. If the water isn't hot enough, your machine will have a hard time doing the job. However, some detergents are rated for a lower water temperature. (For more information on water heaters, refer to the earlier section "Keeping Water Heaters in Check.")

Changing the way you rinse and load

The key to greener dishwashing is to minimize how much water you use. Here are some suggestions to help you do that:

- ✔ **Rinse dishes as little as possible.** In fact, just scraping off large chunks of food without rinsing at all is often sufficient. Most dishwashers do a good job of getting rid of caked-on, hard stuff. New models have special cycles that steam-heat the crud and loosen it up.

- ✔ **Always run a full load.** Your dishwasher uses just as much water to wash a few dishes as a full load, so make the most of the water you use.

- ✔ **Try skipping the prerinse cycle on your dishwasher and using the economy wash cycle.** You probably won't be able to tell the difference.

Eating Up Power with Stoves and Microwaves

Depending on how much you cook in your home, energy costs for your stove and microwave can be significant. You can do a number of easy things to save costs, and in this section, you find the best and easiest candidates.

Checking out efficient ovens

Some ovens (both microwave and conventional) are just plain more efficient than others. Some have features that offer extra efficiency, and some are more efficient even without the extra features.

- **Self-cleaning ovens:** These ovens are more efficient because they have higher insulation levels, which means that less heat is lost while you're cooking.

- **Gas ovens with pilotless ignition:** One of these ovens saves you 30 percent over its lifetime, and the air in your home will be cleaner. With pilot lights, some gas is always being burned. (You can usually see the little blue flame wavering near the burner.) With a pilotless gas stove, a spark plug type device ignites the gas each time the burner is turned on.

- **Convection ovens:** Convection ovens incorporate a small, high-temperature fan that moves the internal air in the oven compartment thereby bringing more heat into contact with the food being baked. Convection ovens are very efficient because they allow you to bake in less time, with less energy.

Altering your cooking techniques

You don't have to use a conventional oven to cook a hot meal. Sometimes the following appliances do the job more efficiently:

- **Toaster ovens:** Use a toaster oven for small jobs. Small toaster ovens (the kind that sit on your countertop) take much less energy than big conventional ovens. And if you know how to use them properly, you can get great browning effects. They don't cost much, but you're better off getting a good one with an automatic timer and temperature controls.

- **Barbecue grills:** Use your barbecue as much as possible in the summer. From an efficiency standpoint, gas models are the best. Charcoal grills waste a lot of energy (you can't turn them off and on, as needed), plus they put out far more pollution. Small propane barbecues work very well and, contrary to what some people claim, they don't make the food stink. Burning petro-based charcoal is no different from burning petro-based natural gas. Look instead for 100 percent hardwood charcoal made from scrap lumber.

- **Crock pots and portable pressure cookers:** In the summer, put them outdoors to save air-conditioning costs and lower humidity.

You can also employ energy-saving strategies like the following:

Book II

Energy Efficiency

- **Bake dishes simultaneously.** Try to fill your oven with a number of dishes at the same time. Doing so lowers the per-item cooking cost. If different items call for different temperatures, relax; there's wiggle room. Put the items that need higher temperatures on the top rack, and items that need lower temperatures on the lower rack.

- **Don't preheat.** Let your food warm up with the oven. And turn your stove off a few minutes before the allotted cooking time — the residual heat will finish the process. In winter, take advantage of the extra heat from your oven by leaving its door open after you turn it off.

- **Don't lay foil on racks.** Foil obstructs the natural flow of heat.

- **Use glass or ceramic pans in the oven.** The food cooks more efficiently, and the texture is better.

- **Match the pan to the size of the heating element on the stove.** This way, no heat escapes around the edges.

- **Contain heat in the summer.** Putting a lid on that boiling pot reduces the amount of heat and humidity that's released into the air, and it brings water to a boil faster. Rinse pans out as soon as practical to cool them down.

- **Release heat in the winter.** In cold weather, let hot pots and pans release their heat into your home. Don't rinse them out because that washes the heat right down the drain.

Enjoying the Fine Life with TVs and Computers

Although the new flat-screen televisions reduce power consumption, the trend toward gigantic screens drives consumption right back up. Combine a big screen with a big sound system, and your entertainment center may be costing you an arm and a leg. Computers and their various components and accessories constitute a similar category of common household energy-eaters. What's a modern person to do?

For starters, be aware that "off" doesn't always mean what it implies. Even when your TV, entertainment system, computer, monitor, DVD player, and so on are sitting idle, they're still drawing power. You can put a halt to this energy drain by plugging these appliances into a power strip and turning off the power strip when you're not using them.

In the same vein, always use the power down feature on your computer and turn your computer off any time that you won't be using it for at least four hours, like at night and on weekends. Remember, even in sleep mode, power is being wasted. Don't forget to turn off your printer when it's not in use, too.

Some processors use a lot more juice than others. Laptop computers use a lot less power than desktops, so if you can, opt for a laptop.

Old CRT monitors draw considerably more power than the new, flat-screen versions. They also put out a lot of extra heat, requiring more air conditioning in the summer. So you may want to update (unless, of course, you're looking for heat in your home office, in which case you may want to keep your old CRT).

Buying New Appliances

Most of the time, you don't have a choice over whether to buy a new appliance. The old one breaks, it can't be repaired, and you come to the difficult conclusion that it's time for a funeral. Many people also decide that upgrading to an energy-efficient model is worth the investment.

Fortunately, the government has made your decision process easy for you with the Energy Star program. (Yes, a government program that actually works the way it's supposed to — take advantage of this rare opportunity!) The Energy Star is awarded to appliances that significantly exceed the minimum national efficiency standards, typically by 20 percent, and by as much as 110 percent. Energy Star ratings apply to nearly all major appliances, plus HVAC systems, natural gas and oil systems, programmable thermostats, and so on.

The Energy Star label shows the product's annual power consumption. Even better, note the annual cost estimates based on different utility rates. On these labels, the highest rate is 12 cents, which is somewhat anachronistic in light of rising energy rates. But multiplying the costs based on your own rates is easy enough. For instance, if you're paying 16 cents, simply multiply the result based on 8 cents by two.

You can easily compare different models of appliances using the Energy Star labels. Simply compare the estimated annual costs. You can then compare the difference in price with the difference in costs.

If you want to buy an energy-efficient appliance, buy one with an Energy Star certification; it's that simple. You can get super-duper-efficient models, but they tend to cost a lot more than they're worth. These are generally for the off-grid crowd, or those willing to pay any price to go green. For the most part, if you buy an Energy Star model and use it efficiently, you're doing very well.

Book II

Energy Efficiency

Chapter 7

Controlling Solar Exposure for Light and Heat

*U*sing sunshine effectively isn't as simple as just letting the sun shine in. Obviously, in the winter, you want both the sunshine and its heat in your home as much as possible. In the summer, you want the sun's light but not the heat — two goals that are almost always at odds.

In this chapter, you find out how to heat your home in the winter and avoid doing so in the summer. We show you how to light your home with sunshine, and how to plan and build sunrooms that increase the value of your home and provide increased living area at an efficient cost. For much greater detail on this subject, check out *Solar Power Your Home For Dummies* (Wiley) by Rik DeGunther.

Lighting Your Home with Sunshine

The more you use sunshine to light your home, the less you need to rely on artificial lighting. Using sunshine to your advantage also creates a kinder, more inviting atmosphere. The following sections outline a variety of ways to manipulate sunlight and reap all the benefits it has to offer. (For details on how to deal with the heat factor, head to the later section "Heating Your Home with Sunlight — or Not.")

Planting a tree

By far the best way to control sunlight in your home is to strategically locate *deciduous trees* (those that lose their leaves in the winter) around your home's exterior. If you plant a single deciduous tree outside a southern-exposed window, particularly a large window, you benefit in many ways.

In the summer, the leaves block most of the sunlight, leaving the room with diffused, subtle, cool light. On a hot summer day, harsh sunlight makes you feel even hotter, but shade creates a sense of calm and well-being, not to mention relief. In the winter, with the leaves gone, direct sunlight enters the room, casting the interior with warmth (due to the greenhouse effect), as well as a bright, yellow tint that feels warm.

Making natural light more effective

You can make the most of whatever natural light is available to you. Here are a number of clever ways to increase the effectiveness of sunlight in your home's interior spaces:

- **Put up mirrors to enhance existing light.** Position your mirrors in corners to broadcast light around the entire room. In essence, mirrors magnify light. Two mirrors positioned catty-corner on opposing walls work even better and make the room seem much larger.

  Before you nail a mirror up permanently, try it out at different times of the day to gauge its effect. If you want more light in the morning than the evening, put the mirror on an eastern-facing wall. Also keep in mind that mirrored closet doors often work wonders to light a bedroom and increase its perceived size.

- **Use glass bricks to let light in.** Cut some high holes through the solid walls of a dark hallway (it doesn't matter whether the walls lead to other rooms or outdoors) and put glass bricks into the spaces so that light enters the hallway. Doing so not only spreads light but also makes the hallway seem larger and less restrictive. In fact, your entire home will feel friendlier and more open. Installing glass bricks is a relatively straightforward and inexpensive do-it-yourself project. (Ask for more details at your hardware store.)

- **Use windowed doors.** Instead of the usual solid wood doors, install French doors between rooms. You can get French doors from most any building-supply stores. Even if you use curtains for privacy, the light will still shine through, and your home will seem more spacious. You're likely to find one location in your home that's a perfect candidate for a French door.

Don't forget the front door. Glass panels can lighten up your entryway, and guests will find them more inviting than a solid, impersonal mass of heavy wood staring them in the face.

✔ **Get rid of overgrowth.** If vegetation is crowding the light through one of your windows, cut it back. Trimming overgrown bushes is especially important with windows facing east because morning sunlight works much better than coffee.

✔ **Clean or tint your windows.** Spotless windows make a huge difference in the way a room feels. Cleaning may not matter much in terms of the quantity of light coming in, but it definitely enhances the quality, which may be even more important.

If your problem is that a room gets too much sunshine (or you want to obscure a view to the outside without using blinds), apply window tinting. Tinting comes in sheet tape form, and anybody can put it up. (Well, pretty much anybody — it helps if you don't have ten thumbs.) You can get a similar benefit from lace or sheer curtains.

Book II

Energy Efficiency

Installing skylights

For those of you with more advanced ambitions, skylights can make a big difference in your home's lighting for a relatively small investment.

Traditional skylights are big, expansive channelers of sunlight, and the large openings in your home's ceiling will make a room bigger and airier, both literally and figuratively. If you're interested in skylights, consult with a contractor unless you're really good with tools and projects.

Skylights are very expensive to install. If you want multiple skylights, consider doing them all at the same time. Installing three or four skylights at one time takes around twice as much time and money (rather than three or four times as much) — food for thought when you're deciding how many skylights to install.

Opting for solar tubes

If you like the idea of skylights but not the amount of dough they require, then consider *solar light tubes*. Also known as tubular skylights, they're a less expensive alternative to skylights. Solar light tubes let in natural light that varies with the clouds and the weather. Solar tubes, which can be installed by just about anybody in half a day for around $250, can have just as much effect as a traditional skylight for around one tenth of the cost. (The typical price, uninstalled, is $200 for a four-foot-long pipe. Extensions cost an additional $20 per foot.)

Here's how a solar light tube system works: Sunlight is collected up on the roof and transmitted down a shiny, silver pipe into a diffuser, which broadcasts the light into the room below.

If you're interested in solar tubes, keep these points in mind:

TIP

✔ **You can make most rooms bright enough to work in during daylight hours, even in the winter.** Large-diameter units (12 inches and more) can output as much light as a dozen 100-watt light bulbs, at one tenth the heat. Because they don't produce as much heat you can use your air-conditioner much less.

One of the best locations for a solar tube is a dark corner in the family room, where the light will be well used and have a dramatic effect. Solar light tubes are also good for dark, isolated bathrooms. The natural light is comforting, and you never have to flip a light switch during the day. If you have a dark kitchen, a solar tube may be the perfect solution, especially if a lot of people come and go during the day. The light switch won't be constantly flipped off and on.

✔ **The intensity of light changes quite a bit because solar light varies with the clouds and weather.** On a partly cloudy day, you can get a lot of fluctuation as clouds move across the sun, making you much more conscious of the outdoors.

✔ **The tubes themselves can drastically change the way decor looks.** Be prepared for a drastically different room because lighting is very influential in terms of how a room "feels." Also, the silver color imparts a certain "cool" mood. Some types of solar light tubes come with filters for creating moods, but the filters cut out light as well.

✔ **Installation isn't easy (you have to go up into your attic space), but it's doable.** When deciding where to install solar light tubes, always keep the installation itself in mind. Just forget about installing these tubes in locations where you can't easily go — like shallow attic spaces or near the edges of the attic. Better to get a professional because you certainly don't want to create leaks.

Heating Your Home with Sunlight — or Not

In addition to being a great light source, sunlight is a great source of heat — which is wonderful when you want heat, but not so wonderful when you want to stay cool. Fortunately, you can regulate how much heat the sun generates in your home.

First, you need to understand the *greenhouse effect.* The best way to describe how sunshine heats a home is to explain how a greenhouse works. Sunlight enters the enclosed space through the *glazing,* or window material, and then gets absorbed and turned into heat. The heat stays in the enclosed space thanks to the glazing's insulation properties.

You can enhance the greenhouse effect — and make your home warmer — by increasing the transmissibility of the window and maximizing its insulation. Double-pane glass works well for this goal, and you can also use a number of window coatings and other optical tricks to good effect. Inexpensive plastic materials that work well are available, although they tend to blur the view.

To maximize the heat generated, the space must be well sealed to prevent air leakage, although the greenhouse effect is often powerful enough to work well even in relatively leaky environments. In fact, sometimes it works so well that the heat is intolerable. (The greenhouse effect explains why your car gets so hot when it sits out in the summer sunshine.) So how do you reduce the greenhouse effect when you don't want all that heat? Easy. By controlling the amount of sunshine that enters your home.

Installing blinds and sunscreens

When you install blinds or shades, you control the amount of sunlight that enters your home. An added benefit is that these things can also increase the beauty of your home and, if you're really smart (of course, you are — you're reading this book), you can use blinds and shades to *insulate,* or maintain heat storage, as well.

Bare glass lets the sun enter freely. Using blinds or sunshades (and even curtains) restricts the amount of sunlight that enters and, depending on how they're hung (whether on the inside or outside of the window, and how far from the window), affects the insulation properties, as Table 7-1 outlines.

Table 7-1	Window Covering Options	
Type of Covering	*Sun*	*Insulation*
Bare glass	Sun enters freely	Minimal insulation
Blind on the inside	Absorbs sun on the inside; controls lighting and enhances decorative qualities in the room; may also completely block view and light	Creates excellent insulation layer inside — good for cold climates and winter

(continued)

Table 7-1 *(continued)*

Type of Covering	Sun	Insulation
Sunscreen tacked outside of window	Stops most sunlight outside; darker inside but doesn't obscure view	Creates insulation layer outside; heat is stopped outside so that the interior of the room is cooler; best for hot climates
Blind hung outside with an air gap	Stops most sunlight outside, but doesn't obscure view	No insulation layer at window; maximum cooling effect, especially in breezy locations

Hanging blinds: Inside or out?

When you hang blinds on the inside of windows, the sunshine comes in through the window, strikes the blind, and gets converted into heat. The heat is trapped in the air gap between the blind and the window and can get very hot because of the greenhouse effect. Of course, heat is desirable only in the winter. In the summer, you may have a cooler room if you just leave the window uncovered and let the sun and air in.

You can use blinds to accomplish several goals:

- ✔ **To warm a room in winter:** Contrary to what you may think, the best way to heat a room with sunshine in the winter is not to open the blinds, but to use special blinds that capture sunlight and insulate at the same time. You can get interior blinds made to do just that. Look for cellular shades, which hold air to provide insulation.

- ✔ **To keep a room cool in summer:** Interior blinds made for summer reflect a lot of light back out the window. They're usually shiny and white, at least on the exterior-facing surface.

    To get the best cooling effect, allow for some ventilation between a blind and the open window it covers. If you can't do that, use a blind that has a shiny, metallic exterior surface that simply reflects all sunlight and doesn't let any heat into the room at all. The room will be completely dark, but this is desirable on a burning hot day.

- ✔ **To maximize the efficiency of an air conditioner:** When your air conditioner is on, it's best to hang blinds so that they create as much insulation as possible *and* banish sunlight. You can achieve this goal by closing your interior blinds all the way. If you have outside shades, all the better. The best scheme for a sunny home that uses a lot of air conditioning is both solar screens (see the next section, "Putting up sunscreens") and interior blinds. The home will be very dark, but it will also be much cooler.

Infrared filtering glass

You can get special glass that filters infrared light out before it gets into your home. In fact, most of the sunlight's heat comes from light that is invisible to the human eye. Some animals (like owls and nocturnal hunters) can see infrared light, but humans can't see it. Infrared filtering glass rejects up to 70 percent of the heat of sunlight, yet you can't tell the difference in the view because it transmits visible light as well as a conventional window. Solar screens and other sunlight-inhibiting processes inhibit the view, which you may not want if your window is a centerpiece to a home that features lavish views. You'll pay more for infrared glass, but it may be just the thing.

Book II

Energy
Efficiency

Putting up sunscreens

Sunscreens, also called *solar screens,* are an inexpensive and effective way to cool your home in the summer. They reflect a lot of sunlight — up to 90 percent — plus they create an insulation barrier on the outside. Most are dark, heavy-duty, fabric screens with a tacky surface. Some are a flexible, tinted plastic film. You can get sunscreens up to 8 feet wide, with unlimited length.

Only windows that get more than a few hours of direct sunlight a day are worth sun screening. The best candidates are tall windows facing south, but east and west exposures can also get very hot. With a solar screen tacked up on the outside of a window, most of the sunlight is reflected before it even gets to the window. The screen gets hot and an insulation barrier keeps that heat trapped, but it's all outside the window.

You don't want sunscreens in the winter, which means you need to mount them in such a way that you can bring them down in the winter. Sunscreens are easy to put up, and most people can do it themselves. Call a screen shop for tools, materials, and installation advice. Easy-to-use mounting hardware is essential. (For automatic sunscreens, you'll need a professional installation.)

Before you go the do-it-yourself route, ask the shop what it would charge to install sunscreens for you. Their employees can do a window in a few minutes, and the bid for the entire job may not be much more than what you'll pay for the material alone.

You can expect at least a three-year lifetime with quality sunscreen, at around 75 cents per square foot. For a 3-foot x 6-foot window, if a screen lasts five years, the cost is only $2 per year (with the cheapest installation method). If your climate is hot and sunny, there's no question you'll get good payback on this small investment. Cheap screen bleaches out and looks perpetually dirty — avoid it unless you like cheap and perpetually dirty.

Covering your windows with exterior awnings

Awnings are great light shades because you can configure them in different geometrical relationships and control the light over the course of a day. They also drastically change the appearance of your home for the better. They add shape and break up monotonous flat surfaces and also complement the color scheme of your home's exterior.

Two common awning styles are the Venetian awning and the hood awning:

- ✔ **Venetian awnings** allow sunlight in the winter, when the sun is low in the sky, and block sunlight in the summer, when the sun is high. Venetians also allow you to see out of the top of your window, and the effect is much more open than that of hood awnings.

- ✔ **Hood awnings** are more decorative. They can be made of nice fabrics that match or complement the house. They work better in rainy climates because they keep cold water off your windows. (You can lose a lot of heat by water-based convection from rain.)

Installing outdoor window blinds

Outdoor blinds, which are designed to cover windows from the outside, stop the heat on the outside of the home. Plus in the winter, these blinds can act as insulators.

Outdoor blinds are usually made of vinyl. Some are prettier than others, which may or may not matter to you. Import shops stock different sizes of roll-up bamboo shades, often priced as low as $5 apiece.

These blinds are also commonly used overhead for patios and porches where late afternoon and evening sunlight can prevent you from using the area. In these situations, leave them up all day, or your floor will heat up. (Concrete or tile floors hold heat for a long time.)

Most outdoor blinds have cords that you pull different ways, but if you don't want to raise and lower the blinds manually, you can find outdoor blinds that retract automatically. Automatic retractable shades are available from specialty suppliers. You can even find solar-powered retractors that work with a hand-held remote controller.

Putting up radiant barriers

A *radiant barrier* is a sheet of thin material that looks like reinforced aluminum foil. It's tacked up beneath your roof joists or simply laid over the insulation on your attic floor. It does a good job of keeping a lot of heat out of your home in summer, but its benefits for keeping heat inside your home during winter are less pronounced.

The material itself costs around 20 cents per square foot. For a 2,000-square-foot house, the material costs $400, and the payback can be very impressive. In hot climates, radiant barriers cool the home down more than enough to pay for themselves in less than a couple years.

Book II

Energy Efficiency

To install a radiant barrier, you simply staple it into place, regardless of whether you mount it overhead or lay it on the floor. (Make sure that you have a good quality stapler.) The design of your roof impacts how easy installation will be. Open rafters are the best candidates; if you have complex trusses, forget it. Installation, however, is a snap if your attic floor is open and easily accessible.

Even if you can cover only a portion of the rafters or floor, it's worth it. Try to cover an entire small area, rather than isolated spots in a number of different areas.

Attics can roast you fast. They heat to over 130°F, easy. Don't kid yourself; if it feels real hot, it can be dangerous. One way to stay safe is to work in the morning, when things are cooler.

Cutting out summer sunlight with overhangs

Overhangs, which are solid constructions built over windows, can provide both financial gain and aesthetic beauty. You can design an overhang to visually complement your home's roofline.

Here's how overhangs work: In the winter, sunlight can enter the home because the sun is lower in the sky. If you have high thermal mass floors (like concrete or tile), your home will heat up nicely. In the summertime, when the sun is higher in the sky, the overhang stops any direct sunlight from entering the home.

Be sure the overhang you install changes your home's appearance for the better. (The best-looking overhangs mimic the pitch of your roof and use the same materials.) Before you nail an overhang up and make it permanent, try to arrange it where it's going to go and see what it looks like. Alternatively, take a digital photo of the window and use a computer program to play around with different ideas. You can find overhang designs in home plan books.

Garnering Sunlight with Greenhouses and Sunrooms

There are two types of solar rooms: greenhouses and sunrooms. *Greenhouses,* which are either connected to your home or separate from it, can help warm your home as well as provide inexpensive, delicious, highly nutritious food or beautiful and soothing decorative plants. *Sunrooms,* which are always part of your home, add living space and square footage for a relatively low cost, increase the efficiency of your heating and cooling efforts, and brighten up your home's ambience and decor.

A well-designed solar room can work efficiently even in very cold climates, giving you a nice, warm escape from the winter. However, a solar room does tend to lose a lot of heat during the night.

Most home additions cost more than your property value increases due to the improvement. But with solar rooms, the variety of designs and the reduced building restrictions make it possible to enjoy profitable appreciations, especially if you do it yourself.

Plant deciduous trees at the same time you build your solar room. They'll cut back the sun in the summer and allow it all in during the winter. Plus, the room will be much prettier with a view of some nice trees. Partnering with Mother Nature brings a benign continuity to the entire project.

Deciding between the different types of solar rooms

So which type of solar room is better: greenhouse or sunroom? That answer depends on what you want to achieve and which type of room you prefer.

Greenhouses invite the maximum amount of sunlight and generally require a glass ceiling or sloping glass walls. In addition:

✔ They're very functional.

✔ They need a water supply.

✔ Their temperatures need to be regulated (the difference between the hottest and coldest temperatures needs to be kept to a minimum, as dictated by the type of plants).

✔ They need adequate ventilation to provide oxygen for plants.

✔ They need floors that can withstand water leaks and mud spillage.

Sunrooms, on the other hand, are designed as extensions of your home's living space. You can leave them partially open to the outdoors, or you can completely enclose them and put in carpeting and fine furniture. Because too much sunlight is uncomfortable and sunrooms are meant to be inviting, they generally have water-tight, solid roofs. They may or may not contain skylights and vents, but both increase the livability factor.

Book II

Energy Efficiency

In both types of solar rooms, most of the southern wall space is taken up by windows or some other suitable glazing material. In addition, both greenhouses and sunrooms can increase a home's privacy by providing a buffer between the outside world and the interior spaces.

The best location in your house is adjacent to the kitchen for attached greenhouses, and adjacent to the living room or family room for solar rooms. These locations afford not only the most efficient use, but also the most use in general. Leaving the doors and windows open between your house and sunroom lends a sense of increased floor space and size to your home. (Building a solar room off your family room is the cheapest way to increase the square footage of your home.)

Building a solar room yourself

A do-it-yourselfer can design and build a sunroom or greenhouse at a relatively low cost with relatively low risk. These rooms can be separate from the house and, as such, don't need electrical wiring or plumbing and don't require that you obey all the building code requirements that are unavoidable inside of a home.

If you don't want to have to apply for building permits or have the property value reappraised (with the commensurate increase in property taxes), build the sunroom against a house, but don't actually nail the frame elements to the home — in this case, it's just a free-standing porch. (Keep in mind, though, that if you ever sell your house, you can't advertise your solar room as part of your house's square footage.)

If you plan to add a solar room to your home, kits are the best bets for do-it-yourselfers. (Greenhouse kits made of plastic sheets instead of windows are easy, cheap, and effective.) Fortunately, an entire industry is dedicated to manufacturing and selling prefab kits that cost anywhere from a few hundred dollars to hundreds of thousands of dollars. You can see samples in showrooms. Remember to touch things before you buy; photos are often misleading and rarely reflect reality the way you expect them to.

Alternatively you can build your own custom design and use the same materials (windows, framing, trim) as the rest of your house. As much as a well-designed solar room can enhance your home's aesthetics, a poorly designed one can make your house look awkward and uninviting.

Easy and straightforward candidates for solar rooms are existing porches and decks that already have the basic support structures and flooring in place. All you need to do is build up and around them.

Book III
Green Cleaning

The 5th Wave   By Rich Tennant

"They're relatively quiet, and they keep food scraps from accumulating on the countertops."

In this book . . .

Aisles full of cleaning products in grocery stores claim to free your family from undesirable elements like bacteria and germs. Who wouldn't want that? But many of these products operate on a "too much is not enough" basis, hurtling powerful and potentially harmful chemicals at your cleaning projects.

Clean doesn't have to mean dangerous, and in these chapters, you find out how to rely on muscle power and green packaged or homemade cleaning products to bring a sparkle to your home. You discover ways to tackle tough kitchen and bath cleaning challenges and even how to green up your laundry process.

Here are the contents of Book III at a glance:

Chapter 1

Bringing "Green" to "Clean" for a Healthier Home

Many conventional cleaning practices add to environmental damage by using energy, wasting resources, and polluting the Earth. Does this risk mean that it's better to skip the cleaning altogether? (Wouldn't that be a great excuse to do away with housework?) By recognizing the relationship between your cleaning practices and the environment, you can identify ways to "green" your housekeeping for a healthier planet and a healthier home.

This chapter shows you that you *can* have a clean house, and green it, too.

Waking Up to a New Awareness

No doubt about it: What happens in Peoria affects Patagonia. And Paris. And Punxsutawney. The water wasted in Scranton hurts villages in the Sahara. The traffic congestion in Atlanta warms the ice caps in the Arctic. If only it were true that what happens in Vegas stays in Vegas. But people there and throughout the world are waking up to the fact that their actions can affect the climate, damage the planet, and use up stuff you may really want to keep.

How you clean has an impact on the environment, too. Greening the way you mop your floors may seem like a drop in the bucket, but each small change accumulates into a larger stream. Maybe you can't save the Antarctic penguins this morning, but you can hold off running the dishwasher until you have a full load. Action by action, you can make positive changes.

Ramping up to a greener clean

Your housekeeping practices intersect with big-picture ecological issues at many junctures. Look for these connections:

✔ **Plugging petroleum consumption:** Plug in, turn on, flip the switch, and press the button. Your home's appliances, temperature control, operating systems, and even water delivery run on energy generated by fossil fuel. Petroleum is also a critical component of most plastic containers that hold everything from ketchup to tile cleaner.

   Modifying your cleaning routine — decreasing the number of laundry loads, updating old, inefficient appliances, and even turning down the temperature on your water heater — can play a big role in reducing your household energy consumption. Throughout this book, you find alternatives to energy-intense cleaning methods.

✔ **Clearing the air:** Not only do many home furnishings and materials include petroleum, some forms can cause harm to the environment and to anyone who lives in your home, contaminating water systems and emitting unhealthy chemicals. Blame it on paint, particleboard in cabinets, vinyl flooring, and carpeting and upholstery, but air quality in the typical American home can be worse than the outdoor air. Commercial household cleaning products are also culpable.

✔ **Blocking the drain on water:** You thought oil was in short supply. Water is being depleted at an alarming rate, through drought, pollution, and commoditization by big business interests. Changing your cleaning habits helps reduce your contribution to water shortage: Using energy-efficient washing machines, taking shorter showers, and using your disposal less all help.

✔ **Taking out the trash:** Landfills climb ever higher as the world population continues to consume. Cleaning practices can contribute to the problem. Choosing reusable dust cloths over paper towels or throwaways; being mindful of the packaging that accompanies new cleaning products; and even purchasing cleaning appliances designed to last help reduce your contribution to the waste stream.

Finding benefits close to home

Cleaning green is good for the planet, but it's also good for you. As you begin making changes to your housekeeping practices, you're certain to discover the following benefits:

✔ **Better health:** Removing harmful chemicals (found in many conventional cleaners) improves air quality in your home, thereby having a positive effect on the health of its inhabitants.

✔ **More savings:** Energy-efficient appliances, although sometimes more costly upfront, mean you spend less on energy and reduce water usage. You gain even more savings when you simplify your cleaning arsenal with homemade recipes concocted from common ingredients that cost pennies compared to commercial cleaners.

✔ **Deeper commitment:** Cleaning green can be one of those "gateway" experiences that lead to a heightened awareness of other ecoconscious practices. Every green step you take elevates you to the next level, where you discover yet other ways to make sustainable changes to your life and to the world.

The sum total of your actions as they affect the environment is referred to as your *carbon footprint*. This footprint is usually measured by the amount of CO_2 that a household generates per year. In the United States, the average annual household footprint is 55,000 pounds. That's more than twice as high as Germany's footprint, and nearly four times that of the average Swedish household. Here's the good news: Just like when you diet to lose weight, you can go on a diet — a low-*carbon* diet — to reduce your carbon footprint. And the way you clean your house, among all the other activities that are part of your life, has an impact on how much weight you can take off.

Looking into greener practices

Making changes, even small ones, takes preparation. And figuring out your plan of attack is an important step when launching your new clean-green assault. Here's what you need to do:

✔ **Employ better tactics.** One of the cornerstones of sustainability is to avoid the *need* to consume resources and expend energy: If you can take a bus to work, for example, why buy a car? A great place to start cleaning green is to consider the stuff you need to clean. A white carpet takes more effort to maintain than a tile floor. Dry cleaning is more costly (from environmental damage to personal budget) than washing at home. You get the idea.

This advice parlays to housekeeping in a bunch of ways: from implementing routines to prevent your home from getting dirty (taking off your shoes at the front door), to recognizing that you don't need separate cleaning formulas for each surface and room in your home.

✔ **Stock better tools.** Choosing tools and cleaning aids that do the least amount of damage to the environment is another important component of sustainable cleaning. Mop systems, for example, are a great convenience for modern housekeepers. But their throwaway mop heads are a green strike against them. Single-use wipes, likewise, are wasteful when an old towel or diaper can do the job again and again.

Simplifying your tools — gathering a few that serve many purposes rather than dozens that all perform a single specialized task — and investing in durable items that last are steps for greening your utility closet.

✔ **Switch to better ingredients.** Cleaning formulas made of petroleum-based chemicals may rid your home of undesirable elements (dirt, mold, grime, germs), but may also introduce unhealthy chemicals into your home. If the same cleaner that kills the germs that were making you sick now emits a fume that makes you sick, are you really ahead?

An easy and inexpensive way to reduce the fossil fuel in your cleaners is to make your own with common household items such as vinegar and salt. Some of the recipes in Chapter 3 of this book take just seconds to make and can clean a host of household surfaces.

Formulating a new green clean

Reducing reliance on fossil fuels is a key step toward sustainability. It's an effort that requires the cooperation of big government and big industry. But individuals who want to be part of the solution are discovering that manageable changes in their own lives can bring about big-impact changes, include cutting down on use of gasoline — whether that means downsizing from an SUV, trading in for a hybrid car, or taking the bus to work — and making their home more energy-efficient.

Changing housekeeping habits also helps reduce carbon impact at home. Petro-whittling moves such as the following can help melt off the pounds:

✔ **Trade in for a newer model.** When it comes to cleaning machines, new is better. The difference in energy efficiency between a 20-year-old washer and a just-off-the-assembly line model is huge. Look for the Energy Star designation on major appliances, including washers and refrigerators. (Visit www.energystar.gov for a full load of information about ways to reduce energy consumption.) Although not Energy Star-rated, the newer models of clothes dryers, vacuum cleaners, and air cleaners rate dramatically better on the energy-efficiency scale.

✔ **Degrease your cleaning formulas whenever possible.** For example, virtually all detergents — even many of the green, vegetable- or plant-based brands — contain varying levels of petro-chemicals. Purists prefer the homemade formulas Grandma would approve of. (See Chapter 3 of this book for recipes.)

✔ **Unplug it.** Instead of behaving — as your dad would say — like you have stock in the electric company, invest in sweat equity. Hang your delicates to drip-dry and give the dryer a rest. Give your wrist a workout and open your tuna with a manual can opener.

Warning: Disinfecting May Be Hazardous to the Planet

Pollution from toxic substances is another negative byproduct of reliance on fossil fuels. Environmental calamities from ozone damage and smog to contaminated water supplies have their roots in the burning of nonrenewables, such as petroleum and coal. And all can result in the following serious damage to the natural world:

- **Smog alert:** Utility plants, coal-burning facilities, and oil refineries are among the biggest generators of acid rain, ozone compromise, particle pollution, and the release of chemicals that shade our skies an ominous gray and brown. This air pollution damages trees and eats away at metal, building materials, and even ancient monuments.

- **Dead in the water:** Chemical runoff from factories, homes, and farms — where petroleum-based pesticides and fertilizers are used — pours into streams and waterways with disastrous consequences, destroying water life and creating algaes that upset the balance of the underwater ecosystem.

- **Dangerous ground:** The same processes and chemicals that cause air and water pollution contaminate soil and threaten vegetation and the creatures (including humans) that depend on them.

Outing indoor pollution

Once they've done their dirty work, tough-acting cleaning products contribute their share to environmental havoc when they're washed down the drain or dumped into the ground. They also do a number on indoor air quality.

In our battles against germs, we often wipe out the enemy only to discover we have a bigger threat. The conventional cleaning formulas employed in housekeeping contain chemicals that can activate or aggravate a spectrum of health problems.

Volatile organic compounds (VOCs), found in certain household products and prevalent in paints, varnishes, household furniture, and carpeting, escape into the air as vapor and contribute to what's been dubbed *sick-building syndrome.* According to the Environmental Protection Agency (EPA), VOC levels can be as much as five times higher indoors than outside. Even at lesser levels, VOCs are known to aggravate allergies and to cause asthma and respiratory illnesses, and they're linked to other health problems. Children and pets are most vulnerable to these conditions.

Ammonia, butyl cellusolve, phthalates, perchlorethylene, benzene: An alphabet soup of ingredients in commercial cleaning formulas has been connected to cancer and other serious conditions.

Breathing easier with greener cleaning

Eliminating or reducing the everyday use of toxic chemicals and keeping them out of our water systems is a step toward a healthier home and environment. Reducing the damage from common household products requires positive changes, such as the following:

✔ To be certain cleaning formulas don't contain chemicals that have been linked to health problems or pollution, choose products that list ingredients on the container. Because they're not legally required to do so, few manufacturers disclose their contents on the label. Search for information by chemical or product at the Household Products Database (http://hpd.nlm.nih.gov).

✔ Dispose of toxic solutions responsibly by taking advantage of hazardous-materials collection sites. Pouring chemicals down the drain means they end up in the water supply (we're hearing a lot these days about the high level of pharmaceuticals in our drinking water) and the soil as well.

Getting into Hot Water

Water is a precious resource on Planet Earth. But if alien beings dropped in on a typical household in the United States, they'd never guess it. American earthlings wash small loads of laundry in large tubs of water; take 20-minute showers; leave the faucet running while brushing and flossing; fill up backyard swimming pools; and excessively hose down lawns to maintain that perfect green grass.

Sure, 70 percent of the earth's surface is covered in water — but only a small percentage is drinkable. And that supply is drying up as the world's population grows and conditions like drought increase. The average American uses 300 gallons of water each day — for drinking, showering, flushing, and washing — yet 1.2 billion people around the globe don't have access to potable drinking water, let alone enough for their animals and crops, which then reduces their food supply and leads to further malnutrition.

Throwing money down the drain

With on-demand access, you can easily take water availability for granted. Residents in certain parts of the country, however, are familiar with the consequences of drought and make sacrifices to reduce water consumption by foregoing watering their lawns and even being cognizant of too much toilet-flushing.

When it comes to cleaning, water is almost always part of the equation, from the content in cleaning formulas to the buckets of hot water for scrubbing the kitchen floor. Letting the water run — running the hose as you wash your car, keeping the faucet on as you rinse dishes, waiting for the shower water to heat up before you step in — hikes up the water bill as it drains valuable resources.

REMEMBER

The bathroom is the home's primary water villain, with the toilet demanding more than a quarter of the monthly water bill and using as much as 8 gallons per flush. The washing machine is the second-biggest guzzler.

Having water available on command comes with an energy cost. That water is pumped into your pipes by means of a system powered by — you guessed it — fossil-fueled electricity. Nearly 5 percent of all electrical energy in the United States goes to moving and treating water, and in some locations, it accounts for more than 50 percent of municipal energy consumption.

Book III

Green Cleaning

Heating up the debate

If wasting water isn't bad enough, the temperature at which you're wasting it can make things even worse. In fact, you don't even have to turn on the hot water to expend electricity. Working around the clock, your water heater keeps a 40- or 50-gallon tankful at the ready. And when you use it up, it generates a new batch — without being asked. Appliances and fixtures that can get you into further hot water include

- **Washing machines:** Washing a full load of clothes in an older-model machine can require as much as 40 to 55 gallons of water. Doing a load in hot water increases energy use by as much as 90 percent, according to Energy Star.

- **Dishwashers:** Older machines suck up as much as 25 gallons per wash, and extra rinse cycles only increase that amount. The cycle uses the same amount of water and energy whether it's a half or full load.

✔ **Showers:** Keeping yourself clean takes energy, too. In many homes, the water heater is located far from the bath plumbing, so the hot water must travel a ways to get to the showerhead. You know what that means: You wait several minutes for it to warm up as water just pours down the drain.

Reducing the water pressure

Being clean and green means being conscientious about taxing the water supply — looking for ways to clean with less water. To green up your house-keeping, incorporate the following practices:

✔ **Turn off the tap.** You can easily treat the faucet like a fountain while soaping up or rinsing the dishes, washing the car, or brushing your teeth. But your plumbing fixtures may be the biggest culprit in water waste.

✔ **Stop the drain on water resources at all source points.** Update your plumbing with low-flow showerheads, faucet aerators, and low-flush toilets and check regularly for leaks.

✔ **Purchase a Star.** Replacing your old clothes washer with an Energy Star model reduces water usage dramatically — as much as 50 percent. Other water-using fixtures, such as toilets, showerheads, and sink aerators, are also much more conservative than their free-spending ancestors.

✔ **Fill it up.** Do full loads of dishes. Your energy and water consumption are the same whether you do a full or partial load. If you need to do small loads of laundry, make sure that you use the lowest water-level setting.

✔ **Keep it cool.** Whenever possible, without sacrificing clean, use a lower water temperature for washing, mopping, and soaking. Also keep the water heater at 120°F or less.

Is Your Home Making You Sick?

The cleaning-product industry seems to view housekeeping as germ warfare: With liberal use of descriptives such as "kills on contact" and "decimates," "destroys," and "wipes out," the manufacturers of commercial cleaning solutions approach their work as a room-to-room battle against bacterial insurgency and house-born illnesses.

Most of this "defenders-of-the-clean-world" positioning is simply part of the advertising hype. But the fact is, your home — and buildings in general — *can* pose a threat to your well-being, and that threat isn't just from the germs and dirt that conventional cleaners vow to protect you against. Within the four walls that make up your sanctuary from the world lurk an army of hazards, hidden in dark corners, under floors and carpets, inside showers, and behind the walls. Your home can make you sick. Literally.

In addition to choosing the right building materials and furnishings, keeping your home dry, well ventilated, and *clean* helps protect against many household health risks. But how effective are *green* cleaning practices? Promoting themselves as "earth-gentle," "ecofriendly," and "safe for plants and animals," they do seem to lean more toward the speak-softly strategists than the carry-a-big-stick camp.

By understanding the potential health threats in your home, you can easily see that among the strategies for combating sick-building syndrome, good *green* housekeeping practices are your No. 1 ally.

Factors in poor indoor air quality

A confluence of forces within your home can create an unhealthy environment. From that old carpet where the dog has slept for the past ten years to the vinyl floor in the kitchen that still gives off the new smell, your home exudes its own *atmosphere* in more ways than one — and I'm not talking about bad feng shui. The combination of all sorts of elements can bombard you on a daily basis with substances unseen but highly potent.

WARNING!

According to the Environmental Protection Agency, indoor air pollution is one of the top five environmental risks to public health. Levels of pollutants inside a private home are often five times higher than they are outdoors; under certain circumstances, they can be as high as 1,000 times more. This pollution can result in a slew of respiratory problems, including asthma. Poor indoor air quality can cause headaches, dry eyes, nasal congestion, nausea, fatigue, and other symptoms. Children and people with respiratory illnesses are at an even greater risk.

Don't count on being able to *see* signs of poor air quality. Although you may be able to pick up on the strong acrid smell of a new furniture stain or "feel" that a room is too humid, indoor air pollution is particularly insidious in that it's often invisible. Primary culprits of poor indoor air quality include

- ✔ **Poor ventilation:** When the air inside a home doesn't have enough circulation, unhealthy particle matter — dust and pollen, for example — and gases from chemicals in furnishings and household products stay in the atmosphere, creating their own form of smog.

- ✔ **Humidity:** Bathrooms, basements, kitchens, and other areas where moisture can collect in dark, warm spots are prone to structural rot and the growth of mildew and mold, which may not be visible when the damage is spreading behind the tiles of a bathroom shower or under the floorboards where a pipe is leaking.

- ✔ **Biological pollutants:** In addition to mildew and molds, bacteria, dust, dust mite droppings, pollen, and pet hair and dander are other biological contaminants that wreak havoc.

Book III

Green Cleaning

✔ **Radon:** A gas created when uranium in the Earth decays, *radon* can enter your home through cracks and other entry points in the foundation. It's the second-leading cause of lung cancer. The good news is you can test for radon — and prevent it from getting into your home. For more information, visit the U.S. Environmental Protection Agency's Web site at www.epa.gov.

✔ **Chemicals in some building materials and furnishings:** Treated wood used in home construction, carpets, flooring, and furniture can emit chemicals known as *volatile organic compounds* (VOCs) — harmful substances, such as formaldehyde, that are released as gases and remain in the air until after the new smell has worn away. Older homes may contain asbestos insulation, which, if it's in poor or deteriorating condition, can release fibers dangerous to lung health.

✔ **Household products:** Personal-care toiletries, pesticides, paints, solvents, and cleaning solutions may be sources of hundreds of potentially harmful VOCs and chemicals that compromise the air quality of your home.

The next two sections tell you what you need to know about these common pollutants.

Dander and dust mites and mold — oh, my!

Some of the worst-offending home pollutants come from biological sources: your beloved family dog and cat (pet hair and dander), pollen, tiny little dust mites that like to snuggle into your pillows and bed linens, and mold spores that reproduce like rabbits in the privacy of your home's dark, damp hiding places.

Most of these contaminants are so small that they can't be seen, but what they lack in size they make up in impact, penetrating into your airways and lungs and potentially producing a string of symptoms. Some effects are as mild as headaches, dizziness, flu or cold symptoms, and fatigue. For those sensitive to respiratory conditions, these contaminants can trigger allergic reactions and asthma attacks. The worst pollutants — such as toxic black mold — have been linked to serious immune deficiencies, attacks on the central nervous system, and, in rare cases, death.

Keys to eliminating these sources of indoor air pollution are good cleaning practices:

- Cleaning bathrooms weekly helps wipe out mildew and mold before it can do damage.

- Vacuuming floors and carpets with a HEPA (high-efficiency particular air) filter picks up irritants. Both bag and bagless models can be effective — but do be careful with bagless vacuums so that you don't accidentally release dust and particles when you open the machine.

- Washing bedding and curtains frequently helps reduce pet hair, dust, dust mites, and other contaminants.

Good ventilation helps fend off the negative effects of pet dander, bacteria, dust mites, and the formation of mildew and mold. And, of course, controlling the humidity in wet-prone areas, such as bathrooms, basements, and kitchens, helps, too.

Chasing down chemical contaminants

You've probably walked into someone else's home and, by your first inhale, known that something in the place was new — the carpeting, the kitchen cabinetry and countertop, a sofa, or even paint. Although sharp, acrid, and sometimes overwhelming, the odor frequently elicits positive feelings — people often equate the new smell with cleanliness and abundance.

To many people, however, that first breath of "new smell" equates to dizziness, nausea, coughing, and difficulty in breathing. Others may not react as strongly, but the chemicals emitting those smells affect all people who are exposed to them at any length.

VOCs are in the air

That new smell whiff comes from VOCs, which are in many of the following materials:

Carpeting	Vinyl flooring
Pressed wood	Furniture
Upholstery	Paint
Varnish	Treated wood
Fiberglass insulation	Solvents
Adhesives	Nail polish remover
Air fresheners	Gasoline
Mothballs	Cosmetics
Insect killer	Cleaning products

VOCs include a variety of chemicals, such as formaldehyde, benzene, and tuolene, found in adhesives in carpeting. The new smell lingers in the air for quite some time as the gases continue to slowly release. This process is called *outgassing* or *off-gassing*, and it's another good reason to keep your home well ventilated.

Eventually, all of the VOCs dissipate — in anywhere from three months to five years or more. But in the meantime, they're known to cause both short- and long-term adverse effects ranging from eye, nose, and throat irritation; headaches; and nausea. They also damage the liver, kidneys, and central nervous system. Some VOCs are suspected or known to cause cancer in humans.

Pointing the finger at the top suspects

Indoor air quality can get worse when you have a mix of chemicals within the confines of your house — the combination of those chemicals can create other toxic compounds. Some of the known offenders are

- **Ammonia:** A common cleaning agent in toilet bowl cleaners and all-purpose sprays, ammonia is regulated by protective agencies, including the Environmental Protection Agency, the Food and Drug Administration, and the Occupational Safety & Health Administration.

- **Chlorine bleach:** Found in laundry bleach, dishwasher detergent, scouring powders, and tub and tile cleaners, chlorine bleach is a byproduct of chlorine, listed in the 1990 Clean Air Act as a hazardous air pollutant. It's on the EPA's Community Right-to-Know list as well. In 1993, the American Public Health Association issued a resolution calling for the gradual phase-out of most chlorine-based compounds.

- **Synthetic solvents:** These chemicals appear in all-purpose cleaners, window sprays, floor strippers, degreasers, and oven, metal, and carpet cleaners under an alphabet soup of names, including ethyl cellosolve, ethylene glycol, ethylene dichloride, butyl cellosolve, and 2-butoxyethanol. Ethylene glycol, for example, is found in everything from window cleaners to antifreeze and is listed in the 1990 Clean Air Act as a hazardous air pollutant and in the EPA's Community Right-to-Know list.

- **Formaldehyde:** Conventional deodorizers, disinfectants, and germicides can contain this compound that is common in household products such as adhesives, permanent press fabrics, particle board, and many others. The EPA has classified formaldehyde as a probable human carcinogen.

- **Optical brighteners:** These synthetic chemicals in laundry detergents make clothes appear whiter but don't actually make them cleaner. They're toxic to fish when washed into the general environment and can create bacterial mutations. Optical brighteners also can cause allergic reaction when in contact with skin that is then exposed to sunlight.

- **Phosphates:** Although phased out of laundry detergents and other cleaners in some states, phosphates are still added to some automatic dish detergents to soften water. When released into the household wastewater, phosphates encourage certain algae to grow, which then upsets the ecosystem balance, killing many forms of water life.

- **Perchloroethylene:** Perc is the chemical used in the dry-cleaning process, but it's also found in spot cleaners and degreasers. Classified as a hazardous air pollutant by the EPA and a probable human carcinogen by the International Agency for Research on Cancer, it's also a primary groundwater contaminant.

Other chemicals, including phthalates and alkylphenol ethoxylates (APEs), have raised controversy as some studies have linked them to cancer and diseases of the reproductive system. Phthalates, a common component of plastic and a petroleum derivative, are commonly contained in fragrance additives, and APEs are often found in detergents, fabric softeners, and products that foam.

Going beyond the ingredients list

Don't bother pulling out your reading glasses: Even if you know which ingredients to avoid, don't expect to find them listed on most cleaning products. Manufacturers aren't required by law to disclose the ingredients in cleaning formulas on the label. Some cleaners may advertise that they're environmentally sound but fail to provide a full list of ingredients.

In choosing products for their health and environmental safety, make sure that you can find a full list of ingredients; that's a good sign, even if you haven't a clue what those polysyllabic mouthfuls of letters means. You can find out more about the formulas by visiting the Household Products Database Web site (http://hpd.nlm.nih.gov) and looking up the Material Safety Data Sheet (MSDS).

Also, be on the lookout for certain claims that may not carry a lot of weight:

- **All-natural or nontoxic:** These terms are unregulated and can't necessarily be validated.

- **Biodegradable:** Referring to a chemical's ability to break down into harmless components, this claim is only meaningful if the product indicates how long it will remain in the environment.

- **Plant-based:** While agents derived from plant sources are better than petroleum-derived agents, be aware that some manufacturers may advertise their plant-derived ingredients — while downplaying their synthetic components.

- **Phosphate-free:** Because phosphates have been phased out of virtually all laundry detergents, this claim is meaningless. Be aware, however, that many more automatic dish detergents still contain phosphates.

Book III

Green
Cleaning

Home Safe Home: Green Solutions to the Rescue

From choosing natural building materials or those without harmful chemicals to building and maintaining an energy-efficient structure that allows for fresh air exchange, environmental practices support a healthy home.

But green *cleaning* techniques, despite their kinder-to-the-planet characteristics, can be just as tough in room-to-room combat with indoor pollution and offer one of the best ways to get toxins out of your space. Here are a few cleaning practices that have a positive effect in reducing poor indoor air quality and other environmental risks:

- **Eliminate the usual chemical suspects.** Avoid cleaning products that contain the most offensive compounds, including the ones listed in the earlier section named "Pointing the finger at the top suspects."

- **Choose safer cleaning agents.** Because most manufacturers *don't* list all the ingredients in the product, this one can be a challenge. Stick with cleaners that disclose all the ingredients or make your own simple and safe formulas included in Chapter 3 of this book.

- **Get the dirt to stick.** Conventional dusting and sweeping can actually make air quality worse by stirring up sleeping dust and dirt into the air. The best solution is to replace your old shaggy-headed dust mop for one with a microfiber pad — dirt sticks to it like Velcro.

- **Suck it up.** Vacuuming regularly helps keep pollutants at bay — as long as the vacuum is actually sucking up dirt instead of spewing it out. A HEPA filter is a critical component of a good vacuum. Look for one that traps 99.97 percent of particulates 0.3 microns and larger, which include some chemical contaminants that bind to household dust.

- **Clear the air.** Use an energy-efficient air purifier to remove dust, pollen, and tobacco particulates from your home. Conventional air cleaners can drain a lot of energy, but to keep it under control, choose an Energy Star-rated model. (You can find listings on www.energystar.gov.) Select the smallest model that meets your needs based on area size.

Counting the Cost of Cleaning Green

In some respects, going green demands a lot more green — you know, the kind with dollar signs? A neighbor just got a quote on installing solar panels to generate his home's energy. The estimate was almost as much as my first home! Tankless water heaters. Hybrid cars. Even free-range eggs and grass-fed beef cost more than their conventional counterparts. Organic towels and sheets? Before you look at the thread count, better count up the extra expense.

Of course, cost is relative. The organic, locally grown tomatoes are a good $1 a pound more than the hothouse brand. But when you weigh in the fertilizers and pesticides used to grow the conventional tomatoes and add the embodied energy from their packaging, storage, and cross-country journey to your grocery store, the environmental price tag offsets any cost savings.

Some green upgrades may require more cash out of your pocket, but cleaning green is *not* one of them. In fact, in most cases, following environmental cleaning practices can save you money.

Shopping for green cleaners

As you stroll down the housecleaning aisle at the grocery or big box chain, you're bound to notice that, in most cases, the earth-friendly cleaning brands are more expensive than the conventional names your mother would be familiar with. A recent shopping expedition in a Midwestern discount chain confirmed that for toilet bowl sanitizer, all-purpose spray, laundry detergent, window cleaner, and dish soap, the green brands were pricier — sometimes by spare change and sometimes by several dollars.

Bottom line: If you intend to stock your utility closet with preformulated cleaning supplies from green-brand lines, be prepared to budget just a bit higher.

If you're willing to take the minute or two to whip up your own recipes from basic household workhorses — baking soda, white distilled vinegar, and salt— you can watch your cleaning budget plunge deeper than a plumber's snake. (For recipes, see Chapter 3 of this book.)

As of late, more commercial brands are advertising cleaning solutions with baking soda, vinegar, and other environmentally safe ingredients. In some cases, these products also contain the offending chemicals that make them environmentally undesirable. But they also cost as much as the other commercial products. So, why buy a window cleaner *with* vinegar when the vinegar alone works at least as well — at one-tenth the price?

Considering your time investment

In addition to the cost of your cleaning solutions, your time has a value, too. If it didn't, why would housecleaning franchises be popping up like dandelions? Plenty of homeowners are willing to pay as much as $100 an hour for a cleaning crew rather than sacrifice hours of their own time.

But if you're cleaning on your own dime, you don't have to worry about adding anything more than negligible increments to your time. Count on a few minutes to mix together your own cleaning solutions — if you're bypassing the packaged products — and a little more time if you opt for old-fashioned, appliance-free cleaning methods, such as dust-mopping instead of vacuuming or hanging your wash to dry in the sun rather than loading up the dryer.

You may have to invest a little more sweat equity into your scrubbing and scouring efforts. Giving your oven a good cleaning may feel like the equivalent of 20 minutes of upper-body exercise.

Reducing the Need to Clean

The best shortcut to maintaining a clean and orderly home is to sidestep the *need* to clean. Making changes that reduce the amount of dirt you bring into the home or the mess you make means cleaning less often and not having to work as hard.

Leaving your shoes at the door

In many parts of the world, particularly Asia, it's customary to take off shoes that are worn in the outside world and leave them at the door, slipping on "house shoes" or shuffling about in stocking feet. Maintaining a shoe-free home is more than a quaint custom, however; it's a wonderful way to keep the crud you pick up on the bottom of your shoes from ending up on your floors. It also reduces scuffmarks, scratches, and wear and tear on floor materials, from carpet to hardwood.

Keep a mat of assorted slippers at the door for guests to put on. This hospitable gesture serves as a signal to folks that they can "get comfortable" and make themselves at home.

Doormats serve a similar purpose. Place a rough-textured mat on the outside of all entrances to the home, including the garage. If caked-on mud is an issue, add a *boot scraper,* a heavy wrought-iron or stiff-brushed device to run the bottoms of your shoes over. Keep another doormat on the inside. Well-used doormats mean extra cleaning, but shaking out or washing a doormat is a lot easier than mopping and sweeping the floors throughout your house.

If you have only one mat, put it by the door you use the most. So many people put them at their front door for appearance, but for function, you may need it most at the garage, kitchen, or back door. If the mat will be rained on, get one specially made for outside.

Wear it again, Sam

The "wear-it-once" school of thought is anathema to environmental advocates. A pair of denims or a sweater doesn't have to go into the wash after one wearing — unless you've been up to your knees in garden muck or running a marathon. Retraining kids or teenagers to hang up their clothes instead of letting them drop where they take them off can help extend the wear before they have to be washed.

You can modify other home habits to reduce the frequency of your washing:

- If just-worn clothing has no discernable stains or dirt, refresh it by hanging it outside in the sun or in a room with well-circulated air.

- If you've switched to cloth napkins to cut down on paper use (a great idea even though you must use water and energy to clean them), consider the European tradition of reusing mildly soiled napkins through more than one meal. In most homes, family members tend to sit in the same seat, so what's the harm if you reuse the same napkin you used with your bagel and juice at breakfast for your soup and sandwich at lunch?

- Putting a glass top on a piece of furniture, such as a wood cabinet holding a television or a table, is a decorator trick. This trick prevents staining from glasses or plants and makes for easier clean up. Glass can be custom cut to fit the particular piece of furniture, and the sides are rounded for appearance and to prevent injuries.

- A clean towel for every shower or bath isn't necessary: Even hotels are catching on and offering guests the option of turning down daily linen changes. Do the same at home. Do, however, change towels at least once a week to avoid bacteria growth that thrives in warm, humid spots. And if allergies are a problem, be sure to change bed linens frequently to get rid of dust mites.

Book III

Green Cleaning

Preventive maintenance

Scheduling a yearly checkup keeps your furnace and air conditioner healthy. Not only does preventive maintenance ensure that everything is in working order, a smoothly operating appliance means more efficient energy use, lower utility bills, and cleaner air.

Keeping the air clean

One of the components of the tune-up is changing the air filter, which you can do yourself more frequently. Change your air conditioner filters monthly during the summer or warm-weather periods and replace your furnace filter in heating season every two or three months, more frequently if you have pets.

Choose a high-efficiency filter over a traditional fiberglass one. According to the American Lung Association, a high-efficiency filter can capture 30 times the amount of indoor air pollutants, including smoke, pet hair and dander, and pollen.

Keeping the air dry

Damp air breeds mildew, particularly in the ever-humid bathroom. A working exhaust fan goes a long way in expelling moisture and discouraging the growth of mold and mildew. But mold can spread anywhere — wood furniture, books, the clothing in your closet — so ensure good air circulation throughout the house.

Ventilate by opening the windows and letting the fresh air do what it does best. You can't always open windows, of course, if it's extremely cold or hot, or you live in an area with frequent smog alert days. When your house is sealed (good for reducing energy consumption), good circulation is more important than ever. Despite the increased energy usage, running the fan or the air conditioner or furnace may be an unavoidable tactic.

Filters, filters everywhere

The furnace and air conditioner aren't the only appliances putting in overtime to filter out dust, pollen, dander, or other elements dirty and undesirable. Plenty of other filtering devices are at work, too. Regularly clean out or replace filters and dirt traps for

- Vacuum cleaners
- Air-filtering machines
- Water filters (whole-house water filters or refrigerator water-in-the-door filters or faucet filters)
- Dryer lint traps
- Hood exhaust fans above the cooktop or stove (these filters can go in the dishwasher)

Tidy up as you go

You may remember yelling at your kids, "Why can't you just put it *away* when you're done with it?" Or "Is it so difficult to take two more steps to the closet instead of throwing your pants on the bed?" Or maybe that was *your* mom yelling at you.

She's right, and you know it. When you replace the book on the shelf when you're done with it, if you place your coffee cup in the sink after you've taken the last sip, when you put the clean clothes back in the drawers as soon as you fold them — just finishing up the job that you've started goes a long way in minimizing on your cleaning effort.

When you're in a hurry getting out the door in the morning, being tidy may be impossible and simply another stressor. If that's the case, resolve to do a quick pickup when you get home or, as many families do, reserve Saturday mornings for a general housecleaning. Tidying as you go is ideal, but slippage (just as in a diet) is normal. Be kind to yourself.

A Lean-and-Mean Plan for Getting the House Clean

When faced with a houseful of rooms demanding to be cleaned, you can become so overwhelmed you don't know where to begin. Maybe you start by picking up the dirty clothes on the bathroom floor and take them to the laundry room, where you stop to fold socks that take you next to your bedroom to put them away. The dirty mirror distracts you, and you head into the kitchen for the window cleaner, and stop to finish up the breakfast dishes and then. . . .

When you hop from room to room, putting a single pair of socks away or wiping down one piece of furniture at a time, you may be multitasking or merely running around in circles.

What you need is a plan. A method. A strategy. There are plenty of great ones: Cleaning strategies are certainly not a one-size-fits-all. Trial and error will tell what works for you. But all good plans have certain components.

A practical sequence

If you were making a shirt, you wouldn't sew the buttons on before you cut out the material from the pattern. Likewise, cleaning necessitates a logical order. You wouldn't, for example, mop the floor before you sweep it. Each home is different, but the order follows some universal principles:

Book III

Green Cleaning

✔ **Clean from the top down.** Dust the ceiling corners and lighting fixtures, then the tops of picture frames, clean the windows, and finally the window frames and sills. Wipe up any smudges on the walls or light switch plates, dust the furniture, and sweep or mop the floor.

If you start from the floor and work up, by the time you get to waist-level cleaning, you're sweeping toast crumbs off the counter onto your clean floor.

✔ **Work your way through the house.** When doing a whole-house clean, move from room to room in a sequential order. Say that you have a two-story home: Start on the second floor in the room farthest from the stairs and work toward them, cleaning the hallway floor as you make your final trip toward the steps.

Then start on the first floor, working from the room farthest from the kitchen or laundry room — whichever place you must return to for more water or cleaning supplies as needed.

✔ **Prioritize "public" areas.** If you have frequent visitors, start with the rooms and areas your guests are most likely to see: the main floor entry area, powder room, living room, and kitchen.

✔ **Go around in circles.** A good strategy for cleaning a single room is to work in a circle. Start to the left or the right of the door or entrance and make a clockwise or counterclockwise circle around the room.

What about the center? Most rooms are small enough that your efforts can be somewhat pie-shaped, stepping from the perimeter to catch any furniture placed closer to the center of the room. By following this methodical path, you're less likely to have overlooked a corner or a piece of furniture.

✔ **Group by task.** Here's another plan of attack: Instead of moving through the house room by room, approach your cleaning one task at a time. For example, begin with your dust rag and wood cleaner and dust everything in several rooms. Put that down and pick up the window cleaner and do the mirrors and so on.

Bundling your chores can be a very efficient approach: After you finish all the vacuuming, for example, you can put away the vacuum instead of leaving it out until you're ready to use it in the next room.

A surefire spring cleaning strategy

Ah, spring! In cultures ancient and traditional, spring holidays have celebrated the renewal of life through food, festivity — and cleaning rituals. Doors and windows are opened, the sun is welcomed in, and homes are given a good airing.

According to a survey conducted by the Soap and Detergent Association, 77 percent of Americans participate in spring cleaning each year. Out with old, in with the new!

And the *new* may include a fresh approach to cleaning. As motivated as you may be to tackle your spring housework, the prospect of overhauling your home from top to bottom is a bit intimidating — overwhelming, even. Try the following to bring it down to a manageable level:

- **Spread it out.** Don't try to power through your entire homestead, from window washing to attic-purging, in one weekend. To do a thorough job of spring cleaning without losing momentum, divide the chores and spread out the work over a month or even more.

- **Practice patience.** Take on the tasks as they make sense. Wait on washing the windows for a cloudy day (fewer streaks than on a sunny day) or cleaning out the fireplace if more winter storm activity is likely. Repaint the living room first and then replace the old carpet with a new bamboo floor.

- **Don't go it alone.** If your housemates and family members aren't reliable members of the housekeeping team, then sign on a free agent: Enlist the help of a cleaning service, especially for the most demanding jobs. Better the licensed experts climb on the ladder to dust your chandelier and clean the skylight, and you polish your heirloom silver.

Seeking Professional Help

The most effective way to reduce your cleaning efforts? Let someone else do the work. There's no shortage of housecleaning services in the phone book or notices on your mailbox. But until recently, most of them, whether national franchises or local businesses, were anything but green. Driven primarily by a clientele who wanted clean at any cost, such enterprises typically chose cleaning products that clean fast and powerfully. No surprise, most services used powerful products with bleach, ammonia, and other fossil fuel-based or eye-watering powerful chemicals.

That's changing, and changing fast. Housecleaning companies that offer green services are popping up from coast to coast. But before you pay a premium for green service, do a little digging to find out exactly how that company differentiates itself.

- If the service claims to use "green" cleaning formulas, find out what they are. If their brand's labeled "nontoxic," "natural," or "biodegradable," be wary as these labels may not mean much. Remember, manufacturers don't have to list ingredients on the label.

Book III

Green Cleaning

✔ Find out whether the company is committed to sustainable business practices. In addition to its choice of cleaning products, does the business attempt to reduce its environmental footprint by considering transportation issues and building operations? Does it offset for the carbon emissions it generates?

✔ Ask what else the business does to define itself as green. Are the employees cognizant of water usage, conserving where possible and using cooler water when it makes sense? Do they clean without electronic appliances? Do they clean with reusable tools — cloth rags instead of paper towels?

If the greenness of the cleaning products is your primary issue, consider sticking with a conventional service and ask that they switch to your cleaning products. Most are happy to use whatever products you specify, whether your homemade recipes or green-brand formulas.

Chapter 2

Building an Arsenal of Green Cleaning Tools

*P*eek into a green cleaning closet, and you won't see a dramatic difference from a conventional collection of cleaning tools and equipment: dust rags, brooms, mops, sponges, and a vacuum cleaner. The sustainable sensibility may be reflected in the *type* of dust cloths, or the *amount* of mops and brooms, or the *content* of the trash bags.

In this chapter, you explore these sometimes-subtle differences as you get a rundown of just what tools and hardware belong in the green utility closet, from stuff as basic as old towels for cleaning rags to the latest gadgets that make quick work of cleaning.

Greening Your Cleaning Closet

The general rule when assembling the greenest cleaning equipment is the environmentalist's first commandment: Thou shall reduce, reuse, and recycle. Just as you question whether you require a multitude of cleaners for countertops, bathroom tile, and floors, you may not need that assortment of brushes or three different kinds of vacuum cleaners. Secondly, work with what you have. Instead of tossing and replacing, repair and reuse. And, lastly, when your old equipment is finally ready to go to the utility closet in the sky, recycle everything that you can.

Remember that *buying* isn't a green activity. But for those tools you must acquire, seek products made of ecofriendly materials or of recycled content. Look for items with minimal packaging — more and more, such wrappings may be identified as recyclable, biodegradable, or compostable.

Tackling dirty jobs: Cleaning cloths

Cleaning cloths are the workhorses of your house-cleaning kit. If you have nothing else in your utility closet but towels and rags, you have all you need to attack most cleaning jobs. (See Chapter 3 of this book for cleaning-agent recipes that pair up well with your cleaning cloths.)

These multipurpose fundamentals can tackle just about any household job, including

- ✔ Dusting, wet or dry
- ✔ Wiping down appliances and furnishings
- ✔ Mopping floors
- ✔ Cleaning tile and kitchen and bathroom surfaces
- ✔ Shining chrome
- ✔ Sopping up spills
- ✔ Polishing silver
- ✔ Cleaning glass and mirrors

Hanging up a damp cleaning towel to reuse risks growing and spreading bacteria. Solve this issue by switching out the towel and washing it often in hot water.

Working with the right material

Options for cleaning cloths are endless: On the market are packages of cloth-like throwaway towels, heavy-duty, purpose-made cleaning cloths; products with antimicrobial properties; microfiber wipes, and paper towels. And you can always repurpose old, worn T-shirts, towels, and sheets.

The best cleaning choice is the cloth that picks up the most dirt without streaking, spreading, smearing, or leaving behind muddy trails. Certain fabrics do a better job than others:

- ✔ **Wool:** Ideal for dusting, wool contains lanolin and has static electricity properties, attracting dust and keeping hold of it more so than other fabrics.

- ✔ **Cotton:** The soft, absorbent nature of pure cotton makes it a great choice for almost any cleaning job.

- ✔ **Microfiber:** Its fine filaments pick up dust, dirt, and oil and boast a high absorbency factor, able to hold up to seven times its weight in water.

Repurposing old clothes: The greenest option

Used fabrics make outstanding cleaning aids. They've been washed to a smooth softness, with less lint and loose fibers. Cut up an old wool blanket or reuse hole-ridden wool socks (just slip them on your hands) for dusting; convert old cotton towels, baby diapers, and soft cotton T-shirts and night-wear into scrub rags. Remove any buttons or zippers because they scratch surfaces.

This standout choice for cleaning rags meets the highest green standards: It requires no additional output of energy (other than your effort to cut it into rag-size pieces); you don't have to buy it; it requires no wasteful packaging; it's not damaging the environment; and you're exercising the principle of reuse. And if you're using old towels or T-shirts made of organic cotton, chalk up even more green points.

Buying new cleaning cloths

One benefit of buying new cleaning cloths rather than repurposing: You can choose colors to separate cloths for different uses — red for dusting and blue for wet-wiping, say. The ability to color-coordinate makes keeping cloths separate a lot easier.

Look for 100-percent organic cotton towels. Organic towels often cost more than conventional towels because the natural materials used are grown without the use of most pesticides, synthetic fertilizers, or genetic engineering. Most organic towels are 100-percent cotton or a blend with cotton and another natural fiber, such as linen or hemp. To verify that the product is organic, look for the USDA certified organic symbol. Another green choice is bamboo. Yes, that sturdy woody rapidly renewable grass can be transformed into the softest fabric. Its antibacterial qualities make it a perfect choice for dishtowels.

Getting attached to microfiber

Microfiber cleaning cloths are available from a number of brands. Though derived from petroleum, polyester-polyamide-based microfiber materials are worth their weight in water — they're super-absorbent and scoop up dirt like iron shavings to a magnet. You can reuse most of them, and some are specialized to tackle

- ✔ **Granite,** picking up dirt and dulling residue, and leaving a shine

- ✔ **Wood,** attracting and trapping dust

Book III

Green Cleaning

- ✔ **Windows/glass,** cleaning and adding gleam
- ✔ **Stainless steel,** removing smudges, fingerprints, and streaks
- ✔ **Floors,** picking up dust, dirt, and debris with mop pads or sweep dusters

Shredding the use of paper towels

Anything that ends up in the trash after a single use doesn't rate very high on the green-o-meter. And paper towels are the ultimate in discard-ability.

Rolled up inside every package of paper towel is a dirty back-story: The paper industry is one of the world's worst polluters, keeping company with chemical and steel manufacturing. And very little paper towel is recycled, of course. Instead, it contributes to the 40 percent of landfill content from paper.

Because wood pulp is the basis for paper, its production has an impact on deforestation, which adds to global warming. And the manufacturing of paper towel, in addition to bearing a heavy environmental footprint, involves bleaching with chlorine-based chemicals, which can lead to the release of toxic emissions, causing further damage.

Cleaning cloths can pinch-hit for virtually any job that paper towels can handle. They're washable, and you can use them again and again. Save your most tattered and faded dishtowels and other soft cloths to use for the dirtiest jobs, giving them one last shot at service before discarding them.

If you decide that your home can't function without paper towels, you're in good company. Some steps do help lessen the environmental impact:

- ✔ **Seek products with the highest percentage of *post-consumer waste* (PCW).** This figure indicates the amount of material that came from paper used and recycled by consumers — mail-order catalogs and magazines you're finished with or the used copy paper from your office, for example. Most recycled-content products include some recycled content from manufacturing waste, referred to as *preconsumer* waste. For example, Seventh Generation paper towels use 80-percent PCW and 20-percent preconsumer.

- ✔ **Choose unbleached paper towels.** They're identified by the label PCF (processed chlorine free) to ensure that no chlorine derivatives were used in the processing of the paper.

- ✔ **Select products free of dyes and fragrances.** Why add chemicals (and potential irritants) when you're working to go green?

- ✔ **Buy the largest quantity with the least amount of packaging.** Double rolls make more sense than single rolls.

An absorbing issue: Sponges

An ideal ally for soaking up wet messes, sponges suck up water so that you can transfer it into the sink with a good squeeze. Once upon a time, the sponges used for cleaning were from the amorphous, faceless sea creatures that float under the ocean's surface like deflating beach toys. Today, the articles you buy in hardware and home stores are rarely made from real sponge, but rather from some sort of polymer with petroleum origins. The microfiber sponges, a relatively new novelty, are likewise synthetic-based.

Reduce the elbow grease and cleaning solution required by choosing sponges with a "scrubbing" side and sponge mops with an abrasive strip — great for scraping away stubborn dried-on food.

The dark side of sponges

Whether plastic- or plant-based, all sponges pose a similar risk: They're germ carriers. Talk about a natural breeding ground: All those little holes and dark crevices are the perfect spot for germs to hide and thrive. When you use a dirty sponge to clean a surface, chances are you're leaving behind a trail of bacteria even as you're picking up the mess.

Some companies have countered the sponge's dirty reputation by soaking their products with antibacterial agents, typically the ingredient *triclosan*. Avoid this ingredient! Triclosan has not been proven to be any more effective than soap and warm water in killing germs. It's also suspected of contributing to the spread of drug-resistant bacteria. Finally, when in contact with chlorine, triclosan can become chloroform, a probable human carcinogen.

Book III

Green
Cleaning

Practicing sponge safety

Don't write off sponges completely. These guys are redeemable and worth the effort because of their super-hero absorption powers. They just require a little more attention. Follow these practices for safe sponging:

- Buy cellulose sponges or long-lasting microfiber products for the greenest options. (The packaging usually identifies the contents as such.)

- After each use, wash the sponge in hot soapy water or spray with a solution of white distilled vinegar.

- Set the sponge on a kitchen windowsill so that sunlight and its magical disinfecting properties can dry it.

- Wash the sponge often in the washing machine. Warmer water is preferred.

- Use common sense: Keep the bathroom sponges only for bathrooms, the kitchen sponges only in the kitchen, and then specify their use for wiping crumbs off the table or range top or rinsing out the sink.

Clean sponges in the dishwasher or boil them in water for three minutes. Another solution is to microwave them for one to three minutes, making sure that they're wet before you "nuke" them. Using hot water to get at the holes and crevices is important for thorough cleaning. Even following these practices, you want to replace sponges frequently. When the dirt discoloration appears permanent and the sponge starts to disintegrate, it's time to toss.

Brushing up on other cleaning tools

No other product in the cleaning closet offers such diversity as brooms and brushes. You can find brushes expressly for cleaning baseboards, cobweb brushes, ceiling fan brushes, carpet rakes, dryer vent and lint trap brushes, grout brushes, and even garbage disposal brush.

Sweeping changes

No green home is complete without the traditional good-luck gift, a broom, for new homeowners. Although more cleanup jobs are handed over to the vacuum cleaner these days, the broom still earns its keep for sweeping up. A broom comes in handy when the power is out, or when you simply find the meditative motion of sweeping relaxing.

The no-plug broom is by its very nature a green cleaning tool. That brooms are traditionally made of natural and abundant material such as straw — from sorghum and often referred to as broomcorn — and wooden handles adds to their sustainable allure.

Many brooms found in hardware and big box stores are plastic-based, with nylon brush and plastic or metal handles, but plenty of the traditional models are available. In fact, Home Depot has committed to using wood certified by the Forest Stewardship Council (meaning that the wood was sustainably harvested from a properly managed forest) down to and including broom handles.

Don't use a broom to sweep a hardwood floor. The brush, whether natural-material or nylon, can scratch the surface. You're better off using the vacuum or dust mop to round up dust bunnies.

Nylon brooms or other lightweight smoother finished brooms are best for inside use, such as tile floors. Straw brooms, however, work fine indoors, too. And the rougher texture of the brush is especially effective on uneven surfaces, such as outdoor brick patios. The unevenness of the straw gets into the cracks and crevices between the bricks. Shake brooms outside to clean them.

Close brushes with green cleaning

When you remove the harsh chemical agents from your cleaning arsenal, you're compelled to use a little more elbow grease to get some surfaces and furnishings as clean as the chemicals do. The tough scrubbing power of brushes can up your cleaning power, using agents as mild as plain water.

A good stiff scrub brush can tackle scuffed kitchen floors, mildewed tile grout, grease-coated ovens, and brick or stone floors and surfaces. You can also use it for sweeping (a push-broom is, in essence, a scrub brush with a handle). You can use soft-bristled brushes for picking up dust and cleaning delicate objects and surfaces.

Every green home should have the following brushes in the utility closet or appropriate spot in the house:

- Stiff-bristled scrub brush for scouring and scrubbing tough surfaces and tougher dirt — both indoor and outdoor scrub brushes
- Soft-bristled brush for cleaning fragile furnishings and for dusting and polishing
- Toilet brush
- Vegetable brush, for cleaning food
- Bottlebrush for thoroughly cleaning long, narrow-necked containers from baby bottles to flower vases and reaching into garbage disposals, drains, and even dryer vents

TIP Before buying a custom-use brush for small jobs, tap your medicine chest and bathroom toiletry cabinet first. Toothbrushes are great for getting into the tiny crevices of blenders or taking lint off hair-dryer vents. Old makeup brushes are soft and gentle for dusting the curves and hard-to-reach spots on antique furniture.

Not your mother's mop

Unless you're partial to housemaid's knee, floor mops and dusters are a must-have. Most floor mops have a sponge on the end that has a scraper edge to get up crusted-on food or dirt. They pair nicely with a bucket of soapy water. Dust mops, on the other hand, are based on a fringy head or microfiber cloth to pick up dry dust and loose particles.

Mops both wet and dry have evolved, overcoming some objections to their performance. One of the biggest trends in floor cleaning is the "mop system." An all-in-one kit includes the mop handle, mop head, and removable cloths that attach to the mop head. Some systems also feature an "onboard" refillable cleaning solution dispenser — as you mop, you can press a button to squirt out cleaning liquid from the mop head.

Book III

Green Cleaning

Until recently, most mop systems used disposable mop cloths: You'd use them a couple times and then toss them. But as consumers and companies become more attuned to sustainability issues, these throwaways are increasingly replaced by reusable cloths, most often made of microfiber material.

Microfiber means harder-working and longer-lasting cloths for both wet and dry mopping. These qualities earn microfiber, while a synthetic material, plenty of green points. Additionally, some makers manufacture their microfiber from post-consumer content, and some cloths are recyclable or biodegradable.

Trashing plastic bags

As more communities, including countries from Ireland to China, impose bans, fines, and restrictions on the plastic grocery bag, its bigger relative, the trash bag, continues to raise environmental debate.

Used for purposes from collecting leaves to gathering kitchen garbage, these larger trash bags have the same drawbacks as the smaller offenders: They're made from petroleum-based synthetics, so both extraction and manufacture contribute to greenhouse gas emissions.

In addition, trash bags are used almost exclusively for disposal, which means that they're adding to the growing landfill and possibly preventing compostable and biodegradable materials from decomposing.

For a number of reasons, trash bags are near essential to even the greenest consumer. Some community trash pickups require that materials be bagged rather than set out loose in trash containers to discourage animals. And few people have been able to reduce their household footprint to the point that they're no longer generating trash. Thus, the trash bag conundrum.

One way to cut down on your use of plastic trash bags is to ratchet up your recycling efforts to reduce your waste output. (See Chapter 3 of this book for ideas on setting up an efficient recycling collection center.) In addition, follow these steps and watch your use of trash bags shrink.

- **Compost kitchen scraps.** You can turn fruit and vegetable trimmings, coffee grounds, tea leaves, eggshells, and some other materials into rich garden soil in your backyard. (See Chapter 2 of Book VI for more about composting.)

- **Limit the use of trash liners to only those receptacles that collect wet or drippy garbage.** For smaller cans, such as those in the bedroom or living areas, eliminate the trash bag. Many waste cans now come with a removable, washable plastic liner (ah, more plastic!) so that you don't have to continue to use small liner bags.

> ✔ **Use bags you already have, such as brown paper bags from grocery stores, tired-looking gift bags, and department store bags for trash.** This option is green because you're recycling, but it's a less green option because you shouldn't have these items in the first place if you've converted to taking your own cloth bags to the store.
>
> ✔ **Designate the lined trash bin as the homes "central" receptacle and empty the smaller bins into this one.** That way, you can limit your weekly bag use to one.
>
> ✔ **Look for biodegradable trash bags.** These bags are made from corn or other renewable sources, and many advertise that they can biodegrade in a compost bin in just days. Even if you set them out for your weekly trash pickup, at least they're breaking down in the landfill.

Plugging in Green Gadgets

The best energy source for green cleaning is, of course, your own muscle power. But some technological tools are too valuable and effective to do without. Especially where indoor air quality is concerned, nothing picks up dirt and filters irritants as well as a well-made vacuum cleaner.

Book III

Green Cleaning

A clean sweep of vacuum cleaners

A regular sweep through the home with your vacuum cleaner does wonders for reducing problems related to poor indoor air quality, particularly with issues of dust mites, dander, and other irritants. Specialized vacuums suck up pet hair.

The new kid on the block is the Halo vacuum. It has a built-in ultraviolet light bulb that disrupts the DNA of viruses, bacteria, flea eggs, and dust mites. When vacuuming, you activate the light. The Halo vacuum is suggested for cleaning carpets and mattresses. Similar technology is being used in heating and air-conditioning ducts. Anywhere it is dark and dusty, the idea is to shine light on the potential problem. (Stay tuned on this one because the scientific tests and reviews are still underway.)

The *micron* is the measure of the microscopic particulates that find their way into air passages. The best machine is one that includes a high efficiency particulate air (HEPA) filter, which can pick up 99.97 percent of particulates as small as 0.3 microns, the size of cat dander, and on up, including such irritants as dust mite droppings (10 to 20 microns), and pollen, weighing in at a whopping 15 to 25 microns. They can also catch chemical pollutants such as flame-retardants, phthalates, and pesticides.

The vacuum cleaner is an investment in your home's air quality, but it won't help much if it isn't routinely put into service and maintained. Be sure to take these steps to properly use and care for your appliance:

- ✔ Vacuum often — once a week or more frequently if someone in your home has allergies, or you have pets.

- ✔ Vacuum more in areas with high foot traffic, such as the area in front of your couch.

- ✔ Change bags or canisters before they're full to avoid spilling dirt when you empty and change.

- ✔ Replace the filters and maintain according to manufacturer's guidelines.

- ✔ Assist your vacuum cleaner with its chore by dusting furniture regularly (less to fall on the floor) and taking off shoes before tracking dirt onto floors and carpets.

- ✔ When carrying, grip the vacuum by the handle, not the hose.

- ✔ Remove hair entangling the brushes.

- ✔ If you're using a bagless vacuum, empty the canister outside to help alleviate any allergen concerns and wipe the vacuum cleaner with a slightly damp cloth.

Investing in the best vacuum cleaner you need and can afford makes environmental sense. The embodied energy that went into manufacturing it certainly warrants its good care and long life. A model with a lifetime warranty is something to look for. Also, buy from a company that you can purchase parts or repairs from rather than simply replace the vacuum down the road.

Heating things up: Steam cleaners

A clean and chemical-free way of cleaning, steam cleaners are especially good for zapping dirt embedded in carpet, rugs, and fabrics, such as draperies, upholstery, mattresses, and bedding.

In particular, steam cleaners are known to wipe out dust mites and clean up the microscopic messes that irritate allergy sufferers. By targeting dirt with steam heat at 240°F, steam cleaners exceed anything that the clothes washer may aspire to.

Use steam cleaners for wiping up all traces of pet stain, mildew, and mold. They clean most surfaces and get into grout like nothing else can. Read and follow instructions carefully before using.

Remember that steam cleaners are not vacuum cleaners: Dust or pick up loose dirt before steaming and vacuum before using the steam cleaners.

The steam generated can cause bad burns. Some reports suggest that some of the smaller hand-helds may be more prone to causing burns because of malfunctions. Be sure to research models carefully and read consumer reviews before purchasing.

Sniffing Out Room Fresheners

Not only do most people measure clean by the looks of a place, but they also judge it by its smell, but nice smells don't equal clean. In fact, they can spell indoor air quality issues. Many of the aerosol spray room fresheners propel the chemicals used to create the scent, dispersing them in such small particles that they can easily make their way into your air passages and lungs. Some of the sprays are merely overbearingly strong.

Even candles are guilty when it comes to indoor air quality. The smoke they produce creates particulates that can enter air passages and cause irritation and distress to those with respiratory problems. And the wire that supports the wick? Some foreign manufacturers use lead. When burned, the substance enters your airways and is no better for you in this form than if you ate lead paint.

To add insult to injury, candles are most commonly made of petroleum-based paraffin, known to burn "dirty" compared to natural candles made of beeswax, palm oil, or soy.

Cleaning the air in your home is better accomplished by the following methods rather than covering up bad odors with yet more fragrances, whether sprayed, burned, or plugged in:

- Open the windows and let in the fresh air.
- Open curtains or blinds to get some sun exposure, which does its part to freshen.
- Get rid of odors by removing the source or cleaning.
- Set an open box of baking soda in the room to absorb odors.

A mixture of ½ cup baking soda and ½ cup cornstarch with 3 drops of essential oil (optional for scent) sprinkled in athletic shoes will absorb odors and moisture.

Book III

Green Cleaning

✔ Limit candle burning to those made of beeswax, soy, or palm-oil, making sure that they contain all-cotton (no-lead) wicks. Avoid burning in a drafty area to prevent fires.

✔ Create your own natural scents with favorites such as lavender buds, citrus oils, and mint oils. (See Chapter 3 of this book for recipes for air fresheners.)

Don't assume that you won't have a reaction to natural scents made from essential oils. These oils are quite strong and may irritate the skin. Don't put these oils directly on your skin. Use in small amounts until you determine whether you or anyone else has a reaction to them.

Chapter 3

Mixing Up Your Own Green Cleaning Solutions

Grocery stores, warehouses, and home-supply stores contain aisle after aisle of commercially formulated products, promising to clean, dust, disinfect, degrease, polish, shine, scour, scrub, swab, mop, and eliminate every last bit of dirt in your home. Who would have imagined that cleaning is such a complex task that it requires dozens of different formulas for each room and surface?

Fact is, these shelves of solutions contain pretty much the same ingredients. And many of them aren't so good for you — or the planet. These ingredients are commonly derived from petroleum, a fossil fuel responsible for greenhouse gas emissions, and many of the chemicals contained in these powerful cleaners are linked to a host of illnesses. And to make matters more confusing, manufacturers aren't required to list the ingredients on their labels. Even products that claim to be "natural" or "gentle" may still contain chemicals that can cause harm.

When you make your own cleaning formulas, you know exactly what's in them. Consider this chapter your green-clean cookbook.

Beginning with the Basics: Elbow Grease and Water

The greenest ingredient is your own muscle power. Add a little water, and you have a highly effective recipe for eliminating dirt. Water is often the *best* first response — with a little scrubbing, the stain or spill is gone.

Water also happens to be the predominant ingredient in most of the recipes in this chapter. Unless otherwise directed, use warm water — in most cases, hot is not necessary to do the job.

Using water in the form of steam is another great way to zap dirt and sanitize floors without chemicals. Steam mops with reusable microfiber pads require no more than ordinary tap water to clean slate, marble, tile, and sealed wood surfaces. Hand-held steamers are perfect for cleaning kitchen counters and combating mold and mildew in bath areas. And using plain steam means no cleaner residue or buildup. (For more information about steamers and other cleaning tools, read Chapter 2 of this book.)

Remember that all chemicals, including water and common table salt, are toxic at some level of exposure. Additionally, some home-grown cleaning remedies are definitely *not* safe. Using mayonnaise or yogurt to clean furniture, for example, can lead to bacteria growth.

Here are a few precautions to take when making, using, and storing home-made mixtures:

- ✔ Keep all cleaning solutions out of reach of children — on a top shelf or in a locked cabinet.
- ✔ Don't store cleaning formulas in reused food or beverage containers.
- ✔ In recipes using perishable ingredients, such as lemon juice, make only enough for immediate use. Don't store.
- ✔ Use steamers or hot water with caution. Take care when carrying full buckets of hot water.
- ✔ Don't leave water buckets unattended, especially in homes with young children or small pets.

Gathering Your Ingredients

Pull together all the ingredients you need to mix up your green cleaning agents. Chances are, you've got a good number of them in your pantry, maybe a couple in the fridge, and one or two under the bathroom sink or in the laundry room. You probably will have to purchase very little to whip up your own formulas. And if you do, you can find most of the ingredients in your grocery store.

Neutralizing with acids or alkalines

Many of the ingredients in do-it-yourself cleaners are either acid or alkaline, and each functions as a cleaning agent in a unique way.

 No need to panic: Understanding the power of acids and alkalines doesn't require an advanced degree in chemistry. The *pH scale* is used to measure the nature of certain elements, with 7 being neutral. Certain household cleaning ingredients rate as

- ✔ **Acid,** which measure at 6 or less on the pH scale
- ✔ **Alkaline,** agents that come in at 8 or higher on the scale

The cleaners in these categories work as a function of the pH level. Here's how: Say that you spill some tomato sauce on your tablecloth. Tomatoes are acidic in nature, so the best cleaner is one that neutralizes the acid: an alkaline agent such as salt or baking soda. On the other hand, if the tablecloth has been washed in an alkaline-based detergent, it may have some soap buildup that a more acidic solution, such as a vinegar rinse can remove.

Acids include

- ✔ **Lemon juice:** This citric acid bleaches, disinfects, deodorizes, and cuts grease. Use the real thing — or bottled concentrate.
- ✔ **Hydrogen peroxide:** An oxygen bleach that doesn't have the harmful properties as chlorine bleach, this mild acid is used as an antiseptic for minor wounds and kills germs when it's used as a cleaning agent, too.
- ✔ **White distilled vinegar:** Count on this wonder cleaner for deodorizing, cutting through grease, removing stains, and freshening.

Book III

Green Cleaning

Alkaline ingredients are equally common and include

- ✔ **Baking soda:** Sodium bicarbonate not only neutralizes the acid in your stomach, it cleans up after acidic stains and messes, works as a mild abrasive, shines up aluminum, chrome, silver, and other metals, and unclogs and cleans drains. It cuts grease and dirt and deodorizes.

- ✔ **Washing soda:** Also known as sodium carbonate, this stronger iteration of sodium *bi*-carbonate (baking soda) looks similar and is sometimes available in the laundry section of the supermarket or hardware store.

- ✔ **Borax:** Another member of the *sodium* family (sodium borate), this natural mineral is a disinfectant, and sold at drugstores, supermarkets, hardware and supply stores.

- ✔ **Cornstarch:** Just as its name implies, this mild and absorbent cleaner is a starch derived from corn.

- ✔ **Cornmeal:** Set aside some the next time you're making corn muffins: This mildly abrasive substance makes easy work of grease stains.

- ✔ **Club soda:** Have a big bottle of bubbly on hand for cleaning glass or tackling wine spills on carpet.

- ✔ **Cream of tartar:** This white crystalline powder sold in the spice section of supermarkets whips up impressive meringue and makes a great paste for scrubbing up cookware.

- ✔ **Salt:** Another member of the sodium family, sodium chloride — or common table salt — is a natural scrubbing agent.

Lathering up with soaps and oils

Soap comes in many forms: bar, liquid, foam, laundry formulas, dish liquid, and hand and body bars. But all contain similar elements, including minerals, which give soap an alkaline nature, and oils that promote lather and add *emollient* (softening) properties. The time-honored recipe for bar soap has been a concoction of animal fat and lye — an extremely corrosive alkaline substance that can cause severe burns. You want to avoid contact with skin, eyes, and mouth and keep away from children and pets.

The basic liquid soaps on the ingredients list are plant-based, and the alkaline list includes products not nearly as harsh as lye. You also find essential oils in a few of the recipes. Here's what to shop for:

- ✔ **Liquid castile soap:** This vegetable-based soap, found in grocery or health-food stores, is a mild and versatile cleaning agent.

- ✔ **Essential oils:** Tea tree, peppermint, grapefruit, and other oils (found in health-food or craft stores) not only smell great, they have disinfecting properties, as well.

- **Glycerin:** This common ingredient in hand-wash and dish liquid is an oil that provides lubrication and is often used in milder cleaners.

- **Castor oil:** The colorless or sometimes yellowish oil, from the castor plant, is a fine lubricant and a worthy ingredient in wood cleaners or polishes.

- **Liquid hand soap and liquid dishwashing soap:** The same ingredients — castile soap, glycerin — are found in both of these mild cleaners.

Singling out two top workhorses

Baking soda and vinegar are the yin and yang of cleaning ingredients. One alkaline and the other acid, the two team up to create a formidable cleaning duo. They can stand on their own against some of the toughest challenges: Baking soda shines metal surfaces and fixtures, unclogs drains, removes odors, and tackles tough baked-on food buildup. Vinegar fights stains, scum, mildew, and germs and can make windows gleam. Both are gentle on most surfaces and materials — but wait until you see them join forces to clean a toilet bowl!

Keep a shaker of baking soda and a squirt bottle of vinegar-water solution at your kitchen sink and turn to them throughout the day for a variety of needs:

- Sprinkle baking soda in an empty sink, give the sink a brief scrub with water and a damp cloth or sponge, and rinse with clear water.

- Dust baking soda on your cutting board to draw out odor and stains — especially if they're acid-based. Let it sit for 15 minutes or so and then rinse.

- Set a box of baking soda in your refrigerator to absorb food odors. Replace every three months. Pour old baking soda down the sink drain.

- Soak rubber gloves in water with a sprinkle of baking soda. Then rinse and dry.

- Add a sprinkle of baking soda to freshen the cat litter box.

- Spray vinegar on counter stains (unless countertops are marble) and let soak a few minutes before wiping off.

- Keep fingerprints and toothpaste spatter off bathroom mirror with a mist of vinegar—just wipe dry with newspaper.

- Pour vinegar in the toilet tank to keep odors away.

As versatile as white distilled vinegar is, it doesn't belong in some places: cleaning marble or marmoleum floors, for example, or washing cotton, linen, rayon, and acetate. Baking soda and other alkaline detergents, on the other hand, should not be used on wool or silk.

Book III

Green Cleaning

Let the sunshine in

Sunshine a cleaning agent? You bet. The ultra-violet radiation in sunlight works to kill germs. No wonder your grandma hung out her wash on the clothesline. Not only did the laundry absorb that sweet scent of outdoors, the sunlight worked to subdue dust mites in the bed sheets and bacteria in your grandpa's socks.

If you live in a sunny area — and a neighbor-hood that doesn't have an ordinance against clotheslines — take advantage of free solar power and let your laundry line-dry. Set freshly washed toys, car accessories, doormats, and outdoor furniture to dry in the sun on an old blanket, quilt, or shower curtain.

Windows filter out much of the ultraviolet rays, but you can still get some assistance from the sun by opening your curtains and letting the sun shine in.

Cleaning Up with Basic Formulas

You've likely bought a spectrum of all-purpose cleaning products that claim to clean everything from tub and tile work to Formica counters and appliance surfaces. You can make general-use formulas with similar powers with a minimum of effort and mess. Several of the recipes in this section include one or the other of the two "workhorse" ingredients covered in the previous section: baking soda and white distilled vinegar. But I introduce a few of the other agents in your new green-cleaning arsenal here.

In the cleaners to come, those with vinegar and water can last a long time, but those with lemon or essential oils have a shorter shelf life. If your recipes contain these last two ingredients, make only a batch and use it up in a day or two.

Try sampling one new recipe at a time, testing it, and seeing how you like it. Mixing up cleaning formulas is a lot like experimenting in the kitchen: Sometimes it takes some tweaks and finessing to get a recipe just where you like it.

Check garden-supply centers, hardware stores, and grocery stores for plastic spray bottles you can use for your recipes. Quart-size bottles are most convenient for big jobs like windows, counters, and showers. Label them so that you know what's in the bottle.

Do-it-all cleaners

These all-purpose cleaners should do everything you need. More abrasive cleaners are available commercially, some are quite gritty. Generally, the larger and harder the particles, the more abrasive.

Here are three easy options:

- ✔ **Mix 4 tablespoons baking soda in 1 quart water:** This baking soda-based formula gently scours away dirt, food spills, stains, and buildup on most surfaces. Its deodorizing properties make it an ideal solution for cleaning refrigerators, microwaves, diaper pails, tiles, coffee pots — even baby and children's toys.

- ✔ **Mix ¼ to ½ cup white vinegar and 1 quart of water in a spray bottle.** Vinegar is a great degreaser and works especially well to remove soap scum in tubs and showers. Spray this mixture on the surface, wait 30 seconds, and wipe away. Rinse off with hot water if you're cleaning soap scum in tubs, showers, or sinks.

- ✔ **In a quart spray bottle, mix 2 tablespoons peppermint liquid castile soap, ¼ cup baking soda, and ¼ cup white vinegar.** Add water to fill the bottle. This cleaner has a minty scent and works on sinks, showers, tile floors — and as a great insect-deterrent when sprayed on outdoor plants and flowers.

A leading brand name in scented castile soap, Dr. Bronner's comes in several size containers, often available at health-food stores. Some sell it in bulk — bring your refillable jug with you.

Tile and vinyl floor cleaner

Both vinyl and tile are tough floorings that clean up beautifully with this simple formula. In a bucket, mix ⅛ cup liquid castile soap, ⅛ cup white vinegar, and 1 gallon water and then damp mop.

If you don't have castile soap, add another ⅛ cup vinegar.

Linoleum floor cleaner

Made from natural products, including linseed oil and cork flour, linoleum is making a comeback because of its green qualities. Care can be more of a challenge, however, as excess water and harsh chemicals can cause damage. For the necessary wipe-down or spot cleaning, this recipe is a safe remedy. Just spray it on a soft mop until it's just damp, and run it over your floors.

In a quart spray bottle, mix ¼ cup white vinegar and 1½ to 2 cups water.

Book III

Green Cleaning

Window, glass, and mirror cleaner

Newspapers do a great job of shining up glass — and they're a great green solution: Reuse before recycling! But if you object to getting the newsprint all over your hands, paper towel is another option. Just be sure to buy a brand that's soft on nature. Do outside windows on an overcast day, as strong sun dries the glass before you can buff the windows clean.

Don't use cotton cloth because it leaves lint behind. A microfiber cloth made for glass and windows works fine.

A squirt bottle of this mixture and a stack of newspapers can wipe away a season's worth of grime and fool resident birds into thinking that the windows are open. In a spray bottle, combine ½ cup to 1 cup white vinegar and 1 quart cool water.

Polishing Wood Furniture, Floors, and Collectibles

Water isn't a friend to wood, so the best way to clean it is to dry-dust. Use a lint-free rag or microfiber cloth — which traps dust, lint, and pet dander — for furniture and collectibles. Dry-mop or vacuum floors to pick up dust and food particles. Steer clear of feather dusters: They simply stir up dust rather than eliminate it, and their quills can scratch wood surfaces.

When furnishings and floors have collected a little more grime than floating dust or lint, you're probably inclined to ratchet up your efforts. In that case, here are some solutions that involve the sparing use of water.

Dust buster for collectibles

White distilled vinegar is a terrific solution for collectibles and fragile items. In a bowl or spray bottle, mix 2 cups water, 1 cup white vinegar, and two drops of lemon oil (optional for scent).

Be cautious when damp-dusting delicate items, antiques, and furnishings with old paint, gilding, or gold leaf. Avoid leaving any water on these pieces and take care not to rub too vigorously. Leave valuable items to the care of professionals in antique care.

Hardwood floor cleaner

Vacuum or dry-mop floors first to remove crumbs, chunks of dirt, and dust. Then follow with this cleaner on a damp rag or mop. In a bucket, mix 3 cups white vinegar, 1 tablespoon castile soap, 3 drops grapefruit essential oil, and 3 cups water.

Wood furniture polish

Traditional furniture polishes contain beeswax and linseed or lemon oil. You can actually take a chunk of beeswax and rub it into your wood furnishings, buffing in with a soft cloth. An easy homemade favorite is to mix 1 pint linseed or olive oil (or a smaller amount if you prefer) with 4 or 5 drops of lemon essential oil (optional for scent) in an open container. Then dab the mixture with cloth and rub the oil into furniture, using sparingly.

Linseed oil seems to be absorbed more easily than olive oil, which requires a bit more elbow grease to buff in. Both oils are expensive to use in large quantities. This recipe is definitely not a good use for expensive extra-virgin olive oil!

Rolling Out the Carpet Cleaner

A good vacuum is a must for maintaining your carpeting, but effective cleaners for spots and shampooing are also important.

Don't wait for spills to settle in: Take action immediately by picking up the debris and follow with a dab of water blotted into the spot gently. Plain water is always the first course of action — cold water is the best solution for bloodstains and most food stains.

Choose a white absorbent cloth or white paper towel to dab out the spot: Printed or dyed materials can leave a stain of its own, especially on white or light-colored carpet. Don't use too much water; you don't want the carpet to be damp for long or water to seep down into the pad.

This solution works well for a number of stains, including chocolate and blood (if cold water alone doesn't work). Simply combine ¼ teaspoon of clear, plant-based dishwashing liquid with 1 cup warm water.

Never use laundry detergent on your carpet. It may contain bleach and be too harsh.

Book III

Green
Cleaning

For a strong-staining substance, such as pet urine, mix 1 cup white vinegar and 1 cup warm water. Dab mixture on spill and blot to dry.

For wall-to-wall carpet with multiple stains, the best solution is to call in carpet-cleaning professionals. (Chapter 6 of this book covers carpet cleaning in more detail.)

Keeping Food Surfaces Clean

Because of spoilage and contamination issues surrounding food, surfaces and appliances in the kitchen pose unique challenges to the green housekeeper. In commercial kitchens — restaurants, institutional cafeterias, and hotels — state health laws require strict standards of upkeep, which include using hot water and strong disinfectants to clean, eliminating the risk of food-borne illnesses. Chlorine bleach is the disinfectant often dictated, but a milder choice is hydrogen peroxide. Solutions made up of hydrogen peroxide and water or borax and water or vinegar and water have disinfecting properties.

Green commercial cleaners can effectively disinfect surfaces as well. These cleaners are suitable for the home environment, and many smell good, too. Look for the following characteristics:

- Nontoxic, phosphate-free and biodegradable ingredients used when possible
- Detergents are plant-based, not petroleum based
- Never tested on animals, sometimes listed as cruelty-free
- Doesn't create harmful fumes or leave harmful residues behind

This book is about home cleaning rather than commercial cleaning, but the same health risks exist in the home as in the restaurant. Many experts insist that ecofriendly disinfectants, such as vinegar and lemon juice, don't stand up to bleach. So if you're determined to keep bleach out of your home, you need to be even more diligent about food contamination in your kitchen, which has as much to do with techniques of food handling as it does with cleaning products.

Oven and stovetop cleaners

Check the oven manufacturer's instructions before cleaning the oven. If you lost them, go online for the answer or call the place you bought the oven. Many manufacturers are adding green suggestions to their instruction booklets.

Here are a few tips to get you started:

✔ Cornstarch is great for absorbing grease and oily spills. Lightly sprinkle cornstarch on your stovetop and allow it to soak up the grease. Wipe away with damp sponge.

✔ After a messy spillover — whether blueberry pie or lasagna — wait until the oven is cool before attempting to clean. Then sprinkle baking soda on spilled food or spray inside of oven with water until damp. Allow to sit for several minutes or even overnight. Remove with cleaning cloth or paper towel.

  If you're out of baking soda or want a little more "scrub" action, salt is a good choice. Simply sprinkle table salt on the spill while the oven is still warm. Wait for the salt and stain to cool and then scrape food away. Wipe with damp cloth.

✔ To clean your microwave oven, mix ¼ cup baking soda and ½ cup water and apply with damp sponge. Let the paste set for several minutes and then wipe away with clean sponge.

Cleaners for cookware

As soon as your cookware has cooled after using, put it in the sink to soak in water, adding a squirt of dishwashing liquid or a sprinkle of baking soda. This method lifts off the burned-on food and makes cleanup easier. After soaking your cookware, scrub it with a sponge and finish with hot soapy water or the dishwasher, if appropriate. You find more dishwashing tips in Chapter 4.

Book III

Green Cleaning

The following combinations are for pots and pans that may have years of buildup and won't come clean with a general washing:

✔ **Stainless Steel Rejuvenator:** Pour water in a pot until halfway to almost full. Add ½ cup of white vinegar and bring to boil. Immediately reduce heat and simmer 30 minutes to 1 hour. Empty and wash as usual.

✔ **Aluminum Illuminator:** You can shine up your aluminum cookware and rub new life into pots and pans. Add water until the pot is halfway to three-fourths full. Add 2 tablespoons cream of tartar or ½ cup of white vinegar to water. Bring to boil. Then reduce heat and simmer 10 to 15 minutes. Empty and wash as usual.

✔ **Burned-On Grease Cleaner:** Baking soda works well at removing built-up grease from any kind of cookware. After the pan cools, scrape out surface grease. Fill pan with water and sprinkle in baking soda. Place pan on stovetop and bring to boil. When grease floats to the top of the water, remove from heat. Let cool. Wash as usual.

Don't make the mistake of putting dishwashing liquid into the dishwasher. You'll end up with tons of suds spilling out all over the floor.

Cleaning metals and silverware

You can wipe the stickiness right off refrigerator door handles, faucets, fixtures, cabinet pulls, and more by mixing ¼ cup white vinegar and ½ cup water. Using a clean cloth, wipe the surfaces with the mixture.

For sinks and silverware, consult the manufacturer's recommendations. Stainless steel flatware can go right in the dishwasher.

If you use your silverware on a daily basis, good for you! Simply wash in the sink with mild soap and hot water, dry, and put away. If you pull out the good stuff only rarely, storing it properly can help cut down on tarnish. Nevertheless, you may need to polish once or twice a year. Apply a low-abrasion white toothpaste (not gel) to a soft toothbrush and gently brush the silverware. Rinse with warm water and dry thoroughly with a towel or silver polishing cloth.

If you prefer to keep your toothpaste in the medicine cabinet, here's another traditional favorite that works equally well. Combine 1 cup water with 2 tablespoon baking soda in a measuring cup. Apply mixture to silver with a soft cloth, rubbing until dry.

This last concoction is great for cleaning stainless steel sinks. It's more to the watery side than a pasty texture. In a bowl or bucket, mix 3 tablespoons baking soda, 1 drop of essential oil (for scent, optional), and 1½ cups water.

Tackling Water-Challenged Areas

No area of the house gets wetter than the bathroom. And along with all that water come the accompanying problems of mold, mildew, mineral buildup, lime and scale, soap scum, and clogs. The traditional solutions to these challenges have relied on some pretty strong chemicals: Caustic lye and chlorine bleach are two of the most familiar agents to plumbing, fixtures, porcelain and tile.

The fact is, these tough chemicals do attack the problems ferociously — you can *see* the scum just fizz away! But if you're committed to retiring these toxic elements, you have other ways to combat those troublesome water-loving blights. Plenty of cleaners that claim to be green are on the market, but sometimes it's hard to read between the lines to determine whether they're really free of the petrochemicals and elements toxic to the residents of your home and damaging to the earth.

Use the mild and medium all-purpose cleaners already covered in "Cleaning Up with Basic Formulas" for countertops, tub, and tile floors. Baking soda with a small amount of water makes a mild abrasive paste that you can apply with a sponge or soft cloth to sinks and faucets.

Battling mold, mildew, and other buildup

Chlorine bleach has been the conventional cleaner of choice for mold and mildew. Eliminating mold and mildew is crucial because they can lead to serious health issues.

A preemptive effort is to keep the bathroom and other areas of the house as dry as possible. Make sure that the air in your home is circulating effectively. Use the bathroom fan during and after showering. You may even consider using a dehumidifier to remove excess dampness.

To keep mold and mildew at bay, mix ¼ cup hydrogen peroxide and 1 cup water in a spray bottle. Spray on problem areas. Do not rinse off.

Removing soap scum, water stains, and lime and mineral deposits

The mild all-purpose cleaners mentioned earlier in this chapter in the "Cleaning Up with Basic Formulas" section are great for eliminating soap scum and water stains. For a bit more punch, increase the vinegar for a 1-to-1 ratio. It works on tile, porcelain, and metal fixtures and drain covers.

For lime and mineral deposits, use vinegar straight-up, wiping on with a rag. For extra-stubborn spots, leave the rag on for several minutes or one hour. Then wipe dry.

Book III

Green Cleaning

Flushing away dirt and germs

The toilet area is another hot spot for bacteria. In addition to store-bought green cleaners, vinegar and baking soda are two tough agents. Use any of the all-purpose cleaners appearing in the "Cleaning Up with Basic Formulas" section in this chapter. You may want to use paper towels to clean the outside the toilet — or be sure the sponges and cloths you use for the toilet aren't used for anything else. One technique is to put the disinfectant in the toilet and let it stand while you clean the rest of the bathroom. Then swish with the toilet brush and flush.

This mix gives you a fun mini-explosion when the alkaline baking soda and acidic vinegar meet up in the toilet:

1. **Sprinkle sides with baking soda and allow to stand for a few minutes.**

2. **Pour in ¼ to ½ cup vinegar and let stand for 15 minutes.**

3. **Scrub with toilet brush and flush.**

Cleaning and Unclogging Drains

One of the easiest ways to keep your drain clean is to pour ½ to 1 cup baking soda down the drain. Follow with dripping warm water. Perform once every week or two. Be sure to let it stand a few minutes before rinsing — if you flush it out too quickly, the baking soda won't have much effect.

To combat rusty drains and dirty garbage disposals, rub the cut side of a halved lemon half on rust around drain and on faucets. Rinse with water. Then put the used lemons in the disposal and grind for freshening — or throw in your compost bucket.

If a clogged showerhead is an issue, remove the showerhead and clear holes with an old toothbrush or unbent paperclip. Rinse with clear water. Then place the showerhead in a bowl or bucket and cover it with vinegar. Soak overnight to remove deposits. Rinse with clear water, dry, and put back in place.

Drain cleaner

For trouble-free maintenance, mix up a batch of this cleaner and use once a week: 1 cup salt, 1 cup baking soda, and ¼ cup cream of tartar.

Pour ¼ cup of this mixture into the drain. Rinse with water. Repeat as necessary or save the rest of the batch for the future.

Drain declogger

If this process doesn't work, try a plunger or call the plumber.

1. **Pour ½ to 1 cup of baking soda down the drain.**

2. **Follow with ½ to 1 cup of vinegar, pouring slowly.**

3. **When you hear a fizzing sound, cover the drain and let stand for 5 minutes.**

4. **Pour boiling water into drain.**

A Laundry List of Solutions

In addition to taking steps to reduce your energy and water consumption, your choice of detergents, soaps, softeners, and spot removers can help you improve your personal environmental report card in the laundry room.

See spot run

Removing stains is a bit tricky, because some fibers are weakened by certain chemicals. Strong alkaline substances, such as washing soda, for example, can ruin delicate wool and silk, but small amounts of washing soda can be good for removing oil and grease stains on sturdier fabrics. Always check the label on your garments to determine their fiber content and washing instructions.

Water is your first solution for most fabrics. So as soon as you drop food or drink or whatever, try to wipe it off with clean water. Here are a few solutions when you need a little more power.

White clothing stain remover

This prewash treatment isn't appropriate for silk, but it's great for handling stains on most other whites.

Mix 1 tablespoon borax and 6 tablespoons water to create a paste. Dab the mixture on stains. Follow with normal washing.

Presoak and fabric softener

A favorite and easy fabric softener is to add ¼ to ½ cup white vinegar to the rinse cycle in an automatic washing machine. If your washer requires you to add the fabric softener at the start of the rinse cycle to and you don't want to be a wash-watcher, try this presoak, which also removes stains.

1. **Mix 2 tablespoons cream of tartar and 1 gallon hot water in a bucket and then let cool.**

2. **Let the fabrics sit in the mixture for a half-hour or until the stain is released.**

3. **Rinse with fresh water.**

4. **Launder as normal.**

Freshening clothes

If a garment doesn't require a washing but needs an airing-out, hanging it out in the sun is a much gentler remedy than spraying it with a clothing freshener — which is, in essence, a perfume masking the musty odor of the clothing.

If fading is concerned, turn the garment inside-out. This tactic also serves to expose the underarm area, which is likely where most of the freshening is needed.

Laundering

As you prepare to launder, always remember to read garment and linen labels and follow the manufacturer's instructions when using a washing machine.

- ✔ Use the proper load setting for the size of each load.
- ✔ Match the temperature setting to type of cleaning desired is also important.
- ✔ When using detergent, measure properly. If you use too much, the load won't rinse properly.

Here are some beginning recipes for cleaning everyday home laundry. Remember that many green product makers offer ecofriendly laundry detergents.

Dry laundry detergent

Mix the following ingredients and store them in an airtight container:

> 1 cup soap flakes or shreds of homemade soap, or any store-bought type without lotion
>
> ½ cup washing soda
>
> ½ cup borax
>
> A few drops of essential oil (optional for scent)

Use ¼ cup to 1 cup detergent, depending on the size of the load and the machine type.

Liquid laundry detergent

Use ¼ to ¾ cup of this detergent per load. You might need to remix it before you use it. It tends to congeal.

> 1 cup soap flakes (homemade soap, or any store-bought type without lotion)
>
> ½ cup washing soda
>
> ½ cup borax
>
> 2 tablespoons glycerin
>
> 2 cups water

Mix soap, washing soda, and borax. Add glycerin and water, stirring until thoroughly combined.

Cleaning Up the Odds and Ends

Beyond the typical household cleaning tasks that involve floors, furniture, fixtures, and more are some unique surfaces or materials that need to be cleaned, too. Here are some ways to address those items:

- ✔ For a gentle paint remover for your hands, use vegetable oil instead of paint thinner.

- ✔ You can use this gentle cleaner for your garage floor or patio or kitchen floor. Mix ¼ cup mild dishwashing liquid with 2 gallons warm water and apply. Rinse with clean water and air dry.

- ✔ When cleaning your vehicle's exterior, do not use anything abrasive on the finish — that means no grit, such as baking soda, or anything acidic like vinegar. Try mixing several squirts or ¼ cup of mild liquid dishwashing detergent with 1 gallon of water in a bucket. Get some suds going, throw in the sponge, and clean away! Rinse with clean water, use a squeegee, and buff the car dry with a clean cloth.

The best way to get your house to smell good is to rid it of sources of bad odor. But when that's not possible, here's a spray with disinfecting ingredients that also seems to suppress unpleasant odors. In a spray bottle, mix 1 teaspoon baking soda, 1 teaspoon vinegar or lemon juice, and 2 cups water.

Try this realtor trick to freshen up your house. Add 3 or 4 cinnamon sticks to 4 cups boiling water. Simmer for an hour or so. (Don't let all the water evaporate out of the pan.)

Book III

Green Cleaning

Chapter 4

Making Green Work of Laundry

*T*hrough the miracles of modern machinery, clothes from not-so-fresh to downright dirty are delivered clean, bright, good-smelling, and ready to be worn and used again. This transformation doesn't occur with the press of a button. A lot of resources go into turning dirty laundry into once-again presentable apparel.

Because laundry-room activity consumes so much energy and water, the green changes you make to your clothes-cleaning practices are sure to have a positive impact on lightening your household's carbon footprint.

Giving Your Appliances a Break

When you replace your old-dinosaur washer and dryer with the most efficient models on the market and maintain them well, you can see your energy use drop. But the most effective way to cut down on their energy consumption? Use your washer and dryer less often.

Hand-washing small loads

Unless you live in a commune or are part of a very large family, you're likely to have some small loads to wash. Socks and undies just don't take up much space in the machine, for example, making the electricity a load of laundry consumes hard to justify. The greener choice is to hand-wash any small loads you encounter in your laundry adventures.

For items that require temperatures a little more *torrid* than tepid (cleaning rags, for example), fill a bucket or the laundry sink with steam-emitting hot water and soap, scrub the clothing by hand, and let the items soak. This practice keeps your hot-water use under control, but gives you the peace of mind that the grimiest, germiest articles get a high-powered cleaning.

Hand-washing is a practical option for lingerie and other garments too delicate for the agitator or even the gentler frontload tumbler. And for any less-than-full-load-sized piles of dirty laundry, a scrub in the laundry tub can be an easy cleaning option that saves the wear and tear on your washer and cuts down on water and electricity.

If you like scent, add a couple of drops of essential oils to hand washables. Lavender is a favorite, said to induce a state of relaxation. Citrus or peppermint offers a fresh, wake-up aroma.

Wash and wear (and wear and wear)

Adherents to the wear-it-once school of fashion assume that a single wearing can dirty or soil an item so badly that it must be washed again. Sometimes that's true, but as long as you're not sweating profusely or rolling around in the mud regularly, many outer garments — sweaters, jackets, even casual pants — can be worn two, three, or more times before they need cleaning.

If you're concerned that your preworn clothing smells "stale" or looks worn, try these tips to freshen up your apparel without dedicating yet another wash cycle to getting it clean:

- ✔ **Air it out.** Hang your clothing on a hanger in a room with good circulation. Better yet, weather permitting, let it hang outside in the sun for a bit. Turn items inside-out to avoid fading and to expose the underside to the disinfecting powers of the sun.

- ✔ **Give it a rest.** When you let your garments breathe between wearings, you can often wear them more times without feeling like a walking laundry hamper. If you allow the jeans you wore on day one to air out on day two, they seem "cleaner" when you wear them again on day three.

- ✔ **Brush it off.** If you see lint, cat hair, grit, or other stuff collecting on the material, take a clothes or a lint brush to the item.

- ✔ **Spot-clean stains.** The sooner you catch stains, the better. Sometimes all it takes is a dab of cold water to get out a bit of dirt. (See the "Removing stains" section, later in this chapter, for more information.)

- ✔ **Hang it back up.** Remind the kids to hang up their bath towels so that they can use them again.

Line-drying, inside and out

Not only does sun-drying cut down on your energy use, the disinfectant properties of sunshine help kill bacteria as clothing and bedding dry, aided by gentle breezes.

Line-drying your clothes outside can be as simple as stretching clothesline (found in most grocery and hardware stores) from one tree to another or as complicated as a kit that includes zinc pulleys, hooks, a clothesline wire, a line tightener, and a line divider. With this technology, you can stand in one place and pull the line to you for hanging up or removing clothes.

You can also install a fold-up pole dryer in your backyard. This contraption usually has an aluminum center pole with folding steel-coated arms that accommodate two to three loads of wash. The arms rotate, and you can place unmentionables so that they're not visible to the street or the neighbors. Also, when the arms are down, the pole itself is fairly unobtrusive in the landscape.

If you or someone else in your household suffers from allergies, hanging bed sheets and towels on the line during pollen season isn't a good idea.

Conditions aren't always amenable to outdoor drying, and some clothes don't do as well when hung out to dry. Follow these suggestions to make the most of your indoor and outdoor space:

Book III

Green Cleaning

- ✔ For towels, bathrobes, and other heavy materials that take a long time to dry — or dry stiff and rough — hang on the line until partially dry and then finish up with a brief spin in the dryer.

- ✔ Knits and sweaters tend to stretch when hung on a line. Better to lay them flat to retain their shape. You can set up a mesh dryer rack so that air circulates around the fabric.

- ✔ When weather permits, hang up damp dishtowels, washcloths, hand towels, and bath towels and let them dry in the sun. Then replace them on your towel bars to be reused.

- ✔ If you live in a wet, humid, or perpetually gray place, you can dry wet clothes in well-circulated rooms. Install a retractable clothesline in your laundry room or get a drying rack.

- ✔ At your house, use the bathtub to stretch out sweaters and items that need to be dried flat. To control inside humidity, you may want to put a fan in your drying area.

Making Sense of Laundry Products

Wander the housekeeping aisle of any grocery store and prepare to be overwhelmed by options for cleaning your clothes, but doing the laundry doesn't have to be complicated. Basically, you clean your clothes with the same stuff you use to clean everything else: soap or detergent. There is a difference between the two; in a nutshell, soap is most often derived from plants, oils, ash, and other natural ingredients, and detergents are commonly made of synthetic surfactants, based on — you guessed it — petroleum-based compounds.

Both are effective cleaners, but when it comes to washing clothes, the popular choice has been detergent. Soaps, many complain, leave a film on fabric that turns the material dull and gray, but they're the greener choice.

Zeroing in on green alternatives

Ecofriendly laundry detergents substitute plant-based oils for the nonrenewable, petroleum-based components. They typically are free of heavy perfumes, although many are scented with essential oils, such as lavender and orange. And they also omit dyes and optical brighteners — for those who prefer their clothes to be *truly* clean rather than coated with something that makes the material *look* whiter. (You want clothes to be clean, not glow in the dark like George Hamilton's smile.)

Many consumers say that plant-based cleaners often don't seem to do as good a job getting clothes really, really clean. Adding a *laundry booster,* which improves the power of other laundry cleaners and are good for presoaking, can give your cleaner the edge: Two are washing soda and borax. (See Chapter 3 for more about these mainstay ingredients of the green cleaning cupboard.) Add ½ cup along with your laundry detergent at the beginning of the wash cycle. Or use as a presoak — 2 tablespoons in a gallon of water ought to loosen up the toughest stains in 30 minutes.

The newest high-efficiency (HE) washers require low-sudsing detergents, and the green aisle offers a selection of them. HE machines also take much less soap than the traditional top-loading agitator models. So go easy on the amount. Follow instructions to avoid suds overflow.

Getting soft on laundry

Fabric softeners reduce friction and static electricity. They give material a soft, fluffy feel and often provide a sweet or fresh smell.

These formulas don't, however, aid the cleaning process in any way. The conventional brands typically contain petrochemicals and ingredients, such as artificial fragrance, that have been linked to air, water, and health concerns. Moreover, liquid softeners and dryer sheets can cause skin rashes and asthmatic reactions.

And don't think you're safe with dryer balls, either. Although advertised as environmentally friendly, the spiky, rubbery devices you throw in the dryer to "naturally" soften your clothes are made of polyvinyl chloride (yes, PVC), which may result in the release of carcinogenic substances.

Even the green softeners may be considered a waste of resources, what with the manufacturing, packaging, and shipping required. But if you love the effect of fabric softener, it's your decision; just choose wisely and use sparingly.

For a similar anti-static, softening result, try one of these ingredients in the rinse cycle:

- ½ cup of baking soda
- ¼ cup of borax
- ¼ cup white distilled vinegar

Material Matters

Your clothing plays a part in your home's energy-consumption habits. Factors such as material, color, and quality all determine how often an item should be washed — and how. Understanding fabric and its care is an important step in making choices that reduce your laundry energy load. Checking out the care label of a garment before you buy can help you select responsibly for minimizing the energy demands for cleaning and maintaining your clothing.

Preparing clothes for the wash

Pre-sorting the laundry is a great tactic for cleaning most efficiently. By dividing your clothing into like loads, you're more likely to wash in a way that requires less energy and less water and maintain your garments so that they last longer.

Of course, if you've switched over to cold-water wash, you've already reduced the risk of making colors run, fabrics shrink and wrinkle, and material wear faster.

Still, follow these tips to ensure the best results when you do your laundry:

- Sort laundry by color, separating whites and light colors from garments with intense color.

- Separate items that are stained or heavily soiled or require special pre-treatment.

- Pull out clothing that must be hand-washed.

- Place delicates in a mesh bag to avoid hand-washing. In the bag, they're less likely to snag during the cycle.

- Check the label for each article: Even in a load of reds, you may want to treat an item likely to bleed separately.

  Imported fabrics and madras can bleed for many, many loads, so don't assume that if it's been washed before, it won't bleed again.

- If you're washing a load in warm or hot water, double-check the labels to be sure that nothing in that batch can shrink or bleed.

- Turn dark-colored clothing, such as jeans and cotton T-shirts, inside out before washing to reduce fading.

- Check pockets before throwing garments in the wash. Those used tissues wreak enough havoc, but heaven forbid that a lipstick or a permanent marker gets by, permanently marking your favorite white shirt.

- Fasten Velcro openings, clasp hook-and-eye fasteners, and zip zippers to prevent snagging and snarling with other garments.

Removing stains

Blood, grass, grease, lipstick. When you discover these stains on your garments, you know a regular wash won't do the trick. You've got to take decisive steps and laser-focus on the stain if you're going to get it out.

Conventional spot removers are good at getting out some of these more challenging stains, but many contain nasty solvent ingredients — the kind that do unfriendly things to your air passages and put groundwater at risk.

You can find earth-friendly spot removers on the shelves of big box stores and even conventional supermarkets. Or you can make your own by pulling these stain-zapping ingredients right off your shelf or out of your refrigerator:

- Baking soda
- Borax
- Club soda
- Lemon juice

- ✔ Liquid dishwashing soap
- ✔ Liquid laundry detergent
- ✔ Salt
- ✔ White distilled vinegar

Best course of action when discovering a stain is to take care of it immediately. Water is always your first and best defense. When in doubt, always use cold water rather than warm water. Many stains, such as blood and tomato, are protein-based, and hot water can set the stain. If a bit of plain cold water doesn't do the trick, try the solutions in Table 4-1.

Table 4-1	Solutions for Specific Stains
Stain	**Solution**
Berries	Soak the spot with cold water and then let it soak in lemon juice for 20 minutes. Rinse with cold water and launder as usual.
Blood	Wash stain with cold water. If that doesn't do it, use a little baking soda, liquid soap, salt, or other alkaline-based agent.
Chocolate	Soak fabric in cold water. If that doesn't work, dab with liquid laundry detergent.
Coffee	Rinse with warm water and then soak in a mixture of half borax and half water. When the stain is gone, rinse with warm water and air dry.
Fruit juice	For a substantial stain, pour boiling water on sturdy fabrics, warm water on delicates. For a light drop or two of juice, a quick once-over with cold water should do the trick. Grape juice may take more effort than lemonade.
Grass	Bring on the liquid dish soap and warm water and then rinse with clear water. For more stubborn stains, try white distilled vinegar or cream of tartar.
Ink	A little dishwashing liquid and water may remove a small stain. For more stubborn spots, try white distilled vinegar. A little white wine or vodka may lift the spot out, too.
Tomato-based foods, such as pasta sauce or ketchup	Rinse immediately with cold water and then rub on liquid dishwashing or laundry detergent. Let it set for a few minutes and rinse again with cold water. If the stain remains, try laundering with a cup of white distilled vinegar in the wash, followed by a cool-water rinse.

(continued)

Book III

Green Cleaning

Table 4-1 *(continued)*

Stain	Solution
Lipstick	Put stained garment or linen on an old white towel and soak with a solution of water and dishwashing detergent. Blot to remove the stain. The lipstick should seep under onto the towel. Follow by laundering. Baking soda and water may work as well.
Perspiration	Make a solution of 4 tablespoons of salt in 1 quart of hot water. Sponge the area with this mixture, rinse well, and launder as usual.
Red wine	Gently dab the spot with club soda until the stain is removed. Follow by laundering.
Sunscreen	Remove any remaining lotion, then sprinkle with baking soda, and allow to sit for an hour or two. Shake off the residue and sponge with a small amount of dishwashing liquid and warm water. Launder as usual.
Urine	Soak in ¼ cup white vinegar in a quart of water, remove, and launder as usual. Works for human and pet urine.
Yellowing	Prescrub with a mild liquid detergent. Then wash as usual in the washing machine.

Some solutions can weaken certain material fibers: Cotton, for example, doesn't take too well to acidic bases, such as vinegar or lemon juice. Always read the care instructions on the inside of a garment before treating with any stain remover. Once stains have become set in the dryer, it may be nearly impossible to remove them. Fresh stains are easier to remove than stains that have dried.

Chapter 5

Bringing Kitchens and Baths to a Green-Clean Sheen

*Y*our green-living philosophy can smoothly align with the tenets of germ-free kitchens and baths. These rooms pose some of the greatest challenges to clean, let alone clean green. The kitchen is the heart of the house — and the stomach. Food preparation and disposal bring to light issues all their own. And bathrooms raise quite a few issues of their own, most of them less than appetizing — from the soap scum that clings to tile walls and shower curtain to the shaving cream and toothpaste detritus that coat the sink.

In this chapter, you find tips for keeping your family healthy and your kitchen and baths clean.

Handling Food Properly

Storing, preparing, and serving food involves more than merely keeping a tidy kitchen: Ensuring that perishable items are stored properly, food surfaces are kept scrupulously clean, and methods of meal preparation eliminate possible cross-contamination is absolutely critical for your safety.

Raw meat and contaminated produce can leave behind dangerous bacteria such as *E. coli* and *salmonella* in preparation areas, on knives, and on towels reused for wiping up after spills. Children and the elderly are especially at risk of food-borne illness. Meat, poultry, and eggs have long been considered the biggest threat, but contamination can come from many sources — even packaged spinach. Clean food-handling practices can't prevent all food-borne illnesses, but they sure cut way down on these risks.

Adherence takes strict attention and can sometimes seem a challenge to your environmental principles. After all, many of these steps involve liberal amounts of *hot* water, or you may be advised to use disposable wipes or towels to avoid contamination. The safe choice may be to throw out quantities of food if its freshness is in question. And your concern about disease and disinfecting may pressure you to use chemicals that are decidedly unhealthy for the planet.

Depending upon how you maintain and care for them, your cleaning implements can serve as your staunch allies for clean — or traitorous enemies. Sponges, dish cloths, mops, and scrubbers tend to be damp mediums that serve as breeding ground for all kinds of gruesome germ life. For more on keeping these items free of bacteria, see Chapter 2.

Fighting food contamination without chemicals

For the most part, you can keep a clean and safe kitchen and still adhere to your environmental principles. Here are general guidelines for protecting your food from contamination.

- Keep your refrigerator at the proper settings (36 to 39°F) to ensure that food is cool enough not to spoil.

- Adhere to the expiration dates on all perishables, especially meat.

- Keep refrigerated food well wrapped.

- Keep meat products separate from fruits and vegetables.

- Place meat on the lowest shelf to reduce risk of juices dripping on other food items.

- Wash any produce that is to be eaten raw — even if you plan to peel it.

- Don't prepare vegetables, fruits, or other foods on the same surface or with the same knife used for poultry, beef, pork, or fish, until it has been scrubbed clean with soap and *hot* water.

- Use separate cutting boards: one for meat, another for fruits and vegetables, and perhaps even another for bread or other food items. (For more on keeping your cutting boards sanitized, see the next section.)

> ✔ Don't reuse the same cloth towel to wipe up spills from food, especially animal products, including eggs. In some cases, you may feel justified in using paper towel to avoid contamination.
>
> ✔ Don't reuse plastic bags or packaging that has held poultry or other animal products. Wash thoroughly and let dry before recycling.

Keeping cutting boards germ-free

In addition to using separate cutting boards for meats and produce, you also need to wash them with dishwashing liquid and hot water every time you use them and dry them thoroughly before you put them away. (This method is the best way to clean wood cutting boards, which don't hold up in the dishwasher and don't take to harsh cleaners — even vinegar can be too acidic.)

Dishwashers have hotter water than your hands can stand, so you can trust that your plastic cutting boards are thoroughly sanitized after a wash. If you plan to clean them in this way, be sure that the cutting boards are dishwasher safe: Most acrylic or plastic boards are.

Bamboo is another cutting board alternative. This rapidly renewable, earth-friendly material is extremely hard and durable and has some antibacterial properties. Bamboo boards are typically formaldehyde- and toxic-finish–free, but check to make sure. (Now if they could only grow bamboo closer to home to skip all that embodied energy from shipping from Asia!) Clean bamboo cutting boards as you do wooden boards: dish soap and hot water.

Book III

Green Cleaning

Doing the Dishes

Is it more environmentally friendly to do your dishes by hand or in the dishwasher? Opinions vary. Most sources weigh in on the side of the automatic dishwasher.

The pros and cons of automatic dishwashers

An automatic dishwasher's efficiency depends on several factors:

> ✔ Newer, Energy Star dishwashers use less energy, less water, and less *hot* water than other models — especially those manufactured before 1994. If you're ready to replace your old model, visit www.energystar.gov for research about the benefits and efficient operation of dishwashers.

- Running your dishwasher with a full load cuts down on the number of loads you do, reducing energy and water usage. If you're single or have a small family, you may need to run it only every other day, or less.

- Taking advantage of the dishwasher's most energy-efficient settings improves energy efficiency, too. Choose the air-dry feature and avoid the heat-dry, rinse-hold, or pre-rinse options.

Do review the manufacturer's instructions for use. (If missing, go to the manufacturer's Web site.) Some models require you to dispense detergent for each load, while others have a place to insert a bottle of detergent, which dispenses just the right amount based on water hardness, cycle selection, and soil level of the dishes.

From a green perspective, dishwashers may have some drawbacks:

- If you find yourself pre-rinsing or scraping your dishes manually before placing them in the dishwasher, you're doing double-duty.

- Water-saving or energy-saving dishwashers may or may not work well. Using the no-heat option may make the cycle longer or leave glasses spotty. Some appliance experts suggest adding a rinse agent, which prevents water from beading and causing marks. However, a rinse agent adds another set of chemicals to the process.

Most conventional automatic dishwashing detergents contain phosphates or chlorine. Green brands eliminate these ingredients, but many find that dishes don't come as clean and spot-free, especially if you have hard water. This factor alone may be enough to persuade you to stick to hand-washing.

Doing dishes by hand

To make the most of washing by hand, follow these tips:

- Use hot water. Protect your hands with dish gloves. (When finished, turn gloves inside-out, sprinkle with baking soda, and allow to air-dry.)

- To avoid running the water while washing, fill the basin with enough hot soapy water to cover or immerse dishes. Then fill a dish tub or the other side of the sink with hot water for rinsing.

- Use a mild but grease-cutting dish soap that contains plant-based surfactants rather than bleach- or ammonia-based cleaners.

- Add a tablespoon or two of baking soda to hot, sudsy dishwater to cut the grease and loosen sticky foods on dishes.

✔ Add vinegar to the tubs of rinse water to eliminate the suds.

✔ Towel dry or, better yet, air-dry on a plate rack next to the sink. Air-drying is the most sanitary practice, as damp dishtowels collect germs.

Getting Down to Clean Floors

The following are the greenest cleaning tips for most floors, unless otherwise indicated.

✔ To keep floors cleaner longer, put floor mats at outside entrances into the kitchen, as well as one in front of the sink and under pet food/water areas.

✔ Vacuum or sweep the floor to remove loose dirt. Brooms have been improved to have bumper guards so that they're less likely to dent cabinets or furniture. When sweeping, use short, powerful strokes and a dust pan.

✔ Damp mop once a week or as needed, using a mild cleaning solution — either a commercial green solution or one of the recipes in Chapter 3. Some of the best recipes include white distilled vinegar and maybe some liquid soap.

✔ Choose a porous sponge mop with an abrasive strip for coaxing stuck-on gunk or use a mop with reusable microfiber head.

✔ Consider an electric steam cleaner, also called a steam mop, which uses nothing more than tap water. This cleaner is especially great for tile, marble, slate, and sealed-wood surfaces.

✔ Do not wax kitchen floors, because that makes them slippery. A properly sealed floor should provide enough shine, which re-emerges on a dry mopping or damp mopping.

Book III

Green Cleaning

Tackling the toughest floor problems

Everyday dirt, such as food and drink spills, clean up easily, but some substances pose out-of-the-ordinary challenges:

✔ **Dried paint:** Carefully chip away with a putty knife and follow with a green all-purpose floor cleaner.

✔ **Shoe scuff marks:** Rubbing with a sock should take them away. If not, apply a green cleaner with a soft cloth and buff dry.

✔ **Chewing gum and candle wax:** Apply ice in a muslin bag or wrapped in an old T-shirt to the gum or wax, and it should flake off with a putty knife. (Don't have a putty knife? A butter knife will do; what you don't want is something sharp that may gouge the floor.)

Cleaning Kitchen Surfaces: From Sink to Stove and Beyond

Green concerns aside, conventional cleaners include abrasive powdered cleansers and chlorine-based formulas, which aren't good for some sinks and other surfaces.

The following sections give you some ideas for treating your kitchen surfaces well but leaving them well cleaned.

Scrubbing (gently) the sink

Kitchen sinks come in many materials. In most cases, a similar cleaning routine applies for all:

1. **Routinely wipe out the sink with water to keep foods, oils, and stains from building up.**

2. **For a good cleaning, add a few drops of the same soap you use for your dishes into your sink.**

   Use hand-washing dish soap, not automatic dish detergent. Baking soda is an alternative to dish soap, or you can use a combination of both.

3. **Lightly wet the sink with a splash from the faucet or use a damp sponge and wipe 'til it shines.**

   Avoid using anything abrasive, including steel wool or caustic powder cleaners that can scar or pit the surface.

4. **Rinse the sink with water.**

5. **Pat the sink dry with a towel or simply allow to air-dry.**

   If you have hard water, you may need to rub down the sink with dry paper towels to remove water spots.

Some sink materials pose unique cleaning challenges:

- **Stainless steel:** Thinner material may mean more stains, dings, and dents, so consider your choice carefully when installing a new stainless steel sink.

- **Porcelain enamel:** If yellowing is a problem, try distilled white vinegar (a tablespoon in a cup of water) and rub the surface with a clean cloth or sponge, let sit for a few minutes, and rinse with water.

- **Solid surface:** More commonly known by brand names such as Corian or Silestone, these surfaces are nonporous and inhospitable to bacteria. For routine care, check with the manufacturer's recommendations.

- ✔ **Copper and brass:** These materials are more often used as bar sinks or accessory sinks. Both are very sensitive materials, so follow the manufacturer's recommendations. For a sink that's heavily stained, try a mixture of salt and water. Use a soft rag or sponge and rub the sink with a mixture and then add a little lemon juice to cleanse. Rinse with water and then dry completely with soft clean towel. Avoid any strong acids or bleaches, even glass cleaners!

- ✔ **Stone:** A bit unusual, but granite, soapstone, and marble sinks do exist. The best advice is to do what the manufacturer recommends. *Don't* use ammonia or strong soaps or detergents.

Attending to faucets, drains, and disposals

Don't forget to clean your faucets, drains, and garbage disposal. For routine cleaning, follow the same guidelines as for sinks: dishwashing liquid or baking soda and a sponge work fine. Pour baking soda down the drain to neutralize odors and rinse with cool water. If the faucets are made of chrome, a vinegar and water mixture works — go for the gleam! Remove any food remnants or soap scum around the base — an old toothbrush helps you get into those cracks and crevices. Attend to the pull-out sprayer. Older ones, especially, get a lot of buildup. You can soak the sprayer in vinegar and water to dissolve the mineral buildup.

While grinding up food in the garbage disposal may at first blush seem green, it's not. First, proper use of the disposal requires a lot of water, an increasingly precious natural resource. And running the disposal requires electricity. If you're on a septic system, you have to worry about sludge buildup, which can lead to serious plumbing problems. And sewage treatment results in a sludge that winds up in a landfill or is used as fertilizer. But with all the poisons tossed down the nation's drains, that material contains a lot of toxins and harmful chemicals. So compost everything you can, throw away anything that can damage your drains, and use your disposal with discretion, following the manufacturer's recommendations.

Book III

Green Cleaning

Bringing on the counter revolution

For most countertop materials — whether the ubiquitous plastic laminate (known to most people by its brand name, Formica) or designer tile — wiping up with warm water and an all-purpose cleaner, such as those presented in Chapter 3, is all it takes to keep them clean.

Keep the following caveats in mind:

- ✔ If you have a wood countertop (which, depending on the source, may or may not be green), avoid vinegar-based cleaning solutions.

- If you have a granite, marble, or stone countertop, mild dish soap and water is the best for cleaning. Keep in mind, though, that granite and marble can be fussy — they don't like harsh solutions or even highly acidic food spills and are sensitive to heat, so use trivets and hot pads to protect counters (a good idea for any countertop regardless of type).

- If you have a solid surface counter top, such as Corian or Silestone, use an all-purpose cleaner or 4 tablespoons of baking soda in 1 quart of warm water, apply with a sponge and dry. Do not use abrasive cleaners or tools.

Hot tips for cleaning stoves

The green way to eliminate oven grease and other cooktop grime is to use a lot of elbow grease along with some traditional cleaning agents. You can also employ a few other tactics to pre-empt some of the buildup:

- Avoid or limit cooking practices that increase grease and grime. Deep-frying meat is a major gunk-producer.

- Install a cooktop backsplash, such as ceramic or glass tile, that you can wipe clean with soap and water.

- Use an all-purpose cleaner for the cooktop, whether one of the recipes in Chapter 3 or an on-the-shelf green product, all-purpose or specially formulated for the stove.

- Don't use abrasive pads on glass or ceramic cooktops.

- Clean removable parts (racks, grates, and grate pans) to wash in the sink or dishwasher, as necessary.

- For grease stains, dampen the spot with water and cover with baking soda or cornstarch — both natural grease absorbers. Give it some time to work and then rinse off with water and wipe dry.

- From the inside of the oven, remove the racks and clean in the sink with soap, water, and a scrub brush. Baking racks can get pretty filthy, so consider taking them outside and rinsing off with the garden hose.

- While the oven is still slightly warm, cover baked-on food with table salt. After it cools, scrape away the salt and spills and wipe with a damp sponge.

- Prevent spills in the oven by using the proper size of baking pan or cookware. If your food is likely to bubble or spill over, place a larger pan or cookie sheet underneath to catch the overflow. Washing one pan in the sink or dishwasher is much easier than scrubbing the inside of your oven.

Many modern ovens have a self-cleaning feature (no chemicals necessary): Essentially, it burns off the spills so that you can easily wipe out the remains. Check your manufacturer's guidelines for use.

The Ins and Outs of Refrigerator Cleaning

The refrigerator consumes the most energy of any indoor home appliance — more than the washer and dryer combined. It probably doesn't help that it's also one of the most frequented places in the home! A constant open-and-close of the door adds dollars to your electric bill and increases opportunity for bacteria growth, for food inside as well as the door handle, which is a bacteria magnet.

A cleaning tip to reduce your utility bill

How you clean your refrigerator can also affect your monthly energy costs. Take a peek at the back of the fridge, and you see a rack-like attachment — those are the condenser coils, and they're a magnet for dust bunnies, pet hair, and lint. Just as the human heart has to pump harder for the overweight person, the refrigerator motor must exert more effort when its coils are coated and clogged with dirt.

A good brushing every couple of months makes your refrigerator more efficient. But take some precaution when cleaning. First, follow any special instructions from the manufacturer. Unplug the unit and then use your vacuum's crevice tool or a coil-cleaning brush. Hardware and home supply stores also sell appliance brushes for this purpose.

Purging and cleaning the fridge

To clean the inside of the fridge, toss any food gone bad and remove the remaining food items. Then, using a top-down approach, start cleaning with the top shelf, wiping with a sponge or rag and a bucket of warm water and dish soap or warm water and baking soda mixture, and work your way down. Finish with a good wipe-down of the outside — don't forget the door handle.

Several times a year, remove the glass shelves and the drawers (for deli, meat, fruit, and vegetables) and clean in the sink using hot, sudsy water, rinse well, drain, and dry before putting them back in the refrigerator.

After the refrigerator is sparkling clean, add a box of baking soda, opened up to absorb odors. You can certainly use one of the baking soda air filters, with a replacement indicator shows when you need to change it out. But why, when a small box of the real stuff is so cheap and easy to use? (Less packaging and plastic means less energy and resources expended).

To plug or unplug the refrigerator and freezer for an exhaustive deep cleaning is a choice you'll have to make based on the condition of the appliance and what the manufacturer says.

Keeping Small Appliances Clean

Microwave ovens, toasters, blenders, mixers — if your kitchen is like most, you have a cadre of small devices that assist with food preparation, often getting a daily workout. These appliances, depending upon their specific service, need cleaning daily or frequently.

Many appliances contain parts that you can remove from the motor. In these cases, treat the components as you do your dishes and cookware and wash by hand or in the dishwasher. Always be sure to unplug the devices before cleaning and follow these tips for specific appliances:

- **Microwave ovens:** All-purpose or glass cleaner works fine for the outside. Wipe the inside with a green all-purpose cleaner or liquid soap and water and dry thoroughly. Wipe the glass turntable often and put in the dishwasher when needed. Depending on the buildup you get, you may want to use a baking soda or cornstarch paste.

- **Toasters and toaster ovens:** Unplug before cleaning with a glass or all-purpose cleaner on the outside. Turn upside-down and dump out the crumbs into the sink. Clean the counter underneath.

- **Blenders:** Wash the container portion after every use. One method is to pour soapy water in and turn on the blender — some models have a dedicated button for this function. You can also remove the container-and-blade portion, take it apart, and then wash pieces separately by hand or in the dishwasher. Wipe down the base with soap and water or a mild all-purpose cleaner. Clean the counter underneath.

  The blades can cut you, so watch your hands.

- **Mixers:** The beaters go in the dishwasher or sink. Wipe the base with soap and water or an all-purpose cleaner. Large, stand-on-the-counter models should be cleaned as recommended by the maker. You can hand-wash stainless steel bowls or put them in the dishwasher.

- **Coffee makers:** Check the manufacturer's instructions. As a rule, simply wipe down drip coffee makers with soap and water or mild cleaner. You can wash the coffee pot in the sink or dishwasher.

Getting Wise to Preemptive Practices in Bathrooms

You can avert, postpone, or minimized major cleanup by incorporating some healthy bathroom habits. The bonus? Changing some of your most basic hygiene practices can go a long way in reducing germs and other unwelcome problems.

Close the lid on toilet spray. I'm not talking about the gender war between "seat up or seat down," but keeping the bowl covered — most especially before you flush. Shut the lid and then flush. Thus, whatever is in there stays there (kind of like Vegas). Some toilets have a powerful force. Even if you can't *see* any spray, you can trust that those bacteria are flying and landing in the area, on the cabinet next to the toilet and perhaps even on the sink ledge where your toothbrush sits.

Diving into the no-flush policy debate

Understanding that the toilet is the home's biggest water hog, is it responsible to flush after every visit? What a dilemma for a person who wants to be clean and green. Fact is, leaving an unflushed toilet — even if only fluid waste — allows time for bacteria-breeding, but every flush consumes as many as 7 gallons of water in older toilets.

If you're living with older-model toilets or in an area that suffers from water shortage, "let it mellow," as they say. *But* only for a few hours: Or from your last visit at night until your wakeup stop in the morning. If only one or two members of the household are using a particular john, a "reduced-flush" policy is probably manageable. Several household members using a single toilet, on the other hand, may require more frequent flushing.

And if you're flushing less often, you want to clean more frequently. One tip is to keep a gallon of white distilled vinegar under the sink and pour a quarter-cup or so into the bowl or tank every other day.

Spending 20 seconds on your hands

In every restaurant restroom, you find a sign that admonishes all employees to wash their hands before returning to their work. Wouldn't you be horrified if you saw your waitperson or chef coming out of a stall and marching right back into the dining room or kitchen?

Book III

Green Cleaning

Research continues to prove how effective soap and warm water are at killing disease-carrying germs and reducing illness. Hand-washing is especially mportant in the bathroom.

Reduce opportunities to spread germs on surfaces from dirty hands: Put a waste can with a pedal opener in the bathroom. You can also install pedal-operated water faucets if you wanted to take it to the next level.

Running the fan

Moisture from showering and washing lingers in the air, promoting the growth of mold and mildew over time. A musty odor is the least of the problems: Some forms of mold can aggravate and cause allergies, and they can spread throughout the infrastructure and framework of the home. In some rare cases, homeowners have had to tear out large areas of the house.

Signs of humidity problems are easy to see or smell. You may spot moisture stains on walls and ceilings, discover the gray tentacles of mildew spreading in your shower grout, or find whitish, powdery mildew on fabric or furniture in or near your bathroom.

A working bathroom fan does a lot more than remove unpleasant odors; it provides needed ventilation and air circulation in a wet, enclosed space. Turn it on as soon as you turn on the shower and keep it on at least ten minutes after you've finished your shower. If the bathroom is an interior room with no windows for air circulation, run it longer.

Other tips for reducing humidity and risk of mildew and mold:

- ✔ Leave the shower curtain or door open after your shower so that the bath area can dry.

- ✔ Keep the bathroom door open after showering or bathing.

- ✔ For rooms that get little circulation and seem to develop mildew quickly, a dehumidifier may help suck moisture from the air. There's an energy cost attached, but the payoff may be worth the effort.

- ✔ Verify that your exhaust fan is connected correctly so that the air is forced outside of the house and not blasted into the attic or another area of the house. Have your ducts checked.

- ✔ Make sure that windows are well sealed: Cold air leaking into the house exacerbates condensation and humidity problems. Replace worn weatherstripping around windows.

For advice on removing mildew and mold from shower walls and bathroom surfaces, see the next section of this chapter.

If you think you have a mold problem, don't let it grow worse and risk permanent damage to your home or your health. To find certified contractors who specialize in mold removal, contact the Institute of Inspection Cleaning and Restoration Certification (www.iicrc.org).

Cleaning the Bath from Top to Bottom

While the bathroom poses some cleaning challenges, its major surfaces are fairly straightforward in terms of cleaning: Start with the least germy and easiest to clean places (mirrors and sinks), working your way from fixture to fixture toward the dirtiest (the toilet) area, and then finally tackle the floor.

Choosing safe, effective cleaning formulas

Bathrooms are a tough clean, to be sure, but don't be oversold on the super-duper germ-obliterators that the commercials insist you need. Manufacturers rarely list the ingredients on the label. But you know you're in trouble when you see warnings such as "Danger," "Warning," "Corrosive."

The safest and greenest course of action is to steer clear of these heavy hitters and stick to the recipes included in Chapter 3 or buy commercial products that identify themselves as plant-based. Don't assume that you're green to go just because the bottle says "nontoxic," "all-natural," or "biodegradable." These terms aren't regulated.

Gathering the best cleaning tools

You won't need to grab many cleaning tools from your utility closet. Your toilet brush is already in place, perhaps in an attractive brush holder sitting unobtrusively behind the commode. (Some of the brush holders I've seen — even in the big box stores such as Target and Lowes — are decorative elements in their own right.) You can keep a pumice under the sink to deal with toilet bowl stains as needed. But otherwise, a bucket, a squirt bottle filled with green cleaner, and lots of cleaning cloths ought to do the job.

For tough mildew stains in the sink or tub areas, you'll need a scrub brush or an old toothbrush for the grout. (For more tips on gathering your equipment, see Chapter 2.)

Book III

Green Cleaning

Be liberal with the number of cloths you use to avoid spreading germs from one surface to another. Clean more benign surfaces, such as the mirror and sink, first. Drop the used cloths in a bucket or laundry basket and then grab clean ones for the next task, whether tub or shower. When it comes to the toilet, change cloths often. Clean the bowl and the underside of the toilet seat first then deposit the dirty rag in the used pile. Then grab a fresh cloth for the seat itself, and another for the lid, tank, or handle.

Identify certain cloths solely for toilet cleaning — perhaps repurpose the splashy red beach towel that's seen better days, cutting it up into workable squares. That way, you can easily identify these as toilet rags and keep them separate from your other rags.

Taking a look at the mirror

The glass cleaner recipes s included in Chapter 3 or store-bought green formulas are good for cleaning bathroom mirrors. Spray and wipe with a microfiber cloth made for glass. If you use a cleaning cloth from your rag pile, choose a lint-free material.

For splatters of toothpaste, soap, or cosmetics, you may want to spot-wipe with a damp cloth and a little liquid soap, if necessary.

Newspaper is the traditional favorite for streak-free mirrors and glass. But some people object to the mess the ink makes on your hands or are irritated by the chemically smell of the inked paper. That said, yesterday's news is certainly an environmentally friendly way to clean glass. The soy-based inks of the black-and-white pages (don't use the comics or the shiny color advertising inserts) are benign, and, in fact, organic gardeners recommend their use in composting and layering under soil to prevent weeds.

Bringing sparkle to the sink

The sink and vanity area of the bathroom sees plenty of traffic. A routine wipe-down with a gentle cleaner is a good practice for keeping up with the daily toothpaste buildup and soap scum that accumulates. Whether the sink is made of porcelain, stainless steel, a synthetic material, or glass, a basic all-purpose cleaner should make short work of sink and faucet grime.

Use one of the recipes included in Chapter 3 or a good green general product to kill germs and shine sink surfaces and chrome fixtures to a gleam. For polished brass and other types of faucets, follow the manufacturer's instructions, but most gentle, all-purpose cleaners are fine.

Use extra elbow grease, however, if you're cleaning a vanity area used for hairstyling. Hairspray tends to leave a sticky coating on sinks and counter-top, but a vinegar cleaner ought to do the trick. Grab a sponge with a scrubby side for especially tacky buildup or soap scum.

Steer clear of abrasive formulas or scrub brushes for most materials to avoid scratching or damage. And *never* use conventional toilet bowl cleaners for sinks, tubs, or shower areas: The chemicals in these products are too harsh and may ruin the materials.

Rubbing the tub and scouring the shower

When it comes to cleaning the tub and shower area, the materials you're most likely to be dealing with are prefabricated tub-and-shower surrounds made of polyester and acrylic, or vitreous porcelain, stainless steel, tile, or stone. Most easily stand up to the basic all-purpose formulas included in Chapter 3, with a few exceptions.

Here are some tips for most bath and shower cleaning:

- Use an all-purpose cleaner to wipe away grime on bath surfaces and fixtures.
- For soap, lime, and scale buildup, bring in the vinegar. Soak your cleaning cloth and rub away on tile, porcelain, and chrome fixtures.
- Clean glass shower doors with the same cleaner you use on mirrors.
- If you have a clogged-up showerhead, simply remove it and let it soak overnight in a bucket with water and vinegar, at a 1-to-1 ratio. Rinse and put back on.
- To reduce soap buildup on glass doors, wipe them down with a squeegee after each shower.
- Battle mildew with hydrogen peroxide.
- Avoid steel wool, scrub brushes, scrub pads, and abrasive cleaners on any bath surfaces — they're just too harsh for the materials and can scratch and damage them.

Book III

Green Cleaning

Some shower and tub materials pose more challenges than others. Stainless steel is prone to dings and scratches. Stone and marble may require special care. And tile, while in itself a breeze to keep clean, the stuff that holds it together — grout — is something else. Sometimes it seems like mildew is holding the tiles together.

A hand-held steam cleaner is handy for cleaning grout. Another approach is rubbing a paste of baking soda or borax on the grout, let it dry, and then wet and remove with a soft-bristled toothbrush.

Toilet talk

Be diligent about keeping the toilet area clean. Getting your household into the habit of closing the lid before flushing and washing their hands helps reduce the risk of spreading bacteria, but routine cleaning of the toilet — at least once a week — is necessary to flush out the germs.

In most cases, a non-abrasive all-purpose cleaner works well for cleaning the outside of the toilet, tank, lid, seat, and bowl. Choose from the cleaners in Chapter 3 or a commercial green product. Vinegar-based solutions help kill bacteria. After cleaning your toilet, remember to immediately set aside cloths for the wash and not use them on any other surface.

If you poured your toilet bowl cleaner first thing as you started your bathroom clean, you've got a head start on a tough job. Ingredients for bowl cleaners are stronger than those used for the other bathroom surfaces.

Let the cleaner sit in the toilet for at least 10 minutes. For a really grungy bowl, pour in a cup of borax, which acts as a water softener, sanitizer, and deodorizer, and let it sit overnight. Then swish and scrub with the toilet brush. Don't neglect the area you can't see just under the rim inside the toilet — where ugly mildew really collects. Tackle stains with pumice, wearing plastic gloves to protect your hands. Then scrub, close the lid, and flush.

When using conventional cleaners with caustic chemicals, be especially careful not to splash when pouring in the cleaner. Ammonia, bleach, lye, and other ingredients can burn your skin and eyes. Even commercially available green toilet bowl cleaners have cautions.

After the inside of the bowl is clean, you're ready to give the outside of the toilet — lid, seat, tank — a good wipe-down with your preferred all-purpose cleaner. Don't forget to clean the handle!

Getting to the bottom of floor cleaning

Bathroom floors tend to be of the same types of materials as other bathroom surfaces: those that stand up well to water and clean with a wipe of a sponge. The other good news is, as a rule, bathroom floors aren't as big as in other areas of the house, so keeping up with the floor cleaning doesn't take much more effort than a quick zip-through with the mop. After all the above-floor surfaces are cleaned, vacuum the floor to pick up loose hair and dust. Then clean with water and a floor cleaner best-suited for your floor type. In most cases, any of the all-purpose cleaners or commercial green cleaners are fine. But do follow the manufacturer's guidelines when choosing a cleaning product.

Other options include

- ✓ A store-bought mop system. Most include an ergonomically shaped mop with washable microfiber head and a gentle squirt-and-mop formula, no buckets of water required.

- ✓ An electric steam cleaner — skip the cleaning formula altogether. Just use water and steam, a great solution for tile and sealed wood floors. Lightweight models heat up in 60 seconds or less, and, with swivel heads, they can reach those corners and hard-to-reach spaces, such as behind the toilet. (For more on steam cleaners, see Chapter 2.)

Book III

Green Cleaning

Chapter 6

Working Outside In for a Clean and Green Home

All the activity and traffic that goes on in living rooms (or family rooms, great rooms, and so on) can mean only one thing to the homeowner: a whole lotta cleaning. The flip side of that coin is the bedroom, a sanctuary that few visitors see but that certainly you have good reason to want spic-and-span. (A third of your life takes place there, after all.) And getting to a whole-house clean starts outside your home.

No matter what its function, any place your family spends its time must be as safe and clean as possible. This chapter shows you how to maintain healthy spaces throughout your home

Making a Green Entrance

Whether you enter from the formal front door, sneak in the side entrance or garage into the mudroom, or track through a sunroom from the backyard, your homes entry points connect your inside space to your outside space — which means that one way or another, plenty of dirt gets tracked in. But each transitional area is used in different ways and demands unique attention.

Leaving shoes at the door goes a long way to keep outside dirt from working its way across your floors. Stock slippers or house shoes so that you and your guests can tread lightly in your home.

Crossing the energy threshold: Doors

Which door in your home sees the most traffic? Whether front, back, or side, give this entrance special attention in terms of weatherproofing. Make sure that the door shuts easily and properly and adjust as necessary to stop the energy leaks.

Cleaning your home's doors is a half-inside, half-outside job. The outside work requires, no surprise, a little more elbow grease as it gets battered with rain, mud, pet paw prints, and the occasional kick from an impatient kid. Unless the manufacturer specifies some unusual cleaning procedure, you can almost always handle the job — inside and out — with a basic all-purpose spray and a cleaning rag.

A storm door reduces the need to clean your entry door. You can clean storm and sliding glass doors as you would any window, with a little vinegar and a lint-free cloth, newspaper, or squeegee.

Wash the glass on a cloudy day to reduce streaking. (Sun dries the solution faster than you can buff it in.) For windows that have been cleaned with commercial window solutions, you may need to mix in a little liquid detergent with your vinegar and water to cut the buildup. (See Chapter 3 to find green glass-cleaning recipes.)

Putting out the welcome mat

The welcome mat is more than an expression of hospitality to guests. Doormats inside and outside entry doors save cleaning time. Mats on the outside of the door are typically of a more rugged material, often a bristly brushlike texture that's great for catching grass, mud, and other gunk you don't want tracked into your home.

Inside doormats don't have to work as hard as the outdoor mats, unless you have kids, spouses, or friends who have to be reminded to wipe their feet. For both inside and outside, doormats come in several ecomaterials:

> ✔ **Coir mats** are made from coconut husk fiber. These thickly woven mats are extremely durable and repel insects naturally. They're not recommended for outdoors, however, unless on a well-covered porch.

- ✔ **Flip flop** doormats are made from — you guessed it — recycled rubber flip-flop material culled from the scraps on the manufacturing floor. They're available through many sources online and start at $20. Simply wash down with a hose whenever called for.

- ✔ **Rubber doormats** are made from recycled car tires. Some of these brands are manufactured in the United States, so you're not adding to the energy cost of the doormat. Mats vary in price, anywhere from $25 to more than $100, based on size.

- ✔ **Jute, seagrass, sisal, and hemp rugs** are sold through environmentally oriented catalog companies, as well as some of the big box and home stores. Just shake to loosen soil, vacuum, and wipe clean with a damp sponge. Expect to find these mats in the $30-and-up range, although they're sometimes less.

Rolling Out the Green Carpet

Carpet, whether area rugs or wall to wall, can be a good choice for living or bedroom areas. But it also presents issues both green and clean. You can resolve most challenges, however, with a little know-how.

Calling pests and pets on the carpet

A particular challenge with wall-to-wall carpeting is its propensity for harboring irritants that cause health problems. Dirt, dust, mold, and other allergens find carpeting just as cozy as humans do:

- ✔ **Dust mites:** Just as they do in bed sheets, pillows, and fabrics in the bedroom, dust mites are likely to burrow into your floor cover and leave their asthma-provoking droppings in your living room.

- ✔ **Carpet beetles:** Wool carpeting, along with leather and wood fiber, is a favorite feast of both the varied carpet beetle and black carpet beetle. Once they get into your home, they can attack carpeting as if it were an all-you-can-eat buffet. Prevent infestations with frequent vacuuming. Once they settle in, they're hard to get rid of and may destroy the carpet.

  Read *Carpet Cleaning Tips For Dummies* by Elizabeth B. Goldsmith for more detail about carpet beetles.

- ✔ **Pet odors and stains:** In addition to pet hair and dander, your beloved four-legged family members are as likely as small children to have "accidents" on carpeting — and these messes do the same damage. Carpeting seems to be a sponge for pet odors; more often than not, you can easily pick out the dog's favorite nap corner simply by smell.

Book III

Green Cleaning

✔ **Mildew and mold:** Anything from a spill to a pet accident to a humid house can result in carpet mold and mildew. (You can usually smell or see mildew and mold.) Once it takes hold, the best cure is to toss the carpet and the pad.

Cleaning and caring for carpeting

The best defense against carpet challenges is prevention: Vacuum regularly, keep carpeting dry, and discourage pets from sleeping directly on the floor. Dogs should have their own beds and area rugs.

For regular maintenance of any carpeting, a good vacuum cleaner is best for the job. A machine with a high efficiency particulate air (HEPA) filter removes tiny particles, such as pollens, dust, and, dander, relieving those who suffer from common allergens. A vacuum with a CRI (Carpet and Rug Institute) Seal of Approval/Green Label passes many tests on soil removal, carpet texture retention, and dust containment. CRI-approved vacuums must not release more than 100 micrograms of dust particles per cubic meter of air.

Getting out common stains and spills

Quick action can save you from massive cleanup jobs or hiring the professionals. Don't ever let a stain set. Address it as soon as you spot it by following these steps:

1. **Absorb the spill with a dry cloth or paper towel and vacuum up solids (such as spilled soil from a plant or food crumbs) or pick up larger pieces with a towel.**

2. **Wipe or blot with a cloth saturated with a one-part-vinegar and one-part-water mix to neutralize the smell.**

3. **Treat or spot-clean the stain with plain water applied with a sponge or cloth.**

   Blot; don't scrub.

4. **If the stain is stubborn, try adding a little dishwashing liquid.**

   For treating specific stains, such as blood, ink, or wine, see Chapter 4.

5. **Blot-dry with a clean cloth and allow to air-dry.**

Never use laundry detergent with bleach to remove carpet stains. Refer to the cleaning instructions from the carpet manufacturer for specific treatment.

Making time for a deep cleaning

When carpeting begins to show a traffic pattern, it's a sign that a deeper cleaning may be due. Most carpeting requires a deep-clean every year or two, depending upon the wear the room sees.

Rather than resorting to harsh carpet cleaners, which contain the same kinds of toxic components that some carpet materials do, limit your deep-clean to a steam-vacuum process, sometimes referred to as *extraction cleaning*. The steam seeps deeper into the carpet, knocking the heck out of dust mites and picking up embedded dirt. If you don't own a steam cleaner, you can find them for rent from many grocery stores.

If you want a thorough clean but don't want to hassle with moving furniture and renting a steam vacuum, consider a carpet-cleaning service. These services use a variety of techniques, including chemicals, but most often they stick to deep steam-cleaning. For information about services in your area, the Institute of Inspection, Cleaning, and Restorations Certification (IICRC) represents more than 4,500 Certified Firms and more than 45,000 Certified Technicians in 30 countries. You can visit its Web site at www.certifiedcleaners.org.

Living with pets

If your cat, dog, rabbit, ferret, bird, snake, or (gulp!) tarantula has the run of the house, these tips are sure to help you keep a leash on your home's cleanliness and show your pet who's in charge:

- Wash the pet bed or favorite blanket weekly. If your dog or cat sleeps on your bed, wash the bedding more frequently. If fleas or dust mites are a concern (and they always are), wash in hot water.

- Discourage your pet from sleeping or sitting directly on upholstery. If you can't persuade Mitzy or Bruno to give up the couch, put down a blanket to keep your furniture from wearing and taking on a permanent pet odor.

- If possible, steer clear of skirting on sofas and chairs. It can take a lot of wear, what with dogs rubbing up against it or cats slipping under the couch to hide.

- Try to keep pets corralled in one or two areas of the house and keep other rooms off-limits. Restricting your pets' roam area reduces the amount of special cleaning attention you have to exert.

- Get your pets to follow the same rule as everyone else: "Wipe your paws before you come in!" Be sure a good doormat is at the entrances they use and give them a little help. Keep an old towel by the door so that you can wipe muddy paws before they head inside and jump on the couch.

- If your pet insists on communing with nature on a regular basis, weekly baths may be a good idea.

- Both dogs and cats benefit from regular brushing, which reduces the amount of pet hair that ends up on your couch and carpet.

For blogs about green pet products and advice, check out Great Green Pet (www.greatgreenpet.com) and Raise a Green Dog (http://blog.raiseagreendog.com).

Book III

Green Cleaning

Upholstery: The Great Furniture Coverup

Most living room furniture — at least the stuff you sit on — is padded for comfort and covered, or upholstered, with fabric. Use the following tips to keep that fabric clean and looking good:

- Remove pillows and cushions and vacuum with the crevice tool, reaching into the dark recesses to suck up popcorn kernels along with all the detritus that gets lost under the cushions.

- Use the upholstery nozzle to go over the cushions. Fluff or punch them to shape up the stuffing, and set them back in place.

- Take care of spots or stains as soon as possible, following the manufacturer's guidelines. If you don't want to use the offensive chemical cleaner recommended, try baking soda and the tiniest bit of water to pull it out.

- Do *not* wash or soak the fabric: You may end up with a permanent water stain *and* get the stuffing wet, which can lead to mildew or mold.

- With natural cushion materials (feathers or wool), fluff daily — but don't overdo it.

Zen and the Art of Dusting

That near-invisible whisper of sediment that's equally happy to settle on houseplants, coffee tables, valuable artwork, or electronics is *dust* made up of things like pollen, lint, pet hair and dander, and teeny particles of dirt that drift in from outdoors or from room to room. Your living room collects more or less dust, depending on the activities inside and outside of your home, the inhabitants, and the air flow.

Because it's light, dust floats around in the air until it settles on surfaces like tables and floors. You want to minimize dust inside because you don't want to breathe it. Air or vacuum filters or a dust mop or cloth are the devices typically used to capture dust and remove it from the home environment.

Walking the labyrinth of dusting

Tables and other flat surfaces covered with knick knacks are useful for collecting dust and keeping it off the carpet or other fabrics so that dust mites and other vermin don't settle in.

The last thing you want to do is whisk all that dust to the floor. Dusting is a *mindful* activity — not a mindless one. And here's a mindful approach to follow:

- ✔ Make a microfiber cloth or a lint-free piece of fabric from your rag pile, your partner in dusting. (Read Chapter 2 for the inside story on microfiber and its role in cleaning.)

- ✔ Skip the feather duster or any other aid that does nothing more than move dust from one place to another, stirring up irritants.

- ✔ As a backup — and especially if you can't reach the ceiling — have a vacuum cleaner with an extension tool on hand, too.

- ✔ If you want, you can use a cleaning product or dampen your cleaning cloth just slightly so that more dust clings to the cloth. (Read Chapter 3 for cleaning recipes for dusting.) But, remember, the act of rubbing, not the cleaning solution, is what picks up and traps the dust. Spray that table all day, and it's not going to eat away the dust.

- ✔ Start dusting from top to bottom, making a circle around the room.

- ✔ Continue to change dust cloths frequently. As soon as one appears to have been grayed by a film of dust and cobwebs, exchange it for a clean one. Hey, you're not using throwaways, but even though using a new cloth increases your wash load, it's important to have clean cloths.

- ✔ Continue your circle around the room, hitting the next highest level and then moving lower.

Attending to the details

Each section of the room and piece of furniture deserves special attention. Consider this approach:

- ✔ **Ceiling:** With a vacuum and a long attachment, pick up the cobwebs clinging to the ceiling corners. You can use an old-fashioned ceiling broom if you prefer.

- ✔ **Walls:** Dust walls the same way as you would the ceiling. No direct spray is needed on the surface, but if you want to use a product, spray lightly into the cloth and wipe down. This procedure is fine for both painted and wallpapered surfaces. (If the wallpaper is special, particularly old, or hand-painted, seek advice from experts for the best way to clean.)

- ✔ **Ceiling fans, ceiling light fixtures, and floor and table lamps:** For safety, turn off the lights, lamps, and ceiling fans before cleaning.

- ✔ **Artwork and framed items:** To avoid damage to unprotected artwork if you're using a cleaner, spray the dust cloth with the cleaner rather than spraying it directly on the picture frame.

- ✔ **Books:** Again, if using a product, spray the cloth, not the item, and use any liquid sparingly when wiping down book covers.

- ✔ **Mirrors and glass:** You can use a microfiber cloth made expressly for glass or opt for a newspaper. A vinegar-and-water solution or one of the other recipes in Chapter 3 works well to capture dust on glass. (Pass up the ammonia-based commercial cleaners because of their toxicity.)

- ✔ **Wood furniture:** If you like a little bit of polish, or even scent, blend a few drops of a citrus essential oil and a few drops of olive oil — you don't need much. Dip your dust cloth in the solution and rub furniture to a sheen.

- ✔ **Plants:** Use your dust cloth or take them outside to clean. Also, keep an eye out for moldy soil (gray on the top) and change it. Skip the leaf-shining sprays, which may emit VOCs.

Keeping electronics dust-free

Dust is a detriment to electronics: Just look what happens when you get a bit stuck on a DVD or CD. When cleaning your living room, you can dust electronics the same as you dust other furniture and items. But leave out the fluid cleaners or water.

Most electronics cleaners — including computer monitor sprays and DVD cleaners — contain elements that you'd prefer not to spray in your home if you're concerned about indoor air quality. Problem is, you don't have many options for cleaning stuck-on gunk.

Start with a purpose-designed microfiber or other cloth. You can find these in office-supply and electronics stores. Sometimes a good rub-down does the trick. If not, you may have to resort to the cleaner. To reduce your environmental impact, try to use a spray product with a reusable cloth rather than the disposable, single-use wipes.

Here are some more tips for cleaning electronic equipment:

- ✔ Turn off computer and TV monitors before cleaning.

- ✔ Avoid using water or excess liquid cleaner on electronics.

- ✔ Gently brush away loose dust before wiping a monitor to scrub off gunk, lest you scratch the screen by scrubbing in a hard piece of dirt.

- ✔ Clean LCD monitors with more care than glass-fronted CRT monitors. They can be scratched or damaged more easily. Use a soft cloth and, if necessary, a spray formulated for LCD monitors.

- ✔ Unless otherwise advised by the manufacturer, gentle green solutions, such as vinegar and water, are probably fine for most electronics.

✔ Most cleaning products recommended by manufacturers aren't likely to be green. Some even come in aerosol cans. But unless you can verify that another cleaning solution can be substituted, it may be best to stick to the recommendation.

✔ Computer keyboards seem to collect a lot of crumbs: While the computer is off, turn the keyboard over and shake the loose debris. An old toothbrush or a cleaned and dried old mascara wand gets between the keys to remove whatever hasn't shaken out.

A Green Well-Lighted Space: Windows

Rare is a living space without windows. Although I have seen them, a room without windows is claustrophobic and undesirable. Home is a haven from the outside world, yes, but it's also your *window* to the world around you, whether rolling fields, dense forest, or urban skyline.

Enjoying the view: Keeping windows clean

A clean window is an energy-efficient window, letting in more light. Window sills and frames seem to attract dirt more so than many surfaces in your home. Dust on and around the window as you dust everything else in the living room, either vacuuming the loose stuff or hand-dusting.

Don't forget the outside views, too. The glass and frame get dirtier, what with the elements, car exhaust, and outdoor activity of bugs and birds. The outside sill may require a heavy scrubbing. Arm yourself with a stronger all-purpose cleaner and a damp sponge to attack it.

You can keep all your glass clean with a window cleaner made of vinegar and water. Look for this recipe and other glass cleaners in Chapter 3.

Choosing and cleaning drapes and blinds

When it comes to window treatments, the green home designer faces several dilemmas: While window coverings can enhance energy-saving efforts, they're often made of undesirable materials (blinds of plastic and vinyl, draperies covered with toxic fabric finishes), and many serve as a magnet for dust mites and other harbingers of allergy misery and respiratory woe. If you opt for window treatments, here are a few of the greener options, along with cleaning advice:

Book III

Green Cleaning

✔ **Heavy draperies** provide a high insulative quality, keeping the room warm in cold weather and blocking solar gain when it's hot. Seek draperies made of natural, unfinished material; linen, cotton, and some wools and silks are machine washable, so you can avoid the cost and chemicals associated with dry cleaning.

✔ **Honeycomb shades** are fabric coverings that fit snugly within the window frame. Their cell-like construction traps air, which provides extra insulation. The more opaque the shades, the better job they do of keeping out the temperature and solar gain. The fabric may be of synthetic content and treated with finishes that repel dust and dirt. Dust or vacuum regularly to prevent dirt buildup. Use a damp cloth and mild detergent for spot cleaning.

✔ **Traditional** *horizontal* **aluminum** or **plastic slat blinds** provide some insulation — but vertical blinds add little insulative value. Blinds can be dusted and vacuumed. Special brushes with "fingers" are available, though far from necessary to do a good cleaning job. Clean with damp cloth and mild solution or remove the entire assembly and stick it in the bathtub.

✔ **Indoor shutters and blinds** made of wood, are better for blocking heat than for lending insulation value. Clean wood or bamboo blinds or shutters as other wood furniture: Simply dust with a dry or slightly damp cloth or use a wood cleaner.

Cleaning the Fireplace: Ashes to Ashes

The more they're used, the more soot and ash fireplaces produce. And because the material can drift like dust into other areas of your home, you want to keep on top of it.

When you're ready for a seasonal clean, get ready for one dirty job and follow these steps:

1. **Make sure that the fire is completely out before you attempt to clean the fireplace.**

   Cleaning out a place that contains frequent fires requires caution, however. Avoid cleaning out the fireplace if a fire has burned recently. Wait two days after the last use.

2. **Close windows and doors to prevent any drafts from blowing around the ashes and soot.**

3. **Don an apron or work shirt, eye goggles, gloves, and a mask to avoid getting stirred-up ashes in your eyes or breathing passages.**

4. **Using your fireplace tool or another scoop, shovel all the ashes into a bucket.**

Carry the bucket outside before dumping to minimize floating soot. (Wood ash may be a great addition to your compost pile if your soil leans toward the acidic end of the pH spectrum.)

5. **Vacuum up the remaining ash in the fireplace.**

Never vacuum within two days of burning a fire in the fireplace, or attempt to vacuum all the ash. Most vacuums aren't capable of handling that volume of debris. Be aware of outdoor conditions and warnings from fire departments of extremely dry conditions.

6. **(Optional) If you want to take it to the next level, you can wash out the fireplace with water and a mild soap.**

On the walls outside the fireplace, brick can take a tougher scrubbing than adobe and stucco, or wallboard, which can be treated as you would your interior walls. With most stone, marble, slate, tile, and cement — baking soda and water is a safe choice.

7. **Clean the grates, irons, and fireplace accessories.**

Like grilling tools, you can take the fireplace accessories outside and hose them down with soap and water or an all-purpose cleaner. If your accessories are brass, polish them with a solution of lemon juice, baking soda, and water and dry with a soft cloth.

Hiring a chimney sweep to clean out the inside of your chimney is important. Let the experts thoroughly — and safely — clean out your fireplace and rest assured that dangerous buildup inside the chimney has been cleared away. Choose a professional certified by The Chimney Safety Institute of America (www.csia.org).

Book III

Green Cleaning

Ensuring a Degree of Comfort

In precentral-air days, folks set up their sleeping quarters so that windows welcomed breezes and high ceilings allowed hot air to collect *away* from sleepers. When the temperatures climbed to sweltering, sleeping porches drew the inhabitants to bunk down in the coolest place in the house.

With the advent of air conditioning, those who live in warm-weather regions no longer have to suffer through sticky-hot nights. But the concerned citizen who wants to minimize energy use can prepare the bedroom to be a more comfortable *and* energy-efficient place to dream away a midsummer night.

Good air circulation in your home helps manage comfort in warm weather, reducing the need for an air conditioner. Cross-ventilation also reduces humidity, discourages mildew, and brings in clean, fresh air.

To encourage good air flow and reduce energy-guzzling air-conditioning and heating, follow these suggestions:

- Install windows that you can open to let in breezes.

- Use floor fans or ceiling fans, which take less energy to run than an air conditioner.

- Hang blinds, curtains, or window treatments that you can open to take advantage of sun and breeze and that you can tightly close to provide insulation and privacy when needed.

- To reduce *solar gain* (when the sun heats up the interior of your home through your windows, making your air conditioner work harder), plant deciduous trees so that they shade your windows.

- Arrange your bedroom furniture so that the bed is positioned in the cross-breeze from the window to the door.

- Adjust your bedding instead of the thermostat: heavier blankets in the winter, light coverings in the summer.

Greening Your Bedding

In days of old, young girls began at an early age to fill big trunks they called *hope chests,* preparing for the time when they'd be running and furnishing their own homes. Bed linens, pillow cases, and blankets filled the hope chests as the girls readied for marriage.

If that tradition continued today, most women would have to switch to a storage unit to contain all the bedding products available. With a wider range of bed sizes and styles and broader selection of materials, bedding must accommodate all sorts of options, from California king–sized beds to futons. Green-conscious consumers choose mattresses, pillows, and bed linens not just for their style, but also on their environmental merits.

A firm understanding of mattress care

Size and firmness level aren't the only considerations in choosing and maintaining the fundamental backbone of your bed. Think natural and organic when selecting your mattress. Pass up the polyurethane foam and chemically treated products for organic-content mattresses. Available through a number of companies, preferred mattresses typically contain organic cotton, wool, and natural rubber, all biodegradable materials.

Green mattresses are commonly wrapped in a wool outer layer. Wool deters dust mites, keeps its shape, wicks moisture, and is naturally flame-retardant — all desirable qualities in a mattress.

After you find the perfect mattress, you need to take care of it to extend its life. Mattresses are designed to last 8 to 10 years, although several of the organic brands advertise a life of 20 years. But you can extend the wear of any mattress by following these practices:

- Cover the mattress with a mattress pad to keep dust and dander from collecting.

- Recycle the mattress pad when it's yellowed or threadbare: At that point, it's no longer doing its job.

- When the bed is stripped, vacuum the mattress to capture loose dust, dirt, and dust mite residue.

- Flip the mattress over every few months — just like rotating your tires, this practices makes for more even wear. (Flipping a large mattress is a two-person job: Watch your back.)

- Clean stains or spills as soon as possible to prevent bacteria or mildew from developing. Use plain cool water or one of the stain remover recipes in Chapter 3. Let the mattress dry thoroughly before replacing bedding.

- Air out the mattress — at least every time you change the mattress pad or flip the mattress. Let the sunshine stream in and do its disinfecting job for a couple of hours.

Pillow talk

Bed pillows sell for $3 and up, so they're affordable to replace often. But frequent replacement doesn't exactly jibe with a sustainable lifestyle. So investing in a longer-lasting pillow, such as wool or latex, is a wise choice, even if they do cost a bit more.

Whatever its content, pillows last longer when well-cared for:

- Use pillow covers or protectors in addition to pillowcases. These zip-up coverings help reduce dust mite invasion and keep other pollutants out of the pillow filling.

- Hand-wash wool pillows; machine-wash cotton and synthetic pillows. Follow manufacturers' instructions.

- Air out pillows frequently. Strip their coverings and lay out in the sun on a blanket. When you make the bed, fluff and flip the pillows.

- Give pillows a rest. If you have extras, rotate them occasionally. But be sure to store in the linen closet only after washing or airing.

Converting to green sheets

Your sheets and pillowcases come in closest contact with your skin. So the greener the content, the less chance you're sleeping with unsafe chemical treatments. Choosing your bed linens from organically grown or cultivated cotton or silk is the first step. But be sure, too, that the materials aren't treated with a chemical flame retardant or easy-care coating.

A new material choice is bamboo. Who knew that the hard, woody grass used to support scaffolding in China could produce such soft, luxurious fabric? Bamboo sheets do feel silky soft. What's more, bamboo is a rapidly renewable resource. (Now, if only U.S. growers would start cultivating it, so green consumers don't have to pay such a high carbon price for bamboo shipped from Asia!) More bamboo benefits? The material is machine-washable, durable, and antibacterial.

Dealing with dirty linens

The best organic materials are also easily washable. Change and wash your bed sheets as needed — more frequently during sweltering weather and certainly during illness to make sure to eliminate germs.

Change your pillowcases more often than you change your bed sheets, but at least once a week. Your pillow is where your head rests, leaving a more tempting feast for dust mites, which favor dead skin flakes, hair, secretions, oils from lotions, and residue from gels and shampoo, cosmetics, and hairspray.

If you or anyone in your home suffers from allergies, wash sheets in water hot enough to kill irritants including dust mites — some recommend 130° or higher. Unless pollen allergies are an issue, hang sheets outside in the breeze for a heavenly sun-kissed scent that no bottle of fabric softener can capture.

Letting linens out of the closet

Never store soiled linens: Dirt and perspiration attract mildew. Whether you stack bedding as sheet sets (bottom and top sheet plus pillowcases) or store them separately, place the most recently cleaned linens on the bottom of the stack so that you rotate usage consistently. This way, the sheets last a lot longer.

Linen closets serve you best if they're dry and cool with ventilated shelves. Mildew can grow in warm, humid environments. If items smell musty, give them a good wash and dry before putting them on the bed. Don't use sealed plastic bags for storage, as moisture gets trapped inside and fabric can't breathe. Cotton, canvas, or muslin bags are better choices.

Covering bedspread basics

Because they're not next to your skin, you can get away with less frequent washing for blankets, bedspreads, and their accompanying bed skirts and sham coverings. (Even hotels don't wash their spreads as often as their sheets, which is why you're advised *not* to come into contact with the covering.)

For easiest care and greenest practices at home, however, follow this advice:

- ✔ Use comforters, blankets, and other bed coverings that are machine washable. Avoid those that must be dry-cleaned, a highly toxic process involving the chemical perchloroethylene.

- ✔ If your spread must be dry-cleaned, seek out a cleaner that uses one of the more earth-friendly processes.

- ✔ If you use a comforter, slip on a *duvet cover* and cut down on care. You can button or zip on this cover and wash it separately.

- ✔ Air out down comforters by hanging them outdoors in the sun or at least toss them in the air some when making the bed to evenly redistribute the contents.

- ✔ Launder washable covers and spreads according to label instructions. Cold water is likely suitable for most materials. If you or someone else in your home has allergies, wash in hot water.

Book III

Green Cleaning

Book IV
Green Remodeling

The 5th Wave   By Rich Tennant

"Sometimes Bill working for the city comes in real handy. Like when we decided to replace the kitchen fixtures."

In this book . . .

Quick: What's in your walls? It's hard telling, frankly, but if you're remodeling (or building brand-new walls), you have a great opportunity to make sure that your house is as healthy, energy-efficient, and ecofriendly as it can be. Doing so contributes to the big picture — a healthy planet — but to the more immediate concern of keeping yourself and your family healthy.

In this part of the book, you get a wealth of ways to put sustainable materials into your building or remodeling plan and get guidance on which products to seek and which to avoid. You discover the latest word on ways to bring green flooring, countertops, and other elements to your design plan and what to look for in heating and cooling systems.

Here are the contents of Book IV at a glance:

Chapter 1

Thinking Sustainability When You Remodel

Given the amount of wood, concrete, and steel needed to create a new home, remodeling your existing home instead of building something new is one of the greenest things you can do. The average new home uses 13,127 square feet of lumber; that's about the size of three basketball courts — and a lot of wood — that you can save by remodeling your home instead.

If your house is architecturally sound and if it has the potential to meet your needs, a well-planned renovation project can transform an ordinary house into your green dream home. If your home is more than 20 years old, chances are, it's missing important features, such as insulation, energy-efficient windows, and water-saving fixtures. A green remodel is your opportunity to fix these shortcomings, saving you money on your monthly utility bills. This chapter shows you how to turn those little annoyances into design opportunities.

Deciding Whether to Remodel

Remodeling has the potential to transform your home into something that you wouldn't even recognize when complete. Most people aren't aware of the possibilities open to them. A good architect or interior designer can help you uncover this potential.

To decide whether a remodel will work in solving your house issues, look at your current home. Do you suffer from any of the following?

✔ **Clutter:** You may think you need a bigger home to hide all that clutter. What you really need is smarter storage (and less stuff), not more space to fill with more clutter.

✔ **Noise:** People often complain that their old house has thin walls, and they can hear noise from the other rooms. Adding insulation to these walls will help make the house quieter.

✔ **Limited use:** If your dining room is too small to allow you to entertain, you may think you need a new home. An addition can convert your dining room into enough space for the perfect dinner party.

✔ **Darkness:** Even the darkest room in your home can probably be brightened with a good remodel. New windows, skylights, or nice lighting can brighten your existing home.

✔ **Problems with temperature (too hot or too cold):** You might think of your house as always uncomfortable: too hot or too cold. Adding insulation and a new heating system can greatly improve the comfort of your existing home.

If your main complaints focus on your personal comfort, a green remodel can easily turn your messy, dark, or drafty house into the perfect place to entertain friends. The following sections outline some of the benefits of remodeling and give you some questions to ask yourself in order to decide whether remodeling is right for you.

Recognizing the benefits of remodeling

Remodeling your existing home instead of building something new offers several cost savings and environmental advantages. Consider these benefits:

✔ Remodeling greatly reduces the amount of raw materials you would use if you built a new home from scratch.

✔ Remodeling involves less work than building, and less work means less construction cost.

✔ You can put the money you save in initial construction costs (over what you would have spent on a new home) toward nicer finishes and appliances.

✔ Upgrading your appliances to energy-efficient models will lower your monthly utility bills.

✔ Choosing green finishes that are low in toxins or are toxin free makes your home healthier for your family.

✔ Green buildings may fetch a higher resale price than their nongreen counterparts.

Sorting comfort from structural issues

If you're not sure whether to remodel or build a new home, ask yourself some questions:

- ✔ Are my rooms drafty?
- ✔ Is my home uncomfortable?
- ✔ Do I need more storage?
- ✔ Were my appliances purchased before 1990?
- ✔ Do I have high utility bills?
- ✔ Does my home contain lead paint?
- ✔ Do I have mold issues?
- ✔ Is there any minor dry rot in the wood in the home?
- ✔ Is my roof old and in need of replacing?
- ✔ Do I have ample space but find myself sick of the appearance?
- ✔ Do I have continual maintenance issues with my home?

Each of these questions addresses an issue of comfort — and the good news is that each of them can be remedied. If you answered *yes* to any of these questions, a well-planned remodeling project can correct these issues.

Now ask yourself the following questions:

- ✔ Does my home need major structural upgrades before work can begin?
- ✔ Does my home contain asbestos (in the shingles, insulation, or tiles, for example)?
- ✔ Does my lot not allow room for expansion?
- ✔ Is my home already overbuilt compared to the other homes in the neighborhood?
- ✔ Am I planning to move in less than five years?

Each of these questions addresses a structural or planning issue. If you answered *yes* to any of these questions, the problems with your home may be too costly to fix, and a remodel may not help.

Of course, if you're planning on selling your home in the near future, a basic remodel may help it sell faster. If you see deficiencies in your home, potential buyers will, too.

Book IV

Green Remodeling

Planning Your Remodel

When you've decided that you're ready to remodel, you may be tempted to dive right in and run out to your local home improvement center. But before you begin, you need a plan. Part of remodeling is working with existing walls, ceiling heights, and window locations. Plus, you need to consider other factors, such as your budget, the resale value of your home, and the return on your investment that you're likely to get when you sell.

For most people, planning isn't much fun. But if you don't plan, you pay for it with added costs — in time and money.

If you plan on doing any of the work yourself, make a schedule and stick to it. Half-completed remodeling projects are surprisingly easy to walk away from and never finish. Divide each task into smaller weekend projects. If you can finish each part over a single weekend, you'll be more likely to get it all done.

Considering all things financial

A key part of planning your remodel is considering the cost of the upgrades and whether and when you'll get your money back from a higher resale value.

Thinking about resale value

Looking at other homes in your neighborhood helps you determine where to focus your remodeling efforts. Look at surrounding property values and comparable homes in the area. If other homes in the area offer large master suites with walk-in closets, but yours doesn't offer much in the way of closet space, consider including a master suite in your remodeling project.

Drive around the neighborhood, talk with your neighbors, and consult a real estate agent to assess what's appropriate for your specific neighborhood.

Older homes can pose a challenge when you're remodeling, but they also have an inherent charm that's missing from most new houses. When you choose to recycle your existing home, you want to make sure that you don't lose the allure and character of your house. Those are the traits that will appeal to a buyer down the road.

Knowing where to get the most bang for your buck

You can spend a fortune remodeling a home, but not every improvement you make will reap rewards when it comes time to sell. You need to know which areas to focus on to get the most for your money.

On average, any money you spend on a remodel should increase the value of your home by one and a half times. So if you spend $10,000 on a remodel, your home should increase in value by $15,000. But certain rooms add more value than others. Here are three rooms that really pay off:

- ✔ **Bedrooms:** Adding bedrooms to your home is a great way to increase your home's value. Loosely speaking, a legal bedroom is any room with a window, access to fresh air, and a closet.

- ✔ **Kitchen:** Upgrading an old, outdated kitchen is the best investment you can make in your home. Although the kitchen is the most expensive room in a home to build, the payback in increased value is enormous.

- ✔ **Bathrooms:** Although you don't want too many bathrooms, having well-located bathrooms adds to the value of your home. A half bath (with just a toilet and sink) is less expensive than a full bathroom (with a toilet, sink, and shower or bathtub), but it carries the same value.

Most older homes have several areas you may have overlooked. You may be able to capture valuable space in the following places:

- ✔ **Attic:** If your attic is tall enough to stand in, consider adding a staircase from the floor below it and finishing the space to make a new room. Dormers are an inexpensive way to add ceiling height and windows to an existing roof. Rooms up that high may also offer a great view.

- ✔ **Basement:** Clear out those old boxes and take advantage of the space in your basement. If you have a high ceiling (or at least a ceiling of standard height — say, 8 feet), finish the space and create the perfect play room for the kids, a spare bedroom, or a movie room for the family.

If you have to excavate the floor to get more ceiling height, the costs won't be worth the added value.

Figuring out how long your payback should be

When it comes to remodeling, the length of the *payback* refers to how long it takes for you to see a return on your investment. For example, if you pay to install solar panels on your roof, how long will it take you to make up the cost of that investment and start reaping the benefits of your lower energy bills?

In general, for upgrades to the energy efficiency of your home, expect a payback of less than five years. The environment enjoys immediate, priceless effects.

Eyeing green remodeling projects

If you don't know where to start with your remodeling and you need suggestions, consider the following green projects:

Book IV

Green Remodeling

✔ **Remove moldy carpet.** Exposure to carpet mold is one of the leading causes of respiratory problems. Keeping your carpets clean and dry will prevent the growth of mold. Remove moldy carpets and fix the source of the water leaks.

✔ **Install dual-flush toilets.** In the average home, the toilet accounts for approximately 30 percent of household water. High-efficiency toilets use at least 20 percent less water than standard toilets. Dual-flush water-saving toilets save you money (about 20 percent on your monthly water bills) and reduce sewer loads, not to mention conserving water.

✔ **Install efficient windows.** Windows are thermal holes. An average home may lose 30 percent of its heat or air-conditioning energy through its windows. Energy-efficient windows save money on heating and air conditioning every month.

✔ **Install energy-efficient appliances.** The typical household spends $1,400 per year on energy bills. And in this typical home, appliances account for about 20 percent of your energy bills. You can save a lot of money — including more than $400 per year on heating bills — with high-efficiency appliances, such as Energy Star appliances.

✔ **Insulate your water heater.** Most people tend to overlook the expense of heating water for their daily needs. But 25 cents of every dollar you spend on energy goes to heat your water. Using an insulated water heater, you can save $156 (or much more, depending on energy costs) on water heating over the life span of the water heater, which is generally around ten years.

✔ **Install a low-flow showerhead.** Inexpensive and easy to install, low-flow showerheads and faucet aerators can reduce your home water consumption and your energy cost as much as 50 percent without sacrificing water pressure. You could save $100 per year on water and energy costs.

✔ **Install natural insulation in your walls and attic.** Natural insulation in walls, such as Coler Natural Insulation (www.coler.com) and Bonded Logic (www.bondedlogic.com), are highly effective and have an exceptionally low impact on the environment. By reducing heating demand, both insulations significantly reduce household carbon-dioxide emissions.

✔ **Use nontoxic cleaning methods.** Today's modern home is loaded with toxic and polluting substances. The effects of these substances range from long-term health concerns for the family to environmental pollution caused in manufacturing and disposal. Alternative, nontoxic cleaning methods are much healthier and environmentally responsible. These methods include baking soda, borax, white vinegar, isopropyl alcohol, and trisodium phosphate.

✔ **Use nontoxic paints.** Indoor paints and finishes are among the leading causes of harmful indoor gases. Recently developed low-VOC and zero-VOC paints are durable, cost-effective, and much less harmful to people and the environment.

VOC stands for *volatile organic compound*. VOCs are the harmful chemicals in paint and the source of that new-paint smell. Not all VOCs have an odor, however: don't assume that something is safe just because you can't smell it.

✔ **Install a programmable thermostat with a timer.** To maximize your energy savings without sacrificing comfort, you can install an automatic setback or programmable thermostat. If you forget to turn down the heat before you leave for work in the morning, a programmable thermostat adjusts the temperature setting for you. You can save 5 percent to 15 percent per year on energy bills by using a programmable thermostat with a timer.

✔ **Test your home for radon.** Radon is a naturally occurring gas that comes from the decay of uranium found in nearly all soils. Long-term exposure to elevated levels of radon increases your risk of lung cancer. Testing for radon is easy and inexpensive and should only take a few minutes through low-cost, do-it-yourself radon test kits, which are available in hardware stores and other retail outlets.

✔ **Insulate your roof.** Roof insulation reduces the amount of heat that flows from a house through the roof to the cold outside air. By reducing this heat loss, roof insulation reduces the amount of energy needed to heat the house in the winter. You can save 13 percent per year on your heating bills by insulating your roof.

✔ **Install solar panels.** The average solar heating system pays for itself in four to seven years. Not only can installing solar panels save you money by reducing or eliminating your electric bill, but it generates pollution-free and maintenance-free electricity. You can save $500 per year on energy bills by installing solar panels on your roof.

✔ **Switch to a solar water heater.** A solar water heater is an environmentally sustainable home energy system that doesn't produce harmful greenhouse gases. You can save 50 to 85 percent per year on your energy bills by using a solar water heater.

✔ **Install sun tunnels.** Also called solar tubes, these mini skylights are easy to install through an existing attic. Because they use flexible tubes to carry the light through your attic, you can place them almost anywhere and bring light to a previously dark corner, thereby saving money on your electric bill.

✔ **Put in a whole-house fan.** You may see up to a 30 percent savings on air-conditioning costs with a powered attic fan — if your home is well-sealed. Otherwise the fan can suck out the expensive cooled air (and suck in hot air from outside) through the leaks in your house.

Depending on the weather where you live, you may even be able to use a whole-house fan in place of an air-conditioning system to bring in cooler outside air and protect against mold or mildew caused by attic humidity.

Book IV

Green Remodeling

Remodeling Room by Room

If you're starting on a journey, you need to know where you're going. The following sections show you how you can create the ideal green kitchen, bathroom, bedroom, and nursery. Think of this section as a green road map.

Kitchens

Your kitchen is the heart of your home. Unfortunately, older homes have small, utilitarian kitchens not designed for socializing. In Figure 1-1, you can see a typical kitchen and the green features to include in your kitchen remodel:

- ✓ **Built-in recycling center:** Set aside space for recycling and composting bins to encourage their use.

- ✓ **Compact fluorescent light bulbs:** Energy-saving light bulbs save energy and money. Light the work surfaces with directional lights.

- ✓ **Energy Star dishwasher and refrigerator:** These two appliances consume more energy than any other. Find the most energy-efficient models available.

- ✓ **Flow reducer:** Save water without sacrificing water pressure with an inexpensive flow reducer or aerator.

- ✓ **Formaldehyde-free materials:** Most cabinetry is made with cheap plywood held together with formaldehyde. Select formaldehyde-free wood instead.

- ✓ **FSC-certified trim:** Choose sustainably harvested wood that is stamped from the Forest Stewardship Council (FSC).

- ✓ **Low-VOC interior paint:** Stay healthy with low- or no-VOC paints.

- ✓ **Range vented outside:** Carry the cooking fumes outside to keep the air fresh.

- ✓ **Recycled-content tile and countertops:** Gorgeous choices in tile are available with recycled metals, glass, ceramics, and paper.

- ✓ **Sustainable flooring:** Cork and linoleum are among the many new durable and comfortable green flooring choices for your kitchen.

- ✓ **Upgraded insulation:** While remodeling your kitchen, insulate the existing walls.

Because most of the energy in the home is consumed in the kitchen, these energy-saving suggestions will significantly reduce your monthly utility bills.

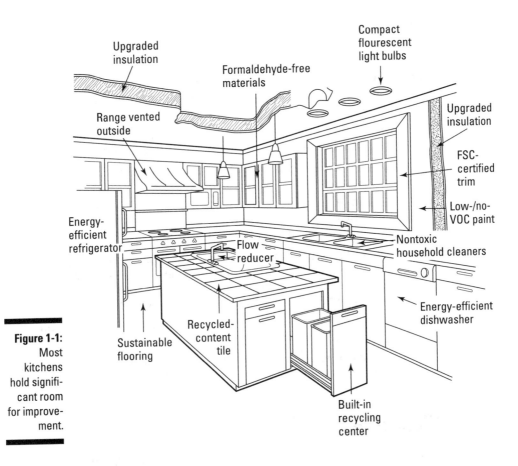

Figure 1-1:
Most kitchens hold significant room for improvement.

Bathrooms

You're in your bathroom every day, several times a day, which makes it one of the most scrutinized rooms in a house. You may focus on those ugly pink tiles from the 1980s, but appearance isn't all that matters when it comes to a green bathroom remodel: You can make some significant changes that won't affect appearance at all, but will save energy and money while helping the environment.

In Figure 1-2, you can see a typical bathroom and the green features to include in every bathroom remodel:

✔ **Water filter:** If needed, filter the water coming out of the tap with an inexpensive filter. It will improve the taste of the water and eliminate the need to buy bottled water.

✔ **Compact fluorescent bulbs:** Save money and energy with compact fluorescent bulbs. Look for color-corrected bulbs to light areas where you put on makeup.

✔ **Double-paned low-E window:** *Low-emissivity* (or low-e) windows use energy-efficient, insulated glass. Keep your heat from leaking out of your home with energy-efficient windows.

✔ **Flow reducers:** You can reduce the amount of water you use without losing water pressure by installing a simple flow reducer.

✔ **Formaldehyde-free cabinetry:** Most cabinetry is made from plywood with toxic glues. Skip the formaldehyde.

✔ **FSC-certified wood:** Buy cabinets using sustainably harvested wood stamped by the Forest Stewardship Council (FSC). Chapter 2 tells you more about FSC-certified options for your home.

✔ **Low-flow, duel flush, or ultra efficient toilet:** You can save thousands of gallons of fresh water a year by choosing a "green" toilet. They look and cost similar as their traditional counterparts, too. Look for efficient models marked with the Environmental Protection Agency's WaterSense label.

✔ **Low-VOC interior paint:** Paint the walls with a low or no-VOC paint to create a healthier room.

✔ **Recycled-content tile:** Dozens of manufacturers offer beautiful tiles made from recycled glass, stone, or ceramics.

Bedrooms

You're not conscious of much of it, but you spend a significant amount of time in your bedroom, so making sure it's a healthy retreat is important. Figure 1-3 shows opportunities for greening your bedroom.

For many people, their bedroom doubles as a TV room, office, and reading room. Avoid sleeping problems by using your bedroom only for sleeping. Design the room specifically for that purpose with black-out curtains and operable windows for fresh air.

Insulate all the walls of the bedroom with formaldehyde-free insulation to block unwanted noise from disturbing you. Turn the thermostat down and use an extra blanket instead. A timed, programmable thermostat can warm up your room before you wake up.

Select a mattress and linens made of natural materials. You can find an incredible selection at stores like Gaiam (www.gaiam.com). Select nonvinyl carpeting and low- or zero-VOC paints. Removing VOCs helps you sleep better.

Keep your electric clock away from your head. The electromagnetic field disturbs dream patterns.

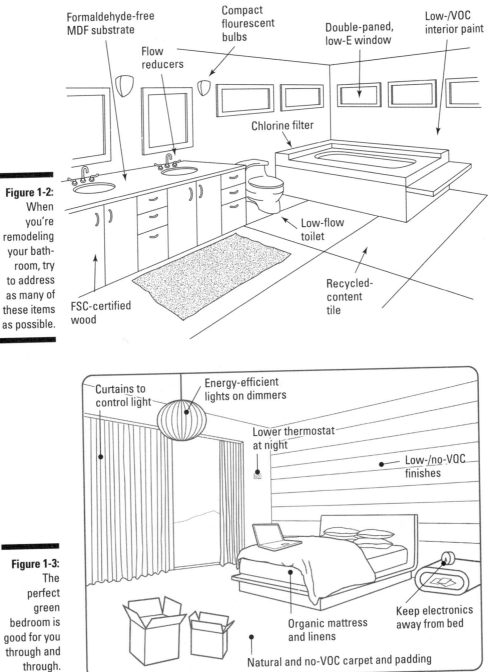

Formaldehyde-free MDF substrate

Compact flourescent bulbs

Double-paned, low-E window

Low-/VOC interior paint

Flow reducers

Chlorine filter

Figure 1-2: When you're remodeling your bathroom, try to address as many of these items as possible.

Low-flow toilet

FSC-certified wood

Recycled-content tile

Curtains to control light

Energy-efficient lights on dimmers

Lower thermostat at night

Low-/no-VOC finishes

Figure 1-3: The perfect green bedroom is good for you through and through.

Organic mattress and linens

Keep electronics away from bed

Natural and no-VOC carpet and padding

Courtesy of GreenHomeGuide.com.

Book IV

Green Remodeling

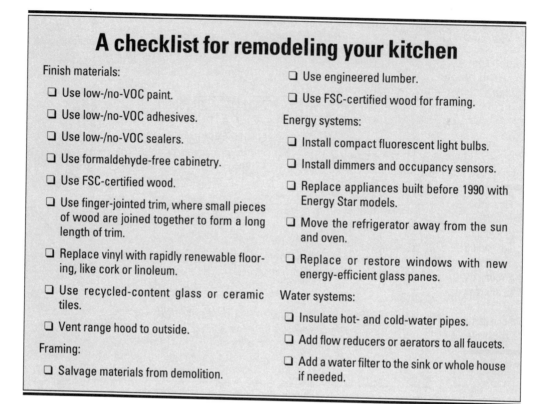

A checklist for remodeling your kitchen

Finish materials:

❑ Use low-/no-VOC paint.

❑ Use low-/no-VOC adhesives.

❑ Use low-/no-VOC sealers.

❑ Use formaldehyde-free cabinetry.

❑ Use FSC-certified wood.

❑ Use finger-jointed trim, where small pieces of wood are joined together to form a long length of trim.

❑ Replace vinyl with rapidly renewable flooring, like cork or linoleum.

❑ Use recycled-content glass or ceramic tiles.

❑ Vent range hood to outside.

Framing:

❑ Salvage materials from demolition.

❑ Use engineered lumber.

❑ Use FSC-certified wood for framing.

Energy systems:

❑ Install compact fluorescent light bulbs.

❑ Install dimmers and occupancy sensors.

❑ Replace appliances built before 1990 with Energy Star models.

❑ Move the refrigerator away from the sun and oven.

❑ Replace or restore windows with new energy-efficient glass panes.

Water systems:

❑ Insulate hot- and cold-water pipes.

❑ Add flow reducers or aerators to all faucets.

❑ Add a water filter to the sink or whole house if needed.

Nurseries

A newborn baby has not yet developed resistance to chemicals. Because babies can spend up to 18 hours a day in their nurseries, the finishes you select are even more important for their health.

In Figure 1-4, you see how to make the perfect green nursery for your newborn baby.

Try to create a nontoxic nursery using zero-VOC paints. Pregnant women should avoid painting altogether — have someone else do it. Paint at least one month before the baby is due and open the window to flush the room with fresh air.

Avoid wall-to-wall carpeting because it traps dust mites and allergens. A natural linoleum floor is the best choice, but wood works just as well. Be sure that the floor has no toxic sealers.

A bathroom remodeling checklist

Finish materials:

❑ Use low-/no-VOC paint.

❑ Use low-/no-VOC adhesives.

❑ Use low-/no-VOC sealers.

❑ Use formaldehyde-free cabinetry.

❑ Use FSC-certified wood.

❑ Use finger-jointed trim, where small pieces of wood are joined together to form a long length of trim.

❑ Replace vinyl with rapidly renewable flooring, like cork or linoleum.

❑ Use recycled-content glass or ceramic tiles.

Framing:

❑ Salvage materials from demolition.

❑ Use engineered lumber.

❑ Use FSC-certified wood for framing.

Energy systems:

❑ Install compact fluorescent light bulbs.

❑ Install dimmers and occupancy sensors.

❑ Install cellulose, recycled-content, or formaldehyde-free insulation.

❑ Caulk around windows.

❑ Replace windows with new energy-efficient windows.

Water systems:

❑ Install insulation wrap around your water heater.

❑ Convert to a tankless water heater.

❑ Insulate hot- and cold-water pipes.

❑ Add flow reducers to all faucets and showerheads.

❑ Replace toilets with high-efficiency (HET) dual-flush or low-flow models.

❑ Add a water filter to your sink if testing your water shows you that it's necessary.

In order to block and control the sunlight, use wooden shutters. Use zero-VOC paints or stains. Aluminum miniblinds work just as well as wood and don't require paint.

Select naturally finished wood furniture with pure, organic cotton and wool linens. Avoid plastic toys; most are made in China and can contain traces of lead and other potent toxins. Cloth and wood toys are a better choice.

Clean your green nursery with natural or nontoxic cleaning products. You can find some homemade cleaners in Chapter 3 of the Green Cleaning section of this book.

Book IV

Green Remodeling

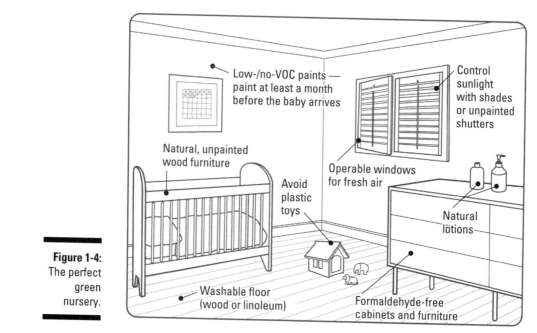

Low-/no-VOC paints —
paint at least a month
before the baby arrives

Control
sunlight
with shades
or unpainted
shutters

Natural, unpainted
wood furniture

Avoid
plastic
toys

Operable windows
for fresh air

Natural
lotions

Figure 1-4:
The perfect
green
nursery.

Washable floor
(wood or linoleum)

Formaldehyde-free
cabinets and furniture

Courtesy of GreenHomeGuide.com.

Surviving Your Remodel

Renovating your home is a stressful process. From the cost to the dust to the interruption, remodeling will turn your daily life upside down. Seeing your family home get torn apart adds to the regular construction stress. Keeping the end result in mind helps you survive these traumatic times. In the following sections, you find tips for surviving your remodel.

Living in the house during construction

Whether due to cost concerns or curiosity, you may want to live in your house during your remodel. If you're doing minor work, staying in the house during construction isn't an issue, but if you're doing an extensive remodel, it can be like living in a war zone.

Talk to your contractor about whether it'll be okay for you to live in the home during construction. If you decide to stay in the house, keep in mind the following suggestions:

- ✔ **Make sure that your contractor alerts you in advance of any interruptions to the power or water.** If you know that the power or water will be turned off, you can plan to take showers or power down your computer beforehand.

- ✔ **Plan a long vacation to coincide with the more disruptive construction work.** You may need a vacation during the remodel just to relax!

- ✔ **Create a backup plan for cooking and showering for those times when things don't go as planned.** Knowing what to do ahead of time will alleviate most of your construction stress.

The majority of the stress people feel from construction comes from having unrealistic expectations. Expect to have dust in your clothes, no access to your stuff, and early mornings when you're awakened by all the noise. If you expect the construction process to be tough, you won't be surprised by it. Set your expectations ahead of time, and you'll find yourself delighted by the result.

Health risks: Handling surprises as they come

When construction begins and the demolition opens up the walls, finding some surprises is common. Be aware of the potential health risks described in the following list:

- ✔ **Asbestos:** Asbestos was commonly used in insulation, tiles, and siding from the 1940s through the 1970s. It's dangerous if it's broken and fibers are released into the air. Don't sand or break up any material you suspect may contain asbestos. Turn to Chapter 5 of Book I to find out more about asbestos.

  Exposure to asbestos dust is dangerous! Check with your local building department for more information on asbestos abatement. You may need a licensed abatement contractor.

- ✔ **Mold:** When moisture gets into a wall and isn't given a chance to dry, mold can form. Even unseen mold can create respiratory illness and other sicknesses. Fix the source of the leak and remove the moldy and damp materials completely.

Book IV

Green Remodeling

✔ **Lead paint:** If your home was built before 1978, you could find some layers of lead paint below the current paint. Originally used as a pigment in paint, lead was found to be hazardous, because it flakes off and turns into dust, which can be inhaled.

Exposure to lead paint flakes or dust is dangerous! Your local building department can provide you with more information on removing lead from your home.

✔ **Vinyl:** Polyvinyl chloride (PVC), or vinyl, is one of the most common synthetic materials. Approximately 75 percent of all PVC manufactured is used in construction materials. It creeps into all sorts of unlikely building products. PVC is the worst plastic from an environmental health perspective, posing great environmental and health hazards in its manufacture and disposal.

Chances are, you've got vinyl in your home. As you remodel, take out the vinyl and recycle it. Your local waste company can tell you how and where to recycle vinyl.

Put some extra money in your budget to pay for these unexpected problems as they arise. Your homeowner's insurance may cover some of the expense of cleanup.

Chapter 2

Thinking about Building Materials in New Ways

*H*ow do you separate fact from fiction when it comes to the green qualities of a product or material? Part of green building and remodeling is examining materials and products and discovering methods to reduce their impact.

In this chapter, you find various methods available for examining products and selecting materials.

Looking at Life Cycle

Everything — every material, every product — has a life cycle. A *life cycle* is the journey a material goes through during its entire life. Every material starts in some raw form, is processed, and is made into a finished product. At some point — five, ten, or dozens of years later — the material reaches the end of its life and is disposed of. (In fact, most construction materials end up in a landfill.)

A life cycle is divided into three phases:

- **Production:** Raw materials are extracted and processed into a finished product. This process occurs before you even get to see the product in your home.

- **Use:** The finished product is used and needs to be operated, maintained, and repaired. The length of this stage varies from one material to the next.

- **Return:** At some point, the product is no longer needed or needs to be replaced. It's thrown into a landfill, recycled, or degrades back into some raw material.

Recognizing What Goes Into and Comes Out of Material Production

In looking at materials, you need to understand the notion of *embodied energy*. Embodied energy is all the energy and effort that went into the making of a material, including all the effort from

- **Extraction:** The material is harvested from nature.

- **Processing:** After it's harvested, the material is processed into a usable form for manufacturing.

- **Manufacturing:** The processed material is fabricated into the final product.

- **Transportation:** The finished product is shipped (often long distances) to a warehouse or store.

- **Installation:** After it arrives on the construction site, the final product must be cut, fit, and installed.

People usually overlook embodied energy when they think about green products, but it's a large portion of the overall impact of a material on the environment.

For example, the chair you're sitting on while reading this book has energy in it. Sure, it isn't plugged into the wall (unless you're sitting in one of those vibrating massage chairs!), but there *is* energy within the chair. Energy is embodied within it. Most likely someone had to farm cotton, chop down wood, forge nails, and shear sheep just to get the raw materials together. Some of these materials may have even traveled a long distance to get to the factory. All these steps involved in making the chair required energy.

After the materials were gathered up, someone had to process them into fabric and cut the wood into a structure. All these steps *also* required energy.

Finally, someone had to ship these products to the store. The store is probably located far away from the factory, so the chair had to travel by plane, truck, or train to get there. All these steps *also* required energy.

All these efforts to make your chair add up to an immense amount of energy and effort. The goal of examining this embodied energy is to find ways to reduce it. For example, if your chair were made out of salvaged scrap wood, no new trees would have to be destroyed to extract the wood. If when the wood was being cut, the leftover scraps were saved for later reuse, it would save future materials. If a local craftsman made your new chair, it wouldn't have to be shipped long distances, saving gasoline and greenhouse gas from the exhaust. Repurposing and buying local are ways that embodied energy can be reduced to lessen the environmental impact of a product.

In addition to the energy that goes into a product, keep in mind the materials that come out of manufacture and production. *Byproducts* are all the leftover materials created from the material's life cycle, stuff like the greenhouse gas that results from the manufacture of steel.

When you think of byproducts, you probably assume that they're all bad. But that's not necessarily the case. For the most part, byproducts are potentially valuable resources — we're just not smart enough to know how to deal with them yet.

 Ask product manufacturers about the byproducts they create and what they do with them. Many products now contain their own scrap recycled back into the product.

Talking to Manufacturers about Materials

Book IV

Green
Remodeling

Whenever you're choosing among various products to use in your building or remodeling project, you want to find out some key information from the products' manufacturers.

For example, say you're getting ready to buy countertops. You start by making a list of the countertops you like best. After you've identified your favorite products, find out which companies manufacture those products. For each product, write down the company's contact information alongside the name of the product and any other identifying information you can find (such as the manufacturer's product ID number). This information is often on the back of the sample you see at a showroom or store.

Not every manufacturer will have the same identifying information for every product. You just want to assemble as much identifying information as possible so that the manufacturer knows exactly which product you have a question about.

After you have your list of products and manufacturers, start by calling the first one on your list and move through your list until you've found the answers you need from every manufacturer. Be sure to ask each manufacturer the questions in the following sections — you want to be able to compare the answers to all the questions from all the manufacturers so that you can get an accurate picture of how they stack up.

You can find many of the answers to these questions from the manufacturers themselves in the form of a material safety and data sheet (MSDS). Every manufacturer is required by law to produce an MSDS for every product it sells. The MSDS includes information about the product, such as ingredients, toxicity, health effects, proper storage, disposal, and special handling procedures. The exact contents of the MSDS will vary from product to product, but they're basically the same.

You can request the MSDS directly from the manufacturer or find the MSDS online at Web sites such as MSDS Search (www.msdssearch.com). In addition, each sales representative should be able to provide some answers about the products he sells. If the sales rep doesn't know, ask him to find out.

Where did this material come from?

From the obvious (wood comes from trees) to the obscure (linoleum comes from linseed oil), this question explores the source of the product. When looking for green materials, try to choose one of the following options:

- **Reclaimed:** Reusing materials salvaged from other uses, reclaimed materials offer old material quality no longer available. For example, the siding of an old barn can be milled into new flooring.

- **Recycled:** Unlike reclaimed materials, recycled materials are put back into the material production and reprocessed into new finishes. Sourced from various materials, recycled materials often have slight imperfections that add to the final appearance. For example, glass tiles can be made from recycled windshields.

- **Sustainably harvested:** Yielding materials without completely destroying the chance for future harvesting, sustainable-harvested materials will be around for future generations. Look for lumber certified as being grown in and harvested from managed forests. The Forest Stewardship Council (www.fscus.org) is a great resource.

✔ **Rapidly renewable:** Instead of needing the 50+ years required to grow an entire forest, rapidly renewable materials grow back within ten years. These resources also offer some unique aesthetic options. For example, cork flooring comes from the bark of a cork tree; cork will grow back in less than seven years. Bamboo is another popular and rapidly renewable resource and great for sturdy flooring.

In addition to helping preserve our resources, these materials also offer finishes that are often more unusual and attractive than their traditional counterparts.

What are the byproducts of the manufacturing process?

The manufacturing of any product brings with it some unwanted results. These byproducts are frequently difficult to measure precisely, but they're easy to identify in a general way. Deforestation, pollution, global warming, and landfill debris are the most common byproducts to look for.

Most manufacturers aren't fully aware of the impact of their own products. By asking the questions in this section, you're actually helping bring green issues to the attention of the manufacturer.

Look for products where the manufacturing process is low in pollution. Make sure that the manufacturer did not destroy something else to get to this material.

How is the material delivered and installed?

The average item on a grocery-store shelf travels over 1,500 miles to get there. (The traveling your groceries do to find their place in the aisles is referred to as *food miles*.) Most of the products people use trek great distances to reach them. Choosing locally produced materials will lessen the energy used. When building, select local materials that traveled less than 500 miles to get to you.

The installation of the materials may require additional finishes, such as sealers on a granite countertop or urethane coatings on a wood floor. These things add to the labor (and the cost) of using this material. Pick materials that don't need these extra finishes.

Book IV

Green Remodeling

How is the material maintained and operated?

From sealers and lacquers to paints and oils, many materials require continual care and maintenance. Other products require constant energy, even when they're not in use. Give preference to products that are durable and easily repaired. Does this product need continual energy by being plugged in all the time, or does it use batteries? Does it need to be painted (and then repainted)?

How healthy are the materials?

Most people in the United States spend 80 to 90 percent of their time indoors, so the healthy aspects of the materials used in home construction is important. From the paint on the walls, to the hidden adhesives under the rug, most people's homes are full of pollutants. Specifically choosing healthy materials will reduce these dangers.

What do you do with the materials when you're done with them?

The product manufacturer should be able to tell you how to safely dispose of their products. Most might just tell you to "throw it in the trash," which isn't a good answer. Look for materials that are recyclable so that they can be reused in the future.

The typical kitchen remodel is good for 15 years. By the time your new kitchen is ready for a facelift, you may have moved to a new home. Designing with durable, recyclable, or biodegradable materials will help ensure safe reuse, even if you aren't around. Look for the following traits in the materials you use in your home:

- ✔ **Durability:** If the product is durable, it will have a longer life, and you'll use it for a longer period of time.

- ✔ **Recyclability:** If you don't mind taking special care to recycle a material, then choose something that will be recyclable, which is the best choice.

- ✔ **Biodegradability:** If you think you'll just end up throwing the product in the trash, at least choose a biodegradable material. *Biodegradable* means that the product can break down naturally and not spread toxins into the ground.

Putting Standard Materials to the Life Cycle Test

Buildings consume a whopping 40 percent of the world's materials. The construction of a typical 2,000-square-foot home uses approximately

- ✔ 1,397 tons of concrete
- ✔ 13,127 board feet of framing lumber
- ✔ 6,212 square feet of plywood sheathing
- ✔ 2,325 square feet of exterior siding material
- ✔ 3,100 square feet of roofing material
- ✔ 3,061 square feet of insulation
- ✔ 6,144 square feet of drywall
- ✔ 2,085 square feet of flooring material (carpet, tile, or wood)

With all the materials that go into a single home, the impact on the environment is immense. In the following sections, you find some of the more traditional and common construction products put to the life-cycle test.

Concrete

From the walls of the foundation to the mortar in the tile, concrete is used in nearly every construction project. You can't avoid it. Here's a look at the life cycle of concrete:

- ✔ **Where does concrete come from?** Concrete is natural, made up of sand, Portland cement, stone, and water. *Verdict:* Good.

- ✔ **What are the byproducts of making concrete?** The production of the chief ingredient — Portland cement — requires an immense amount of energy, and the byproduct is greenhouse gases. *Verdict:* Bad.

- ✔ **How is concrete delivered and installed?** Concrete can be made locally or even right on the job site. *Verdict:* Good.

- ✔ **How is concrete maintained and operated?** Concrete is durable, can be left unpainted, and is virtually maintenance free. *Verdict:* Good.

- ✔ **How healthy is concrete?** Concrete is stable and does not release any harmful chemicals. *Verdict:* Good.

- ✔ **What do we do with concrete after we're done with it?** Concrete is technically recyclable and could be reused. However, reuse and recycling don't happen with concrete as often as they should. *Verdict:* Fair.

Book IV

Green Remodeling

By asking these simple questions, you can see the only real issue with using concrete comes from the byproducts created from Portland cement. But instead of using Portland cement, you can use fly ash. *Fly ash,* the soot byproduct of coal-fired electric plants, can substitute for 15 percent to 50 percent of the Portland cement in the concrete. This substitution saves 44 trillion BTUs of energy annually in the United States, while preventing the mercury content of the fly ash from seeping into the food and water supply.

Bottom line: Fly ash concrete is the most responsible choice. After it's mixed with concrete, the mercury in the fly ash is safe and completely contained. Any concrete contractor or structural engineer can find sources of fly ash. For more information, visit www.flyash.com.

Wood

Nearly all (some 90 percent) of the homes built in the United States are framed out of wood. Plus, if you consider trim, furniture, cabinets, and doors, wood is used throughout the design of a home. Here's how wood stands up to the life cycle test:

- ✔ **Where does wood come from?** Wood is natural and renewable, coming from various species of trees. *Verdict:* Good.

- ✔ **What are the byproducts of harvesting wood?** Most wood is sourced from the clear-cutting of forests. Cutting down the forest just to get to the wood is like shoveling up the lawn to get the blades of grass. *Verdict:* Bad.

- ✔ **How is wood delivered and installed?** Most wood comes from the Pacific Northwest and Canada and is shipped around the United States and Canada. Energy is required to ship and mill the wood. Wood is installed easily, and the most junior person on the construction site knows how to work with wood. *Verdict:* Fair.

- ✔ **How is wood maintained and operated?** The wood itself is durable and easily refinished, but it's traditionally covered with sealers and coatings that release harmful chemicals. *Verdict:* Fair.

- ✔ **How healthy is wood?** The wood itself is very healthy, because it's a natural material. However, it's often finished with chemical sealers. *Verdict:* Good.

- ✔ **What do we do with wood after we're done with it?** Wood can be reclaimed and milled into other uses. It can be recycled and turned into particle board. *Verdict:* Good.

The source of wood has the greatest environmental impact. Instead of using wood from destructive sources, you can get sustainably harvested wood. Certified by the Forest Stewardship Council (www.fscus.org), this wood has been certified to come from well-managed sources. Expect to pay 20 percent more for sustainably harvested wood than you would pay otherwise.

Glass

You probably couldn't imagine your home without glass. The windows and doors of your home rely on glass to let in light and provide you with the views of your yard or neighborhood. Other products, such as glass tile and lighting fixtures, make glass one of the most common materials in your home. So how does glass stack up on the life-cycle test?

- ✔ **Where does glass come from?** Glass is made from sand, specifically silica. It comes from a natural and abundant raw material. *Verdict:* Good.

- ✔ **What are the byproducts of producing glass?** The formation of glass requires heat and molten tin, which requires energy and produces some greenhouse-gas emissions in the process. *Verdict:* Fair.

- ✔ **How is glass delivered and installed?** Unlike most other construction materials, glass is often produced locally and is available everywhere. *Verdict:* Good.

- ✔ **How is glass maintained and operated?** Except for protection from the occasional flying baseball, glass is durable and easily maintained. It requires only simple cleaning. *Verdict:* Good.

- ✔ **How healthy is glass?** Glass is completely inert and does not release any chemicals. It is also mold resistant, unlike other exterior materials like wood. *Verdict:* Good.

- ✔ **What do we do with glass after we're done with it?** Glass is one of the most commonly recycled materials on the planet. Americans recycle 20 percent of the glass we use. *Verdict:* Good.

Glass is already a very green material, but using recycled glass lessens its minimal impact further. Producing recycled glass requires less energy because the crushed recycled glass melts at a lower temperature. Recycled glass products are readily and easily available and often aren't even advertised as recycled. The costs are the same as new glass.

Book IV

Green Remodeling

Steel

The high strength of steel makes it ideal for use in structural beams and foundations. But steel is also used in everything from cabinets, to furniture, to doorknobs. You find steel everywhere. Here's how steel measures up on the life-cycle test:

- ✔ **Where does steel come from?** Structural steel is an alloy produced from iron ore. Mined out of the earth, the production of steel creates extensive environmental destruction. *Verdict:* Bad.

- ✔ **What are the byproducts of producing steel?** The steel industry is one of the largest energy consumers in manufacturing. The intense heat required in steel production comes from the burning of coal and releases thousands of tons of greenhouse gas as a result. *Verdict:* Bad.

✔ **How is steel delivered and installed?** Steel is produced in a relatively small number of plants around the United States. Due to the weight and size of most steel elements, it requires a great deal of energy to transport. *Verdict:* Fair.

✔ **How is steel maintained and operated?** The strength and durability of steel is unsurpassed. It requires little, if no, maintenance. *Verdict:* Good.

✔ **How healthy is steel?** Steel is inert and doesn't release any chemicals. *Verdict:* Good.

✔ **What do we do with steel after we're done with it?** Steel is highly recyclable. Steel has risen in price in the last decade, making it one of the most valuable resources to save from the demolition pile. (In fact, many contractors have to lock up their construction sites at night to prevent the steel awaiting installation from being stolen.) *Verdict:* Good.

The embodied energy of steel creates a great deal of environmental impact. Because of the cost of the energy required to mine and produce it, most structural steel contains up to 80 percent recycled content in order to lower costs. If you're using steel in your construction project, look for the highest recycled content available.

Brick

Bricks add a rustic and human scale to a home. In the U.S. Northeast and Midwest, brick is a common finish material in buildings. Bricks also make attractive walkways and fireplaces. Here's where brick comes out on the life-cycle test:

✔ **Where does brick come from?** Dating back nearly 10,000 years, brick is a ceramic material created from the firing of clay. It's a natural material and doesn't have the same impact as the mining or quarrying of stone. Aggressive clay mining can destroy farmland. *Verdict:* Fair.

✔ **What are the byproducts of producing brick?** Because of the heat required to fire the clay, brick production demands high energy and generates some greenhouse gases. *Verdict:* Bad.

✔ **How is brick delivered and installed?** Bricks are produced at locations across the country, meaning that in general they don't travel far to get to you. Their relatively small, modular size makes them very resource efficient and encourages use of the entire brick. *Verdict:* Good.

✔ **How is brick maintained and operated?** The thermal mass of brick helps maintain the temperature of the building. The brick itself requires little maintenance. *Verdict:* Good.

✔ **How healthy is brick?** Brick is inert and does not release any chemicals. *Verdict:* Good.

✔ **What do we do with brick after we're done with it?** Although technically recyclable, most people don't pay much attention to protecting bricks during demolition. If preserved, reclaimed bricks have a certain charm. *Verdict:* Fair.

The durability, strength, and natural material of brick make it a good choice for green building. Reclaimed bricks don't require the embodied energy of new bricks.

Drywall

Drywall is one of the most common materials used in construction today. Walls are typically covered with drywall, making it one of the most common materials in a home. Here's how drywall stacks up on the life-cycle test:

✔ **Where does drywall come from?** Drywall, often referred to as *gypsum board,* is the traditional wall finish for interior walls and ceilings. This rigid panel consists of an inner core of gypsum plaster, wrapped with paper. *Verdict:* Fair.

✔ **What are the byproducts of producing drywall?** The gypsum is mined and creates some substantial environmental impact. *Verdict:* Bad.

✔ **How is drywall delivered and installed?** Formed into wide boards, drywall lends itself to leftover pieces created in the course of installation. (Up to 17 percent of drywall is wasted during construction.) Because it generally comes in 4-foot widths, designing (or having your architect design) rooms to be some module of 4 feet reduces waste. Drywall can't be left unfinished; it's typically painted. Use a zero-VOC or low-VOC paint to reduce the release of chemicals. *Verdict:* Good.

✔ **How is drywall maintained and operated?** Drywall is easily patched and repainted. *Verdict:* Good.

✔ **How healthy is drywall?** Drywall is a relatively healthy material, especially when a healthy paint is used to finish it. *Verdict:* Good.

✔ **What do we do with drywall after we're done with it?** Drywall is easily damaged in the demolition process, making it difficult to recycle into a reusable form. Scrap pieces of drywall can be recycled if separated from the other construction waste. *Verdict:* Fair.

Given the impact of gypsum mining, using recycled-content drywall is a great idea. Several manufacturers offer recycled-content drywall paper as well.

Book IV

Green Remodeling

Vinyl

Vinyl creeps into a surprising number of construction products. It can be found in everything from pipes, to floor tile, to windows. Here's where vinyl comes out on the life-cycle test:

- ✔ **Where does vinyl come from?** Vinyl, also referred to as *polyvinyl chloride* (PVC), is a type of plastic polymer made from petroleum, and is one of the most common synthetic materials. *Verdict:* Bad.

- ✔ **What are the byproducts of producing vinyl?** Often referred to as the "poison plastic," vinyl has been linked to numerous rare cancers occurring in the factory workers and in neighborhoods surrounding the production plants. *Verdict:* Bad.

- ✔ **How is vinyl delivered and installed?** So toxic it is only produced in a handful of locations, raw vinyl is shipped to thousands of manufacturers around the world to be made into everything from siding to children's toys. It has to travel vast distances, using immense amounts of energy. *Verdict:* Fair.

- ✔ **How is vinyl maintained and operated?** Vinyl is incredibly flexible and durable. It does not require additional painting or finishing. *Verdict:* Good.

- ✔ **How healthy is vinyl?** In its final state, vinyl is inert and does not release chemicals. In a fire, however, vinyl produces smoke fumes so toxic that they can kill the inhabitants in 20 minutes. The health issues surrounding the production of vinyl are severe. *Verdict:* Bad.

- ✔ **What do we do with vinyl after we're done with it?** Although technically recyclable, vinyl is so *difficult* to recycle that most recycling plants will not accept it. Even if it does manage to find its way to a recycling center, it can only be made into more vinyl. *Verdict:* Bad.

When most people think of vinyl, they probably think fondly of their old vinyl LP records. But the truth about vinyl is less romantic. PVC appears in thousands of different formulations and configurations. Approximately 75 percent of all PVC manufactured is used in construction materials. PVC is the worst plastic from an environmental-health perspective, posing great environmental and health hazards in its manufacture, product life, and disposal. Fortunately, healthier alternatives exist. For a list of alternatives to vinyl, visit www.healthybuilding.net/pvc.

Looking to Trusted Green Certification Programs When Shopping for Materials

Several wonderful green certification programs have emerged as well-respected, trusted names. Similar to the Good Housekeeping Seal, these programs give you some assurance of product claims:

- ✔ **Cradle to Cradle Certification** (www.c2ccertified.com): Cradle to Cradle (C2C) certifies a high standard for "environmentally intelligent" design. C2C examines the entire life cycle of a material to ensure the most environmentally friendly material available.

- ✔ **Forest Stewardship Council** (www.fscus.org): The FSC seal of approval is something you find on wood products certifying that wood has been *sustainably harvested,* meaning the forests have been protected to last for future generations. Look for the FSC logo as the greenest choice in purchasing wood products.

- ✔ **GREENGUARD** (www.greenguard.org): GREENGUARD is an independent organization that has developed standards for adhesives, appliances, ceiling, flooring, insulation, paint, and wall-covering products. The GREENGUARD logo indicates interior materials with low chemical emissions.

- ✔ **Green Seal** (www.greenseal.org): Green Seal's environmental standards for paints, household cleaners, and window products date back to the mid-1990s, and the products are independently tested so there's no bias. The Green Seal logo indicates the product has gone through the rigorous Green Seal testing standards. The seal is used on paints, paper, cleaners, and even on hotels to certify the overall environmental quality.

- ✔ **Scientific Certification Systems** (www.scscertified.com): Scientific Certification Systems (SCS) has developed a certification program for environmentally preferable products and services, such as adhesives and sealants, cabinetry and casework, carpet, doors, flooring, paints, and wall coverings. The SCS logo is an independent certification that the product lives up to its environmental claims, including the amount of recycled content and the amount of chemicals released.

Book IV

Green Remodeling

Setting Priorities and Goals for Your Home

Green building is riddled with contradictions. For example, should you choose the bamboo that was sustainably harvested but came from 3,000 miles away? Or should you opt for the wood from trees that *weren't* sustainably harvested but were grown locally?

Evaluate each decision on a project-by-project basis. For example, if you plan on remodeling again in just a few years, using the bamboo wouldn't be the most environmentally correct choice. But if this floor will be around for the next foreseeable decade or so, bamboo may be a wise decision.

Here's a recommended list of priorities when it comes to choosing products for your green building or remodeling project. The items at the top of the list in this example are more important than the ones at the bottom of the list. Look for

- **Natural, nontoxic:** These products are healthy, nonsynthetic, and grown (not mixed).

- **Low embodied energy:** These products are easy to gather and nonpolluting.

- **Sustainably harvested:** These products are gathered without completely destroying the source.

- **Recyclable/biodegradable:** These products can be reused or fed back into the earth.

- **Recycled content:** These products contain a high percentage of materials that used to be something else.

- **Locally harvested:** These products didn't travel more than 500 miles to reach you.

- **Durable:** These products are built to last and don't require ongoing maintenance.

Feel free to rearrange these priorities to fit your own values. The key is to set these priorities before you find yourself standing in your home-improvement store or talking about products with your contractor. That way, you're prepared for all the decisions you need to make.

Today, you have the option of dozens of green, healthy, and more responsible new materials. For every traditional, unhealthy finish you normally find in a building, a green substitute exists. In most cases, you can play this substitution game on a one-for-one basis. Table 2-1 provides some examples. (**Remember:** This list isn't exhaustive — these items are just a few examples.)

Table 2-1	Green Material Substitutions
Instead of . . .	**Try . . .**
Latex wall paints	Zero-VOC paints
Vinyl floor tile	Natural linoleum
Oil-based floor sealers	Water-based sealers or natural linseed oil
Drywall wall panels	100 percent recycled gypsum panels
Vinyl wallpaper	Natural fabrics, such as hemp, jute, sawgrass, or bamboo
Melamine plastic cabinets (white)	Formaldehyde-free medium density fiberboard (MDF)
Carpet with vinyl backing	Carpet with natural fiber backing
Plastic carpet padding	Natural jute carpet padding
Plastic tiles and plastic laminate countertops	Recycled glass tiles, recycled quarry tiles, recycled paper resin panels, bamboo, or other green materials

Instead of seeing the lack of simple, straightforward answers about materials as a problem, try to look at them as opportunities. At each stage of the life cycle, you have the opportunity to improve on the impact and save money. Table 2-2 lists some of these opportunities.

Table 2-2	Opportunities throughout a Material's Life Cycle
Stage of the Life Cycle	**Opportunities**
Raw-material source	Choose sustainably harvested wood.
	Use products made of reclaimed materials.
	Choose finishes with a high recycled content.
Supply-chain process	Avoid mined materials, such as granite and gypsum.
	Avoid synthetic polymers.
Manufacturing process	Use fly-ash concrete.
	Use products with a low embodied energy.
	Select materials you can create on-site, such as mixed concrete.
Delivery/receiving	Use local materials.
	Hire local craftspeople.

Book IV

Green Remodeling

(continued)

Table 2-2 (continued)	
Stage of the Life Cycle	Opportunities
Installation	Design modular sections to reduce construction waste.
	Focus on standard sizes (2 x 4, 4 x 8, and so on) to save money and speed up construction time.
Operation	Opt for solar or alternative energy.
	Install low-flow plumbing fixtures.
	Avoid painted finishes.
Repair	Use modular fixtures.
	Use tiles instead of full carpet.
Reuse	Salvage what's there instead of demolishing it and starting over.
	Use existing buildings.
Disassembly	Use recyclable materials.
	Avoid PVC — it's nearly impossible to recycle.

Remodeling an Old Home with Green Materials

Older homes pose certain challenges in remodeling. But not only do older buildings have a certain charm that their newer counterparts can't fake, but remodeling an older home can save thousands of pounds of new items.

In the following sections, you find some of the common issues that come up in remodeling old homes. Don't panic! These are normal issues for you to be on the lookout for.

Salvaging the wood

The studs in an older home are typically old growth wood, in true size 2-x-4-inch studs, and they're very easy to salvage and reuse. The walls you remove may be over the existing wood floor and a simple refinishing will revive those old floors. But watch out! You can't simply take old wood and use it to build a new structural wall. Consult with your architect or structural engineer before doing anything structural with salvaged wood.

Demolishing a few old walls is minor, but you'll probably need a permit from your local building department.

Being aware of asbestos

Asbestos is a durable, insulating, fire-resistant material widely used from the 1950s through the 1970s. When certain unusual cancer cases were attributed to asbestos, its use was banned. Old asbestos tiles may be lurking under your carpet or wood floor. That old resilient sheet flooring in your home may not be vinyl — if it's more than 30 years old, the floor may be vinyl asbestos tile (VAT). Covering the side of your home may be asbestos shingles.

Asbestos is only an immediate threat if the material is broken, releasing fibers into the air. But exposure to asbestos dust is dangerous! If you own an older home and you're planning to do any remodeling, check with your local building department for more information on asbestos *abatement* (removal). You may need a licensed asbestos abatement contractor to do the job. Asbestos cannot (and should not) be recycled. The licensed abatement contractor will dispose of it for you.

Looking out for lead paint

For centuries, lead was used as a pigment and binding agent in most paints. Banned in 1978, lead-based paints were found to cause nervous system damage, hearing loss, stunted growth, reduced IQ, and delayed development. It's especially dangerous to young children whose immune systems are still developing. Lead affects every organ in the body. And children aren't the only ones at risk. Adults are not immune from the dangers of lead paint; for example, it can cause reproductive problems in men.

You've probably heard that lead-based paint is harmful to children because they eat large flakes of broken lead paint. That's true, but a more insidious danger is that you and anyone else in your household may unknowingly inhale microscopic dust.

The most practical method of protecting everyone in your home from lead-based paint is to keep any old paint intact. Do not sand, scrape, or remove any old paint until you're sure it isn't lead based. You can buy a lead testing kit at your local hardware store. A licensed paint contractor can also help.

A professional lead-abatement specialist can remove lead-based paint in your home. Your local painter can provide referrals for these professionals.

Book IV

Green Remodeling

Chapter 3

Green Finish and Construction Materials

*P*erhaps no other aspect of green building garners more attention or excitement than the finishes inside the home; the multitude of tile, paint, and counter finishes make homeowners' heads spin. In this chapter, you find out about your options for covering floors, walls, and ceilings. You also explore the necessary adhesives, caulks, and other materials lurking behind your walls. This chapter makes the daunting task of finding and selecting green finishes easier.

Identifying the Dangers in Traditional Finishes

Most standard construction materials contain a wide array of unhealthy or toxic chemicals. You don't need to put these materials in your mouth to be affected by them; they release harmful chemicals into the room — a process called *off-gassing*.

Figure 3-1 shows some of these common chemicals hidden in your home, lurking behind the walls. Because you can't see the chemicals, preventing them from entering your home is more of a challenge.

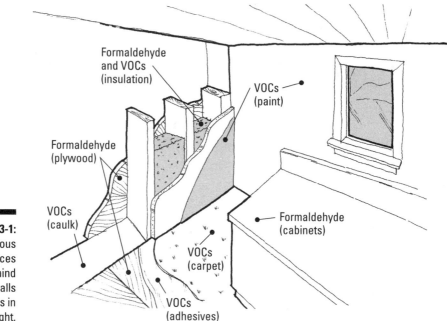

Figure 3-1:
Hazardous
substances
lurk behind
your walls
as well as in
plain sight.

Volatile organic compounds

You know that new carpet or new paint smell? Not a good thing. In fact, what you're sniffing are harmful chemicals known as volatile organic compounds (VOCs). When you install traditional products, they begin to evaporate and release these VOCs into the air, which results in that familiar odor. Even after the odor goes away, though, these materials continue to release VOCs.

Just because you can't smell anything doesn't mean the air is clear. The drying of paints, stains, caulks, and adhesives all can release VOCs into the air.

VOCs can refer to a large number of potentially harmful chemicals. The long-term effects of exposure to VOCs are still not fully understood. Because the VOCs come from dozens of sources around your house, it's impossible to point to one specific chemical or side effect.

Although you can't see VOCs, if you build or remodel your home with low or no-VOC finishes, you notice a difference. A healthy, green home doesn't smell.

Formaldehyde

One of the most common indoor pollutants is formaldehyde — the same chemical scientists use to preserve dead bodies. Formaldehyde is a known *carcinogen* (cancer-causing chemical). Formaldehyde-based adhesives are used throughout the construction process, from kitchen cabinets, to insulation, to furniture. Small particles of formaldehyde continue to be released into the air years after these products have been installed.

Hidden Materials: What's Behind the Walls

Hidden within your home, behind the walls and under the floors, lay dozens of materials that you probably don't even think about. But these materials can have a major impact on your health and the environment. Finding healthier and more sustainable substitutes for these unseen materials is important.

Insulation

Inside the walls of your home is some sort of insulation, which helps hold in temperature to lower your heating and cooling bills and is the best way to save energy in your home. Generally, insulation is like a coat on a cold day — the thicker it is, the more comfortable you are inside.

For a new house, you should add as much insulation as will fit into the walls. For an existing home, adding insulation to finished walls is much more difficult. In either case, choose the insulation best for the health of you and your family.

Many different types of insulation are available. Generally, formaldehyde is used as a binding agent in most insulation products. Look for formaldehyde-free products instead:

- ✔ **Batt insulation:** Choose formaldehyde-free and recycled cotton insulation. Bonded Logic (www.bondedlogic.com) offers recycled cotton insulation made from old blue jeans, making the insulation batts blue in color.

- ✔ **Loose-fill cellulose:** Choose natural cellulose made from recycled newsprint. It's treated with natural chemicals to make it fire resistant. Cellulose is naturally formaldehyde free.

- ✔ **Spray-in foams:** Choose natural soy-based foams. They're healthier and offer all the benefits of spray foam.

Book IV

Green Remodeling

Sheathing

No matter what type of siding you have on your home, underneath it sits a hidden layer of plywood called *sheathing*. Sheathing adds strength to your walls and serves as a barrier to moisture.

The typical type of sheathing used is plywood, which comes from trees and is glued together with a toxic formaldehyde-based binder. As a green substitute, select plywood that's certified by the Forest Stewardship Council (FSC) and is formaldehyde free.

Oriented-strand board (OSB) is an efficient alternative to plywood. OSB is made of small scraps of low-grade wood. As with any wood product, choosing FSC-certified wood with formaldehyde-free glue is a good idea. Because plywood adds strength to your walls, you should check with your architect or structural engineer to see if OSB will provide enough strength for your project.

Certified wood: A look at the Forest Stewardship Council

The Forest Stewardship Council (FSC) is an international agency that promotes the use of *sustainably harvested wood,* which is wood gathered from well-managed forests.

Not all wood is created equal. Although structural lumber is stamped to indicate the quality and strength, you can't determine whether a forest was clear-cut in order to get the wood. The FSC was created in 1993 to provide an independent certification for just this reason. The FSC stamp is a guarantee that the wood came from a sustainably managed forest.

The FSC is an independent, not-for-profit, non-government organization. The FSC sets standards that reflect agreed-upon principles for responsible forest management and accredits organizations that certify the achievement of those standards by specific forests or woodlands. These certifiers track each company and their supply chains back to FSC-certified sources. This *chain of custody* certification assures that consumers can trust the FSC seal.

The term *chain of custody* refers to the path taken by raw materials harvested from an FSC-certified source through processing, manufacturing, and distribution until it is a final product ready for sale to the consumer. In the case of a house, this includes framing lumber, trim, or plywood. Any product made of wood is now available from an FSC-certified source.

The FSC has developed the following list of the Ten Principles of Forest Stewardship to address the issues and impacts surrounding forest management:

Principle #1: Compliance with Laws and FSC Principles: Forest management shall respect all applicable laws of the country in which they occur, and international treaties and agreements to which the country is a signatory, and comply with all FSC Principles and Criteria.

Principle #2: Tenure and Use Rights and Responsibilities: Long-term tenure and use rights to the land and forest resources shall be clearly defined, documented, and legally established.

Principle #3: Indigenous Peoples' Rights: The legal and customary rights of indigenous peoples to own, use, and manage their lands, territories, and resources shall be recognized and respected.

Principle #4: Community Relations and Workers' Rights: Forest management operations shall maintain or enhance the long-term social and economic well being of forest workers and local communities.

Principle #5: Benefits from the Forest: Forest management operations shall encourage the efficient use of the forest's multiple products and services to ensure economic viability and a wide range of environmental and social benefits.

Principle #6: Environmental Impact: Forest management shall conserve biological diversity and its associated values, water resources, soils, and unique and fragile ecosystems and landscapes, and, by so doing, maintain the ecological functions and the integrity of the forest.

Principle #7: Management Plan: A management plan — appropriate to the scale and intensity of the operations — shall be written, implemented, and kept up to date.

The long-term objectives of management, and the means of achieving them, shall be clearly stated.

Principle #8: Monitoring and Assessment: Monitoring shall be conducted — appropriate to the scale and intensity of forest management — to assess the condition of the forest, yields of forest products, chain of custody, management activities, and their social and environmental impacts.

Principle #9: Maintenance of High Conservation Value Forests: Management activities in high conservation value forests shall maintain or enhance the attributes which define such forests. Decisions regarding high conservation value forests shall always be considered in the context of a precautionary approach.

Principle #10: Plantations: Plantations shall be planned and managed in accordance with Principles and Criteria 1–9, and Principle 10 and its Criteria. While plantations can provide an array of social and economic benefits, and can contribute to satisfying the world's needs for forest products, they should complement the management of, reduce pressures on, and promote the restoration and conservation of natural forests.

For more information on the Forest Stewardship Council, go to www.fsc.org.

Caulks and adhesives

The thousands of cracks and leaks in a typical home are filled with a sealant called *caulk*. Sealing these cracks is an important part of saving energy in a building, but these products are typically made from chemicals containing VOCs and are blown in using ozone-depleting chlorofluorocarbons (CFCs). Adhesives are also used throughout a building in hundreds of hidden locations. These adhesives typically contain toxic chemicals containing VOCs.

Look for products with non-ozone-depleting blowing agents. Look for the term *ozone-safe* on the label. Also, choose water-based products with low-VOC or zero-VOC content.

Stains and sealers

The countless stains, sealers, and lacquers used in a home typically go unnoticed. Because they're traditionally oil-based, when you use these products, you have to wear gloves and a mask. After installation, they continue to give off fumes for years — sometimes many years — and unless you're wearing a mask 24/7, you're breathing in those fumes.

Choose water-based and low-VOC or zero-VOC products instead. You'll be thankful for the headache you *don't* get after using them.

All-natural linseed oil (made from flaxseed) is a healthy and effective sealant for wall and floor surfaces. Just make sure to avoid linseed oils mixed with drying agents; these add unnecessary toxins to the air. Natural beeswax is a wonderful finish for plaster, concrete, and furniture.

Constructing and Covering Your Walls

Whether the walls of your home are constructed out of traditional wood framing or built green out of straw bales, all your walls must be completed with some protective and decorative finish. This section introduces you to the various types of wall finishes available and lets you know what to look for when you're shopping.

Paints and coatings

Some 40,000 years ago, people covered their walls with early cave paintings drawn with natural pigments of red ochre and charcoal. Although we still decorate our walls, paint has evolved into the ubiquitous finish for all our interiors.

Paint poses some potential health concerns because it consists of pigments held together with a binding agent. These binding agents contain VOCs, which are released into the air.

Nearly all the major paint manufacturers now offer a low-VOC line of paints, but be careful: The term *low* is hard to define. Check the labels for the exact content of VOCs. Instead of low-VOC, purchase zero-VOC paints from healthy-paint manufacturers such as AFM Safecoat (www.afmsafecoat.com or Mythic (www.mythicpaint.com).

Always wear gloves and a respirator mask while painting, especially if you're using a paint sprayer. After painting, open the windows and flush the home with fresh air for a few days. All these measures will lead to a healthier and happier home.

Recycle or donate all your leftover paint. Your local salvage yard or hardware store may take back your remaining gallons. *Never dump paint down the drain.* You can dispose of it safely, however, by letting it dry first. After it has completely solidified (just leave off the lid for several days), you can put it in with your regular trash.

Earthen plaster

As an alternative to paint, earthen plaster is a beautiful finish for your walls. Made from a pure mix of clay and natural pigments, earthen plaster is also healthy and naturally mold resistant.

The plaster is applied directly onto drywall with a trowel and can be finished smooth or with a heavy texture for a variety of looks. Applying earthen plaster is surprisingly easy to do yourself, and you can keep any leftover plaster and reuse it in the future simply by adding some water.

You can use plaster in a damp area such as a bathroom, but make sure that you seal with a water-based sealer any areas that may get splashed.

Wall coverings

For something more interesting than a solid color of paint, wall coverings offer a way to introduce patterns and textures into your home. Unfortunately, most wallpaper is made of vinyl, an environmentally harmful product.

Skip the vinyl and instead look at the large number of beautiful options available. Natural fibers, such as jute and raffia, create a soft texture on your walls. Natural paper wall coverings are available from several manufacturers, with an incredible assortment of colors and patterns. Old-fashioned wallpaper paste is already natural and healthy, so choose it over synthetic brands.

Book IV

Green Remodeling

If you're thinking about putting wallpaper in a damp location such as a bathroom, you may want to reconsider. If water seeps into the wallpaper, mold can grow undetected under the paper, creating a health hazard.

Drywall

Drywall, also known as gypsum wallboard, is one of the most common materials used in construction today. All the walls in your home are likely covered with drywall, which you've coated in paint or wallpaper. Drywall accounts for more than a quarter of all construction waste. Its chief ingredient, gypsum, has to be mined out of the earth and requires an immense amount of energy to produce. All this effort gives off carbon dioxide and other greenhouse gases.

Drywall made from recycled and synthetic gypsum is readily available; you just have to ask for it. The backing is made from 100 percent recycled, unbleached paper that's bonded without adhesives onto a gypsum core.

Keep in mind that the boards come in standard heights of 8 feet, 9 feet, and 10 feet. Designing to those ceiling heights will reduce cutting and waste, and save you money as well.

Wood paneling and cabinetry

Wood adds a warm and visually interesting finish to any room. A thin *veneer*, or skin, of real wood is typically glued over a panel of compressed particleboard to create wood paneling. Although this process uses less wood than solid pieces, the particleboard is commonly held together with urea-formaldehyde, a known carcinogen and health hazard.

Request formaldehyde-free particleboard for your panels and cabinets as a healthier option. For the veneer, select woods certified by the Forest Stewardship Council (FSC) to ensure that the wood has come from a sustainable source. Avoid tropical hardwoods — they come from the rain forest and contribute to its destruction. Panels of solid bamboo, a grass, are a greener and unique alternative.

Wall base and trim

The trim molding lining the walls at the floor, and possibly the ceiling, of your home serves two purposes:

- ✔ Trim adds elegance and style to any room.
- ✔ Trim covers the edges of the wall plaster where it meets the floor or ceiling.

Use trim made from small scraps of wood finger-jointed together. After you paint it, you'll never see the joints.

Avoid vinyl and fiberglass trim entirely; both are bad for your health and the environment.

Choosing Greener Floor Finishes

The floors of your home reflect the function and purpose of each room. A wood floor conveys a more formal feeling; carpet is more about comfort and walking around with your shoes off.

Because the floor covers such a large area, it has a huge influence on the indoor air quality in your home. Your kids, guests, and pets walk on your floors, wearing them down and breathing in the chemicals they give off. In this section, you find greener and healthier alternatives for flooring.

Wood flooring

Because they're easy to clean, hardwood floors are great for indoor air quality and for people with allergies. Traditional wood flooring comes from — drum roll, please — trees. (Shocking, isn't it?) Although wood is a renewable resource (people can plant more trees), wood used for flooring is typically harvested from the *clearcutting* of forests — removing all the trees in an area. More sustainably harvested options are available, coming from sources where no trees were clearcut or harmed to make your floor.

Look for wood certified by the Forest Stewardship Council (FSC). Anything certified by the FSC came from a managed forest — not from clearcutting. Expect to pay 20 percent more for sustainably harvested wood.

If you choose floors that have been prefinished at the factory, those chemicals won't have to be brought into your home. If you do stain or seal the floors, choose low-VOC or zero-VOC, water-based products.

Reclaimed wood

Reclaimed wood is salvaged from unusual sources, such as old barns, train trestles, or bridges in the process of being demolished. Although all wood flooring is warm, these recycled woods add particular warmth to a room because of their weathering and flaws. Because it's salvaged from older buildings, reclaimed wood was originally from old-growth trees, so the quality of the wood is far superior to anything available today. The rich wood grain of this old-growth wood is incredibly beautiful. Reclaimed wood commonly contains old rust stains, nail holes, or patched joints, all of which add character and charm to the wood's appearance.

Book IV

Green Remodeling

With the rising cost of new wood, more building suppliers now offer reclaimed and salvaged wood options. The energy needed to salvage the wood is still far less than the impact of clear-cutting new trees.

Bamboo

In the past few years, bamboo has become the best known and most popular of the green flooring options. Technically, bamboo is not wood — it's a grass, and some species can grow up to 3 feet in a day. To harvest it, the stalks are cut, leaving the plant intact to continue to grow. Unlike with wood, nothing is killed or destroyed in the process, which is what makes bamboo such an environmentally attractive option.

Unfortunately, most bamboo comes from Asia, and shipping it such long distances requires a great deal of energy. More local sources are now becoming available.

Although many people imagine an island hut when they think of bamboo, the finished bamboo floor closely resembles traditional wood flooring. It installs in the exact same way, and you may not even notice the distinctive knuckle pattern in the bamboo. The grain is incredibly durable, and it's stronger than oak, one of the strongest woods.

Like most floors, bamboo flooring is available in a prefinished surface, reducing the need to add sealers or coatings. Be sure to select water-based and low- or zero-VOC sealers.

Laminated wood

Laminate flooring is a durable particleboard base covered with a plastic photograph of wood grain. The result is an incredibly durable, nearly indestructible floor perfect for high-traffic areas. The planks arrive already finished, so no extra sealing is required.

 Although the particleboard is mostly compressed sawdust, it is held together with a binder of formaldehyde, a known toxin. Look for formaldehyde-free wood, sourced with wood certified by the Forest Stewardship Council (FSC). Seal the cut edges of the planks to prevent the formaldehyde from being released into the air.

Laminate flooring options made from bamboo are also available.

Carpeting

Carpeting is the ubiquitous floor covering in the United States, desired as much for its texture as for its ability to cover a variety of hidden sins. Carpet provides a soft, warm, and sound-absorbing surface. Combine all that with carpeting's low cost per square foot, and you see why it's the most-selected floor covering in the country, covering 70 percent of American floors.

However, in its short life span, carpet attracts dust and allergens. Once considered the status symbol of a luxurious home, carpet is now among a long list of related indoor air-quality problems and material-waste issues. (Nearly 5 billion pounds of discarded carpet end up in landfills each year.)

In the 1990s, after receiving more than 500 complaints about carpet-related health effects, the U.S. Consumer Product Safety Commission (CPSC) commissioned a study examining carpet chemical emissions. The landmark study identified dozens of toxic chemicals released from carpets, many of them known carcinogens. That "new carpet smell" is the smell of chemicals being released into the air.

Carpet, especially wall-to-wall carpet, has several inherent environmental issues:

✔ **It is typically made from synthetic, oil-based materials.** These materials are considered toxic, they release harmful chemicals, and we're depleting natural resources to utilize them.

✔ **Carpet is typically backed with vinyl (PVC).** Vinyl is harmful at every stage of its life cycle.

✔ **The synthetic and mixed materials make carpet (nearly) impossible to recycle.** Efforts are afoot to create recycling opportunities; however, at this point billions of pounds of carpet are ending up in landfills each year.

✔ **Carpet requires a great deal of energy to maintain, because it must be vacuumed.** More electricity to vacuum means more burning of fossil fuels, in most cases.

✔ **Vacuuming alone does not clean carpet and instead creates an environment in which pests, mold, and mildew can reside.** Carpet is host to numerous indoor air-quality issues, including the spread of asthma.

Luckily, a select group of carpet manufacturers have addressed some or all of these issues. Some of these initiatives include such wonderful ideas as

✔ Carpet made from natural, renewable fibers and materials.

✔ Carpet backed with natural, healthy materials like wool.

✔ Take-back programs, where the manufacturers accept the carpet at the end of its use and recycle it back into their supply chain.

✔ Carpet tile, which is an environmentally preferable alternative to wall-to-wall carpeting, because damaged tiles can be individually replaced without having to replace an entire floor (Although it takes more energy to produce the tiles, several manufacturers, such as FLOR [www.flor. com], produce a recycled content and recyclable carpet tile in a wide array of interesting colors and patterns.)

Used sparingly at entranceways, you can use carpet to control pollutants being tracked into a building.

Cork

Harvested from the bark of an oak cork tree, cork is considered a *rapidly renewable material,* because it grows back in just five to seven years without harming the tree. Most people imagine a corkboard when they think of cork floors, but in reality, cork flooring comes in a wide array of gorgeous patterns and styles and has been in use for well over 50 years. (The famed architect Frank Lloyd Wright often installed cork in his kitchens.) Cork flooring is surprisingly durable, providing an attractive, healthy, and biodegradable surface for your home.

The prefinished tiles provide a soft and comfortable walking surface, giving off a pleasant hickory smell. The cork naturally resists water, making it a great choice for kitchens and bathrooms.

Although all-natural cork is sustainably harvested, it typically comes from Mediterranean countries, requiring a lot of energy to transport it. Several manufacturers now offer cork flooring made in the United States from recycled wine bottle corks, reducing the travel distance.

Be sure to avoid cork flooring backed or mixed with vinyl. Choose a zero-VOC adhesive to install and seal the surface with a natural wax twice a year.

Vinyl tile

At first glance, vinyl flooring seems like a great material. Inexpensive, easy to install, and durable, vinyl is one of the most popular flooring choices — 14 billion pounds of it are produced each year in North America alone. But the reality of vinyl shows it to be a health hazard at every stage of its life: Vinyl releases poisonous dioxins into the atmosphere when it's produced, gives off very harmful chemicals after it's installed, and is nearly impossible to recycle.

Vinyl is the most environmentally destructive material used in buildings today. Unfortunately, vinyl is found in hundreds of building products. From plumbing pipes to flooring to wall base, vinyl is everywhere. Because it's so bad throughout its life cycle, avoid it at all costs.

Linoleum

Invented in 1860 by rubber manufacturer Fredrick Walton, linoleum quickly became the floor and wall covering of choice for Victorian homes, and has been in use ever since. Though vinyl tiles replaced linoleum in popularity back in the 1960s, the surging interest in green materials is helping linoleum make a comeback.

Linoleum is a natural product made of linseed oil, pigments, pine rosin, and pine flour (sawdust). It's covered with a natural jute backing. The finished material is thin and incredibly durable. It becomes harder in areas of high traffic. A linoleum floor can last 50 years.

As a green alternative to vinyl, linoleum offers numerous other advantages. The color and patterns are dyed all the way through to the backing, ensuring that the floor will not wear away. Linoleum is natural, making it biodegradable as well. Linseed oil is a natural antimicrobial agent, making it a great choice for kitchens.

Be sure to purchase only "natural linoleum," because the term *linoleum* is sometimes mistakenly used to refer to a generic vinyl floor. Avoid installing linoleum in damp areas, such as basements. Use only low-VOC or zero-VOC adhesives to install it.

Concrete

Sometimes you don't need to install any floor at all. Leaving the concrete slab exposed is a great way to save money on additional flooring. Generally, your contractor takes more care in finishing concrete that will remain exposed. In addition, numerous finishing options — from stains to pigments to acid etching — offer a wide variety of design flexibility.

In order to control cracking, a small joint is cut into the concrete every 20 feet or so. You can arrange these cuts, called *control joints,* in interesting patterns and angles for more visual interest.

Earthen floors

Perhaps the most environmentally friendly flooring option is good, old-fashioned dirt or earth. Called an *earthen floor,* it offers some interesting options.

Technically, a true modern-day earthen floor comes in various mixtures. Some are a mix of cement and earth (as in rammed-earth construction). The type of earth chosen makes a large difference in the durability. For example, the more clay content in the earth, the more susceptible it is to cracking from changes in water content. (The clay expands and contracts quite a bit.)

If you're buying commercial-grade soils for this floor, you can select a *plasticity index* to select the exact amount of clay content. Most single-family houses just collect soil left over from the excavation for the house. The correct soil will stabilize and prevent cracking — but there are no guarantees.

Be sure to seal the floor when it's complete. The best sealer available is simply boiled linseed oil, thinned with turpentine and brushed on in several coats. Its odor is gone in a week.

Earthen floors are the perfect complement for radiant heat. The thermal mass of the earth stores the heat and maintains a nice, consistent temperature all winter long. You could also use the same system for radiant cooling, by running cool water through the same tubes.

Checking Out the Options for Countertops

No other finish seems to get people as excited as countertops. Most people don't have strong feelings about toilet fixtures, roofing material, or exterior siding, but their eyes always light up when they talk about countertops.

People have an intimate connection with their countertops; you touch them and look at them every day. In recent years, countertops have become a bit of a status symbol for homeowners — granite, for some reason, has become the countertop of choice for high-end builders and, thus, for high-end kitchens. Granite is both lovely and natural, but many equally beautiful alternatives are out there. This section runs down the options.

Granite and stone

Stone has a natural and timeless quality. It has a reputation as being too expensive for the average person, but the truth is that stone comes in a wide range of varieties and prices. Stone also has varying degrees of environmental impact. Marble and granite are mined deep out of the earth, but other stones (such as sandstone, slate, and soapstone) can be locally quarried without the same damage to the earth.

Natural stone is an elegant and durable finish. Unfortunately, stone is *nonrenewable* (we can't make more of it), and it requires huge amounts of energy to quarry, finish, transport, and install. The most popular stone types — granite, marble, sandstone, and limestone — must be transported long distances, using large amounts of energy. The impact from quarrying, cutting, and polishing the stone requires even more energy. The dust from the stone cutting is irritating and polluting.

As an alternative, look for salvaged stone. Your local salvage yard carries some countertops saved from demolition. Salvaged stone is much less expensive, but provides a limited choice of colors.

Stone is sold in large slabs, not in pieces. When only a part of a slab is used, the remaining pieces are left behind. Every stone and marble yard has what they call a *boneyard* where these leftovers are placed. These pieces save you money, and they offer more variety. As long as you don't need a large amount of the same type of stone, the boneyard is a great place to find stone.

Seal the stone as needed with a low-VOC and water-based sealer or select stone that doesn't require sealing.

Many types of stone — especially marble, sandstone, limestone, and slate — are surprisingly soft, and they scratch and absorb stains easily. Granite is stronger and more scratch- and stain-resistant.

Dispose of leftover and discarded stone by giving it to a salvage yard. Stone tiles can be reused or crushed into aggregate for concrete.

Terrazzo

Terrazzo is made up of small pieces of marble set into cement and highly polished. Odds are, you've walked on a terrazzo floor. They're common in public buildings — museums, airports, hotels, and so on — so you know terrazzo countertops are durable. Countertops made from glass instead of marble are often called Vetrazzo (from vitreous glass), or glass terrazzo, and it reflects light in the most beautiful way. The result is a surface so beautiful you won't notice that this particular glass happens to be made from recycled beverage bottles. You can choose the colors of the glass and the cement binder, giving you an endless list of possibilities. The surface is durable, heatproof, and easy to maintain. The cost is similar to granite, and it can be cut into shapes just like stone.

Paper resin

Made from paper and a resin binder, composite countertops have a warm, neutral look that fits well with most decorating styles. This material looks similar to other popular solid-surface countertops like Corian, but because it's only about one-third plastic, it has a more natural look and feel. Many people compare paper resin to soapstone. The material is very practical — it's not hard enough to dull knives, but it's dense enough to resist slice marks that can harbor bacteria.

Book IV

Green Remodeling

Companies such as Richlite (www.richlite.com/countertop) and PaperStone Products (www.paperstoneproducts.com) offer products made out of recycled paper, so ask for the highest recycled content available.

As with concrete or any formed surface, special features can be incorporated into the countertops, such as a drain board next to an under-mount sink, or casting metal rods near the stove, creating a built-in trivet.

Concrete

Concrete is a natural product and, as such, has a natural beauty. A chemical mixture of cement, sand, and water, concrete is durable and doesn't release harmful chemicals.

Because concrete is a formed material, you can have special features incorporated into a concrete countertop, such as a drain board next to an under-mount sink, or a small depression cast into the surface to create a soap dish. With an infinite variety of colors, shapes, and textures, concrete is one of the more interesting surfaces you see in a kitchen. The drawback is that it can be expensive, depending on the shape.

Solid surfacing

Solid surfacing is a type of acrylic epoxy plastic mixture formed into large, continuous surfaces. Because the entire counter can be formed at once, other elements are often formed into it as well, such as sinks and back-splashes. The color runs through the entire material, so it won't show wear. Inexpensive and durable, solid surfacing is one of the most popular counter-top materials.

Because these products are made from plastic, issues around health and sustainability have been raised. Every major manufacturer of solid surfacing now offers a line of recycled-content products. Typically, the recycled material comes from their own scraps that have been reground back into the mixture (post-industrial content). Pick the brand with the highest recycled content; unfortunately, even the highest is still fairly low, around 15 percent.

As an inexpensive alternative to granite, solid surfacing is now available mixed with chips of real stone, usually quartz. Often called *engineered stone*, the surface looks like granite but feels different to the touch and uses much less energy to produce. The surface has a more uniform appearance, a give-away that it isn't real stone. Because quartz can't be cut into large slabs, crumbling bits of quartz are instead used in this mixture.

Although pure solid surfacing is 100 percent plastic, engineered surfaces are mostly stone, usually around 94 percent. (The rest is plastic.) Choose the product with the highest amount of recycled stone available, such as those manufactured by Silestone (www.silestoneusa.com). Although engineered stone is not the greenest product available, it is greener than pure solid surfacing.

Plastic laminate

In the 1950s, plastic laminate was all the rage, but by the 1960s, it was beginning to shows its age. Strange patterns, toxic glues, and frayed edges began to show the drawbacks of plastic laminate, but people still ask for it.

To make plastic laminate, slim layers of acrylic plastic are bonded onto a wood backing. This thin sheet is glued down onto a plywood base to create a countertop. The plastic, adhesives, and resins pose potential health risks.

If you must choose a laminate, abaca is a wonderful alternative. Made from recycled banana fibers on a hemp backing, abaca laminates have an organic, natural texture. Use nontoxic adhesives to glue the laminate to the plywood. As a nice detail, place a solid strip of wood along the edge for a more finished appearance.

Countertop refacing

Give the countertops you have a facelift without having to chuck the old ones (or suffer through time-consuming installation) by refacing them. A water-based spray sticks to your old laminate or formica countertops, contains no VOCs, and takes just a few hours to apply. You can choose from a whole slew of colors and feel good about working with what you have instead of buying new. Find out more or locate a dealer at www.ecocountertopsusa.com.

Book IV

Green Remodeling

Running Down Other Finishes

From accent tiles to wall panels, countless other green finishes are available to decorate your home.

Be sure to explore the life cycle impact of any product you're considering for your home (see Chapter 2).

Ceramic tile

For thousands of years, ceramic tiles have been used for flooring and wall tiles. Although it requires a great deal of energy to produce, ceramic tile is durable and recyclable, made from natural clay.

Look for locally sourced quarry tiles — they require less energy. Make sure that natural glazes have been used; unglazed tiles are course and porous. As a fun alternative, ask your local tile warehouse for any damaged or dropped boxes. You can arrange broken tiles into a mosaic pattern for a beautiful finish.

Set the tiles into cement grout instead of adhesives to avoid adding VOCs into the air. Choose a colored grout instead of white to hide dirt; the grout lines are difficult to keep clean. Seal the completed tile and grout with a water-based sealer.

With careful planning, you can design the bathroom to fit the spacing of the tile. Doing this lets you avoid cutting, looks much better, and reduces waste. If you must cut tiles, do it outside to keep the dust out of the indoor air.

If properly installed, ceramic tile can last 50 years or more, and it biode-grades after removal. Tiles can be reused if carefully removed or crushed and recycled into aggregate filler for concrete.

Glass

Glass is an all-natural product, made of silica (sand) and melted into a variety of shapes, colors, and types. Because glass is healthy and can be found locally, glass is a fairly green product. Manufacturing glass does require some energy, so recycled glass is an even better option.

Recycled glass tiles are gorgeous and gemlike, and they're a great choice for a backsplash or shower wall. Recycled glass is produced from recycled wind-shields, bottles, and windows crushed to a sandlike texture and mixed with other ingredients, including minerals that add color. This mixture is then heated until the glass particles soften and fuse on their edges. This process uses far less energy than standard glass or ceramic tile manufacturing. Made from a mixture of sources, these recycled tiles contain slight imperfections and bubbles, adding character.

The color of the grout shows through some of the clear tiles, so choose a grout color carefully.

Metal

Environmentally speaking, metal is incredibly durable and easily recyclable. Unfortunately, metal production is incredibly harmful to the environment. From mining the minerals to the energy needed to melt it down to the greenhouse gases released from this process, metal has a huge negative impact.

Different types of metal vary in their impact. Copper, for example, is destructively mined using slave labor in South America. Aluminum requires mining of bauxite, an incredibly polluting process. Stainless steel is different from steel — it's a combination alloy of steel, chromium, and nickel designed to resist rust, and the chromium is highly polluting and toxic.

Because of high manufacturing costs, most metals now contain some amount of recycled content, so just be sure to look for the highest amount available. Several companies produce tiles, sinks, and other finishes made of 100 percent recycled metal.

Both durable and hygienic, metal finishes resist heat and staining. Using flat stainless steel sheeting and adding a natural wood edge reduces costs and eases installation.

Metal scratches and shows fingerprints very easily, so be sure you like that look before you buy.

Resins and plastics

Rigid plastic panels are typically produced from a polyester resin, made from oil, toxic in their production, and difficult to recycle. Several companies now offer greener alternatives with recycled and recyclable options. One company, 3-Form (www.3-form.com), refers to its product as an *eco-resin* to describe its patented, environmentally friendly manufacturing processes.

Choose panels with the highest recycled content available. An infinite array of options, colors, shapes, and thicknesses is available. Panels are a stronger and more colorful alternative to fragile glass, making them a great choice for kid-proof windows, attractive shower enclosures, and unusual cabinet doors. Ask the manufacturer about standard panel sizes to reduce cutting and waste.

Finding Ecofriendly Furnishings

No home is complete without furniture, and several green options are available. Shop carefully and don't be afraid to ask questions. Although finding a green floor may be easy, furnishings are more difficult. With so many options available, knowing what to ask or where to look is tough. This section points you in the right direction.

Furniture

Chairs, tables, and sofas are typically made of cheap particleboard, finished with oil-based lacquers, and stuffed with toxic foam. You can smell these chemicals when you unwrap a new piece of furniture.

With any furniture, look for the following green features:

- ✔ **Reclaimed:** Reusing materials salvaged from other uses, reclaimed materials offer old-material quality no longer available. *Example:* Wood from old wine barrels milled into chairs.

- ✔ **Recycled:** Unlike reclaimed materials, recycled materials are put back into the material production and reprocessed into new finishes. Sourced from various materials, recycled materials often have slight imperfections that add to the final appearance. *Example:* Metal tables from recycled metal.

- ✔ **Sustainably harvested:** Yielding materials without completely destroying the chance for future harvesting, sustainably harvested materials will be around for future generations. *Example:* Bamboo furniture, Forest Stewardship Council (FSC) certified.

- ✔ **Natural materials:** Instead of cushions stuffed with synthetic materials containing harmful chemicals, look for those with natural latex.

- ✔ **Nontoxic finishes:** Most furniture is finished with oil-based lacquers; instead, use water-based finishes and adhesives free of VOCs.

Looking for these options will also ensure a healthier home. Companies such as Vivavi (www.vivavi.com) and Furnature (www.furnature.com) offer only products with these green features.

The most sustainable choice is buying used furniture. Haunt garage sales, flea markets, resale shops, and antique stores to find your greenest furniture options.

Draperies and fabrics

The fabrics making up your drapes, curtains, and sofa coverings are typically dyed with polluting pigments on synthetic fabric.

Natural fabrics, such as organic cotton, hemp, linen, and natural wool, offer healthier alternatives. Exciting new fabrics made from polylactic acid (PLA) are becoming more available. PLA is a natural material made from corn; it's recyclable and biodegradable. Companies like Terratex (www.teratex.com) offer PLA-based fabrics.

Examining Exterior Finishes and Trim

Although you don't need to worry about indoor air issues with exterior materials, you have other issues to consider. Anything outside is exposed to the weather, so you need to choose durable materials. Outside, anything painted needs to be repainted every few years, so save yourself the work and choose materials that can be left exposed and unpainted.

Siding

For many people, vinyl siding is considered the best material to use in covering your home. After all, it's durable and cheap, and it never needs painting. Unfortunately, the environmental issues with the manufacturing and disposal of vinyl make it a terrible choice. The following sections run down some alternatives.

Aluminum siding

Popular in the 1940s and 1950s, aluminum siding offered a maintenance-free option for your home. When less expensive vinyl siding was introduced, it forced aluminum siding from the market. Older aluminum siding is easily recycled, but finding a source for new siding made of recycled content is difficult.

Wood siding

Both vinyl and aluminum siding are designed to copy the look of real wood siding. The best choice is wood certified by the Forest Stewardship Council (FSC) to be sustainably harvested. Instead of paint, finish the planks with a water-based stain to allow the beauty of the wood to show through.

Cedar shingles

Cedar shingles are an attractive and natural option for siding. Cedar forests are disappearing rapidly, so look for shingles made from reclaimed or FSC-certified wood.

Shingles don't need to be placed in straight lines. Arranging them in curves can be a fun and interesting way to cover your home.

Fiber cement boards

Fiber cement boards are rigid panels made of Portland cement, sand, wood fiber, and clay. They're a durable and attractive siding option. Although they hold paint well, the panels can be left unfinished if you don't mind the gray color. James Hardie (www.jameshardie.com/homeowner) is the largest manufacturer of fiber cement boards, but several other manufacturers offer fiber cement boards as well. The product is available in shingles, boards, and long planks for a variety of design options. Many manufacturers offer a wood grain or sand finish.

Stucco

Stucco is a cement-based product and must be applied or sprayed on by hand. Traditional stucco is really just cement-based plaster — a mixture of Portland cement, lime, sand, and water.

Stucco is typically applied in three coats: a rough scratch coat, a secondary base coat, and then a finish coat, for a total thickness of about 3/4 inch. If you apply the stucco over a brick or concrete wall, you don't need a scratch coat.

Synthetic stucco, made from acrylic, is now typically used in place of cement-based stucco. If you use synthetic stucco, you have to use a thin fiberglass mesh. Stick with the natural cement stucco instead.

Although stucco can be painted, an integral color can be mixed into the finish coat, making painting unnecessary. Don't be afraid to select bright colors. Stucco is available in much more than tan, with a wide palette of fun colors. Although the cement requires a great deal of energy to produce, the long life and ease of maintenance make stucco a very green choice for your home.

Decking

A well-designed deck can open up a room and allow you the chance to get some fresh air. From staining to dry rot and splinters, traditional decks can be a maintenance headache. Green options can solve some of these issues. Encourage outdoor living with the durable, low-maintenance decking alternatives in the following sections.

Certified wood

If you go with wood, be sure to use wood certified by the Forest Stewardship Council. The FSC stamp ensures this wood has been sustainably harvested. The most popular traditional decking material, redwood, typically comes from old-growth trees and cannot be replaced. Save these irreplaceable redwood trees and look for FSC-certified redwood instead.

Wood framing used outside is typically pressure treated with chromated copper arsenate (CCA) — a form of arsenic (not exactly healthy for you or anyone else). The Environmental Protection Agency (EPA) has now banned CCA wood, but it's still in use, especially in children's playgrounds. Look for wood treated with the healthier ammoniacal copper quaternary (ACQ).

Composite lumber

Combining recycled plastic and sawdust, composite lumbers are much healthier and more environmentally friendly than wood. They don't warp, splinter, or need staining.

The maintenance savings alone is reason enough to consider composite lumber. Composite lumber is available from dozens of manufacturers; look for the companies that offer the highest recycled content planks.

Ipe wood

Ipe wood is an attractive alternative to the typical redwood or teak decking. The strength and natural water resistance of ipe makes it a great choice for a durable deck. As always, FSC-certified ipe wood is the greenest option.

Reclaimed beams (railroad ties)

Salvaged ties from old railroad tracks are available and attractive, and they don't require any new trees to be made.

Because they were manufactured to be used outside, railroad ties are pressure-treated with CCA. Coat them with two coats of a water-based sealer to seal in the CCA. Sealants will keep most of the harmful chemicals from soaking into your skin when you touch the wood. Maintain the coat every few years to stay protected.

Roofing

A roof's job is to keep out the water, but the choice of roof can greatly alter the appearance and energy efficiency of your home. Here are some options for keeping out the rain:

- ✔ **Asphalt shingles:** Nearly two-thirds of all roofs, both new and existing, are clad in asphalt shingles. Each year, about 11 million tons of asphalt roofing shingle waste is generated in the United States. Although recycled shingles are available, they aren't the best choice. Their dark color absorbs heat in the summer, heating up your home.

  If you plan on collecting the rainwater from the roof, the oil in the asphalt shingles will make the water undrinkable. Opt for another type of roofing instead.

- ✔ **Recycled rubber roofing:** Nearly 300 million car tires are thrown away in the United States each year — that's nearly one per person. Dozens of companies recycle these tires into rubber shingles. These durable and resource-efficient shingles are a good choice. However, like asphalt, these shingles will contaminate the rainwater as it falls on the roof.

- ✔ **Recycled plastic and metal shingles:** The large amount of recycled plastic and metal available has prompted manufacturers to create some great roofing products. Recycled plastic shingles look surprisingly like natural slate. Lightweight and affordable, they're a great option for your roof. Recycled metal shingles are also available, offering a reflective and attractive pattern.

WARNING!

When installing metal outside, never mix your metals. A copper roof must be installed with copper nails; a zinc roof with zinc nails.

✔ **Spray-on foam roofing:** Spray-on foam roofing, such as poly-isocyanurate (or poly-iso, for short) is the perfect choice for flat roofs. Once dry, these foams provide a seamless, continuous roof surface that will never leak and that's durable enough to walk on. The light yellow color of the foam is not very attractive, so you'll probably only want to use it on flat roof locations that aren't visible from ground level. But the light color *does* reflect heat to keep your home cool.

No matter what type of roof you choose, select the lightest color available. A dark roof absorbs heat, adding to your cooling costs in the summer. If you live in a warm climate, this issue is even more important.

Remodeling: Bringing Old Materials to Life

Remodeling your home is a form of recycling. Reusing an existing building, instead of building something new, saves energy and resources.

The old appliances you remove are easily salvaged or sold. The sinks and tubs removed can be reused. If your existing toilet is a low-flush model, keep it and reuse it; if not, these old fixtures can be ground up and added as an aggregate into concrete.

Salvage yards offer possible treasures waiting to be found. Antique light fixtures, claw-foot tubs, and historic fireplace mantles are common finds in a salvage yard.

While paint strippers can bring new life to old furniture and fixtures, the chemicals they use are typically some of the harshest you can imagine. Although they require more elbow grease, electric sanders and strippers are a healthier choice. For stubborn or hard-to-clean surfaces, new products, such as SoyGel (www.franmar.com), offer a natural and chemical-free alternative to paint strippers.

Before the remodeling work begins, seal all the existing ducts and vents, which prevents dirt from traveling through the home. In order to remove the dust and chemicals stirred up by the remodeling project, tell your contractor to seal off the area to be remodeled with plastic sheeting and leave it up until the project is finished. Finally, when the project is complete, open all the windows to flush the home with fresh air for a few days; doing so removes a large portion of the VOCs and chemicals in the home.

Chapter 4

Exploring Options for Heating and Cooling Systems

*O*ne of the best ways to make your home healthy, comfortable, and energy efficient is to choose the correct heating and cooling system. Just keeping yourself comfortable uses up to two-thirds of the energy in your home. And if you're using an inefficient or faulty mechanism to heat or cool your home, you're burning through money and energy faster than you can say leaky ducts.

In this chapter, you find out about the pros and cons of various heating and cooling systems — some tried and true, some you might well not have run into yet.

Examining Forced-Air Systems for Heating and Cooling

A *forced-air system* (also called a *whole-house system*) is one of the most common types of heaters used in homes. Gas or electricity is used to heat air, which is then blown around the house via metal ducts and into different rooms through vents on the floor or ceiling. You can use the same system for cooling your home as well. A thermostat controls the air flow. The vents are usually located in the draftiest parts of the room, typically near the windows and doors.

Although they sound simple enough, forced-air systems have some disadvantages:

✔ **Uneven heating and cooling:** Air is blown into the room, causing some areas to be warmer or cooler than others.

✔ **Pollen and dust:** Forced-air systems bring in fresh air from the outside, carrying with it pollen and allergens. These systems also spread dust around the home — especially if the home has floor vents, where dust and dirt are easily trapped. If you have asthma or allergies, a forced-air system is the worst choice for controlling the air around you.

If the air coming out of the vents smells funny, consider having your ducts cleaned by a licensed mechanical contractor. Not only will your system operate more efficiently, but you'll notice an immediate improvement with dust and allergies.

✔ **Noise:** You can hear when the fan is on because of the sound of the air blowing through the vents.

✔ **Inefficiency:** Most homes have only one thermostat monitoring the system, resulting in some rooms being warmer or cooler than others. Plus, you typically have to heat and cool the entire home rather than just the room you're using.

If your current heater was built before 1980, it's time to upgrade to a new system. Even if you stick with a forced-air system, current models are much more efficient than older ones; the upgrade will pay for itself in energy savings in less than three years.

Finding Energy-Efficient Heating Systems

Most building departments require you to install a heater in your home, but a cooling system (or air conditioner) is not required. Even in warmer climates, you need to install a heater, whether it will be used or not. This section runs down a variety of energy-efficient heating systems for your home.

Electric baseboard heat

Individual room units can be a great alternative to a large system for the whole house. Small electric baseboard heaters run along the base of the wall and are relatively inexpensive to operate.

If your home is well insulated and doesn't require a lot of heating, electric baseboard heaters may be the best option. You can control the heat in each room, allowing for great flexibility.

Gas room heaters

Similar to electric baseboard heating, individual room heaters are usually wall-mounted, self-contained units. Running on natural gas, they're an efficient option for small homes or for heating one room at a time.

Select a model with an automatic ignition instead of a pilot light. Pilot lights waste energy and often blow out, potentially leaking gas into your home.

Solar thermal water heater

A solar heater is a wonderfully simple device. This 2-x-4-foot box sits on your roof. It has no moving parts, just a coiled pipe entering at the bottom and exiting at the top. When the sun shines on the box, it heats the water in the pipe. The heated water rises through the coiled pipe automatically, where it's stored in a standard water heater tank.

Although you can use the heated water to meet the hot water needs in your house (showering, dishwashing, and so on), you can also use it for heating your home. The hot water can be converted into heat in the form of

- **Radiators:** Pipes carry hot water to a typical radiator.
- **Forced-air fan:** A fan blows air over copper tubes filled with the hot water. The hot water, in turn, heats the air.
- **Radiant heat (see the following section):** The hot water is used for a radiant heating system.

Powered solely by the sun, the solar thermal heater provides hot water for free, greatly reducing the operating costs for all these heaters. Because it relies on the light and not heat to warm the water, the system even works in the winter. When the sun sets at night, the hot water is stored for later use. If carefully planned, this system can provide for all your hot water and heating needs.

Be sure your roof is strong enough to support the weight of the solar heater before you install it. If your home was built before 1980, ask your architect or engineer to confirm the strength of your existing roof.

Radiant heat

In a *radiant heating system* (also called *hydronic*), hot water flows through tubes hidden beneath the floor to slowly warm the room. Unlike traditional forced-air heating, where hot air blows to heat the air, radiant heat uses the principle of radiation to heat the surface. Radiant heat warms the occupants, not the space — an important distinction. The result is a wonderfully comfortable and cozy feeling of warmth.

The advantages of radiant heat have brought it to the mainstream market in the United States. (It's already commonplace in Europe.) A radiant heating system is

- ✔ **Comfortable:** Because the heat source is under the floor, temperatures are warmer at floor level (where you are) and the heat rises to the ceiling. Because the floor is warm, walking barefoot and sitting on the floor are cozy possibilities.

- ✔ **Dust-free:** No air is pushed around in radiant heating, which makes it a dust and pollen-free alternative particularly advantageous for anyone suffering from allergies or asthma.

- ✔ **Not drying:** Unlike forced hot air, radiant heating doesn't dry out the air.

- ✔ **Safe for kids:** Children are safe from contact with hot radiators or dirty vent ducts.

- ✔ **Quiet and maintenance free:** A radiant heat system is virtually noise and maintenance free.

The hot water in the tubes can be produced through a gas or electric boiler or hot water heater. If you're generating your own electricity with solar panels, the electric version is a better choice. The best and most energy-efficient option is to add a solar water heater on the roof to preheat the water and reduce the operation of the boiler.

Although you can adapt a radiant system for any floor type, an earthen floor or concrete slab works best. The thermal mass of these floors holds in the heat from the tubes and maintains a much more consistent temperature. Radiant heat can be installed in both floor-joist systems and slab floors, but installing it into a slab is easier and therefore slightly less expensive.

Special products are now available to make installing a radiant heat system over wood floor joists easier. Products such as Warmboard (www.warm-board.com) are plywood panels with precut grooves. The tubes are set into the grooves for quick installation.

As a general rule, a radiant heating system costs about $1.50 to $1.75 per square foot installed, not including the heat source. Although electric radiant heat systems are expensive to operate normally, your costs are zero if you're producing your own electricity with solar panels.

For areas where tubing isn't an option, electrical radiant heat companies, such as Nuheat (www.nuheat.com), provide a thin wire mesh you can install in the thin space under tile or carpeting. These items warm the floor slowly, just as with a tube system, and are a great addition to a single bathroom.

Ground source heat pumps (geothermal)

Ground source heat pumps (also called *geothermal systems*) are a fairly new and innovative method of heating and cooling a building, but the idea is simple: The earth below ground maintains a consistent temperature of around 55°F. Instead of heating the building from the freezing air outside, or cooling the building from the blistering air outside, you heat it or cool it from this 55°F. Because this geothermal temperature is much closer to people's normal comfort zone, it requires much less energy to use. In Figure 4-1, you can see how this system works.

The U.S. Environmental Protection Agency (EPA) credits geothermal as "the most energy-efficient, environmentally friendly heating and cooling technology available."

The only byproduct of using a ground source heat pump is warm water. With this ground source water, you can heat both the air and the water for your building.

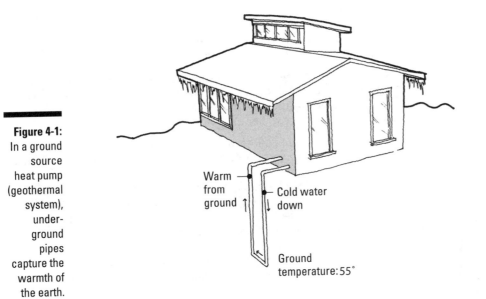

Figure 4-1:
In a ground source heat pump (geothermal system), underground pipes capture the warmth of the earth.

Warm from ground

Cold water down

Ground temperature: 55°

Geothermal systems come in two standard configurations:

- **Vertical closed loop** is the most common system. In this system, loops of piping are fed several hundred feet into the earth, which requires a great deal of boring. Given the depth, the ground source temperature remains consistent throughout the year. On a site with expansive soils or bedrock, vertical systems are too expensive.

- **Horizontal closed loop** systems are installed in trenches only 5 feet below the surface of the earth. This shallow installation means the system is affected by seasonal ground temperature changes. Although horizontal loops are much easier to install and work with for bedrock sites, they do require significantly more surface area (approximately 2,500 square feet of surface area per ton of cooling) in order to work effectively.

The advantages of geothermal include the following:

- **Cost savings:** Homeowners with geothermal units typically realize energy savings of 25 to 50 percent over conventional gas, oil, or above-ground heat pump systems (which work much like an air conditioner in reverse). As a general rule, a 2,000-square-foot house can be heated or cooled for as little as $1 a day. Because a geothermal system also produces hot water as a byproduct, it's up to 30 percent less expensive to operate than a traditional gas or electric water heater.

- **Absence of pollen and dust:** A geothermal system doesn't draw spores and pollen into the building as a forced-air heating system does. If you have allergies or asthma, this relief is a welcome change, and you'll notice a marked improvement in your indoor air quality.

- **No fumes:** Because the geothermal system doesn't involve combustion, a pilot light, or a chimney, it doesn't add an odor or fumes to the house.

For smaller buildings, installation cost is the main drawback. Drilling holes for the vertical system can be prohibitive for single-family homes. Another possible roadblock is the lack of qualified contractors who know how to properly design, install, and service these systems.

Look for equipment certified by the Air-Conditioning and Refrigeration Institute (www.ari.org), a nonprofit organization that rates residential and small commercial systems.

Fireplaces

No other feature provides as strong an image of home as a fireplace does. When they think of holidays and family gatherings, many people picture people sitting around a hearth. For centuries, a fireplace was the sole source of heat in a home; today, it's used only occasionally.

Be sure to close the chimney flue of your fireplace when you aren't using it. If you don't, valuable (and expensive) heated or cooled air will fly right up and out of your home, wasting money.

Here are your fireplace options:

- **Wood:** Wood-burning fireplaces have long been a sentimental vision of home. The sounds of the crackling fire and the warmth of the hearth are comforting and romantic. But in recent years, local building codes have banned their use, in favor of cleaner-burning gas fireplaces.

  According to the U.S. Department of Energy, wood-burning fireplaces emit nitrogen oxides, carbon monoxide, organic gases, and particulate matter. These pollutants can cause serious health problems for children, pregnant women, and people with respiratory problems. Some of these are even known carcinogens.

  If you have an existing wood-burning fireplace, an EPA-certified clean-burning fireplace insert and a glass screen will protect your family from the gases entering the room. Instead of using petroleum-based premanu-factured logs, look for ecofriendly versions, like a fire log made from recycled, dried coffee grounds. You can buy them from Java-Log (www.java-log.com).

- **Gas:** Gas fireplaces are cleaner burning and mean you don't have to clean up ash from the bottom of the fireplace. The burners can be set into sand, stones, or glass for a modern, high-tech look. Most models are even available with remote controls. However, gas fireplaces still use a fossil fuel as their energy source, making them less than ideal.

- **Pellet stoves:** The most efficient fireplace available is a pellet stove, which uses small cylinders of compressed sawdust as a fuel. The combustion chamber is sealed, so instead of a crackling fire, you see a flame behind glass. Though not as romantic as a wood fireplace, pellet stoves provide the most heat with the least amount of fuel.

- **Open fireplaces:** If you don't like the sterile flame or fake wood inserts of gas fireplaces, EcoSmart Fire (www.ecosmartfire.com) has introduced an environmentally friendly open fireplace. Fueled by renewable methylated spirits (fermented sugar cane), the EcoSmart doesn't require a flue. Imagine having a fireplace in the center of your dining room table.

Book IV

Green Remodeling

Cooling Options for the Hottest Months

On a hot day, nothing beats walking into a nice, cool, air-conditioned home. Unfortunately, running your air conditioner is expensive and eats up energy. Fortunately, some simple decisions can help you reduce the amount of energy you use to cool your home, even on the hottest days.

Air conditioners

Central air conditioning is the biggest single user of energy in your home, and the most wasted one as well. Most people set the thermostat lower than necessary, because they think it'll make the cold come out faster. (It won't.) Compare your utility bills from March with those in August, and you can see firsthand how much air conditioning is costing you.

Ironically, air conditioning produces more heat outside than it relieves inside. During the summer, it's estimated that air conditioning is responsible for nearly half the electricity used in the United States.

Although you may think you can't live without your air conditioner, in truth, a home can be built to never need air conditioning. If you're still considering a central air-conditioning system, purchase an Energy Star–rated unit, with a Seasonal Energy Efficiency Ratio (SEER) of 12 or higher. Also, look for units with a fan-only option and a replaceable filter.

The following list details your air-conditioning options.

- ✔ **Individual window units:** Instead of installing central air (see "Forced-Air Systems: Heating and Cooling," earlier in this chapter), consider individual window units. They cost less to operate and cool only the areas you need.

  Be sure to properly size the unit for the room; people tend to buy the biggest air conditioner they can find, wasting money and energy. Place the unit in a window away from direct sunlight or plant a tree outside to shade that window.

- ✔ **Ductless units:** A more attractive and less noisy option, ductless air conditioners use a simple outdoor condenser unit to run power and refrigerant to small, wall-mounted fans. Instead of filling a window, the ductless unit can go anywhere on the wall. Because the refrigeration takes place outside, ductless units are much quieter than a central or window unit system. But expect to pay double the cost of a simple window unit for a ductless unit.

- ✔ **Ice energy:** Ice energy is an innovative and cost-effective system for cooling a building. A large box in your yard produces a block of ice at night, when the temperature is cool and electricity costs are lower. During the day, a fan blows air over the ice, creating air conditioning. By time-shifting most of the energy use to night, an ice energy system can save you hundreds of dollars on your utility bills. Commercial units have been around for some time, and smaller residential units are now finally available as well from companies like Ice Energy (www.ice-energy.com).

Ceiling fans

When it's warm, most people really just need to feel comfortable. Air conditioners blow cold air, taking a long time to cool the entire home. A ceiling fan offers the same level of comfort, but costs must less to operate. It circulates the air, generating a feeling of comfort and carrying cooling breezes through the home. Save the air conditioner for the really hot days and use the ceiling fan instead.

 Because warm air rises and collects around the ceiling, ceiling fans have two settings: winter and summer. That little switch on the side of the fan controls the setting. The default summer setting pulls air upward, sucking in breezes from open windows and cooling things down. The winter setting pushes the warm air gathered at the ceiling down onto you. Make sure that you have your fan on the correct setting.

Whole-house fans

A whole-house fan is installed in the ceiling of the top floor of your home. The fan sucks air into the attic, drawing in cool air from the outside. Open the windows of the rooms you want to cool and close the doors of unused rooms to help the system work most effectively.

Highly effective and much less expensive than central air conditioning, a whole house fan can keep you cool through the summer.

Solar attic fans

If your home has an attic space, install a solar-powered attic fan. These inexpensive fans turn on automatically when the attic gets too hot, siphoning hot air out of the attic. Using an attic fan lowers the temperature of the attic, reducing strain on your air conditioner and saving you money.

Book IV

Green Remodeling

Using Nonmechanical Methods to Keep Your Home Comfortable

Believe it or not, nature provides its own methods of maintaining a regular temperature. For thousands of years, human beings used the systems of nature to stay comfortable. But in traditional modern homes, when the temperature gets too hot or cold, people just pump in energy. Before consuming energy to heat or cool your home, consider the following methods.

Insulation

A well-insulated home holds in temperature, lowering your heating and cooling bills. Insulation keeps your heat from leaking out through the walls. The more you have, the better it works, and the lower your heating and cooling bills will be.

Nothing you do has as big an impact on your monthly utility bills as insulating your home sufficiently. When it comes to insulation, if some is good, more is definitely better. (Check out Chapter 2 of Book II for more on insulation.)

Insulation doesn't just go in the walls. Be sure to insulate the following places, too:

- ✔ **Attic:** Insulate the floor and roof of your attic.

- ✔ **Foundation:** More than half of the heat in the average home leaks out of the edges of the foundation slab. Insulate the edges prior to erecting the walls.

- ✔ **Crawl space:** An average of 80 percent of the air in a home's moldy, dank, cold crawl space will end up in the house. Insulate your home's floors to prevent air from creeping in.

- ✔ **Hot-water pipes:** Adding insulation wrap to the hot-water pipes is simple and especially important for pipes in crawl spaces. Try to avoid running ducts and pipes through unheated attics or crawl spaces.

Thermal mass

If insulation is the ability of a material to *hold in* temperature, thermal mass is the ability of a material to *absorb and store* temperature. Sometimes referred to as a *heat sink,* this characteristic can keep a building cool in the summer and warm in the winter in one of the simplest methods to reduce heating and cooling costs.

If you've ever gone swimming at night, you've experienced thermal mass. The sun heats up the pool water all day, and the water stores that heat. At night, when the surrounding temperature drops and the water releases this heat, the pool feels like bathwater. You're feeling the stored heat being released in the water. This is thermal mass in action. (Water has a very high thermal mass.)

Heavy, massive materials, such as concrete, brick, and stone, have a high thermal mass. Thermal mass is why your basement is always so cool in the summer, and why your dog sleeps on the tiles. The mass of the concrete basement and tile floor store the cold and release it when the air around it is warm.

An exposed concrete slab is a simple way to utilize thermal mass. In the winter, let the sun come through the windows and warm up the concrete. In the summer, use curtains or overhangs to block the sun from coming in, keeping the concrete cool. This simple method helps your home maintain a consistent temperature year-round.

Utilizing thermal mass is ideal in a climate where it's warm during the day and cool at night. Build the south-facing walls of your home out of adobe, rammed earth, or concrete. The sun warms the walls all day and keeps the house warm at night.

You can use thermal mass to maintain a consistent temperature in your home. Materials with a high thermal mass aren't affected by sudden temperature swings; they take a long time to heat up and cool down. Using thermal mass in the winter requires positioning a mass wall so that the sun warms it all day). At night, after the temperature drops, the wall will release heat and keep you warm.

Because thermal mass requires changes in temperature in order to work, it won't work in areas that are always hot or always cold. In fact, thermal mass works against you in these areas. For example, a concrete building in a hot desert, where it's hot all day and night, never has the chance to release heat. This building will be even hotter inside from the saturated thermal mass.

Passive cooling

Through the physics of convection, heat rises. Warm air is lighter than cool air, and as the warm air rises, cooler air rushes in to take its place. Passive cooling uses this principle to create ventilation.

You can use this idea to keep cool in the summer by funneling air through your home. Using something called a *thermal chimney* (a tall, vented space), this rising heat is directed up and out of the house. As wind passes over the building, it pulls more air through the chimney. Cool air from the outside is pulled into the lower part of the house.

Book IV

Green Remodeling

A tall, open stairwell can function as a thermal chimney. Place operable skylights at the top of the stairwell to allow the heat to escape on warm days. You can create air movement even if there is no breeze.

Ventilation

The movement of air, even slightly warmer air, across your skin causes a cooling sensation. The air removes heat and evaporates perspiration, creating the illusion of a comfortable temperature. By simply moving air through your home, you can reduce the need for air conditioning.

Here are three simple ways to move air through your home:

- **Operable windows:** The easiest way to create natural ventilation is to install operable windows. Locate windows at different heights and on opposite walls to encourage cross-ventilation. Windows placed at the same height allow air to pass only straight across the room.

- **Bathroom fans:** Bathroom fans exhaust the hot, steamy air from your bathroom to the outside. Not only do fans lessen the need for air conditioning, but it reduces potential problems with moisture and mold.

- **Switch boxes for clothes dryers:** Install a switch box on the hose of your clothes dryer. In the summer, the hot air is pumped outside, as it normally would be. In the winter, flip the switch box to redirect the heat back into the room. These inexpensive boxes are available at any hardware store.

Earth berms

Earth sloped near or against the house protects it from cold winters and hot summers. Called *berms,* these mounds use the high thermal mass of the earth to keep your building cool. Berms can be an attractive addition to your landscape.

Passive solar

Passive solar integrates insulation, thermal mass, and passive cooling into one cohesive approach. When used correctly, a passive solar home can use the sun to provide the heating, cooling, and daylighting of most of your needs.

The process is simple: Passive solar design takes advantage of the fact that the summer sun is higher than the winter sun. Overhangs shade the building from the summer sun, keeping it cool. The same overhangs allow the lower winter sun to enter the building and heat an interior thermal mass wall.

Passive solar design works in most climates, but it works best in areas with seasonal changes in weather. When a sun-facing, thermal mass wall is placed behind some glass, it's called a *trombe wall*. The space between the glass and the wall fills with hot air. Vents at the top and bottom of the wall control this hot air, allowing it to be used to heat the building.

The best approach to passive solar is to use the principles to influence and shape the design of your home. Although considering passive solar during the initial design of your home is best, even an existing building can benefit from these ideas. Passive solar systems don't add to the cost of the building, and you'll see an immediate improvement in your energy use.

Active solar

Active solar is a strategy for designing high-performance, ultra-energy-efficient buildings. Active solar incorporates all the elements of a passive solar design (see the preceding section), but with additional mechanical equipment, such as pumps or fans, to take advantage of the heat from the sun. This equipment can include some elaborate technologies such as:

- ✔ **Motorized shades:** Timers and sensors control when window shades are raised and lowered, which controls heat gain from the sun.

- ✔ **Solar trackers:** Solar panels are turned throughout the day to follow the path of the sun. This increases the output of the solar panels.

- ✔ **Vents:** Thermostats and sensors control vents, which open to allow warm air into the house.

Book IV

Green Remodeling

Book V

Sustainable Landscaping

The 5th Wave — By Rich Tennant

"Of course, when we landscape the place, we'll get rid of that old washing machine and replace it with one that's indigenous to these parts."

In this book . . .

*E*ven the lushest landscape may fail to be green. (In terms of ecofriendliness, that is.) In fact, landscape designs that necessitate a whole lotta chemicals and watering are the very opposite of green.

No worries, though: You can create a great-looking, functional landscape that doesn't tax our planet's resources. You get tips for doing just that in the chapters to come, wherein you find out how to design and maintain a truly green landscape.

Here are the contents of Book V at a glance:

Chapter 1

Pursuing a Smart, Sustainable Landscape

. . . .

In This Chapter

▶ Getting an overview of sustainability

▶ Figuring out how you fit in

▶ Designing your sustainable landscape

▶ Building hot landscape action

. . . .

*W*hat's your dream garden like? Is it a place of frantic activity, pollution, noise, constant struggle, endless expense, butchered and dying plants, and menacing weeds? Or do you imagine a peaceful retreat: serene, wholesome, bursting with color and thriving with little effort?

Sadly, most gardens are dependent on *adversarial horticulture:* the war-like practices of hacking, decapitating, shearing, poisoning, ripping, tearing, and swearing that characterize many homeowners' relationship with landscaping. In fact, the American culture seems to encourage the false idea that a garden is a battleground, a place where special skills and violent activities are necessary to keep things in line. What a shame. You shouldn't have to become a weed warrior or an herbicide-wielding killer just to have a nice yard. Who thought up this crazy mess, anyway?

Nobody gardens nature. Nature quietly thrives while down in town everyone takes up arms every Saturday morning. What's the difference, and where did we go wrong? And most importantly, how can we change things so that this doesn't happen again? This chapter shows you how to develop your landscaping along natural models that have proven themselves over tens of millions of years. When you do things the right way, you enjoy lovely, environmentally friendly surroundings and you get a break from the battle.

Getting Up to Speed on Sustainability

At one time, all gardens were simple. They were made up of plants, soil, and natural building materials. They didn't cost much to create or care for. Their impact on the environment was positive because they didn't cause strip mining, release poisons into the atmosphere, or consume huge quantities of fossil fuel. They were sustainable before the word was popular because they could go on essentially forever.

Gardens can be that way again. All over the world people are getting wise to the fact that they have an alternative to the dysfunctional industrial/commercial landscaping model that's been jammed down our throats by advertising and ignorance. There is a better way. It's not 100 percent perfect, but by doing things the sustainable way, you'll make a huge and important difference. Your land is your opportunity to help create a better future.

What the heck is sustainable landscaping anyway?

A few key ideas describe how sustainable landscaping works. They're simple and easy enough that you can put them into practice in your home landscape without an advanced degree in botany.

A *sustainable landscape* includes the following features:

- ✔ **A living, integrated system:** Nature is a system of interrelated subsystems that work together to form a smoothly operating whole — like your body, for example, made up of its various organs, or a forest filled with many kinds of plants and animals, or the ocean teeming with millions of interdependent life forms. By making your landscape a highly functioning system patterned after the ways of nature, it will operate like nature: without the need for much control or intervention and without harming any other living system.

- ✔ **Homeostasis:** *Homeostasis* is a fancy word for stability. It's the balance of forces in a living system, with no force getting out of control to cause harm. Consider your body, which more or less functions automatically. You don't need to will your heart to beat or your eyes to see; it just happens. A little care from you, and everything is groovy. The landscape system can work this way, too, if you set it up right.

- ✔ **Deep design:** Homeostasis in the garden doesn't happen by accident. It's a product of good design. Not the too-common kind of superficial design that creates pretty but dysfunctional gardens, but design that looks beneath appearances to develop a beautiful landscape that also really works. It takes special skills to create a sustainable design, but you can discover those skills booking this chapter. (Here's a tip: They're not hard at all.)

✔ **Cyclical:** Nature recycles everything. There's no waste in nature. As the Buddhist master Thich Nhat Hanh once said, "When I look at a rose I see compost; when I look at compost I see a rose."

Conventional manmade systems are linear: Get a virgin material from nature (usually with disastrous effects at the source), use toxic and energy-intensive processes to alter it so much that it will never go back to nature again, use it one time, and when its usually too-short useful life comes to an end, dispose of it in a landfill where it plugs up the works of yet another formerly living system.

Nature has been very patient with us, but this linear game is just about up. She hates it, and besides, she's nearly out of merchandise. By going back to the infinite and ancient cyclical way of life, our gardens become one with nature, less troublesome, and more enduring.

✔ **Harmony with local environment:** Your property is unique in all the world, with a particular soil type, microclimate, exposure, vegetation, and other factors. By choosing plants and other elements that are well suited to these particulars, you're setting up a robust ecosystem that will be happy with its lot in life.

Conventional gardens rely on ill-adapted plants and other elements and then depend on a constant input of resources to keep them from failing.

✔ **Careful management of inputs and outputs:** The sustainable landscape thrives on what nature offers. It makes efficient use of resources, such as building materials, water, fertilizer, fossil fuels, and others. What goes into it and what comes out are minimized so that as many impacts as possible are beneficial.

✔ **On-site impacts:** What happens on site is carefully considered at the design stage. Natural features, such as soil, native plants, and animal habitat, are preserved. All improvements must meet the test of being a good player. Each element in the newly formed ecosystem must play a beneficial role: making oxygen, sequestering carbon, providing food, improving the climate inside dwellings, preventing erosion, protecting against wildfire, to name a few. To minimize negative impacts, toxic materials aren't part of the scheme, nor are energy-intensive processes, noise-generating machinery, or thirsty plantings.

✔ **Off-site impacts:** What happens off-site is important, too; your landscaping practices should cause no damage at the source of materials. Your landscape won't be truly sustainable unless it leaves forests intact, mountains unmined, oil unburned, and workers safe and happy.

Work toward taking your landscape beyond mere sustainability. As visionary architect William McDonough has observed, we shouldn't just be less bad, we should be good. Landscapes offer so many benefits to users and to nature that it's easy to use the power of the sun and rain and soil to create a paradise for all living beings. You, too, can do that, and there's no reason not to.

What does a sustainable landscape look like?

Sustainable landscaping isn't about a look. A Japanese garden can be sustainable. So can an English garden or a desert garden or a woodland garden. A sustainable landscape can be formal or informal, geometric or naturalistic, simple or complex.

Other than planting vast swaths of mowed lawn in a dry climate, you're pretty much free to choose whatever look you want as long as you follow the principles of sustainability, setting up a smoothly functioning ecosystem that makes minimal demands and creates minimal problems.

Why sustainable landscaping matters to the environment

The traditional landscape is an environmental train wreck. Some of the ways that it damages the environment include the following:

- Fragmenting and destroying native habitat.

- Consuming natural resources.

- Strip mining, clear-cutting of forests, and other impacts at the source of materials.

- Introducing non-native plants that invade and devastate wild ecosystems.

- Wrecking waterways and groundwater through leaching of pesticides, herbicides, and fertilizers. (Much — to the tune of 40 to 60 percent — of the nitrogen applied to lawns ends up in the water.)

- Increasing runoff, which results in further damage to waterways and also causes urban flooding.

- Filling canyons and landfills with waste.

- Increasing global warming through the use of fossil fuels.

- Wasting precious water to keep useless ornamental plants and lawns alive.

- Decreasing the peace; outdoor power equipment creates noise in every neighborhood.

- Harming living soil with heavy machinery and toxic chemicals.

- Disturbing the natural animal order. Pesticides kill 60 to 70 million birds each year, not to mention its impacts on beneficial insects and other wildlife. And, get this: U.S. landscape pesticide use is applied at a rate of ten times more per acre than that of agriculture.

Busting some sustainable myths

As with anything new, concerns come up about sustainable landscaping practices. You'll be making a big, expensive, long-term commitment to your landscaping, and you need to know sustainable landscaping isn't some goofy new-age idea that doesn't really deliver the goods. Here are some facts to set your mind at ease.

✔ MYTH: Sustainable landscapes are ugly.

TRUTH: Plants in a sustainable landscape are healthy and vigorous, and they have room to grow into their beautiful natural form. Structures are made from natural materials with their inherent beauty showing through. Sustainable landscapes are green, flowery, fresh, and lovely.

✔ MYTH: Sustainable landscapes are expensive.

TRUTH: All landscaping takes some cash, but sustainable landscaping is less expensive than traditional landscaping for a couple of reasons. First, because the sustainable approach emphasizes plants over hardscape, you save money on the installation. Plants are cheaper than concrete. Second, and even more important, the ongoing care of the landscape will be much less because it's undemanding of resources and labor.

✔ MYTH: Sustainable landscapes don't work.

TRUTH: The whole point of developing a landscape sustainably is to create an ecosystem that functions smoothly without much effort from us. When you look at what you need to keep a conventional landscape in one piece — the mowing, watering, pest control, pruning and all the rest — you can easily see that it's conventional landscaping that doesn't work.

Human well-being doesn't escape the effects of traditional landscaping, either. The health of one in seven people is affected by pesticides. Air pollution caused by pesticides and fossil fuel use damages the health of everyone. Between 60,000 and 70,000 severe accidents and fatalities occur each year just from lawn mowing. We can do better!

Sustainable landscaping addresses all these issues by cleaning up the system, making these impacts unnecessary, and respecting the environment.

What's in it for you

The case for taking sustainable action to preserve our planet is strong, but if you need even further reason to pursue a sustainable landscape, go ahead and think of yourself: A sustainable landscape is cheaper, easier to care for, more satisfying to live with, and much more interesting.

You save money because your inputs are significantly reduced. You spend less on materials, water, fertilizer, gasoline, labor, dump fees — the works. Compared with traditional landscaping practices, sustainable landscaping is a penny pincher's delight.

Because your landscaping will make so few demands on you, you're able to spend less time keeping it from falling apart and more time enjoying it (or enjoying something else you love). If you've busted your chops on a conventional landscape for a while, you know how much work it can be. Imagine that work not happening. That's what converting to a sustainable landscape can do for you.

Finally, after you see how beautifully everything works, you'll come to admire the elegance of a finely tuned system. It's soothing to know that things are working smoothly without much help from you.

Doing Your Part: What It Takes to Make a Sustainable Landscape

Sustainable landscapes occur naturally all around you, but taking over Nature's job requires some thought and effort on your part. The following sections provide some tips on how to take your sustainable landscaping project from good idea to beautiful, low-maintenance retreat.

Taking the time to do it right

Slow down. Creating a sustainable landscape is a big project. And more important, the practice of deep design demands careful observation and attention to detail.

In ancient times, Japanese garden designers would sit on the site every day, all day, for a year, carefully noticing the way the sun moved, how the trees responded to wind, what animals visited, and many more subtleties that can be grasped only by quiet, intense scrutiny. As the seasons changed, they learned in summer what they could never learn in spring, and so on through the full annual cycle. Only after that apprenticeship would they dare to begin the design process.

Consider taking a year of your own to develop a deep bond with your property. You'll discover quite a lot, and your work will be enriched by your understanding. Plus, you'll get to put off all that hard physical work a while longer.

Getting buff: Your sustainable DIY fitness course

If you're planning to do the work of building your new landscape, you can look forward to a lot of very hard physical effort. Building a landscape isn't crocheting doilies. You can end up in the best physical condition of your life or in the chiropractor's office.

First, take stock of your ability to dig ditches all day, lift heavy stuff, and generally grunt out, weekend after weekend. Balance that against the cost of paying someone to do some or all of the work. If you do want to tackle it, be sure that you know how to work safely and check with your doctor if you have any qualms about your fitness level. Stay safe, OK?

Skills that lower your bills

Doing the work yourself can save up to half the total cost of the project. But before you leap in, assess your abilities. You can learn new skills, true enough; but you can also get in over your head and end up with a really crummy job because you didn't actually know what you were doing.

Tackle work that you're experienced with and stretch yourself to learn some new things. The rest? Hey, don't let your ego get in the way of hiring an expert. It's cheaper than doing it all over.

Setting a budget

Developing a good tight budget is tough when you're not exactly sure what you'll be doing. You have a lot of variables to consider, and costs vary wildly depending on the kinds of improvements you'll be making. For example, a flagstone patio can cost 20 or 30 times what a ground cover would for the same area.

Generally speaking, landscaping an entire yard front and rear can set you back the price of a new car or two, but the sky's the limit. (Conversely, you can save tons of money by doing the work yourself and by tapping the waste stream for materials whenever you can.) Develop a rough budget by talking to contractors, shopping for materials, and also considering the value of your own time. Don't get too detailed at this stage.

Scheduling your project

Consider the scope of the work and how much time it will take you to do it or have it done. If you'll be getting professional help with some or all of the job, talk to your contractor about the timing from their perspective. And remember that many landscaping tasks are dependent on the time of year. Think, too, about your cash flow if that's a consideration. Develop a project calendar using the sequencing information in Table 1-1. Of course, things can get off track, but at least you'll have an action plan to work from.

Some steps are done concurrently with others. For example, you may (and probably will) still be designing certain aspects of the project while you're building others. Whatever the particulars of your project, Table 1-1 can help give you an idea of how things usually go.

Certain sequences are pretty hard to argue with. You have to do your demolition before you build anything new. And it's a whole lot easier to do the grading before the plants are planted and the irrigation is in. Others are more flexible. You may be installing a patio in one corner of the yard before you even touch another corner. And as for design, it can be a continuing process of thinking, learning, and reconsidering throughout the course of the entire project. Overall, though, if you follow the chain of events in Table 1-1, you'll do okay.

Table 1-1	Order of Operations
Category	*Tasks*
Planning and design	Site analysis, landscape plans, budgeting.
Permits and approvals	Building permits, zoning approval, and so on.
Grow and kill	Weed control.
Utilities location	Call 811 for line location.
Demolition	Remove plants, structures, and so on.
Tree trimming	Prune existing trees.
Earthwork	Grading, excavation, import soil.
Drainage	Underground drains, dry streambeds, and so on.
Erosion control	Netting, hydromulching, and so on.
Water mains	Piping, backflow prevention device/s, valves.
Electrical	Irrigation control wires, lighting wires.
Flatwork	Paving, patios, walkways, and so on.
Plantings	Trees, shrubs, ground covers.
Mulching	Cover ground with mulch.

Category	Tasks
Lighting	Install fixtures, transformers. (Check out Book VII to find out about going solar in your landscape.)
Site furnishings	Benches, tables, artwork, and so on.

Planning and Design: The Key to a Sustainable Landscape

When it comes to making your landscaping work properly, good design is everything. It determines once and forever how the system will work. It's important, it's detailed, and it's a lot of fun.

Getting to know the site and your needs

Responding appropriately to conditions is essential to developing the kind of finely tuned landscape that's easy to live with. The first step is to make friends with the site so that you understand what you're dealing with.

But understanding the site isn't enough. You have to learn what you want and need, too. Rushing into the design phase without going through this process will leave you without the information you need to make good decisions.

First, plan on spending some quality time with your yard. Go outside when you have the time to just hang out, quietly observing the many characteristics of your property: the path of the sun, the condition of the soil, the health of existing plants, good and bad views, and so on. Take photos, make notes, move around to see things from as many perspectives as possible. Get professional advice if you have special concerns, such as an unstable hillside or soil problems.

Make a simple list that details what you want from a finished landscape. Include your family in the process. Create this list while outdoors so that you can better imagine the possibilities. For example, suppose that you were to stand in your back yard and dream about what you need. You might list privacy, a shady place with a hammock or a patio, a play space for the kids, a vegetable garden, a few fruit trees, secure fencing, a butterfly garden, a wildlife habitat, and a water feature. Take the time to get it all down on paper and be sure everybody gets heard.

Developing a design

Design deserves your best thinking because it determines the outcome of the project and how it will function over time. Design goes from the general ("I think I want a vegetable garden") to the specific ("I want four 4 x 10-foot raised stone beds in the northeast corner of the back yard with 6 kohlrabi plants and 5 Bad Boy tomatoes."). It's a rigorous process, but anyone can do it.

Here's an overview:

1. **Develop the conceptual design.**

   After you've learned about the site and about your own needs, you're ready to take a first pass at putting it all together. This step is called a *conceptual design* because it looks at the general approach to laying things out.

2. **Refine your design.**

   After you have a good understanding of how the elements fit together, you can begin to work on all the little details. What will that patio be made of, and precisely what will its shape and location be? Exactly which tree will go on the east side of the house and what size will it be at planting time? What species of perennials will go in the front border, how many of each kind, and what size? You'll develop a series of plans to detail the construction, planting, irrigation and other phases of the work. These plans help you refine your ideas and also guide you through the long process of constructing the landscape.

3. **Revisit the budget.**

   After you know exactly what you'll be doing, it's time to crunch hard numbers, adding up all the materials, equipment, outside labor, and other costs to determine your total budget. If you'll be doing an entire property, this number will be big. If it's too big, consider how you can lower costs without compromising quality (by using smaller plants or less hardscape, for example) or how you can break up the project into phases that you'll spread out over a few years.

Starting with Simple, Sustainable Projects

Designing a sustainable landscape from scratch takes time, but you can do several things right away to improve your landscape's environmental record. They require little or no money, are easy, and don't require the use of heavy equipment, chiropractors, or bad language.

Axing your overgrown plants

Take note of how many hours per month you spend keeping plants from growing too big for the space they're in. This is time you could be enjoying a nice sustainable activity like loafing.

Plants never, ever figure out (much less obey) how big you want them to be. When they're programmed to get 100 feet tall, they always try to do so. If you want an 8-foot-tall plant, you need to choose one that gets 8 feet tall at maturity. You will never have to trim it. It will look better and be healthier for being left alone. And you'll look so relaxed in that hammock.

Getting rid of the weaklings

Sorry, rose lovers, but hybrid tea roses really stink when it comes to taking care of themselves. It hurts sustainability-minded landscapers to ponder the rust and the leaf spot and the bugs and all the other ills and ailments these pitiable creatures suffer from — and all the chemicals homeowners use to keep these ills and ailments under control.

Consider putting the roses out of their misery and replacing them with something a little more durable.

Go around your yard with a shovel, swiftly and mercifully ending the lives of namby-pamby plants of whatever kind. Or, if they just need a better location to thrive (if they aren't getting enough sun, for example, or are too exposed to wind), move them to a spot where they'll do better. Probably 80 percent of gardening problems are caused by 20 percent of the plants. You know who they are. Go get 'em.

Dumping your chemical arsenal

Exactly what excuse does anyone have for holding on to that smelly collection of gummy bottles of insecticide and scary containers of weed killer and leaky bags of fert-n-hurt? C'mon. You know you'll never use that stuff again. You're a sustainable gardener now! Put those old jugs into a sealed container and take it to your local hazardous waste collection center. They'll safely dispose of it for you.

Some herbicides, pesticides, and fertilizers are truly treacherous, so be sure and wear protective gear and be very careful not to spill anything as you purge.

Trading your power tools for hand tools

The thing about power tools is that they don't actually save that much effort. First of all, you had to work pretty hard to earn the money to buy them, right? Then you have to store them somewhere. And do tune-ups and repairs. And fuel them and oil them and wipe them down and sharpen the blades and adjust the dang carburetor over and over again because nobody but the high priests of internal combustion can get it right the first time.

And think about the number of times you've pulled the starter cord with no results. Must be in the thousands, right? Remember how frustrating that is? And the language! Shoot, you could have had the lawn mowed with a simple push mower by the time you got that wheezy old putt-putt running and regained your composure. Power tools are a heck of a lot of work.

Shop around for some truly good, lifetime-quality hand tools and then leave the power ones out at the curb for some other fool to struggle with. You'll be glad you did.

Mulching

Naked beds don't work. The soil dries out too quickly, root systems suffer heat and cold, weeds come up everywhere, rain washes earth away, beneficial soil microorganisms suffer, mud sticks to your boots. In nature, organic material constantly rains down from the plants, creating mulch while also returning valuable nutrients to the soil. The sustainable landscaper mimics this elegant system by practicing chop-and-drop pruning (let the pieces fall where they may) and by spreading some form of organic mulch on the surface of the soil.

Be sure you use an organic mulch (in most situations), not crushed rock or other nondegradable material. Many communities offer mulch made from green waste for free or very cheap. You can also purchase mulch made from many different local materials, many of them from the waste stream.

According to the ASPCA, cocoa mulch is toxic to dogs. If you have a dog, use an alternative material.

Growing food

What better thing to use your land for than growing your own food? Home-grown food offers the following advantages over supermarket food:

✔ It's stunningly fresh.

✔ It didn't get shipped from far away.

✔ It's organic (assuming that you grow it that way).

✔ It's made use of few resources (assuming that the crop is adapted to your local conditions).

✔ It's not dependent on fossil fuel.

✔ You can share it with your friends and neighbors.

✔ It tastes really, really good.

Some food is easier to grow than others. Once established, most fruit trees and perennial crops, such as asparagus, strawberries, and rhubarb, are less work than annual crops like broccoli, tomatoes, and onions.

Look for crops that are easy to grow in your area. If you live in a cool microclimate, you may find that it makes most tomato plants unproductive. Buy your tomatoes at the farmer's market and use your land to grow potatoes, leaf crops, asparagus, artichokes, and other climate-adapted varieties. It's so much easier than struggling to make something happy that's really out of its element. Book VI tells you much more about growing your own food.

Chapter 2

Making Sustainable Decisions for Your Landscape Design

*O*ne of the coolest things about landscaping your property sustainably is that you, personally, benefit from it. Heck, even if you don't give a hoot about the environment, you're going to save big bucks and a whole lot of hard work that you don't really want to do anyway. Sustainable landscaping is good for your lazy side, and the planet still gets what it needs.

In this chapter, you find out how to make good decisions about what to include in your landscape and how to select materials and features that make sense for you and the environment and create a dream landscape that's beautiful and easy to live with. And then you get tips for putting it all together in a landscape design that delivers.

Maximizing Materials, Minimizing Waste

When you create a garden that minimizes the need for *inputs* (whatever you bring into it, like building and maintenance materials) and makes use of the most efficient and earth-friendly inputs, and that also generates few or no *outputs* (what we erroneously call "waste"), you get a highly tuned, very efficient system that rewards you with decades of pleasure and beauty. (This section talks about inputs. Check out the "Generating few (or no) outputs" section, later in this chapter, for more info about minimizing outputs.)

The following sections explore, on an item-by-item basis, how you can optimize inputs.

Building material inputs: Turning so-called trash into landscaping treasure

You need to build the landscape out of *something*, of course, but there are huge differences in materials and many really great sustainable options.

When trying to minimize building material inputs, first consider how much hardscape (stone, wood, or other nonplant parts of your landscape) you really need. Don't build a huge deck that you'll never actually use or pour a patio that would accommodate a wedding reception when you really just need someplace for the family to have dinner. Ask what you need, not what you want. Get into the habit of self-restraint. When you do, you give the poor old planet a break and save big bucks.

The first place to look for materials is in your own backyard, where what you have is free, doesn't need to be transported from elsewhere (burning up fossil fuel in the process), and isn't doing much just sitting in your side yard by the trash cans.

Do you have native stones, undesirable trees that can be harvested for lumber, an old patio that could be broken up and turned into stepping stones? Go look around your property and make a list of anything that you could possibly transform into a landscape feature. If nothing else there's always soil, which you can turn into handsome earthen walls and benches. And don't overlook the neighbors either — their so-called trash may be just what you need for your garden.

Consider re-using things that come from the community's waste stream, such as broken concrete (now called *urbanite,* a brand-new mineral!), which you can easily turn into a lovely patio or handsome dry-stacked low retaining wall. Try turning old timbers on their way to the landfill into edging for a raised bed or a handsome footbridge.

The following sections provide a sampling of waste-stream landscaping materials that you can probably find floating around your community

Salvaged and reclaimed materials

Salvaged and reclaimed materials aren't really waste because people recognize that they have value. They're resources that could have been wasted but are instead carefully saved and sold to willing buyers.

Look for redwood that's been taken out of old barns (with the barn owner's permission, of course), for example, or even logs dredged up from underwater where they sank a century ago and were left behind.

Modern portable lumber mills are circulating around some communities, making usable lumber out of urban trees that had to be cut down for one reason or another. You can find used bricks in nearly any community. A search of the Web can often turn up amazingly cool things for sale that you can use to create a one-of-a-kind refuse-chic landscape feature.

Recycled content materials

The difference between waste-stream or reclaimed materials and recycled ones is the degree of processing involved. You can use a waste-stream material, such as urbanite, as-is, with no special alchemy to make it into something else. It's still just concrete when you're done with it: concrete then, concrete now. But a recycled material, such as plastic lumber, goes into a factory as a big load of sticky pop bottles and comes out looking like a 2 x 4 — you'd have a hard time guessing what it's made from.

Recycling often isn't actually recycling. Some people call it *downcycling* or *remanufacturing* because the end product is so different from the ingredients that went into it, and because in most cases you can never take it in the other direction — for example, you can't make soda bottles out of old plastic lumber. A few materials, such as aluminum and steel, are truly recyclable, but their use in the landscape is minimal.

Despite these imperfections, using recycled materials is a big improvement over buying new ones, because it makes use of what had been considered trash and reduces the need to cut down trees, strip-mine raw materials, and do other environmentally nasty things.

Some recycled content materials, such as plastic lumber, may cost somewhat more than conventional products. Others, like wood chips, are free or available at a very low cost.

Low-impact materials

If you have to go with a virgin material, be sure it's produced in an environmentally sustainable way. Look for lumber that's been certified as having been sustainably grown and harvested by an independent organization (such as the Forest Stewardship Council or The Sustainable Forestry Initiative). Or consider straw bale or earthen construction instead of using lumber. Grow your own wood or bamboo for a truly low-impact and ultra-local resource. Substitute high-density polyethylene (HDPE) or galvanized piping for PVC. (Avoid copper because it is strip mined.) If you must use paint and finishes, choose low-VOC ones that don't emit as much junk into the atmosphere.

Renewable materials

Simply put, a renewable resource is one that you can keep going back for more of. Trees are a renewable resource; oil is not. By choosing renewable materials, you can be sure that future generations will be able to enjoy them, too. Renewable materials are those that come from living sources, because they're the only things that replicate themselves. Here are some examples:

- ✔ Animal manures
- ✔ Bamboo
- ✔ Lumber and other wood products
- ✔ Organic fertilizers such as bone meal, fish emulsion, kelp
- ✔ Straw

You can expedite the renewal process by planting trees after you purchase lumber or by donating to tree planting through a carbon-offsetting organization, such as Carbonfund.org Foundation (www.carbonfund.org) or TerraPass (www.terrapass.com).

Heritage materials

Heritage materials are produced so that they can be re-used over and over again as circumstances change. An example is the interlocking concrete paver block systems that are popping up in driveways all over the place. Because they can be taken up and re-used, your driveway could become a neighbor's driveway 40 years from now and then end up, another few decades out, in the next block as a patio in the back yard of somebody who wasn't even born when you first built your driveway.

When you create things that last and then make them modular so that they can be used again or repurposed, you're doing something very sustainable indeed because the initial environmental impact can be spread over many decades of use. Any durable and movable item — bricks, stones, paving blocks, segmental retaining walls — can fall into the category of heritage material, as long as you understand their long-term potential and avoid cementing them into place so that they can't be re-used.

Pseudo-sustainable materials busted

As with so many things these days, some of what passes for "green" materials is anything but. For example, phony plastic lawns are all the rage in some circles. Some communities even give rebates to homeowners who replace their living lawns with artificial ones. Manufacturers point out that a fake lawn uses no water and needs no mowing, fertilizer, or pesticides. But they ignore the fact that nonliving turf worsens the urban heat-island effect, uses materials that are made from fossil fuels and in some cases may contain toxic elements, eliminates even the paltry life-giving benefits of real grass, and creates a potential waste-stream nightmare at the end of its service. Add to that the fact that synthetic turf does require some water to keep it clean and contributes to stormwater pollution because it offers no biofiltration, and you can see that plastic lawns are a bad idea.

Real lawns are a huge part of the negative environmental impact of landscaping, but substituting a sea of plastic is going in the wrong direction. Far better is to install a meadow of native grasses or other perennials. Better yet, put in a diverse garden of useful plants that will be appreciated by wildlife and enjoyed by you for food, with far fewer problems.

Maintenance inputs: Planning ahead to reduce the need for upkeep

There is no such thing as no-maintenance landscaping, but by designing for sustainability and building things so that they last, you greatly reduce the materials, effort, and money that go into keeping the place looking good and functioning well. The upcoming sections give you ideas for making the most of the materials that your landscape may require.

Water

We think of water as being abundant, yet out of the 326 million cubic miles of water on the planet, only about .03 percent is usable by humans. Overall, that's not much.

Water is a renewable resource, of course. In fact, the water that falls from the sky in the form of rain and snow is about as renewable as you can get — plus, it's free. Rain even picks up nitrogen on its way down, delivering nice organic fertilizer right to your plants and then watering it in, all at no charge. But water is in short supply in most places now, and it's not right to use potable water to irrigate lawns and decorative plants when people are going thirsty. Fortunately, you can greatly reduce your landscape water use without materially compromising the appearance and function of your garden.

Here are some simple strategies to set up your landscaping so that it's water-thrifty:

- ✔ **Design smart.** Group plants into *hydrozones*, which are areas containing plants with similar water needs. (Chapter 4 tells you more about choosing plants for a sustainable landscape.)

- ✔ **Choose drought-tolerant plants.** Select species that are climate-appropriate and that will thrive on rainfall alone, or with very little supplemental irrigation.

- ✔ **Downsize your lawn.** The lawn is the big water-sucker in the landscape. Try reducing the size of your lawn to just what you actually use. Consider a long, skinny lawn that's great for throwing a Frisbee or running around on but that eliminates the excess turf you never use anyway.

> ✔ **Mulch.** Mulch is a layer of organic matter — usually wood chips or bark — that you put on top of the soil. It conserves water by reducing evaporative loss from the soil surface, keeping the roots of the plants cool, and reducing weeds that compete with desirable plants for water.

Fertilizer

Nobody fertilizes the mountains or the forests, yet they grow perfectly well century after century. If you suspect that there must be something haywire about the constant need for "feeding" garden plants, you're right.

If a plant is well adapted to local conditions, it's going to be satisfied with the nutrients that are naturally available in the soil. And if you can manage to resist raking up all the leaves, you allow valuable nutrients to remain in place, which means you don't have to replace them with expensive, imported fertilizer.

If you just can't stand to see leaves lying on the ground, then compost them and return them to the soil. (But hey — they call them leaves because you're supposed to leave them there.) Oh, and when you do fertilize, be sure to use organic fertilizers, which come from natural, renewable, nonpetroleum sources, are less likely to burn plants, and are a lot kinder to the soil.

Pesticides

Plants in nature get pests and diseases just the same as the ones in your garden. In nature, though, there's a better balance of pests and predators, and because the system is in a state of equipoise things are less likely to go wildly out of control. And, of course, nature doesn't have the same attitude about pests and diseases as the average gardener. Humans tend to judge roses as beautiful and aphids as unbeautiful.

Even if you want to stay within the bounds of proper suburban order, you can control most pests pretty easily without resorting to wicked chemicals and warlike ways. Refer to Chapter 3 of Book VI for complete details on pest management.

Herbicides

Herbicides kill weeds. Weeds are plants that are both undesired and inclined to self-replicate to a troublesome degree. A lot of them are imported, but opinion makes a plant a weed, so natives don't escape the designation.

Despite decades of herbicide use, you may have noticed that you still have as many weeds as ever. Something's not working. Although you'll never entirely get rid of weeds, there are some simple, sustainable strategies that work at least as well as the big chemical guns. See Chapter 3 of Book VI tells you more about this important subject.

Fossil fuels

Petroleum products (oil, gasoline, natural gas) are used everywhere in the garden. The first thing that comes to mind is gas-powered lawn mowers and other power garden equipment.

According to the EPA, Americans use over 800 million gallons of gas a year just mowing their lawns. Incredible. But there's a whole lot more oil in those gardens. Have a look:

- ✔ Transportation of imported materials

- ✔ Transportation of tools, equipment, and workers

- ✔ Manufacturing of nearly everything used in the landscape

- ✔ Pumping water from its source to your house

- ✔ Chemically based fertilizers

- ✔ Many pesticides

- ✔ Plastics of all kinds, including irrigation pipe and materials, garden structures, furniture, and plant containers

- ✔ Construction processes that require power tools and heavy equipment

- ✔ Maintenance, including the use of power equipment

- ✔ Disposal, including trash hauling, green-waste processing and landfill management

By using hand tools, organic fertilizers, natural materials, and other low-impact inputs, you can significantly reduce your garden's dependence on fossil fuels. And if you use some of your property to grow food, you'll reduce your own dependence on fossil fuels for food production and shipment.

In fact, many sustainable processes don't just make things less bad, they make them a lot better than they were. Take this approach far enough, and your landscaping will go beyond sustainability to become a net producer of great stuff — food, fresh air, cooler homes, more wildlife, happier people and more. That's when things get really good.

Time

Sustainable landscaping is stable landscaping, which means it isn't always trying to blow itself to pieces if you leave it alone for a few days. With its own elegant system of checks and balances, it doesn't really need much from you. A little benevolent nudging now and then is sufficient for the routine care of the landscape, with perhaps a long day in the garden once or twice a season. Know what that means? You have time to enjoy the garden instead of working in it every weekend!

Money

When you construct your landscape sustainably and maintain it sensibly, you spend less money on it over time. It may or may not cost you less to put in, but certainly it will cost less to care for because it makes fewer ongoing demands. Table 2-1 gives you a rough idea about how the costs differ.

Table 2-1	Conventional vs. Sustainable Costs*	
Element	*Conventional Garden*	*Sustainable Garden*
Original design and installation	5,000 sq. ft. × $4 per foot = $20,000	5,000 sq. ft. @ $4 per foot = $20,000
Professional maintenance labor (excluding lawn)	3,000 sq. ft. @ $0.03/ft./mo. × 20 years = $21,600	3,000 sq. ft. @ $0.02/ft./mo. × 20 years = $14,400
Lawn mowing and care	$50/week × 50 weeks × 20 years = $50,000	Zero (no lawn)
Pesticides (traditional) and soil amendments (sustainable)	$10/mo. × 20 years = $2,400	$2/mo. × 20 years = $480
Water	10 units/mo. @ $5 each (inc. sewer charges & tax) × 20 years = $12,000	3 units/mo. @ $4.50 each (inc. sewer charges & tax) × 20 years = $3,240
Replacement of short-lived plants	10 per year @ $40.00 inc. removal & disposal × 20 years = $8,000	None
Totals	$114,000	$38,120
Maintenance as a percentage of total cost	82%	48%
Net cost savings of sustainable garden		$75,880

Prices are not adjusted for inflation.

Generating few (or no) outputs

Outputs — the so-called waste products of the landscape — occur because of inefficiencies in the design of the system. When a landscape is designed as a *linear system* (like an industrial process where materials are taken from nature, used once, and then thrown away), a lot of waste is inevitable. Nature is a *cyclical system*. Each element in a cyclical system stays within that system, eliminating the need for both inputs and waste.

You can minimize or even eliminate most outputs by optimizing your inputs. This give-and-take is the synergy of a finely tuned system at work. The following sections focus on less desirable outputs, but, of course, some outputs are good — the oxygen given off by living plants, for example, or the food you grow in your garden. Never forget that a sustainable garden is a very fine thing to have around.

Green waste

Green waste is a fancy term for the plant parts we cut off and send to that magical place called "away." Sometimes green waste ends up in a landfill, and sometimes it comes back to us as mulch.

Excess growth that just needs to be cut off and thrown away creates problems without any attendant benefits. Putting the wrong plant in the wrong place is one common cause of green waste — so much trimming to try to overcome a plant's genetically determined size. Overwatering and overfertilizing both make plants grow faster and bigger (and lead to more green waste).

When you design your garden, carefully check the ultimate size of the plants you select and then locate them so that they have enough room to grow. Consider how much time you may be spending now just keeping overly large plants in place and then imagine a garden that required little or no pruning to control the size of things.

Polluted runoff

Polluted runoff is caused by rainfall or irrigation water moving pesticides, herbicides, fertilizers, dog poo, and other nasty stuff into streets, storm drains, and eventually bodies of water. Polluted runoff is a major problem all over the world, and you can correct it by simply not using all that junk in the first place. Nothing in, nothing out. You can deal with what little remaining pollution there might be on your property, mainly in the form of atmospheric pollution that settles on your land and rooftops in between rains, by keeping rainwater on site when it's safe and practical to do so. You can use dry streambeds, underground percolation chambers, bioswales, green roofs, pervious paving, and other strategies that allow water to soak in rather than run off and bioremediate pollutants through the natural action of plants and soil microorganisms. *Sustainable Landscaping For Dummies* (Wiley) gives you information on all these techniques.

Air pollution

Also consider the emissions produced by humans engaged in pernicious gardening activities, such as operating power lawn and garden equipment, spraying volatile pesticides and herbicides, and so on. In fact, the small engines used in powered outdoor gear emit enough hydrocarbons, carbon monoxide, and nitrogen oxides to qualify as the largest single contributor to nonvehicle hydrocarbon emissions. Not only that, 17 million gallons of gasoline are spilled each year by people trying to refill their lawnmowers; that's more than was spilled in the Exxon Valdez incident!

Here's what you can do to cut back your landscape's contributions to air pollution:

✔ Reduce lawn areas and oversized plants so that you don't have to trim and mow as much.

✔ Use hand tools whenever you can.

✔ If you must use power tools, use electric ones.

✔ Trade in your old gas mower on a newer, less polluting one. The same goes for other power equipment.

✔ Keep equipment in proper operating condition.

✔ Stop using pesticides and herbicides.

Reconsidering Your Sources

One of the best ways to mess up your sustainable game plan is to mindlessly drive over to Home World and get a bunch of the same old stuff without asking yourself or the clerks where it came from and what the impacts of the purchase will be, both in your landscape and at the source of the materials. There's such a wide range of impacts that it's essential to consider where all your materials and supplies will be coming from.

Suburban lawns and gardens receive more pesticides per acre than agriculture. Some of the unfortunate outcomes include cancer, birth defects, reproductive effects, neurotoxicity, liver and kidney damage, endocrine disruption, and others. Children are especially susceptible because they absorb more pesticides in relation to their body mass. This effect is in addition to the harmful effects on birds, fish, bees, and other wildlife. Amazingly, only a tiny percentage of the lawn and garden chemicals sold are tested for safety or for the environmental side effects of their use.

Additionally, some of the building materials common to landscaping projects offer their own toxicity problems. Table 2-2 shows some toxic and harmful landscape materials and nontoxic alternatives.

Table 2-2	Toxic Materials and Alternatives
Toxic or Suspected Toxic	*Safer Alternative*
Arsenic-treated wood	ACQ-treated wood
Railroad ties	Recycled plastic landscape ties, salvaged timbers
PVC	High-density polyethylene or other plastics, non-plastic alternatives

Toxic or Suspected Toxic	Safer Alternative
Glues	Alternative glues, mechanical fasteners like nails, screws and bolts
Paints, finishes, and solvents	Low-VOC finishes, or best of all, materials that don't need finishing

Toxic materials are rarely, if ever, necessary. There were beautiful gardens long before there was PVC and solvents and all that. By choosing natural materials you end the problem of toxics before it begins.

Building Your Sustainable Landscape: Concepts for Design

A sustainable landscape can also be a fun landscape. There's no reason to give up the things you love or become the eyesore of the neighborhood in order to be sustainable. You just have to make sensible choices and design for sustainability as well as for the other aspects of the landscape.

Chances are that you already understand good design on some level. It's not that much of a leap from appreciating a well-designed landscape to creating one. Apply these principles to your project, and you'll soon see a wonderful garden emerge.

Unity

Any garden that's a chaotic mish-mosh of all sorts of plants, ten kinds of paving materials, and a zillion different colors is more disconcerting than relaxing. Conversely, a space that's composed of harmonious elements, with a consistent and comprehensible color scheme and an overall sense of hang-together, is pleasing to both the eye and the mind — a place where one wants to linger.

How do you create unity? First, decide on a style for the garden: formal, natural, geometric, curvy, rectilinear — whatever you like and whatever is appropriate to the surroundings. Then pick plants and hardscape elements that look good together and use them repeatedly throughout the design. Choose a suitable color scheme — more on that in the upcoming "Color" section.

Unless you're a master of design, keep the number of elements in your plan fairly minimal — a few kinds of plants, one or two hardscape materials, not too many precious trinkets. Think Zen.

Balance

Nobody likes a loudmouth. Yet some landscapes have one or more elements that scream at you and overshadow their counterparts instead of working in concert with them. If the purpose of your garden is to create a sense of anxiety, go ahead and color your patio hot pink. Sometimes an outrageous approach can be wonderful. But most of us want a soothing place to hang out, which means keeping the rude surprises to a minimum. Unity and balance go hand in hand.

In a formal garden, balance is achieved through right-left symmetry: one lilac on the left and an identical lilac on the right. In an informal garden, balance is asymmetrical, with varying elements skillfully combined into a composition that has overall balance without being rigid.

Repetition

Don't be afraid of repeating strong design elements; doing so makes the design that much stronger. Think of a forest with a million of the same kind of tree, each with the same understory vegetation. We find this beautiful, yet most people seem timid about using repetition in their landscaping.

Of course, each of these principles depends on sensitive application to be successful. Repetition carried too far creates a tedious scene, while lack of repetition works hard against unity. Think about a piece of music, how it keeps coming back to a refrain and how phrases repeat throughout the piece but only at the appropriate moments and within a comprehensible, pleasing pattern. That's how a well-designed landscape should work. The idea is to keep it interesting, intriguing, and understandable.

Contrast and variety

The dance between repetition and variety is a delicate one. Including elements that contrast with one another in color, form, shape, and overall character can add a lot of life to the composition. Light-colored foliage against a dark background, rough natural stones abutting very refined smooth concrete, patterns of sun and shade — all these combinations contribute to a lively scene.

Scale

Keep things in proper proportion. An overly large tree can dwarf a house, dominating the whole environment (and also perhaps making the house dank and gloomy, as well as using a lot of water, needing very costly professional care, and maybe even presenting the danger of falling over). Similarly, a patio that's too small looks silly and probably doesn't meet the needs of its users.

Shape

Decide on a shape family for your layout — rectilinear, curvilinear, angular, or free-form. A landscape made up of strongly geometric shapes can be very formal (if it's symmetrical) or elegantly restful (such as a Japanese garden). On the other end of the spectrum, a free-form approach is best suited to the naturalistic garden. But even the free-form is not free of form, it's just more subtle. Study wild natural areas to see how this works.

Line

Lines in the garden are created by plantings, hardscape, and other elements. Lines can be very explicit, such as an *allée* (long double row) of trees, or subtle, such as a gently curving path. Line leads the eye through the scene and helps make sense of the elements it contains.

Lines can run parallel or perpendicular to buildings and other existing structural elements, or you can place them at angles. This latter approach usually has more visual energy and creates a feeling of movement and depth. It's especially useful in making small spaces seem bigger. Curves are also quite lively and can make for a delightful sense of movement.

Focal points and vantage points

Imagine sitting out in the back yard on a balmy summer's evening, watching the water dance in your fountain. Or coming around a corner and seeing a gorgeous persimmon tree laden with fruit, its leaves starting to turn color. Those attention-grabbing elements are called *focal points*. Any strong and striking visual element, such as a piece of sculpture or a particularly stunning plant, can be a focal point in your composition. Without good focal points, the eye searches in vain for a place to rest.

Every focal point has at least one *vantage point* — that is, a place from which it is viewed. This spot may be your patio, the living room sofa, or a bench. When you design, make the creation of focal points and vantage points one of the first things you think about.

Too many focal points weaken the design and create the same confusion as having none at all: The eye has no place to land.

Form

Think of *shape* as the two-dimensional arrangement of the elements of the landscape when viewed from above and *form* as the three-dimensional space that things occupy when viewed from ground level.

For example, a sheared boxwood hedge has a strict rectilinear form, whereas an Italian cypress or poplar tree will have an upright columnar form, and a spreading oak tree grows in the form of a broad canopy. Each form has a particular role to play. The boxwood leads one along a path, the upright cypress is like a giant exclamation point, and the oak embraces and shelters the area beneath it. Study plants and books about plants to learn the vocabulary of forms you can use.

Be sure to include some plants with strap-shaped leaves, such as Iris, or some bold succulents like Agaves in your plantings. Strap-shaped plants act as points of emphasis, and their contrast to leafier textures and shrubbier forms really enlivens a planting.

Texture

A tropical Philodendron with leaves 6 feet across is said to have a coarse texture. A tiny-leaved thyme plant has a very fine texture. Designers contrast textures for appealing combinations, playing coarse against fine, and repeating the play of textures using different plants. Different textures, when combined skillfully with nicely partnered colors, is a key element in what makes plantings work well.

This principle also applies to hardscape. Sometimes a surface made of large tiles looks great in a small space because the texture is unexpected and makes the area seem roomier than it is. The texture of paving, walls, woodwork, and other manmade elements contributes much to the overall effect.

You can use texture to create a sense of depth by placing finer textures in the background, or to create drama by purposely placing a coarse-textured plant in an unexpected location.

Color

Color works to create many different effects. A multicolored planting is upbeat and happy — or chaotic, if handled poorly. A monochromatic color scheme can be elegant or boring, depending on the context. Contrasting colors create an assertive look, and harmonizing colors make for soothing surroundings. Bright colors advance, and cool ones recede. Hot colors are stimulating, and pastels are restful and calming.

Don't forget that foliage colors play a strong role, too. And don't overlook the seasonal changes that can be challenging to a novice designer but that can also reward with interesting color shifts as the year progresses from spring through summer, fall, and winter. Match the fresh green leaves of spring with brightly colored flowers and then later in the year key the autumn foliage to more somber autumn colors by using fall-blooming plants. The tricks you can play are endless. Use the plant lists in gardening books to plan your color schemes by season. And visit nurseries and gardens to see real plants in bloom.

Hardscape has a color scheme, too. Sometimes it's really fun to use an outrageous bright red or purple or yellow piece of art in a focal point where it will have a stunning impact amid subtle plantings.

From a sustainability perspective, the color of pavement can affect the livability of the area. The relative reflectivity (or *albedo,* as fancy-pants landscape architects like to call it) of a surface can make it hot or cool, pleasant or otherwise.

Chapter 3

Hardscaping: Beauty and Function from Patios, Walls, and More

· ·

In This Chapter

▶ Getting your yard ready for the changes ahead

▶ Adding outdoor rooms for any purpose

▶ Finding the right "flooring" for patios and decks

▶ Making good spaces (and good neighbors) with walls

▶ Putting a roof over your head when it's on the patio

▶ Introducing a soothing soundtrack with water features

· ·

*H*ardscape is a fancy term for parts of the landscape that are not plants or irrigation. Patios, decks, and fences are hardscape. So are lighting systems, art, retaining walls, ponds, and plaster lawn squirrels.

Sustainable hardscape is a part of a living landscape, emphasizing plants and biological elements over industrial elements made of concrete, steel, plastic, and other manmade materials. Conventional hardscape, on the other hand, can be needy and troublesome. It's made up of materials that are taken from the planet in often abusive ways, leaving behind a trail of devastation. Hardscape materials are often toxic, nonrenewable, and high in embodied energy and transported from far away using climate-wrecking fossil fuels. Their operation and upkeep can require toxic finishing substances and energy-intensive processes. Finally, hardscape is not self-renewing like plants; you can't grow a patio from seeds.

Despite all the negatives, hardscape can be done in less damaging ways, and it certainly has its place in the sustainable landscape. Every garden needs basic hardscape features, such as paths, places to sit and entertain, safe ways to get up and down hillsides, and enclosures. Hardscape adds so much to the visual quality of the landscape as well. With the right approach, you can have great hardscape features without all the environmental problems.

Preparing Your Site

If you take the time to design a truly sustainable landscape, you're selling your yard short by taking shortcuts when the time comes to get down and dirty. To get your landscape ready for the changes ahead, you need to keep your own safety in mind and — as in all matters sustainable landscape — stay alert to how you're treating the earth.

First, make a mess: Demolition

The old-school approach to demolition was to push the old yard into a dumpster and send it away to the landfill. But there is no "away": Everything we dispose of causes problems somewhere. Instead of treating the unwanted parts of your existing landscaping as waste, look for ways to use it in constructing your new landscaping. Set aside soil, trees, broken concrete, useful plants, and even artsy junk for later use. Find homes for re-usable castoffs, such as the bricks from your old patio or excess soil. Recycle where appropriate, sending green waste to the local composting operation instead of mixing it with other materials in a dumpster.

Keep nature safe, too. Don't park equipment or store heavy materials under trees where it will compact soil in the root zone. Protect against erosion by installing *straw wattles* or *silt fencing* at the base of piles of soil that might wash away in the rains. Avoid working in wildlife habitat or nesting sites. Keep soil out of waterways.

Locate utilities

Utilities come into your property underground as well as overhead. Before you start digging, you need to determine the exact location of gas and water mains, power lines, telephone and television cables, sewer pipes, and any other utilities serving the site. You may also have *utility easements* running through your property and transmission lines or pipes within those easements.

Why call the utility company to locate your utility lines before you get started? Umm . . . well . . . is the potential for death enough reason for you? A lot of nice folks have blown themselves up hitting gas lines, fried themselves poking into underground electric wires, disrupted phone service to whole neighborhoods, and had other highly humbling misadventures. Don't be one of them.

Fixing damaged utilities is incredibly expensive, and so is paying the fines for not following the law that says you have to find your utilities with something other than a backhoe or pickaxe.

You need to locate underground items, including water and gas lines, drain pipes, sewer lines, and possibly electric or phone lines. To ease the process, look up your state's free One Call service (dial 811 or visit www.call811.com); with one call from you, it contacts all the utility providers serving your property and arranges to have them come out and flag everything. Within a couple of days, everything will be identified, and you can dig with confidence.

Earthwork: Grading and drainage

Grading determines how long water remains on the land, its path across the surface of the ground, and whether it soaks usefully into the ground or runs off to cause erosion, flooding, and pollution. Grading keeps the house safe from flooding, creates usable areas, and sculpts dull terrain into elegant, sensual forms.

You do grading just once, and you need to do it properly because you can't change it unless you remove all the plants.

The sustainable approach is to do as little grading as possible because soil is damaged when it's moved around, and the heavy equipment that's required compacts soil and may damage tree roots. You should also only grade for good reason, such as conserving water on site, preventing erosion, or keeping the house from flooding.

Avoid bringing soil in or taking it away if you can. Both can be disruptive to off-site locations and involve the usual pollution and fossil-fuel dependency of trucking and heavy equipment use. In addition, when you import topsoil, you run the risk of also importing new kinds of weeds, diseases, and even toxic substances.

Sometimes you can't avoid moving soil on or off the site. In those situations, try to find a good home for your soil so that it can used to repair a damaged site rather than to create new problems. And ask about the source of imported soil, perhaps even requesting a complete soil test as a condition of purchase. You probably won't get far with this tactic, but it's worth a try.

Control weeds the safe way

Pretty much every site has weeds. Weeds are hard to control because they've evolved to be aggressive, sneaky, virile, and just plain annoying. If you don't get the weeds under control before you install your landscaping, they'll come right through and make a mess of your lovely work. *Annual weeds* come back from seed, and *perennial weeds* poke up from old root systems.

We won't mention any names, but certain herbicides have been applied to our poor suffering planet for decades now, and yet there seem to be just as many weeds as ever. Seems like we're losing the battle despite all the poisons. It's just another example of how conventional methods don't really work.

Sheet mulching is the practice of killing weeds by smothering them. Hoe out any surface weeds, cover the soil with two or three layers of corrugated cardboard salvaged from the waste stream, overlap the cardboard and wet it down thoroughly, and then cover the whole funny-looking mess with at least 4 inches of organic mulch, such as wood chips. Leave it there for a few months if you can. Sheet mulching has proven to be more effective than herbicides, which can also take months to fully kill weeds.

Horticultural vinegar is another keen way to kill weeds without nasty chemicals. It works best on young weeds and doesn't kill every weed in the book, but it's pretty effective on many. Horticultural vinegar is stronger than the vinegar you cook or clean with, so treat it with care as you would any other strong acid. Weeds will often die within a couple of hours. Your yard will smell like a salad for a short while, but other than that, it's utterly harmless.

A 3 to 4-inch thick layer of organic mulch, such as shredded bark or wood chips, will create the conditions to keep most weeds out and will weaken the ones that make it through so that they're easy to pull by hand. Turn to Chapter 3 of Book VI to find out more about the wonders of mulching.

Low ground covers and bare ground attract weeds like crazy. Choose plants that grow tall and provide a dense canopy of foliage, and weed seeds never make it to the light. I call these *knee-high plants,* and they're the most sustainable way to keep the weeds down without using herbicides.

Trim the trees

Get your big trees in shape before you start any landscaping. Your project will be easier and cheaper if workers don't have to pussyfoot through new plantings. Choose your tree care company carefully. A hundred years of growth can be destroyed in minutes by improper care.

Invest in the expertise of an arborist certified by the International Society of Arboriculture or the American Society of Consulting Arborists. An arborist really knows how to look at trees and can identify health or safety problems that you'd never see on your own.

Using Sustainable Hardscape Features to Build an Outdoor Room

The idea of the *outdoor room* goes far back in the history of landscape design. Cro-Magnon cave owners in the Paleolithic Era had spacious outdoor rooms that they used for eviscerating woolly mammoths and entertaining visiting troglodytes. Over time, the idea evolved into the modern outdoor room equipped with 50 square feet of barbecue grill surface, two convection ovens, a big-screen TV, spa, fitness center, and maid's quarters. Somewhere between these two extremes lies the sensible, sustainable Outdoor Room of the Future.

Just as the rooms in your house are specialized for certain activities — eating, entertaining, bathing, sleeping, storage — so can the landscape be divided into areas with particular functions. Many outdoor rooms are more versatile than indoor ones, combining functions that you'd never pair up indoors, such as providing a place for lounge chairs, bouncing light into the house, and soaking up rainwater. (*Permaculture,* a methodology of holistic design, calls this multiple-use approach *stacking functions,* and it's a hallmark of sustainable design.)

The ideal outdoor room should feel like it's a part of nature. An overabundance of manmade structures and appliances is not only environmentally unsound, it creates a setting that's too much like the indoors. The whole appeal of having landscaping in the first place is to be closer to natural things, so why muck it up with a lot of hardware? After all, the Garden of Eden didn't have a spa and an 8-burner barbecue.

Coming home: Entry space

Getting to your front door is an important daily act for your family and others. The experience should be comfortable, safe, and welcoming. You want a pathway that leads unambiguously to the house, that's wide enough to accommodate two people walking side by side (so at least 4 feet, 6 inches), and is smooth, safe, and well lit. Sidewalk pavement must be durable and free of hazards, which means a solid, smooth path of concrete, brick, tile, grouted flagstone or some other permanent, hard-wearing surface.

To reduce the environmental impact, use bricks or paver blocks securely set on sand (so that they can be re-used), or high-volume fly ash concrete (which makes use of a waste stream product and reduces production of CO_2).

Here are some other tips for entries:

- Provide safe paved landings in the planter space between the curb and sidewalk so that passengers can alight onto a passable surface and not have to step on your flowers or leap over stickery junipers.

- If possible, avoid making people walk up the driveway. Provide a completely separate entry path, or at the very least widen the driveway to accommodate pedestrian traffic, using a contrasting and classier-looking material for the paths.

- Consider using shrubs and trees to partially screen the view of the street from the front door and create a gentle transition between outside and in.

- Avoid an excessively direct or indirect path to the front door. Change directions a couple of times, providing wider landing spaces at turning points and offering an attractive focal point or two such as a fountain, piece of art, or special plant.

- If your situation and zoning regulations permit it, incorporate outdoor living space, such as a patio, in the front yard. Use fencing or shrubbery to conceal it from the street. A front-yard patio works especially well where the back yard is small or when the front yard offers a pleasant microclimate.

- Keep grades gentle (no steeper than 5 percent) or provide safe, well-designed steps.

- The landing at the front door should be large enough for a small group of people to gather briefly when coming or going and be free from steps or level changes. The landing should be just a couple of inches lower than the floor inside the house.

- If you're part of a homeowners association, check to see what you're permitted (and required) to do in the front yard. Also check zoning regulations and setback requirements.

Keeping the cars happy: Parking

The automobile is with us for the foreseeable future, and both yours and those of your guests need to be parked somewhere. Your driveway is probably already in place, but ponder the possibilities of reorienting it or making it smaller or more environmentally friendly. Here are some tips:

- Make your driveway *pervious,* meaning that water can find its way through. Runoff from driveways causes flooding and pollution. Use pervious concrete, pervious paver blocks, gravel, or a vegetated paving system so that water soaks in and is used by plants rather than going into the gutter.

✔ Mulch or gravel guest parking and turn-around space instead of paving it. Mulch and gravel are permeable and much lower impact than concrete or other formal paving (but gravel attracts weeds).

✔ Allow at least a 9-x-18-foot space for each car and also allow room beside parking spaces so that doors can be opened and people have a place to alight when getting out of the car.

Living and entertaining space

The patio is usually the heart of the garden and can serve many purposes. Here are a few things to keep in mind when planning a patio:

✔ Your main patio should be large enough to accommodate whatever size group will be using it frequently. Don't make it big enough for your largest parties; those happen only once in a while, and you can accommodate them by setting up tables and chairs in lawn or meadow space. A couple of lounge chairs require a space at least 8 feet by 8 feet. Generally, a family-sized patio should be around 12 feet on each side. Breaking up the patio into subspaces is okay — for example, dining in one area, sitting area nearby, cooking not far away, and so on.

✔ Look for places other than right outside the house to put your patio. Outdoor furniture isn't usually so attractive that you want to make it the focal point of the yard from inside the house, so if the furnished area is off to one side, you'll have a clear view (and clear passage for foot traffic) into the back yard. Think about making the main patio an "away" place, somewhat distant from the house, so that you feel you're more immersed in the garden and less connected to the hubbub of indoor life.

✔ Place smaller patios at other locations: a spot for a couple of chairs outside the master bedroom, a meditation nook half-lost in the back of the property, a zone for the teenagers to hang out.

✔ Think about microclimate when you choose the location for your patio. If you'll be using it mainly on summer afternoons, and if your climate is a hot one, place your patio on the north or east side of the house away from the scalding sun. If you plan to use the patio for breakfast in a cool climate, put it on the east side of the house where morning sun will warm chilly bones.

✔ Evaluate wind conditions, sheltering the patio from prevailing winds by locating it in the lee of existing structures or vegetation, or by creating new fences, walls, or plantings to provide a windbreak.

✔ Consider proximity to neighbors, street noise, trash cans, and other odor sources, traffic patterns, and immediate and distant views.

✔ Take the relationship to indoor rooms into account. Locate the dining patio fairly close to the kitchen and not so close to the bedrooms, for example.

✔ Decide whether you want to surround your patio with walls or vegetation or have it covered by a canopy of manmade structures or overhanging trees. Enclosed spaces are intimate and room-like; if there are no views or they're unpleasant, then the enclosed approach works well. If you have a great view, locate the patio to take advantage of it. An overhead covering can be dense or open, rainproof or not, and it can extend over all or only part of the patio space to allow for shady and sunny areas.

✔ Patio surfaces are usually made of solid material, such as concrete, tile, or flagstone, or wood decking where the terrain is too steep for a masonry surface. But consider lower impact (and also less costly) materials, such as mulch, gravel, or other pervious materials where use will be light.

Dining areas

This function is often accommodated by the main patio, but a separate area is tidier and can be near the main patio area, which you can use as temporary overflow dining space for large parties. Here are some planning tips:

✔ A dining table and chairs takes up a minimum 10 feet by 10 feet space.

✔ Make sure that the patio surface is smooth and nearly level.

✔ Allow room for a counter or side table to use as a buffet.

✔ Overhead lighting makes evening dining easier.

✔ Conceal the dining area from view of neighbors and the public.

✔ Screen to keep out bugs if they're a problem in your area.

Recreation and sports

Kids, adults, and pets all need recreation spaces. Generally, these areas should be on level ground, on safe surfaces, and away from quiet spaces or fragile plantings.

Formal recreation courts (tennis, basketball, and so on) are not all that sustainable, using up lots of resources and requiring impermeable surfaces and regular maintenance. Similarly, swimming pools are pretty over-the-top, with their immense demands for energy and water. Why not save yourself big bucks by enjoying the local public facilities and use your yard to grow food instead?

Work spaces

Garden work space can be as simple as a potting bench or as complex as a greenhouse for getting a head start on the veggie season. Work spaces include storage areas, an outdoor extension of a garage workshop, vegetable prep areas, or a spot for a special hobby. Try these tips for setting up a work space:

✔ Work areas aren't always so tidy looking, so site them for both convenience to related indoor rooms and concealment from the rest of the garden.

✔ Keep them away from living areas and neighbors if they're sources of noise.

✔ Provide enclosed storage that blends with the surroundings; add a lean-to storage compartment onto the side of a building, for example.

✔ Provide power, water, and other utilities. If you include a sink, have it drain into an underground soak zone in the garden (assuming that you won't be using any toxics but just washing off pots and veggies).

Floors: Patios and Decks

Unlike the other elements of the hardscape system, floors get walked on and stuff gets dragged across them, stored on them, and displayed on them. They need to withstand traffic, but they don't necessarily need to be solid to do so. A resilient floor of mulch is quite suitable for many uses, and it's natural and sustainable and cheap. Other situations demand something more durable. Each of the many available materials has its own characteristics, uses, and degrees of sustainability. They vary from the extremely natural (mulch, gravel, flagstone, wood) to the clearly manmade (tile, concrete). They can be loose and re-usable (brick or pavers on sand) or permanent (the not-very-sustainable poured concrete).

Individual pieces, such as bricks or paving blocks, are referred to as *unit pavers.* You can often install unit pavers many different patterns. Living paving materials, such as turf and ground covers, vary in their ability to withstand foot and vehicle traffic and in their maintenance requirements.

From a sustainability point of view, many paving choices have unacceptable negative impacts. Concrete used to make paving comes from materials that are strip-mined, the processes used to convert raw materials to cement are energy-intensive and generate gobs of CO_2, and transport of the material to the site depends on big trucks that get lousy gas mileage. Even things as simple as crushed rock, decomposed granite, and mulch create damage at their sources and use petroleum for processing and transport.

Some aspects of hardscape production are improving. The manufacturing of cement for concrete production is incredibly energy-intensive and generates 5 to 10 percent of the world's CO2 emissions, but improvements in the processes are dramatically lowering that figure. Newly developed technologies like *nano-concrete* are very promising, and a new type of concrete actually absorbs huge amounts of air pollution.

There are also some pretenders to sustainability — materials with questionable or fraudulent environmental credentials. These materials include (perhaps debatably) plastic lumber and (not at all debatably) mulch made from ground-up tires and phony plastic lawns.

Stick with materials that are as close to a state of nature as possible and ones that require a minimum of processing and maintenance. Build something that lasts, because durability is a supremely sustainable strategy, dividing the initial inputs over many decades of usefulness.

Don't forget *heritage materials*, ones that can be re-used over and over again. These items include bricks, concrete pavers, or flagstone — as long as they're laid on sand and not permanently mortared in place. And, of course, tap the waste stream for *urbanite* (broken concrete) and other materials that can be rescued from an eternity in landfill hell.

Because solid paving sheds water, it can be an unfriendly part of the watershed, causing flooding and pollution from runoff. Choosing pervious surfaces is one way to deal with that concern, but you can also use (and even purposely choose) impervious surfaces to act as water catchment zones that spill their captured water into a bioswale, planted area, or other spot where it will be put to use.

Safe, sustainable surfaces

Here are some surfaces that you can feel good about. None is perfect, but they all get you a floor with less impact than many materials.

✔ **Living ground covers:** Making a living floor follows the key principle of choosing biological solutions before technological ones. Options include low-growing plants, such as thyme, chamomile, or yarrow, as well as conventional turf. Unmowed, these plants make a gorgeous natural meadow; mowed, they form a walkable, playable turf. Nearly all require some watering and fertilizing, but almost any ground cover is less needy than turf. Of course, living plants won't take the kind of abuse that a harder surface will, and they can be troublesome to walk on, especially when wet. Reserve them for low-traffic and play areas.

✔ **Mulch:** Biodegradable, and beneficial for the soil beneath your feet, mulch is the daddy of all sustainable pavements — so darn natural it could have come from your own back yard (and if you got the chips from tree trimming, perhaps it did). It looks good, smells good, and lets water through. It also keeps the weeds down and the roots of your plants happy.

Mulch does have some shortcomings: It isn't the best for sitting chairs on, as the legs can sink, and it's not so great for handicapped access.

✔ **Gravel or crushed rock:** Taken from riverbeds or quarries, gravel or crushed rock do come at an environmental price. And surfaces covered with them tend to attract weeds. Use them sparingly, where their simplicity, perviousness, and nice crunchy sound underfoot are welcome.

✔ **Urbanite:** This newly discovered "mineral" is nothing more than old broken concrete paving, used like flagstones to make what the British call *crazy paving*. Urbanite is the ultimate waste-stream material, with no environmental impact other than transport. It can be stained or used as is, and it makes a lovely surface. Urbanite is available nearly everywhere.

✔ **Pervious concrete:** This one's great for driveways and other heavy-traffic surfaces. It's regular concrete without the sand; just crushed rock, portland cement, and water. It comes out looking like a giant rice cake, and the voids between the bits of rock slurp up water at up to 350 inches per hour — that's *hallelujah!* level. Pervious concrete can take plenty of weight. It can be colored. The top can be ground for a more attractive and smoother surface. (Visit www.perviouspavement.org or www.concretenetwork.com for details.)

✔ **Vegetated paving systems:** Imagine a honeycomb of recycled plastic panels supporting the weight of a vehicle, with turf or wildflowers growing out of the soil-filled, open-topped cells or a similarly open concrete grid. Vegetated paving systems go by many names and offer a wonderful solution for driveways, overflow parking areas, and fire lanes. Because of their open surface they're not suited to patios, but they make your driveway look totally rad.

✔ **Paver blocks:** All the rage for the past few years, paver blocks aren't very permeable, but specially designed ones absorb rainfall at the rate of around an inch per hour. This level isn't even close to the perviousness of pervious concrete, but it's better than a solid surface. Paver blocks are good for driveways, paths, and patios, and re-usable.

✔ **High-volume fly ash concrete:** This concrete looks and acts like regular concrete but is made with a waste product of coal-burning power plants. *Fly ash* makes concrete stronger and taps the waste stream. Specify high volume fly ash concrete for nearly any concrete application.

Considering maintenance

Most paved surfaces require little maintenance as long as you don't make the mistake of painting them. For most applications, don't waste your money on sealers and stains; leave surfaces to age naturally and gracefully. If you start applying finishes, there's no end to the scraping, sanding, sandblasting, priming, and painting that you have to do.

Of course, living surfaces require weeding, watering, and other normal plant care. Choose species that are adapted to your area and learn their needs before your make your decision.

Choosing between a patio and a deck

Decks are made from renewable natural materials, for the most part, or from plastic lumber made from soda containers, grocery bags, and wood waste. Their embodied energy is fairly low, and if you avoid toxic finishes, a deck can be a reasonable addition to your landscaping.

Still, decks come with environmental problems. They're made from wood, and trees generally have to be cut down to get the wood out. That means partial or total destruction of a forest somewhere. If you use wood for a deck (or for any other garden structure), be sure it's certified as sustainably harvested by the Forest Stewardship Council in the United States. The other approach, the plastic wood route, can set you up for a smelly deck on hot days (and for hot feet if the wood is dark), and for potential off-gassing issues (though no one seems to know whether the stuff is bad for you or not). Finally, being made of wood, decks don't last very long.

If you live in a high fire hazard area, check with local authorities about special regulations for decks, which can be a fire magnet if not built right.

Patios can have nasty impacts, too, but generally speaking, they're easier, more durable, and cheaper. The rub comes when you have a hillside that has to be leveled and stabilized before it will support the weight of a patio. That can mean a very costly retaining wall system and still more environmental impact. That's when decks start to look good.

The bottom line? If you have a steep slope, consider a deck. If your ground is stable and close to level, stick with a patio.

Walls: Free-Standing and Retaining

Walls come in two basic flavors: Free-standing walls enclose space to create privacy, make an area secure, or improve the microclimate; retaining walls do the hard work of holding back slopes.

Creating privacy with walls and fences

Use walls or fences to block views of neighbors, creating an enclosed court-yard or walled garden. For complete privacy, make your enclosure at least 6 feet high and solid. Lower, more open walls may be suitable where you want to feel less boxed-in or where regulations prevent you from building a taller wall. Walls don't have to be out at the boundaries; use interior walls to create outdoor rooms and break up the space into interesting subspaces.

Solid enclosures change the microclimate. They create shade on one side and sun on the other, block or channel winds, and sometimes absorb or reflect heat. Handled properly, these characteristics can be desirable, but if you aren't aware of the changes you'll be creating, you may end up with trouble.

Adding walls and fences for security and safety

Keeping people and animals in or out of your property requires sturdy bar-riers. The most sustainable of these is thorny or otherwise impenetrable shrubs, but small or determined interlopers can still make their way through. For complete security, choose a solid wall of masonry, adobe, or other truly impenetrable material or use chain-link fencing, which is made of recyclable steel. Don't forget secure gates.

Windy sites call for something to intercept or divert the wind from use areas, which not only increases comfort but reduces heating and cooling needs. Trees and shrubs are good at blocking wind because they're noncontiguous and flexible, absorbing energy efficiently. Solid fences and walls can actually worsen wind on the lee side by creating an eddy effect. Slatted or louvered fencing does a better job, as does a fence with an angled top to change the flow characteristics. If you choose a wooden fence, try to find certified sus-tainably harvested lumber, which still lessens the impact considerably, and avoid using posts that have been pressure- treated with arsenic; nontoxic treated wood is commonly available these days. Earthen berms or mounds can also direct wind. And, of course, there's nothing more sustainable than simply piling up earth that's already on the site.

Using walls for retaining slopes

Retaining walls are really in a category of their own. Because they support impressive loads, they need to be treated as a structural element as well as a visual and functional one. Cutting and filling soil to create level ground on a slope may call for retaining walls on the high and/or low sides to hold the disturbed soil in place. This can be a wonderful, if expensive, way to increase the usable space on your property.

The most basic kind of retaining wall is the *gravity wall,* which is simply a mass of solid material, such as concrete or dry-laid stone. Gravity walls are suitable for level changes of up to 3 feet in height and are a good DIY project. Sustainable materials include dry-stacked urbanite, stones from the site or nearby, or rubble. The newer mortarless individual stacking block systems, called *segmental retaining walls,* are made from concrete but can be re-used, making them a good heritage material.

You can also fashion gravity walls from wooden timbers, landscape ties, reclaimed redwood, or logs. You can use treated wood as well, but be sure to choose the kind that is free of arsenic. Adobe can be used for very low walls with little pressure on them, but keep in mind that holding back soil with more soil isn't going to be all that much stronger than no wall at all.

For taller walls, and where there is a *surcharge* above the wall (that is, a slope rather than level ground), you need to use a *cantilever wall*, which is made up of two parts: a big flat concrete foundation called a base, and the vertical, visible portion called a stem. Together they form a T or L shape that's very good at resisting the pressure of the soil it's holding up.

For any cantilevered wall, any wall taller than 4 feet (including the base or footing), or any instance where there is a surcharge of soil behind the wall, get the help of a civil engineer to be sure the wall is designed properly — and don't forget to look into building permit requirements.

Ceilings: Topping Off Your Room

The sky is a nice ceiling: It's time-tested, colorful, attractive, durable, made from local materials, goes well with nearly any architectural style, and is very inexpensive. Consider sky for an expansive, interesting overhead.

Still, sometimes sky isn't quite what you want. It doesn't keep out the sun or rain, modify the microclimate, or give you that cozy, snuggly feeling of being sheltered by a room-height ceiling. That's when you turn to other alternatives.

Ceilings, living or manmade, offer shelter, shade, enclosure, privacy, architectural interest, and a place to hang your wind chimes. Take into consideration the following factors when pondering what kind of ceiling to include in your plans:

- ✔ Be sure you really need one. A very cool or foggy climate calls for openness to let in light and heat, not a shade-casting overhead.

- ✔ Check local zoning ordinances to be sure that you don't put an overhead structure in a location on your property where it isn't permitted. And ask whether you need a building permit for your structure.

- ✔ Choose a rainproof roof if you live in a wet climate or enjoy being outside during wet weather. Select a shady but open overhead to protect against heat and allow breezes to move through the area.

- ✔ Determine how much shade you want, because you can use the density of the structure to control the amount. If you use parallel louvers to cast shade, place them perpendicular to the rays of the sun; this placement is especially important for overheads located in the path of the setting sun.

    Take the path of the sun into account in placing your structure and don't forget to estimate where the sun will be at different seasons as well as different times of the year.

- ✔ Think about leaving part of the area open to the sky so that you have a choice of sun or shade.

- ✔ Set the height of your ceiling so that it's in scale with surrounding elements, and so that it creates the kind of feeling you want: tall ceilings feel open, low ones cozy.

- ✔ Don't paint overhead structures. It costs money, uses resources, and, worst of all, is a huge pain to re-paint when the time comes, especially if you have to remove a covering of mature vines first. Stains are okay, as they're water-based or made from an ecofriendly material like soy or beeswax.

- ✔ If you want a vine on your overhead, choose something that looks good from underneath, not just on top. (Most vines carry a lot of dead stuff beneath them.) Make sure that they don't drop litter on your dinner. Use a deciduous vine if you want the sunlight to penetrate in winter. Try something edible, like grapes, to get more use out of the structure.

Living ceilings: trees

What's more sustainable, durable, or beautiful than a tree? Name another overhead that creates oxygen, sequesters carbon, cools by evaporation, operates by solar power, costs practically nothing, provides habitat for birds and other organisms, is fun to climb, and makes flowers and fruit.

Avoid messy or weak-wooded trees, ones that might blow over, and certainly trees with root systems that lift pavement. As with all plantings, be sure that the tree you choose is adapted to your climate, soil, and other conditions and place it carefully so that it casts shade where you want it.

Deciduous trees (ones that lose their leaves in winter) automatically provide shade during summer and allow sunlight to penetrate in winter. Evergreen trees can make a good overhead, too, as long as you can use the shade all year.

Constructed ceilings

Attractive, sustainable overhead structures can be made of salvaged wood, driftwood, tree branches, canvas, or metal (especially good in high fire hazard areas). Unlike trees, constructed ceilings require skill to design and build and are usually subject to building codes in order to make them safe.

Making a living ecoroof

One of the coolest sustainable landscape elements is the living *ecoroof*, also known as a *green roof*. Made of drought-tolerant plants growing in a shallow layer of lightweight soil held in place by a waterproof membrane and supporting structure, or by individual recycled plastic bins, the ecoroof turns your roof into a beautiful living ecosystem.

Ecoroofs are showing up all over the place, from tiny sheds covered in succulents to the world's largest, which covers 10 acres over a Ford Motor Company plant in Michigan. Some areas even offer tax credits for ecoroofs.

Ecoroofs offer any number of environmental advantages in addition to their special quirky charm. They

- Absorb rainwater, keeping it off the streets.
- Trap and bioremediate 70 percent of pollutants that fall on the roof.
- Produce oxygen and sequester carbon.
- Provide wildlife habitat, especially where native species are used.
- Reduce the *urban heat island effect*, which is the overheating of cities because of the huge expanses of dark pavement and rooftops.
- Lower temperatures inside the building.
- Increase the life of the roof.
- Can even produce food as well as ornamental plants.
- Offer positive benefits for human users: tranquility, delight, comfort, and improved mental health.

There are two types of ecoroofs: extensive and intensive. The *extensive ecoroof* is planted with very drought-tolerant plants, such as Sedums and other succulents, and is rarely watered or managed. The extensive ecoroof is on its own, undemanding, and environmentally optimum. The *intensive ecoroof* is more of a roof garden, with a wider variety of plants, often watered and highly groomed, and producing flowers and possibly even food.

Before you go dragging a bunch of plants up to your roof, here are some important considerations:

✔ Ecoroofs aren't a do-it-yourself project. Hire an expert to help you, because they require a lot of know-how.

✔ Ecoroofs are heavy, and so first you need to be sure your house can handle the extra weight. A structural engineer can help you; don't scrimp on this step because nothing will spoil your day like a squashed house, especially if you're in it.

✔ Ecoroofs can slide off if not properly anchored in place. This issue is not quite as bad as a squashed house, but it's still no picnic.

To decide whether an ecoroof is for you and to find qualified ecoroof professionals in your area, visit Green Roofs for Healthy Cities at www.green roofs.org or Greenroofs.com at www.greenroofs.com.

Creating Paths and Steps

Moving from one part of the landscape to another should be as close to effortless as possible. Yet, paths can also be an exciting element, leading you on a journey that's full of interesting focal points and discoveries.

Practical paths should be straight or gently curved and as level as possible. Locate paths along natural lines of travel so that passage is comfortable and people don't cut corners. For high-traffic areas, choose solid, wear-resistant paving; for secondary and occasionally used paths select something inexpensive and organic, such as wood chip mulch.

For a good-looking design, keep your materials simple and avoid mixing too many kinds of materials. Match the material for the paths to those of other paved surfaces.

You can build steps from stone, reclaimed wood, landscape ties, or concrete. Proper steps should be wide (at least 3 feet), even, and well marked. Ramps are handy when the slope is gentle enough that steps aren't necessary. The ideal slope for ramps is 5 to 8 percent, which is 6 to 10 inches of rise for every 10 feet of run.

Level changes can be treacherous if you don't handle them properly.

Here are some tips for creating safe transitions between one level and another:

- ✔ Never have a single step. It's hard to see just one step and therefore easy to trip on it. Group steps together or eliminate them entirely by gently ramping your path from one level to the next. Nobody ever caught his toe on a ramp.

- ✔ Use handrails wherever you have four or more steps.

- ✔ Make stairs visible by changing materials, placing distinctive plants nearby, and providing ample lighting.

- ✔ All steps must be perpendicular to the direction of travel and evenly spaced.

- ✔ Make the surface of the treads textured to prevent slipping and slope the treads slightly towards the front of the steps so that they shed water.

Special standards apply for wheelchair and walker use. Naturally, paths need to be smooth and level or gently sloping, without steps or sudden grade changes. Avoid sharp curves and drop-offs alongside the path. Paths need to be at least 4 feet wide, and slopes should be no steeper than a 5 percent grade. See the Americans with Disabilities Act site at `www.ada.gov/std spdf.htm` for the official standards.

Considering Water Features

People gravitate to water. Maybe it's because our lives depend on it. Maybe it's because we ourselves are mostly water. Or perhaps it's just because it's so darn beautiful. Nothing can really substitute for water in the garden.

Water features use resources for their construction, require regular topping off with fresh water (at about the same rate as a lawn), and consume electricity for pumping. Water features may seem like an unsustainable indulgence, but another look reveals some real benefits to the environment that compensate for at least some of the impacts. After all, water is the source of life, and soon after you put a water feature into service, you can expect to find it used by dragonflies, thirsty honeybees, and native insects of all kinds, as well as native animals, and many species of birds. In fact, manmade water features are often the only source of life for miles around because natural bodies of water have often been destroyed to create neighborhoods.

Elements of landscape water features

Water features are simple: You need a vessel of some kind to hold the water or a running streambed. Some water features are kept free of plants and fish, but the sustainable garden is about nurturing life, so do consider populating your water feature. Plants and fish provide for each other and keep the system in balance so that it requires little input from you.

An *active water feature* is one that uses a pump to move water for filtration purposes or for the beauty of sound and movement of water. A *passive water feature* is still and pumpless, such as a lovely urn with standing water and a plant or two. Naturally, passive water features are the more environmentally friendly choice, and they create a serene mood without any negative impacts and for very little money.

Water features can be formal or informal, manmade looking or naturalistic, simple or complex. A bubbling spring can spill into a small running stream that runs down into a still pond reflecting the sky and overhanging tree branches. A waterfall can create pleasant sounds to screen traffic noise. A tiered fountain can be the centerpiece of a courtyard. The possibilities are endless.

Working with and around natural water features

If you're fortunate enough to have a real stream or pond on your property, you have some special responsibilities. Generally speaking, you don't have legal or ethical grounds to mess around with natural waterways. It's usually against federal and local laws to modify, pollute, excavate, harass, fold, spindle, or mutilate natural bodies of water and the life in them. Be content with enjoying them as they are.

If a natural waterway has been damaged and you want to restore it, first check with your local flood control agency to see what regulations apply. You'll probably have to work with numerous agencies, such as the Department of Fish and Game, Army Corps of Engineers (bet you didn't know they were looking after your little creek!), flood control, as well as biologists and other professionals. Sometimes the government even helps pay for restoration work.

Natural waterways are delicate, complex, and deserving of the very best of care. Take advantage of your awareness to do the job right.

Pumping, filtering, and other mechanical considerations

The most effective water filter is a 10-inch deep layer of coarse (1 to 2 inches in diameter) gravel in the bottom of the pond, with a set of suction lines on the very bottom to draw water down through the gravel and return it to the pond via a jet of water or waterfall. Bacteria come to live in the gravel — good bacteria that eat gunk for breakfast and keep the water nice and clear.

Use a small, low-volume, high-efficiency pump and run it all the time to keep the bacteria alive. Naturally, running a pump constantly uses some electricity, but a 50- to 100-watt pump usually moves enough water for a small pond. Larger ponds and thundering waterfalls require larger pumps, of course, which is a good reason to keep your pond small. The benefits are the same no matter what the size. Ideally, you use solar power so that operating the pump isn't a drain on the power grid. Some small pumps have their own solar panels; these pumps are fine for moving tiny quantities of water but not for running an under-gravel filter or powering a rushing stream.

Caring for your water feature

Bringing a new water feature into balance takes a little time. High nutrient levels and alkalis leaching from the pond shell must dissipate before you introduce permanent organisms. You'll have a big algae bloom at first, but that should diminish with time.

You have many plant species to choose from and be sure to include some mosquito fish or goldfish to keep the mosquitoes from breeding. Over time, your little ecosystem will become nearly self-reliant.

Chapter 4

Selecting Plants for a Sustainable Landscape

· ·

· ·

*B*eginning gardeners are often overwhelmed by the huge variety of trees, shrubs, and plants and the mysteries of creating and managing the living portion of the landscape. You're smart to take this responsibility seriously — the wrong tree in the wrong spot can do more damage than good — but doing right by your landscape isn't surgery. This chapter shows you how to choose plants and trees to create a sustainable, attractive, and healthy landscape.

If you're a "green" person, you've probably heard that food travels 1,500 miles from farm to plate, and you've read about the 100-mile diet, re-localization, and permaculture. But sustainable landscaping has more to it than just the environmental benefits. Growing food gets you and your family outside, provides great exercise, teaches valuable lessons about life, nature, and patience to kids and adults alike, builds community through sharing the food you grow, and makes you a little more secure and a little less dependent on the supermarket and corporate food. It's a heck of a lot of fun, too. Chapters 4 and 5 of Book VI give you details about growing fruits and vegetables.

Choosing Perfect Plants

If you pick plants well, and combine them skillfully, they'll be an asset and a delight for decades, even centuries. Choose poorly, and they'll torment you forever, growing too large, becoming invasive or hazardous, or suffering from poor growing conditions. Awkward combinations will make the place look busy and unkempt no matter how well the plants do or how much love you give them. The selection of plants should be given the utmost attention. Choosing the perfect plants for your space means learning plants well, visiting them in real-life situations, reading about them, talking to experienced gardeners, and getting advice from pros when necessary.

Size does matter: Give them room to grow

This section may just be the most important thing you read in this book, so listen up. Plants aren't just pretty things to put around the yard; they're living organisms with their own way of getting along in the world. They have a very specific destiny – a set of genetic instructions that determine their height, width, growth rate, and many other characteristics. Plants are indifferent to our needs. That's hard for a plant lover to accept, but there it is. Plants don't give a hoot about you and your landscaping. Sorry.

This indifference on the part of plants means that your job as a landscaper is to figure out what plants need and to make sure that they get it. For example, suppose that you put a 20-foot wide shrub where you actually wanted a 4-foot one. The shrub, in its blissful ignorance, will keep trying to grow to 20 feet wide, and you'll have to keep cutting it back. Now, a plant can't be trained as if it were a dog, and your relationship with it will go on unchanged, with much labor on your part, until you finally take it out and put in something that grows to the proper size and no more.

The implications of not giving plants room to grow are many. You work harder, the plants always look cut back instead of natural, some plants may never flower under these conditions, they'll often suffer from the abuse necessary to keep them in bounds, your green waste can will be full of clippings all the time, energy use and noise from power tools and hauling clippings away will be troublesome, and you'll find yourself in a constant battle with your yard that's worse the more oversized plants you have. I (Owen Dell) call this *adversarial horticulture,* and believe me, it's an epidemic. In some gardens, 80 percent of the work consists of cutting things back all the time. It's unnecessary, and it's a sign of terrible, unsustainable planning.

The remedy, of course, is simple. Believe the gardening books when they list sizes. Choose plants that grow to the size you want for any given application. Then enjoy watching the garden develop into a graceful state of equipoise, getting easier to live with rather than harder.

Choosing healthy plants: What to look for when shopping for plants

Suppose that you had to choose between three plants at the nursery, all the same variety and in the same size containers. One is huge and in luscious bloom, the second is mid-sized, and the third hasn't even grown out to the edges of the pot. Which would you pick? Most people would pick the first one, thinking it was the better deal because it was already fully grown. That would be the very worst choice in most cases, because it's probably root-bound. Roots that circle in the pot, as they do when confined for too long, will continue to circle in the ground and will never grow out into the soil. The plant that looked so great at the nursery will slowly decline, and when you pull it out after a couple of years, you'll find little or no root development.

The best choice in most cases would be the mid-size plant: not too big and not too small. If you were to carefully remove such a plant from its container, you'd find roots that are just beginning to emerge from the root ball and touch the sides of the container. There would be no circling roots, but the soil would be solidly knitted together and wouldn't fall apart as it would with a younger plant.

Consider also the following plant-buying guidance:

- Check out the *crown* of the plant, which is where the stem enters the soil. There should be no circling roots there either. (In that case, they're called *girdling roots* because they can choke one another out as the plant grows.)

- Beware of plants with roots growing out of the drainage holes in the bottom of the pot; these plants belong on the compost heap.

- A plant should have no broken, crossing, or rubbing branches, and the overall shape of the plant should be roughly symmetrical in most cases.

- Be sure there are no pests or diseases evident and watch out for yellowing of the tissue between the veins or any other abnormal coloration that could indicate nutrient deficiencies or other problems.

- Look for an abundance of growth buds, indicating vigor.

Select problem-free varieties

Buying a right-sized, healthy plant is a good start, but choosing varieties that are strong and well adapted to your growing conditions is also important. Some species, and even entire genera, of plants are going to be weaklings, either because they're so far out of their element in your climate that they'll never get what they need to thrive, or because they've been hybridized for appearance at the expense of performance. (Like some exotic breeds of dogs, these poor plants don't have a chance of a long, happy life.) Some people love to challenge themselves by trying to grow difficult plants, but that's not for the sustainable landscaper, who knows better than to throw resources at plants for years when suitable plants demand so little.

If you want a truly sustainable landscape, find out which species of plants really work in your neighborhood. Start with those types and move on to experimental things in small quantities if you're so inclined. But make sure that the backbone plants in your yard are survivors, not wusses. Walk your neighborhood to see what does well and talk to nursery people and others who really know plants. Don't give yourself an uphill battle by choosing plants that will never thrive. What's the point of that?

Native plants versus exotic plants

Which is better, native plants or non-native plants? Like so many aspects of landscaping, there isn't always a simple answer. It depends.

What's a *native plant,* anyway? Here are a few key points to understand:

- Natives are plants that have evolved in place and, in the case of North America and other colonized areas of the world, were present prior to European settlement. Native plants weren't introduced or dispersed by humans; they developed on their own.

- A native species doesn't exist in a vacuum; it's part of a *plant community* of interconnected species that have all grown up together. In turn, the plant community is part of a larger *ecosystem* made up of plants, animals, insects, bacteria, fungi, bodies of water, soil, and even weather patterns and other nonmaterial things. Ecosystems are highly complex and even contain sub-ecosystems, such as streams, hilltops, and valleys.

- Native plants are highly adapted to local conditions. In fact, in many cases, they're adapted to very specific parts of the local ecosystem, growing in a wet spot or on a sunny slope.

- Because of their specificity to a particular environment, they'll generally work well in similar environments in the region, but may be touchy about being moved to a different environment.

- Because they're so well adapted to local conditions, they'll thrive under those conditions with little or no tending by humans. Properly located, they won't need supplemental watering, fertilizing, or other special treatment. A plant's easygoingness is important in developing a sustainable landscape because sustainable is all about minimizing inputs.

- The destruction of ecosystems makes it important to restore as much as possible. Therefore, using natives in a landscape setting (although it may not be an exact replica of nature) will help bring things back into balance. Native plants provide food for native animals and insects, so inviting those plants into your garden will benefit many species.

So does this information mean that you should plant only native plants in your sustainable landscape? In many cases, an all-native garden is an excellent option. If you've come to love the wild areas in your region, by all means consider planting natives. Bring in the whole ecosystem or just the parts that meet your needs. Every little bit helps. If your design is well handled, the natives will make gardening much easier than using ill-adapted non-native plants.

 On the other hand, in an urban or suburban area that's far from a wild condition, you can feel free to mix in well-adapted plants from regions with a climate similar to yours. These *exotic plants* (another word for non-natives), if they're accustomed to similar conditions, will be very sustainable and will mix well with natives. Incorporating non-native plants can add diversity and interest to the plant community you'll be creating. (We all call it a landscape, but it's really an ecosystem, isn't it?) And when there just isn't a native plant that will do what you want, a well-adapted exotic is particularly appreciated.

Working with native plants

If you're considering natives for some or all of your project, first learn about them. Visit a local botanic garden that features natives, take a class in native plants, read up on natives, or join a local native plant society.

 And above all, spend time in truly wild places in your region to understand what a native plant community is, what makes it tick, and what plants are associated with one another and to find out whether it's really something you want on your property. Next, check to be sure that the conditions on your property are really right for the plants you're considering. Soils, exposure, water, and other elements often have to be just so, and not all sites are suitable for natives. If you're not sure how to proceed, consult with a professional who specializes in native landscaping.

When you plant natives, do so in the proper season (often fall, but it will vary depending on location) and be careful to avoid fertilizers, soil amendments, and other modifications unless you know that the plants you've chosen really need them. During the establishment period, keep an eye on watering and other care because even native plants need a little babying when they're pups. Over the long haul, avoid killing your natives with kindness, keeping in mind that they're quite happy with what nature delivers.

If you live near wild land, be careful about introducing natives that aren't present in the immediately local plant community. If such plants are genetically similar to the truly local natives, they can hybridize with the locals and cause genetic pollution.

 Never dig plants from wild places, even on private property, unless you're sure that it won't disrupt a native ecosystem or if you're saving them from approaching bulldozers. Buy natives from reputable growers who propagate them in their nursery and can guarantee that they're not dug in the wilds.

Avoiding invasive plants

Some plants are so nasty that they should never show up in your garden. A particular species may be just fine in its native habitat where competition, browsing animals, or insects keep it under control, but taken elsewhere it runs everything else out of town. Many are the instances of this happening worldwide, and if you're already a gardener, then the names of the locally accursed plants in your area may come easily to your lips. People have been moving plants around the globe for centuries, and while most introductions are benign, quite a few have made a mess of things, out-competing native plants, increasing fire danger, destabilizing slopes, ruining habitat for indigenous animals, and more.

Look to your local native plant society, botanic garden or university, or visit The United States National Arboretum at www.usna.usda.gov/Gardens/invasives.html for information on troublesome plants in your area. Many plants are actually outlawed because they've created so many problems.

Some invasive species are still sold at nurseries. Just because you see a plant for sale doesn't mean it's been tested for good behavior. Learn which species are invasive and never plant them, no matter how cute they look in the pot.

Getting to the Root of a Tree's Purpose and Placement

Trees and shrubs form the basic structure of the landscape and can live for decades or even centuries. As the biggest living things in the garden, trees and shrubs can demand more than their share of attention and resources if they're ill-suited to your growing conditions, too big for the space they've been given, or susceptible to problems. Choose trees and shrubs carefully, give them a good home, and provide the minimal care they need to thrive. They'll reward you with an abundance of valuable services.

A tree is here for — well, not forever, but for a very long time. Choosing and placing it wisely is important to you and to future generations.

Make sure that you run through these points before you buy any tree:

- ✔ **What's it gonna do?** Are you looking for shade, privacy, wildlife habitat, flower or foliage color, wind protection, food, or what? Of course, one tree can conceivably fulfill all those functions and more. Make a list of your needs and then pick a tree that meets them.

- ✔ **Where's it gonna go?** Do you have a spot picked out? Why did you pick it? Will shade be desirable there at all seasons and times of the day? Is there actually room for a tree in that location, and is the tree you're considering the right size at maturity? If it will grow over a driveway or into the street, will there be clearance for vehicles? Does it work well with the architecture of your house? Does it fit with other trees and the overall landscaping in the neighborhood? Is it compatible with other plants in the landscape?

✔ **What's it gonna mess up?** Are you sure a tree in that location won't create more problems than it solves? Will there be adequate clearance from power lines, underground utilities (never plant a tree directly over water mains, sewer lines, or other plumbing), pavement, and foundations? Avoid trees with aggressive or lifting roots anywhere near any improvements that may be damaged. Don't plant a tree that drops a lot of leaves, flowers, and fruits over pavement, especially if it creates a hazard, such as slippery things on the sidewalk. Think about the effect of the tree on your view and on the views your neighbors enjoy; some communities outlaw trees that grow into a neighbor's view.

✔ **What's it gonna look like?** Trees are a big visual presence, and the right tree can really make a property swing. Ponder the many shapes of trees: broad crown, spreading, narrow crown, pyramidal, vase, columnar, *fastigiate* (very tall and narrow), and, of course, the distinctive shape of palm trees. Each has a place. Go look at the shapes of some trees and imagine how they'd fit in your yard. Think about foliage texture and color, flower color and season, branching habit, and even wind movement; all these have a strong visual presence.

✔ **What's it gonna need?** What's the water requirement of the tree? (Remember that a tree is a huge plant, and a thirsty one will run your water bill sky high.) Is it a heavy feeder? How much will it cost to prune? Does it have to be treated regularly for pests and diseases (not sustainable!)? Will it get the kind of soil and weather conditions it needs?

How do you find out enough about a tree to answer all these questions? Read up on it in a good gardening book, check it out at a local botanic garden, or visit the U.S. Department of Agriculture at www.csrees.usda.gov/ Extension/ to find a local extension office. One of the professionals at the extension office can give you great information on choosing the right tree. And visit real, mature trees to get to know them better.

Making Trees Happen

Plant a perennial in the wrong spot, and it's no big whoop to move the plant somewhere that's better suited — or to get rid of it entirely. Trees are not quite so easy: Selecting the right tree, planting it correctly, and giving it good followup care are essential to any tree's success. Messing up a tree means years of lost time or a permanently disfigured or inappropriate (and very large) element in the landscape. Choose, plant, and care for your trees with the utmost loving attention.

Bigger is not always better

Unless you have a huge budget and a genuine need for instant shade, plant a relatively small tree. You can buy trees in all sizes, from a 1-gallon pot (or even a seed) up to a fully mature giant specimen in a huge wooden box that has to be planted with a crane. Costs run from a few dollars to thousands.

In terms of the actual size of the tree, what we in the biz call a *one* (which refers to the size of the container, as in 1-gallon) is a foot or two tall — not too impressive a start but a good way to go if you want fast growth and low cost. A *fifteen* is 5 to 8 feet tall in most cases and has a *caliper* (the diameter of the trunk) of between 1½ and 2 inches; it's a great choice for a reasonably sized and still pretty inexpensive tree that will grow well when planted. (Of course, the size can vary a lot, depending on the species of tree.)

Larger containerized trees come in tapered wooden boxes running from 24 inches to 72 inches and even bigger. Boxed trees need to be planted with heavy equipment and are stunningly expensive. A tree in a 24-inch container isn't a bad way to go, planting out at around 12 to 15 feet tall and still young enough to establish well.

The smaller tree won't give you instant gratification, but in the long run, it'll be the fastest growing. You see, those big specimen trees are way past the age for travel. Their roots are old and set in their ways, and in many, if not most, cases, a big tree will just sulk in your yard, showing little vigor and growth. Some of them die after a number of years. Compare that with a young tree in, say, a 15-gallon container, which will take off and grow like a puppy, rooting vigorously into the soil and developing like you'd hoped. The bottom line: Save your money and buy a smaller, better tree.

Finding a healthy specimen

Trees are sold in several forms. Popularity of different tree "packages" varies from region to region. There is no one right way to buy a tree; it just depends on what's available in good condition.

Here's what you're likely to find:

- ✔ **Containers:** Trees are often planted in plastic pots of varying sizes, expressed in gallons (though the containers don't seem to reflect actual capacity). The smallest are 1-gallon size, and the largest are 15-gallon size.

✔ **Balled and burlapped:** In many regions, trees are grown in the ground and dug up at the time of sale. The root ball is then swathed in burlap and fastened with twine or cradled in a wire basket. *B&B trees* (the landscaper's affectionate term for them) come in various sizes, starting at about the size of a 15-gallon container tree. B&B trees are most often of the deciduous kind, dug in the *dormant season* when they're leafless, and planted as soon as possible after purchase.

✔ **Bare root:** Deciduous fruit and ornamental trees are often sold as *bare root trees* in winter when they're dormant and leafless. Bare roots are dug and sold to you naked as a fish, with their roots hanging out for all to see. Needless to say, they need to be planted very quickly. Bare root trees tend to be small (no more than 8 feet), a snap to evaluate for condition because of their exposed roots, lightweight and therefore easy to plant, and quite vigorous after they're in the ground. They're inexpensive, too.

✔ **Transplanted:** Using ordinary hand tools or huge tractor-mounted *tree spades* for larger trees, you can dig up established trees and move them from one place to another. The best practice is to pre-dig around part of the root system 6 months to a year in advance, to allow new roots to develop within the future root ball. Transplanted trees are at a high risk for loss, but can be a good way to go if you or a neighbor has a good tree in an undesirable location.

A few nurseries grow stocky, robust real trees, but most commercially available trees suck. They're grown too tall and skinny, placed too close together in the nursery, trained to be top-heavy (big canopy on a feeble little trunk), and are nothing like what a young tree looks like if it's grown naturally in the ground from seed. It's an unfortunate reality that we have to put up with garbage trees. Bare root and B&B trees tend to be better than containerized ones.

Here are some things to look for in a healthy tree:

✔ **Good roots:** The root system should be proportional to the canopy, well branched (looking similar to the canopy in form and extent), and free of broken, twisted, or girdling roots. The roots should be fresh and juicy and show a lot of young root shoots. You can easily see all these details with a bare root tree, and impossible otherwise. For containerized trees, avoid ones with roots coming out the drainage holes in the bottom of the pot. The root ball of a B&B tree should be firm.

With all trees, grab the trunk and push it back and forth; a well-rooted tree will be immovable, while a poorly rooted one will wiggle around in the soil. Finally, examine the trunk where it enters the soil to be sure that it doesn't have *girdling roots,* which circle around one another (a sure sign the tree has problems).

✔ **Trunk flare:** The trunk of a healthy tree widens out as it enters the ground. If you see a trunk that plunges straight into the soil like a telephone pole, that tree has been planted too deeply to ever do well.

✔ **Happy branches and good crotches:** The canopy of the tree should be nicely proportioned, with evenly spaced branches that are attached to the trunk at nearly right angles rather than pointing upwards. Examine the crotches where branches come together; they should be wide and strong. V-shaped crotches with *included bark* (bark that wedges into the crotches) indicate weak attachment and the probability of catastrophic failure in some future windstorm. Avoid trees with wounds and clumsy pruning cuts that left stubs, and with cracks where branches meet the trunk. Finally, if the tree is tied to a stake, be sure the ties aren't girdling the trunk.

Caring for established trees

Trees quickly grow beyond the ability of a home gardener to care for them safely and effectively. It's best to hire a professional to perform an annual tree health and safety inspection, which identifies any signs of damage, health problems, dangerous limbs, and poor growing conditions. If your trees need work, let the pros handle it rather than trying to save a little money by doing it yourself. Stay on the ground where you belong.

Anyone with a chainsaw can claim to be a tree expert, but real professionals are certified by the International Society of Arboriculture (ISA), the Tree Care Industry Association (TCIA), or the American Society of Consulting Arborists (ASCA). Don't jeopardize your trees by putting them in the hands of a self-appointed expert or a gardener. That's like letting your hair stylist do brain surgery. Real arborists have to pass rigorous exams for their certification. Ask to see their credentials, get a certificate of insurance so that you're protected if there's an accident, and, of course, get a written estimate. If a tree expert advises you to *top* a tree, send them packing.

Tree care myths

People believe a lot of nonsense about trees, and unfortunately much of it is started or perpetuated by incompetent tree trimmers. Get a limb up on the tree experts so that you can spot the phonies. Here are the most common myths:

✔ **Trees can be topped to control their size.** *Topping* is the practice of whacking the upper portion of limbs off to make the tree smaller. It has been discredited and will never be proposed by any qualified professional. Topping trees ruins their structure and creates the danger of falling limbs. A tree that has grown too big can be controlled by *crown reduction,* careful and correct pruning that removes branches around the tree's top, or it can be replaced with a right-size tree.

✔ **Newly planted trees should be heavily pruned.** Poppycock. A young tree needs every leaf in order to develop a healthy root system.

✔ **Trees should be staked at planting time.** If the tree is robust and well grown, it won't need staking unless there are extreme wind conditions.

✔ **Pruning cuts should be covered with tree sealer.** Wrong. Sealing cuts is ineffective and can even seal in problems. Leave 'em naked.

✔ **The roots of a tree are equal in size to the crown.** Actually, the majority of roots of most trees are in the top 18 inches of soil (where all the good soil, beneficial microorganisms and oxygen are) and spread much farther than the extent of the canopy. Imagine a wine glass sitting on a dinner plate and you have an idea of the geometry of a typical tree.

Shrubs in the Sustainable Landscape

Shrubs are long-lived and often one of the easiest groups of plants to care for, assuming that you choose varieties that aren't pest-susceptible or too big for the space you give them. (All that cutting back will drive you nuts — and it will never end.) Properly used, shrubs demand little in the way of fertilizer, water, or other resources. In fact, a good shrub will be as sustainable as anything you could ever imagine, getting all it needs from sun, soil, and rain.

What shrubs can do for you

Shrubs can screen out undesirable views, create private spaces, exclude unwanted visitors, block wind, define boundaries, subdivide large spaces, create a stunning accent, soften the lines of your house, provide a background for smaller plants, act as erosion-controlling ground cover, provide food and concealment for wildlife, and bear fruit and other food for you.

Here are tips on a few key uses of shrubs:

✔ **Screens and hedges:** Using shrubs as untrimmed screening plants is a lot less work than planting a sheared hedge. If you have the space, choose evergreen shrubs of the proper size for boundary plantings and let them do their thing unmolested by hedge clippers. If space is limited or if you're looking for a formal effect, a clipped hedge is the way to go. Unfortunately, Mother Nature didn't make very many plants that are 2 feet wide and 8 feet tall, so the gardener is forced to try to train larger plants into that form — a losing battle. If space is really limited, try a fence covered with vines; you get the effect of a hedge with much less width and less care.

✔ **Specimen shrubs:** A striking plant, when used individually at a focal point in the landscape, is called a *specimen*. Choose something with an open habit, interesting branch structure, fabulous flowers, or some other attention-getting characteristic. Keep it separated from adjacent shrubs, and place compatible perennials at its feet for a lovely scene.

- **Massing:** To cover large areas with tall, easy plants, use masses of shrubs, mixing a few different varieties that vary in texture, foliage color, flower color and season, and habit. Consider the year-round appearance of the planting and make sure that you have something for every season, whether it be foliage, flowers, fruit, or attractive bare branches. Avoid random one-of-each plantings; repeat varieties through the area.

- **Foundation plantings:** The old idea of planting shrubs all around the house, popularized in Victorian days when the bottoms of houses didn't always look so cute, has been out of fashion for quite a while. But shrubs located strategically to soften or accent the lines of the house are still welcome. Try planting shrubs far enough away from the house that they you can enjoyed them from both inside and out.

Buying quality shrubs

Shrubs are long-lived plants and, along with trees, form the backbone of the garden. For that reason, choosing well is important. Buy shrubs in smaller container sizes unless you need mature plants immediately for a party or a wedding. A 1-gallon shrub will often overtake a 5-gallon or 15-gallon shrub of the same variety in just one or two growing seasons.

Choose varieties that are well adapted to your climate, that will thrive without any inputs of water and fertilizer, and that are the right size for the space you have.

Make sure that your shrubs aren't poisonous, especially if little kids are around. Some shrubs, such as yew, rhododendron, and oleander, are highly toxic.

Enhancing Your Landscape's Sustainability with Smaller Plants

You could create a lovely planting of just trees, shrubs, and mulch (done right it would be almost zero maintenance, by the way), but small-scale companion plants add a lot to the personality of the garden. If you're interested in the many charms of plants, you'll quickly tire of just trees and shrubs and yearn for something more interesting. Many kinds of nonwoody plants serve practical functions in addition to being ornamental. Perhaps most important of all, diversity increases stability and therefore sustainability.

Perennials

Perennial plants are those that live for more than two years. They're generally nonwoody, and most of them die back in winter, at least in colder areas. You grow perennials mainly for their colorful flowers, but many are valuable for foliage interest, as well. Perennials sit at the feet of trees and shrubs, covering the ground, and attracting the eye to the lower levels of the garden. Perennial plants offer waves of color throughout the growing season and a lot of interest in exchange for very little care.

Perennials are perfectly attuned to the low-impact, low-maintenance philosophy of sustainable landscaping. They're among the easiest of flowering plants, requiring only occasional *deadheading* (removing the dead flowers) and an annual hard pruning to remove old foliage at the end of the season. And, of course, the well-chosen perennial planting will be adapted to your climate and soil, so it will require little supplemental watering or fertilization and will be resistant to attacks from pests and diseases. Finally, if given adequate space to grow, perennials won't need to be pruned to control their size.

What do you get in exchange for so little input? Tons o' color, beneficial insects, honeybees, hummingbirds, fragrance, cut flowers, and lovely beds full of interesting plants.

Considering color

Perennials are the color kings of the garden. Color is what they're about, and they do it well. To get the most from your perennial plantings, be extra careful with your arrangement of colors. A meaningless mish-mosh of flower and foliage color isn't satisfying; a controlled and purposeful color scheme is a delight to behold.

Choose an overall approach to color. Decide whether your colors will be *harmonizing* (a mixture of similar colors, such as yellows, oranges, and reds), *contrasting*, also called *complementary* (opposite colors, such as blue and yellow), or *monochromatic* (subtle variations on one basic color). Consider a white scheme for a simple, soothing effect. Contrasting color schemes can be intense, which is useful in small doses to counterbalance an overall soft color scheme, or use darker values of contrasting colors for a gentler effect. Try kicking in a little contrast here and there, such as a dollop of bright red or yellow, in an otherwise subtle planting.

Choosing and using perennials

As with any plants, perennials vary widely in their tolerance for sun or shade, wet or dry, cold or mild climate, and soil type. They also come in a wide range of sizes from creepy crawly ground covers to big guys that grow higher than an elephant's eye. Finally, they have a range of flowering periods, from spring through fall, and some varieties even bloom in fairly cold winters. If you live in a mild Mediterranean or other semitropical climate, you can enjoy perennial flowers all year long.

Avoid *Saturday Morning Syndrome* — choosing plants impulsively because they look cute at the nursery. Even though relocating most perennial plants is easy if you don't get the size, location, or color scheme right, why not nail it the first time around? Take the time to make a plan before you run off to the nursery:

✔ Decide on a color scheme. (For ideas, see the previous section.)

✔ Research climate-adapted varieties that might work. Make a long master wish list and then choose the most compatible plants from that list, being sure that they combine well culturally (not whether they read the same books but whether they have the same growing requirements) as well as aesthetically.

✔ Repeat varieties throughout your planting so that you don't get the one-of-each look. For example, compose a 4 x 20-foot bed of six to ten varieties, using at least three plants of each variety, spread throughout the bed.

✔ Mix varieties with contrasting foliage color and texture and also take into account the overall form (mounding, spiky, and so on) of the plants and season of bloom.

✔ Vary the height and width of the plants you choose. Keep it lively, but not too busy.

Mail-order nurseries are a great source of unusual perennials and other non-woody plants. Specialty growers ship right to your door. The plants often cost more than what you'd find locally, but it's the only way to obtain some of the thousands of hard-to-find species, including natives, that you'll never run across at Vern's Plant World.

Annuals and biennials

Annuals live one year, set seed for the next generation, and croak. Live fast, die young is their philosophy. Some examples of annual plants are petunias, cosmos, and pansies. *Biennials* take a slightly different tack, hanging around for one year as somewhat unimpressive green blobs and then doing the flower-and-kick-the-bucket thing the second year. Examples are sweet William and foxglove. Annuals and biennials are grown for three reasons: color, color, and color. Unlike perennials, which pick a (usually short) window during the season to show off their stuff, most annuals and biennials continue blooming all summer long.

Many plants considered annuals in cold winter climates are actually perennial where winters are mild. That doesn't make any real difference unless you're uptight about botanical accuracy. After all, a dead plant is a dead plant. So whatever they call annuals in your neck of the woods can be treated as such, even if they're not technically annuals per se.

Book V

Sustainable Landscaping

Are annuals sustainable?

When you think about those massive beds of marigolds and petunias that are laboriously renewed every spring with robotic devotion by some gardeners, you may conclude that annuals are about as far from a sustainable landscaping element as you can get.

But there are all sorts of annual plants, and some of them are most welcome in the sustainable landscape.

Many native wildflowers are annuals; they come up on their own, thrive on natural rainfall, and reseed themselves to come back year after year. You can't get more sustainable than that. In fact, the whole annual strategy is about exploiting current resources to the max and then getting out of the way when conditions change.

Choose appropriate annuals, ones that fit with your overall planting scheme and can take care of themselves. Check the hardiness and *earliest planting date* information on the seed packet if you're planting from seed (the most sustainable way to go). *Hardy annuals* (ones that are cold tolerant) can overwinter as seeds in the ground; *tender annuals* that can't take freezing winters should be planted in spring whether from seed or plants. There are also *half-hardy annuals* that put up with yucky cold weather but not frost.

The true story behind meadow magic

No doubt you've seen the ads: An elegant woman in a long gown is sashaying through a stunning alpine meadow, leisurely shaking wildflower seeds from what looks like a parmesan cheese container, and a blindingly colorful carpet of wildflowers of every description is popping up behind her as she walks. You, too, can have this bliss, the ads imply, and you don't even have to get your hands (or gown) dirty. Sounds great, doesn't it? If only it were true!

A wildflower meadow is one of the most daunting challenges in all the gardening world. Yes, you can sow those seeds, but if you haven't eliminated the weed seeds first, and if you don't follow up with diligent weeding and protection from browsing animals and other pests as the young meadow develops, you'll end up with something fit only for a pass with the rototiller. Many is the disappointed gardener who has fallen for this tempting illusion. Adding insult to injury, most of the so-called wildflower mixes available for sale aren't remotely true to the mix of species found in any real meadow and certainly aren't tuned to your particular location.

That doesn't mean that you can't succeed with a small wildflower meadow. Make sure that you choose a custom mix of truly local wildflowers; see a reputable local seed dealer for this and spend at least several months sheet mulching (see Chapter 3 of Book VI) before you sow your seed. Plant the meadow at the right time of year for your location; this timing will vary depending on climate and the type of plants you'll be introducing. And plan on spending some time on your knees handpulling tiny weeds out of tiny wildflower seedlings.

If you're successful, you'll have a great display of color in spring, and maybe some plants will come back the following spring. But it's an awful lot of work for a dicey outcome.

 Instead of going for the carpet-of-color effect, try sowing smaller quantities of wildflowers into established perennial borders and turf-type meadows. This approach is more akin to what nature would do, making a plant community of a diverse mix of permanent and annual plants. Remove little patches of mulch to expose bare ground, loosen it up a bit with a cultivating fork, sow a few seeds (just a few, okay?), and top-dress with a quarter-inch thick layer of fine compost or similar organic matter. Nature will do the rest.

Bulbs and bulb-like plants

Not all the things we call "bulbs" actually are. To most gardeners, anything with strap-shaped leaves and colorful flowers is a bulb, whether it's a true bulb, such as onions or daffodils, rhizomes like iris, tubers like tuberous begonias, corms such as gladiolas, or tuberous roots like Dahlias. These botanical differences are of little interest to the gardener because they don't really change how you use or care for the plants.

Whatever their strict botanical classification, "bulbs" are among the loveliest and easiest garden plants. Their vertical, strap-shaped foliage and stunning flowers add a lively bit of punctuation (think exclamation point) to perennial beds and meadows.

Bulbs are easy. Here are some tips for using them successfully and enjoying them without a lot of effort.

- ✔ Use bulbs in drifts and masses for a stunning effect or salt them amongst other small plants or in low-growing ground covers. Bulbs belong in meadows, where they'll co-exist happily with typical meadow plants and add diversity.

- ✔ Many bulbs are among the first plants to bloom in spring. You can plant bulbs in mixed borders for an early show before the perennials get going.

- ✔ Plant bulbs with other low-growing plants so that there's something to look at when the bulbs are dormant.

✔ Many bulbs will *naturalize,* increasing their numbers annually until they form sizable, dense populations that need no care from you other than an annual cutback of dead foliage and flowers.

✔ Most bulbs can remain in the ground; you don't need to dig them up and put them in storage every year as people sometimes do. If a bulb needs that kind of treatment, it's not adapted to your climate.

✔ Follow package instructions on the depth to plant your bulbs; it can be critical to their success. Ask at the nursery if you're not sure which part of the bulb should be up when you plant them; it's not always easy to tell.

✔ Plant in chicken wire baskets and cover the soil with wire as well, to protect the bulbs from squirrels, gophers, and birds.

✔ The foliage of most bulbs needs to die down naturally in order to feed the bulb for the following year's performance. Curb your impulse to cut back the leaves until they turn yellow.

Ground covers

In some ways, "ground cover" is a dubious term. Many plants cover the ground, after all. But *ground cover* as commonly used means a low, often creeping *herbaceous* (that is, not woody) plant that will sprawl across a wide area. The idea of ground covers seems to be twofold:

✔ Playing the role of lawn, visually and sometimes functionally by using ground-cover plants that you can walk on. In this task, the ground cover makes a sort of living wall-to-wall carpet.

✔ Outcompeting weeds for a low-maintenance sward of greenery and flowers.

Both of these ideas are lovely, and they actually work in some situations. Other times the solution becomes the problem because of poor plant selection. Tread carefully in the world of ground covers and learn what really succeeds before committing to a plan of action.

The main pitfalls of the ground-cover approach have to do with the nature of the chosen plants. Following the "right plant, right place" dictum can result in a successful planting. But a careless choice can create a disaster. Here are the major ills of common approaches:

✔ **Weeds:** Nature is competitive, always pitting one force against another, flinging the seeds of opportunistic plants into every open space. Weeds show up in two ways: via underground or above-ground runners and, most commonly, by way of seeds. If the ground-cover planting is too low to the ground, or if there are bare spots in it, weeds and germinating weed seeds are able to get right to the sunlight and quickly take control. At that point the gardener is faced with laborious hand weeding or the use of herbicides (which may kill the desirable plants as well as the weeds). At some point, despair sets in, and the whole thing tanks.

The sustainable approach is to plant things that are at least a foot tall (preferably taller, ideally around knee-high) so that they shade the soil. The other strategy is to use a soaker hose to irrigate rather than keeping the soil surface constantly moist with an overhead sprinkler system, which creates a perfect environment for seed germination. Of course it helps to have drought tolerant plants and to water little or not at all; then seeds will germinate only during the wet season.

✔ **Invasiveness:** Many ground covers are viney by nature and try to grow out of bounds. Some, like ivy, are so aggressive that you'd swear they're going to grow into the next zip code. With invasive plants, you can't do anything except keep cutting them back.

The obvious solution is to replace invasive varieties with plants that have a *determinate growth habit*, meaning that they grow to a certain relatively predictable size and stay there. (Your county extension office can give you plant suggestions.) Be sure to keep them far enough from the edges of the space so that they don't grow beyond it despite their limited size. In other words, keep a plant that grows to 4 feet in diameter at least 2 feet from the edge of the bed it's in.

✔ **High water use:** Many ground covers achieve their verdant good looks by sucking up literally tons of water. There's rarely any need for high water use when so many drought tolerant ground covers are available. Pick one.

✔ **Bees:** Bees are good. They pollinate crops and make honey and are smart and cute and utterly essential to life on this planet. Really. However, stepping on bees is good for neither man nor bees, and if you happen to be allergic to them, it can be very nasty indeed. Avoid bee-attracting varieties like clover or Lippia for walk-on ground covers.

Ornamental grasses

Time was when grasses in the yard were either lawn or weeds. Then some folks in Europe began growing grasses for their beauty, not perpetually crew-cut and indistinguishable from one another as in a lawn but placed as individual plants in flower beds and allowed to grow into their full glory. This idea came as a shock to a lot of people, and it took a while for gardeners to get used to seeing a fully grown grass plant without having the urge to walk over and yank it out by the roots. But their charms prevailed and eventually ornamental grasses came to be loved by many gardeners.

Ornamental grasses range in size from 6-inch tall *Fescues* to clumps of *Miscanthus* 8 feet or more in height. Even bamboo is technically a grass. Grasses can be a sustainable element in the landscape if they're climate-adapted, non-invasive, and right-sized. In fact, many grass species tolerate or prefer poor soil, require little or no fertilizer, and — unlike lawn grasses — they don't need much in the way of water. Grasses are generally pest-free, too.

Grasses sequester a lot of carbon, which helps to mitigate global warming. They're fast-growing, live a long time in most cases, and even resist browsing by deer and other animals. (Grasses grow from the base rather than the tops, and so they recover well from being gnawed on. That's why they're tolerant of grazing and lawn mowing.)

On the other hand, grasses have some problems. The most vexing is what happens when weeds, especially undesirable grasses, get into them. If you've ever tried to pull two grassy plants apart, you know it's like trying to break up a dog fight. Multiply this task by a whole yard full of grasses, and you've got yourself a hobby. The answer is to choose drought-tolerant varieties and be very diligent about not letting weeds go to seed or creep into the grass.

Certain ornamental grasses should be avoided at all costs because of their invasive tendencies. They become garden weeds, and some can even harm wild ecosystems. After they're introduced, they can be nearly impossible to get rid of. What's harmless in one area can be pernicious in another, so you need to check for locally troublesome species. Your county extension office keeps a list of plants you should avoid in your area, and they'd be thrilled to know you're taking it seriously. Check in with them.

Some grasses can be highly flammable. In fact, most wildfires start in dry grasses and move on to larger plants. Irrigate enough to keep them green and periodically use your hands to remove the dead foliage or cut the plants back hard in early spring.

Integrating grasses into the landscape

Ornamental grasses make great specimen plants, ground covers, and mass plantings. They even grow in containers. Mixing grasses with perennials and shrubs gives a natural feel to your landscaping. (Most wild plant communities have a grassy element.)

Here are some basic considerations for working grasses into your plantings:

- ✔ **Cool and uncool grasses:** Grasses fall into two categories: *cool season* (which are most active when temperatures are low) and *warm season* (which do better in that other time of year). Mix cool and warm season grasses for year-round interest. Winter brings a fourth season of beauty to many grasses if you wait until spring to cut them back.

- ✔ **Runners and clumpers:** *Running* grasses spread, often vigorously, by underground shoots; they can be handy for erosion control, but many of them can get out of hand quickly and become a nuisance. *Clumping* grasses hang out in one place and don't get in anybody's face; they're easier to live with.

✔ **Light:** With a few exceptions, grasses like full sun, so plan on using them in open areas where they get at least half a day of the stuff. In shadier areas, try grass-like rushes and sedges.

✔ **Special effects:** Exploit the unique charms of grasses — their fountain-like growth habit, the graceful way they move and rustle in the wind, the way morning and afternoon light settles in the foliage. Plant grasses to the west of a bench or patio for a wonderful back-lit sunset show. Use the showy blooms in flower arrangements. Plant a tall specimen grass where you want an eye-catching vertical element.

✔ **Soil stabilization:** Take advantage of the extensive root system of grasses to knit unstable soil together.

Maintenance: Avoiding a pain in the grass

Choose your grasses well and give them an appropriate home, and you shouldn't have much trouble with them. Here's a rundown of tasks:

✔ **Watering:** Know the water needs of your grasses. Many are quite happy with rainfall alone, but some need supplemental irrigation. Even drought-tolerant grasses can take wet soils if need be, but they often grow too lush and floppy and lose much of their charm in wet soil. Overwatered grasses may end up being short-lived, too. Wet the soil to a depth of 12 to 18 inches at each irrigation, and water as seldom as you can get away with.

✔ **Fertilizing:** Most grasses don't need to be fertilized, and, in fact, overly fertile conditions encourage weak growth. Especially avoid excess nitrogen, which produces lush foliage to the point where it can be a problem.

✔ **Pests and diseases:** Overwatering and overcrowding can encourage diseases, but absent those conditions, you should have no problems. Gophers eat grasses from below ground, and other critters will browse on your grasses from time to time; remember that grasses are here for just that purpose and can't be hurt by a little grazing, so chill out and let the other species have their fun, too.

✔ **Weed control:** Pull young weeds, roots and all, carefully out of the grass clump. Wetting down the ground first helps a lot. Don't let the weeds get too big or you end up lifting and dividing the grass just to get the weeds out, or removing it altogether.

✔ **Cutting back:** Some grasses can go along for years with no pruning, but most look better (and be safer in a fire) if you cut them back hard annually in early spring. You may also want to try combing dead foliage out with the hands (wear gloves). Meadows can be mowed — or grazed if you happen to have a few head of cattle around.

Walking a vine line

Vines have a special place in the landscape. The form they take can be useful, especially when you need plants for small or narrow spaces. But they can also be problematic, growing into trees and invading spaces not meant for them. Using vines well can result in a richer garden environment; misusing them can cause grief.

Vines developed as a way to exploit limited sunlight in forested, mostly tropical, environments where trees beat small plants to the light. Vines tolerate shade when young and scramble quickly to the tops of the trees to get to the sun, spreading out as soon as they reach the canopy. All vines compete with their host trees, and some, like the strangler fig of tropical rainforests, ultimately kill the tree and become one themselves by developing huge trunks and branches. Some introduced vines, such as the famous kudzu in the southern United States, have become a severe problem with no solution in sight. If all this domination by vine sounds kind of violent, or at least rude, it is. "Natural" isn't always gentle.

Properly chosen and planted in a suitable location, the right vine can be just the ticket for special garden needs. Vines need more trimming than other plants, but sometimes that's a small price to pay to get a lot of function. Here are some tips for using vines without risk:

- ✔ **Conceal and cover:** Make use of vines to cover fences where you don't have space for a hedge. Plant them on walls to help insulate the house and conceal bad architecture. Send them over the hill to control erosion.

- ✔ **Climbing styles:** Some vines twine around their support, others hold on using small tendrils that wrap around wire or the stems of other plants, and still others stick to the side of your house with little *holdfasts* that look like teeny lizard's feet. Some just sprawl. Choose a vine type that will grow on the support you plan to offer it. Holdfasts, by the way, are well named; they can be nearly impossible to get off if you want to paint.

- ✔ **Evergreen or deciduous:** Some vines hold their leaves all year; others lose them in winter. Choose one of the former kinds if you need consistent coverage for screening purposes.

- ✔ **Speaking of support:** Make it strong, since mature vines can be surprisingly heavy. A building will do, as long as you're willing to keep the vine trimmed away from eaves and openings where it may cause damage. Install horizontal stainless steel wires on fences and hand-train the vines onto them. Make trellises out of natural materials, such as the whip-like branches pruned from deciduous fruit trees.

There's always the temptation to grow big vines on overhead pergolas. What usually happens is that all the leaves and flowers are on top where all the light is, and you end up sitting underneath looking at dead leaves and wondering when the rats are going to start jumping on your head. And when the time comes to paint it, you wish you'd never heard the word "vine." If your pergola is ugly, tear it down. Don't make things worse by trying to hide it with a vine. Another thing: Go ahead and let a vine climb up to the second story if you like spending your weekends teetering high on a ladder with electric hedge clippers in your face.

Avoid growing vines on power poles. It draws attention to the pole and makes the utility companies unhappy because they have to constantly cut them back. Keep them out of trees, too.

✔ **Vines and wildlife:** Many vines attract and nurture butterflies, birds, and bees. This is good (unless you're allergic to or afraid of bees). They also provide rodents food, shelter, and a handy ladder into your house, which is not so good unless you happen to love rodents.

✔ **Vine combinations:** Try planting two vines that bloom at different seasons for a longer display of color.

Everyone knows the grape vine, but many other vines produce edible fruits, including passion fruit, kiwi and cold-hardy arctic kiwi, berries, hops, and chayote. Don't forget annual vines, such as peas, beans, squash, and melons. Food-bearing vines can grow in places where fruit trees and vegetable beds would never fit, and they often put the fruit at a nice pickable level to eliminate stooping and climbing.

Succulents and cacti

You either love or hate *succulents* and *cacti* — the fleshy, water-storing plants that thrive in drought conditions. If you hate them, you don't have to read this section; you'll still be welcome in the sustainable landscaping club. We'll see you at another chapter of the book.

Okay, now that they're gone — hey, how 'bout those succulent plants, huh? What an amazing array of shapes and forms! And they can't be touched when it comes to sustainability.

Getting to know succulents and cacti

Generally, succulents and cacti like sun, but there are some shade-tolerant ones as well. They prefer warmer climates (USDA zones 8 to 10), but some can grow as far north as parts of Canada. Because they hold water in their tissue, they're very drought-tolerant, though many can accept limited regular watering under otherwise good growing conditions. They use one third to one half less water than turf. Pests and diseases are fairly rare. And there are few, if any, invasive varieties. Overall, succulents and cacti are among the easiest, most bulletproof plants for the landscape.

Choose and use succulents effortlessly with a few guidelines:

- ✔ **Placement:** Especially if you get frost, locate succulents on the sunny south side of a house or building where reflected heat and the warmth retained in the walls helps them endure cold nights. Choose a location with good air circulation as well. Place thorny plants away from paths and other traffic patterns.

- ✔ **Arrangement:** Use succulents and cacti in contrast to leafier drought-tolerant plants, keeping in mind that they rarely grow only with others of their kind in nature. It's okay to have an all succulent/cactus garden, but it's okay to mix plants, too. Just be sure to group them with plants that have similar water needs. Use the bold forms as specimen or accent plants. Silhouette them against walls. Play with the many foliage colors.

- ✔ **Drainage:** Without good drainage, succulents drown. They grew up in places with gravelly soil and fast internal soil drainage. Give it to them. Give them drought. Give them sun. Leave them the heck alone. They'll love you for it. If you're one of those people who waters everything every day, stay away from succulents; they hate that kind of attention.

- ✔ **Feeding and watering:** Go easy on the fertilizer and apply it only during the active growing season and in small doses. Use none unless you see actual nutrient deficiencies. Keep in mind the required rest period during fall and winter and withhold fertilizer and water then.

Handling thorny plants

Work with thorny plants carefully! Wearing thick leather gloves! Try wrapping them in the Sunday newspaper or a piece of old carpeting. Wear a heavy, long-sleeved shirt or jacket even if it's hot out. Oh, and no flip-flops; heavy boots are de rigueur. Eye protection isn't a bad idea, either.

Keep in mind that spines can cause infections or painful injuries that take a surprisingly long time to heal. Clean all wounds promptly and thoroughly. (How's your tetanus booster doing?) Succulents are much heavier than other plants because of the water in their tissue, so they can be top-heavy. Many are also brittle and need to be handled with care. This is extreme gardening.

Chapter 5

Finding Greener Ways to Work Around (or with) Lawns

*T*oday, lawns are a major industry — $30 billion a year is spent just on professional lawn care. That figure doesn't include the efforts of homeowners themselves and the vast array of technologies that are thrown at modern lawns. Devotion to lawn technologies wouldn't be so bad if it weren't for the negative impacts of all this lawn care: global warming, noise, cancer and other diseases, water and air pollution, fossil fuel use, habitat destruction, soil degradation, excess water consumption, mountains of clippings, and golf.

Lawns have become a symbol of consumerism gone mad, and they pretty much deserve their bad reputation. Still, how many people can resist the lure of the lawn? In this chapter, you find good reasons to try to resist, anyway, along with lawn substitutes and — if you can't give the sucker up — ways to maintain your lawn with less environmental impact.

What's So Bad about Lawns, Anyway?

If you have a lawn, you're not exactly alone. In the United States, lawns take up 50,000 square miles, which is nearly twice the size of the 100 largest U.S. cities put together. If only turf were a truly beneficial element of gardening, Americans could be proud of the accomplishment. Unfortunately it hasn't worked out that way. Here's a look at some of the downsides of lawns:

✔ **Effects on air quality:** Lawn-care equipment (mowers, edgers, and so on) account for 2 percent of American fossil fuel use, and because they operate without smog devices, they're responsible for at least 5 percent of U.S. air pollution. In fact, a lawnmower emits the same amount of pollution as eight new cars driving 55 miles an hour. Each mower emits 80 pounds of CO_2 per year, generously contributing to global warming. Pesticides also evaporate into the air, causing still more pollution.

✔ **Water use:** Lawns suck water like crazy. Between 30 percent and 60 percent of household water in the United States is used to keep lawns alive. If every American lawn were watered optimally, it would use 200 gallons per person per day. (To put that number in perspective, you probably use around 40 to 80 gallons per day for all personal uses, such as cooking, laundry, bathing, drinking, and so on.) Lawn water use amounts to 270 billion gallons per week, which is three times what is put on irrigated corn and enough to grow 81 million acres of organic food. So is it better to have 31 million acres of lawn or 81 million acres of pure fresh food? Well, go graze on your lawn and then you tell me which is better. Oh, and by the way, that's water that people could be drinking.

✔ **Fossil fuel consumption:** The EPA says 800 million gallons of gas are burned in lawn mowers each year, and mower operators spill 17 million gallons just fueling those suckers — more than was spilled in the Exxon Valdez disaster.

✔ **Pesticides:** Sixty-seven million pounds of synthetic pesticides go on American lawns each year, at a cost of $700 million. That's ten times more per acre than U.S. farmers put on their crops. This pesticide use leads to water and air pollution, global warming, loss of wildlife and beneficial insects, and numerous diseases (cancer, birth defects, and heart disease, to mention a few).

Only 35 percent of those pesticides actually reach the plants; the rest drifts off to do harm. One in seven people are negatively affected by pesticides. In fact, according to the National Academy of Sciences, a 5-year old has already absorbed half his lifetime dose of pesticides. And yet some people still believe that a poisoned yard is a better yard. (Check out www.beyondpesticides.org for more info.)

✔ **Fertilizers:** Chemically based fertilizers are made from nonrenewable fossil fuels and other environmentally hazardous ingredients. They leach into the water supply, and they kill lakes by nourishing algae blooms that suck all the oxygen out of the water. A substantial percentage of the fertilizer applied to lawns ends up leaving the area, but even the portion that stays in the root zone is troublesome, killing the beneficial soil microorganisms on which the grass depends for its health.

Unlike natural fertilizers made from organic sources, chemical fertilizers are salts that have a negative effect on soil well-being. Most fertilizers applied by spray are fast-acting and disperse quickly; this boom-and-bust cycle is just as hard on a lawn as living on candy bars and whiskey would be for you.

- ✔ **Lack of biodiversity:** Chemically treated lawns are dead zones for wildlife. Compared to a mixed planting of trees, shrubs, perennials, and annuals, a lawn contains almost no biodiversity and offers little or no habitat value. Add in the fact that 11 of the 30 common lawn chemicals are toxic to bees, 24 are toxic to fish, and 16 to birds, and you've got a bright green desert (except that's an insult to the highly diverse and lively deserts). Even the family dog isn't safe; a study of Scottish Terriers by Purdue University determined that four to seven times the incidence of lymphoma and bladder cancer occurs in those dogs that lived around pesticide-treated lawns.

- ✔ **Green waste production:** A typical American one-third acre lawn generates almost two tons of clippings a year. That's just shy of 190 million tons, just in the United States. Depending on where you live, a good portion of that green waste may be taken away in a fossil fuel-consuming truck and put in a landfill where it will never again be part of a living system.

- ✔ **Injuries:** There are between 60,000 and 70,000 severe lawnmower accidents per year in the United States alone. A rotary mower can fire rocks at 200 miles per hour. Not to mention what happens when you try cleaning out the chute while the mower is still running.

- ✔ **Noise pollution:** Stop already with the racket! Imagine your neighborhood on a Saturday morning without all the lawnmowers going at once. How peaceful that would be. It's not an impossible dream.

- ✔ **Cost:** Suppose that you pay a gardener 50 bucks a visit to mow your lawn. Suppose that you live in a mild climate where mowing is a year-round job. If you do that for 20 years, you'll spend $50,000 — not accounting for inflation (or if you're just very cheap and never give the poor gardener a raise). And that's just for the mowing. Factor in also the water, fertilizer, sprinkler repairs, replacement, weed control, and all the rest.

Finding some good news about lawns

A lawn does have some advantages. A recent independent study found that if lawn clippings are left on the lawn after mowing (see the upcoming "Grassscycling" section), lawns can sequester significant quantities of carbon, which helps mitigate global warming. That's a big plus. Here are a few more:

- ✔ Grassed areas absorb water readily and so can soak up some of storm water in a rain, reducing urban flooding and allowing groundwater recharge.

- ✔ They produce oxygen, cool the air, and trap dust and crud.

- ✔ They're soft and safe to play on.

- ✔ They reduce glare.

- ✔ And, sure, they're pretty. (But mostly because we're conditioned to think so. A meadow is darned pretty, too, and a more sustainable option.)

The question is, are these benefits justified in light of the problems that lawns create? There are differing schools of thought on this question, and there is no solid data that takes into account the mitigating effects of organic lawn care.

Does a truly sustainable lawn exist?

If the test of sustainability is that a lawn could maintain itself with no watering, feeding, mowing, weeding, or pest control — no inputs of any kind — then, no, lawns aren't sustainable. If the test is whether the lawn gives back more than it takes, then the answer also is probably no.

Not having a lawn is preferable for a green home, and the upcoming section "Exploring Lawn Alternatives" shows you ways to make your land greener, in the figurative sense.

But the reality is that lawns are here and probably not going away any time soon — if at all. (For crying out loud, some homeowners associations *require* them.) If you do have a lawn, maintaining it with a minimum of destructive effects at least takes some of the ecological sting out of it. You get tips for doing just that in the next section.

Minimizing the Negative Impact of the Lawn

If you're not ready to go lawn-free, you do have options. You can change your lawn, and the way you manage it, with significant positive results for the planet. Most of the changes are simple and inexpensive. Some of them are even free and result in immediate savings in water and labor. None of these improvements is rocket science.

Reducing lawn size

How much lawn do you really need? Assuming that you have an actual need for lawn, such as playing on it, a third of an acre usually is plenty unless you host regulation tackle football games on weekends.

Figure out how much lawn you really need (for a badminton court, if that's what you're into, or maybe just a lane for cut-throat bocce ball games) and then whittle down your lawn as much as possible. Shoot for reducing your lawn area by half.

You don't necessarily have to get rid of your lawn. But if you could please, please, please just make it a teeny bit smaller, Nature would be awfully grateful! And so would your bank account.

Changing to a low-maintenance variety

You find many kinds of lawn grasses, some less troublesome than others. Choose a low-care variety suited to your region, one that's resistant to pests and diseases, and maybe even uses less water. Hybrid tall fescues are the current candidate in many areas, but the best choice for your lawn depends on where you live. Talk to one of the professionals at your local cooperative extension service; they're amply familiar with local conditions.

Many of a lawn's problems stem from its being a *monoculture* — that is, composed of only one type of plant. Adding a mix of native plants is a much more sustainable option that cuts back tremendously on the effort and maintenance products your lawn requires. And it creates a more attractive environment for birds and frogs and other visitors.

Clover, for example, brings a wealth of benefits to a lawn but is regarded as a weed by many homeowners. Mix in clover with your grass, and you not only draw a wider range of beneficial insects (including bees, so watch your step) but practically ensure that you'll have some green in your lawn during even the driest seasons when the grass dries out.

Improving water management

Most people are overwatering their landscaping, and lawns are the biggest culprit. Managing water better involves a bit of learning and some careful attention to changing conditions rather than watering on a fixed schedule that ignores actual water need. But it doesn't cost a penny, and you'll start seeing lower water bills right away.

Lawns do best when they're watered deeply but infrequently; err on the dry side. If your grass takes on a blue or gray tint and starts showing footprints, the time to water is now. Water too much, and you encourage fungal disease.

So much of the water applied to lawns is wasted that you have a huge opportunity to save water (and money) just by tuning up your irrigation system. Simple adjustments, such as re-aiming heads, cleaning plugged nozzles, and moving heads to improve coverage and eliminate overspray onto pavement, can make a big difference. As you delve further into sustainability, you'll most likely want to give up your irrigation system, but in the meantime, at least make sure that it's functioning at its most efficient.

Grasscycling

Bagging grass clippings is unnecessary and wasteful. It removes valuable nutrients and organic matter from the system for no reason.

Grasscycling, also known as *mulch mowing*, is the practice of leaving the clippings on the lawn so that they return to the soil through the process of decomposition. Special *mulching mowers* cut the grass blades more finely than regular mowers, helping them to break down faster, but any mower will work. Grasscycling can reduce the need for nitrogen (the key element in lawn fertilizer) by 30 to 50 percent. You're basically giving your lawn a free fertilizer treatment just by leaving the clippings on the lawn.

By the way, it's a myth that leaving the clippings on the lawn causes *thatch* (the thick, spongy layer of dead material that sucks up water before it gets to your grass's roots), so cross that one off your worry list. Thatch's real culprit is overfertilizing and overwatering.

Using a reel mower

Reel lawnmowers use no fuel, unless you count what you had for breakfast. They're quiet. They always start. They let you mow the lawn *and* get your exercise at the same time, which is perfect for busy people. They work great for the small urban lawn as long as you don't let it grow too long before mowing.

If you must use a power mower, choose an efficient electric model. They are just right for the average suburban lawn, and they reduce fossil fuel consumption, are quieter than gas mowers, and cost one-tenth as much to operate as a gas mower. Or try sheep; they're a classic solution.

Exploring Lawn Alternatives

Suppose that you're ready to 86 your lawn and do something more sensible. Bravo! It's a smart move, especially considering that so many better alternatives are out there. First, consider how much turf-like area you actually need. Use a lawn substitute in that area and integrate the remainder into your overall landscape design, creating perennial beds, an orchard, vegetable gardens, native plants, or some other appropriate use. Your costs will go down, benefits will go up, and the environment will love you.

The following sections detail some great ideas for antilawns.

The meadow idea

Everywhere you look, people are taking out their lawns and replacing them with meadows. The transformation has been described as a revolution, and it's surely one of the bright spots in modern horticulture.

Instead of fertilizing and watering to make grass grow and then ruthlessly decapitating it every week with snarling fossil-fuel-powered lawnmowers, the meadow owner enjoys a more tousled, natural-looking turf made up of native or climate-compatible non-native grasses, sedges or herbaceous plants such as yarrow.

Better yet, meadows need mowing only rarely — or never. For example, a sedge meadow can be mowed a couple of times a year to freshen it up or left to its own devices. (And if you do want a clipped look, many meadow plants can take regular mowing.)

Meadows in general require much less water than lawns and need very little fertilizer. Properly chosen plants, put in favorable locations, will have little if any trouble with pests and diseases, so their overall impact is very low. (Chapter 4 tells you more about choosing plants.) Yet after they're established, they offer a tough, playable, beautiful surface. Finally, meadows can be more diverse than lawn, providing habitat for beneficial and native insects.

Meadow plants

Meadow plants fall into three basic categories:

- ✔ **Grasses** have an attractive unmowed appearance and overall low maintenance. You can choose grasses that are native or otherwise, as long as they're easy to live with.

- ✔ **Sedges** look like grasses but are in a different family of plants. They're handsome and fresh-looking, tolerant of a wide range of conditions and easy to live with. A few species can be moderately invasive and should be surrounded by an underground plastic root barrier to keep them where you want them.

- ✔ **Perennials,** such as yarrow, clover, violets, and roman chamomile are flowering plants that develop a tight covering of foliage; many of them are very showy. Don't forget that you can (and really should) use a mixture of several different kinds of plants in your meadow to make it more adaptable to varying conditions, create a richer habitat, and provide a more interesting look.

How to make a meadow

Creating a meadow isn't that much different from putting in a lawn. Soil preparation is the same, and depending on the species you choose, you can plant from seed or small pots. In some regions, certain meadow mixes are available as sod.

If your climate is dry during the growing season, you may need to water a few times until the plants are established.

Establishment of some meadow species can involve more work than a lawn because the plants are slower to mature, meaning you'll have to pull weeds for a while longer than usual. But that's a small price to pay for a lifetime of easy care and low impact.

Meadow management

Living with a meadow is pretty easy, given that they don't care whether you pay much attention to them or not. Mowing can be challenging if the plants are very overgrown; using a weed whacker or hand shears can work better than a mower in some cases.

As for watering, try letting it go until you see signs of stress (slowing of growth, change in color, droopiness) and then water. Chances are, the interval will be longer than you think. Fertilize once or maybe twice a year but only if growth is slower than you like — meadow plants are tough and, after they're established, under normal conditions you don't need to fertilize. It's supposed to be easy and is.

Walk-on ground covers

You can use various kinds of ground covers in place of a lawn. The main difference between a ground cover and a meadow is the degree of traffic the plants can tolerate: Meadows are okay with normal lawn use, and ground covers are better off with only occasional foot traffic because they're more easily injured or recover more slowly. Ground covers provide the look of a lawn where you want a broad swath of something low to set off other, taller plantings and can tolerate limited access and use.

As a general rule, ground covers offer fewer benefits and take more care than meadows, but how well they function in your yard depends on which ground cover you choose. As with other plants, look into varieties that are suited to your region and then choose ones from that list that will thrive in your particular conditions. Your local cooperative extension service can direct you to plants that meet your needs and thrive in your area. Chapter 4 tells you more about choosing ground covers.

Making use of mulch

Organic mulch is an ultra-low care surface that's well suited to paths and open areas where you don't need a living element. Sometimes mulching is a temporary solution while you're killing weeds or waiting to decide how to develop a space. Other times, it's a great permanent element in the landscape, offering weed control, water conservation, soil improvement, erosion protection, and a nice natural appearance. Cheap, too.

What about artificial turf? (Yecch!)

Maybe you're starting to see your resource-greedy lawn as more of a thorn in your side than a benefit, but you're not ready to commit to a meadow. Could artificial turf be the answer to your problems? A resounding no answers that question.

Sure, phony plastic lawns require no fertilizer, water, or mowing, but they originate from fossil fuels and may include toxic ingredients. Because they soak up no water, they contribute to runoff problems.

Nonliving turf worsens the *urban heat-island* effect — any densely populated area is hotter than a wide-open rural area, partly because of all that concrete.

Check out Chapter 2 to find out further reasons to avoid artificial turf, in case you're not deterred by the stink-eye you get from your neighbors after you install the stuff.

Reducing Your Lawn's Environmental Impact

The shift to organic lawn care has been huge. People are fed up with spreading poisons all over their yard. According to Popular Mechanics magazine, the number of U.S. households purchasing natural fertilizers increased from 2.5 million to 11.7 million between 1998 and 2003. During the same period, households practicing natural pest control went up from 1.8 to 10.9 million. That's a revolution!

People wouldn't be taking the natural approach if it didn't get results. Organic lawn care isn't just for hard-core enviros; it's a well-developed system with a lot of great science behind it. Organic lawn care saves you time and money and delivers a great-looking, robust lawn. The upcoming sections show you how to make that happen in your yard.

Smart mowing means good growing

Mow high. No, not *you* — the mower. Set your mower to keep the grass at least 3 inches high for most *cool season grasses* like fescues, bluegrass, and rye (1 inch or less for *warm-season grasses* like Bermuda grass; they're a special case). Not cutting your grass too short is the Most Important Lawn Care Practice. Maintaining grass at the proper height preserves plenty of leaf surface so that photosynthesis is maximized and plenty of sugars go into the roots to strengthen them (plants are sugar junkies, too); it helps shade out weeds, encourages grass to spread by sending underground runners, discourages pests, and keeps diseases at bay. Mowing high is the right thing to do.

Keep in mind the following tips for mowing:

- ✔ Never cut more than one-third of the total height at any one time; losing too much off the top is shocking to the grass. If your grass is 4 inches high, for example, don't cut more than 1.33 inches.
- ✔ Keep your mower blades sharp to avoid damage to the grass.
- ✔ Mow in late afternoon when the lawn is dry so that the clippings don't clump.
- ✔ Cut in a different direction each time you mow to prevent wear and to keep grass blades upright.
- ✔ Mow when the grass needs it, not just because it's Saturday morning.
- ✔ Use a mulch mower or mulching blade to return the clippings to the lawn. You can also mow right over fallen leaves and they too can return to the soil.

Lawn watering secrets

Nearly everybody waters too much. A few people water too little. Very few people water just the right amount. Remember the following key points to water your lawn properly:

- ✔ Most lawns need about an inch of water per week, including rainfall. That inch will penetrate 6 to 12 inches depending on your soil type (deeper in sandy soils than in clay soils).
- ✔ Brown grass isn't necessarily dead grass. Cool season lawn grasses go dormant and turn brown during hot, dry summer weather. You don't need to water these lawns to keep them alive, and when they do get adequate water again (from rain, preferably), they green back up and start growing again.
- ✔ Watering should replace what's been used and no more.
- ✔ Use a soil probe to examine soil moisture. If the root zone is damp, there's no need to irrigate. If you step on the grass and it doesn't spring back when you remove your foot, you might want to water.
- ✔ Water in early morning. Never water at night or in the heat of day.
- ✔ Among cool season grasses, fescues are the most drought tolerant; bluegrass and rye are the least. Warm season grasses tolerate more drought than cool season ones.

Fertilizing the sustainable way

The major nutrient required by lawn grasses is nitrogen, followed by phosphorous, potassium, and some trace elements like iron in certain situations. Many soils are abundant in everything *except* nitrogen, which is volatile and needs to be applied regularly in any soil to keep grass vigorous. However, many people overapply lawn fertilizers thinking that more is always better. The smart approach is to test soil to find out exactly what yours needs. Chapter 2 of Book VI tells you more about soils tests and about fertilizing.

Proper fertilizing replaces what your grass has used up rather than dumping on a set amount each time. Overfeeding your lawn can result in damage to waterways and ground water through leaching of nutrients, and it means more watering and mowing — unfortunate outcomes all around.

Be sure to use only organic fertilizers, not chemical ones.

Aeration and dethatching

Aeration is the practice of removing plugs from the root zone of turf to reduce compaction and allow air and water to penetrate. Clay soils are especially susceptible to compaction. *Dethatching* is a method of combing *thatch* (built-up dead grass) from the turf. Thatch inhibits the penetration of water, organic fertilizer, and air, and it can encourage certain diseases and pest problems. Thatch is most prevalent in overfertilized and overwatered lawns, especially those that are Kentucky bluegrass.

If the *soil food web* (the balance of organisms that make their home in your soil) is in good shape, the beneficial microbes, including bacteria and fungi, insects, and earthworms will consume thatch and keep the soil open, and you won't have to bother with the relatively laborious practices that are aeration and renovation. But even with the best of care, conditions are sometimes less than ideal because of inherent soil conditions, such as heavy clay, compaction due to heavy use, or regrettable lapses of good practice. That's when you're prudent to step in and fix the situation.

Dealing with weeds

The best way to head off the weed problem at the pass is by doing all the right things to make your grasses dense and vigorous so that they outcompete the weeds:

- ✔ Plant the right varieties for your area.
- ✔ Provide great soil and growing conditions.

- Mow high and as needed (when grass is tall enough that you'll cut down only a quarter of its height — 4 inches if you're mowing to 3 inches) to prevent seed set on annual weeds.

- Water deeply when necessary.

- Reseed bare spots quickly with disease and drought-resistant varieties. Any vacancies will be likely fill up with weeds, not desirable grasses.

- Monitor weed development and eradicate newcomers early.

Of course, you'll still get some weeds. This ain't the Garden of Eden. Outsmart them. For example, dandelions like a pH of around 7.5 (slightly alkaline soil), so if you adjust the pH, the dandelions will diminish.

Clover absorbs nitrogen from the air and puts it into the soil where grasses can use it. It was a common feature of lawns until chemical company propaganda convinced people it was a weed.

Turn to Chapter 3 of Book VI to find out more about green methods of weed control.

Working with a lawn-care company

Choose a lawn-care company that has a genuine commitment to sustainability. Some of them use the same equipment for chemical and organic lawn care, resulting in contamination. Others don't really understand the principles behind organic lawn management and won't deliver good results. The organic approach has been around long enough and enough training is out there that there's no excuse for poor performance.

Ask questions about the program the company is proposing. Get specifics about the materials they'll use and the strategies they recommend for your particular situation. Get a detailed written management plan and a fixed price as well as the usual references and written contract.

Maintain open communication with the workers to be sure you understand what they're up to and are aware of any problems that come up. Remember that no gardening service — organic or otherwise — can keep things 100 percent perfect all the time; nature isn't perfect, but it does provide a heckuva strong system when you work with it instead of against it.

Book VI
Organic Gardening

"That should do it."

In this book . . .

How does your garden grow? With pesticides, packaged fertilizers, and ample doses of water? That's one way to grow tomatoes and petunias, but you can find a more ecofriendly way in these chapters, which show you how to take an organic approach to creating a glorious home garden that's healthy for the planet and your family.

Gardening is all about getting in touch with the earth, so what better notion than doing it without damaging the earth? You have great methods at your disposal — ways to increase your soil's nutrient value and texture, tactics for keeping pests and diseases at bay, plans of attack for fighting weeds, and keep close tabs on what goes into your food by growing it yourself.

Here are the contents of Book VI at a glance:

Chapter 1

Sowing the Seeds of Organic Gardening

*O*rganic gardening means different things to different people. All agree that it means avoiding synthetic fertilizers and pesticides. But the philosophy and practice of organic gardening often goes far beyond that simple concept. Growing organic food, flowers, and landscapes represents a commitment to a sustainable system of living in harmony with nature. For many people, organic gardening is a way of life.

The way that people use — and misuse — soil, water, and air affects the lives and habitats of plants, insects, birds, fish, and animals, as well as humans. Dedicated organic gardeners adopt methods that improve soil health and fertility, decrease erosion, and reduce pests and diseases through cultural and natural biological processes. They encourage plant and animal diversity in their landscapes.

Tuning in to Organic Methods

Observing your natural environment — watching the weather or noting the arrival of migrating birds and emerging insects — helps you choose the most appropriate ways to plant and nurture your vegetables, flowers, and landscape plants. When you see white butterflies fluttering around your garden, you know it's time to protect your cabbages, broccoli, and cauliflower from cabbageworm. Instead of sprinkling on a pesticide after the caterpillars hatch, you can cover the plants with a special fabric to prevent the butterflies from laying eggs in the first place.

Organic gardening is about preventing and treating problems in the least toxic and least invasive ways.

Working with nature's cycles

Plants and animals live in *ecosystems* — communities in which each part contributes to and affects the lives of the other parts. In a balanced ecosystem, each plant and animal species has enough food, water, and *habitat* (place to live). The predators have enough prey, and the prey have enough predators.

When one part of an ecosystem dies out or becomes too scarce, the plants and animals that depend on its function in the environment get out of balance, too. If honeybees disappeared, for example, the plants that need bees for flower pollination wouldn't be able to produce seeds. If predators, such as ladybugs, become scarce, the insects they normally prey upon — aphids — could become so numerous that they would seriously injure or even kill the plants upon which they feed.

Some call this cycle the *web of life,* but ecosystems contain important nonliving parts, too. Soil nutrients, sunlight, water, and decaying plants and animals also contribute to the community health. When decayed organic material, called *humus,* becomes scarce, the soil microorganisms that feed on it die. Many of these microorganisms help release soil nutrients that plants need for growth. Without them, plants starve. Humus also holds moisture in the soil and helps soil particles stick together. When humus becomes depleted, the soil dries out too quickly, parching the plants and risking erosion.

Organic gardeners observe and use these natural relationships to grow healthy crops and landscape plants. For example, a gardener might shred the leaves that fall from his landscape trees and use them to mulch perennial flowers. The leaves suppress weeds and, as they decompose, they release plant nutrients and feed earthworms, which loosen and aerate the soil. When plants grow in such a balanced ecosystem, they receive all the nourishment they need from the soil and sun, and they bear plentiful flowers, fruits, and seeds. Insect pests and diseases do little long-term damage.

Taking from the soil without giving anything back breaks that natural cycle. Harvesting crops, bagging the lawn clippings, and raking fallen leaves removes organic material that's ordinarily destined for the soil on which it falls. If the organic material isn't replenished, the soil loses humus and its natural fertility. Substituting synthetic chemical fertilizers for naturally occurring nutrients may feed plants, but it starves the soil.

Pesticides also upset the natural balance. Using pesticides to kill insects deprives the pests' natural predators of food, which causes the predators to decline, necessitating more pesticides to achieve pest control. It's a vicious cycle. In addition, pesticides often kill more than their intended targets.

Beneficial insects and spiders that prey on plant pests and pollinate flowers die, too. And if pesticides drift on the wind or water away from their target, fish and birds may become poisoned, as well.

Gardening for the future

Depleting soil fertility, damaging and polluting ecosystems, and consuming excess water threatens the future of earth's safe and abundant food supply. The way that farmers and individual gardeners and homeowners choose to farm, garden, and maintain their landscapes makes a difference in whether our land can continue to house, feed, and clothe us.

Organic gardeners grow plants using sustainable methods. According to Webster's dictionary, *sustain* means "to keep in existence, to provide sustenance or nourishment." Sustainable gardening practices, such as composting, conserving resources, and using nontoxic pest controls, ensure safe and plentiful food for future generations.

Organic doesn't always equal nontoxic

Organic pesticides are derived from plant, animal, and mineral sources. *Synthetic chemical pesticides* come from petroleum and other chemical sources, and that's the main difference between the two types.

Traditional farmers worldwide have used plant, animal, and mineral-based pesticides for centuries. Indeed, home gardeners continue to use concoctions of garlic, hot peppers, onions, and other plants and substances to discourage pests.

Many people assume that *organic* means nontoxic, but that definition isn't really correct. Some commonly accepted organic pesticides are just as toxic, if not more so, than some synthetic chemical pesticides. Although organic pesticides generally have far fewer health side effects than synthetic pesticides, that's not always the case. Nicotine, for example, although derived from a plant and used as an organic pesticide, is highly toxic to humans and many other species.

Pesticides pose another problem. Some hang around in the environment long after their job is done. Chemists measure this persistence of chemicals by their *half-life,* or number of days it takes for half of the original quantity to break down into its components. Sunlight, water, soil microorganisms, and composition of the pesticide influence the half-life of these chemicals. Organic pesticides, and some synthetic ones, have half-lives of only a few days. Others, however, remain toxic in the environment for months, or even years, after the farmer or homeowner uses them.

Going Organic for Land's Sake

The earth's population continues to grow, but the amount of land available for growing food is rapidly disappearing. Erosion, development, pollution, dwindling water supplies, and other human-induced and natural disruptions threaten safe food and water supplies. Plant and animal species continue to disappear at alarming rates as humans damage and encroach upon their habitats. Many gardeners work to improve this grim picture by making personal choices that, at the very least, do no harm to the environment.

The way you choose to grow flowers and food and maintain the landscape can actually improve the quality of the soil, air, water, and lives of the organisms that depend on it. Organic gardening is based on the principle of working with nature instead of against it.

Erosion

It takes 500 years to produce one inch of natural *topsoil,* the rich matrix of humus, minerals, and microorganisms that plants depend on for growth. Plants, in turn, hold the topsoil in place with their roots and shelter it with their leaves. Soil without plants *erodes* easily — washing away with runoff from rain and snow or blowing away in the wind.

When soil washes into streams, rivers, and lakes, it significantly disrupts those ecosystems and pollutes the water. In fact, sediment accounts for nearly half of all lake pollution and 22 percent of river pollution, according a 1991 United States government report. Erosion devastates farmland, playing a major role in the 2 million acres of *arable land* (land that's suitable for growing crops) that the United States loses each year. The Iowa Department of Agriculture reported that half of that state's topsoil had eroded by the early 1980s. Experts report that 30 percent of arable land was lost worldwide in the past 40 years of the 20th century due, in part, to erosion.

What happens in your own small garden plot may seem insignificant compared to these mind-numbing statistics, but how you garden does play a role in the bigger picture. Gardeners can help reduce erosion by keeping plants growing on or covering the soil throughout the year, preserving and encouraging humus formation, and avoiding excessive tilling, disruption, or compacting of the soil.

Wildlife and habitat

Pesticides kill pests, but unfortunately they harm innocent bystanders, as well. Some pesticides are highly toxic to fish and aquatic organisms, birds, and beneficial insects, such as bees.

Poisons harm innocent animals in two ways — either immediately or slowly over a period of time. A fast-acting pesticide, such as pyrethrum, kills bees and fish, as well as pests, on contact, but it breaks down rapidly in the environment. Within a few days, it's harmless.

Other pesticides, such as the infamous DDT, accumulate in the bodies of animals, harming them over a long period of time. In the case of DDT, which was banned in the U.S. in 1972, the chemical accumulated in fish, rodents, and other animals. When predators, such as hawks and eagles, ate the animals, they accumulated increasingly larger quantities of DDT, too. As a result, they laid eggs with thin shells that broke before they hatched, destroying generations of birds and sending many species to the brink of extinction.

Pesticide contamination of wildlife has serious implications for humans, too. In its report, *Chemicals in Sportfish and Game Health Advisories 2000–2001,* the New York State Department of Health lists 73 bodies of water within the state from which fish shouldn't be eaten at all by women of childbearing age and children under the age of 15. At most, the department recommends eating no more than a half pound of fish per month from the least contaminated of these waters. You can find the full report at www.health.state. ny.us/nysdoh/environ/fish.htm or call 800-458-1158, extension 27815. Sadly, advisories such as this one exist throughout the United States. The U.S. Environmental Protection Agency gathers all state fish advisories at www.epa.gov/waterscience/fish.

Pollution

The U.S. Environmental Protection Agency (EPA) reports pesticide contamination of groundwater in 39 states. *Groundwater* flows below ground in the cracks in bedrock and between soil particles where it collects in large, saturated areas called *aquifers.* The EPA estimated that, as of 1994, 1 percent of the country's groundwater was already contaminated, and that the percentage was increasing rapidly. A 2006 report by the United States Geological Survey found at least one pesticide in about half of the wells in urban areas.

Half of the U.S. population uses groundwater sources for their drinking water — the other half gets their drinking water from *surface water,* such as rivers, lakes, and reservoirs. Surface waters are even more vulnerable to pollution than groundwater and become polluted from *runoff* — water that runs over the ground, carrying pesticides, fertilizers, and soil with it.

Excess nitrogen and phosphorus fertilizers from lawns, farms, and gardens wash into streams, lakes, and oceans where they contribute to excess algae growth. Densely growing algae depletes the oxygen in the water, which can kill fish and suffocate the native plant species. Nitrogen, the main element in most fertilizers, also moves easily through the soil, especially when mixed with water from rain, snowmelt, or irrigation. Depending on soil conditions, nitrogen percolates down through the soil and enters the groundwater, contaminating wells and other sources of drinking water. High concentrations of nitrate — a common nitrogen compound — can be toxic to children under the age of 6 months and to other mammals, including horses.

Disease

One of the main reasons to garden organically is to provide safe, wholesome food and a toxic-free environment. Despite extensive testing by chemical companies in controlled trials, it's hard to know exactly what pesticides will do in the real world. It seems that every time you turn around, another pesticide is making headline news and hastily being pulled off the market. *Chlorpyrifos* is the sixth most commonly used pesticide in the United States. Although used extensively in homes, yards, and farms to kill fleas, roaches, ants, termites, lice, and agricultural pests, the chemical is now banned for home use because of its effects on humans. Agricultural use of chlorpyrifos also is being curtailed. As it turns out, chlorpyrifos harms the central nervous system, cardiovascular system, and respiratory system. Children are particularly vulnerable because they crawl around and play on the floor and soil where the chemical is sprinkled and sprayed.

Ponder this: The EPA now considers 60 percent of all herbicides, 90 percent of all fungicides, and 30 percent of all insecticides to be potentially *carcinogenic,* or able to cause cancer. A study conducted by the National Cancer Institute found that farmers exposed to chemical herbicides had six times greater risks of developing cancer than farmers who were not exposed. Scary stuff.

Strategies for Organic Gardening

The most successful organic gardeners use a combination of strategies to grow healthy food and ornamental plants. They monitor and increase soil fertility, observe and emulate nature, and make planting decisions based on the needs of the plants and opportunities of their site. Organic gardeners see their gardens as a small part of the larger natural world and understand that their gardening practices have an impact that goes far beyond the borders of their yards.

If you're just getting started, though, all these practices can seem daunting — even discouraging. Keep in mind that gardening is a process and take it one step at a time. Here's a rundown of important strategies for making your garden organic:

✔ **Enrich your soil.** Enriching your soil instead of pouring on fertilizer is similar to eating healthy foods instead of popping vitamin tablets. Get your diet and soil right, and many other potential problems are apt to be less troublesome. Organic matter, which decomposes into humus, increases soil's ability to hold moisture and drain efficiently, feeds the beneficial soil organisms, and adds important plant nutrients. You can increase the amount of organic matter in your soil by adding compost and using plant-based mulches, such as shredded leaves, bark, and straw.

✔ **Let nature do the weeding.** Preventing weeds is so much easier than getting rid of them when they're all grown up. Weeds flourish on open ground, but mulch can slow them down — even stop them in their tracks. Surround your garden and landscape plants with bark, pine needles, grass clippings, shredded leaves, straw, and other organic materials to shade the ground and keep weeds from sprouting. Use landscape fabric — not plastic — or newspaper in paths and around trees and shrubs, covering them with loose mulch materials.

Book VI

Organic
Gardening

Starting a new garden or reclaiming an old one usually involves ridding the land of weeds. Instead of reaching for a bottle of herbicide, use the power of the sun to solarize your soil with weed-killing heat. See Chapter 3 of this book for step-by-step instructions.

✔ **Choose healthy and disease-resistant plants.** Your plants won't get sick if they're immune to or at least tolerant of the nastiest diseases. Plant breeders work long and hard to develop varieties of your favorite fruits, vegetables, flowers, and landscape plants that fight off devastating diseases. Read catalog descriptions and plant tags to find resistant plants whenever possible.

Buying and planting only healthy plants also pays off. Struggling plants attract diseases and insects, but thriving plants fight them off. Take time to examine trees and shrubs and look for virus-free fruits. Don't bring home any insect-infested plants, either. If you have any doubts about a plant's health, quarantine a new plant in a separate area before adding it to your landscape or garden.

✔ **Put plants in the right place.** Give your plants the soil, sun, and moisture conditions they prefer to keep them healthy and thriving. That advice is especially important for long-term landscape and fruit plants.

✔ **Encourage beneficial insects.** Most bugs are good bugs for your garden. Each harmful insect has a predator or parasite that attacks it, making your work easier. You can cheer these helpmates by planting flowers and other plants that they're attracted to and by avoiding the use of pesticides.

✔ **Practice integrated pest management.** These big words describe a simple concept. *Integrated pest management* (IPM) is the practice of looking at all the costs and options before deciding on a course of pest treatment. Instead of merely eradicating pests, you manage them. (For more on this approach, see the sidebar "Practicing IPM in everyday life.")

✔ **Use companion planting.** Some plants naturally grow better in the company of another species. In some cases, one plant repels the pests that affect the other, or it attracts beneficial insects that attack its companion's pests. Other plants add nitrogen to the soil that benefits their neighbors. Deep-rooted plants bring nutrients closer to the soil surface where shallow-rooted plants can reach them.

✔ **Add traps and barriers to your arsenal.** Sometimes, protecting your crops from insects is as easy as throwing a fabric row cover over them. If the cabbage moths can't reach your broccoli to lay their eggs, for example, you won't find caterpillars in your vegetables. A strip of newspaper wrapped around the tender stem of a seedling can prevent a cutworm from chewing through it. You can foil many common pests with specially colored, sticky-coated traps. You can also use insects' own attractants against them. *Pheromones,* which are scents secreted by insects to attract a mate, are among the most powerful tools in your pest-control kit.

Pheromone baits combined with traps are the downfall of millions of Japanese beetles and other pests every year. They attract only the pest you want to eradicate, so they're safe to use around beneficial insects.

✔ **Promote diversity.** Natural plant populations contain many species scattered over a large area, making them less vulnerable to insect and pest eradication. Plants also benefit their neighbors in a number of ways. Use the same concepts in your garden by mixing crops within a row and avoiding large patches of the same variety.

Practicing IPM in everyday life

Most of the time, reaching for pesticide to eradicate pests isn't the best move. In fact, you should focus on managing the pests instead of annihilating them. For example, in an apple orchard, several serious pests and diseases affect the quality and quantity of the harvest. An orchard manager who practices IPM deals with them in several ways:

✔ **Monitors the weather carefully:** The appearance of many insects and diseases is tied closely to the temperature, humidity, and time of the year. Anticipating a problem gives you more options than does reacting.

✔ **Monitors pests:** Keep a sharp eye out for trouble. It doesn't make sense to treat for pests unless they're causing serious damage. A few pests may be insignificant and tolerable in the big picture.

✔ **Keeps it clean:** Good plant managers discourage problems by practicing good cultural techniques, such as rotating crops from one part of the garden to another, destroying harmful weeds, and cleaning up infested plant debris.

✔ **Uses the least invasive and least toxic control methods first:** For persistent problems, first use a nontoxic control, such as a weed flamer (a device that burns weeds; see Chapter 3) or strong blast of water. Move to traps and barriers and then as a last resort to pesticides that affect only the particular pest.

Use this information to help choose the most appropriate plants for your soil. Keep in mind that adding organic matter, such as compost, to the soil can improve the drainage of both sandy and clayey soils. See the section "Organic Matter: The Soul of Soil," later in this chapter.

Finding soil pH and nutrient content

After you know the type of soil you have and how well it drains (see the previous section), you need to know its pH and nutrient levels. The *soil pH* measures the *alkalinity* (sweetness) or *acidity* (sourness) of the soil.

Soil is acidic if it's below pH 7 on a scale from 0 to 14 and alkaline if it's above pH 7. Knowing your soil's pH is important because some nutrients are available to plants only within a specific pH range. Most plants prefer soil that's between pH 6.0 and 7.0.

A simple rule is that if your plants are growing, flowering, and fruiting well, the levels of nutrients your plants need are fine. If you're just starting out or if you aren't satisfied with the growth of your plants, a little testing can help you get to the root of the matter. Too high or too low pH or unbalanced nutrient levels can result in yellow, stunted, and unproductive plants. Unhealthy plants are more prone to insects and disease attacks, which translates into more work for you and less satisfaction from your garden. And that's not what you want!

Using a home soil test kit is simple and gives you a basic pH reading and an estimation of the major nutrients in your soil. You can buy a range of test kits at nurseries and garden centers. The more sophisticated tests cost more but give you more accurate results.

You can also send a soil sample to a lab for testing. You simply take a representative sample of the soil from your garden, fill out a form, and mail or take it to the lab. The results are more accurate and detailed than if you do the test yourself with a home kit, plus testing labs can look for things that home kits can't, such as organic matter and micronutrients.

Lab reports give you the current levels of nutrients and soil pH and also offer specific recommendations about which nutrients to add to your soil and in what quantity for your plants' optimum growth. Lab tests can get costly, however, especially if you have many different types of plantings, such as perennial flowers, vegetables, and lawn, and you do separate tests for each type. Run a Google search or check the phone book under "Soil Testing" for private soil labs in your area or contact your state university's extension service. Many state universities test soil for a small fee or can recommend a private testing lab.

Chapter 2

Improving Your Soil and Feeding Your Plants Organically

*B*uilding healthy soil is the single most important thing you can do to ensure the success of your garden and landscape plants. Healthy soil is alive with microorganisms that feed upon and decompose organic matter and release nutrients for plants to use. Beneficial microorganisms in the soil prey on harmful ones and protect plant roots from diseases and pests. Earthworms and other soil creatures tunnel through the soil, opening up spaces for oxygen, water, and nutrients to move freely. Many pesticides and synthetic fertilizers destroy that subterranean life, while organic gardening practices promote it. In this chapter, you find out how to provide the best growing medium for your plants and how to keep them going strong with compost and organic fertilizers.

Getting to Know Your Soil

Several factors contribute to soil health, including pH, organic matter and nutrient levels, drainage, and soil type, and you need to understand a little about each of them.

Soil health is so important that before you start a vegetable, perennial, or annual flower garden, consider spending one growing season just building the fertility of the soil — *before* planting. One season spent adding organic matter and nutrients and adjusting the pH may save you years of struggling to produce healthy plants.

Identifying soil type

The most basic factor you need to know about is *soil type,* which is the composition of the soil's particles you inherit in your garden. Knowing your soil's type helps you determine what you need to do to build healthy soil.

Soil comes in three main types, each with its own strengths and weaknesses:

- ✔ **Clay:** Clay soil has the most potentially high natural fertility but can be difficult to work with. Clay's individual soil particles are so small that water and air have little room to squeeze between them. Clay soil stays wet longer, contains little oxygen, and dries as hard as concrete.

- ✔ **Sandy:** Sand particles are large, leaving plenty of room for water and air to move between them but allowing sandy soil to dry out quickly. Nutrients leach through sandy soils quickly, too, making them naturally less fertile and more prone to drought.

- ✔ **Silt:** Silt soils have moderate-sized particles that hold some water and air but also allow the water to drain. They have moderate amounts of fertility, are easy to work with, and make life easy for the gardener.

You may have heard some gardeners singing the praises of *loam* — soil that consists of roughly the same amounts of sand, silt, and clay. It holds optimum amounts of water, oxygen, and nutrients for most plant growth. If you're lucky, it's in your yard already. More likely, you need to amend your soil to work toward loam's balance.

Your soil is probably a mixture of sand, silt, and clay, but to find out the predominant type of soil in your garden, reach out and touch it. Take a small handful of damp soil in your hand and rub a pinch of it between your thumb and pointing finger. If it feels gritty, it's mostly sand; if it feels slick and slimy, it's mostly clay. If it feels like something between those two, it's mostly silt.

For a more accurate measurement of the amounts of clay, silt, and sand in your soil, do the jar test. Here's how:

1. **Collect soil from several places in your garden.**

2. **Mix the samples thoroughly and measure out 1 cup of the mixture.**

3. **Let the soil air-dry on a sheet of paper until crumbly.**

4. **Crush chunks until the soil is very fine, removing any stones and debris as you do so.**

5. **Place soil in a narrow glass jar, such as a pint-sized canning jar, and add 1 teaspoon of nonsudsy dishwasher detergent.**

6. **Fill jar ⅔ full of water, seal, and shake vigorously to mix the contents.**

7. **Put down the jar and start a timer.**

8. **Measure and mark the level of settled soil after 1 minute.**

   This soil is sand.

9. **Measure again in 2 hours and subtract the sand layer to find the amount of silt.**

   After several days, the clay settles out on top of the sand and silt.

10. **Measure this top layer, subtracting the sand and silt to find the amount of clay.**

11. **Divide the height of each level by the total height of the settled soil and multiply by 100 to find the percentage of each.**

    For example, if the total settled soil is 6 inches high and the sand portion is 3 inches, the percent of sand is 50 percent:

    $$\tfrac{3}{6} \times 100 = 50\%$$

Evaluating drainage

Knowing your type of soil helps you determine how well water will drain through it. What's the big deal with drainage? Well, certain plants, such as lavender, need soil that drains quickly to thrive, while other plants, such as willows, can survive and flourish in wet soils.

Sometimes drainage is obvious. Puddles in your lawn a day or two after heavy rains certainly indicate poor drainage. But, sometimes a layer of clay lurks underneath a loamy or sandy soil, which causes water to linger in otherwise well-drained soil. So, before you plant — especially trees and shrubs — dig a hole to check what lies beneath the surface.

Here's how to check for *percolation,* or soil drainage:

1. **Dig a hole 1 foot in diameter and 1 foot deep.**

2. **Fill the hole with water.**

3. **Time how long it takes for the water to drain.**

   If the water drains in

   - 10 minutes or less, your soil drains too fast and probably dries too quickly.

   - 10 to 30 minutes, your soil is well-drained.

   - Less than 4 hours, the drainage is okay for most plants.

   - More than 4 hours, the soil is poorly drained.

pH test results

Soil tests measure two components: your soil pH and its major nutrients. Most plants grow best in the range between 6.0 and 7.0. Some plants, however, such as blueberries and rhododendrons, like a highly acid soil (pH below 5.0), so you may need to adjust the pH to individual plants.

In general, you add lime or limestone to raise the pH and sulfur to lower it. How much lime or sulfur you need to add depends on the type of soil you have and its current pH. A soil-testing lab can make a specific recommendation based on that information.

You can spread the material by hand or use a drop spreader made to spread grass seed on a lawn. In the garden, work the lime or sulfur into the top few inches of soil with a rake or shovel after spreading.

When adding lime or sulfur to your soil, remember to wear gloves and a dust mask because this material can be very dusty and irritating if you inhale it.

Don't expect results right away. Most limestone or powdered sulfur products take a few months to react with the soil enough to change the pH to the desired levels — another good reason to prepare your soil a season before you plan to plant. Keep tabs on your pH with an annual test and make adjustments as necessary.

Nutrient test results

Soil tests also show the quantities of soil nutrients that are available to plants, especially the three nutrients that plants use in the greatest amount — nitrogen (N), phosphorus (P), and potassium (K). These three nutrients are the ones you see listed on the front of fertilizer or compost bags. Soils also contain many micronutrients, such as magnesium and calcium, that plants need in smaller amounts. If any nutrient is insufficient, plants don't grow to their maximum potential.

The balance of nutrients is more important for the proper functioning of your plants than the actual levels of the nutrients. For example, too much of one nutrient may create a situation where other nutrients, though plentiful in the soil, aren't taken up by the plants.

Book VI

Organic Gardening

Organic Matter: The Soul of Soil

Organic matter is basically material that was living or was produced by a living thing, including grass clippings, leaves, hay, straw, pine needles, wood chips, sawdust, manure, and anything else that used to be alive. It's a miracle worker that improves soil by

- ✔ Feeding microorganisms and other soil life
- ✔ Improving the soil structure
- ✔ Increasing soil's reserve of nutrients

Add organic matter to your plantings any time you can — whether it's straw mulch between vegetable garden beds, compost around perennial flowers, or bark mulch around trees or shrubs. Try adding a 3- to 4-inch layer of dead leaves to your garden, either in the fall or up to one month before you start your vegetable or annual flower garden, and work it into the soil.

Soil microbes, such as fungi and bacteria, don't work efficiently when soil is cold and wet, such as in early spring. They also use nutrients in the soil to fuel their eating, so if you give them too much material to work with at once, they tie up the nutrients, creating a deficiency for the plants. If you live in a cold-winter climate, add straw, leaves, and other raw organic matter in the summer or autumn when the soil is still warm to allow them plenty of time to decompose before plants need the nutrients.

Dung ho!

Few things get organic gardeners as excited as a good pile of aged animal manure. If you're not yet a connoisseur of manure, think of it as processed organic matter that has already begun decomposing. It does wonders for soil health and plant growth.

You can add the droppings of many different farm (and sometimes wild) animals to your garden, giving the soil all the benefits of organic matter plus a little higher boost of the N-P-K nutrients. (See the "Nutrient test results" section, earlier in this chapter.) Like a fine wine, however, manure is best aged. Fresh manure may be too potent for tender plants and can contain bacteria that make people sick. It's a good idea to let manure age for six months to a year before using, or you can compost it. (See the "Compost: The prince of organic matter" section, later in this chapter). If you add fresh manure to your garden in the fall and mix it into the soil, it will be ready for planting in the spring.

Keep these rules in mind when using manures:

- ✔ **Compost fresh manures before using.** Mix into a compost pile and age before using or spread on the garden and work into the soil at least a month before planting.

- ✔ **Select manure from the oldest pile at the farm.** Many farm manure piles contain a lot of additional organic matter such as sawdust from horse or chicken bedding. Manure from the oldest pile probably has naturally decomposed this bedding the most and can be used directly on your garden.

✔ **Use bagged manures.** They're usually composted and ready to use. If you need a lot of manure, however, buying bags can be costly.

✔ **Apply composted manure annually.** In general, add a 2- to 3-inch layer of manure to garden beds and around perennial plants at least once a year.

Cat, dog, pig, and human manures have no place in composting. They can carry diseases that affect humans, and so you should never use them in your garden.

Green manure

Another great way to get organic matter into your garden is to grow your own. *Green manures* are plants that you grow specifically to cut down and mix into the soil to add organic matter and nutrients. Farm-supply stores and mail-order catalogs usually offer the widest selection of green manures, but many garden centers sell the common ones. The following plants are some of the valuable green manures that you can grow in your garden:

✔ Alfalfa

✔ Annual ryegrass

✔ Barley

✔ Buckwheat

✔ Cowpeas

✔ Crimson clover

✔ Fava beans

✔ Hairy vetch

✔ Oats

✔ Winter rye

✔ Winter wheat

To grow green manure, broadcast (apply uniformly) the seed as you would for a lawn and let the crop grow through the gardening season. If you want to prevent the plants from returning next season, turn the plants under the soil before they produce seeds,. In addition to adding organic matter, green manures

✔ **Control erosion:** Hardy crops, such as winter rye and wheat, cover the soil over the dormant season, preventing wind and rain from eroding precious topsoil.

- ✔ **Loosen compacted soils:** Some green manures, such as alfalfa, have aggressive roots, which can grow 3 feet deep into the soil. They break up compacted soils and even "mine" nutrients deep in the soil, bringing them to the surface where other plants can use them.

- ✔ **Balance nutrients:** Some green manures, such as clover, vetch, peas, and beans, are *legumes,* which means that they have the unique ability to take nitrogen from the air and make it available to plants — often in the same year. These crops are great to grow right before you grow a heavy nitrogen-feeding crop, such as sweet corn.

- ✔ **Control weeds:** Some green manures, such as buckwheat, grow so quickly and aggressively that they can shade or crowd out weeds growing in the same ground.

- ✔ **Maintain high levels of soil microorganisms:** When the plants are incorporated into the soil, they feed the essential microbes that make nutrients available to plants. The plant residues also provide surfaces on which the microbes can live.

- ✔ **Attract beneficial insects:** Some green manures, such as clover, have flowers that beneficial insects love. These insects help with pollination and insect pest control in your garden.

Compost: The prince of organic matter

The best and most refined of organic matters is *compost,* which is organic matter and/or manures that have decomposed until they resemble loamy soil. Thoroughly decomposed compost contains a lot of humus — the beneficial, soil-improving material your plants need. Whether the original source was grass clippings, sawdust, animal manure, or vegetable scraps from your kitchen, all organic matter eventually becomes compost.

Whether you make your own compost (see the "Composting: Turning Waste into Garden Gold" section, later in this chapter), or buy it ready-made, you can add finished compost anytime to the garden or around plants. Pile on a 2- to 3-inch layer annually around plants and on garden beds.

Why not just add raw organic matter to your garden instead of composting it? By composting the materials first, the final product is uniform in color, nutrients, and texture; is odor free; and contains fewer viable weed seeds and potential disease organisms (depending on how it was composted). Your plants will be happy with you for treating them so well.

You can buy compost from a number of sources either in bulk or bagged, depending on where you live. Bagged compost is the easiest way to go, especially if you have a small yard or container garden. The down side is that you don't really know the quality of the compost until you get it home.

For larger quantities of compost, buy in bulk. The price is lower, and you can check the quality of the compost. Many private companies, municipalities, and community groups make and sell compost. Often, they even deliver the compost to your yard for a fee.

Use these tips to evaluate bulk compost:

- **Consider the source.** Before buying the compost, ask about the primary organic matter sources that were used to make the compost. Compost made from yard waste (leaves and grass clippings) is usually considered the safest and best. Other compost may contain ingredients that had contaminants, such as herbicides from agricultural crop residues and heavy metals from municipal wastes, which may affect the growth of your plants or accumulate toxins in your soil.

- **Look at the color and texture.** Finished compost should look dark and have a crumbly texture without any large pieces of undecomposed organic matter, such as branches or pieces of wood.

- **Squeeze it.** If water oozes out when you squeeze a handful of the material, it's too wet; if it blows away easily, it's too dry.

- **Give it a whiff.** The smell should be earthy without a strong ammonia or sour smell.

Making your own compost is probably the simplest way to ensure high quality compost and save some money. (To find out how to make your own compost, see the next section.) It's really not as complicated as you may think: The many commercial composting bins and containers on the market make it a mess-free and hassle-free process.

> **Book VI**
>
> **Organic Gardening**

Composting: Turning Waste into Garden Gold

At least two schools of thought exist on building composting piles:

- The active school makes uniform piles, mixes materials thoroughly at the correct ratios of carbon (brown stuff) and nitrogen (green stuff) — see the "Getting ratios right" section for more on carbon/nitrogen ratios — and keeps the pile watered just enough to keep it moist, but has enough air to breathe. They enjoy finished compost a month or two from the start.

- A second school says, pile it in the backyard somewhere, and eventually (within six months or so) it'll turn into usable compost. After all, everything rots doesn't it?

Although the second school of thought is technically correct, you may find advantages to building a pile by the rules espoused by the first school. A well-constructed pile — built with the proper dimensions and maintained correctly — heats up fast; decomposes uniformly and quickly; kills many diseases, insects, and weed seeds; doesn't smell; and is easy to turn and maintain. Conversely, a pile just thrown together rarely heats up and, therefore, takes longer to decompose. This type of *cold composting* doesn't kill any diseases, insects, or weed seeds; may smell bad; and definitely looks messy. Still, it's far better than not composting at all, so if cold composting is all you care to do, by all means go for it.

Containing your compost pile makes it look neater, helps you maintain the correct moisture, and prevents animals from getting into it. You can build your own, as shown in Figure 2-1, or buy a commercial home composting unit. The advantages of a commercial composter include the availability of a wide range of attractive sizes and shapes and ease of use. Choose from box-shaped plastic and wooden bins and barrels or elevated and easy-to-turn tumblers, as shown in Figure 2-2. Buying bins is costly, however, and most bins produce only small quantities of compost at a time, especially compared to a homemade bin that's built from scrap lumber or wire.

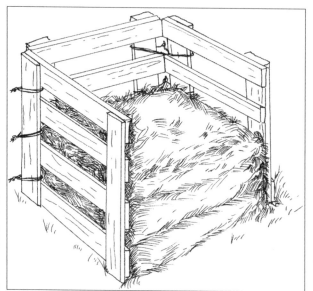

Figure 2-1:
Build a simple wooden bin to hold your compost pile.

Book VI

Organic
Gardening

Figure 2-2:
Commercial
compos-
ters help
you make
compost
yourself.

Wire composter   High-rise composter   Tumbler composter

Here's what you need to know to build a good compost pile:

1. **Choose a well-drained, partly shady location, out of the way, but still within view so that you don't forget about the pile.**

2. **Make or buy a bin.**

   Create a wire cylinder that's 3 to 4 feet in diameter or build a three-sided box (similar to the one in Figure 2-1), that's 4 to 5 feet high and wide.

3. **Add a 6-inch layer of "brown" organic matter, such as hay, straw, old leaves, and sawdust, to the bottom of the container.**

4. **Add a 2- to 3-inch layer of "green" organic matter, such as green grass clippings, manure, table scraps, or even high-nitrogen fertilizer, such as cottonseed meal, on top of the brown layer.**

5. **Repeat these layers, watering each one as you go, until the pile is 4 to 5 feet tall and fills the bin.**

   A smaller pile won't heat up well, and a larger pile can be difficult to manage.

6. **Within two days, mix the layers together thoroughly.**

7. **Cover the pile with a tarp to keep rain away and preserve moisture.**

   If the pile gets too soggy or too dry, it won't heat up.

Good additions for great compost

What you put in the compost pile is up to you — just remember that it needs to be from an organic material. Here's a short list of possibilities:

- ✔ Hay
- ✔ Straw
- ✔ Pine needles
- ✔ Leaves
- ✔ Kitchen scraps (egg shells, old bread, vegetable and fruit scraps)
- ✔ Animal manure, except for dog, cat, pig, or human
- ✔ Old vegetables, flowers, or trimmings from trees and shrubs
- ✔ Sawdust
- ✔ Wood chips
- ✔ Weeds
- ✔ Shredded black and white newspaper

Poison for compost piles

Some items don't belong in your compost pile. Hot compost piles can kill off many diseases, weed seeds, and insects, but it's not a sure thing; some of these unpleasant guests may survive to invade your garden again. Certain materials can also invite unwanted wildlife to the pile or spread human diseases.

Avoid adding the following to your compost bin:

- ✔ Kitchen scraps like meats, oils, fish, dairy products, and bones. They attract unwanted animals, such as rats and raccoons, to the pile.
- ✔ Weeds that have gone to seed or that spread by their roots, such as quackgrass.
- ✔ Diseased or insect-infested vegetable or flower plants.
- ✔ Herbicide-treated grass clippings or weeds.
- ✔ Dog, cat, or pig feces.

Getting ratios right

In composting corners, you often hear about the *C/N ratio* or *carbon to nitrogen ratio*. Basically, all organic matter can be divided into carbon-rich (brown stuff) and nitrogen-rich (green stuff) materials. Using the right mixture of brown to green stuff when building a compost pile encourages the pile to heat up and decompose efficiently. Although nearly any combination of organic materials eventually decomposes, for the fastest and most efficient compost pile in town, strike the correct balance (C/N ratio) between the two types — usually 25 to 1.

Table 2-1 shows which common compost materials are high in carbon and which materials are high in nitrogen. Notice that the softer materials, such as fresh grass clippings, tend to be higher in nitrogen than hard materials, such as sawdust. Mix these together to form a pile with an average C/N ratio of 25:1 to 30:1, and you'll be well on your way to beautiful compost.

Use the ratios in Table 2-1 as guidelines. Actual ratios vary depending on the sources of the materials and other factors. And speaking of sources — be sure that your compost materials haven't been contaminated with pesticides or other chemicals.

Book VI

Organic Gardening

Table 2-1	Carbon/Nitrogen Ratios of Various Materials
Material	*C/N Ratio*
Fresh alfalfa hay	12:1
Table scraps	15:1
Grass clippings	19:1
Old manure	20:1
Fruit waste	25:1
Corn stalks	60:1
Old leaves	80:1
Straw	80:1
Paper	170:1
Sawdust	500:1
Wood	700:1

Keeping your pile happy

A hot pile is a happy pile: Heat makes the ingredients break down faster and kills weed seeds and diseases. If you follow the method of just throwing everything together, the pile rarely heats up. If you follow the method of building the pile carefully with the recommended C/N ratio, as you find in the "Getting ratios right" section, the pile will start to cook within a week. Now you need to keep it cooking. Here's the procedure:

1. **Keep the pile moist by periodically watering it.**

   Dig into the pile about 1 foot to see whether it's moist. If not, water the pile thoroughly, but not so that it's soggy. The pile needs air, too, and adding too much water removes air spaces. If you built the pile with moist ingredients, such as kitchen scraps, it won't need watering at first.

2. **Turn the pile when it cools down.**

   Using a garden fork, remove the outside layers and put them aside. Remove the inside layers into another pile and then switch. Place the outside layers in the center of the new pile and the inside layers along the outside of the new pile.

3. **Let it cook again.**

   How hot it gets and how long it cooks depends on the ratio of C/N materials in the pile and whether you have the correct moisture levels.

4. **When it's cool, turn it again.**

   You should have finished compost after two to three turnings. The finished product should be cool, crumbly, dark in color, and earthy smelling.

Sometimes, a compost pile smells bad, or contains pieces of undecomposed materials, or never heats up. Chances are that one of the following conditions occurred:

- ✔ The pile was too wet or dry.

- ✔ You added too many carbon materials and not enough nitrogen materials.

- ✔ The pieces of material were too big or packed together. Shred leaves, branches, and pieces of wood to decompose more quickly.

- ✔ The pile was too small.

You can find a lot of compost aids on the market. *Bioactivators* — packages of concentrated microbes — are one of the most popular because they can speed the decomposition process. These microbes occur naturally, however, and many are already present in a well-constructed compost pile. Save your money and use microbe-rich compost materials or add a scoop of healthy soil instead.

Addressing Plants' Nutrient Needs

Plants need 16 essential elements or nutrients for proper growth. The nutrients that plants need in the largest quantities are carbon, hydrogen, and oxygen, which plants get from the air and from the water in the soil. Others come from minerals in the soil. Even if the soil contains enough nutrients, environmental conditions, such as soil temperature, nutrient imbalance, and high or low pH, can make some of them unavailable for plants. For example, if the pH is below 5.0, phosphorus combines with iron, aluminum, and manganese to form compounds that plants can't use. Most nutrients are available when soil pH is in the ideal 6.0 to 7.0.

Before you add fertilizer to your soil, take a soil sample to a soil testing lab or farm and garden store or use a home test kit to find out the soil pH and exactly which minerals your plants need and in what quantities. (For more on this topic, see the section "Identifying soil type," earlier in this chapter.)

Book VI

Organic Gardening

The big three nutrients

Nitrogen, phosphorous, and potassium are often called *macronutrients* or *primary* nutrients because plants need them in the largest quantities. Healthy, fertile soil naturally contains these three elements and plants can easily take them up. But in many cases, you must supplement the soil with fertilizers, especially if you're growing vegetables, fruits, or other demanding crops.

Complete fertilizers contain all three macronutrients — nitrogen (N), phosphorous (P), and potassium (K) — but don't let the term "complete" fool you. It doesn't mean that the fertilizer has all the nutrients that plants need, just that it contains all three of the major ones.

Bags of complete fertilizers contain three numbers, such as 5-3-3, for example. Each number represents a percentage of N-P-K in that bag, as measured by weight. In this case, a bag of 5-3-3 fertilizer contains 5 percent nitrogen, 3 percent phosphorous, and 3 percent potassium. To determine the amount in pounds of each nutrient in the bag, multiply the weight of the bag (say 50 pounds) by the percentage of each nutrient: 50 pounds x .05 = 2.5 pounds of nitrogen. You need to know the actual amount of nutrients in the bag because a soil test often recommends pounds of *actual* N-P-K to add per square foot to your garden.

Each of these nutrients plays a critical role in plant growth and development. Here's what they do and their deficiency symptoms to watch for:

✔ **Nitrogen (N):** This critical element is responsible for the healthy green foliage of plants, as well as protein and chlorophyll development. (*Chlorophyll* is the pigment that makes plants green and is a vital component in photosynthesis.) Nitrogen moves easily in the soil and leaches out rapidly, especially from sandy soils and in high rainfall areas or irrigated gardens. Plants use a lot of nitrogen during the growing season, so it's commonly the most deficient element. If you add too much nitrogen, however, plants will have dark green, leafy growth but less root development and delayed flowering and fruiting. Symptoms of nitrogen deficiency include slow growth and yellowing leaves, especially on older foliage. Animal manures, soybean meal, and cottonseed meal provide high levels of nitrogen.

✔ **Phosphorous (P):** Plants need phosphorus for strong root growth; fruit, stem, and seed development; disease resistance; and general plant vigor. Phosphorous doesn't move in the soil as easily as nitrogen does so you don't have to add it as frequently. Depending on where you live in the country, your soil may have plenty of phosphorous, but it may be unavailable to plants. Phosphorus availability depends on warm soil temperatures, pH range, and the levels of other nutrients, such as calcium and potassium, in the soil. Maintain the soil pH between 5 and 7 to keep phosphorous available. (For more on pH levels, see the section "Finding soil pH and nutrient content," earlier in this chapter.) Work phosphorous-rich fertilizers into the soil around the root zone at planting time to make them readily accessible by the plant roots. Deficiency symptoms include stunted plants with dark green foliage, reddish-purple stems or leaves, and fruits that drop early. Rock phosphate and bone meal are good sources of phosphorous.

✔ **Potassium (K):** This nutrient, sometimes called *potash,* is essential for vigorous growth, disease resistance, fruit and vegetable flavor and development, and general plant function. Potassium doesn't move around in the soil, so work the fertilizer into the root zone. Potassium also breaks down slowly, so you won't need to add it often. Annual applications of organic matter may supply enough potassium fertilizer, but a soil test is the surest way to determine need. Avoid adding too much potassium fertilizer because it can upset the N-P-K balance in the soil and make other nutrients, such as magnesium, unavailable. Deficiency symptoms include yellow areas along the leaf veins and leaf edges, crinkled and rolled up leaves, and dead twigs.

Secondary nutrients

Calcium, magnesium, and sulfur are called *secondary* nutrients. They're essential not only for plant growth but also for adjusting and maintaining soil pH. Calcium and magnesium, found in *dolomitic limestone,* help raise the pH of acid soils toward neutral where most plants grow best. In alkaline soils, sulfur helps lower the pH to the optimum level. These nutrients are also vital to plant functioning and, if excessive or deficient, can upset plants' ability to use other nutrients in the soil.

Although home garden soils rarely are deficient in these nutrients, keep your eye out for these deficiency symptoms:

 ✔ **Calcium:** Twisted, dark green new leaves and leaf tip burn. Flowers may have weak stems, and fruit may develop rotten spots on the bottom (opposite from the stem end).

 ✔ **Magnesium:** Curled leaf edges and discolored older leaves.

 ✔ **Sulfur:** Slow growth and small, spindly plants.

Micronutrients

The essential nutrients that plants need in the smallest quantities are called *micronutrients,* and they include iron, manganese, copper, boron, molybdenum, chlorine, and zinc. Adding too much of any one of these micronutrients can cause more problems than adding none at all. Luckily, organic matter usually supplies adequate amounts of these nutrients.

Micronutrient deficiency is often hard to spot because plants vary in their specific needs and symptoms. Maintaining the pH between 6.0 and 7.0 and adding manures and compost often is enough to make micronutrients available for plant use. (For more on pH levels, see the section "Finding soil pH and nutrient content," earlier in this chapter.) The microorganisms that feed on organic matter help plants take up these and other nutrients — another good reason to use compost and other organic fertilizers! Other micronutrient sources include kelp/seaweed, bone meal, and blood meal.

Considering Sources of Organic Fertilizers

Organic fertilizers generally come from plants, animals, or minerals. Soil organisms break down the material into nutrients that plants can use. Some organic fertilizers contain significant amounts of only one of the major nutrients, such as phosphorus in bone meal, but they often have trace amounts of many other beneficial nutrients. As a general rule, organic fertilizers release about half their nutrients in the first season and continue to feed the soil over subsequent years.

Commercially formulated fertilizers list specific nutrients levels on the package, but bulk products, such as compost and manure, have widely variable contents. The nutrient levels for each fertilizer in this section are approximate because they vary depending on the product and supplier.

Plant-based fertilizers

Fertilizers made from plants generally have low to moderate N-P-K values, but their nutrients quickly become available in the soil for your plants to use. Some of them provide an extra dose of trace minerals and micronutrients. If you don't find plant-based fertilizers at the garden center, check out your local feed store. The most commonly available plant-based fertilizers include

- ✔ **Alfalfa meal:** Alfalfa meal is beneficial for adding nitrogen and potassium (about 2 percent each), as well as trace minerals and growth stimulants. Roses, in particular, seem to like this fertilizer and benefit from up to 5 cups of alfalfa meal per plant every ten weeks, worked into the soil. Add it to your compost pile to speed up the process.

- ✔ **Compost:** Compost is mostly beneficial for adding organic matter to the soil. It doesn't add much in the way of fertilizer nutrients itself, but it does enhance and help make available any nutrients in the soil. (For more on compost, see the section "Composting: Turning Waste into Garden Gold," earlier in this chapter.)

- ✔ **Corn gluten meal:** This powder contains 10 percent nitrogen fertilizer. Apply it only to actively growing plants because it inhibits seed germination. Use it on lawns in early spring to green up the grass and prevent annual weed seeds from sprouting.

- ✔ **Cottonseed meal:** This granular fertilizer is particularly good at supplying nitrogen (6 percent) and potassium (1.5 percent). Look for organic cottonseed meal because traditional cotton crops are heavily sprayed with pesticides, some of which can remain in the seed oils.

- ✔ **Kelp/seaweed:** You can find this product offered in liquid, powder, or pellet form. Although containing only small amounts of N-P-K fertilizer, kelp meal adds valuable micronutrients, growth hormones, and vitamins that can help increase yields, reduce the plant stress from drought, and increase frost tolerance. Apply it to the soil or as a foliar spray.

- ✔ **Soybean meal:** Used in pellet form, soybean meal is prized for its high nitrogen (7 percent) content and as a source of phosphorous (2 percent).

When looking at organic fertilizer products, you'll invariably come across those containing *humus, humic acid,* or *humates* — organic compounds often found in compost. These products have no fertilizer value, but rather are used as stimulants to support soil microbial life that, in turn, supports the plants. Use them as supplements, not to replace proper soil building and nutrition.

Animal-based fertilizers

Animals, fish, and birds all provide organic fertilizers that can help plants grow. Most animal-based fertilizers provide a lot of nitrogen, which plants need for leafy growth. Here are some of the most commonly available ones:

- **Manures:** Animal manures provide a lot of organic matter to the soil, but most have low nutrient value. A few, such as chicken manure, do have high available nitrogen content but should be used only composted because the fresh manure can burn the roots of tender seedlings.

- **Bat/seabird guano:** The poop from bats and seabirds, *guano* comes in powdered or pellet form and is actually high in nitrogen (10 to 12 percent). Bat guano provides only about 2 percent phosphorous and no potassium, but seabird guano contains 10 to 12 percent P, plus 2 percent K. The concentrated nitrogen in these products can burn young plants if not used carefully. Use them to make manure tea, as described later in this section. They tend to be more expensive than land-animal manures.

- **Blood meal:** It's a bit gruesome, but blood meal is the powdered blood from slaughtered animals. It contains about 14 percent nitrogen and many micronutrients. Leafy, nitrogen-loving plants, such as lettuce, grow well with this fertilizer. It also reportedly repels deer, but may attract dogs and cats.

- **Bone meal:** A popular source of phosphorous (11 percent) and calcium (22 percent), bone meal is derived from animal or fish bones and commonly used in a powdered form on root crops and bulbs. It also contains 2 percent nitrogen and many micronutrients. It may attract rodents.

- **Fish products:** Fish byproducts make excellent fertilizers. You can buy them in several different forms. *Fish emulsion* is derived from fermented remains of fish. This liquid product can have a fishy smell (even the deodorized version), but it's a great complete fertilizer (5-2-2) and adds trace elements to the soil. When mixed with water, it's gentle, yet effective for stimulating the growth of young seedlings. *Hydrolyzed fish powder* has higher nitrogen content (12 percent) and is mixed with water and sprayed on plants. *Fish meal* is high in nitrogen and phosphorus and is applied to the soil. Some products blend fish with seaweed or kelp for added nutrition and growth stimulation.

Book VI

Organic Gardening

 You can use animal manures and compost to make liquid fertilizers called *manure tea* or *compost tea*. The nutrients in these teas are readily available for plant use; the teas are gentle enough to use on young plants or spray on the plant foliage to give them a quick boost.

Here's how to make manure or compost tea.

1. **Place a shovelful of composted manure in a burlap or other porous cloth bag and secure the top.**

2. **Submerge the bag in about 10 to 15 gallons of water.**

3. **Let the liquid steep for one week or until the water takes on the color of brewed tea.**

   Pour off the manure tea as needed.

4. **Dilute the liquid until it resembles the color of weak brewed tea.**

5. **Use the diluted tea to water around plants.**

   Dilute it some more to half-strength tea for young seedlings and as a fertilizer spray.

Rock on with mineral-based fertilizers

Rocks decompose slowly into soil, releasing minerals gradually over a period of years. Organic gardeners use many different minerals to increase the fertility of their soils, but it's a long-term proposition. Some take months or years to fully break down into nutrient forms that plants can use, so one application may last a long time.

Rock on with these fertilizers:

- ✔ **Chilean nitrate of soda:** Mined in the deserts of Chile, this highly soluble, fast-acting granular fertilizer contains 16 percent nitrogen. It's also high in sodium, however, so don't use it on arid soils where salt buildup is likely or on salt-sensitive plants.

- ✔ **Epsom salt:** Containing magnesium (10 percent) and sulfur (13 percent), Epsom salt is a fast-acting fertilizer that you can apply in a granular form or dissolve in water and spray on leaves as a foliar fertilizer. Tomatoes, peppers, and roses love this stuff! Mix 1 tablespoon of Epsom salt in a gallon of water and spray it on when plants start to bloom.

- ✔ **Greensand:** Mined in New Jersey from 70 million-year-old marine deposits, greensand contains 3 percent potassium and many micronutrients. It's sold in a powdered form but breaks down slowly.

- ✔ **Gypsum:** This powdered mineral contains calcium (20 percent) and sulfur (15 percent). Use it to add calcium to soils without raising soil pH.

- ✔ **Hard-rock phosphate:** This mineral powder contains 20 percent phosphorous and 48 percent calcium, which can raise soil pH — avoid it if your soil is already alkaline. It breaks down slowly, so use it to build the long-term supply of phosphorous in your soils.

✔ **Soft-rock phosphate:** Often called colloidal phosphate, soft-rock phosphate contains less phosphorus (16 percent) and calcium (19 percent) than hard-rock phosphate, but the nutrients are in chemical forms that plants can use more easily. This powder breaks down slowly, so one application may last for years in the soil. It also contains many micronutrients.

✔ **Limestone:** This mined product has various nutrient levels, depending on its source. It's used primarily to raise pH, but *dolomitic* limestone, is high in calcium (46 percent) and magnesium (38 percent). This powder also comes in an easier to spread granular form. *Calcitic* limestone is high in calcium carbonate (usually above 90 percent). Conduct a soil test for pH and for magnesium to find out which kind of lime and how much to add to your soil.

✔ **Rock dusts:** Mined from various rocks, these powders often contain few major nutrients but are loaded with micronutrients and other essential elements needed in small quantities by plants. Use them as supplements to regular soil building and fertility programs.

✔ **Sul-Po-Mag:** Also known as K-Mag, this mineral source provides plants with readily accessible potassium (22 percent), magnesium (11 percent), and sulfur (22 percent). Use it to add magnesium to high pH soils without raising the pH.

✔ **Sulfur:** This yellow powder contains 90 percent elemental sulfur, which is used not only as a nutrient for plant growth, but also to lower the pH. Go easy on the application, however, because overuse can decrease soil microbe activity.

Chapter 3

Controlling Weeds, Pests, and Disease

*W*eeds, pests, and disease set a challenge for gardeners that the good health of their plants depends on. Weeds compete with your lawn and garden plants for food, water, and sun; they harbor injurious pests and diseases; and they run amok, making the yard look unkempt. Insects are a mixed bag; most of the insects in your garden and yard won't harm your plants, but the ones that do cause damage accomplish more than their share to keep gardeners on their toes. And pests like rabbits and deer harvest your plants before you get a chance. Disease may prevent that harvest from even getting started.

This chapter introduces you to common garden invaders and shows you how to fend them off without doing damage to the environment — and how to make your garden unattractive to them in the first place.

Winning the Weed Wars

Weeding is not a favorite gardening activity — it's just not glamorous. Most gardeners prefer almost any other chore to crawling around on their knees in the dirt and pulling weeds. A better approach is to prevent weeds from sprouting in the first place.

Use the techniques in the following sections to prevent and control weeds in your landscape and garden. Choose the methods that match your needs, whether you're starting a new garden or maintaining an established planting.

Mulch

Just like other plants, weeds and their seeds need air and light to grow, and if you deprive them of these crucial requirements, they will die or fail to sprout. One of the best ways to keep weeds in the dark is to put mulch over them. *Mulch* is anything that covers the soil for the purpose of preventing weeds, conserving moisture, or moderating the soil temperature. Many materials make good mulch: The ones you choose really depend on what's locally available, how much you want to spend, the appearance factor, and where you plan to put it.

The best mulch materials for organic gardens and landscapes also feed the worms and add organic matter to the soil as they decompose. Usually, 2- to 4-inch layers are sufficient to do the job, depending on the density of the material. Take a look at the following popular mulches and their uses:

✔ **Tree bark:** Bark is the ubiquitous landscape mulch. Available in shreds or various-sized chunks, bark lasts a long time, depending on the particle size, and gives your landscape a finished look. Be sure you're buying real bark, however, by checking the bag label or asking the seller for the content. Wood chips that are dyed to look like bark are becoming prevalent in some areas.

✔ **Wood chips, sawdust, and shavings:** Although suitable for mulch, these products break down more quickly than bark and compete with your plants for nitrogen as they decompose. If you use these around food and landscape plants, be sure to add another nitrogen source.

Never use materials from chemical- or pressure-treated wood, which contains pesticides that may cause cancer.

✔ **Shredded leaves and pine needles:** These items are among the best sources of free, attractive, and nutrient-rich mulch for flowerbeds, fruits, and vegetables. Be sure to shred leaves before using to prevent matting in the garden. In fact, I run over fallen leaves with the lawn mower, discharging them into easy-to-rake mounds.

Pine needles and leaves of oak and some other trees acidify the soil. Use them freely around acid-loving plants, but monitor the soil pH around less tolerant plants. Some plants are sensitive to the chemicals in certain tree leaves. Cabbage-family plants, for example, don't like oak leaves. Many plants are incompatible with walnut leaves.

✔ **Seed hulls and crop residue:** These attractive, locally available, light-weight materials include cocoa bean, buckwheat hulls, ground corncobs, and other materials left over from processing an agricultural crop. Use on top of newspaper or other sheet mulch to increase suppression of weeds.

✔ **Straw and hay:** Be wary of these traditional vegetable garden and strawberry mulches. Hay contains weed seeds that add to your problems. Straw from grain crops, such as oats and wheat, may contain some crop seeds but is a better choice as weed-suppressing mulch. Allow the soil to warm up in spring before putting mulch around tomatoes and other heat-loving crops because straw keeps soil cool.

✔ **Lawn clippings:** Clippings cost nothing and work best in flower and vegetable gardens where they decompose quickly. Allow the clippings to dry on the lawn and then rake them up before using. Fresh clippings may mat down and become slimy as they decompose. If you're getting clippings from a well-meaning friend, be sure the clippings don't come from a chemically treated lawn.

✔ **Newspaper and cardboard:** Use cardboard or several layers of whole newspaper sheets in pathways or around landscape plants to smother weeds. (Avoid the colored glossy pages.) Cover with a thick layer of loose mulch, such as bark, shredded leaves, or straw. Depending on rainfall, you may have to replace newspaper during the growing season.

Some organic mulches can go sour if they get too wet and packed down and begin to decompose without sufficient air. If your mulch smells like vinegar, ammonia, sulfur, or silage, mix and aerate it with a garden fork. Don't apply sour mulch around flowers, vegetables, fruits, or young shrubs and trees — its acidity can damage or even kill the plants. Cover unused mulch piles with a tarp to keep them dry.

No matter what kind of organic mulch you use, keep it away from direct contact with plant stems and trunks. Pull it several inches away from the plants to prevent moisture buildup around the trunks and to deter insects, slugs, rodents, and diseases. Be sure to loosen the mulch with a rake periodically to allow water to penetrate easily.

Some mulches don't decompose but are useful in some situations:

✔ **Gravel and stone** are best for landscapes in fire-prone areas and around buildings where termites and carpenter ants pose problems. They don't add significant nutrients to the soil, however, and usually need landscape fabric under them to prevent weeds. Avoid sand, which attracts cats, ants, and weed seeds.

✔ **Landscape fabrics** allow water to pass through but shade the ground and prevent weeds from coming up. They also prevent organic material from reaching the soil, however. While the fabric will last for a long time, it may need to be replaced at some point. Shallow-rooted plants, such as blueberries, grow roots into the landscape fabric, making it difficult to remove later. Use it around trees and shrubs or under decks where you don't want weeds, but avoid using landscape fabrics in gardens.

Book VI

Organic Gardening

✔ **Plastic sheeting** is useful mainly in rows because clear and colored plastics heat the soil, while white plastic keeps it cool. Don't use plastic sheeting around landscape plants because it prevents water from reaching roots.

IRT (infrared transmitting) plastic lets in the warming rays of the sun but blocks the rays that stimulate seed growth. *SRM (selective reflective mulch)* is a special red plastic that warms the soil, increases some crop yields, and may repel some pests but doesn't prevent weeds as well as other plastics.

Solarization

One of the niftiest ways to beat the weeds is to *solarize* or use the heating power of the sun. The concept is simple: Capture the sun's heat under a sheet of clear plastic and literally bake the weeds and waiting seeds to death.

Use solarization to clear existing plants from new gardens. (Clear plastic works best for this endeavor.) This technique takes several weeks in warm, sunny climates. If you garden in a cool, cloudy climate, try it during the warmest or sunniest times of year and allow up to eight weeks for the process to work.

Here's how to solarize:

1. **Mow closely or till the ground to remove as much of the existing vegetation as you can.**

2. **Dampen the soil.**

   Moisture helps speed the process.

3. **Spread a sheet of heavy-gauge clear plastic over the area.**

   Stretch it tautly to keep it close to the ground.

4. **Anchor with stones.**

   Place a few stones or other weights on the plastic to keep it from blowing around and to hold it near the soil.

5. **Seal the edge of the plastic to hold in the heat by covering it all the way around with soil or boards.**

Avoid tilling the soil after solarization, or you may bring new seeds to the surface. If the soil gets hot enough, solarization also eliminates some soil-dwelling pests and diseases.

Cover cropping

Open ground is an open invitation for weed seeds to take root and for creeping plants to expand their territory. You can prevent and smother weeds, protect the soil from erosion, and enrich it at the same time by planting crops that you can till into the soil later. Thickly planted cover crops prevent weed seeds from sprouting and crowd out the ones that do. When the cover crop has done its job, you simply rotary till it into the soil, where it decomposes and adds organic matter.

Cover crops fall into two broad categories. Within each group, some live for a single season, and others are *perennial,* coming back year after year.

- ✔ **Legumes:** Plants that have the ability to convert nitrogen from the air into nitrogen in the soil are called *legumes.* These plants increase the fertility of the soil while they grow and add rich organic matter when rotary tilled under. Some of them, especially alfalfa, have deep roots that bring water and other nutrients to the surface. Legumes provide an excellent source of nectar for bees as well as habitat for numerous beneficial insects. Legumes for cover crops include several types of clover, hairy vetch, soybeans, and alfalfa.

- ✔ **Grasses and buckwheat:** These cover crops grow quickly, allowing you to till under some of them just a few weeks after planting; others can remain in place for months. Either way, they add large amounts of organic matter to the soil. Buckwheat flowers are also valuable for bee nectar. Other cover crops in this group include annual ryegrass, oats, winter rye, and sudangrass.

Cover crops can serve your garden needs in different ways, depending on your goals and time frame, but unlike some other weed-control measures, you do have to plan ahead when using them:

- ✔ **New garden preparation:** The year before you intend to plant a vegetable, fruits, or flower garden, turn over the soil and sow a thick cover crop. Depending on the crop used and on whether you have time, turn under the first cover crop and grow another before tilling the garden for food or flowers.

- ✔ **Between gardening seasons:** After you harvest the last of your vegetables and remove the crop residue from the garden, sow a cover crop for the winter. If you live in a cold-winter climate, choose a fast-growing grass and plant it at least several weeks before the ground freezes. Turn it under in the spring. In warmer climates, prevent the cover crop from going to seed. Otherwise, it may become a weed itself.

- ✔ **During the garden season:** Some cover crops, especially white clover, are useful as permanent ground covers in orchards and in the aisles between permanent planting beds. Clover encourages beneficial insects and adds nitrogen to the soil while preventing noxious weeds.

Flaming

One of the latest and most effective weed killers to hit the market, propane-fueled flamers make quick work of weeds. Instead of setting plants on fire, they have special nozzles that work by literally boiling the sap inside the plants and bursting their cells. The least expensive flamers cost little more than a high quality rake and are a worthwhile investment for large gardens, yards, and orchards. Expect to pay from $30 to more than $100 for a flamer hose, fittings, nozzle, and valves. They attach to any standard propane tank. The most expensive models allow the fuel tank to be worn as a backpack and include convenient squeeze-control valves.

For the most effective control, use your flamer when weeds are small. Large weeds and tough perennials may need repeat treatments. You can purchase flamers at farm- and garden-supply stores and mail-order companies.

Avoid using flamers in windy or dry conditions, especially if you live in an arid region. Keep a hose or other water source handy to douse unexpected flames.

Cultivating

Good old-fashioned hand-pulling and hoeing aren't among gardeners' favorite garden chores, but they work — especially if you follow these two basic rules:

- **Disturb the soil as little as possible.** This first rule is really important because many weed seeds lie dormant in the darkness just under the soil surface. When you churn up the soil, you expose them to the light and air that they need in order to sprout and attain pest status.

- **Get them while they're small.** Little weeds with fragile roots and stems take little effort to destroy. Large weeds take more work, disrupt more soil, and potentially contribute to the seed population in your soil, if you leave them long enough. Also, the longer the weeds live, the more water and nutrients they rob from your food and landscape plants.

The most effective and all-around useful weeding tools disturb very little soil as they work. The best hoes for weeding have sharp blades that slice the plants just below the soil surface, as shown in Figure 3-1:

- **Collinear hoe:** The collinear hoe, designed by organic farmer Eliot Coleman, allows you to stand up straight as you weed.

- **Stirrup hoe:** I use the stirrup hoe frequently because it cuts both on the push and pull action.

- **Swan neck hoe:** The swan neck hoe gets into tight spots easily.

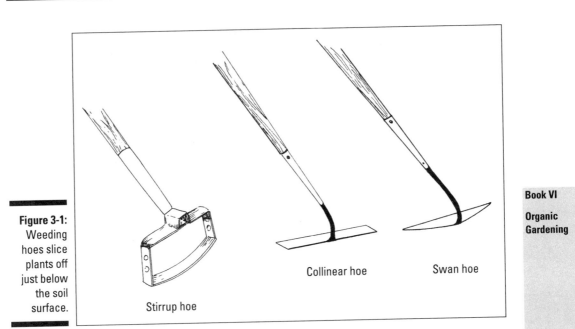

Figure 3-1:
Weeding
hoes slice
plants off
just below
the soil
surface.

Stirrup hoe

Collinear hoe

Swan hoe

Smaller hand tools and those with shorter handles exist, too, and let you weed raised beds or weed from a sitting or kneeling position.

All weeding hoes need occasional touching up with a sharpening stone.

Organic herbicides

When all else fails, gardeners turn to herbicides to kill the weeds. Sound like blasphemy? Take a look at some organic weed control chemicals. As with any chemical treatment — organic or synthetic — use the most powerful ones only as a last resort.

Herbicides work in several different ways that depend on a particular plant life stage or characteristic to be effective:

✔ Sprouting seeds send out roots first and then the stem and first leaves. This vulnerable time is the best and easiest stage to knock them out. *Pre-emergent herbicides* kill these tiny seedlings as they sprout and are especially useful on lawns and other places where mature weeds are difficult to remove. The timing of application is critical, however. If you put them on too early, they may wash away before they have a chance to work. Put them on too late, and the seedlings will be too big to be affected.

The most promising organic pre-emergence herbicide is corn glutenmeal, a highly concentrated corn protein extract. It can control weeds for up to 6 weeks, if applied in early spring and again in late summer, and, as a bonus, is high in nitrogen. Trade names of the product include Safe Lawn and WOW!.

✔ Plants have a waxy coating on their leaves, which prevents moisture loss. Herbicidal soap damages the waxy layer, allowing the plant to dry out and die. This type of herbicide works best on young, tender, actively growing weeds in hot, dry weather. Herbicidal soap is less effective on mature plants and perennial weeds. Safer's Superfast Weed Killer is a commonly available product.

✔ Plants are sensitive to changes in pH. Some products use vinegar, which is acetic acid, or pelargonic acid, which is derived from fruit, as their active ingredient. These acids lower the plant's pH dramatically, killing the sprayed plant parts in a matter of hours. For best results, remove as much of the plant top as you can before treating with the herbicide. Don't use these products where you intend to grow plants again for a few months because they can sterilize the soil. One product that contains pelargonic acid is Scythe. Bradfield Natural Horticultural Vinegar is a product with 20 percent vinegar.

Managing Pests

Sharing your vegetables, flowers, trees, shrubs, and lawn with insects is a balancing act. On the one hand, you want a safe, attractive landscape and bountiful, pesticide-free harvest. On the other hand, armies of marauding insects and other pests may seem intent on destroying your dreams. What's an organic gardener to do?

The answer is *integrated pest management,* called *IPM* for short. Success with IPM depends on careful and regular observation of your plants, the weather, soil conditions, and other factors that influence plant and insect growth. You also have to get very familiar with each important pest. Here's what you need to know:

✔ **Pest identification:** You have to know exactly which insect(s) you're dealing with. Capture a few in a jar to get a good look at them. Use a magnifying lens for small pests. Ask your local extension office for a color guide to common pests and their symptoms for your particular crop or ornamental plants. Extension *entomologists* (people who study insects) can also identify pests for you.

✔ **Understand the pest:** Learn as much as possible about when the pest appears, on which plants, what factors contribute to its abundance, what kind of damage it does, at what life stage it is easiest to control, where it lives when it's not on your plants, and what controls it naturally (beneficial insects or disease, for example).

✔ **Population size:** Knowing whether you have just a few aphids or a cast of thousands makes a difference in how you deal with them. After you spot a particular pest or symptoms of its damage, examine as many similar plants in your garden as you can to determine the extent of the population and its distribution. Traps can help you evaluate the population of some pests.

Deciding whether to control the pest or let it be

After you identify and profile a pest, you have a choice about how to control it — and whether to control it at all. Consider the following factors when making your decision:

Book VI

Organic Gardening

✔ **Crop value:** Are you looking at a small planting of annual zinnias or your family's strawberry patch? Obviously, a valuable fruit crop warrants more intervention than an easily replaced ornamental.

✔ **Extent of the damage:** Is the pest confined to a single plant, to the one end of one row, or to the entire crop? Is the damage mostly cosmetic, will you lose a significant percent of the harvest, or will the tree's or shrub's health be significantly reduced?

✔ **Your tolerance threshold:** Can your family live with blemished apples, using them for sauce and cider? Or do you plan to sell them for fresh eating at a roadside stand? Are your roses going to be entered in a contest, or will they simply grace your own house and garden?

You have many control methods from which to choose. Organic gardeners choose the least invasive and least toxic methods first and graduate to harsher steps as necessary.

Making the garden less inviting to pests

Your garden may be unintentionally rolling out the red carpet for insect pests. Bugs are opportunists that take advantage of weak or stressed plants. They also take up residence where the eating is easy. Keep pests at bay with the following prevention strategies:

✔ **Give plants the advantage.** Choose the right location for each plant, taking into account its particular needs for water, sunlight, and nutrients. When plants don't get their needs met, they become stressed, and the longer the stressful situation continues, the greater the decline in plant health. Think of insects as opportunists waiting for a weakened plant host to hang out the welcome mat. Of course, even a healthy plant can fall prey to insects and diseases, but it will be better able to survive the attack than will a plant that's already weakened.

Damaged bark or leaves are ideal entryways for insects and diseases. You can't lessen the ravages of weather, but you can protect plants from mechanical damage from lawn mowers, trimmers, and rotary tillers. Encircle trees, shrubs, and perennial beds with a wide band of mulch to keep equipment away from plants.

✔ **Confuse insects by mixing plants.** Insects have chemical receptors that help them zero in on their favorite foods. If you mix different types of plants instead of planting each type in large blocks, insects have a harder time finding all of them. Plant smaller patches of each crop and scatter them throughout the garden or yard.

✔ **Keep time on your side.** Young plants, with their tender, succulent stems, are easy prey for pests. As plants grow and become more vigorous, their tissues become more fibrous and less prone to damage. Plant a crop so that it's growing strong by the time its predominant pest insect hatches. In some northern regions, for example, early plantings of corn can protect against corn earworm and fall armyworm, which migrate from the south and arrive in the north later in the season. You can also time your plantings for a couple of weeks *after* the pest eggs hatch so that the young larvae will die from lack of food before your plants are up and growing. Talk to local growers and your local extension office about pest emergence predictions and recommended planting times.

✔ **Rotate crops.** Moving each vegetable crop family (the Solanaceae family, for example, includes tomatoes, eggplant, peppers, and potatoes) to a new location in the garden every year can help foil pests. At the end of the season, many insects leave eggs or pupae in the soil near their favorite host plants. If the young emerge in the spring looking for food and find their favorite crop is nearby again, they'll have a feeding frenzy. If, on the other hand, their food is on the other side of the garden, they may starve before they find it. Use this technique especially with annual flowers and vegetables that you replant each year.

✔ **Don't overdo a good thing.** An excess of nutrients is as harmful to plants as nutrient deficiency. In fact, excess nitrogen causes stems and leaves to grow rapidly and produce juicy growth that's a delicacy for aphids and spider mites because it's easy to puncture and consume. Aphids, as well as other pests, also are attracted to high levels of amino acids in plants, which can be caused by too much nitrogen in the soil. Similarly, an imbalance of phosphorus encourages egg production in spider mites. The easiest way to avoid nutrient imbalances is to provide nutrients in the form of organic matter and organic fertilizers, which make nutrients available gradually.

Encouraging beneficial insects and other predators

The average square yard of garden contains over a thousand insects. For the most part, that's a good thing. Some pollinate plants, some help break down organic matter, and some prey on other more damaging pests. Most of the insects in your gardens help — not hurt — your plants. Only a small fraction cause much damage.

The following sections help you sort out the predators from the pests and give you tips for keeping the good bugs where you want them — in your garden.

Book VI

Organic Gardening

Identifying the good guys

Those insects that prey on, or *parasitize,* insect pests are called *beneficial insects.* You rely on these allies to help keep the insect balance from tipping too far in the destructive direction. If you familiarize yourself with these good guys, you can encourage their presence in the garden and avoid killing these innocent bystanders just because they happen to be the insects you spy on your favorite dahlias.

You can buy many of these beneficial insects from mail-order catalogs to increase your local populations.

The following are some beneficial insects worth befriending:

- ✔ **Beneficial nematodes:** These microscopic, worm-like creatures live in the soil and are effective against the scourge of many gardens: Japanese beetles. Nematodes prey on the grubs, the larval stage of the beetle, as well as on armyworms, cutworms, onion maggots, raspberry cane borers, and sod webworms. Mix nematodes (available by mail order) with water and apply them to your lawn and garden soil. According to Ohio State University, beneficial nematodes are most effective in moist soil and at soil temperatures between 60°F and 90°F. They can be killed by exposure to the sun, so they're best applied in early evening or on cloudy or rainy days when the soil temperature is at least 55°F.

- ✔ **Big-eyed bug:** These fast-moving, ⅛- to ¼-inch bugs have tiny black spots on their heads and the middle part of their bodies, as shown in Figure 3-2. They resemble the pesky tarnished plant bugs, which are a favorite food of the big-eyes. They also dine on aphids, leafhoppers, spider mites, and some small caterpillars. Because these bugs aren't commercially available, look for them on nearby weeds, such as goldenrod or pigweed, and relocate them to your garden.

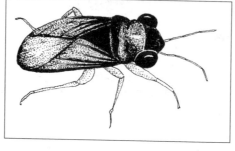

Figure 3-2:
Big-eyed bugs eat many pests including tarnished plant bugs, aphids, and leafhoppers.

✔ **Braconid wasps:** Several species of braconid wasps, shown in Figure 3-3, parasitize pest insects. Both the slender adults and tiny, cream-colored grubs feed on a range of pests, including aphids, cabbageworms, codling moths, and corn borers. Purchase these ⅒- to ½-inch wasps from suppliers and plant some parsley-family flowers to help keep them around. Adults require carbohydrate food, such as the *honeydew* secreted by aphids, tree sap ooze, or flower nectar.

Figure 3-3:
Braconid wasps and their larvae prey on caterpillars and aphids.

✔ **Centipedes:** Indoors and out, multilegged centipedes feed on many insect pests. Most species don't bother humans, and while some southwestern species inflict a temporarily painful bite, none are dangerous. You can't do much to encourage their presence, but if you leave them alone to do their job, you'll have fewer insects.

✔ **Damsel bugs:** These slender, ⅜- to ½-inch bugs have strong-looking front legs, and they prey upon aphids, caterpillars, leafhoppers, and thrips. They're common in unsprayed alfalfa fields, where you can collect them in a net and relocate them to your yard. Plant flowers in the sunflower family, goldenrod, or yarrow to keep them around.

✔ **Ground beetles:** Many beetle species live in or on the soil where both their larval and adult stages capture and eat harmful insects. They vary in color — black, green, bronze — and in size. Most live close to the ground, feeding on aphids, caterpillars, fruit flies, mites, and slugs; the 1-inch-long caterpillar hunter climbs trees to feed on gypsy moths and other tree-dwelling caterpillars. Because these beetles aren't available commercially, the best thing you can do to encourage their presence is avoid using herbicides and insecticides and learn to distinguish them from other unwanted insects. Ground beetles bear an unfortunate likeness to cockroaches, but the latter have longer antennae and a different overall shape. Most of the helpful ground beetles are large, dark, and fast moving. They often have nasty-looking mandibles and eyes on or near the fronts of their heads.

✔ **Hover flies:** Also known as flower flies or syrphid flies, hover flies got their most common name from the adults' habit of hovering around flowers. The adults, resembling yellow jackets, are important pollinators, while the brownish or greenish caterpillar-like larvae have an appetite for aphids, beetles, caterpillars, sawflies, and thrips. If you grow an abundance of flowers, you're likely to see hover flies.

✔ **Ichneumonid wasps:** Ichneumonid wasps are a valuable ally in controlling many caterpillars and other destructive larvae. The dark-colored adult wasps (see Figure 3-4) vary in size from less than 1 inch to 1½ inches, and they have long antennae and long egg-laying appendages — called *ovipositors* — that are easily mistaken for stingers. The adults need a steady source of nectar-bearing flowers to survive.

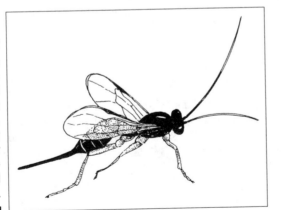

Figure 3-4: Ichneumonid wasps look threatening, but only spell danger for caterpillars and grubs.

✔ **Lacewings:** The delicate, green or brown bodies and transparent wings of these ½- to -¾-inch insects, shown in Figure 3-5, are easily recognized in the garden. Adults live on nectar, while the spindle-shaped, alligator-like, yellowish or brownish larvae feed on a wide variety of soft-bodied pests, such as aphids, scale, thrips, caterpillars, and spider mites. The distinctive, pale green oval eggs each sit at the end of its own long, thin stalk on the undersides of leaves. You can purchase lacewings as eggs, larvae, and adults. To keep the welcome mat out for the adults, allow some weeds to flower nearby.

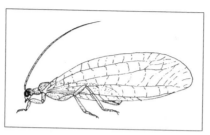

Figure 3-5:
Lacewings look delicate, but have voracious appetites for soft-bodied insects.

- **Lady beetles:** You may be surprised to learn that not all lady beetles (also called ladybugs) are beneficial — the damaging Mexican bean beetle is a type of lady beetle! The convergent lady beetle, however, is what most people think of when they praise lady beetles' appetite for aphids. (This species is distinguished from her pest cousin by two converging white lines on its *thorax* — the segment between the head and the abdomen. The number of spots varies widely.) Both adults and larvae prey on soft-bodied pests, including mealybugs and spider mites. The convergent lady beetle larvae look like small black, segmented pillbugs with rows of knobby or hairy projections and four orange spots on their backs. Although lady beetles are commonly purchased and released into the garden, they often do like the song says and "Fly away home." You can help keep them around by setting out another food source, such as an artificial yeast/sugar or honeydew mixture, which is commercially available from lady beetle suppliers.

- **Minute pirate bug:** These bugs, which are available for purchase, have an appetite for soft-bodied insects, such as thrips, corn earworms, aphids, and spider mites. A single bug can consume 30 or more spider mites a day! The adults are ¼-inch long, somewhat oval-shaped, and black with white wing patches. The fast-moving, immature nymphs are yellow-orange to brown in color and teardrop-shaped.

- **Predatory mites:** Similar in appearance to pest mites, such as the two-spotted spider mite, predatory mites are tiny (smaller than ½ inch) and quick. They feed primarily on thrips and pest mites and are widely used to control these insects in commercial orchards and vineyards. They're available to home gardeners, too.

- **Rove beetles:** These beetles, which resemble earwigs without pincers, have the distinctive habit of pointing their abdomens upward as they walk. Decaying organic matter is their home, where they feed on soil-dwelling insects, such as root maggot eggs, larvae, and pupae, especially those of the cabbage and onion maggots. In mild, wet climates, they also eat slug and snail eggs.

✔ **Soldier beetles:** The favorite diet of both adults and larvae of these common beetles consists of aphids, caterpillars, corn rootworms, cucumber beetles, and grasshopper eggs. The adults, shown in Figure 3-6, are slender, flattened, ⅓- to ½-inch long. The larvae have the same shape and are covered with hairs. They spend much of their life cycle in the soil, so they're more prevalent in areas where the soil is undisturbed.

Figure 3-6: Soldier beetles live in the soil where they eat caterpillars and damaging larvae.

Book VI

Organic Gardening

✔ **Spiders:** All spiders are predators, ridding the garden of many common pests. You can provide a good habitat for spiders by mulching with hay and straw, which has been found to reduce insect damage by 70 percent due solely to the numbers of resident spiders. Just make sure that you use old hay: Fresh bales tend to contain a whole lotta weed seeds.

✔ **Spined soldier bugs:** Adult spined soldier bugs dine on the larvae of Colorado potato beetles, Mexican bean beetles, and sawflies, as well as European corn borers, cabbage loopers, and tent caterpillars. The adults, shown in Figure 3-7, resemble tan, shield-shaped stinkbugs with prominent spurs on their shoulders immediately behind the head. They pierce their victims with a harpoon-like mouth. You can purchase them for release in your garden.

Figure 3-7: Spined soldier bugs resemble stinkbugs with armored shoulders and harpoon-like mouth.

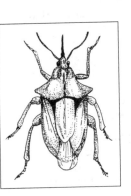

- **Tachinid flies:** These large flies feed on tent caterpillars, armyworms, corn borers, cutworms, stinkbugs, and other pests. The adult fly is about the size of a housefly and may hover above squash plants in search of prey. It has a bright orange abdomen, black head and thorax, and a fringe of short black hairs on its hind legs. Coriander, coyote brush, evergreen euonymus, fennel, goldenrod, and white sweet clover attract these flies to your yard.

- **Tiger beetles:** A variety of brightly colored and patterned ½- to ¾-inch beetles fall into this group, and they all have distinctively long legs. Some have shiny metallic green bodies and run fast when disturbed. They feed on a wide range of soil-dwelling larvae. If you use an electric bug zapper light, you're inadvertently killing these garden allies.

- **Trichogramma wasps:** Tiny as a pencil point, these parasitic wasps inject their eggs inside the eggs of more than 200 species of moths, such as cabbageworms, codling moths, corn earworms, and cutworms. Their developing larvae consume the host. Buy these wasps commercially and release them during their hosts' peak egg-laying times. Suppliers can give you more specific directions on release times.

- **Yellow jackets:** It's hard to think of these annoying insects as beneficial, but they do help rid your garden of flies, caterpillars, grasshoppers, and many larvae by taking them home to their young. Yellow jackets are fond of white sweet clover and ivy, so expect to see them near your house if you have either nearby.

Attracting beneficial insects

You can take important steps to welcome beneficial insects to your yard and encourage those you purchase to stick around. To keep the good guys from flying the coop, try these tips:

- **Wait to release beneficial insects until you've seen their favorite prey in the garden.** If beneficial insects don't find any food in your garden, they move elsewhere. You can even purchase food for lady beetles (from the companies that sell the beetles) to encourage them to stay even after aphid populations decline.

- **Grow some plants that attract beneficial insects.** With a constant supply of nectar, adult beneficial insects can live much longer than they would without it. Shallow-throated flowers are easier for many of the tiny beneficial insects to feed from than deep-throated flowers. Goldenrod is a favorite, attracting more than 75 different species of beneficial insects. Include this and other plants from the parsley and sunflower families, such as artemesia, aster, coriander, cumin, daisy, dill, Florence fennel, gazania, goldenrod, marigold, alyssum, sunflower, yarrow, and zinnia.

- **Include a diversity of plants in your yard to attract a diversity of insects.** Plant different species, including evergreens, and plants of different sizes and shapes. A mixture of trees, shrubs, perennials, and annuals in the yard provides lots of options for food and hiding places.

✓ **Avoid using broad-spectrum insecticides, which kill a wide range of insects, including beneficial ones.** Even some organic insecticides, such as pyrethrin and rotenone, are toxic to beneficial insects. Often, these insects are even more susceptible to the insecticide than pests because, as predators and parasites, they must move quickly over leaf surfaces and thus they come into contact with insecticides more readily. Many insecticides are also toxic to bees. If you must use a chemical as a last resort, spray only in the evening when bees have returned to the hive.

✓ **Provide a water source for beneficial insects by filling a shallow birdbath or bowl with stones and water and placing it near the garden.** Change the water frequently to discourage breeding mosquitoes.

Attracting other insect predators

Many creatures depend on insects for food, and you can enlist them in your pest-control efforts. Birds, bats, frogs, toads, lizards, and even small mammals can eat surprisingly large numbers of insects. Offer them the habitat they enjoy and let them get to work.

Keep in mind the following points:

✓ **Bats are beneficial, too.** Bats are often underappreciated. Their steady diet of insects — beetles, moths, and, of course, mosquitoes — makes them worth a gardener's tolerance. Some gardeners put up bat houses to help keep bats nearby. Bat houses look like birdhouses with entrance slots in the bottom and are available at many garden-supply outlets.

✓ **Welcome your fine, feathered friends:** Granted, birds do snare valuable, soil-enriching earthworms, but they also consume huge numbers of insects. A house wren, for example, can gobble more than 500 beetles, grubs, and insect eggs in an afternoon. Welcome birds to your yard by providing food, such as fruiting trees and shrubs, bird seed, suet, water from bird baths, and shelter that includes a diversity of trees and shrubs, including evergreens. Put up birdhouses to encourage your favorite feathered friends to raise their families nearby.

✓ **Tolerate toads and lizards:** If you're lucky enough to have a resident toad in the garden, consider him an ally. He'll consume up to 100 insects — cutworms, grasshoppers, grubs, slugs — every night during the gardening season. He may even hang around for years if you make your yard hospitable. Toads lay their eggs in water, so a water garden or pond will ensure future generations. You can easily provide drinking water by setting a low dish or birdbath on the ground near some tall plants that offer shelter.

Practicing good outdoor housekeeping

Getting rid of insects can be as simple as handpicking or even vacuuming them. Incorporate these easy techniques into a stroll around your yard:

✔ **Handpick insects:** When you go out to tend your plants, take along a can of soapy water — the future final resting-place for any Japanese beetle you encounter. In the early morning, beetles are sluggish and can be easily picked or knocked off your plants into a can. You can make this habit an after-dinner routine as well, when the beetles have slowed down and settled in for the night.

Use this technique on many other insects, as well. As an alternative to the catch can, spread plastic under plants and shake them to dislodge insects. Then pour the insects from the plastic into a pail of soapy water.

Tiny insects are difficult to pick off, but a little judicious pruning can remove masses of them. Aphids tend to cluster near flower buds and growing tips, so cutting off those portions will help reduce the population and control damage spread. Pick off leaves that have leaf miners and other insects and remove portions of branches infested with tent caterpillars.

✔ **Vacuum the leaves:** You can use your hand vac to bust more than dust. Pest insects tend to congregate on the upper portions of plants, while beneficial ones frequently hide on the lower leaves and branches. You can use these tendencies to your advantage by vacuuming the upper leaves with a low-suction vacuum (you don't want to lose the leaves, too) whenever you see pests accumulating. Afterward, dispose of the vacuum bag in a sealed bag or covered container so that insects can't crawl back out.

✔ **Give plants a brisk shower:** You can deter many an aphid and spider mite (and other crawling insects) from feeding on your plants with a strong blast from the garden hose. Simply knocking the insects off onto the ground can greatly reduce their damage, especially if you spray plants every day or two, before the insects have time to make the journey back up. Avoid spraying leaves in the evening because wet foliage at night can encourage disease organisms to spread.

✔ **Clean up debris:** Fallen leaves, dropped fruit, and other debris can harbor insects, so at season's end, pick up and destroy fallen fruit and till plant residues into the soil or add them to your compost pile. Burn diseased plants, dispose of them in trash bags, or add to a compost pile that reaches 160°F degrees. Even if you compost your spent plants, cultivate the soil to work in any debris that can shelter insects through the winter. Cultivating also exposes pests to cold temperatures and predators.

Outwitting Critters

A discussion of garden pests wouldn't be complete without considering the animals that may plague your gardens — birds, deer, rabbits, ground hogs, gophers, and moles. While insect feeding is subtler and causes incremental damage over time, some of these larger critters can eliminate an entire plant — or row of plants — almost right before your eyes. You can, however, keep damage to a minimum by getting to know their habits:

✔ **Birds:** Birds in the yard are a mixed blessing. You appreciate their appetite for insects, but when they nibble on the tomatoes and devour the ripe blueberries, they cross the line into nuisance territory. You can keep birds away from your plants by draping bird netting or row covers over them, but this practice isn't always practical.

Fortunately, birds can be startled by noise, fluttering objects, and, of course, anything resembling a predator. Try bordering your garden with string tied to stakes and fastening aluminum pie plates or unwanted CD disks to the string. The noise and flashing of the sun on the shiny surfaces can scare birds away. Or instead of string, use only a thin nylon line, which will vibrate and hum in the breeze. You can even use the modern version of the scarecrow — balloons and kites with images of predators, such as owls and hawks. Place them in the garden to convince birds that their enemy is on guard. Birds catch on quickly, though, so change your scare tactics regularly.

✔ **Deer:** Deer tend to travel the same routes day after day. If your yard is in the path of their customary travels from sleeping quarters to a water source, you'll be spending some evenings discussing deer-repellent strategies. Deer do, however, have some quirky tendencies that gardeners can use to their favor. Try some of the following remedies:

- **Fencing:** Deer have been known to jump a 10-foot fence, but apparently, they're intimidated about jumping when they can't tell how much distance they have to clear. Deer are less likely to jump a fence over a narrow, long garden than a fence that surrounds a large, wide garden. The two long sides appear too close together for the deer to see a place to land. You can create the same illusion by installing a fence so that it slants outward away from the garden. This technique can intimidate the deer by making the fence appear wider than it really is. You can even make a 5-foot-fence more deer proof by using taller posts and attaching strands of wire above the fence.

  If all else fails, you may need to resort to low-voltage electric fencing. Bait the strands of wire with peanut butter to encourage the deer to take a taste and get the message.

- **Row covers:** In early spring, spread fabric row covers over tender new growth, supporting the covers with wire cages or hoops, if necessary. This trick can deter the deer long enough to give your plants a head start and allow time for wild food plants to become plentiful.

- **Repellents:** Hang bars of soap from low tree branches or from stakes so that the bars are about 30 inches off the ground. Tallow-based soaps work best. Or spray plants with hot pepper solutions made from Tabasco pepper sauce or another hot sauce mixed with water and a little insecticidal soap or nonsudsing dishwasher detergent (to help the spray stick to the foliage). Another spray worth trying consists of three raw eggs in one gallon of water, which apparently smells worse to the deer than it does to you.

You can purchase repellent sprays, such as Hinder, Deer-Away, Repellex, and Tree Guard, to spray on foliage. For best results, spray plants before the deer develop their feeding habits. You need to reapply most sprays after heavy rain. Avoid spraying fruit and vegetables — you don't want to eat the stuff yourself. Follow label instructions on commercial repellents carefully.

✔ **Rabbits:** Rabbits are homebodies. They tend to stake out a territory of 10 acres or less and not wander elsewhere. They make their homes in natural cavities in trees, other animals' abandoned burrows, brush piles, and under buildings. They nibble foliage of almost any plant, returning again and again — day and night — to finish off the job. Here are some techniques to foil their feeding:

- **Fencing:** The best way to keep rabbits away from your plants is to fence them out. Because they burrow, a fence must also extend underground. Choose a 4-foot-high chicken wire fence with 1-inch mesh. Bury the bottom foot of the fence, bending the lowest 6 inches into a right angle facing outward.

- **Repellents:** Try repelling rabbits with hair gathered from hair salons and dog groomers. Sprinkle it around the boundary of your garden and replenish it every few weeks. You can also purchase commercial repellents made to spray on the ground or directly on plants.

✔ **Groundhogs:** These slow-moving rodents, also called *woodchucks,* live in an extensive system of underground dens and tunnels, and they defy you to find all their tunnel entrances. A tunnel can extend nearly 70 feet. Groundhogs generally stay within about 100 feet of their dens, venturing out to find food — your tender veggies — usually in the morning and evening. To deter them, try

- **Fencing:** Groundhogs can climb up almost as well as they can dig down, so use a sturdy 4- or 5-foot fence and bury the bottom 18 inches underground. Bend the top of the fence outward so that the groundhog will fall over backward if it attempts to climb over.

- **Repellents:** Spray plants with hot pepper solutions, such as the one recommended in the Deer listing, earlier in this list.

- **Traps:** You can use a Havahart trap to capture a live groundhog and then release it into the wild. Be sure to check with local and state ordinances about restrictions on live trapping and releasing of wild animals.

✔ **Gophers:** These burrowing rodents live in underground tunnel systems extending as far as 200 yards. They feast underground on plant roots and bulbs, occasionally emerging to eat aboveground parts of those plants located near the tunnel openings.

You can plant gopher spurge (*Euphorbia lathyrus*), a natural repellent, as a protective border around the garden. Castor oil sprayed on the garden also repels them. Vibrating devices, such as large whirligigs, stuck in the ground near tunnels can send them packing. If gophers are a serious problem, you may want to go to the trouble of lining the sides and bottom of your garden (at a depth of 2 feet) with hardware cloth to keep the gophers out. Gopher-resistant wire baskets, which you can place in planting holes prior to planting, are commercially available. For persistent problems, use traps.

✔ **Mice:** Mice cause the most damage to plants in the wintertime, when food is scarce and the bark of your favorite tree makes an easy meal. Even during the summer, if you have a thick layer of mulch surrounding the tree right up to the trunk, a mouse can hide in the mulch and feed undetected. To guard against this problem, leave a space of several inches between the trunk and the mulch to deter feeding. During winter, the snow cover provides a similar hiding place, so wrapping the trunk with a tree guard made of wire or plastic provides the best protection.

✔ **Moles:** These critters are the innocent bystanders or innocent burrowers of the garden pest realm. They simply love to burrow in search of grubs, earthworms, and other insects. In the process, they inadvertently expose plant roots to air or push the plants out of the ground, both of which kill plants. Field mice or voles also use the mole tunnels to reach plant roots and flower bulbs, which they eat. Traps are the most reliable method for getting rid of moles. Use them in the spring or fall, when moles are busiest, and make sure that you place them directly into a runway.

✔ **Cats:** Roaming cats enjoy loose soil and mulch and frequently use gardens and landscaped areas as litter boxes. Laying rough-textured or chunky bark mulch or ornamental rocks on the soil may repel them because these materials are uncomfortable to soft paws. You can also lay chicken wire on the soil and cover it with mulch. Cats also don't like the smell of dog hair or anise oil, so try spreading these items on the soil. Shredded lemon or grapefruit peels also deter cats. Look for a commercial product, such as Bad Cat, that contains citrus oils.

Book VI

Organic Gardening

Running Down Pesticide Types

An *insecticide* is any pesticide used to kill insects. Some are nontoxic to all but the intended pest, while others affect any insect that comes in contact with it. Insecticides that kill a wide range of insects are called *broad-spectrum insecticides,* and they should be used only as last resort because they kill beneficial insects as well as the harmful ones.

The easiest way to classify all the different kinds of pesticides is to put them into groups based on how they work and, to some extent, where they come from. Organic pesticides come from plants, animals, minerals, and microorganisms, such as bacteria and fungi. Each of these pesticide groups — and individual products — kills pests in different ways. Some are more effective against insect larvae; others affect adults, for example. To get the best result from any product, you have to know as much as you can about the pest you hope to control: its life cycle, where it lives and at what times of the year, and when it's most vulnerable.

Many people mistakenly believe that organic and nontoxic mean the same thing. *Organic* simply means that the product came from naturally occurring sources, such as plants, animals, and soil minerals. But some organic pesticides — nicotine, for example — are highly toxic and every bit as dangerous to humans and other animals as they are to insect pests. Whether you grow plants organically or not, avoid the most toxic pesticides whenever possible.

Dust to dust

Insects don't have skeletons and skins like animals. Instead, a waxy cuticle covers their bodies, holding in moisture. Some insects have hard plates covering some of their body parts; others have almost entirely soft bodies. Dusts work by disrupting the waxy cuticle, which causes the insects to dry out and die. Unfortunately, these dusts harm beneficial insects, too. Although they're not toxic to humans, use the following dusts with caution to avoid harming the innocent bystanders of the bug world.

- **Diatomaceous earth:** Called *DE* for short, this well-known and widely used white powder consists of the fossil remains of microscopic water creatures, called *diatoms,* and is mined from areas where ancient oceans or lakes once existed. DE resembles microscopic shards of broken glass, which pierce the soft bodies of insects, slugs, and snails. DE kills beneficial as well as harmful insects, so it may not be the best choice in all situations. Some DE products contain nontoxic bait that attracts pests and induces them to eat the dust, which is also fatal.

- **Iron phosphate:** This mineral product, when mixed with bait, attracts and kills slugs and snails. You apply it to the soil in pellets and, although it won't hurt people or animals, it interferes with calcium metabolism in slugs, causing them to stop eating and die within days.

- **Boric acid:** For cockroaches, ants, and silverfish, look for boric acid powder. If kept dry, the powder remains effective for years without harming animals, people, or the environment.

The pesticides in the preceding list are very low in toxicity, but you still need to use them judiciously and keep them out of reach of children.

Watching the soaps and other oily characters

Insects breathe through pores in the cuticle that surrounds their bodies. If you plug up the pores, the insects suffocate and die. That's where horticultural oils enter the picture. Disrupt the cuticle with special soaps and poof! — the insects can't maintain their internal moisture. Soaps and oils kill a wide range of pest insects, but affect beneficial insects, too. Use them with caution to avoid harming beneficial insects.

- ✔ **Horticultural oils:** These oils are made from refined mineral or vegetable oils. Although oils effectively kill any insect that they cover, including eggs, larvae, pupae and adults, they don't differentiate between good and bad bugs.

  Use horticultural oils in the winter to suffocate over-wintering pests, such as aphids, mites, and scales, on dormant fruit and ornamental trees and shrubs. During the growing season, horticultural oils work against aphids, mites, lace bugs, corn earworms, mealybugs, leafminers, scale, and many others.

- ✔ **Citrus oils:** The oils from the skin of citrus fruits kill a broad range of insects on contact by poisoning them. The oils continue to repel pests, such as fleas, ants, and silverfish, for weeks and are safe around people and pets. The *active ingredient* — chemical that does the damage — is d-Limonene. Look for it on the label or try the commercial product Orange Guard.

- ✔ **Plant extracts:** Many herbs, spices, and plants, including tansy, nasturtium, garlic, onions, marigolds, rue, mint, rosemary, sage, and geranium, contain chemicals that repel or kill insects. Garlic is one of the most well-known and effective extracts against thrips and other leaf-eating insects: The strong odor disguises the true identity of the host plant, so pests pass them by. Look for the commercial product Garlic Barrier.

- ✔ **Insecticidal soaps:** The active ingredient in insecticidal soap, called *potassium salts of fatty acids,* penetrates and disrupts the cuticle that holds moisture inside insects' bodies, causing soft-bodied pests like aphids to dry out and die. Some pests, however, especially beetles with hard bodies, remain unaffected. To make soaps more effective, products such as Safer's Yard & Garden Insect Killer, combine soap with pyrethrins, a botanical insecticide that's covered in the "Becoming botanically correct" section, later in this chapter.

Getting small with microbes

Everybody gets sick at one time or another — and that includes bugs. You can help them along the path to their destruction with a variety of infectious microorganisms or *microbes* that target specific pests. The beauty of these disease-causing microbes is that they're completely harmless to most beneficial insects, humans, and other animals. Microbes take time to work but often remain active in the environment long after you apply them.

- ✔ **Bacteria:** Several insect-infecting bacteria, or *Bacillus* species, that exist naturally in most soils have become important tools in the battle against damaging caterpillars, beetles, and other pesky bugs. In the 1960s, scientists began using the bacteria *Bacillus popilliae,* also called *milky* *spore disease,* to control the Japanese beetle and other closely related beetles. The disease affects the soil-dwelling larvae or grubs. After the grubs eat the bacteria, they become ill and stop feeding, dying within days. They often darken in color when infected. When the insects die, the disease organism spreads in the soil where it can infect others.

It takes several years for the bacteria to spread and achieve good control, however, and it is less effective in very cold-winter climates. In warmer climates, one treatment can remain effective for at least ten years. For best results, entire neighborhoods should participate in spreading the milky spore product.

Another very important group of bacteria, *Bacillus thuringiensis,* known as *B.t.* for short, infects many insect pests, especially their larval stages. Different strains or varieties of the bacteria affect different kinds of pests. One of the most widely used products contains the strain *B.t.* 'Kurstaki' or 'Aizawai', which infects and kills young caterpillars, including many major pests of vegetables, ornamentals, and trees. Product names to look for include Dipel, Thuricide, Javelin, and Safer Caterpillar Killer.

The strains *B.t. tenebrionis* and *san diego* infect leaf-eating beetles, such as Colorado potato beetle. The bacteria are most effective against young larvae because the bacteria more easily rupture their stomach linings. Colorado Potato Beetle Beater is a *B.t. tenebrionis* product. Another strain, *B.t. israelensis,* is effective against mosquitoes, fungus gnats, and blackflies. Products include Mosquito Dunks and Mosquito Attack.

All bacteria-containing pesticides degrade when exposed to sunlight and high storage temperatures. Also, insects must eat the pesticide to become infected.

✔ **Fungi:** Many naturally occurring fungi infect and kill insect pests, and one of the most promising for farm and garden use is *Beauveria bassiana,* commonly known as the white muscadine fungus. The fungus lives in the soil and affects aphids, caterpillars, mites, grubs, whiteflies, and others. Insects don't have to consume the fungus — mere exposure can lead to infection. For this reason, avoid using it whenever bees and beneficial pollinators could be affected. It may also be toxic to fish and shouldn't be used around fish-containing waters. To encourage the native *Beauveria* population in your garden, avoid using fungicides. Products that contain *Beauveria* include Mycotrol O and Naturalis H & G.

✔ **Viruses:** Two other groups of promising microbes include *granulosis virus* and *nuclear polyhedrosis virus,* which infect many caterpillar pests. Although still unavailable for home gardeners, granulosis virus is proving to be an important tool for commercial orchardists. These viruses can control codling moths, armyworms, gypsy moths, oriental fruit moths, and cabbageworms.

Becoming botanically correct

Insect and disease killers that come from plant extracts are called *botanical pesticides* or *botanicals.* Although derived from natural sources, botanicals aren't necessarily safer or less toxic to nonpest insects, humans, and animals than synthetically derived pesticides. In fact, most botanicals are broad-spectrum insecticides, which kill both good and bad bugs indiscriminately.

Some botanicals cause allergic reactions in people, others are highly toxic to fish and animals, and some may even cause cancer. All pesticides — including botanicals — should be used only as a last resort after thoroughly reading the label on the package. See the "Using pesticides safely" section, later in this chapter.

Book VI

Organic Gardening

The following pesticides are listed from least to most toxic to humans:

- ✔ **Hot pepper wax and powder:** The chemical *capsaicin* causes the heat in hot peppers, and it's the active ingredient in these useful botanical products. In low doses, hot pepper wax repels most common insect pests, from vegetables and ornamental plants. It doesn't cause the fruit or vegetables to become spicy hot but stays on the surface of the plant where it remains effective for up to three weeks. Stronger commercial formulations kill insects as well as repel them. Hot pepper wax is even reportedly effective in repelling rabbits and tree squirrels. You can find it at garden centers.

- ✔ **Neem:** This pesticide is made from the seeds of the tropical neem tree, *Azadirachta indica,* and it comes in two forms — azadirachtin solution and neem oil. Unlike the other botanical insecticides in this section, neem doesn't poison insects outright. Instead, when insects eat the active ingredient, it interrupts their ability to develop and grow to their next life stage or lay eggs. It also deters insects from feeding and is effective against aphids, thrips, fungus gnats, caterpillars, beetles, leafminers, and others. Amazingly, plants can absorb neem so that any insects that feed on them may be killed or deterred from feeding.

    Neem oil, the other seed extract, also works against some plant leaf diseases, such as black spot on roses, powdery mildew, and rust diseases. Mix the syrupy solution with a soapy emulsifier to help it spread and stick to the plants.

    Neem has very low toxicity in mammals.

- ✔ **Pyrethrins:** These insecticidal compounds occur naturally in the flowers of some species of chrysanthemum plants. The toxins penetrate the insects' nervous system, quickly causing paralysis. In high enough doses or in combination with other pesticides, the insects die. Powerful synthetic compounds that imitate the natural chrysanthemum compounds are called *pyrethroids.* Pyrethroids aren't approved for use in organic farms and gardens. Also avoid any pyrethrins that list "piperonyl butoxoid" on the label. This additive isn't approved for organic use.

Pyrethrins have low toxicity, but can induce some serious sneezing, headaches, and even nausea if you inhale too much of an insecticide that contains them.

✔ **Ryania:** This pesticide comes from the tropical *Ryania speciosa* plant. Although it controls fruit and codling moths, corn earworm, European corn borer, and citrus thrips, it's also moderately toxic to humans, fish, and birds. It's very toxic to dogs. Seek other botanical pesticides before considering ryania.

✔ **Sabadilla:** Made from the seeds of a tropical plant, sabadilla is a powerful broad-spectrum insect killer especially useful for controlling thrips, aphids, flea beetles, and tarnished plant bugs, but it also kills bees and other beneficial insects. Some people have severe allergic reactions to the chemical. Use it only as a last resort.

Using pesticides safely

As an organic gardener, you have already made the commitment to eliminate synthetic chemical pesticides from your garden and yard. Many of the insect, weed, and disease controls that organic gardeners use, however, are still toxic, especially if improperly used. Broad-spectrum botanical insecticides, such as pyrethrins and sabadilla, kill beneficial insects, destroy aquatic animals, and can injure pets and people. Knowing when, where, and how to apply these chemicals is part of responsible gardening.

Before you grab that spray bottle or can of dust off the shelf and head out to the garden, pause to check your personal attire. No matter how innocuous the pesticide, you must protect yourself from potential harm. Here's what you need:

✔ **Long sleeves:** Cover your arms and legs completely. If you're spraying trees, wear a raincoat with a hood for extra protection.

✔ **Shoes:** No sandals, please, and don't forget the socks.

✔ **Hat:** Your scalp easily absorbs chemicals. Also, remember to cover your neck.

✔ **Gloves:** I use disposable rubber gloves, especially when measuring and mixing concentrated pesticides with water.

✔ **Goggles:** Eyeglasses aren't enough. Use safety goggles that enclose your eyes and protect them from spray.

> ✔ **Dust mask or respirator:** Protect your lungs and sensitive membranes from damage. Use a special respirator with filters (available from garden centers, farm-supply outlets, and mail-order catalogs) when spraying pesticides. A dust mask is only helpful when applying nontoxic dusts to prevent inhalation.

Most pesticide injuries occur during mixing while you're preparing to spray. Put on your gear before you get started. Always mix and pour chemicals, including organic pesticides, in a well-ventilated area where accidental spillage won't contaminate or damage food or personal property. Even something as nontoxic as diatomaceous earth can irritate your lungs, while spilled oil can ruin your clothes. Don't use your kitchen measuring cups and spoons, either — buy a separate set for garden use.

Book VI

Organic Gardening

Clear all toys and other stuff out of the area you plan to spray, including the areas where the spray may drift. (Check wind direction.) Don't allow pets or other people into the area while you're spraying, and keep them out for the duration recommended on the product label.

Read the pesticide label carefully and apply the chemical only to listed plants. Relatively harmless pesticides can injure some plants. For example, horticultural oil isn't safe to use on Colorado blue spruce and many thin-leafed plants. Protect them from harm if you spray other nearby plants.

Consider weather and overall plant health, too. Some chemicals more easily injure drought-stressed and insect- or disease-weakened plants. High temperatures or intense sunlight can also increase the chances of plant damage.

Some botanical pesticides, such as pyrethrins, are very toxic to fish and beneficial insects. When you apply chemicals, follow the label directions very carefully. Never spray or dump pesticides near bodies of water or pour them into the sink or down the storm drain. Mix up only as much as you need.

Check the weather, too. Don't spray or apply dust in breezy conditions because the chemical may drift away from the target area and harm nearby plants or animals. If you expect rain, don't bother to apply pesticides that will wash off before doing their job.

Use a calendar with plenty of space on it to write notes and record everything that affects your garden. Seed planting and first harvest dates, rainfall amounts, unusual temperatures and weather events, the appearance of pests and diseases — everything goes on the calendar. Note the fertilizers and pesticides you use and on which plants. After keeping calendars for a couple of years, you may see patterns emerging that help you anticipate problems and keep them from becoming too troublesome. Good records show you what works and what doesn't, allowing you to make informed changes to your gardening practices.

Addressing Common Plant Problems

Sorting out what ails your plant can be difficult, but the following sections give you a good place to start. Compare your observations to the disease and environmental problems in the sections that follow to narrow your list of suspects.

Recognizing dastardly diseases

Several different kinds of organisms cause plant diseases, just as they do in people. Viruses are the toughest ones because they're incurable — all you can do is try to prevent them. Bacteria are nearly impossible to eliminate, too, after the plant is infected. Fortunately, fungi cause most plant diseases, and effective control chemicals exist, although prevention is still the best course of action.

The following list describes some of the most common diseases of trees, shrubs, vegetables, flowers, and fruits:

- **Anthracnose:** This group of fungi can attack many plants (beans, vine crops, tomatoes, and peppers) and trees (dogwoods, maples, ash, and sycamores). Look for small, discolored leaf spots or dead twigs, especially on the youngest ones. The disease can spread to kill branches and eventually the whole plant. Many plant varieties are resistant to anthracnose fungi — choose them whenever you can. It spreads easily by splashing water and walking through wet plants. Prune off affected plant parts, if possible, and dispose of the debris in the trash, not the compost pile. Fungicides containing copper can help.

- **Apple scab:** This fungus attacks apple and crabapple trees, producing discolored leaf spots and woody-brown scabs on the fruit. The leaf spots start out olive colored, eventually turning brown. Plant scab-resistant varieties. Rake up and destroy fungus-infected leaves to prevent the fungus from reinfecting the trees in spring. Spray with copper- or sulfur-based fungicides during wet spring and summer weather.

- **Armillaria root rot:** This fungus infects and kills the roots and lower trunk of ornamental trees, especially oaks. Symptoms include smaller than normal leaves, honey-colored mushrooms growing near the base of the tree and declining tree vigor. Trees may suddenly fall over when the roots weaken and decay. Keep trees growing vigorously and avoid damage to their roots and trunks. If you live in an area where the disease is prevalent, plant resistant tree species. Consult local nursery or local extension office experts.

✔ **Black spot:** This fungus causes black spots on rose leaves. Yellow rings may surround the spots, and severe infections can cause the shrub to lose all its foliage. The disease spreads easily by splashing water and overwinters in fallen leaves and mulch around the plant. Remove old mulch after leaf fall in the autumn and replace it with fresh mulch. Prevent black spot by choosing disease-resistant roses and cleaning up and destroying any diseased leaves that fall to the ground. Avoid wetting the foliage when you water.

Neem oil (not neem extract) is the best organic fungicide against black spot. Use it at the first signs of the disease, but spray either early or late in the day to avoid harming beneficial insects. Fungicide sprays containing copper or sulfur or potassium bicarbonate can also offer some protection.

✔ **Botrytis blight:** This fungus attacks a wide variety of plants, especially in wet weather. It causes watery-looking, discolored patches on foliage that eventually turn brown. Infected flowers, especially roses, geraniums, begonias, and chrysanthemums, get fuzzy white or gray patches that turn brown, destroying the bloom. Strawberry and raspberry fruits, in particular, develop light brown to gray moldy spots and the flesh becomes brownish and water-soaked. Discourage Botrytis by allowing air to circulate freely around susceptible plants and avoid working with wet plants. Remove and destroy any infected plant parts.

✔ **Cedar-apple rust:** Rust diseases, including this one, often have complicated life cycles in which they infect different plant species and exhibit very different symptoms on each, depending on their life stage. Cedar-apple rust fungus appears as bright orange spots on the leaves and fruit of apples and crabapples. On its alternate hosts — juniper and red cedar — it develops yellow to orange-colored jelly-like masses in the spring. The fungus needs both hosts to reproduce and spread. Prevent the disease by planting resistant apple varieties and keeping the alternate hosts several hundred yards away from susceptible trees. A related fungus, western pear rust, affects pears similarly.

✔ **Club root:** This fungus mainly infects cole crops, such as cabbage, broccoli, and collards, and grows best in acidic soils. Symptoms include stunted growth, wilting, poor development, and swollen lumps on the roots. Practice good garden hygiene by keeping tools clean and picking up plant debris. Raise the soil pH to 7.2 and avoid planting susceptible crops in infected soil for at least 7 years. Some vegetable varieties are immune.

✔ **Corn smut:** You can't miss this fungus disease because it causes large mutant-looking, white to gray swellings on corn ears. When the swellings burst open, the fungus spreads. Prevent the disease by planting resistant corn varieties and rotating crops so that you don't grow corn in the same place year after year. Dispose of infected plant parts in the trash. Or, go with the flow and work corn smut into your recipes — chefs have been making use of its earthy flavor since pre-Columbian times, especially in Mexico.

✔ **Cytospora canker:** Cankers appear as oozing, sunken or swollen areas on the bark of susceptible trees, such as peaches, apples, maples, spruces, and willows. The new shoots turn yellow and wilt and then die back. The disease attacks woody stems on susceptible plants, such as fruit trees, spruces, and maples, forming cankers that can kill infected branches. Plant resistant or less susceptible plants and keep them growing vigorously. Avoid bark injuries that provide an entrance for infecting fungus. Remove and destroy infected branches, cutting back to healthy wood that doesn't contain any black or brownish streaks.

✔ **Damping off:** Mostly a problem in young plants and seedlings, this fungus rots stems off near the soil line, causing the plant to keel over and die. Prevent damping off by planting seeds and seedlings only in pasteurized planting soil and avoiding overwatering. Air circulation helps prevent the fungus, too. Clean your tools in isopropyl alcohol to prevent the spread.

✔ **Fusarium wilt:** This fungus is fatal to many vegetable crops. The first symptoms are yellowing leaves and stunted growth, followed by wilting and plant death. In melons, the stems develop a yellow streak, which eventually turns brown. Choose Fusarium-resistant varieties. After plants are infected, there's no cure. If you build your soil's health so that it contains lots of beneficial microorganisms, you should rarely be bothered with this disease.

✔ **Galls:** These appear as swollen bumps on leaves, stems, and branches. Gall wasps, aphids, and mites infest oaks and other landscape trees and shrubs, causing unsightly swelling on leaves and twigs. In other cases, bacteria and fungi are the culprits. Usually the damage is simply cosmetic and not life-threatening to the plant. Control depends on what's causing the problem. Take a sample of the damage to a plant expert at your local extension office or contact your local master gardener program.

✔ **Leaf spots and blights:** Several fungi show up first as circular spots on leaves of tomatoes, potatoes, peppers, and other vulnerable vegetables, flowers, and ornamental plants. The spots increase in size until the leaves die and fall off. The fungi spread easily in damp weather and in gardens where overhead watering wets the foliage, especially late in the day. The best control is to remove all plant debris at the end of the gardening season, clean tools between uses, practice crop rotation, buy disease-resistant varieties, and avoid contact with wet plants. Copper-based fungicides offer control as a last resort.

✔ **Mildew (downy and powdery):** These two fungi produce similar symptoms: white, powdery coating on leaves. They infect a wide variety of plants, including roses, vegetables, fruit trees, strawberries and raspberries, and lilacs. A different species of mildew attacks each kind of plant. A mildew that attacks lilacs, for example, won't harm roses. The fungi disfigure plants, but may not kill them outright. Instead, they weaken their hosts, making them unattractive and susceptible to other problems. Downy mildew attacks during cool, wet weather. Powdery mildew appears during warm, humid weather and cool nights, especially when the soil is dry.

Many vegetable and flower varieties are resistant to mildew — read package and catalog descriptions carefully. Remove infected plant debris from the garden and avoid getting the leaves wet. Use superfine horticultural oil or neem oil to treat infected plants. Use copper- and sulfur-based fungicides as a last resort.

✔ **Root rots:** This broad term covers a number of fungal root diseases, which cause susceptible plants to turn yellow, wilt, and sometimes die. Nearly all plants are susceptible under the right conditions, such as excessive soil moisture, poor soil aeration, and wounding. The fungi can survive in the soil for many years without a host. Prevent root rot by building healthy, well-drained soil. Microbial fungicides can help foil many root rot diseases.

✔ **Rust:** Many different fungi cause rust, and the symptoms of this disease vary widely, depending on the kind of plant they infect. Usually, the symptoms include yellow to orange spots on the leaf undersides, with white or yellow spots on the upper leaf surface. Susceptible plants include brambles, hollyhocks, roses, pines, pears, bluegrass and ryegrass lawns, wheat, barberry, beans, and many more. Each rust species infects a specific plant species, so that the rust on roses can't infect beans, for example. Some rusts, such as white pine blister rust, have complicated life cycles and must infect two different plants — in this case, white pines and *Ribes* species, such as currant and gooseberry. Symptoms of this disease include yellow, orange, reddish-brown, or black powdery spots or masses on leaves, needles, or twigs.

Rust fungus is most prevalent in humid and damp conditions. Provide good air circulation to keep foliage as dry as possible, remove and destroy infected parts, and keep your tools clean. Plant disease-resistant varieties.

✔ **Slime flux:** This bacterial rot inside infected trees, usually elms, maples, and poplars, causes oozing and often bad-smelling sap to run from old wounds or pruning cuts. There's no control after the symptoms appear.

✔ **Verticillium wilt:** This fungus affects many plants, including tomatoes, eggplant, potatoes, raspberries, strawberries, roses, Japanese maples, olives, and cherries. Look for wilting and yellow leaves, especially older ones. In some plants, the leaves curl up before falling off. Prevent future infections by cleaning up all garden debris, cleaning tools thoroughly with disinfectant, and avoiding susceptible species. Choose resistant varieties and practice crop rotation.

✔ **Viruses:** This group of incurable diseases infects vegetables, brambles, strawberries, trees, and flowering plants. Usually the leaves develop mottled yellow, white, or light green patches and may pucker along the veins. Flowers may develop off-color patches, and fruit ripens unevenly. Aphids, leafhoppers, nematodes, and whiteflies spread the virus as they move from plant to plant. Viruses often live in wild bramble plants and weeds. Smoking or handling tobacco products around susceptible plants can spread tobacco mosaic virus, which infects tomatoes, eggplants, peppers, petunias, and other plants. Prevention is the only strategy. Buy only virus-free plants and keep pests in check. Eradicate wild brambles near your garden.

Preventing problems

Your gardening methods can go a long way toward keeping diseases out of your vegetable and flower patch and away from your fruits and landscape trees:

- ✔ **Choose disease-resistant plants.** Many popular flowers, vegetables, perennials, turf grasses, trees, and shrubs have varieties available that resist common diseases and even some pests.

- ✔ **Mulch to reduce insects, weeds, and diseases.** A thick layer of organic mulch around your garden plants and shrubs keeps weeds from gaining an upper hand. It also helps to maintain consistent soil moisture and temperature, which keeps plant roots healthy and better able to resist disease.

- ✔ **Choose plants that are adapted to your climate and site.** If your soil drains poorly, for example, don't plant shrubs that require well-drained soil.

- ✔ **Space and prune plants to provide good air circulation.** Fresh air helps leaves dry quickly and thwarts diseases.

- ✔ **Water the soil, not the plants.** Early-morning watering is best because the sun will evaporate any water on the leaves. Avoid evening watering because the foliage will stay wet all night, giving fungus spores a chance to grow and infect plants.

- ✔ **Avoid working with wet plants because diseases spread easily when the foliage is wet.** Many diseases spread through splashed water. Beans, strawberries, raspberries, and other plants are particularly susceptible.

- ✔ **Avoid excess nitrogen fertilizer.** Nitrogen makes plants grow fast and juicy. As a result, the outer layers of the leaves and stems (similar to human skin) that protect the plant are thinner than usual and more susceptible to insect damage.

- ✔ **Keep your yard clean.** Dispose of diseased leaves, fruit, and wood in the garbage, not the compost pile. Keep your yard tidy to discourage pests that live in dead plant debris, log piles, and other hidden places. Some insect pests — such as aphids, bark beetles, and tarnished plant bugs — can spread diseases between plants. Keep them under control, and you'll help prevent disease.

- ✔ **Inspect plants frequently.** You have a better chance of preventing a serious outbreak if you catch it early. Look for stem and leaf wounds and damage, off-color foliage, wilting, leaf spots, and insects whenever you work among your landscape and garden plants.

- ✔ **Practice crop rotation.** Many insects and diseases live in the soil from one year to the next, waiting for their favorite host plants to return. Foil them by planting something different in each spot each year.

Understanding disease-control methods

Preventing plant stress and environmental imbalances are the most important first steps in controlling disease. Beneficial microbes, especially in the soil, usually keep the populations of plant-disease-causing organisms in check, but environmental factors can tip the balance in favor of the bad guys. High humidity and soil moisture, as well as temperature extremes, encourage fungi to grow. Stress from transplanting, pruning, and insect infestation can weaken plants and make them more vulnerable to infection from fungi, bacteria, and viruses. And sometimes the pesticide you choose to use against one problem can make another problem worse. Broad-spectrum fungicides, such as copper and sulfur, for example, kill beneficial fungi as well as harmful ones.

Book VI

Organic Gardening

The only plant diseases you can effectively control after the plants become infected are those caused by fungi. Except for solarization and copper, the following control methods target mainly fungi. The treatments are listed in order of toxicity, starting with the least toxic method.

- ✓ **Solarization:** Heating the soil with the rays of the sun works to kill fungi and bacteria. Unfortunately, it kills both good and bad microbes. Use this technique in gardens where disease has been a problem in the past; find out how in the solarization section earlier in this chapter.

- ✓ **Antitranspirants:** These waxy or oily materials are designed to help evergreens maintain leaf moisture during winter months. By coating the leaves, they also prevent fungus spores from attacking. Look for Wilt-Pruf and similar products and follow the instructions on the label.

- ✓ **Potassium bicarbonate:** This natural chemical controls powdery mildew on roses, grapes, cucumbers, strawberries, and other plants. It also supplies some potassium fertilizer when sprayed on foliage, which strengthens plant cell walls and makes them harder for pests and diseases to penetrate. Look for the products called Kaligreen by Toagosei and Remedy by Bonide Company. Mix the powder with water and spray all leaf surfaces thoroughly to ensure contact with the fungus. Note that repeated applications can burn or stunt the leaves.

- ✓ **Microbial fungicides:** Some of the newest fungicides are fungi themselves. These good guys grow in the soil on plant roots and protect the plants from harmful root-rot fungi. Apply them to the soil before planting or water them into lawns and gardens. Products to look for include Mycostop, Serenade Garden Disease Control, RootShield, PlantShield, and TurfShield. These products contain viable fungi and must be stored properly and used carefully according to label instructions for best results

- ✓ **Neem oil:** This multipurpose pesticide thwarts black spot on roses, powdery mildew, and rust fungi as well as insects and mites. Look for a product called Trilogy and others that contain neem oil, not neem extract. Warm the syrupy solution to make it easier to mix.

- ✔ **Sulfur:** Useful for controlling nearly all fungus diseases on leaves and stems, sulfur is one of the oldest pesticides known. You can dust the powder directly on leaves or mix finely ground dust with water and a soapy wetting agent that helps it adhere to leaf surfaces. It can cause leaf damage if applied within a month of horticultural oil, however, or when temperatures exceed 80°F. It also lowers soil pH and harms many beneficial insects. Inhaled dust can cause lung damage. Take precautions to protect yourself. Products include Bonide Sulfur Plant Fungicide, Safer Garden Fungicide Liquid and Britz Sulfur Dust.

- ✔ **Copper:** Copper sulfate is a powerful fungicide that controls a wide range of leaf diseases, including fungal and bacterial blights and leaf spots, but it's much more toxic to humans, mammals, fish, and other water creatures than most synthetic chemical fungicides. Use copper-containing products only as a last resort and take full precautions to avoid poisoning yourself and others. It can also build up in the soil and harm plants and microorganisms.

Chapter 4

Raising Organic Vegetables and Herbs

As more and more news comes out about the dangers of chemical pesticides and fertilizers, more people are choosing to grow their own food — and in the process are discovering that homegrown vegetables and herbs are fresher and taste better than store-bought. Nothing tastes better than a sliced red, ripe, sun-warmed tomato in a leafy salad with sweet basil or your own fresh peas picked right off the vine.

In this chapter, you find out about designing and starting your vegetable garden. You get tips to make your garden more productive and information about growing and harvesting the most popular home garden vegetables and herbs.

Planning Your Vegetable Garden

When you're starting your first garden, you may have more questions than answers — where to put the garden, when and how much to plant, which vegetables to choose. It's no wonder that problems can pop up before you know what's happening! This section shows you how to get off to a good start and how to prevent troublesome pests, diseases, and other plant stress-related problems along the way.

Finding a place to grow

You may dream of a big garden filled with all types of fresh and inviting vegetables, but getting to that stage takes experience and preparation. For the first timer, small is beautiful — take time to get it right on a small scale before launching a market-garden-sized project. Keep the following ideas in mind to save yourself a lot of work and frustration later in the season:

- ✔ **Start small.** Little plants and seeds turn into a big commitment as they grow. A 10-feet by 20-feet garden is plenty to grow a variety of vegetables such as lettuce, beans, carrots, tomatoes, and peppers. If you want to grow vining crops or space hogs, such as corn or pumpkins, you can expand it to 20 feet by 30 feet. Planting more space than you can keep well tended is probably the No. 1 cause for gardener frustration and burnout.

- ✔ **Make it convenient.** Place the garden in a location where you see it every day. Your garden is more likely to thrive when you visit it regularly.

- ✔ **Put the garden in full sun.** Vegetable plants need at least 6 hours of full sun each day. Plan the garden so that tall plants, such as corn and tomatoes don't cast shade on shorter plants, such as beets and cabbage.

- ✔ **Choose a well-drained spot.** Vegetables are more prone to disease in soggy soil.

- ✔ **Grow a variety of crops.** Planting a number of different vegetables ensures that something will produce. Plus, diversity in the garden encourages good insects and helps to reduce problems from harmful ones.

Preparing the soil

Healthy soil is the key to the success of your vegetable garden. Soil rich with fertile organic matter, beneficial microorganisms, nutrients, and air spaces produces the most vigorous and productive vegetable plants. Keep the soil pH between 6.0 and 7.0 and work a 3- to 4-inch layer of compost or composted manure into the soil before each planting season. Compost adds organic matter, and it's the organic gardener's mantra (see Chapter 2)!

For all but the sandiest soils, raised beds are the best way to grow vegetables. *Raised beds* are plots of soil that has been mounded to form a large flat surface usually 3 to 4 feet wide, 6 to 12 inches tall, and as long as needed. Raised beds offer many advantages, especially if you have poorly drained or clay soil:

- ✔ Soil drains faster.

- ✔ Soil warms up faster in the spring. Drier soil warms more quickly than water-saturated soil.

- Because you don't step on raised beds, the soil doesn't compact as much, and plant roots grow better — especially on root crops, such as carrots, beets, and radishes.

- They enable you to concentrate and conserve fertilizer and water in the growing zone.

- More ideal growing conditions enable you to plant a little closer together than normal, which reduces watering and weeding and gives you more productive plants.

You can build two types of raised beds:

- *Contained raised beds* have permanent walls around them made from wood, bricks, or stone. These beds look neat and tidy and don't have to be reformed each year.

- You make *freestanding raised beds* from soil in the garden each year. They don't have walls made from other materials, so they tend to flatten and lower with time. Freestanding raised beds are good for flexibility and changing garden designs each year and to rotate crops.

Regardless of the type you make, amend the soil in your raised bed each year with several inches compost. Work it into the top 12 inches of soil with a garden fork. Smooth the top of the beds with a garden rake.

Designing your vegetable garden

You can be as creative or traditional as you like in your vegetable garden design. Plant everything in straight rows or create imaginative curved raised beds. Make a heart-shaped garden plot or whatever else strikes your fancy.

Draw a diagram of your garden plan on graph paper, laying out rows and raised beds with a ruler and pencil. To figure out how many plants will fit into a row or bed, follow the guidelines on the seed packets and make little dots or circles to indicate the larger veggies, such as broccoli, tomatoes, and squash. Leave room for walking paths at least 24 inches wide to harvest and work the beds, and don't be afraid to mix in herbs and flowers. The more color and variety, the more beautiful the garden, and the more likely you'll strike an ecological balance with birds and beneficial insects, helping to keep harmful pests in check.

For even more garden success, try a few of the following techniques:

- **Be creative with the garden design.** Don't plant all the same type of vegetables in one spot. For example, plant two small patches of beans in different spots in the garden. Even if animals or insects destroy one patch, they may not find the other.

✔ **Rotate crops every planting season.** Follow crops that use a lot of nitrogen, such as sweet corn and tomatoes, with crops that add nitrogen to the soil, such as beans and peas. Avoid planting crops from the same family, which tend to share the same insect pests and diseases, in the same spot. Allow at least 3 years before planting a vegetable family in the same spot again.

Plants have family trees, too. Check out http://vegetablesonly.com/ VegFamilies.pdf to find out which plants have the same genetic roots — pun totally intended — and therefore share susceptibilities to disease.

✔ **Use succession planting.** Crops, such as lettuce and beans, are quick to mature, so you can plant them several times throughout the growing season for a constant supply of tender new vegetables. This technique works best when you plant small patches of each vegetable every two weeks. That way you won't ever have a glut of lettuce, and you enjoy a longer growing season.

✔ **Try companion planting.** Plants may benefit another plant by repelling certain insect pests, making nutrients more available, giving shade, or providing a habitat for beneficial insects. Table 4-1 shows some favorable and unfavorable combinations. Keep in mind, most of this theory isn't scientifically proven, so experiment in your garden and see what happens.

Table 4-1	Companion Planting Table*	
Crop	*Companion*	*Incompatible*
Asparagus	Tomato, parsley, basil	
Beans	Most vegetables and herbs	Onion, garlic
Beets	Cabbage, onion families, lettuce, radish	Pole beans
Cabbage	Celery, beets, onion family, spinach, chard	Pole beans, lettuce
Carrots	English pea, lettuce, rosemary, onion, sage, tomato	Dill
Celery	Onion and cabbage families, tomato, bush beans, nasturtium	Carrot
Corn	Potato, beans, pea, pumpkin, cucumber, squash	Tomato
Cucumber	Beans, corn, English pea, sunflower, radish	Potato
Eggplant	Beans, marigold	
Lettuce	Carrot, radish, cucumber	Broccoli, wheat, rye

Crop	Companion	Incompatible
Onion family	Beets, carrot, lettuce, cabbage, strawberry	Beans, English peas
Pea, English	Carrots, radish, turnip, cucumber, corn, beans	Onion, garlic, Irish potato
Potato, Irish	Beans, corn, cabbage family	Pumpkin, squash, tomato, cucumber
Pumpkins	Corn, beans on trellis	Irish potato
Radish	English Pea, lettuce, cucumber, squash	
Squash	Corn, beans on trellis	Irish potato
Tomato	Onion family, asparagus, carrot, cucumber, parsley	Irish potato, dill
Turnip	English pea	Irish potato

Compiled from traditional literature on companion planting.

Planting the right seed at the right time

Most vegetables are *annual plants,* which die after one season of growth. These plants generally fall into two groups:

- ✔ *Cool-season* vegetables grow best during cool weather and include broccoli, spinach, lettuce, carrots, peas, and potatoes. You can usually plant them in the garden 1 to 2 weeks before the last frost date. Not only can they tolerate cool weather, they need cool weather to grow and mature properly. If you plant these crops too late in spring, they won't thrive in the heat of the summer. You can even plant some, such as peas and lettuce, in mid to late summer for a fall harvest.

- ✔ *Warm-season* crops, such as tomatoes, squash, peppers, sweet corn, melons, and cucumber, grow best in hot weather. Plant them 1 to 2 weeks after the last frost date for your area or when the soil is at least 60°F. These plants don't like the cold, so don't rush to plant them before the soil warms up. Contact your local weather service to determine your average last frost date, if you aren't sure when it usually occurs.

Winter is the quiet time between gardening seasons in most parts of the country. But in mild winter and hot summer areas of the country, such as southern California, Texas, and Florida, the cycle is reversed. There, you plant warm-season crops in spring and fall and cool-season crops in winter. Summer is the time for you and the veggies to take a break from the hot weather. In rainy, mild areas, you can grow some crops, especially those that enjoy cool weather, year 'round. Plant warm-season crops so that they mature during the warmest months of the year.

Some crops, such as beans, peas, carrots, and squash, are normally sown directly in the garden soil where they'll grow. Other plants, such as tomatoes, peppers, and eggplants, which take a long time to mature, grow best if they get an early start in greenhouses or indoors in your house 4 to 6 weeks before you set them in their permanent garden location. This head start is critical in cold areas with short summers.

Some vegetables, such as cucumber, broccoli, onion, and lettuce, go either way. You can find already started *transplants* (seedlings) at local garden centers, or you can sow them directly in the garden. Base your decision on how much time you have and whether your favorite varieties are more readily available as transplants or seeds.

Sorting out seed types

When choosing vegetable varieties to plant, you may come across the terms *hybrid, open pollinated,* and *genetically modified.* The first two are important for home gardeners, while the third is a new type of plant that, to date, applies mainly to commercial farmers.

✔ *Open-pollinated* or *heirloom* varieties are those that produce offspring similar to the parents. The flowers are naturally pollinated in the fields with little or no interference from the farmer. Some classic open-pollinated varieties include Brandywine tomato, Kentucky Wonder bean, and Golden Bantam sweet corn. Many of these varieties are locally adapted and have unusual colors, shapes, and flavors. Gardeners have relied on these varieties for generations because they can save the seeds and grow the plants easily.

✔ *Hybrid varieties* have been around since the 1900s. Researchers found that breeding different corn varieties together resulted in offspring with better traits than either parent, plus they grew vigorously and more uniformly. Although you can't successfully save seeds from hybrids, many varieties exhibit important characteristics, such as improved disease resistance, vigor, and consistent quality. Some classic examples of hybrid varieties include Big Boy tomato, Gypsy pepper, and Premium Crop broccoli.

✔ *Genetically modified* plants are those bred through gene splicing where certain characteristics are taken from unrelated plants or even other organisms and inserted in the vegetable. Most of these varieties are in the corn, soybean, cotton, and potato groups, and most are available only for farmers to purchase. While genetically modified plants offer many benefits, such as decreased dependence on pesticide sprays due to inserting an insecticide into the plant, many questions still exist about the long-term health risks and environmental safety of manipulating the gene pool so dramatically and quickly.

Which type of vegetable variety you grow is a personal decision based on trial and error and recommendations from fellow gardeners. The key is to experiment in your garden with a range of varieties to find the right ones that grow, produce, and taste best to you.

Growing Veggies 101

Growing a garden is like learning to run a marathon — start one step at a time, take it slowly at first, and build on your successes. The following sections outline the steps that create a successful and abundant garden.

Sowing seeds

After your raised beds and garden soil are raked and ready (see the "Preparing the soil" section, earlier in this chapter), it's finally time to plant. The general rule for planting seeds is to plant them twice as deep as the seeds are wide. For big seeds, such as beans and corn, that means about 1 to 2 inches deep, while small seeds, such as lettuce, may be planted only ¼-inch deep. After they're in the soil, keep the soil evenly moist, especially the soil surface. If the surface dries out, it can form a crust that prevents seedlings from emerging.

Book VI

Organic Gardening

You should see signs of life within a few days for quick sprouters, such as radishes. Slowpokes, such as carrots, may need a week or two to germinate. Be patient — as long as you use fresh seed, labeled for the current year, they should come up eventually.

In unusually wet and cold or hot and dry soil, however, seeds may rot or fail to sprout. Replant, if necessary, when the weather improves.

When you put transplants into the garden, you can set them a bit deeper in the soil than they grew in their pots. Try planting peppers, eggplants, tomatoes, and cabbage-type plants right up to their first set of *true leaves,* the ones that look like miniature adult leaves and grow above the fleshy *seed leaves.* Planting more deeply gives plants stability and, in some cases, a stronger root system. Loosely wrap a 2- to 3-inch-wide strip of newspaper around each stem before planting to prevent cutworms from chewing through the tender stem. The paper should extend at least an inch above and below the soil.

Starting plants with a hearty meal

When seeds are up and growing and the transplants are planted, give them a dose of fertilizer. Mild, liquid organic fertilizers, such as fish emulsion and seaweed mix, provide nitrogen and other essential nutrients for early growth. Water your plants with 1 tablespoon each of liquid fish emulsion and liquid seaweed fertilizers mixed into 1 gallon of tepid water one week after seeds sprout and at planting time for transplants.

You may also consider applying a complete organic fertilizer, such as 5-3-3, to keep them growing strong. (See Chapter 2 for more on organic fertilizers.) *Heavy-feeding* vegetables, such as corn, tomatoes, and broccoli, may need monthly doses of fertilizer, while *light feeders,* such as beans, radishes, and peas, may need little or no additional fertilizer.

How much you use depends on the size and type of plants. (Follow package instructions.) Sprinkle it 6 to 8 inches from the stems and scratch it gently into the soil. Water the soil to dissolve and disperse the fertilizer. If you use liquid fertilizer, follow the recommended dosage on the label and apply it with a watering can around the bases of the plants.

Don't go overboard on the fertilizer. Even organic fertilizers can accumulate in the soil, causing a salt buildup that harms plant roots. And excess fertilizer can run off into streams, causing water pollution. If you give plants too much nitrogen at the wrong time, you may even prevent some vegetables from forming fruit. Tomatoes, peppers, and eggplants, for example, grow loads of lush foliage, but few flowers or fruit.

Battling weeds

Almost as soon as you see signs of vegetables germinating, you're probably going to see weeds, too. Get familiar with what your vegetables look like when they're small so that you don't pull them out instead of the weeds. The best way to control weeds is to hand pull or slice them off with a hoe when they're young because you disturb less soil and they're easier to pull at that time than when they're more mature. Then mulch around the vegetables, as follows:

- ✔ For heat-loving crops, such as tomato, cucumber, and squash, use black landscape fabric mulch to stop weed growth, heat the soil, and conserve moisture. Lay the fabric down on the planting bed *before* planting, and then poke holes in the fabric with scissors or a knife to plant your transplants or seeds.

- ✔ For cool-loving crops, such as lettuce, broccoli, and spinach, mulch with organic materials, such as hay, newspapers, grass clippings, or pine straw, after planting. A 3- to 4-inch layer keeps most weeds at bay throughout the summer, keeps the soil cool, and conserves moisture. In warm summer areas, you may need to reapply the organic mulch in mid-summer because it does degrade quickly in heat and moisture.

Keeping plants well-watered

Watering is critical during the early stages of plant growth, but it's also essential when the plants are forming and ripening fruits. Mulching is an excellent way to keep the soil moist throughout the summer, but you may need to do some supplemental watering, depending on your weather and where you live. Lack of water can cause small, deformed fruits. Also, some conditions, such as blossom end rot on tomatoes, are due to fluctuating soil moisture, so be consistent about watering and mulching.

Vegetables from Allium to Zucchini

Book VI

Organic Gardening

Seed catalogs have so many delicious veggies to choose from that you may have a tough time knowing where to start — and stop! If you're growing your first garden, grow just a few different vegetables from among your favorites and stick to one variety of each. As you gain experience, add more kinds and experiment with one or two different crops each year. If something doesn't work out the way that you expected it to, try a different variety or growing method or abandon it and give the garden space to another crop. That's one of the beautiful things about vegetables gardens: You get to start with a clean slate each year and have a chance to improve and change your garden based on last year's experiences.

In the following descriptions of each vegetable, you find choice varieties, planting and care recommendations, harvest tips, and specific pests you need to watch out for. Many organic gardeners prefer to buy seeds and young transplants that were produced organically. Although many seed companies don't grow organic seeds, some specialize in them, and others offer them in addition to non-organically grown seeds. See the "Organic seed sources" sidebar in this chapter.

Alliums: Onions, shallots, garlic, and leeks

Onions, shallots, garlic, and leeks all belong to a group of pungent plants called *alliums*. These plants generally form bulbs or enlarged below-ground stems. Many members of the allium family make lovely additions to the flower garden.

Choosing an onion variety is more complicated than choosing most other vegetables because they fall into different groups based on sulfur content and the day length they need to form bulbs. *Pungent* varieties contain more sulfur, which makes them keep longer in storage and produce more tears when you cut them. *Sweet* varieties don't have as much sulfur and need to be used sooner after harvest. Adverse growing conditions, such as weed competition, drought, and poor fertility, can increase onions' sulfur content, even in the sweet varieties.

Onions are also referred to as short, long day, or intermediate. *Short-day* varieties form bulbs when they receive 11 to 12 hours of daylight. *Long-day* varieties need 14 to 16 hours of daylight to form bulbs. Choose long-day varieties, such as Walla Walla (sweet) and Copra (pungent) for northern climates. Go with short-day varieties, such as Granex (sweet) and White Bermuda (sweet) if you live south of 35 degrees latitude, which runs from northern South Carolina through Oklahoma and Arizona to central California. When in doubt, try an intermediate variety, such as Candy (sweet). You can start onions from seeds, transplants, or *sets,* which are small dormant bulbs.

Garlic varieties come in two types — soft-neck and hard-neck. *Soft-neck* kinds produce 12 to 18 small cloves and are best for long-term storage. *Hard-neck* types produce 6 to 12 cloves and don't keep as long in storage. Some favorite soft-neck varieties include Silverskin, while a good hard-neck variety is German Red. Ask around at farmers' markets for advice and choose a variety that suits your climate and soil type.

Shallots are mild tasting, small onions and the easiest to grow of all the edible alliums. Try Gray or Brittany varieties. Another onion relative, leeks, are indispensable in European cooking and are easy to grow in raised beds. Varieties include King Richard and Winter Giant.

Here are the basics about alliums:

- ✓ **Planting and care:** Alliums like well-drained, fertile, loose soil and appreciate raised beds. They grow well in cool weather and can take a light frost. Sow onion seeds indoors a few months before transplanting into the garden and keep the tops trimmed to about 3 inches high until transplant time. In moderate climates, sow seeds in fall for a spring harvest. In colder climates, sow seeds in early spring for a summer harvest. Plant shallot and onion sets in the spring. Cloves of garlic are best planted in fall, even in cold climates, to overwinter and mature the following summer. Start leeks indoors in spring 8 to 10 weeks before setting transplants into the garden. They mature in fall.

  Keep your alliums weed-free, well watered, and fertilized with a high phosphorous fertilizer, such as bone meal, to promote large bulb growth.

✔ **Harvesting:** When the tops begin to yellow, the bulbs are usually ready for harvest. After pulling them out of the ground, either use fresh or allow them to cure in a warm, airy room for a few weeks before storing in a cold basement. Use sweet onion varieties within a few weeks. Shallots, pungent onions, and some garlic varieties, however, can last for months in storage. Pull leeks as needed in fall, after cool weather "sweetens" their taste. Many varieties can withstand 20°F temperatures.

✔ **Pests and diseases:** Onion maggots are probably the worst pest of the allium family crops, feeding on onion roots and bulbs. Mulching, crop rotation, including carrots as a companion plant, and row covers help reduce the risks from these pests.

Asparagus

Asparagus plants are either female or male, and the best varieties of asparagus are the ones dubbed *all-male.* The female plants produce seeds, which reduce the amount of spears they produce. The males don't produce seeds and, therefore, produce more edible-sized spears. Good all-male varieties include Jersey Giant, Jersey King, and Jersey Knight. UC 157 is a good one for California.

Keep in mind the following asparagus-growing guidelines:

✔ **Planting and care:** Asparagus is a perennial vegetable that can live for 20 years, so take special care to create a proper planting bed. Choose a sunny location with well-drained soil. Dig a 1-foot-deep trench and add 6 inches of compost or well-rotted manure. Form 8-inch-high mounds, 18 inches apart, in the trench and lay the spider-like asparagus roots over the mounds, as shown in Figure 4-1. The *crowns,* where the roots meet the stems, should be about 5 to 6 inches below the soil surface. Cover them with 2 inches of soil and gradually backfill the trench, an inch or two at a time, as the asparagus spears grow until the trench is level with the surrounding soil. Fertilize the bed each spring with compost and a complete fertilizer. Keep the bed weed-free and well watered.

✔ **Harvesting:** Don't harvest any asparagus spears for the first year after you plant them. Let the crowns build up strength. The second year, harvest in spring only those spears larger than a pencil diameter for 3 to 4 weeks. In subsequent years, harvest pencil-diameter sized spears for up to 2 months. Let the remaining spears grow to rejuvenate the crown.

✔ **Pests and diseases:** Asparagus beetle is a hard-to-kill pest of asparagus. The adults damage the spears, and larvae eat the fern-like asparagus leaves. Control them by removing the ferns in late fall and spray with pyrethrins (see Chapter 3) in spring at first signs of this pest.

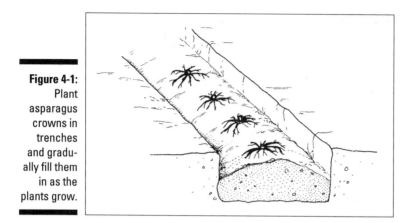

Figure 4-1:
Plant
asparagus
crowns in
trenches
and gradu-
ally fill them
in as the
plants grow.

Cole crops: Broccoli, cauliflower, cabbage, and company

These closely related plants share the same growing requirements, diseases, and pests. All thrive in cool spring and autumn weather and tolerate frost. Some of the best broccoli varieties include Premium Crop, Packman, and Green Comet. For good cauliflower, try Snow Crown and Fremont.

Cabbage varieties that perform well include Red Acre, Savoy Ace, Stonehead and, Dynamo. Some favorite kale varieties are Red Russian, Lacinato, and Vates Dwarf Blue Scotch Curled. Other not-so-common cole crops to try include Bubbles Brussels sprouts and Winner and Superschmeltz kohlrabi.

Heed these pointers when growing cole crops:

- **Planting and care:** Sow seeds directly into the ground or start transplants indoors 4 to 6 weeks before transplanting them outside. Cole crops need a moderate amount of fertilizer and water throughout the growing season to grow well but also like well-drained soil. Fertilize at planting and one month later with a complete fertilizer. Organic mulch, such as straw, placed around plants after transplanting helps keep the soil cool and moist.

  Take advantage of cool weather by sowing cole crops in early spring for an early summer harvest or late summer for a fall harvest. You can grow some varieties of broccoli, cabbage, and cauliflower through the winter in mild winter areas for harvest in spring.

  Be patient when planting Brussels sprouts. You want to plant them late enough (late May or even June) so that they don't mature until late fall. For best flavor, Brussels sprouts need to mature through several frosts.

- **Harvesting:** Harvest broccoli when the heads (clusters of flowers) are tightly packed and still green by cutting just below the head. In most cases, new, but smaller broccoli heads will grow further down the stem. If the yellow flowers begin to open, the taste becomes bitter and the plant will stop producing more heads. Harvest cabbage when they're firm when squeezed. Cut them as described for broccoli. To harvest white or *blanched* cauliflower, wrap the upper plant leaves around the developing, 3- to 4-inch heads. Harvest within 4 to 10 days. Harvest Brussels sprouts after cool weather in fall when the sprouts are still firm by twisting them off the stem. Pick kale leaves as needed.

✔ **Pests and diseases:** Cabbageworms and cabbage loopers are the two primary pests of cole crops. The larvae feed on the leaves, decimating the plant quickly. Handpick the caterpillars or spray *B.t.* (see Chapter 3) to control them. Cabbage maggots attack the roots of cole crops. Place row covers over the plants to prevent the fly from laying eggs at the base of the plant. Black rot and club root damage the roots and heads of cole crops — crop rotation is the best control for these diseases.

Eggplant

Eggplant, like its cousins, peppers and tomatoes, loves hot weather, plenty of water, and full sun. Eggplants come in many size and color varieties. A few favorites include the large, oval shaped Black Beauty (purple), and Rosa Bianca (lavender streaked). Long, narrow varieties include Ichiban (purple) and Thai Long (green). For small, round eggplants try Easter Egg (white) and Turkish Orange (orange).

Check out these eggplant-growing points:

✔ **Planting and care:** Start seeds indoors 8 weeks before transplanting outside. Wait until the soil has warmed to at least 60°F before transplanting. In colder climates or in small space gardens, consider planting eggplant in large containers to save space and get them to grow faster. Eggplants in containers also are very ornamental and look great as a decorative plant as well.

Eggplants like moderate fertility and water, so fertilizer monthly and mulch with black landscape fabric, but go easy on the nitrogen fertilizer or you'll have all foliage and few flowers and fruits.

✔ **Harvesting:** Harvest eggplant when they've reached the desired size for eating. Harvest before the skin color becomes dull-looking — a sign of over maturity and mushiness.

✔ **Pests and diseases:** Verticillium wilt disease is a main problem for eggplant and causes the entire plant to wilt and die in summer. The easiest solution to this soil-borne disease is to plant in containers filled with sterilized potting soil. Colorado potato beetles also love eggplant leaves. Handpicking adults, crushing eggs, and spraying with *B.t.* San Diego will control the larval stage of this pest.

Leafy greens: Lettuce, Swiss chard, spinach, and friends

Leafy greens are easy crops to grow because you don't have to wait for the flowers or fruits as with cucumbers or tomatoes — you just eat the leaves! Lettuce varieties are categorized by the way their leaves grow. *Head lettuces,* such as iceberg types, form compact balls of leaves. *Looseleaf lettuces,* at the other end of the spectrum, have loosely arranged leaves that don't form tight heads. Other types, such as butterhead, romaine, and oakleaf, fall somewhere in between. Popular varieties include Buttercrunch looseleaf, Rosalita red Romaine, Summertime crisphead, and Red Salad Bowl looseleaf.

Other leafy vegetable garden staples include Swiss chard, spinach, and an array of less well-known salad and cooking greens. Swiss chard varieties include Ruby, Bright Lights (with an array of multicolored stems) and Fordhook Giant. Good spinach varieties are Space, Tyee, and Bloomsdale Longstanding.

In the specialty greens category, grow arugula, dandelion, cress, chicory, mache, and mustard to give salad a zippy flavor. Many of these greens are blended together in mixes called *mesclun.*

For Asian cooking, grow pac choi, tatsoi, and mizuna. You can add these leafy vegetables to stir-fries or mix them into the salad bowl. Pac choi forms a loose cluster of juicy stems and dark green leaves. Tatsoi grows in a low rosette of spoon-shaped leaves that will regrow if you cut the leaves. Mizuna has slender stalks and fringed leaves.

Here are the basics of growing leafy greens:

> ✔ **Planting and care:** Most are cool-season crops, so you want to sow seeds or set transplants outdoors a few weeks before the last frost date. You can start some leafy greens, such as lettuce, indoors 3 to 4 weeks before setting them outdoors, giving plants a jump on the growing season. Stagger your crops of greens by planting small patches a couple weeks apart throughout the season: These plants mature quickly, and you'll want a consistent harvest of greens.
>
> Leafy greens need nitrogen first and foremost. Add compost before planting and add a supplemental nitrogen fertilizer, such as fish emulsion, every few weeks. Mulch the plants after they're established with an organic hay or straw mulch to keep the soil cool and moist. Keep the plants well watered to help prevent leaf-tip burn on lettuce.

✔ **Harvesting:** Harvest lettuce and greens when you're hungry and whenever leaves are big enough to eat. Pick off the lower leaves first so that new, younger leaves will continue to grow from the center of the plant. When greens such as arugula and lettuce *bolt* (send up a flower stalk), the leaves are probably too bitter tasting for most tastes, and you should pull up and compost them.

✔ **Pests and diseases:** Snails and slugs can devour a patch in no time. You can trap them, set up barriers, bait them, and, of course, handpick them to keep the populations low. Rabbits and woodchucks can also be a problem and fencing is the best cure for them. Leaf miner insects, especially on spinach, can ruin individual leaves. Just pick off and destroy the damaged leaves and the plant will be fine. (See Chapter 3 for more about how to discourage and prevent pests.)

Book VI

Organic Gardening

Legumes: Peas and beans

Legumes have a unique ability to make their own nitrogen fertilizer through a relationship with soil-dwelling bacteria called *rhizobia*. Beans enjoy warm weather, but peas produce better in cool weather.

You can eat beans fresh or allow the pods to mature for dry beans used in cooking. Popular dry bean varieties include Pinto, Yellow Eye, Midnight black turtle, and Red Kidney. Bean plants grow two different ways, either forming low bushy plants or climbing up a pole or trellis. In some cases, you can find pole and bush versions of the same variety. Good varieties include Blue Lake, Kentucky Wonder, Romano, and Improved Golden Wax bush beans and Blue Lake, Kentucky Wonder, Purple Pod, and Goldmarie pole beans.

Pea varieties also fall into two camps — those with edible pods and those grown just for fresh or dried seeds, called English peas. Good English pea varieties include Alderman, Daybreak, Lincoln, and Green Arrow. Peas with edible pods either have flat pods, called snow peas, or fat, juicy pods, called snap or sugar peas. Try Sugar Snap and Sugar Ann snap peas and Dwarf Gray Sugar for the classic snow peas used in stir-fries.

Check out the following tips for successful legume-growing:

✔ **Planting and care:** Legumes are easy to grow; sow them directly in well-drained soil. Plant beans when the soil has warmed to at least 60°F. Peas, however, need to be planted as soon as the soil has dried out in spring because they grow best before the summer heat arrives. Pole beans need poles for support, while tall pea varieties such as Sugar Snap, need a fence to climb. Keep the beds well weeded and watered. They generally don't need supplemental fertilizer.

✔ **Harvesting:** Harvest bush and pole beans when the pods are about 6 inches long and before the pods get bumpy from the seeds forming. Harvest dry beans after the pods have yellowed and withered. If they don't dry in the garden, you can pull up the whole plants and hang them to dry in an airy garage.

Harvest snap and English peas when the pods fill and are firm to the squeeze. Keep checking and tasting when the pods begin to size up to be sure you harvest at the peak of sweetness. Harvest snow peas at any point after the pods form.

✔ **Pests and diseases:** The Mexican bean beetle causes the most trouble. The adults are ladybug look-alikes, but they produce yellow colored young that love eating bean leaves. Handpick or use predatory insects, such as soldier bugs, to control them. Pea aphids attack pea plants and are easy to kill with just a stream of water from a hose. Watch out for rabbits and woodchucks — fences work best.

Rust fungal disease attacks beans and spreads quickly, especially if you work in the bean patch while the leaves are still wet. The plants and beans will develop yellow colored spots, which can kill the plant. Clean up plant debris in fall and stay away from the bean patch in wet weather.

Peppers

Peppers are warm-weather crops and are generally grouped according to their taste — sweet or hot. Hot peppers contain a chemical, especially in the seeds and ribs, called *capsaicin,* which makes peppers hot. This chemical can get on your hands during harvesting and processing and, if you rub an open wound or your eyes, can cause a painful burning. Harvest hot peppers with gloves and wash your hands after preparing to remove any capsaicin. Some hot pepper varieties to try are Ancho, Hungarian Hot Wax, Super Cayenne, and Super Chili.

Sweet peppers lack the bite of their hot-seeded brethren. Both hot and sweet varieties come in a rainbow of colors when mature. Some sweet pepper varieties to try include bell-shaped Arianne, California Wonder, Golden Summer, and North Star. Some elongated-shaped sweet pepper varieties are Corno di Toro, Gypsy, and Sweet Banana.

Peppers are great plants for container growing. Some varieties, such as Pretty in Purple with its colorful purple to red fruit and purple-tinged stems and leaves, are very ornamental.

Follow these guidelines for perfect peppers:

✔ **Planting and care:** Start seeds indoors 6 to 8 weeks before setting plants outside. Wait until the soil has warmed to 60°F before transplanting. Peppers need fertile soil and plenty of water to grow well. In cool areas, consider growing them in black fabric mulch to heat the soil and keep weeds away. Fertilize monthly with a complete fertilizer and add 1 tablespoon of Epsom salts to the water to help the peppers grow better. However, don't overfertilize peppers with nitrogen fertilizer, or you'll have all foliage and few flowers and fruits.

✔ **Harvesting:** Pepper fruits turn a rainbow of colors, depending on the variety, as they mature. You can pick them at the green stage or let them mature, when they reach their sweetest flavor. Hot peppers also can be harvested at any stage, but the flavor is hotter and better developed when you allow the pepper to mature on the plant.

✔ **Pests and diseases:** The pepper maggot is one of the more frustrating pests on sweet peppers. The adult fly lays an egg on the developing fruits; the egg hatches into small, white worms that tunnel into the fruit and cause it to rot. Cover the plants with row covers early in the season to discourage the adult from laying eggs. Sprays are of little use because the worm is inside the fruit. Fruitworms (see the "Sweet corn" section) and wilt disease (see the "Eggplant" section) also cause trouble.

Root crops: Carrots, beets, and radishes

Root crops provide good eating well into the fall and winter and are easy to grow. Raised beds filled with loose, fertile, stone-free soil provide just the right environment. Some great carrot varieties to try include Scarlet Nantes, Danvers Half Long, Sweetness II, and Sweet Sunshine. Some good beet varieties include Detroit Dark Red, Ace, and Chioggia. A few choice radish varieties to grow include Easteregg, Cherry Belle, and French Breakfast.

Grow great root crops with these tips:

✔ **Planting and care:** To thrive, root crops generally need loose soil that's well-amended with compost, weed-free growing conditions, and water. Directly sow root crop seeds a few weeks before the last frost date for your area. Sow them lightly and cover with sand, potting soil, or grass clippings and keep moist. Radishes germinate within a few days; carrots may take 2 weeks. Try mixing radish and carrot seeds to help mark the row and harvest the radishes before the carrots need the space.

Thin seedlings so the eventual spacing is about 2 to 4 inches apart, depending on the crop. If you don't thin root crops when they're young, they won't get large enough to eat. You can eat the thinned beet greens.

  ✔ **Harvesting:** Pull up radishes when the roots get large enough to eat. Leave carrots and beets in the ground to harvest as needed. Their flavor gets sweeter after the soil cools. You can even cover carrots in late fall with a cold frame, fill it with hay mulch, and harvest carrots all winter.

  ✔ **Pests and diseases:** Other than four-legged critters such as rabbits, which love to eat the carrot and beet tops, the biggest pest of carrot is the rust fly. The adult fly lays an egg near the carrot, and the small larvae tunnels into the carrot root. Cover the crop with a row cover to prevent the fly from laying an egg. Swallowtail butterfly larvae also like to munch on carrot tops, so try to grow enough for both of you!

Potatoes

Look for early-, mid-, and late-season potato varieties to stretch out your harvest. Early potatoes are ready to harvest about 65 days after planting — perfect for summer potato salads. Midseason varieties mature in 75 to 80 days, and late ones take 90 days or more to harvest. The later varieties keep longer in storage. Potatoes are also roughly divided into baking and boiling varieties. Baking potatoes, such as Butte and Yukon Gold, have drier, more mealy-textured flesh, while boiling potatoes, such as Kennebec, Carola, and Red Norland, are moist and waxy.

If you're looking for something new to try, plant fingerling potatoes. These varieties produce long, slim, tasty tubers and tend to yield more per pound planted than regular potatoes. Favorites include Russian Banana, which has yellow flesh and skin, and French Fingerling and Rose Finn Apple, which have pink skin and yellow flesh. Colorful varieties of regular potatoes include All Blue, All Red, and lavender-skinned Caribe.

Here's the lowdown on growing potatoes:

  ✔ **Planting and care:** Potatoes are another cool season root crop that can be planted a few weeks before your last frost date. They grow rather unpretentiously and without much maintenance until late summer when you dig the roots. Potatoes grow best in loose soil that hasn't been amended with fertilizer. Too much nitrogen fertilizer in particular can lead to poor tuber formation. Keep the soil moist by watering or applying organic mulches, such as hay or straw.

  Purchase potato tubers or *seed potatoes* and cut large potatoes into smaller pieces with at least one "eye" or bud. Place them in 1-foot deep trenches about 1 foot apart. Fill in the trench with soil as they sprout and grow, eventually mounding or hilling around the plants with soil. Hilling the soil around the plants allows the roots to form more potatoes, kills weeds, and protects the tubers from the light. Tubers exposed to light turn green (and in doing so produce mild toxins that can hurt you if you make a steady diet of green potatoes) and have an off flavor.

✔ **Harvesting:** When the potato tops turn yellow and begin to die back, it's time to dig up the tubers. With a shovel or iron fork, carefully dig around the potato plants and lift up the tubers. Let them cure in a dark, airy, 50°F-room for a few weeks, and then store them in a cool basement at about 40°F. Eat any damaged potatoes immediately and never store potatoes and apples near each other because apples give off ethylene gas, which causes potatoes and other vegetables to spoil.

✔ **Pests and diseases:** The Colorado potato beetle is the most famous pest. This yellow and black-striped beetle lays orange eggs on the undersides of leaves, which hatch into voracious orange-red larvae that devour potato and eggplant leaves. Handpick the adults and crush the eggs. Spray *B.t.* SanDiego to control the larvae. Wireworms attack potato tubers under ground, causing tunneling and rotting. They're mostly a problem in new gardens created from lawns.

Fungal diseases, such as potato scab and blight, can ruin a crop. Your first defense is to buy resistant varieties. Control potato scab by lowering the soil pH to below 6 and avoid using manure fertilizer. Control blight by planting your potato crop in a new place every year, buying certified disease-free tubers, mulching, and keeping weeds under control.

Book VI

Organic Gardening

Sweet corn

As soon as you harvest corn, the sugars in the kernels begin to turn to starch, making the corn less sweet as time goes by. But many new sweet corn varieties stay sweeter longer after harvest because plant breeders breed them to contain *supersweet* characteristics. These varieties, which include Bodacious (yellow), Honey NPearl (bicolor), and How Sweet It Is (white), must be planted at least 25 to 100 feet from other, nonsupersweet varieties. If another variety pollinates a supersweet variety, the kernels may be tough and starchy.

If you're satisfied with regular, old-fashioned varieties, choose from those with yellow, white, or both-colored kernels called *bicolor.* If you plant yellow and white varieties near each other, you may get bicolor corn, anyway. Some favorites include Silver Queen (white) and Early Sunglow (yellow).

Corn requires the following care:

✔ **Planting and care:** Sweet corn needs a well-drained, highly fertile soil and warm weather to grow well. Sow seeds in blocks of 4 to 5 short rows after the soil has warmed to 65°F. Separate blocks of different corn varieties from each other by at least 25 feet so that no cross-pollination occurs. Hoe soil up around the plants when they're 8 inches tall to support them during windy days and to destroy young weeds that compete with the corn plants. Fertilize at planting (with compost) and again when the corn is knee-high (with a high nitrogen fertilizer, such as soybean meal). Fertilize a final time with the same fertilizer when the silk emerges at the tips of the ears.

✔ **Harvesting:** Start checking for maturity when the corn ears feel full and the silks are brown. You can take a peek under the husks at the corn ear tip to see whether the kernels have matured. The kernels should still appear glossy, not dull, and any juice from pricking the kernel should be milky. Pick the ears on the young side for the sweetest and most tender flavor.

✔ **Pests and diseases:** Major corn pests include the corn earworm and corn borer. The earworm larvae tunnel into the tip of the corn ear, causing only cosmetic damage. The ear is still edible. Spray *B.t.* on the silks or apply a few drops of mineral oil when ears are young to kill the earworm larvae. Varieties with extra tight husks, such as Tuxedo, resist damage.

The corn borer larva causes more major damage to a plant by tunneling into the leaves and stalk. *B.t.* sprays and crop rotation can lessen the problems from corn borers. Raccoons are the other major corn pests. An electric fence is the best — and maybe the only — defense against these clever animals.

Tomatoes

Tomato, easily the most popular garden vegetable, boasts varieties with fruit available in many sizes, shapes, and colors. The plants, however, fall into two categories. *Determinate* varieties stop growing taller when they reach a certain height and need minimal support, making them ideal for containers. *Indeterminate* varieties just keep on growing taller and taller, like Jack's beanstalk! Indeterminate tomatoes require trellising, but yield more fruit per square foot of garden space.

Most gardeners grow tomatoes for three main purposes — slicing, snacks, and sauce. Some of the popular standard, round-shaped, slicing tomato varieties include Celebrity and Early Girl (red), Brandywine (pink), Lemon Boy (yellow), Big Rainbow (striped yellow and red), and Big Beef (red). For snacking, try cherry tomato varieties Sun Gold (gold), Super Sweet 100 (red), Sweet Million (red), and Yellow Pear (yellow). Great plum-shaped tomatoes, which gardeners use to make sauce, include Amish Paste, Roma, Bellstar, Heinz 2653, and Viva Italia.

Use the following guidelines for growing tomatoes:

✔ **Planting and care:** Tomatoes grow best when transplanted into 60°F soil and kept warm. Mulching with black landscape fabric in cool areas helps speed along their growth. They need fertile soil, so amend the soil with compost before planting and then side-dress plants monthly with a complete fertilizer. Keep plants mulched and well watered to avoid blossom end rot (rotting of the end of maturing tomatoes) as fruits mature.

TIP

Plant tall and leggy tomato transplants up to within 4 inches of their tops in a deep hole or lay them on their side in a trench, as shown in Figure 4-2, and the stem will root. Place a tomato cage or trellis support around the plants at planting time. Tie or wind indeterminate varieties around their supports as they grow and prune off extra side shoots to keep the plant from getting too bushy.

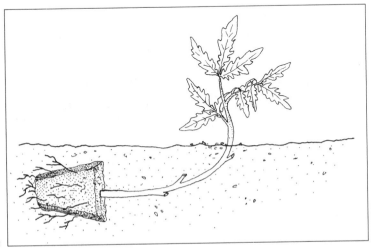

Figure 4-2: Plant leggy tomato transplants horizontally in a trench.

✔ **Harvesting:** Let the fruits turn red (or whatever color was intended). The longer you leave them on the vine, the deeper the color and sweeter and fuller the fruit flavor. However, even if you pick too early, fruits continue ripening indoors if you put them in a warm, airy room.

✔ **Pests and diseases:** The main insect pests are tomato hornworms and tomato fruitworms. You can control both of these caterpillars with *B.t.,* although you can easily handpick hornworms. Nematodes can also attack tomato roots, causing the roots to be deformed and the plants to be stunted and unproductive. Choose nematode resistant varieties if these microscopic soil pests are a problem in your area.

Leaf blight diseases often start as small spots on leaves and then expand to yellow areas, killing leaves and the plant if unchecked. To control these diseases, clean up crop debris at the end of the growing season, rotate crops and mulch to prevent the disease spores from splashing onto leaves during rains. Wilt diseases, such as Verticillium and Fusarium, can cause plants to suddenly wilt and die in midseason. Purchase plants that are wilt resistant (usually indicated in the variety description) and remove and destroy infected plants as soon as you can to prevent the disease from spreading.

Organic seed sources

One way to support organic farming is to purchase organically grown vegetable seeds for your garden. Some seed companies and mail-order catalogs specialize in organic seeds or at least offer as many organically grown seed varieties as they can. Here are a few sources to get you started:

✔ **Abundant Life Seed Foundation** works to preserve heirloom seeds and promote sustainable agriculture worldwide. It offers seeds through its Web site and a mail-order catalog. Visit ALSF at its Web site (www.abundantlifeseeds.com) for more information about its mission.

✔ **Seeds of Change** sells only organic, open-pollinated seeds and plants and is dedicated to preserving sustainable agriculture.

Visit its informative Web site at www.seedsofchange.com.

✔ **Seed Savers Exchange** is a not-for-profit organization that preserves and offers over 11,000 varieties of heirloom seeds through its membership exchange program. Nonmembers can also order seeds through its catalog. Visit its Web site at www.seedsavers.org.

✔ **Fedco Seeds** is organized as a cooperative with workers and customers sharing in their profits. It sells seeds, potato tubers, and lots of gardening supplies. In its very informative and extensive catalog, it discloses the sources of the seeds it offers, some of which are grown specifically for the cooperative. Download a catalog from the co-op's Web site, www.fedcoseeds.com.

Vining crops: Cucumbers, squash, pumpkins, and melons

All these crops share the common trait of growing their fruits on long, trailing vines, although some varieties now grow more compact and bush-like. Many of these species can pollinate each other, too, making it nearly impossible to get seeds that grow fruit resembling the original varieties.

Cucumbers are classified as either *slicers* (long and thin) or *picklers* (short and prickly). Good slicing varieties include Fanfare and Suyo Long. For pickles, try Bush Pickle or Calypso.

Squash are grouped as either summer squash (for example, Black Zucchini, Sunburst patty pan, and Yellow Crookneck) or winter squash (Table King [acorn], Burgess Buttercup, and Waltham Butternut). Winter squash fruits develop hard skin and dense flesh, making them good for storing through the fall and early winter.

Pumpkins range in dimension from apple-sized to something resembling a small Volkswagen Beetle. Some are used for cooking, while others are better for carving and ornament. For pies and soup, grow New England Pie, Baby Pam, or Small Sugar. For carving, Howden and Connecticut Field are among the standards. Grow Atlantic Giant or Big Max for the big pumpkin contest at the county fair.

And finally, a few good melons include Earli-Dew and Burpee Hybrid muskmelon, Crimson Sweet and yellow-fleshed Yellow Doll watermelon, and French Orange, a muskmelon/Charentais cross. Cantaloupes, by the way, have smoother skins and smaller seed cavities than muskmelons, but they taste pretty much the same. Charentais are orange-fleshed French melons that resemble muskmelons. For something delicious and unusual, grow green-fleshed Passport cantaloupe.

Here are tips for vining crops:

- ✔ **Planting and care:** These warm-weather crops need heat, water, and fertility to grow best. Directly sow these vegetables 1 to 2 weeks after your last frost date when the soil is at least 60°F. In colder areas, start seedlings indoors 3 to 4 weeks before setting them outdoors.

    Even though many bush varieties are available, most squash-family plants need room to spread their vines, so space them according to seed packet instructions. Amend the soil at planting with a layer of compost and side-dress the plants with a complete fertilizer when they start vining. Keep the plants well watered.

    Squash-family crops need bees to pollinate the flowers in order to get fruit. Plant bee-attracting flowers around the garden to ensure fruit pollination. If fruits form but rot and drop off before enlarging, it's probably due to poor pollination.

- ✔ **Harvesting:** Pick cucumbers when they are 4 to 6 inches long, before the seeds enlarge. Harvest summer squash when they're small and the flowers are still attached for best flavor and to keep the plants producing well. Harvest winter squash and pumpkins when the varieties turn the desired color and your thumbnail can't puncture the skin when pressed.

    Harvest muskmelons when they easily slip off the vine when lifted. Watermelons are harvested when the skin color turns from shiny to dull and the spot where it rests on the ground turns from white to yellow. Also, check the last *tendril* (curlicues coming off the stems) before the fruit. When it turns brown, it's harvest time. Protect all squash family plants and fruits from frost.

- ✔ **Pests and diseases:** Squash-family vegetables have their own whole set of insects and diseases — many named after the plants they attack. The most prominent ones include

    - Cucumber beetles, which are yellow and black-striped

    - Spotted beetles, which feed on young cucumbers, melons, and squash

- Squash vine borers, which attack mostly squash and pumpkins

- Squash bugs (turn to Chapter 7 for more detailed information on these bad guys)

Bacterial wilt disease attacks mostly cucumber and melons. The plants wilt during the day and are slow to recover even if well watered. Control this disease by planting resistant varieties and controlling cucumber beetles that spread the disease.

For more about growing vegetables, check out *Vegetable Gardening For Dummies* by Charlie Nardozzi and the Editors of the National Gardening Association (Wiley).

Growing and Using Herbs

How and where you choose to grow herbs is limited only by your imagination and, of course, the needs and characteristics of the plants themselves. Most herb plants aren't too fussy about the soil they grow in as long as it's well drained. Soggy soil spells trouble for herbs, but young plants need moisture after transplanting until they begin growing vigorously. Water mature plants during times of drought to prevent wilting and stress. If you're growing herbs simply for their ornamental flowers or foliage, give them fertile garden soil. Herbs grown for fragrance and flavor, however, are more pungent if grown in less fertile soil, so go easy on the fertilizer.

You can fit herbs into your garden and landscape in myriad ways. Tuck herbs into your flower garden, plant them among your vegetables, or give them a special garden of their own. Take advantage of their flowers or leaves to add spark to container gardens and window boxes. Use creeping kinds between paving stones or let them trail over retaining walls. Even if you're challenged for space, you can grow some herbs on a sunny windowsill as houseplants. If you need a few ideas on where to grow herbs, here's a list for inspiration:

- ✔ **Herb garden:** Take an herbs-only approach and design an intricately patterned garden. A typical arrangement consists of a geometric border of tidy, compact plants, such as basil or lavender, which surrounds groupings of herbs with contrasting foliage colors and textures. For a simple, utilitarian herb garden, try a four-patch design that features four same-size triangles, squares, or rectangles separated by 2-foot walkways.

- ✔ **Ground cover:** Creeping herbs, such as thyme and mint, can cover large areas quickly or fill in the gaps between stones in a path. Let them trail over a wall to add color and soften the effect of the stone.

✔ **Vegetable gardens:** Some herbs make natural companions for vegetable plants. Basil, for example, is said to improve tomatoes, while dill and cabbages complement each other. Stick to well-behaved herbs that don't spread by roots or rhizomes, however, or else your garden may be overrun by too much of a good thing.

✔ **Flower gardens:** Many herbs have beautiful flowers or foliage that add color and texture to flower borders. As a bonus, some attract butterflies and provide food for their larva. Good additions to your flower garden include catnip, lavender, chamomile, borage, and oregano.

✔ **Containers:** Treat them as ornamental plants or bring your culinary herbs closer to the kitchen by planting them in pots, tubs, or baskets. Use trailing thyme or rosemary to hang over the side and add colorful sages, parsley, oregano, and chives. In cold climates, grow tender herbs, such as rosemary and bay, in pots that you can bring indoors for the winter. Be sure to give these Mediterranean-climate plants 14 to 16 hours of bright light year 'round to keep them happy. Be careful to keep the soil moist, but never soggy.

Although many herbs are ornamental, most people grow them to harvest. Most herbs have fragrant or pungently flavored leaves or flowers that make them useful for cooking, crafts, and potpourri and adding aroma to cosmetics. Some have attractive stems, leaves, or other plant parts that can be dried or preserved for wreaths and arrangements. Consider the following ways to use harvested herbs:

✔ **Food and drink:** Herbal teas, from soothing chamomile to refreshing mint, offer alternatives to stronger brews, and no supper is complete without seasonings for soup and salad, meat, and vegetable. Indispensable edible herbs include basil, chives, coriander, dill, horseradish, marjoram, mint, oregano, parsley, sage, and thyme.

✔ **Fragrance:** Homes and people haven't always smelled as pleasant as they do today. In the days before frequent bathing, central vacuum cleaners, and indoor plumbing, herbs played a large role in odor control. Sweet Annie, peppermint, chamomile, and lavender, for example, can scent a room or a closet, masking the odors of cooking, wet dogs, or any other smelly aroma. *Aromatherapy,* the art and science of affecting mood with scent, makes liberal use of dried herbs in little pillows and bowls of potpourri.

✔ **Crafts:** Dried wreaths, arrangements, and other crafts depend on herbs for color, structure, and fragrance. The long silvery stems of artemesia, for example, make excellent wreath foundations. Dried lavender flower spikes add elegance to everlasting arrangements. Some herbs lend their colors to fabric and paints.

- ✔ **Medicine:** People have used herbs to treat every ailment known to mankind. Many herbs do contain chemicals, such as those used for heart medicine and to treat pain. Laymen can safely use aromatic herbs to add zip or tranquilizing effects to ointments, massage oils, and baths. Check out *Herbal Remedies For Dummies* (Wiley) by Christopher Hobbs to find more ways to use herbs as medicines.

Another, often overlooked way to use herbs is as landscape and garden plants. They serve several important functions:

- ✔ **Ornament:** Flowers, attractive leaves, and shapes from sprawling to towering give herbs a place in any garden. Several varieties of sage, for example, have colorful golden, purple, white, or gray-green leaves. Rue and compact artemesia varieties with silvery leaves are prized in decorative herb gardens.

- ✔ **Companion plants:** Some herbs reputably aid the growth of other plants by repelling insect pests, discouraging disease, and helping nutrients become more readily available. Members of the onion family, such as chives, for example, may keep bugs away from roses and other flowers.

- ✔ **Insect habitat:** Most insects are good for your garden, so it pays to encourage them to come on in and stay awhile. Herbs with small, nectar-rich flowers, such as dill, fennel, thyme, caraway, and parsley, attract some of the most important beneficial insects.

Planting Popular Herbs

Useful herbs number in the hundreds, at least. This section highlights a few of the most commonly grown herbs, providing tips for tending and using herbs from basil to thyme.

Basil

Easily one of the most popular culinary herbs grown, basil is an annual that comes in more than 30 varieties that include both ornamental and tasty forms. For plenty of pesto, grow sweet basil varieties, such as Mammoth or Large Leaf, in your vegetable garden. Or try some with unusual foliage, such as purple-leafed Dark Opal and Purple Ruffles or frilly Green Ruffles. To edge a garden or spice up a patio planter, grow compact, small-leafed varieties, such as Spicy Globe or Green Globe. For an alternative taste sensation, grow lemon, anise, cinnamon, and Thai basil varieties.

✔ **Planting and care:** Give basil moist, fertile, well-drained soil and space plants about 1 foot apart in full sun. Water them in dry weather and pinch off young flower buds to prevent bloom and encourage more leaves. Sow seeds directly in the garden or start indoors and protect from frost, which will kill basil.

✔ **Special uses:** Plant with tomatoes to discourage tomato hornworms. Dry the leaves or use fresh to flavor food.

Chamomile

Choose from 2- to 3-foot-tall German chamomile *(Matricaria recutita)* or creeping, 9-inch Roman chamomile *(Chamaemelum nobile),* depending on your garden desires. The perennial Roman species is hardy through Zone 3 and thrives in cool, damp climates. German chamomile is an annual. Both plants have lacy, aromatic, apple-scented foliage and small, daisy-like flowers.

✔ **Planting and care:** Sow seeds directly in the garden and keep moist until well established. Chamomile can tolerate some drought after that and appreciates full sun. Harvest the flowers when fully open and dry them on screens in an airy place. Plants self-sow prolifically, so after you plant some, you'll have chamomile for a long time.

✔ **Special uses:** The dried flowers make a popular tea for relieving stress and heartburn. They're also used in many cosmetics and toiletries. Roman chamomile makes an excellent ground cover or mowed lawn in mild, moist climates similar to England or the Pacific Northwest.

Chives

Grassy, onion-flavored foliage make chives popular in the culinary arts, but this perennial plant makes a good 1-foot-tall addition to the ornamental landscape and vegetable garden, too. The dense tufts of lavender-purple flowers bloom in early summer. The related species, garlic chives, grows about 2 feet tall and has starry white flowers in late summer to early fall. Both species self-sow freely.

✔ **Planting and care:** The best way to obtain chives is to divide a clump into groups of slender bulbs and plant in any well-drained garden soil. It prefers full sun, but isn't fussy. If you sow from seed, cover the seeds lightly with soil, keep moist, and be patient — they may take 2 to 3 weeks to sprout. Keep weeds away to make harvesting easier. Harvest by shearing the stems to within a few inches of the ground.

✔ **Special uses:** The pungent foliage reportedly repels some injurious pests, especially around roses, tomatoes, carrots, grapes, and apples. Puree the leaves in the blender with water, strain, and use as a spray to prevent powdery mildew. The flowers attract beneficial insects. Use in cooking as you would onions or serve fresh in salads, dips, and sauces.

Coriander and cilantro

This herb is so versatile that it bears two names — cilantro for the roots and leaves and coriander for the seeds. The flat, parsley-like leaves add pungency to Latin American and Asian dishes. The seeds play a major role in curry and other Middle Eastern fare. It's an annual herb that ancient Mediterranean people prescribed for many medical ailments.

✔ **Planting and care:** Sow directly into fertile garden soil where seeds will sprout in a couple of weeks. Plant every 2 to 3 weeks for continuous harvest because the plants tend to set seed quickly, especially in hot weather, and stop producing new foliage. Harvest young tender leaves before the plants send up flower stalks. Harvest seeds when seed heads turn brown, but before they scatter, and dry thoroughly before using for best flavor.

✔ **Special uses:** Use leaves and seeds in cooking. Plant near aphid-prone crops to help repel pests. The flowers also attract beneficial insects.

Dill

Another member of the aromatic carrot family, dill's seeds are an essential ingredient in pickles, breads, and other savory dishes. The fine, thread-like foliage is rich in vitamins and flavor for fish, sauces, and dips. Tall, narrow plants of this annual herb grow 2 to 3 feet tall. Choose the variety Bouquet for seeds or Dukat or 18-inch-tall Fernleaf if you want mainly leaves.

✔ **Planting and care:** Sow seeds directly into fertile, sunny garden soil. Barely cover the seeds and sow again every few weeks for continuous harvest. Protect from strong winds.

✔ **Special uses:** Flowers attract beneficial insects and the foliage is a favorite of swallowtail butterfly larvae. It reputedly makes a good companion for cabbage crops and can be planted with low-growing lettuce and cucumbers. Use seeds and leaves in cooking.

Fennel

Useful in cooking and in the garden, 4- to 8-foot-tall fennel has a tropical look and resembles giant dill plants. The common fennel is hardy in Zones 6 through 9, but you can grow it as an annual in cooler climates. It self-sows and can become a nuisance weed in warm climates. Try the bronze-red-leafed variety Purpureum as an ornamental plant. If you want to eat the root, look for the annual or biennial plant called finocchio or Florence fennel.

- ✔ **Planting and care:** Sow directly in fertile, sunny soil where you want it to grow. Its long taproot makes it difficult to transplant. Protect from strong wind.

- ✔ **Special uses:** You can use all parts of fennel — from the bulb-like root to the leaves, stalks, and seeds. Harvest seeds when they turn brown and snip leaves and stems as needed and use fresh or cooked lightly in soups and sauces. Flowers attract many beneficial insects.

Lavender

One of the most recognized and popular scents for cosmetics, toiletries, and aromatherapy, lavender also adds drama to your flower garden. A number of different species exist, but all have needle-like foliage and spikes of purplish blue flowers. The English lavender varieties, such as purple Hidcote and Munstead, grow up to 24 inches high and are hardy through Zone 5. Pink-flowering varieties include Hidcote Pink and Miss Katherine. Other species are less hardy, but equally appealing and include spike, French, and fringed lavenders.

- ✔ **Planting and care:** Start from stem cuttings because seeds may not give you plants of uniform quality. Plant in compost-enriched, very well-drained, even gravelly soil in full sun. Space plants 2 to 3 feet apart for a low hedge or mass planting. Prune in early spring to encourage bushy growth.

- ✔ **Special uses:** Harvest flowers as they begin to open. Dry them in bundles hung upside down in an airy place. Flowers attract bees and beneficial insects.

Mint

With 20 or so species and more than 1,000 varieties, you should find a mint to suit any taste. Peppermint and spearmint are the most popular, but other fruit-flavored varieties exist. Some also have variegated foliage, including pineapple mint Varieagata. Some mints creep along low to the ground, such as Corsican mint, and others grow 2 to 3 feet tall. Hardiness varies with the variety and species.

- ✔ **Planting and care:** Start new plants from stem cuttings of the varieties you want so that you're sure to get the flavor or scent you expect. Plant just below the soil surface and keep them moist until they begin to grow. Mints can be invasive, so contain them or plant where you don't mind a carpet of fragrant foliage.

- ✔ **Special uses:** Harvest the fresh leaves and add them to Middle Eastern dishes, soups, vegetables, and beverages. Mint flowers attract beneficial insects, and the fragrant plants reportedly repel some damaging insects and improve the health and flavor of nearby cabbages and tomatoes.

Oregano

Small fragrant leaves on sprawling 1 to 2-foot stems topped by loose spikes of white to pink flowers give oregano a casual appeal for planting in vegetable and flower gardens or trailing over a wall or basket. Choose plants carefully by pinching a leaf to test flavor and pungency. Some varieties, such as Aureum Crispum and Compactum are more ornamental than edible. It's a hardy perennial in Zones 5 and warmer.

- ✔ **Planting and care:** Start new plants from stem cuttings to guarantee the best flavor. Seed-grown plants may lack their parents' pungent flavor. Any average, well-drained soil in full sun will do. Harvest leaves as needed or cut the plant down to a few inches from the ground and hang the sprigs to dry.

- ✔ **Special uses:** The tiny flower clusters attract bees, butterflies, and other beneficial insects. The fresh and dried leaves add classic flavor to many Latin American and Mediterranean dishes. Some varieties look good in hanging baskets, patio containers, and flower gardens.

Parsley

A common garnish on restaurant plates, parsley is probably the most recognized herb. The leaves contain loads of vitamins A and C and help sweeten garlic breath. Although both varieties are edible, the flat-leafed variety has stronger flavor while the curly-leafed kind is more commonly used as garnish. Plants are biennial, hardy through Zone 5, and bloom only in their second year. The 1-foot-tall plants form tidy bright green mounds of ornamental foliage. Plant in vegetable and flower gardens or in container gardens.

- ✔ **Planting and care:** Soak seeds overnight before sowing and plant directly in the garden. If you start seeds indoors, plant them in *peat pots* (biodegradable compressed peat moss containers) so that you don't have to disturb their taproot when transplanting them later. Give the plants fertile garden soil and a cool, slightly shady spot in hot summer climates. Snip fresh leaves as needed or cut the whole plant to a few inches high and dry the leaves on screen.

- ✔ **Special uses:** Use for cooking, especially in Greek and Middle Eastern dishes. Makes an attractive ornamental garden plant and serves as food for swallowtail butterfly larvae. Flowers attract beneficial insects.

Rosemary

Two species of this tender perennial evergreen shrub exist — upright and prostrate — and both are fragrant and edible. The short, needle-like foliage gives off a heady, distinctive aroma when lightly bruised. Ornamental varieties include those with golden or variegated leaves, pink or bright blue flowers, and especially sprawling or upright forms.

- ✔ **Planting and care:** Start from rooted stem cuttings and plant in well-drained garden soil. Rosemary doesn't tolerate soggy soil or complete drought. Although hardy only to Zone 8, you can grow rosemary in a greenhouse or indoors under strong light. Plant it in a pot at least 1 foot deep to accommodate its taproot and maintain humidity by setting it over moist pebbles or misting the plant a few times a week.

- ✔ **Special uses:** As an ornamental, rosemary excels in the low shrub border or trailing over a low wall. Its aromatic foliage is said to repel flying insects from cabbages and other vegetables. Use fresh sprigs in meat stews; use dried rosemary for either culinary use or to scent rooms and linens.

Sage

In Zones 5 and warmer, sage is a perennial that grows into a shrubby mound of fragrant leaves. It can grow up to 2 feet tall. The 2- to 3-inch-long leaves are fuzzy and oval and range in color from silver-green, purple, golden to mixed white, green, and pink, depending on the variety. Sage is equally at home in the herb garden and amongst the ornaments in a container or flowerbed. In late spring, sage has spikes of blue flowers, although some varieties have white flowers. A number of different sage species exist and they range in hardiness, pungency, and size. A favorite, pineapple sage is only winter hardy to Zone 8, but its soft-textured, fruity pineapple-scented foliage and red flowers make a beautiful addition to a flower garden.

- **Planting and care:** Starting sage from stem cuttings is easier than starting from seeds. Plant in organically rich, well-drained garden soil and give it full sun. Avoid soggy soil. Prune to keep the growth compact.

- **Special uses:** The spiky flowers attract bees and other beneficial insects and look great in the garden. Use it to scent dresser drawers and to help prevent damaging clothes moths. Use the leaves, either fresh or dried, in poultry and meat dishes.

Thyme

Hundreds of thyme species and varieties exist and they range in height from creeping, 1-inch-high mats to 18-inch shrubs. They all have tiny, roundish leaves, and their colors range from wooly gray to smooth green to golden to white-edged. Even their fragrance varies from very mild to pungent and includes lemon, caraway, coconut, and more. Creeping thyme makes a fragrant and attractive groundcover and excels between paving stones, while shrubby types are useful low hedges. Clusters of tiny white, pink, or crimson flowers bloom in summer, sometimes covering the plants. The creeping thymes are the hardiest and survive in Zone 4.

- **Planting and care:** Start with rooted stem cuttings to guarantee the flavor and appearance of your thyme. Plant in organically enriched, well-drained soil in full sun. Divide the plants every few years and keep them pruned to encourage dense growth.

- **Special uses:** Flowers attract bees and many beneficial insects. Much folklore exists on the use of thyme as a helpful companion plant for roses and vegetables. Use between patio and walkway stones or plant as a groundcover to replace lawn in small areas. The trailing kinds look good in hanging baskets and planters. Harvest the leaves and young stems for cooking.

Chapter 5

Finding Organic Success
with Fruit

*F*ew plants give you more bang for your buck than berries. Homegrown raspberries, strawberries, blueberries, and grapes take little space and return months of mouthwatering fruit salads, pies, pancakes, and fresh-eating goodness. Some of these berries are easy to grow organically, while others present a real challenge. Choosing disease-resistant varieties, using pest and disease control methods, and planting correctly goes a long way toward producing healthful, pesticide-free berries.

Freshly picked fruit from your own trees and shrubs is juicy joy — and easier to grow than you may think. Sure, some fruit trees need more attention than many other plants, but the harvest is worth the effort. Many fruit varieties that you can grow at home taste far better than supermarket fruit.

Better flavor is reason enough to grow your own fruit. But if you're concerned about pesticides, you have another compelling reason, as well. Cherries, peaches, apples, strawberries, and apricots are among the 12 most pesticide-contaminated foods, according the Environmental Working Group, compiled from FDA and EPA data (www.njenvironment.org/organicproduce.htm).

Even if you have nothing more than a large patio planter, you can grow your own fruit; on a half-acre lot, you can plant an orchard large enough to provide fruit for yourself and half the neighborhood. As a bonus, most fruit trees and shrubs are ornamental, too, especially when blooming.

Finding Your Zone

Unlike vegetables, most fruit plants come back year after year, which means you need to choose the right plant for where you live. (Forget about growing pomegranates in Vermont, for example.)

The United States Department of Agriculture (USDA) divided North America, Europe, and China into 11 zones based on each area's expected average annual minimum temperature — its *hardiness zone.* The USDA Plant Hardiness Zone Map for North America (see Figure 5-1) enables you to find your hardiness zone, which you can find on plant tags and in the information throughout this section.

Figure 5-1:
The USDA Plant Hardiness Zone Maps indicate each zone's expected average annual minimum temperature.

Discovering Berry Patch Basics

Site selection and preparation are more critical with berries than with nearly any other food crop you may grow because most of these plants stay in place for years. The varieties you choose, where you plant them, and how you prepare and maintain the soil determine whether your berry patch produces bumper crops or becomes a disappointing chore.

As you make decisions about where to plant your berry patch, keep in mind the following requirements:

✔ **Sun:** All fruits need at least 6 hours — preferably more — of full sun each day to produce large, flavorful crops.

✔ **Air circulation and drainage:** Moving air helps prevent disease organisms from settling on vulnerable fruits and leaves, so choose a slightly breezy site, if possible. High winds cause damage, however, so protect crops with a windbreak, if needed.

Cold air settles at the bottom of slopes, where it may damage early blooming flowers in the spring or ripening fruit in the fall. Plant your fruits on the slope of a hill instead of at the bottom.

✔ **Soil moisture and drainage:** With the exception of elderberry, all small fruits need well-drained soil. Soggy soil encourages root diseases, which are among the most serious problems for fruits. If your soil drains poorly, however, you can still grow fruits in raised beds. Make beds 6 to 10 inches high and 4 feet wide and amend with plenty of organic matter.

✔ **Soil amendments and fertility:** Fruiting plants need fertile, moist, richly organic soil to produce the best crops. Improve the soil with several inches of compost or composted manure and any needed pH amendments and nutrients before planting. If you must significantly alter the soil pH, allow several months to a year before you plant. Do a soil test for pH and fertility before you plant and again each year, especially if fruits fail to produce well or plants look stressed. See Chapter 2 of this book for more on soils and drainage.

✔ **Locally adapted varieties:** Some plant varieties grow better in particular situations than other varieties. Check with your local extension office (find yours at www.csrees.usda.gov/Extension/) or nurseries in your area for recommendations.

Plant your fruits close to the kitchen door, garage, or some other place that you visit daily. Frequent inspection helps you see potential pests and diseases before they become a problem. Picking and maintenance feel like less of a chore, too, when the patch is just outside the door. Many of these plants can also do double duty as landscape specimens — use them in mixed borders and foundation plantings whenever you can.

Controlling weeds

Controlling weeds is critical for small fruits because they have shallow roots that can't compete for water and nutrients with more aggressive weeds.

Book VI

Organic Gardening

Weeds also harbor insect pests that feed on your fruits. Weed control needs a double-barreled approach to succeed:

- ✓ **Before you plant:** Get rid of weeds completely before you plant your fruits and allow yourself plenty of time. If you have a year to prepare, grow weed-smothering cover crops and till them into the soil. Got only a few months? Use soil solarization with clear plastic.

- ✓ **After planting:** Mulch, mulch, and mulch again. Use materials that add organic matter to the soil as they decompose. Pull individual weeds by hand and hoe only in footpaths.

Weeding a mature berry patch is a strenuous chore because most of these plants have shallow roots that don't allow cultivation or grow in such a way that handpulling each weed is the only solution. Weeding thorny brambles is an especially onerous job. Using a propane-powered flame weeder can make this job easier. See Chapter 3 of this book for details.

Buying plants

Buying the best quality plants that you can find really pays off. If you're fortunate enough to have a local nursery that grows its own fruit plants, by all means, pay them a visit. They usually offer the best varieties for your area and can give you valuable advice on growing them in your particular situation. Local nurseries usually sell potted plants, which transplant well, provided that they've been well cared for and not allowed to dry out before you buy them.

Specialty mail-order nurseries are often the best source of virus-free, disease-resistant fruits in many parts of the country. They carry the widest selection and usually offer the most complete description of each variety and its requirements. When shopping for virus-prone fruits, such as raspberries and strawberries, buy only those guaranteed to be virus-free. Read the catalog carefully to find varieties that resist common diseases. Your local extension office can give you a list of recommendations.

A last piece of advice from someone who's been there and done that — don't plant more than you have time to harvest and maintain. It's easy to get excited about all the promising fruits that you can grow and end up buying more plants than you need.

Presenting Popular Small Fruits

Growing berries is one of my most rewarding gardening activities. The season begins with strawberries. Then, raspberries, blueberries, and grapes ripen in succession through the summer and early fall. Pick your own favorites from this chapter and get growing!

Beautiful blueberry

As an ornamental plant, blueberry (*Vaccinium* species) offers small white flowers in spring, glossy green leaves in summer, and spectacular crimson fall foliage. As an edible fruit, it can't be beat for fresh eating, pies, pancakes, dessert sauce, and jam. Blueberries grow in Zones 3 to 10, but the species and best varieties vary from one extreme to the other:

Book VI

Organic Gardening

- ✔ **Lowbush blueberry** (*V. angustifolium*) is the hardiest for Zones 3 to 6. These 8- to 18-inch tall plants form spreading mats and produce small, intensely flavored berries. Grow them as ground-covering landscape plants in well-drained acidic soil and enjoy the fruits as a bonus or leave them for wildlife. Prune only to remove dead, damaged, or diseased plants. Varieties include 'Northsky' and 'Putte'.

- ✔ **Highbush blueberry** (*V. corymbosum* and hybrids) can grow from Zones 4 to 10, but some varieties are better suited to either extreme. Choose highbush blueberries for plenty of large, flavorful, easy to pick fruit. Shrubs grow 2 to 6 feet tall and produce more fruit when you plant at least two different varieties. In the northern United States, try 'Bluecrop', 'Blueray', 'Earliblue', 'Northblue', 'Patriot', and 'Northland'. In the south, plant 'Gulf Coast', 'Misty', 'O'Neill', and 'Reveille'.

  Flower buds, which appear larger and rounder than leaf buds, form in the summer the year before they bloom. Prune in late winter to remove unproductive canes, leaving the most vigorous 15 to 18 canes.

- ✔ **Rabbiteye blueberry** (*V. ashei*) grow in the warmer Zones 7 through 9. Growing up to 10 feet tall, the varieties of this species have thicker-skinned berries. You need to plant two different but compatible varieties to get fruit. Good companions include 'Beckyblue' and 'Bonitablue' or 'Powderblue' and 'Tifblue'.

Blueberries belong to a group of plants that have very specific soil needs, including a lot of decomposed organic matter and an acidic pH of 4.5 to 5.2. They grow where azaleas and rhododendrons naturally thrive, but you can also alter your soil with acidifying peat moss and sulfur to accommodate their needs. It takes at least six months to a year or more for amendments to significantly lower soil pH, so plan ahead and test the soil before planting. Test on an annual basis and amend your soil as necessary to maintain the pH level you want. See Chapter 2 of this book for more on soil amendments and pH.

All blueberries have shallow roots and need moist, well-drained soil. Mix ½ cubic foot of peat moss per plant into the soil at planting time. Cover the soil around the shrubs with organic mulch, such as pine needles, shredded oak leaves, or hardwood bark, to maintain the soil moisture and prevent weeds. Keep the soil moist throughout the growing season. Avoid deep cultivation.

Blueberries have relatively few serious pests or diseases, but good sanitation practices are a must. Mummy berry fungus causes trouble in some areas and spreads from fallen fruit. You can avoid other fungus diseases by pruning to encourage air circulation through the plant and keeping the foliage dry. Birds are the most serious pest — cover the plants completely with bird netting before the berries turn blue.

Ramblin' brambles

If you love fresh raspberries or blackberries, you'll be glad to know how easy they are to grow. These delicate and perishable fruits are expensive in the market, but you can plant your own small patch and produce enough for fresh eating and freezing, too.

When planning your patch of *brambles* (as these fruits are known), follow the instructions in the "Discovering Berry Patch Basics" section, earlier in this chapter. Pay special attention to air circulation and soil drainage. Taking weed-control precautions before you plant is also important because most brambles sport hooked thorns that make weeding the mature plants difficult and shallow roots that hoes easily damage. Raised beds work well with brambles. Allow at least 8 feet between rows of plants. Don't plant where other brambles or potatoes, tomatoes, or eggplant have grown in recent years due to risk of Verticillium root disease infection. It's also best to eliminate nearby wild brambles, if possible, because they often spread disease. (For more on plant diseases, see Chapter 3 of this book.)

Brambles range in growth habit from upright to sprawling — some stand up on their own, but most need trellis supports to keep the fruiting canes off the ground. A typical arrangement consists of a T-shaped post and crosspiece at either end of the row with taut wires or heavy twine running between them down the length of the row. You can also tie trailing varieties of blackberry to wire fence or other flat support.

Shoots called *canes* grow from either the roots or crown of the plant. Brambles are biennial, which means that plants flower on second-year canes, which subsequently die. Canes are called *primocanes* the first year they sprout and *floricanes* in their second year. Floricanes die after fruiting and should be pruned out. Most raspberries and blackberries produce fruit only on the floricanes and are called *summer-bearing*, but some raspberry varieties, often referred to as *everbearing*, also produce on primocanes in the fall. Although most raspberries produce red berries, some varieties have yellow or purple fruit.

Depending on your personal preference and climate, you can choose from several bramble types and many different varieties for your garden:

Book VI

Organic Gardening

- **Red raspberries:** This delicate fruit grows best in cool climates. Most varieties bear one crop per year, but others produce two.

  Prune summer-bearing raspberries twice a year. After summer fruiting, remove all the floricanes. In early spring, prune out winter-damaged and weak canes, leaving about 3 to 4 vigorous canes per square foot or roughly 6 to 9 inches between canes. Cut these remaining canes back to about 3 to 4 feet high, as shown in Figure 5-2. You can treat the everbearing types similarly or prune all the canes to the ground in late autumn or early spring. This severe pruning forfeits the summer crop, but yields a bumper crop in autumn.

  Summer-bearing red varieties include 'Latham', 'Boyne', 'Killarney', 'Milton', 'September', 'Canby' (nearly thornless), and 'Nordic'. Everbearing varieties include 'Heritage', 'Autumn Bliss', and 'Indian Summer'. Yellow varieties include 'Fall Gold', 'Amber', and 'Honeyqueen'. Purple varieties share red and black raspberry parentage and may resemble either one. 'Royalty' is the most common variety.

- **Black raspberries, black caps:** The fruits of this plant have a rich flavor and lack the core that characterizes blackberries. Plants grow new primocanes from the crown instead of the roots, and thus are easier to contain within a row because they don't grow shoots several feet from the mother plant as red raspberries do. Plant 3 feet apart in raised hills.

  To control their length and encourage *lateral branches* or side shoots to form, prune 3 to 4 inches off the primocane tips when they reach 24 to 30 inches high in mid-summer. The following spring, prune the lateral side branches to about 6 to 10 inches in length. At that time, also remove all but the strongest 4 to 6 canes. Black raspberry varieties include 'Black Hawk', 'Mac Black', 'Bristol', and 'Jewel'.

  Purple raspberries result from crosses between red and black raspberry varieties, but they are much less commonly grown. Their growth habit is similar to black raspberry and the fruit is excellent for jams. 'Royalty' is the most common variety.

✔ **Blackberries:** Preferring hot southern summers, blackberries grow in Zones 6 and warmer, although some varieties make it into Zone 5 and warmer parts of Zone 4. Prune blackberries as described for summer-bearing raspberries, but leave the floricanes about 4 to 5 feet high.

Blackberries fall into two main categories: bush or upright types and trailing. The trailing varieties make less appealing plants for most home gardeners because they require more trellising and maintenance, have more thorns than the uprights, and are less cold hardy. Thornless blackberries are now available, including 'Arapaho', 'Black Satin', 'Chester', 'Navaho', 'Hull', and 'Triple Crown'. Of the thorny upright varieties, 'Illini Hardy', 'Darrow', 'Lowden', and 'Ebony King' are among the cold hardiest.

WARNING!

Some diseases cause serious damage to raspberries and blackberries, leading to their decline and reduced fruiting. Root rots, Verticillium wilt, and leaf rust are among the worst, but some varieties are less susceptible than others to disease. Choose a resistant variety whenever possible, such as the ones listed in this section. Another way to prevent the spread of disease is to plant the different kinds of brambles away from one another. Black and purple raspberries, for example, can get mosaic virus from red raspberries, which can get it from blackberries. If possible, burn or shred prunings and remove them from the site to prevent the spread of diseases and pests. Don't prune, harvest, or walk among plants when the foliage is wet.

Figure 5-2:
In spring, prune raspberry canes to 3 or 4 feet to encourage more fruit.

Going ape for grapes

Growing organic grapes (*Vitis* species) successfully depends on your climate, cultural strategies, and the varieties you choose. Arid climates provoke fewer diseases than humid climates. You can grow grapes nearly anywhere in Zones 3 through 10, and they tolerate a wide range of soil conditions; well-drained soil in the pH range of 5.5 to 7.0 is best. Grapes need full sun and very good air circulation to hamper diseases.

At least three different grape species and countless varieties exist in North American gardens and vineyards. The European grape, *V. vinifera*, grows best in a Mediterranean climate, such as California and parts of the southwestern United States. In hotter, humid climates, many people grow muscadine grapes, *V. rotundifolia*, which thrive in Zones 7 through 9. The native North American species, *V. labrusca*, and its hybrids are the hardiest and best for most other regions of the country.

To sort out the complicated lineage, divide grapes into two broad categories: table grapes and wine or juice grapes. Table grapes have tender skins suitable for fresh eating and may contain seeds or be seedless. Wine and juice grapes may have tougher skins, but plenty of sweet juice for liquid consumption or making into jelly. Ripe fruit colors range from green to pink and red to deep purplish black.

Before planting young grapes, prepare the soil thoroughly as described in the "Discovering Berry Patch Basics" section (earlier in this chapter) and install a sturdy trellis consisting of 2 or 3 heavy wires strung 24 inches apart on sturdy posts. Brace the end posts.

Several pruning and training systems exist, but the basic idea in all of them is to establish 1 or 2 main trunks per vine. Each trunk grows horizontal lateral branches, which you attach to the wires. The flowers and fruit appear on wood that grows in the current year from the laterals that grew in the previous year. Starting in winter after the first growing season, begin the pruning and training as follows:

1. **In the first winter, choose two healthy, vigorous canes to keep and remove the rest.**

   Prune these main trunks back to 3 or 4 buds each.

2. **The next summer, select the most vigorous shoot from each trunk and remove competing shoots.**

   Train the shoots on a string until they reach the top wire and then pinch them to encourage lateral branching, as shown in Figure 5-3.

3. **In the second winter, remove all growth from the trunk and lateral branches.**

   Cut laterals back to 10 buds. Let vines grow unpruned through the summer.

4. **In the third winter and subsequent years, choose the laterals for the current year as well as replacement laterals for next year.**

   Leave 10 buds on the current year laterals and 2 buds on the replacements. Remember that grapes grow fruit on wood that grows in the current year from last season's laterals. Prune off all other wood, removing as much 90 percent of the previous year's growth.

Prevalent diseases and pests include berry moth, mites, leaf hoppers, and Japanese beetles, as well as Botrytis bunch rot, powdery mildew, and black rot. Some varieties are less sensitive to infection than other varieties. Grape varieties often grow best in specific regions of the country. Consult your local extension office or reputable nursery for recommendations.

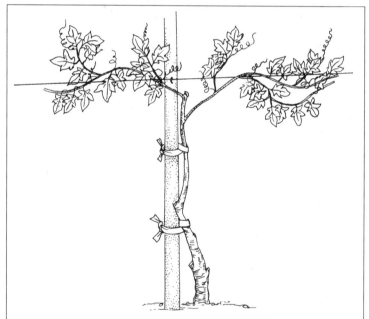

Figure 5-3:
Train grapes
on a trellis
and prune to
a main stem
with lateral
branches.

Sublime strawberries

Probably the most popular small fruit for the home garden, strawberries are also among the hardest to grow organically. Strawberries have many insect pests and diseases that damage plants and berries alike. Establishing your planting in well-drained, fertile soil, and maintaining a weed-free patch is essential for success.

You can choose from three kinds of strawberries, depending on when you want fruit. Consult your local extension office or nurseries for the best varieties for your area. Here are the options:

- ✔ **June-bearing** varieties produce one large crop of berries in late spring to early summer.

- ✔ **Everbearing** varieties produce two smaller crops — one in the early summer and another in early fall.

- ✔ **Day-neutral** berries, the newest type, can produce fruit continuously throughout the growing season.

Plant dormant, bare-root strawberry plants 18 to 24 inches apart in 3- to 6-inch high, 3- to 4-foot wide raised beds. Set the plants so that soil covers the roots, but the crown remains above the soil, as shown in Figure 5-4. Keep the soil moist, but not saturated. Pinch off all flowers until midsummer for the first season to encourage strong root and top growth.

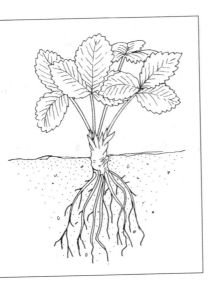

Figure 5-4: Plant strawberry plants so that crowns are just above the soil.

The plants that you set out are called the *mother plants*. They send out runners that take root and develop new *daughter plants* in mid to late summer. Space the daughter plants evenly around the mothers to give each plenty of space to grow. Daughter plants flower and fruit the year after they grow. In the second summer, you can remove the original mother plants to make room for new daughter plants. Another method is to rotary till the sides of the bed in midsummer of the second or third year, leaving plants only in the 18- to 24-inch wide center strip. Train new daughter plants into the tilled soil. Plan to replace your strawberry planting every 3 to 5 years. Cover the planting with straw mulch after the ground freezes in cold-winter climates and remove as the weather warms in spring.

One of the most serious insect pests that affect strawberries is the tarnished plant bug, which can severely damage the developing fruit. These insects spend the winter in plant debris and live on weeds in and around your yard. Covering the strawberry plants in the fall with a floating row cover can offer some, but not complete, protection from the bugs in the following spring and early summer. Early ripening varieties often suffer less damage than late-season berries.

The strawberry clipper or bud weevil is another significant pest in some areas. This insect flies into the planting from neighboring woodlots and hedgerows about the time that the flower buds swell. Adults destroy the developing buds by laying eggs in them. Many other insects, slugs, mites, and nematodes attack strawberry fruits and plants, reducing vigor and production and introducing disease. Birds and ground squirrels will also take their share.

Strawberries are also subject to many fungus, bacteria, and viral diseases. Fungal infections include leaf spot, leaf scorch, leaf blight, powdery mildew, red stele, Verticillium wilt, root rot, and several berry rots. Avoid planting strawberries where tomatoes, eggplants, or potatoes previously grew to avoid wilt diseases. Buy only virus-free plants from a reputable nursery.

Choosing and Caring for Fruit Trees

Most people grow fruit trees primarily to produce food. To make these fruit factories more and more efficient, plant breeders continue to develop special techniques, such as reducing the size of the trees, to make trees produce at an earlier age and yield more fruit per acre. That's good news for home gardeners.

Size does matter

Trees are easier to harvest and maintain when all the branches are within arm's reach. Unfortunately, many fruit trees can grow up to 40 feet tall or even higher when left to their own devices. To keep them in bounds and to produce more high quality fruit, most fruit varieties are *grafted* onto roots of smaller-growing varieties. Tree nurseries slip a bud, called a *scion,* from a desirable fruit variety, such as 'Delicious' apple or 'Bing' cherry, under the bark of a *dwarfing rootstock* variety in early spring. Plant breeders and tree nurseries graft fruit trees for a variety to

✔ Reproduce exact copies of desirable trees.

✔ Reduce the mature size of the tree.

✔ Encourage fruit bearing at an earlier age.

✔ Increase disease and pest resistance.

✔ Adapt to different soils.

✔ Determine hardiness to particular climates.

Roots are one of the most cold-sensitive parts of a tree. Some rootstocks increase the trees' hardiness to cold temperatures.

Some rootstocks influence the size that the tree will ultimately attain, although the mature size of the tree also depends on the standard height that's normal for the scion or main variety. Dwarfing rootstocks are categorized by the amount of dwarfing they provide. Apple tree sizes, for example, fall into several categories:

✔ **Standard-sized** apple trees, grown on seedling or nondwarfing roots may reach 25 feet.

✔ **Semi-dwarf** is about 75 percent of the standard height or about 18 feet at maturity.

✔ **Dwarf trees** are about 50 percent as high as standard or 12-feet tall.

✔ **Miniature trees** are only about 15 percent of the standard size. At a mere 4 feet in height, these trees are the best ones for growing in containers.

As an organic home gardener, consider dwarf to semi-dwarf size trees for several reasons. Monitoring and controlling pests is easier to do when you can reach the top of the tree. On very small trees, you can even use a barrier fabric to help prevent insect infestations. You can also harvest fruit years sooner and pick the fruit more easily.

Book VI

Organic Gardening

Whether you have a large yard or a half whiskey-barrel container, you can find a fruit or nut variety that fits your available space, soil, and climate by choosing the right rootstock. Specialty nurseries that ship by mail have the largest selection of varieties and rootstocks, while local garden centers usually offer only dwarf or semi-dwarf trees in a handful of popular varieties.

Sex and the single tree

Many fruit species, such as apples, sweet cherries, European pears, and Japanese plums, require *cross-pollination* to bear fruit. That means that you need two different but compatible varieties planted near one another so that the pollen of one fertilizes the flowers of the other.

The trees must bloom at the same time for cross-pollination to occur, and some varieties are fussy about who they mix with. Other fruit species are *self-fruitful*, which means that they can pollinate their own flowers, but even those trees often produce larger crops when they mix pollen with a friend. Reputable nurseries or your local extension office can tell you which varieties can pollinate each other.

Feeling the chill factor

Fruits have another peculiar requirement — most need a certain number of hours below 45°F — called *chill requirement* or *chill factor* — in order to produce plenty of flowers and fruit. As you may guess, fruits, such as oranges, that grow mostly in the warm climates have lower chilling requirements than some cold-climate fruits, such as apples. The chill factor isn't related to cold hardiness, however. Even some frost-tender plants, such as fig trees, need some time below 45°F to bear fruit properly.

Crops fall into several categories, depending on how many hours of chilling that they need. Each variety is different, however. Some peach varieties need only 200 hours, while others require more than 1,000. Look for specific varieties that match your climate:

- **Low chill** fruits need fewer than 400 hours below 45°F. In the United States, warm pockets in California, southern Texas, and Florida fall into this category.

- **Moderate chill** fruits need between 400 and 700 hours of chill. Look for varieties with this requirement if you live along the Gulf coast, southeastern seaboard, or Pacific coastal areas.

- **High chill** varieties need more than 700 hours and often more than 1,000 hours of temperatures below 45°f. Most of the United States and Canada easily fall into this range.

Low winter temperatures and timing of autumn and spring frosts play important roles in your selection of fruit species and varieties for your organic orchard. Local nurseries generally sell plants best suited to your local climate. Reputable mail-order nurseries and your local extension office can also steer you toward appropriate varieties.

Budding genius

Fruit trees grow different kinds of buds: The *terminal bud* grows at the end of branches, and that's where new branches and twigs grow from each spring. When the terminal buds expand, they leave *bud scars,* which look like slightly raised rings around the twig. You can measure how much a tree has grown each year by looking at the distance between bud scars. *Leaf buds* appear along the twigs and expand into leaves. *Flower buds* are usually fatter than leaf buds and swell first in the spring. Some trees, such as most apples, pears, cherries, plums, and apricots, produce their fruit on *spurs,* which are short, modified twigs. Spurs usually live and produce flower buds for several years or longer before becoming unproductive. See Figure 5-5 for examples of these bud types.

Book VI

Organic Gardening

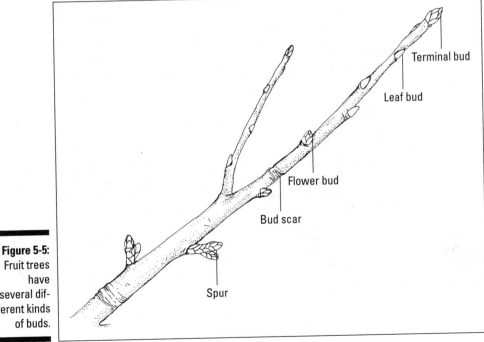

Terminal bud

Leaf bud

Flower bud

Bud scar

Spur

Figure 5-5: Fruit trees have several different kinds of buds.

For the best-quality apples and pears, leave only one fruit on each spur and pinch off the others in early summer. Spurs and flower buds develop best on limbs that are angled slightly above horizontal. Branches that grow upright and those that dangle below horizontal produce little, if any, fruit.

Planting for success

All fruits need moisture-retentive but well-drained soil. Soggy sites spell doom for these species. Adequate water is also critical, especially when the fruit is developing and expanding. If you live in a drought-prone area, consider irrigating your fruit trees for the best yield. Drip tubes, which deliver water directly to the soil around the trees, are best. Avoid sprinklers that spray water on the leaves and contribute to disease.

Professional fruit growers also consider air movement when they plan their orchard placement and layout. Air affects fruit and nut plants in several ways:

- **Wind:** Too much wind can keep pollinating insects, such as bees, from flying and pollinating the flowers at critical times. It also knocks fruit off the tree and can damage the branches. Plant a windbreak, if necessary, or put the trees where a building shields them.

- **Frost pockets:** Cold air flows downhill and collects at the bottom of a slope. Trees that bloom in early spring are especially vulnerable to cold temperatures at that time, and the flowers may be severely damaged if planted where cold air collects. Plant fruit trees and shrubs *on* the slope instead of near the bottom, but avoid the windy top of a slope.

- **Circulation:** Constantly but lightly moving air helps prevent disease organisms from getting a foothold on your trees. Many fungus diseases that infect leaves need water and moisture to spread and grow, so keeping the leaves dry is important.

If you buy your plants locally, they'll usually be already growing in a container. If you order them from a mail-order nursery, however, they'll arrive in a *dormant* or nongrowing state and *bareroot,* without any soil around their roots. Be sure to plant bareroot trees and shrubs right away.

After planting, establish a wide ring of organic mulch around your trees to conserve soil moisture, prevent grass and weeds from competing with the tree roots, and reduce insect pests. See Chapter 3 of this book for the low-down on mulch.

Because producing heavy crops of fruit stresses trees and shrubs, fruit-bearing species need additional nutrients. The texture of your soil, its current nutrient levels, plant age and type, climate, and amount of fruit your tree bears all have an effect on the amount of additional nutrients you need to add to the soil. Soil tests and leaf analyses are the most accurate methods used to determine which nutrients your trees need. Consult your local extension office for information on taking leaf samples and where to send them.

Pruning fruit trees and shrubs

Producing bushels of high-quality fruit and developing a sturdy tree that can support the crop are the twin goals of pruning and training fruit trees. If you end up with an attractive landscape specimen, too, that's a bonus! Although you use the same basic pruning techniques on all fruit trees, each kind of fruit tree has unique timing and methods for reaching your goals.

Book VI

Organic Gardening

You need to prune fruit trees regularly for several reasons. Keep these goals in mind as you make decisions about which limbs to remove:

- **Removing dead, damaged, and diseased wood:** Do this step before any other pruning and whenever necessary.

- **Controlling tree and shrub size:** Keep fruit down where you can harvest and care for it without a ladder.

- **Providing air circulation:** Circulation helps ward off pests and diseases. Crowded limbs invite fungus diseases and provide habitat for damaging insects.

- **Increasing exposure to sunlight:** Sunlight makes fruit develop a sweeter flavor and deeper color. Fruit that's exposed to direct sunlight tastes better than fruit shaded by leaves and branches.

- **Increasing the quality and quantity of fruit:** Branches trained to 60-degree angles where they meet the trunk develop the most flower buds. Spacing the limbs up and down and around the trunk provides the best conditions for the fruit to mature.

Professional fruit growers use several different pruning and training methods, depending on the type of fruit they grow. The following styles apply mainly to temperate-climate fruit — tropical fruits, such as citrus, are trained differently. See Figure 5-6 for examples of each style.

- **Central leader:** Used mainly with apples, European pears and plums, and dwarf cultivars, this method yields trees with single, upright trunks. The main limbs should be spaced about 8 inches apart and extend in all directions around the trunk so that no limb is directly above another. If you looked straight down from the top, the limbs should resemble a spiral in which no two branches are at exactly the same level on the trunk. To maximize sunlight penetration, prune the limbs so that those at the top of the tree are shorter than branches under them.

✔ **Modified central leader:** In this system, trees are trained to a single, upright trunk with evenly spaced limbs until they reach a desired height, usually 6 to 10 feet. At that point, you prune out the leader and maintain the tree at that height. All fruit trees can be trained to this form, and it's especially useful for keeping fruit within picking distance of the ground.

✔ **Open center (also called vase shape):** Peaches, nectarines, sour cherries, apricots, Asian pears, and Japanese plums produce easy-to-reach, high quality fruit when pruned to this form. In this style, you select four or five well-placed main branches and then prune out the central leader. This technique limits the height of the tree and creates a spreading crown. You can use this method with any fruit tree, especially those that normally grow too tall to harvest comfortably.

TIP

Choose young *deciduous* fruit trees — trees that lose their leaves in the autumn — with good structure to start with and shape them as they grow.

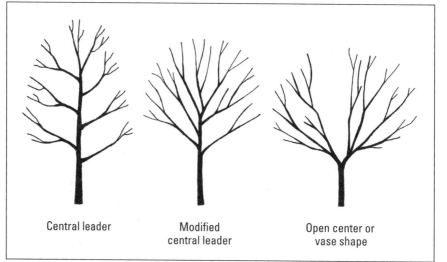

Figure 5-6: Train deciduous fruit trees to one of three forms, depending on the type of fruit and desired tree size.

Central leader   Modified central leader   Open center or vase shape

The first few years are the most critical time to develop a healthy tree structure that will provide years of tasty fruit. Here's how to get your trees off to a good start:

✔ **At planting time:** Remove damaged and dead limbs, those under 25 inches from the ground, and any with narrow crotch angles of less than 45 degrees. Leave branches with crotch angles between 45 and 80 degrees. If the tree has two shoots competing to be the leader, choose one and remove the other.

✔ **First winter:** In late winter, select three to four limbs to keep as main branches. They should be about 8 inches apart vertically, be well spaced around the trunk, and have approximately 60-degree angles at the trunk. Prune off all other limbs. Prune remaining limbs back by one-third of their length to encourage side branching. Prune the central leader to 24 to 30 above the uppermost limb for a central-leader-style tree. If pruning for an open center or vase shape, remove the central leader just above the top branch.

✔ **Second summer:** In midsummer, remove *water sprouts* that grow upright from the branches and *suckers,* which grow up from the base of the tree. In central-leader trees, choose the strongest, most upright leader and remove competing ones. Using the criteria mentioned for the first dormant season, choose the next tier of limbs beginning about 15 to 18 inches above the top branch of the lower tier. Remove undesirable limbs. In open center trees, remove competing, crowded, and upright shoots.

✔ **Second winter:** Remove undesirable limbs, competing leaders, water sprouts, and suckers and prune the new growth of side branches back by one-third. Use notched sticks, called *spreaders,* to spread the remaining limbs to 60-degree angles where they meet the trunk. Leave the spreaders in place until mid to late summer. In open center trees, prune new shoots by one-third to *outward-facing buds* — buds that face away from the trunk — to encourage branching. Thin out crowded shoots by removing the weakest ones.

✔ **Continuing care:** Continue to follow the directions for the second season year after year. To develop a modified leader tree, remove the central leader just above the uppermost branch you wish to keep. Do this step in the summer to inhibit vigorous sprouting.

Picking Temperate-Climate Trees and Shrubs

Popular and easy-to-grow in USDA Hardiness Zones 8 and northward, these fruits find their way into lunch boxes, fruit salads, and pies from coast to coast. All require some dedication to their cultural needs, but richly reward your efforts.

If you have limited space or just don't need bushels of fruit, try growing dwarf or even miniature versions of these trees.

Apples

With hundreds of varieties available, at least one apple *(Malus sylvestris)* is available to match nearly any climate and set of taste buds. Apples are among the most popular fruit trees to grow, but to harvest high-quality fruit, you must be prepared to regularly prune them, feed them, and deal with pests. Apples require cross-pollination, but some nurseries offer trees with two or more varieties grafted onto one rootstock. You can also use ornamental crabapples to pollinate apple trees.

Several serious pests make apples a challenge to grow organically. Plum curculio, apple maggot, and codling moths damage the developing fruits, frequently making them inedible. (For more on pest control, see Chapter 3 of this book.)

As trees increase in size, they become harder to prune and spray, so choose trees on semi-dwarf and dwarf rootstocks that reach only 8 to 12 feet tall. You can also use pruning techniques to control tree height. Prune apple trees in late winter, while they are dormant, and follow up in midsummer to remove overly vigorous sprouts.

Disease resistance is key when choosing apple varieties for organic orchards. Apple scab, cedar apple rust, powdery mildew, and fire blight devastate many common and older varieties, which makes them unsuitable for home orchards. Although the names of improved varieties may be unfamiliar, the fruit is just as flavorful. Some disease-resistant apple varieties worth seeking out, listed from those that ripen earliest (late summer) to latest (mid to late autumn), include 'Redfree', 'Prima', 'Novamac', 'JonaFree', 'Priscilla', 'Freedom', 'Liberty', 'Nova Easygro', 'Enterprise', and 'GoldRush'.

Apples ripen from late summer through late autumn, so choose a variety that ripens its fruit before freezing temperatures in your area have a chance to damage the crop. Varieties also vary considerably in their chill requirements, with some better suited to colder climates and others to milder seasons.

European and Asian pears

Pears *(Pyrus* species) share many of apples' quirks and characteristics, and they grow in similar climates. Like apples, pears are usually sold as grafted trees and require similar pruning and training. Pears, with their glossy dark green foliage, make especially good landscape specimens in addition to providing delicious fruit.

Unfortunately, pears also share many of apple's diseases and insect pests. Fireblight is its most devastating disease, while pear scab can render the trees and fruit unsightly. Avoid planting fireblight-prone varieties and keep insect pests, which spread the disease, under control. Pear psylla, an insect that resembles a winged, yellow- to orange-colored aphid, sucks the juice out of new foliage and excretes sticky droppings that support a black, sooty looking fungus. You can control it with dormant spray oil.

You can choose from two kinds of pears — European and Asian. They share most cultural attributes, but differ in some other ways:

Book VI

Organic
Gardening

- **Pollination:** Most European pears require another variety planted within 50 feet for cross-pollination. Asian pears are mostly self-fruitful, but produce heavier crops when cross-pollinated.

- **Shape:** European pear fruits have the traditional pear shape — a wide bottom and narrower top. Most Asian pears resemble round apples.

- **Texture:** European pears have soft, melting flesh when ripe. Asian pears have crisp, apple-like flesh.

Fireblight-resistant varieties of European pear, listed in order of ripening, include 'Harrow Delight', 'Harvest Queen', 'Starking Delicious', 'Moonglow', 'Stark Honeysweet', 'Magness', 'Seckel', and 'Harrow Sweet'. The earliest varieties begin ripening in mid-August in Zone 5, with the latest finishing up in late September.

Disease-resistant Asian varieties include 'Shinko', 'Shinseiki', 'Large Korean' (also known as 'Dan Beh'), 'Korean Giant', and 'Olympic', all of which ripen from September through October. Ripening begins earlier in Zones 6 and 7.

Pears are best picked when still somewhat hard and allowed to ripen at room temperature or in the refrigerator. Fruit that overripens on the tree develops hard, gritty spots in the flesh and may turn brown and mushy near the core. Asian pears and late-season European pears keep for months in the refrigerator if picked just before ripeness.

Sweet and sour cherries

Cherries are glorious in their spring bloom — the fruit seems just like a bonus. In Zone 5, cherries ripen from June into July, providing the first tree fruit of the season. Most cherries are red when ripe, but some sweet cherries are yellow. Cherries belong to the *Prunus* genus along with peaches and plums.

Although sweet and sour or tart cherries are similar in many respects, they differ from each other in significant ways.

- ✔ **Pollination:** Sweet cherries need cross-pollination, except for the variety 'Stella', so you need two compatible varieties. Sour cherries, also called pie cherries, are self-pollinating. Sour cherries can pollinate sweet cherries, but may not bloom at the same time. Trees must bloom at the same time for them to cross-pollinate.

- ✔ **Hardiness:** Sweet cherry trees grow reliably only in Zones 5 to 8, but some sour cherries thrive in Zone 4.

- ✔ **Culinary use:** Sweet cherries, common in supermarkets in early summer, are best when eaten fresh. Sour cherries make the best pies and jams, but you have to grow your own — markets rarely offer them. Some varieties are sweet enough to eat fresh, too.

The pests that plague apples, including plum curculio and apple maggot, also infest cherries, as do the cherry fruit fly and Oriental fruit moth. Birds will also take a portion of the crop, if not the whole thing, unless you cover the ripening fruit with a net. Birds tend to bother tart cherries less than sweet cherries, but it's better to be safe than sorry. Fruit of some varieties tend to crack in the rain as they ripen, but others resist this bad habit. Of the diseases that affect all *Prunus* species, black knot fungus, bacterial canker, and leaf spot are the most serious. Practice good sanitation by raking up foliage and dropped fruit and prune out any infected wood immediately.

For best flavor, let sweet and sour cherries fully ripen on the tree before picking, but keep them covered to prevent bird theft!

'Montmorency' is the most widely grown commercial sour cherry, but other varieties, such as 'Morello', 'Meteor', and 'Northstar' are good choices for home orchards.

Good sweet cherry varieties for home-grown fruit include 'Stella', 'Lapins', 'Glacier', 'Surefire', and 'Sunburst', which are self-pollinating. 'Bing', which is the most common commercial variety, is susceptible to canker and fruit splitting. Good varieties that require cross-pollination include 'Van' and yellow cherries 'Emperor Francis', 'Stark Gold', and 'Rainier'.

Peaches and nectarines

Peaches and nectarines are actually the same species *(Prunus persica)*, but peaches are fuzzy and nectarines are smooth-skinned. They share the same diseases and pests as cherries, but are worth growing for the juicy flavor and aroma that comes only from freshly picked, sun-ripened fruit. They are self-pollinating, so you need only one tree.

Peaches, nectarines, apricots, and plums are called *stone fruits* after the seed pit in their centers. These fruits fall into one of two camps, called *freestone* and *clingstone*, depending on whether or not the flesh separates easily from the seed. In general, freestone fruit has softer, melting flesh and is best for fresh eating, while clingstone fruit has firmer flesh that holds up well in baking and canning. Generally, fruits ripen from mid-July through August, depending on the climate and variety.

Geography and climate influence peach growing rather significantly. Diseases and pests that are prevalent in some parts of the United States cause little concern in other areas. Plum curculio, bacterial leaf spot, and fungus diseases, for example, present problems for peaches in the eastern part of the United States from a line that runs approximately from Fort Worth, Texas, to Fargo, North Dakota. Gardeners west of that line have an easier time growing peaches organically, except in the Pacific Northwest where the damp climate encourages diseases. If you're in the eastern United States, vigilant housekeeping, pruning, and choosing a site that encourages air circulation, as well as using natural pesticides, can help you grow this problem-prone crop.

Book VI

Organic Gardening

Peaches and nectarines grow reliably only in climates with mild winters and fairly dry summers, preferably Zones 6 to 9, although some varieties produce fruit in warmer parts of Zones 4 and 5. The hardiness of their overwintering flower buds is the limiting factor in cold-winter climates — several consecutive nights of –13°F will kill them. Mild weather in winter or early spring followed by a return to freezing weather also spells disaster for their blooms. Plant breeders have developed varieties, such as 'Reliance' and 'Veteran', that withstand temperatures as low as –25°F, but they're usually less flavorful than peaches grown in warmer climates. If you want to try growing peaches in Zones 4 or 5, choose varieties with high-chill requirements because they bloom later in the season.

Gardeners in Zones 9 and 10 can successfully grow peaches if they choose varieties with low chill requirements. Some varieties developed for Florida, for example, need only 150 to 400 hours below 45°F to bear fruit.

Peaches and nectarines bloom on wood that grew in the previous year, so prune them in June after flowering. Maintain an open-centered form and encourage lots of new growth each year. Maintain a vigilant pest- and disease-control program, too, because peach and nectarine trees are among the most susceptible to attack of all fruit trees. Peach leaf curl — a serious fungus disease — causes leaves and fruit to drop prematurely. Look for varieties that resist canker, brown rot, bacterial leaf spot, and pit splitting. Catalog or plant-tag descriptions will usually tell you whether a variety is resistant to particular diseases.

Peach varieties that resist bacterial leaf spot include 'Harrow Diamond', 'Harrow Beauty', 'Delta', 'Southern Pearl', 'Desert Gold', 'Candor', 'Sweethaven', 'Redhaven', 'Reliance', 'Harbrite', 'Harken', and 'Veteran'. Nectarine varieties include 'Sunraycer', 'Fantasia', 'RosePrincess', 'Mericrest', 'Hardired', and 'Harko'.

European and Asian apricots

Members of the *Prunus* genus, European and Asian apricots enjoy the same mild climates and well-drained soils as peaches and sweet cherries. Although plum curculio, codling moth, and brown rot can infest the fruits, the trees are more vigorous and resistant to disease than peaches. Prune apricot trees to a modified central leader or open-center form. If you can grow them in your climate, give apricots a try because they have beautiful early spring flowers followed by luscious fruit that supermarkets just can't match. Unfortunately, spring frosts damage the tender blooms in cold regions.

European apricots that you may see in your grocery's produce section grow on 10- to 30-foot trees that thrive in the warmer, drier parts of Zones 6 to 8. Trees grown in cool, humid climates produce less fruit, and it tends to be of poorer quality. Choose varieties that are suitable for your specific climate. Local nurseries and your local extension office can make knowledgeable recommendations. Choose a freestone variety (discussed in the "Peaches and nectarines" section), if you wish to dry the ripened fruits for storage. Good varieties include 'Harcot', 'Harglow', 'Hargrand', 'Harlayne', 'Puget Gold', 'Veecot', and 'Goldcot'. For best flavor, allow the fruits to ripen on the tree before picking in July and early August.

Plums

Plum is one of the most genetically complicated fruits in the *Prunus* group because it has a number of species, all which are commonly interbred. The resulting fruits fall into several broad categories, including European, Japanese, and prune plums. They differ in important ways:

- ✔ **Japanese plums** are round, usually require cross-pollination to set fruit, and are pruned to an open-centered shape. They're generally hardy to Zone 6 and warmer parts of Zone 5, although some hybrids are hardier. Varieties include 'Shiro', 'Early Golden', 'Burbank', 'Redheart', 'Santa Rosa', 'Methley,' and 'Beauty'. Hybrids 'Elite', 'Superb', 'Tecumseh', 'Perfection', and 'Brookgold' are hardy through Zone 4.

✓ **European plums** are oval, and most don't need a second variety for pollination. Train these trees to a modified leader form. Most varieties are hardy through Zone 5, and some produce fruit even in Zone 4. Varieties include 'Damson', 'Seneca', 'Verity', and 'Green Gage'.

✓ **Prune plums** are European plums with drier flesh and a high sugar content that makes them suitable for drying. Common varieties include 'Stanley', 'French Prune', 'Fellenberg' or 'Italian Prune', 'Valor', 'Earliblue', 'Sugar', and 'Mount Royal', which is hardy in Zone 4.

Japanese and European plums can't pollinate each other, so if your trees require cross-pollination, be sure to choose compatible varieties. Thin the fruits to hang 4 to 6 inches apart, 5 to 8 weeks after bloom. Fruits ripen from July through September, starting with Japanese plums and ending with prune plums, depending on the variety.

Plant breeders have also crossed apricots with plums to create hybrids called apriums, plumcots, and pluots. These are hardy wherever European apricots grow, require cross-pollination, and have characteristics of both parents.

Book VI

Organic Gardening

Growing Warm-Climate Fruit Trees

These trees grow where winter temperatures remain mild — generally in Zones 8 and warmer. Evergreen species, such as citrus, perish when the thermometer reaches or goes more than a few degrees below freezing, although some citrus varieties can grow in colder climes. Deciduous fruits, such as figs and persimmons, are somewhat hardier, especially if you give them a favorable site. Gardeners in colder climates can grow some of these fruits successfully in containers, moving them to sheltered places in the winter or growing them as houseplants.

Citrus

This large _tropical_ and _subtropical_ group covers a wide range of juicy fruits that require almost frost-free climates to produce fruit (most can take 25°F to 28°F for several hours) and hot summers to help ripen and sweeten the fruit. These trees need temperatures between 70°F and 90°F for best growth. In the United States, the citrus-growing region is limited to Florida, coastal areas of the Gulf coast states, and parts of Arizona and California.

Citrus trees have evergreen foliage, and most have thorny limbs. Trees are usually grafted. (See the "Size does matter" section, earlier in this chapter.) Most species bloom in early spring and don't require cross-pollination. Fruit ripens from autumn to spring, but some everbearing trees produce fruit year 'round. Allow fruit to ripen on the tree for best flavor. Here's a look at some of the popular citrus fruits:

- **Grapefruits:** Grown primarily in Florida and southern Texas, the trees reach 30 feet in height. Varieties include both seeded and seedless types and those with red, pink, or white flesh.

- **Kumquat:** A bit hardier and smaller than most citrus trees, kumquat can tolerate temperatures as low as 18°F to 20°F and also make good houseplants. You can eat the small fruit whole — rind and all.

- **Lemons and limes:** Among the most cold-sensitive citrus, this group grows best in frost-free climates. Some varieties do well as houseplants, producing the sour fruit indoors.

- **Mandarins:** Members of this large group have somewhat flattened shapes and loose, easy-to-peel skins. Varieties include tangerines, clementines, and tangelos. The 'Calamondin' variety makes a good houseplant or container shrub and produces loads of small fruit with edible rinds. Most mandarin varieties need Zone 9 and warmer, although 'Calamondin' and 'Satsuma' varieties tolerate temperatures down to 20°F.

- **Oranges:** You can choose from many varieties, which vary in ease of peeling, sweetness, number of seeds, hardiness, quality of the juice, color, and time of ripening. Although most types ripen during December and January, some are ready to pick in November, while others, such as juicy Valencia varieties, don't ripen until late winter to spring. Navel oranges are among the hardiest varieties.

Annual pruning isn't necessary for citrus trees — a good thing, given that most of these trees sport long, sharp thorns. They require pruning just to keep the centers of the trees open to light and air and to remove dead branches. If trees get too big to pick easily, you can cut back the limbs with thinning cuts every year or two. Wait to prune frost-nipped trees until new growth shows the extent of damage. To prevent sunburn after pruning, paint exposed branches that were previously shaded by foliage with whitewash made from a 1:1 mix of water and a white, water-based paint.

Citrus demands moist but well-drained soil and regular applications of nitrogen fertilizer beginning in January and ending in late summer. Make sure that trees have adequate water when they're actively growing and developing fruit. Pests and diseases infrequently cause problems, except when trees are stressed from drought or other weather-related factors. Scale, mites, thrips, and whiteflies may infest these trees, and so can cankers that infect the wood.

Figs

These attractive trees have smooth, gray bark and large, lobed, tropical-looking leaves. Figs *(Ficus carica)* can take winter cold down to 15°F, but freezing temperatures kill the upper branches and even the trunk of the tree, after which the tree sprouts up from its roots and forms a shrub with several stems. Following such a freeze, the plants may not produce fruit in the following season, depending on the variety. Figs grow best in subtropical climates with mild winters and long, hot summers to ripen their fruit. They need well-drained soil.

Figs make good container specimens for climates where they can't survive outdoors year 'round. Move the containers into a cool, protected location where temperatures remain above freezing. Bring the plants into a warm, sunny location in early spring when the buds begin to swell.

Figs typically ripen two crops per year in warm climates. Leave the fruit on the trees to fully ripen before picking, but protect them from hungry birds. Prune to encourage new shoots, prevent branch crowding, and remove dead wood. Encourage the plant to form 3 to 5 main stems. If you prune when the trees are dormant, you decrease or eliminate the first crop but increase the second crop of the year.

Fig trees have no serious pests except for fruit flies and ants, which attack the fruit in some climates. In some areas, the trees are prone to fig rust, which can be controlled with Bordeaux mix sprayed on the leaf undersides every 2 to 3 weeks from June through August. 'Brown Turkey', 'Celeste', 'Magnolia', and 'Mission' are common varieties.

Book VI

Organic Gardening

Persimmon

This lovely landscape tree grows up to 25 feet tall and wide, with bright yellow, red, and orange fall foliage and gracefully drooping branches. Its orange fruit dangles from the ends of the limbs as it ripens. Although this tree can withstand winter temperatures to 0°F, in colder regions, it tends to break dormancy and begin growing before the cold weather has fully departed. Plant persimmons in well drained, acidic soil, but keep the soil moist, especially during the summer when the tree is carrying fruit. Prune only to establish a modified central leader branching structure of young trees and to remove dead and damaged limbs from mature trees.

Persimmons have few serious pests or diseases, although fungus disease can affect the fruit late in the season and trees are susceptible to wilt disease in some areas. Control scale insects with dormant oil spray in late winter. They need little pruning.

Japanese persimmon *(Diospyros kaki)* fruit fall into two different categories — astringent and non-astringent. Fruit of the astringent varieties are eaten when the flesh is soft and almost jelly-like, while non-astringent varieties can be eaten when firm. Some varieties have seeds, and others are seedless. The best astringent varieties include 'Saijo', 'Tanenashi', and 'Yomato Hyakume'. Good non-astringent varieties include 'Fuyu', 'Hanagosho', and 'Hana Fuyu'. Female trees don't need male trees to set fruit and, in fact, produce seedy fruit with dark streaks in the flesh when pollinated. Harvest in autumn when the fruit feel slightly soft. Protect from birds.

The American persimmon *(Diospyros virginiana),* which is native to the United States, grows vigorously from Zones 4 to 9 and spreads easily from seeds eaten by birds and animals. The trees tend to form thickets of suckers. Fruits measure 1 to 2 inches across and are sweet and edible after they mature, especially after a frost. Some varieties have larger fruit.

Book VII
Solar Power

The 5th Wave   By Rich Tennant

"Go ahead. It's like a mudroom, only better."

In this book . . .

Quick: What readily available energy source provides power without losing power, doesn't add pollution to the atmosphere, and brings your utility bills down? Give yourself a gold star if you answered "the sun." The very orb that keeps life on earth going can keep your household going, too.

This book gives you the goods on how solar can work for your house, giving you the basics of ways you can make the sun's power work for you and places to turn for financing (rebates, anyone?) solar projects around your house.

Here are the contents of Book VII at a glance:

Chapter 1

Soaking Up the Pluses and Minuses of Solar Power

*P*roducing energy can be dirty work. Carbon emissions, coal slurry, nuclear waste, and other pollutants can wreak havoc on the environment, cause health problems, and make people hopping mad. And many energy sources are in limited supply. Not only these conditions drive up prices, but they also lead to political conflicts when people decide they're not willing to share. You're probably not ready to go completely unplugged, but you do want to play your humble part to save the environment, help the country become less dependent on outside energy sources, and save money. Tall order? Maybe not. Of all the energy sources in use today, solar shows the most long-term promise for solving the world's energy problems.

On any given day, 35,000 times the total amount of energy that humans use falls onto the face of the earth from the sun. If people could just tap into a tiny fraction of what the sun is providing each day, society would be set. Of course, some problems do crop up, but they're solvable, and going solar can be well worth the effort.

To understand the role solar energy can play in your home, you need to have a good understanding of where your own energy comes from, where it's used, and how much pollution each of your energy sources generates. In this chapter, you find out how solar fits into your day-to-day life — and why it's such a good energy option.

Looking for Sustainable Energy

The words *renewable* and *sustainable* are being knocked around quite a bit, and both are strongly associated with energy conservation. *Renewable* forms of energy constantly replenish themselves with little or no human effort. Solar energy is just one example — no matter how much you use, the supply will never end. (Okay, it may end after billions of years, but your using solar power won't make the sun burn out any faster.)

Other examples of renewables include firewood, water (through hydroelectric dams), and wind power. Note, however, that firewood is notoriously polluting; the term *renewable* doesn't necessarily imply good environmentalism. Firewood also has another potentially severe drawback in that people go out into forests and cut down trees, often without much thought to the overall health of the forest (a good example of not seeing the forest from the trees).

To make sure that resources last, humans need to focus on conservation, recycling, environmental restoration, and renewable energy sources. Sustainability is commonly associated with such a holistic approach to personal lifestyle. Not only are sustainable forms of energy renewable, but they also have the ability to keep the planet earth's ecosystem up and running, in perpetuity. Sustainable energy, such as solar, is nonpolluting to the greatest extent possible.

The basic notion behind sustainable energy sources is that by their use, society is not compromising future generations' health and well-being, nor their ability to use their own sustainable resources to any less capacity than we have.

Understanding Why Solar Is King

Solar power has historically been more expensive than other energy options, but that's changing fast because of government investment in technologies, as well as the simple fact that many more people are investing in solar, which results in economies of scale. Solar energy equipment increases your financial standing in basically two ways:

- Savings on your monthly bills
- Appreciation of your home's value

The following sections cover reasons why solar is a great investment, both financially and environmentally.

Reaping financial rewards

Solar is an investment; you must actively go out and purchase solar equipment and install it at your home. However, after the initial costs, not only do you save money from lowering your energy bill, but you also may see the value of your home increase.

So how does investing in solar compare to other investments, such as the stock market, a savings account, or a new kitchen?

To compare, you need to calculate your payback period. *Payback period* is a measure of how long it takes to recoup your upfront investment with the costs you save. If you install a solar water heater system for $4,000 and it saves you $50 a month on your power bill, the system will pay for itself in 80 months, or 6⅔ years. (Though you may easily cut that time in half if the price of oil skyrockets and utility rates double, for example, during a war in the Middle East.)

Now consider other ways you can spend that money. With investments in remodeling, such as a new kitchen, you get no monthly cost reductions at all unless you're installing new appliances that are more energy efficient. If you put the same $4,000 into an interest-bearing bank account, you may get $20 a month in interest. After 80 months, you'd make $2,000 in compounded interest, or half your investment. And if you put the same money into the stock market, you may enjoy a return of $3,400. Of course, you can also lose the entire thing and drive yourself nuts with regret!

When you go solar, your home *appreciates*. Realtors can give you statistics that estimate how much the value will go up, given the type of investment and the area you live in.

According to the National Association of Real Estate Appraisers (NAREA), for every dollar you save annually in energy costs with solar equipment, the value of your home increases by up to 20 times your annual energy savings, depending on the type of system you install. For a solar water heater investment of $4,000, the value of your home may increase by at least that much! How can this be? Solar is catching on, and homebuyers are willing to pay more for solar homes that promise energy savings.

Right now, a wide range of government and industry programs are available to help you finance your solar investments. Governments are giving out tax breaks, utilities are offering rebates, and low-interest loans are available for solar investments. The net effect is to make your solar projects less expensive and more attractive on the bottom line.

Erasing your carbon footprint

Most energy resources are burned. The worst offender is coal, and the United States gets around 50 percent of its electrical power from coal-fired plants. Your carbon dioxide footprint is a measure of how much carbon dioxide you're releasing into the environment by virtue of your energy-consuming habits. A typical *carbon dioxide footprint* is around 36,000 pounds (18 tons) per year. That's a lot!

Solar, however, has no carbon footprint. For each kilowatt-hour (kWh) of energy-generating capacity you install with solar, you save that much from other sources, most likely the electrical power grid. Among other alternative energy resources, only wind power and hydro can offer this impact, but solar is far more versatile and widely available.

These numbers are valuable for calculating cost versus gain for installing solar systems because — face it — even though pollution isn't costing you directly in your wallet, you need to factor it into your thinking.

When you generate solar electricity, you don't need transmission lines and all the associated inefficiency. Solar is right there, where you use it. When you install a 3kWh active solar system, you're offsetting the need for that much power from your utility company. But you're *saving* about 9kWh of total power consumption because of inefficiencies. Therefore, you're actually saving much more than 3kWh, as well as the associated carbon footprint.

Table 1-1 can help you calculate your own carbon footprint. Table 1-2 provides an example of a calculation.

Table 1-1	Carbon Emissions for Burnable Energy Sources	
Type	*Pounds CO_2/Unit*	*Unit*
Oil	22.4	Gallons
Natural gas	12.1	Therms (Btus)
Liquid propane	12.7	Gallons
Kerosene	21.5	Gallons
Gas	19.6	Gallons
Coal	4,166	Tons
Wood	3,814	Tons

Table 1-2	Carbon Emissions for Your Car (Example)	
Questions	Your Numbers	Example:
How many miles do you drive per year?	_____	15,000 miles
Mpg?	_____	23 miles per gallon
Divide to yield number of gallons/year	_____	652 gal/yr
Multiply by 19.6 (from Table 1-1)	_____	12,782 lbs/yr (ouch!)

To find how much carbon dioxide you produce by using home fossil fuels, multiply the amount of fuel you use by the value in the second column, the pounds of CO_2 per unit. For example, suppose you use 400 gallons of home heating oil; you produce 8,960 pounds of carbon dioxide per year:

$$400 \text{ gal/yr} \times 22.4 \text{ lbs. } CO_2/\text{gal} = 8,960 \text{ lbs. } CO_2/\text{yr.}$$

And here's your carbon emissions for the 50 gallons of liquid propane you may use for your barbecue:

$$50 \text{ gal./yr} \times 12.7 \text{ lbs. } CO_2/\text{gal} = 635 \text{ lbs. } CO_2/\text{yr}$$

And here's the footprint for using 1 ton of firewood in a year:

$$1 \text{ ton/yr} \times 3,814 \text{ lbs. } CO_2/\text{ton} = 3,814 \text{ lbs. } CO_2/\text{yr}$$

Add those together, and your home fossil fuel consumption produces 13,409 pounds of carbon dioxide per year. You can cut way down on that if you switch to solar heating and cooking.

Calculate also your carbon emissions from electricity use. This number depends on how your local power generators operate. Nuclear reactors emit very little carbon, and coal-fired generators emit quite a bit. The average North American value is 1.33 pounds of CO_2 per kWh. If you're using nuclear energy, you can reduce this number to about 1.0 or less. If you're strictly relying on coal-fired electricity, the number could go as high as 2.0.

Here's how you find out the carbon dioxide output if you use 10,000 kWh of energy:

$$10,000 \text{ kWh/yr} \times 1.33 \text{ lbs. } CO_2/\text{kWh} = 40,000 \text{ lbs. } CO_2/\text{yr (Youch!)}$$

Book VII

Solar Power

Enjoying solar's unlimited supply

At sea level, on a sunny, clear day, 1 kWh of sunlight power is falling onto a 1-square-meter surface. Over the course of a sunny day, you can realistically expect to capture around 6 kWh of total energy from this same surface area. That's 180 kWh per month. Five square meters is enough to completely replace a typical monthly power bill! If only it was so easy.

If you were to build an active solar panel measuring 100 miles by 100 miles in sunny Nevada, you'd be able to produce enough power to handle all the United States' electrical requirements (except when it rained a lot!).

Exercising your legal rights to sunlight

You have legal rights to your sunlight; nobody can build up so that your solar exposures are affected. Government acknowledges value in the amount of sunlight that hits your home.

You have a legal right to demand that your neighbors remove trees and other impediments to your solar access. If a neighbor's trees are shading your property, you can do something about it. Remember, though, this right goes both ways. If you're shading somebody else's property, he can force you to remedy the situation. Check with your local governments to see what sorts of laws apply to your specifics.

Appreciating solar energy's versatility

You can use solar energy in many ways, each with different costs and complexity. Solar power enables you to do any of the following:

- **Generate electricity for general use:** You can install a solar electric generating system that allows you to reduce your electric bills to zero.

- **Cook:** Using the sun and your vivid imagination, along with a few easy-to-build ovens and heaters, solar power can help you put dinner on the table.

- **Practice passive space heating:** The sun can heat your house by strategic use of blinds, awnings, sunrooms and the like.

- **Heat water:** Use solar energy to heat your domestic water supply — or let sun-warmed water heat your house. You may need no electrical pumps or moving parts other than the water itself.

- **Pump water:** You can slowly pump water into a tank when the sun is shining and then get the water back anytime you want. You can also make your tank absorb sunlight and heat the water.

✔ **Heat your swimming pool:** A solar blanket heats your pool cheaply and efficiently. Or you can install solar hot water heating panels on your roof that can heat your pool year-round.

✔ **Light up your landscape:** You can put small, inexpensive solar lights around your yard and eliminate the need for high-priced overhead lighting powered by the utility company. With advances in technology, these lights actually look and work better than hard-wired versions.

✔ **Provide indoor lighting:** The technological boom in light-emitting diodes (LEDs) — small, electronic lights that take very little current and provide long lifetimes — has enabled a number of effective solar lighting systems for in-home use with very low power requirements. You can light your porches and even rooms in your house with a small, off-grid photovoltaic system connected to a battery. During the day, the battery charges so that you have enough juice at night to do the job.

✔ **Power remote dwellings:** You can completely power a remote cabin, RV, or boat with solar.

Acknowledging the Dents in the Crown

Solar sounds great! You're ready to go! But solar isn't all fun and games. The pros outweigh the cons — especially when you look at the big picture — but you should still understand the drawbacks. This section explains a few things to remember when working with solar energy.

Initial costs and falling prices

Going solar requires an upfront expense. When you go solar, you get a good payback on your investment, but you do have to put out cash upfront. Most people don't want to bother, and many don't have the cash. (Chapter 4 of this book gives you ideas for financing your solar investments.)

Reliability and timing

Solar works only when the sun is shining. If you want energy at night or on a dark day in the winter, you need either batteries or other energy resources. What makes sense in Phoenix doesn't necessarily make sense in Seattle. Ultimately, solar relies on Mother Nature's generosity, and this varies from region to region. In fact, it even varies over different locations at your home.

Also, timing of energy use is everything. In a typical scenario, solar energy availability is often at its peak when the household power demands are minimal.

It's out of phase with need. This scenario isn't much of a problem with solar water heaters because they inherently store the energy for later use. But solar electric requires either batteries for energy storage or a special system called an intertie, which connects to your public utility.

On a typical winter day, for example, the heater is on all night but turned low, and the lights and appliances are off. In the morning, the family turns up the heater, turns on lights, takes hot showers, cooks breakfast, and gets ready for school and work. Then everybody leaves, and the day warms up so the heater shuts down. At the end of the afternoon, when the sun is on its way down, everybody returns. Lights are turned on, the heater's turned up, a log is tossed into the fireplace, cooking begins in earnest, the kids play video games and make a big mess, the vacuum is run, and so on.

Red tape and aesthetically minded neighbors

You may have to work around building codes. Bureaucrats are a big hassle, and interfacing with government agencies is frustrating. In addition, only qualified contractors should install complex electrical systems.

Also, most solar panels are ugly. Nobody wants to look at them. If they're your own and you're benefiting, it's acceptable. If they belong to your neighbors, it's a different story. In some communities, solar panels are forbidden. Many homeowners associations have covenants that prohibit solar panels altogether, but this situation is changing; in fact, most legal challenges to solar panels are being stricken by the courts in favor of environmental conscience. At some point, the federal government will likely enter the picture and prohibit all banning of solar panels. Several ongoing efforts are working to make solar panels less obtrusive, so this problem will become less important over time.

Effort and upkeep

Going solar takes work. Making good decisions about solar power can be difficult unless you've done your homework. And not only do you have to do some research, but you also have to work with the equipment itself. Here are some issues to consider:

> ✔ **You face some dangers.** Active systems can shock you if you don't know what you're doing. Water heating systems can scald you. You're much safer sitting in front of your TV than climbing around installing solar equipment.

✔ **You face equipment challenges in freezing weather.** Solar water heating panels can freeze up in the winter. You have to pay attention to how they're working. Most new solar thermal heating systems get around the freezing problem by using some form of anti-freeze, but a good number of existing and new systems still use water. The antifreeze systems are more expensive. If you don't need one, you don't want to pay the extra cost, so water-based systems will always be available.

✔ **You're on your own for upkeep and repairs.** If you get your power from the power company, keeping things maintained and running is its problem. If you have a big array of solar panels on your roof, it's your problem. If they break, you pay. When they get old, you update.

Small to Supergiant: Choosing Your Level of Commitment

No matter where you start, you can always expand your solar system. For example, you can invest in a small photovoltaic system for your rooftop and then expand it as you go, spreading the investment costs over a long period of time. The following sections show you ways to get involved.

Small- to midsized projects

From installing landscape lighting to a stand-alone photovoltaic powered attic vent fan, you can begin investing in solar today with minimal cost and effort. The small-scale projects feature safe operating levels. (Typical voltages in a photovoltaic system are so low that you won't be able to get a shock.) And if you're no good with tools, have no fear. Some of the projects don't even require a screwdriver — you can buy off-the-shelf solutions that you can use out of the box.

You can also do a number of things in your yard to improve the solar exposure of your home. Deciduous trees (which shed their leaves in the fall) planted strategically about your house can ensure summertime cooling while allowing solar energy to help warm your house in the winter. Planting bushes in the right spots can reduce the cooling effect of wind, especially around your pool. And you can also increase the breezes flowing through your house by strategically arranging trees and bushes.

Pick up a copy of *Solar Power Your Home For Dummies* (Wiley) by Rik DeGunther for instructions on tackling a range of solar projects and to find out about some of the larger projects you might want to hire a specialist to add to your home.

Book VII

Solar Power

If you're intending to install a full-scale solar energy system in your home, a great way to find out about the character of solar energy is to start with the simpler projects. You discover the importance of good solar exposure, and you determine when and how solar works the best — as well as the worst. You'll be in a better position to make good decisions on how to invest the big bucks when the time comes.

Large projects

Full-scale photovoltaic energy generators are the king of the mountain these days. You probably won't be able to install one of these systems on your own.

Greenhouses are attractive, and you can grow your own food in them, year-round in some climates. But you can also use a greenhouse or sunroom to provide a warm room in the winter.

Off-grid living means there's no utility company power coming into your home at all. You can use a solar power system, backed up with a gasoline-powered generator, to provide all the power you'll ever need. It's not for everybody, and it really doesn't make much sense unless you're living so far away from the utilities that just running the lines to your house would cost a ton. But for some of the more independent-minded readers, it's the only way to go.

Designing a solar home from scratch

Designing a solar home from scratch is clearly the most efficient way to achieve solar energy advantages. Most existing homes are inefficient in a number of ways. Insulation may be lacking. Sunlight exposure was not thought out — it's just what happened when the house was built on the lot. But when you design your own home, you can control all the variables. You can achieve excellent sunlight in the morning, for example, while blocking off the afternoon heat.

You can shelter for wind by taking advantage of existing trees and cover. Best of all, you can build your roof to achieve perfect solar exposure.

You can also ensure energy efficiency by using the right materials and building techniques. The fact is, a good house design can make it so that you don't need much energy at all. What could be better for the environment?

Chapter 2

Preparing for a Switch to Solar

· ·

· ·

*N*o matter how giddy the possibilities of solar make you, no matter how desperately you might want to run out and get started on bringing cleaner, cheaper energy into your life, careful thought is warranted before you take your green self down to the showroom to start picking out equipment. This stuff is expensive, in a lot of cases, and you may be entering into extensive changes to your biggest investment — your home. All that's worth careful consideration, eh?

In this chapter, you find out a little bit about how solar works and a lot about how your location might limit your possibilities and how you can ascertain the potential benefits of your investment.

Using Sunlight Converted into Heat

When a *photon* (light particle) strikes a surface that absorbs light, the photon's energy is transformed into heat. *Heat,* or *thermal energy,* is simply motion. A hot surface has a lot of molecular motion, and hot objects can burn you because they pass their excessive energy right into your skin.

Many solar applications require sunlight to be converted into heat. Then you want to transfer that heat and change it into a usable form, usually in a location removed from where the heat is captured. Heat can move from one spot to another in several ways:

✔ **Conduction:** In *conduction,* energy is transferred between molecules within a substance. Only heat moves, not the molecules. (Well, molecules are always moving, but the molecules tend to vibrate in place rather than switch places.) Heat always moves from a hotter surface to a cooler surface. (Technically speaking, heat moves in both directions, but statistically the most movement occurs from hotter to cooler.) Copper is an excellent conductor of heat. In fact, most good conductors of electricity are also good heat conductors. Glass is a poor conductor of heat and electricity and is therefore considered an insulator.

✔ **Convection:** *Convection* is the transfer of heat between a fixed, rigid surface and a moving fluid in contact with that surface or the transfer of heat as molecules move from one point to another within the fluid. A *fluid* is any substance that can flow, so air is also considered a fluid. As opposed to conduction, the hot molecules themselves move and switch places.

Water flowing over a hot surface becomes hot. In a tank of water, the hotter molecules expand and weigh less and move upward while gravity draws the colder, heavier molecules down. This heat exchange is called *thermosiphon,* and it's a type of convection.

✔ **Radiation:** A hot object emits infrared radiation. The sun is a perfect radiator. Fires radiate heat, a lot of which you can see. A really hot fire glows white; all wavelengths in the spectrum are present. As the fire cools down, the color changes to orange, then to red, and finally, when you can't see the embers anymore but can still feel the heat, the radiation is entirely infrared. The colors reflect the energy content of the fire.

Keeping the heat where you want it

Solar heat collectors are designed to collect as much solar radiation as possible. Not only do you want to maximize surface area, but you also want to orient the collector in a way that maximizes the amount of solar radiation gathered over the course of a day. Solar heat collectors also ought to do the following, all of which affect what kind of materials go where in your solar collector:

✔ **Convert that radiation into heat as efficiently as possible.** This conversion almost always entails the use of a black surface, which absorbs radiation efficiently.

✔ **Transfer the heat into a usable medium.** In most cases, you want to heat water. If you collect the heat in a black tube, you can simply run water through that tube, and the heat naturally transfers into the water. You can also use other fluids, such as antifreeze fluid.

To move heat effectively, a material needs to be a good conductor (or as physicists like to say, it needs to have *high thermal conductivity*).

✔ **Insulate to prevent heat loss.** For insulators, you want to use materials that make for poor conductors. Converting radiation into heat in the wintertime is easy, but then the cold weather and wind simply steal the heat right back. In order to prevent this loss, people insulate the collector from the outside world with materials, such as fiberglass insulation, or double-pane glass windows.

✔ **Store a sufficient amount of heat.** *Heat capacity* is a measure of how much heat energy (in British thermal units, or Btus) is required to raise the temperature of a given volume of a material by 1°F. To be effective at storing heat, a material needs a high heat capacity. Table 2-1 shows some materials of interest.

Table 2-1	Heat Capacity of Common Materials
Material	*Heat Capacity (Btus per Cubic Foot — °F)*
Air	0.018
Plastic	0.57
Wool, fabric	2.2
Concrete	22
Brick	25
Wood, oak	26.8
Steel	59
Water	62.4
Copper	78

Book VII

Solar Power

So the ideal material for storing and moving heat needs to have a high heat capacity and also has to be a good conductor. Although wood and concrete store a lot of heat, you can't move it into or out of these materials very easily. Steel is very good, but it rusts. Of course, water is the cheapest, so it's used to store and transfer heat, but the problem is that it doesn't absorb radiation because it's clear. Copper painted black absorbs, stores, and conducts heat extremely well, so copper is used extensively in solar heat collectors.

Converting sunlight into electricity: Photovoltaic cells

Most people are familiar with photovoltaic cells (PV cells). You see them on calculators, the kind that don't require batteries. You see PV panels on people's roofs and on businesses and schools and government buildings. Remote telephones along the interstates have PV panels poised overhead.

A standard PV cell, shown in Figure 2-1, is a thin semiconductor sandwich, with two layers of highly purified silicon. A *semiconductor* is a crystal that is constructed in such a way as to yield certain specific properties that can be used in electrical circuits. Transistors are made of semiconductors. Microprocessors are as well. In fact, the entire field of modern electronics uses various forms of semiconductors, so the implications are worldly. If you connect an electrical circuit to your semiconductor sandwich when sunlight is shining on it, electricity flows.

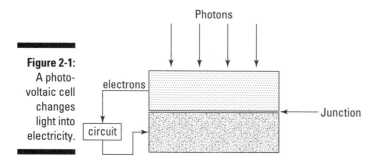

Figure 2-1:
A photo-voltaic cell changes light into electricity.

Photovoltaic arrays are nothing more than huge matrices of interconnected semiconductor sandwiches. The color appears shiny blue. Usable PV systems are comprised of all sorts of equipment that protects the user from electrical shock, stores the electricity in battery banks, and converts the direct current (DC) into alternating current (AC), which is what people use in their houses. But at the heart of each system is a simple conversion process like that shown in Figure 2-1.

Evaluating Your Solar Potential

Depending on where you live geographically — and the orientation and exposure of your particular house or business — you get more or less usable sunshine. Even within small, localized regions, weather patterns vary because of topography and landscape details like trees and ponds. So two identical solar systems separated by a few miles but otherwise built and operated identically may yield different energy outputs averaged over a period of time.

Weather is today's phenomenon, but *climate* is a description of the general weather patterns over a long period of time. It may be cold and rainy in Los Angeles today, and that's the weather, but the climate is warm and temperate. Good solar designers assess climate particulars to enhance system performance. Climate includes elements such as temperature, precipitation, and wind speed.

Here's a look at how climate can affect your solar system:

✔ **Sunlight:** Climate dictates how much sunlight you can expect annually. That the Southwest gets the most sunshine per day — and that Canada and the northern states get the least — should come as no surprise. The sun is higher in the sky in the southern states, so the days are longer.

✔ **Snowfall:** You want to locate your panels so they avoid being inundated with heavy layers of snow. For example, some locations on your roof will experience very shallow snow buildups as compared to other parts of your roof. Also, some parts of your roof may be warmer than others due to proximity to heaters, exhausts, chimneys, and so on.

✔ **Cloud cover:** If you're living in a cloudy region, you still have solar energy, and it's generally diffused (spread out). As a result, collector panel orientation isn't so critical because light will be coming in at many different angles rather than just directly overhead from the sun.

✔ **Smog:** Air pollution and smog affect the amount of sunlight you can expect to receive. If you do live in an area with heavy air pollution, expect less system output over an extended period of time.

✔ **Air density:** You get better solar exposure in the mountains than near sea level simply because the air is thinner and scatters less sunlight. You can make an approximate estimate of how clear your air is by simply observing how blue the sky is on a clear day. Thick air scatters more red light, and so the appearance of the sky is less blue and more white.

✔ **Temperature:** With PV systems (not solar water heaters), the lower the temperature, the happier the semiconductors, and the greater the output. You can get more system output on a cold, clear day than a warm, sunny day.

✔ **Frequent fog:** If you're living in an area that's foggy and misty in the morning (in the San Francisco Bay Area, for example) but the mist burns off into a clear sky by noon, you want to orient your solar panels more westward to optimize the amount of sunlight you can achieve over the course of a day.

✔ **Wind:** If you have a lot of wind, you need to consider where you mount your solar equipment for a couple of reasons:

- Wind can tear equipment off of its mounting hardware and result in expensive repairs, not to mention dangerous conditions. If you're in a windy climate, you need to make sure that you specify heavy-duty mounting equipment. Mounting schemes all have wind speed specifications; pay close attention because mishaps are expensive.

- Wind cools surfaces very efficiently. If you have a swimming pool, one of your best bets is to install landscaping that breaks the rush of wind that will cool the pool water much more than your intuition would indicate. Solar water heating panels may heat the water very effectively, but it doesn't make much sense to install expensive solar panels without addressing wind cooling first, because adding a few bushes and trees will be much cheaper than adding extra collector capacity. Plus, living things frankly look nicer than solar equipment and good for the environment, to boot.

Book VII

Solar Power

You can obtain generalized information and maps about the nation's solar resources from the following The National Renewable Energy Laboratory (www.nrel.gov), which has a solar resources section on its Web site, and from National Climatic Data Center (www.ncdc.noaa.gov).

Analyzing Solar Investments

An important factor to consider when deciding how much money to earmark toward each investment is the *risk profile*. Some investments entail more risk than others. A bank is much safer than the stock market, for example. When an investment entails more risk, it needs to offer more of a chance for gain to offset the increased risk.

The following sections outline a system for analyzing solar investments. The goal is to compare different investment options using the same criteria of costs, gains, and risks and then choose the best one.

Calculating net costs

The first step in calculating payback is to calculate costs. Here you find out how to calculate *net costs,* the total net amount that you're paying for your solar investment. These days, most solar investments are eligible for rebates and tax advantages, which are subtracted from the "retail" cost of a system.

Collecting cost data

The typical solar system has many cost components, and the sum total of all the individual costs must be added up to yield the total cost. Note also that the timing of the costs is important, as well as the timing of the rebates and tax advantages. Timing is important because of the basic idea that a dollar today is worth more than a dollar in one year, the difference being given by current interest rates. So the result of a cost compilation will usually be a timeline rather than a single number.

Consider the following factors:

- ✔ **Equipment:** Sometimes equipment costs are spread out over time — for example, if you get financing from a supplier or different parts of a system are delivered at different times. You need to specify the timeline, as well as the dollar value of each outlay.

- ✔ **Installation costs:** If you're a do-it-yourselfer, you won't have to worry about installation. If you hire out, installation costs may be either fixed or an hourly rate, depending on the complexity of the job.

- ✔ **Refuse:** Add in costs if you'll pay to have project trash hauled away.

- ✔ **Maintenance:** Consider the likelihood that you'll have to pay for servicing — and when that may occur, so you know whether it's likely to be covered by warranty.

- ✔ **Taxes, permits, fees:** Note when such charges are due.

- ✔ **Interest:** If you finance your equipment, the interest is a cost.

- ✔ **Taxes:** Many states have legislation that lets you install solar equipment without paying higher property taxes, but you should find out whether it applies to you. (See Chapter 4 for details on state incentives.) In rare cases, property taxes may go up as a result of a solar investment.

Subtracting estimated gains and discounts

You recover some of your expenses right away, so you can subtract that amount from your costs. For example, you may be able to take advantage of rebates and subsidies offered by utilities, state and federal governments, manufacturers, and so on. Or if you're installing equipment for your home business or office, you may be able to depreciate certain items. (See Chapter 4 of this book for details.)

You also need to consider both salvage (if you can sell some of the old equipment you'll be taking out) and *appreciation* — the value of your home goes up when you install solar. The appreciation amount depends on the following:

Book VII

**Solar
Power**

- ✔ **The cost for a homebuyer to put in new equipment personally:** Don't expect to get much more than that. However, if the cost of new solar equipment increases, the value of your equipment can also go up. Equipment can increase in value if inflation becomes significant or if the demand for solar equipment increases (supply versus demand).

- ✔ **The amount of documentable energy savings achieved with the equipment:** Your energy bills provide proof of the energy savings achieved.

- ✔ **Changes in energy costs:** The more energy costs rise (all energy), the more your equipment — and thus your property — is worth.

- ✔ **Popularity:** Some things sell because they're trendy. In some real estate markets, a solar home is worth a lot more than the same model with conventional energy.

Giving a ballpark about how much appreciation you can expect is impossible, but the most likely case is that you'll get around 25 percent more than new equipment costs. Best case, you may double your original investment after five years. Worst case, you may not get anything at all if the equipment is old and obsolete.

Figuring out monthly savings

With most solar investments, lowering monthly utility bills is the ultimate goal. Here's how to calculate your potential savings:

1. **Look at your power bills and determine your average monthly energy use (gas or electric).**

   Use the electric bill if the new system will reduce your use of electricity, the gas bill if it'll reduce your gas use.

   Suppose, for example, that you want to replace an electric water heater with a solar one. You look at your power bills and find that you use an average of 1,000 kWh of electricity per month.

2. **Out of that number, estimate how much energy the system you're replacing uses or how much energy the new system produces.**

   In the example, perhaps an energy audit tells you that water heating makes up 20 percent of your total electric bill. (See Chapter 2 of Book II for more on energy audits.)

   To estimate output of a PV system, use the specifications given for the proposed equipment and modify them up or down depending on your solar exposure. Ultimately, you're going to be making an educated guess. The best way to get a good estimate is to ask your professional contractor because he has experience and local empirical data. If you're a do-it-yourselfer, the problem is more difficult. The best way to account for the inescapably hazy nature of projections is to be conservative and see how the economics come out. Then redo the calculations with optimistic numbers and see how the payback calculations turn out.

3. **Multiply your average monthly energy costs by the percentage you found in Step 2 to figure out how much you save per month.**

   At $0.15 per kWh, suppose the total monthly bill is $150:

   $$\$150 \times 20\% = \$30$$

   The solar water heater therefore saves you $30 per month.

As energy costs rise, your savings increase even more. The Energy Information Administration reported that from 1996 to 2007, electricity energy costs increased an average of 2.2 percent per year (www.eia.doe. gov/emeu/steo/pub/contents.html), and the change may be even greater in the future — or in your region of the country.

Figuring payback

Payback is the amount of time you need to hold on to your investment for it to pay for itself. In the case of solar, almost the entire investment is upfront, meaning you have to invest cash before you see a single dime of savings.

Payback is measured in years or months. You simply take the net costs of your solar system (costs minus discounts and appreciation — see the earlier "Calculating net costs" section) and divide it by your anticipated monthly savings (see "Figuring out monthly savings"). For example, if you invest $2,000 in a solar water heater that saves $30 a month in electric costs, here's your payback period:

$$\$2{,}000 \div \$30/\text{month} \approx 67 \text{ months, or } 5.6 \text{ years}$$

Analyzing risk

No investment is risk-free. The following elements can affect the returns you get on your investment:

✔ **Repairs and maintenance:** Solar equipment is not simple when it's doing a big job. And being outdoors all the time is wearing, especially in extreme climates. (How'd you like to be strapped to a roof 24/7?) You can't always anticipate when something will break down, and if your equipment has problems after the warranty expires, your costs go up.

✔ **Efficiency decreases over time, just as it does for autos and humans and pretty much everything.** PV panels may see a 15-percent decline in ten years. It's harder to estimate the decline in water systems, but it's on the same order, unless you're using hard water or have well water with a lot of sediment. Use 15 percent per ten years in your calculations for a good approximation.

✔ **Lifetime:** Eventually, every system will simply not be worth running anymore. PV systems are warranted up to 20 years, water systems for up to 15. However, it's not as bad as that, because what the warranties really cover is guaranteed performance. You will probably be able to run your systems for much longer than the warranties, but they simply won't be putting out the same performance.

Book VII

Solar Power

✔ **Inexperience:** If you design and install a system yourself, the performance may not be as good as you planned. The experts know all the little tricks, but you don't. Savings can suffer, and you may have to pay an expert to come in and set things straight.

✔ **Newer, more efficient technologies:** People like new things because they're new. The bottom line with a solar system is the performance it's putting out, but it may be true that a homebuyer simply doesn't like a system that's 10 years old simply because it's 10 years old. Newer equipment is always more efficient as well. This increased efficiency rarely results in a situation that merits tossing out old equipment that is still working, but it may make a difference to a prospective buyer.

Accounting for the intangibles

Good decisions aren't just predicated on dollars and cents. You also need to consider the intangibles, such as aesthetic beauty and pollution mitigation, among others. Not everything comes with a price tag, but you certainly need to factor in how much these elements are worth to you. You can do this calculation by either assigning dollar values, as best you can, or making a list of priorities so that if two potential options have the same numerical score (payback calculation), one option will win over the other based on the intangibles.

Allowing for drawbacks

You should account for any inconvenience. Note whether your system is going to require more work on your part. Solar water heaters, for example, take maintenance. Decide whether you're going to do it or hire someone else to do it for you. In addition, when you install a solar system, you're introducing dangers into your house: electrical shocks. Scalding water. Falling off a roof. Discovering stepladder malfunctions. Think about whether you're okay accepting these risks.

Also factor in your feelings about the look of your house and how that may affect resale value. Some solar equipment can be ugly. Do the pipes running up the side of your house look industrial? Do photovoltaic panels make your house look unearthly?

Considering priceless benefits

Think about visual improvements. For example, if you invest in a maple tree, you get shading in the summer, which is a form of solar system performance, but the greater pleasure is having a nice tree near your house. When you invest in window coverings, you enjoy better insulation by virtue of the fact that you can shade your home's interior from solar radiation, but the greater gain is probably in the remodel.

Don't forget environmental improvements: When you invest in solar, you're saving a lot of carbon dioxide, and you're also helping with national energy independence.

Examining Real-Life Scenarios

Compare your own solar investment decisions with these examples and you can get a good idea of how your investment stacks up. In most cases, just substitute in your own numbers. In some cases, you may have to adjust the model to fit your exact situation.

Decisions often come down to the details of your rate structure. You can find it on your power bill. You may be able to change your rate structure with a simple call to the utility. Some allow for choices. In fact, you may be able to save some money simply by changing your rate structure.

Supplementing an existing water heater with solar

Book VII

Solar Power

To calculate payback, first find the monthly energy savings. Suppose Household X uses an average of 1,000 kWh of electricity per month. At $0.15 per kWh, the monthly cost is $150. An energy audit determines that water heating makes up 18 percent of the total electric bill, at a cost of $27 per month. (See the earlier "Figuring out monthly savings" section for details on such calculations.) With the solar water heater, that amount drops to zero, so $27 is its monthly savings.

Then determine the net cost of the equipment. A solar water heating system costs $2,000, including parts and installation. A federal government tax credit of 30 percent is available, for a total of $600. The net cost is $1,400. The warranty is for five years, so the homeowners won't have to pay maintenance costs for the first 60 months.

To recover the initial investment of $1,400, Household X will need

$1,400 ÷ $27/month ≈ 52 months

That's a good investment. A solar water heater may last about 20 years, and Household X is making a profit within the first 5 years.

Putting money in a bank or stock market

Here's how some other investments stack up: Put $1,000 in a savings account at 6 percent, and you gain compounded interest. You have $1,000 in interest *12 years* after you make your original investment, which is the payback period. At any point in time, you can pull your money back out of the bank, with zero risk.

If you put your money into the stock market and get a return of 12 percent, the payback period is only six years. But the value of your stock could also go down in value, maybe all the way to zero. Because the risk is much higher in the stock market, you insist on a higher potential gain or else you'll just put your money into a bank.

A good general rule is the *Rule of 72:* To find the number of years required to double your money at a given interest rate, just divide the interest rate into 72. For a 12-percent return:

$72 \div 12 = 6$ years

Accounting for pollution

Suppose that you're installing a solar water heater in an area where the climate is northern. There isn't as much sunshine, and the winters are colder. Cost savings are $13.50 per month (or half as much as in the preceding section). For this example, assume constant energy costs, which is probably a simplification. (The point here is to illustrate how you can account for pollution.) When the monthly savings are cut in half, the payback period for a $1,400 water heater is twice as long — about 104 months. This number isn't much different from the return (or payback) you can get at a bank, where there's zero risk and you can take your money back out whenever you want. When you invest in solar, you're stuck with what you've got. This is a bad investment.

But how much is it worth to reduce pollution? Ten dollars a month? Twenty? How much would you pay to completely eliminate your carbon footprint altogether? $1,000 a year?

Out of your total carbon footprint (see Chapter 2 of this book), figure out how much CO_2 the old water heater contributes. The typical carbon footprint is around 40,000 pounds per year. The typical footprint from a water heater is 3,000 pounds per year, or 7.5 percent of the total.

If you're willing to spend $1,000 a year on pollution mitigation, you'd spend 7.5 percent of this on heating water. That's $75 per year, or $6.25 per month. Add this amount to the savings column, and instead of only $13.50 per month, the real savings is $19.75. This number makes the payback 71 months, which is a better proposition:

$1,400 \div (\$13.50 + \$6.25) \approx 71$ months

If you'd spend $2,000 a year eliminating pollution, total cost savings are $27 per month, which is all the way back to the original example with a payback of 52 months (see the preceding section). This is a good investment.

Reaping rewards of rising energy costs

What if energy costs rise 12 percent per year instead of staying flat? That percentage is higher than historical norms, but it's not difficult to imagine how this might come to be, with all the pressure coming to bear on the energy markets. When energy costs rise, each year the savings grow. Perhaps your $1,400 solar water heater saves you $27 per month the first year. But the next year the savings grow to $30.24 per month ($27 × 1.12). Then $33.87 ($30.24 × 1.12), then $37.93, then $42.49, and so on. Look at the yearly savings to see how they add up:

Year	Monthly Savings	Annual Savings	Cost Left to Recoup
1	$27	$324	$1,076
2	$30.24	$362.88	$713.12
3	$33.87	$406.43	$306.69
4	$37.93	$455.20	–$148.51

The payback in this case is 44 months (down from 52 months if the energy costs were to stay the same).

Regardless of how high energy costs go, the amount that you spend on heating water is locked in at zero. This is a form of *hedging*, or making an investment that reduces risk.

Thinking about tiered rate structures

In a *tiered rate structure*, the more energy you use, the more you pay per kWh. So in California, for example, not all watts are created equal. Some tiered rate structures are very punitive, with the highest rates three or four times the base rate. Solar system savings come from the highest tier first. In such a rate structure, cost savings can easily be twice as much. Payback is therefore half as long.

A solar water heater may offset 18 percent of the household energy use, but this may account for more like 35 percent of the total dollar value in a typical tiered rate structure.

Book VII

Solar
Power

In a tiered rate structure, small investments work best. As the size of your investment grows, the payback gets worse because you get less and less return on your investment.

Appreciating a solar home's increase in value

Suppose that some homeowners decide to sell five years after installing a solar water heater. Energy costs are rising, and monthly savings from the solar water heating system are now $48 per month, or $600 per year. A home buyer will pay more for the home because of this built-in cost reduction.

How much more? New systems cost $2,800, and tax rebates are a thing of the past because everybody and their brother are now in the market for solar. A lot of work is involved, and most buyers don't want to do it. They'd have to read some highly technical books, for example. (Unfortunately, they didn't know about this handy guide.)

Even more importantly, most homebuyers use mortgages, where balancing monthly payments with a fixed income is the game. Forty-eight dollars per month in cost-savings translate into $48 that can be spent somewhere else. A buyer could get a larger mortgage, for example. For $50 a month, after taxes, you can borrow $14,000. So although putting in their own solar system may be an option (after the purchase) for homebuyers, they also have a strong incentive to purchase existing solar equipment with their mortgage.

In terms of appreciation, the homeowners are likely to get about 125 percent of the price of new equipment. For the example, a 25-percent appreciation would be $3,500 (that is, $2,800 times 125 percent). Suppose that with rising energy costs, the original investment of $1,400 paid for itself in 44 months (see the preceding section). After that, the cost savings were all pure profit. At 60 months, the sellers get a further profit of $2,100 at the sale of the house.

Financing solar investments with a home equity loan

 Many solar investments end up saving their owners more on energy costs than the payments on a mortgage equity loan used to purchase a solar system. You pay no upfront cost when you finance an investment. You do have to pay off the loan at some point, but from day one, you save more than you pay. Your cash flow is in the black.

Suppose that you borrow $1,400 for a solar water heater with a promise of $27 per month in savings. An interest-only home equity line of credit at 6-percent tax-deductible interest for the $1,400 is only $8 per month (from mortgage payment tables). That's a net gain of $19 per month.

Here's the payback period for this scenario:

$1,400 ÷ $19/month = 74 months

At some point the loan is repaid (principal payments usually kick in after five to ten years), although most equity loans get paid off when the house is sold or refinanced. When it's sold, you often get more for your solar equipment than what you paid. (See the preceding section for details.)

Replacing broken water heaters

When your water heater crashes, doing nothing is not an option. Now you must spend money, probably a good chunk. How much more do you have to spend for a solar system? Probably not much. Now's really the time to go for it.

For example, a solar water heating system costs $3,000, and a conventional water heater costs $1,400. The difference is only $1,600 (And if you factor in rebates and subsidies, the difference may be zero.), whereas if you take out a working water heater in order to upgrade to solar, the real investment is the entire $3,000.

Book VII

Solar Power

Diving in to swimming pool solar heaters

A solar pool heater does *not* save money — except when you compare it to all the other options. Solar collectors load the filter pump (make it run harder) so it costs more to run — sometimes a lot more. If you want a lot of heat, you have to run the filter pump for upwards of 8 hours a day. This extra pump time is solar-system cost, and if you're in a tiered rate structure, it can add up to quite a bit. If you're in a *time-of-use structure* (pricing that varies according to when you use electricity), you also get dinged because you need to run your pump at peak times (midafternoon, when it's sunniest).

When you invest in a solar pool heater, the only gain is comfort, and that's hard to value. But people pay a lot for solar pool heaters. In some areas, they're on every roof. Ask an owner, and he'll probably tell you they're great. Pools cost upwards of $25,000. Another $3,000 to make it much more enjoyable isn't a bad investment. Your swimming season will be extended — a solar heater may triple the amount of time swimmers actually spend in the pool, as opposed to around it.

The other options are insane: a big, gas heater that gobbles propane, or electric, with a 24/7 spinning power meter. (You could light a big fire and boil water, but that's labor intensive.) A solar pool heater not only heats your pool much cheaper than the other options, but the pollution effects are infinitely better.

Blowing hot air

The investment: an attic vent fan powered by PV panels. Equipment costs $350, and installation takes two hours and requires brains, ladders, roof climbing, and decent tools.

An energy audit determines that the fan will save $25 per month in air-conditioning costs over a four-month summer period. At $100 per year, the payback is only 3.5 years.

You also boost your comfort. The house is a lot more comfortable on the days when it isn't hot enough to turn the AC on. And because the fan lets hot air escape, you get more of these days.

The alternatives to installing a solar fan? Not installing anything at all and paying for all that extra air conditioning or installing a hard-wired fan for more than $1,500 because you need a licensed electrician to do the installation, as well as county inspections and permits.

Working with solar in your home office

You can go off the power grid with a home office. A remote cabin solar power kit costs $1,000, with 12 volts DC (direct current) output and a battery so power is always available. You can use the system to run DC lights, a vent fan, coffee maker, radio, and a PC laptop computer with printer. A small inverter provides minimal 120 volts AC (alternating current) power for telephones and other support gear.

The total investment, including wiring and DC equipment (lights, fans, and an AC voltage adaptor), is $1,500. Installation is extra, but with the kits available, a do-it-yourselfer can tackle the job. And because the solar equipment is used for a business, it's depreciated, which reduces taxes.

The system saves around $30 per month in utility-provided electricity, so the payback is 50 months. When all taxes are taken into account, the payback can be as low as 30 months.

Investing in a full-scale PV system

Suppose that some homeowners have good roof exposure for solar equipment, and they want to install a full-scale, *intertie* (connected to the grid so that extra generated power is credited to your power bill) PV system in a three-bedroom, two-bath house. Their monthly average electric bill is $240, and energy consumption is 1,600 kWh's per month. The home is all electric.

After an audit, they employ conservation measures to decrease the bill 15 percent to 1,360 kWh's per month, or $204. (Chapter 1 of Book II discusses energy audits.) The goal is to reduce the average monthly electric bill to zero.

A TOU rate structure will apply when the system is in place. The owners believe they can use 90 percent of their electricity in off-peak hours, so they'll be selling most of their solar production back at the top rate and using it at a much lower rate. In California, utilities are required by law to pay you for your excess generated power the same rate they charge you. In some states, the utilities pay you only a percentage of the rate they charge. Look for this scenario to change in the future, because it's a way to encourage solar investment.

A 5 kWh system that'll do the job costs $40,000. The state will give a rebate of $10,000 directly to the PV system contractor so it's not even billed to the homeowners. The total out-of-pocket cost is $30,000. On top of that, the feds will give a $2,000 tax credit for the system, which now costs only $28,000.

The warranty is 20 years on the panels, less for some of the other equipment. Reliability is good on the brand chosen, which isn't the cheapest. In theory, maintenance and repair costs should be very low.

The owners finance this with an equity loan at $140 per month, tax deductible. They're immediately saving the difference between the power bill they've erased ($204) and the cost for the loan — in this case, $84 per month after taxes. From day one, this deal is in the black.

Using 7 percent as the energy inflation rate, the payback is 11 years, but this doesn't account for the fact that the value of the equipment is also rising because demand is rising. With this factor included in the equation, the payback goes down to 7 years.

The potential savings in carbon footprint are 13,000 pounds per year. Not bad!

What will happen to the value of your equipment if rebates and subsidies dry up? Homebuyers will have to pay a lot more if they choose to install their own equipment. The seller providing that equipment with the house has become much more attractive.

Installing both a water heater and PV

Household Y uses 12 kWhs of electricity per month. A solar water heater supplement costs $4,000 and will save 18 percent of the power consumption. A full-scale PV system will offset the entire electric bill for a cost of $30,000. If both systems are installed, the capacity of the PV system can be 18 percent less, for 18 percent less cost.

Here's what installing both a water heater and a PV system will cost:

$4,000 + 82% of $30,000 = $28,600

Going with the PV option costs only $30,000. That's a savings of $1,400.

But is it worth it? Maybe not. Water heaters need maintenance. Some water heaters are very reliable and work for decades, but PV systems are relatively trouble-free. You also have two investment projects to contend with instead of one. With these numbers, you might want to install only the PV system. Your calculations may indicate a bigger divergence, in which case your decision may be different. This decision may also depend on financing. For example, you may be able to finance a big PV system, but not both, so your decision may be to install only PV for this reason.

When does it make good sense to install a solar water heater? A $4,000 investment is reachable in cash for most homeowners. You get a good payback, especially if you're in a tiered rate structure. You can always add PV later, after you've determined how much cost savings you've achieved with the water heater, or when your finances allow for a larger investment.

Or perhaps you can get a solar tax credit of 30 percent of the cost of your system, at a maximum of $2,000. This credit means you get a $1,2000 tax credit for a $4,000 solar water heater, as well as a $30,000 PV system. The percentages are a lot better for the water heater, making its payback much better.

If tax credits or rebates are limited in any given calendar year, you're better off installing hot water and PV in different years.

Chapter 3

Jumping In to Small Projects with Big Results

S tarting out with small projects makes sense because you find out how solar works through experience. When you move up to bigger and more powerful systems, you get to understand the ropes. In payback terminology, you decrease risk by starting out simply.

Installing Sunscreens for Summer

Installing sunscreens is the cheapest way to prepare a window for the summer season, and it's also one of the best. Sunscreens reflect a lot of sunlight and create an insulation barrier on the outside.

Most sunscreens are dark, heavy-duty fabric screens with a shiny surface. Some are a flexible, tinted plastic film. They can reflect up to 90 percent of all sunlight.

Only windows that get more than a few hours of direct sunlight a day benefit from sunscreen installation. The best candidates are tall windows facing south, but east and west can also get very hot. Of course, part of the effect is the psychological comfort of shading, and you may want that anywhere.

You don't want sunscreens in the winter, so they're only temporary, which means you need to mount them in removable frames or tack them up. You can also roll them up like a blind or buy a finished blind that has solar screen. Or get automatic, electric controllers so that with the push of a single button, you can command every solar screen in your house.

Call a screen shop directly for tools, materials, and advice on how to install sunscreen. Sunscreens come up to 8 feet wide, in huge rolls, so that you can get as much length as you want. You can do the installation with nothing more than tacks, a hammer, and a box cutter, but a good stapler ensures a quality, consistent job and is much easier.

Getting framed

You can buy frames for sunscreens in a range of colors, and they come either loaded with screen or empty. Most are aluminum. Easy-to-use mounting hardware is an essential. Buy that when you get the frames because it's one and the same problem; the frames are useless without mounting hardware.

Houses with wooden window frames work the best because they accept nearly every mounting scheme. If your house is stucco or you don't have wood around your windows, you're limited to prefabricated frames with appropriate mounting hardware. The job is more expensive but still potentially worthwhile. Calculating the cost savings is difficult, so use your budgetary constraints to decide whether it's worthwhile.

To find out what the effect will be, get some cheap screen and tape it up to see how it changes your room; you may not like the effect, which will govern how much you're willing to spend.

If the frame is wood, the fastest and cheapest way to cover a window is to tack the screen right onto the window frame by using a hammer and tacks. Cut the piece of sunscreen down to a few inches bigger than what you need, tack it up, and then trim it with a scissors or a box cutter.

If you want a better look, consider cutting some planks of wood to frame the window, painting them, tacking them up over the screen (the screen is already tacked up over the window — the frames are only for appearance, not functionality), and trimming the excess screen to match.

Get the wood from a lumber store — you can probably find a store that cuts the wood for you, and the pieces will be exact and square. (Cabinet shops are usually willing to do a small cutting job if you can't find a lumber store that does it.)

Using screws for installation is best because taking the screens down and then putting them back up next year is easier. You need a drill to predrill holes for the screws and a screwdriver. The lumber store staff can show you the best screws and drill bits to use.

Creating a manual screen retractor

Figure 3-1 shows a way to make a manually operated screen retractor that works reliably, is easy to use, and costs very little.

You need a wooden mount that's slightly wider than your window; three eyelets; a sunscreen; tacks; a dowel rod as long as the mount; and screws or nails (to install).

Here's how to create a manual screen retractor:

1. **Drill three holes in the mount and attach the eyelets.**

   The first two holes are 6 inches from each end of the mount; the remaining hole should be 1 inch from the end. Screw in the eyelets, making sure that all three holes are lined up, facing the ends of the mount.

2. **Using a box cutter, cut the sunscreen to size.**

   You want to make the sunscreen larger than the window by about 4 inches, although if you don't have the room, any size will work, even if it's smaller than the window. A size smaller than the window will just be unsightly from inside, looking outside.

3. **Tack the sunscreen onto the roll-up rod (dowel) and the mount.**

4. **Put the cords in place.**

   Tie a cord to an eyelet that's 6 inches from the end, loop the cord over the top of the mount and under the rod, and go back up through the eyelet. Repeat on the other side. Then thread both cords through the end eyelet, the one that's 1 inch from the end of the mount.

5. **Screw or nail the mount onto the window frame.**

   To retract the screen, simply pull the cords.

If you like, paint the wood to match your house. You can use pulleys instead of eyelets and get smoother performance. If wind is an issue, get some fishing weights (the kind with holes so that you can get a nail through) and nail them into the ends of the roller dowel, equal weight on each side.

Book VII

Solar Power

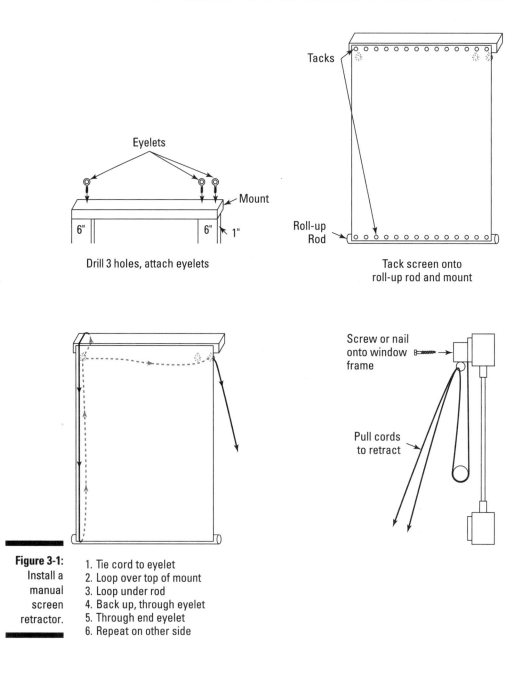

Eyelets

Mount

6"   6"   1"

Drill 3 holes, attach eyelets

Tacks

Roll-up
Rod

Tack screen onto
roll-up rod and mount

Screw or nail
onto window
frame

Pull cords
to retract

Figure 3-1:
Install a
manual
screen
retractor.

1. Tie cord to eyelet
2. Loop over top of mount
3. Loop under rod
4. Back up, through eyelet
5. Through end eyelet
6. Repeat on other side

Securing Your Home

You can make some easy, solar-powered security systems for very little cost. You can also have a lot of fun at somebody else's expense.

By using strategic combinations of motion-activated sprinkler heads and security lights, you can keep just about anything or anybody away from your house. The great news is that both of these products come solar-powered, so they work even in a power outage. These security devices are far from foolproof, but they deter 99 percent of potential offenders. The trick is placement. Plan for maximum surprise and dramatic result.

Hosing down your problems

The idea is simple: Aim a stream of water into a region being sensed by a motion detector — upon detection, the water triggers on. The entire thing is powered by a solar panel, so you can set it up anywhere you have a hose.

Here are some intriguing applications:

- **Security:** A burglar stalking a house who suddenly is hosed is likely to leave.
- **Pest deterrence:** Neighbor's dog like your yard late at night? Deer eating your landscape? Daughter's boyfriend pushing it? Not if they have to take an unplanned shower.
- **Practical jokes:** You can get some laughs out of this one, but you better make sure that the intended victim has a sense of humor and is dressed appropriately. Set up your video camera first.

Book VII

Solar Power

Blasting the bad guys with light

The device is called a security light, but you can find other applications. A PV module connects via a length of wire to a battery, a spotlight, and a motion detector. The module needs to be mounted in direct sunlight — the more the better — but you can mount the light itself anywhere. Wire lengths of 15 feet are common, but you can go a lot longer if you need to. The typical price is around $80.

On the other hand, if you pay an electrician to install an electric junction box, you're looking at over $400, easy. And that location may not really be the best location after all. With solar, you can position anywhere, easily and quickly. And you can hang one of these inside your house just as well as out. The trick is to get the PV panel in the sun — that's all that matters.

Engaging in Small Power Projects

You can run just about anything off of PV panels. The biggest questions are

- ✔ **Whether you need a battery:** A battery is required whenever you'll be using a device when the sun is not shining, such as night.
- ✔ **Whether you need an inverter:** PV panels put out DC voltages only; if you need AC voltages, such as the kind that appliances take, you need an inverter.

Battery power: Charging up your life

PV modules are ideal for charging batteries. The electronics are minimal, and the costs are low because of it.

Leaving dead car batteries behind

Got an old truck, car, or RV that sits around and doesn't get started very often? How about a boat? If they've been giving you problems starting, a solar charger may be a very cheap and effective solution. When a vehicle sits around without being started up for a while, its battery grows weak. If the battery is old, it's even worse.

For $40, you can get a solar battery charger. A PV module plugs in to the car's power outlet, and you lay the module out on the dashboard in the sun. While you're gone, it trickle charges your battery. A solar charger won't overcharge your battery, so you don't have to worry about removing it, even when the vehicle is running. It probably won't revive a dead battery, although it won't hurt anything to try.

Auto batteries cost around $80. With the $40 solar charger, you get more lifetime, up to 50 percent more, so you get a reasonable payback. But how much is it worth (in peace of mind, not to mention the costs of a tow-truck visit) not to get stranded when you can't get your car started?

Charging your electronics batteries with the sun

Standard, off-the-shelf batteries cost around $0.75 apiece. The cost for 100 throw-away alkaline batteries is $75, plus trips to the store to buy them. And batteries have nasty chemicals, such as lead and acids. You run across an environmental issue with 100 batteries.

Rechargeable batteries cost $4 apiece, and the good ones issue the same charge as a throw-away. A solar charger costs $40, but the charge cycles are free. You can charge a good rechargeable battery over 500 times. (Note that the number 500 applies to devices like remote controllers, which don't take much current; if you're drawing a lot of current and running the batteries down to their minimum, expect more on the order of 200 times.)

The cost for a rechargeable battery and 100 charges is $44, which is already a better deal than alkaline. But here's the best part: The cost to charge the next 100 times is zero. And the next, and the next. After 500 free charges, you may need a new battery, but that's only $4.

Alkalines cost about 20 times as much as quality rechargeables to operate. (Cheap rechargeables have much worse payback, so avoid them.) Spend some extra money on quality batteries, and it's a good investment.

The time to charge batteries (most devices charge four at a time) depends on how much direct sunlight you receive. Setting up near a window is often good enough if you don't need a lot of batteries. If you use a lot, you need direct sunlight. Kitchen bay windows are convenient candidates.

Keep a reserve of charged batteries. Buy twice as many as you need — it doesn't cost more because you go twice as long before you need to buy new batteries.

Small-scale PV systems: Using just a modest amount of power

For $1,000, you can get a solar power system big enough to run anything in your house aside from the major appliances. You can power a home office, where you may be able to write off some costs as a business expense. Or use a solar power system in a remote cabin or a boat cabin or an RV.

About $1,000 can get you 500 watt hours, or $1/2$ kWh, or a 60-watt light bulb for 8 hours — plenty of power to run an office or all the equipment other than power tools at a construction site. At this size (on the order of a small end table), you won't be toting your solar system around in a case, although you can find units on sturdy wheels.

Working with RV appliances

Small appliances for RVs, boats, and camping are widely available, and any of these appliances work with 12VDC solar power systems.

You may even be able to run some appliances without batteries, which makes things a lot cheaper and easier. Heaters don't care how the power looks (it can fluctuate, the voltages and currents can change, there can be ripples galore); how much heat you can generate is all that matters. Fans may blow directly from a PV module; the more sun, the harder the fan pushes. Water pumps don't need batteries, and some portable coolers are made to connect directly to solar panels.

You can also get a power system with a 120VAC outlet so that you can use your existing household electrical devices. You give up efficiency, but it may be worth it. If you have a 12VDC system, you can buy a really cheap 120VAC inverter from an auto-supply store. The AC power is dirty, but it works for certain things just fine. It's difficult to specify a list for what will work and what won't without giving it a try. Radios may be noisy, as well as TVs, but some have good internal power regulators. Anything with an internal battery won't mind the noisy AC power.

Going Off-Grid on a Piece-by-Piece Basis

You can go off-grid with small functions — you don't need to go off-grid with your entire home. You'll save on your power bill, plus enjoy some interesting independence and help save the environment — all in one.

Making your reading lamp go off-grid

If you like to read, you can spend $50 to get a small, battery-charged light (LED) that works for four hours on a four-hour charge. A PV module with a length of wire attaches to a battery/light/switch housing with Velcro backing. Apply the matching Velcro anywhere you may want light. During the day, plug in the PV module and set that in the direct sunlight. At night, press the light into the Velcro and use it.

Solar lamps put out a lot of light, but it's focused on a spot. The trick is to get that spot on your book, and you find you have plenty of light. For reading, you want a lamp with an arm that extends out, over your book.

Stick Velcro onto the bottom of a conventional lamp head employing a gooseneck adjustment arm and press the solar light into that. You'll be able to position it directly over your book, about a foot and a half away.

If you're using the solar lamp only in one location, run a cord over to a window and tape the solar module flat onto the inside, facing out. You'll probably get enough sunlight to meet your needs. If not, look for more direct sunlight. If the lamp isn't bright enough, use two. You can also buy more expensive designs with better lights, color, focusing, and battery.

Installing solar light tubes (tubular skylights)

A *solar tube* lighting system collects sunlight on the roof and transmits it down a shiny, silver pipe into the diffuser, which broadcasts the light into the room below. You can make most rooms bright enough to work in, and they stay a lot cooler.

Solar light varies with the clouds and weather, changing the intensity of light in the room quite a bit. You're much more conscious of the outdoors. When the sky is partly cloudy, you can get a lot of fluctuation. Personally, this is my favorite aspect of solar tubes.

The light creates a certain cool mood due to the silver color. Some light tubes come with filters for creating moods, but they cut out light as well. You can change the nature of a room very dramatically with a filter.

Costs and payback

The typical price (uninstalled) is $230 for a 4-foot pipe length. After that, you need to buy extensions for $20 a foot.

Large-diameter units can output as much light as a dozen 100-watt light bulbs at one-tenth the heat. If a $250 solar tube displaces only three 100-watt light bulbs for eight hours a day, it pays for itself in 19 months. If you factor in the cooling effect, payback is even faster.

Book VII

Solar Power

Location

The best locations are dark corners in family rooms. That way, the light gets used the most and has the most dramatic affect. They're also good for dark, isolated bathrooms. The natural light is comforting, and you never have to flip a light switch during the day. Beware, though. They can drastically change the way decor looks, maybe making the existing facades obsolete. Be prepared for a much different bathroom.

If you have a dark kitchen, a solar tube may be the perfect solution, especially if a lot of people come and go during the day. The cool tone of the light goes especially well in a stainless steel kitchen.

Installation

You need a jigsaw, a sheetrock saw, screwdrivers, and basic tools. You also need the requisite nerve to saw a hole through your roof; if you don't know what you're doing, you can hire experts to install solar tubes. Chin up, however — solar tubes come with very good installation instructions and the appropriate sealing materials. The manufacturers rely on the do-it-yourselfers, so they bend over backwards telling you how to do it (as well as how not do it, which is just as important).

Here are some tips for handling some of the installation challenges:

- Don't try to buy separate parts; get a complete kit, with however many extension tubes you think you need. You may want to get an extra and leave it in the box for return. Otherwise, when you find that you don't have enough extension tube, you'll probably have holes cut in ceilings and roofs, and you won't want to stop everything and go to a store.

- The hardest part of the job is probably in the attic space, so plan your route up and then over to where the work is going to be done and then how you'll sit and stand when you get over there. Also, realize that you'll be toting tools with you; the best bet is a tool belt, but if you don't have one, use a sturdy bag.

- You may want to look at the installation instructions before you buy a unit for a list of tools you'll need. If you're going to have to buy one or rent one, add that to the cost of the project.

- Cutting through a typical roof takes more than a toy saw, so use a good jigsaw. Composite shingles eat jigsaw blades, so get extra.

- Take extra precautions to seal against the weather. (Use a good silicon sealant, although most kits will come with appropriate sealant.) If the elements can possibly get in, they will — maybe not this year, but Mother Nature has infinite patience.

- You can botch a few things on this job and nobody will ever notice, but you need to get the hole in your ceiling right. Measure twice; cut once.

- The key to a successful project is to locate the hole properly in your ceiling before you start cutting. Installation instructions are very explicit for this step, so follow them closely.

- You're going to want to make sure that you have enough extension tube. (Most solar tubes come with 4 feet of extension tube, with 2-foot extensions as options.) Get more than you think you need, save the receipt, and take back the extra. The last thing you want is to get halfway through the job, with holes in your ceiling and roof and discover you don't have enough extension tube.

Using tabletop solar fans

Simply take a small 12VDC room fan and a suitable PV panel and wire them directly together. The hotter the sun, the more the air moves — no need for batteries. At $150, a solar fan isn't a cheap option, but it may be reasonable if your energy costs are high enough. Plus, you can use one anywhere; you don't need a plug.

These fans work nicely on porches, where you can position the panel right outside to catch the most sunlight. They're great for RV or even tent camping when the weather's hot enough. Solar fans are perfect for a pleasure boat in the hot sun. Pool houses, as well as remote casitas (small guest houses), likewise benefit.

Purifying Your Drinking Water

Not only can you build a solar water-purification system, such as the one in Figure 3-2, but you can also design it. Designing is just as much fun as building, and it's more rewarding because the system's entirely yours (unless it doesn't work, of course — then you need to figure out how to blame somebody else).

The system uses distillation, a process that can remove salts, microorganisms, and even chemicals such as arsenic, leaving you with pure H2O. Here's how it works: If you leave salty or contaminated water in an open container, the water evaporates and leave the contaminants behind. If you heat the water, the process speeds up considerably.

After the water evaporates, the water vapor condenses on the glass window and drips down into the catch trough. Tilt the catch trough just slightly and put a bottle or other container underneath the low end, and you have purified water.

You can make a purification system as cheaply or as expensively as you want. People in Third World countries use large, efficient versions of this same exact device that are capable of purifying hundreds of gallons a day. A system the size of a microwave oven can yield up to 3 gallons of purified water on a sunny day.

Here's what you need for a basic solar still:

- A wooden (or even better, sheet metal) enclosure, as shown in Figure 3-2; if you want to get imaginative, find a good metal box and cut a hole for the glaze cover

- Reflective material such as aluminum foil (shiny side out)

- Black paint (the kind used for barbeque pits works best)

- Glass (you don't need glazed glass; just use plain old window glass if you like — you can get pieces of discarded glass from window shops for little more than a smile)

- Insulation (the white foam stuff is cheap, effective, and easy to work with)

> ✔ Glue (silicon sealant or similar weather-resistant material)
>
> ✔ A tray that's black or has some other quality that absorbs heat

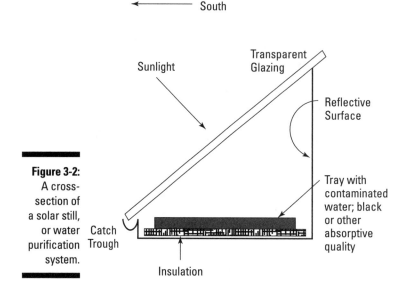

Figure 3-2:
A cross-section of a solar still, or water purification system.

Now take a look at the assembly:

1. **Paint the exterior of the box black to enhance absorption.**

2. **Install the reflective surface at the back and side walls of the enclosure and glue the insulation to the bottom.**

3. **Put a tray of contaminated water inside the enclosure, place the glass on top, and aim toward the sun.**

   That's it — you're done!

The first few times you use this device, the water may taste a little odd. Let the system "sweat" for a few weeks, and the bad taste will go away.

When designing or improving your unit, make filling the inner tray with water convenient. Position it by a hose, for example. Then you don't have to carry water to your system. Configure some kind of funnel through the sidewall so that you can pour the water right into the tray without spilling. Make the unit so that you can remove the glazing top and clean out the tray because the contaminants are going to remain behind.

Chapter 4

Financing Your Solar Investments

. . . .

In This Chapter

▶ Looking in to the various subsidy options

▶ Using loans to finance your solar projects

▶ Looking at the various loan programs available for solar energy

▶ Getting the biggest bang for your buck

. . . .

*T*he fact is, solar power is not a cut-and-dried winner in terms of investments. (Chapter 2 details payback analysis techniques that you can use to calculate the value of a solar investment to compare it with other types of investments.) The bottom line for a solar investment depends on three things in particular: cost of energy (which will rise); amount of sunlight available (which varies greatly from region to region); and cost of solar equipment

Although basic equipment costs don't vary much between regions, one thing that does affect how much you pay for your system by region is government subsidies. This chapter details the basic ideas behind subsidies and then shows you how to do your own research to determine how best to obtain and use them. You also discover other ways to finance your solar projects.

Exploring the Different Types of Subsidies

Governments have recognized the value of solar energy, especially in achieving a more pollution-free energy consumption. Plus, solar power has the potential to free North America from reliance on foreign oil, which is desirable from a political stability standpoint. (Getting oil from the Mideast creates a lot of problems.) Governments also recognize the marginal nature of a solar investment, and they've resolved to do something on the cost end of the equation. (Some politicians may claim to be able to do something on the sunshine supply end, but as usual they're just blowing hot air.)

Subsidies, where the government helps you pay for part of the cost of your solar system, are very powerful incentives to invest in solar, and a solar customer can see up to a 50-percent cost reduction by using all the subsidies available. However, the subsidies scene is constantly changing, so it's impossible to specify the precise details of subsidies and rebates simply because they're apt to change without notice.

The following sections describe the types of subsidies available.

Rebates

A *rebate* is money given back to a customer after he or she makes a purchase. Manufacturers' rebates work the same as they do for other products. You buy a solar system or component, and the manufacturer gives you either an instant rebate at the checkout or one that you need to mail in with proof-of-purchase.

Government solar rebates operate basically the same way. The rebate is paid directly to the professional solar contractor, so the customer doesn't need to finance the entire investment and then wait to get the rebate back. This is, in effect, a secondary rebate because it allows solar customers to more easily purchase their systems. But because these rebates come from government sources, they're also laden with overwrought details generally incomprehensible to the average layperson.

For example, here's how rebates work in California. For a PV system, you can get up to 25 percent of the cost of a system in rebates, but the amount depends on the system's productivity. So the state has a very specific computer program that potential customers use to predict system performance. Inputs are the following:

✔ **Your geographical area:** Data banks show your area's statistical weather patterns, including cloud density and frequency, average temperatures, air density, and the like. Your latitude also gives an indication of sunlight exposure. All these numbers combined yield a measure of how much sunlight you can expect in a given year. Some *microclimates* (a climate that, because of terrain, landscaping, and other factors, may differ from a climate only a mile away) may have much less sunshine than a nearby area, so be prepared for some surprises here.

✔ **The size and orientation of your solar collectors:** The greatest solar exposure comes from a specific roof angle (depending on your latitude) and a specific azimuth angle, namely true south. For any other angles, you get a lower rebate. If your roof is all wrong, not only do you get a lower rebate, but you also get less productivity as well.

To maximize your rebate, you may be able to mount your solar collectors on the ground and get all the angles just perfect. You can also get a higher rebate by employing adjustable mounts that track the sun over the course of a year — and result in greater productivity.

✔ **Any shading issues inherent to the collector location:** A special hemispheric reflector device is used to measure the relative location and shading effects of trees, mountains, chimneys, other buildings, and so on. The device can tell whether these impediments will affect your solar exposure at any time of the year. A computer program translates this data into a single number that tells how much solar potential your collector site has.

✔ **The efficiency of your system:** This is also related to a system's productivity. Manufacturers must define a system's efficiency, but this number also depends on where the collectors are located. (If they're on the northern side of your roof, the score goes down.) The overall system productivity is what's of interest; this is the total amount of energy a system will produce in a given year. The government is subsidizing energy production, not a system. It's a fine point of distinction, but it makes sense. (As a matter of interest, in California, you may choose to get your subsidy after the system is installed instead of using forms and paperwork to calculate a theoretical efficiency when the system is installed. In this way, the actual performance is used to gauge how big the subsidy will be, which often results in a larger subsidy than the necessarily conservative theoretical.)

For a perfect solar location, the state rebates 25 percent of the cost of your solar system. (Acceptable market costs are specified so that you can't get a higher rebate for a system that's out of market pricing guidelines.) In actuality, 25 percent is rare. Most numbers come in around 20 to 24 percent. When they come in much lower, your solar investment quickly loses allure.

You may run into a *buy-down* caveat: As time progresses, the rebates are scheduled to decrease, which encourages solar customers to buy now instead of later. The reason is reasonable: The basic idea with subsidies is that they'll force the cost of solar to come down over time, so why invest now? Why not just wait until prices do come down? But if everybody were to have this philosophy, prices would never drop. Ideally, as the rebates diminish, prices will come down, so the net cost of a system won't change over time. (Well, okay, but when do government programs ever work the way they're supposed to?)

The effect of this rebate has been wildly popular in California, which has some of the highest power rates in the country, plus the prospect of seeing greater increases in energy rates than the rest of the country due to the robust environmental laws that the state legislature is passing. In addition, Californians remember (not fondly) the energy price spikes that resulted in companies like Enron playing with energy prices, resulting in higher profits for the company at the expense of the energy consumers. There were blackouts and brownouts and power outages in the middle of steamy, sunny afternoons.

Book VII

Solar Power

Tax credits

Tax credits, which are subtracted from the amount you owe on your state or federal taxes, are an increasingly common form of subsidy. You must buy a certain type of system to qualify, and the credit is taken on your tax return, either state or federal. As a result, you must carry the cost until your return is filed, and any refund comes back to you. This wait can take more than a year, depending on when you buy a system.

A tax credit is far better than a tax deduction because a *tax deduction* is subtracted from your taxable income. So if you're paying a marginal tax rate of 28 percent and you get a deduction of $1,000, you save $280. But tax credits come out of the amount you owe, so a $1,000 tax credit saves you $1,000.

Both tax deductions and tax credits may be available for a solar system. Many times, both the federal and state governments are offering programs, and the terms will vary. You need to understand the distinction between credits and deductions because they make a big difference on the bottom line.

Here's an example. The U.S. federal government allows a 30-percent tax credit for both solar PV systems and solar water heating systems, up to a maximum of $2,000 per year. If your solar water heater system costs $6,000 to install, you get $1,800 off the price. If your solar PV system costs $30,000, you get only $2,000 off the price. This savings encourages smaller solar investments because you save a greater percentage.

To maximize your tax credits, spread your solar investments out over time. Install a solar water heater this year and a PV system the next. And if possible, install two smaller systems instead of one larger.

No property tax increases

Many states have laws that prevent your property taxes from rising due to the increase in value of your home from a solar investment. So if you install a $40,000 PV system, your county can't reassess your property and charge you extra taxes for having a home that's worth $40,000 more. Very few other investments qualify for this exemption, and because it's basically being paid for by the government, it's a tax break.

Net metering

Utilities aren't particularly enthusiastic about offering rebates, nor do they really want residential customers to hook solar equipment up to the grid. Recognizing this issue, the 1978 federal Public Utility Regulatory Policy Act (PURPA) mandates local utilities to pay "avoided" or wholesale costs to entities that want to sell it. This is the basis for net metering. It makes solar PV investment very viable. Without net metering, solar PV would be no more than a rare novelty.

States often have even more stringent net metering rules. In California, the utilities must pay you the same rate that they charge for power. For example, if you're on a TOU (time of use) rate schedule, the utility must pay you the same rates it's charging its customers at different times of the day.

This arrangement is a very strong incentive for using solar power because the highest power rates always apply in the middle of the afternoon. Midafternoon is the highest demand period because businesses are all using air conditioners at the same time, but it's also the time when solar PV systems are outputting at the maximum rate. So if you have a PV intertie system, you can plan your power consumption to take advantage of the non-symmetric exchange of energy.

Incentives for home-operated businesses

The incentives for businesses are even greater than those for residences, so if you have a home business or office, you may qualify for higher tax credits and rebates. Why? One reason is that businesses use most of their energy in the middle of the afternoon, so they're less apt to go for solar energy when there's *net metering* (a system that lets you sell your excess power back to the utility company). Another is that the green spirit that motivates many solar investments (thereby making the investment more attractive than mere numbers would imply because you save pollution as well as money) doesn't exist for businesses.

Businesses can also take advantage of accelerated depreciation schedules for solar equipment. This stuff can get complex; ask your tax preparer for the details.

Book VII

Solar Power

Tax-deductible home equity loans

Although they may not be a direct subsidy of solar power systems, tax-deductible home equity loans are akin to a government subsidy. If you take out a second mortgage to pay for your solar equipment, the government lets you deduct the interest on that loan from your taxes. So if you're making a monthly payment of, say, $300 for a second mortgage, your net cost may be only $200. The tax-deductible home equity loan works exactly like a subsidy, but it's called something else.

Researching All the Subsidy Options

 Things are changing so fast that it's impossible to keep up with all the government programs. This chapter can only nudge you in the right direction. Your job is to poke around and get all the details for yourself.

Here's how to research the subject further:

- ✔ **Talk to your tax preparer.** Tax preparers should be versed in the details of solar tax credits, but if not, they can still access the information sources they need to process your rebates and tax credits. Solar is relatively new, so give preparers a break if they don't know the details upfront, but keep at them to find out if they don't. Expect to pay more for your tax preparation because your tax preparer will have to complete more forms. (These forms are practically indecipherable to the average layperson, so if you're thinking about preparing your own, be forewarned.)

- ✔ **Ask contractors.** Solar contractors need to know about subsidies because they help sell systems. PV contractors are experts at tax credits and rebates, and they'll usually help you process them as well. Even if you're going to do the installation yourself, you can get good information from contractors when you ask them for competitive quotations.

- ✔ **Contact utility companies.** Utilities will give you information, although they don't necessarily want to. But they have to — it's required by law — so if you push a little, you can get all kinds of information, and it's almost always free. You can find a customer service number on your utility bill. When you call, ask whether a particular department is dedicated to subsidies.

- ✔ **Search online.** Of course, the Internet is a great source of information. Use a search engine to look up key words like "solar energy tax incentives," "solar power rebates," and so on. One thing will lead to another, and who knows where you'll end up?

When doing research, keep in mind that you can find subsidies for all kinds of other systems besides solar. For example, if you install an energy-efficient front door, you may qualify for a 10-percent tax credit. Gas fireplaces may get you a credit. Be expansive in your search, and you can find all kinds of little goodies.

Financing through Loans

The government is interested in promoting solar power, so it has a wide range of loan subsidies available. In essence, the government accepts part of the risk of a loan, so a bank can offer you a lower interest rate. It's worth your while to spend some time looking into the various government programs because you can often get a loan for better terms.

Borrowing money the old-fashioned way

When people need large amounts of money, they either look to a bank or whip out their credit cards. To finance your big solar projects, you can pursue several types of loans:

✔ **Home equity loans** are the most common loans and the best options. If you're contemplating a large solar project, you probably own your own home. (Why would anybody install a big solar system on a home she's renting?)

Home equity is the difference between what a homeowner owes in mortgages on the home and the home's market value (or appraised value, which should be the same but rarely is). You can use your equity to get a loan at a much lower interest rate because the bank's risk is greatly reduced by using real estate as *collateral* (the goods the bank will take if you don't pay on your loan). The bank won't need to come after the equipment you've financed because the bank can go after the house itself. (Banks generally don't care what you do with the money, so they may not even know about your solar equipment.) Homeowners plan to pay off their debt long before they let a bank take their home away. Home equity loans are generally tax deductible. (Consult your tax preparer for details.)

✔ **Supplier loans** are available from manufacturers and suppliers who provide solar equipment. However, solar vendors generally sign up with an equity loan broker and simply act as the sales outlet for somebody else's loans. You can probably find a better interest rate if you go directly to a bank, but the convenience may offset the cost. Or solar vendors may actually offer better terms because they have a strong incentive to close a sale, and making inexpensive financing available helps considerably.

These companies use the equipment itself as collateral for the loan. Supplier loans are similar to automobile loans that dealerships offer when you buy a vehicle. The car is collateral, and if you don't pay the loan, a repo man (or woman) comes to your house late at night and takes back the car — perfectly legal. If you default on a supplier loan for your solar equipment, the company may send someone in the middle of the night to grab the collectors off your roof — you probably won't mistake him for Santa Claus!

✔ **Consumer loans** don't require any collateral, so the lender's risk is high. You can get a credit card with a $30,000 credit limit far more easily than should ever be possible. The reason it's so easy? The interest rate is sky high; the bank expects a number of defaults and lets the customers who don't default cover the losses from the ones who do. Plus, you don't get any sort of tax deduction on the interest.

Consumer loans are the modern version of loan shark products, although the creditors no longer break your fingers when you default. If you're a good credit risk, avoid consumer loans like the plague.

Exploring home energy ratings

A less traditional option of financing your major solar project is through an energy-efficient financing program, but your home has to qualify for the program. To qualify, you need to have your home audited and rated by a licensed expert. He will do an energy audit (see Chapter 2 of Book II) and write a report that estimates annual energy use and costs. You can also expect some recommendations for improvements that you'll have to implement as a loan-approval condition. To get the best loan terms, you have to convince the financing institution that the improvements you plan to fund with the loan proceeds make sense in the grand scheme of things. That's reasonable.

If things look good, you can get special energy-efficient financing programs that have lower interest rates than conventional loans. Keep in mind, however, that with these loans, you'll be required to pay for the energy audit and deal with government agencies.

Residential Energy Services Network (RESNET) is a network of mortgage bankers, builders, and others. RESNET has solar loan programs available for the right customers. Check them out at www.natresnet.org.

Pursuing energy-efficient mortgages

Energy-efficient mortgages (EEMs) give you credit for the energy efficiency of the home you're buying, and you also can use it to refinance so that you can improve your home's energy efficiency. The first step toward getting this type of mortgage for an existing home is to have a home energy rater evaluate the home. You get credit for the savings the home will provide through its efficiencies. If you're planning to upgrade, you use the rating to show how your planned improvements will affect your home's energy usage.

An EEM takes into account the money that an energy-efficient home saves a homeowner and therefore enables you to get a bigger loan than you otherwise could. You also can use it to refinance and get money that you can put toward energy-efficiency improvements in the home you already own. You apply for an EEM just as you would a conventional mortgage (and most of the same companies and government agencies are involved).

Thinking about other mortgage options

Here are some other potentially useful government agencies when you're looking for a mortgage:

- ✔ Federal Housing Administration at `www.fha.com`
- ✔ Department of Housing and Urban Development (HUD) at `www.hud.gov`
- ✔ Department of Veterans Affairs (VA) at `www.homeloans.va.gov`

State agencies often provide subsidized loans as well. Check out the prospects at `www.naseo.org`, the Web site for the National Association of State Energy Officials.

Book VII

Solar Power

Considering Alternative Financing

You also may want to look at some other financing programs. In the following sections, you find out more about a couple of your options: leasing equipment or buying remote parcels of land so that you can generate power and sell it back to the power company.

Leasing solar equipment

In one new idea that's taking hold, companies install solar equipment on your roof, but they retain ownership of the equipment. You lease the equipment from them for a fixed monthly cost or a percentage of the system's production, which works nicely if you save more on your power bill than the monthly cost of the lease. Or alternatively, you can use these programs to lock in the cost of your energy so that when it rises, you won't be bitten like everyone else. You don't have to have any cash upfront, and leasing is often a very popular way to finance a big purchase, as evidenced by how many vehicles are leased on the same basic principle.

 Ultimately, it's almost always a better investment to finance the equipment yourself and purchase it rather than lease it. But many people simply don't have the cash, they want to put their money into something else, or they don't want to sign up for a loan that appears on their credit report.

Be aware that, just as with cars, solar equipment has a *residual value* (the defined value that is estimated at the beginning of the lease; this amount may or may not be the actual market value) at the end of the lease. If your solar equipment has decreased in value for some reason (not super-likely, but it can happen), you may have to pay a big chunk of change to get out of the lease.

Buying an energy-producing plot of land

Another concept that's likely to grow in the coming years is an ownership concept in which you don't actually install your solar equipment at your residence. Instead, a company buys land in Nevada or somewhere really sunny. The company divides the parcel up into small plots, each around 40 feet x 40 feet. Using cash or some other kind of financing package, you buy the plot of land and a solar PV system that's installed on your plot and connected to the grid. The energy production belongs to you, and the equipment belongs to you. In practical terms, using offsite solar equipment is really no different than if the equipment were at your house, except nobody can see it, and you don't have to maintain it. Plus, the equipment is probably in a sunnier location without any shade hindrances.

Whether this concept works or not in your area depends on whether a utility company will allow it. Most won't pay you for excess power averaged over the course of a year. When you install an intertie system at your house, if you generate more power than you use, you've wasted that power because you won't get anything for it. Obviously, with this remote location setup, there's no power use, only generation, so the entire thing earns credit. The good news is that the idea makes so much sense that governments are beginning to require utilities to accept the program, whether they want to or not. (Okay, they don't want to; why would any business agree to reduce its market?)

Remote ownership plans have plenty of advantages for the average home-owner. You can buy your solar equipment for much less. The company doesn't have to come to your residence to install the panels. All the systems are basically the same construction but in different sizes. Maintenance is straightforward and cheap, and the land is cheap. The productivity is high, and because the electric circuits are conjoined centrally, efficiency is much better. It's estimated that if 100 square miles of Nevada desert (of which there's no shortage) were covered with solar PV panels, the nation's electrical needs would be met with almost zero carbon emission.

Considering the Best Overall Investments

You want the most return for your investment. Or maybe you're looking for the quickest payback for the least amount of effort and cost. These projects are the winners in this category. And in a stroke of good luck (unless you're not the hands-on type), many of them also show up Chapter 3 of this book.

Perform an energy audit and perform all the energy conservation measures that your audit suggests. Energy conservation saves money, reduces pollution, and helps make going solar much more practical. See Chapter 1 of Book II.

Nurturing Mother Nature with landscaping

Okay, landscaping isn't strictly solar if what you're looking for is technology that grabs sunlight and puts it to work in a constructive way. But you don't always need to grab photons and train them to get the most benefit out of the sun. Landscaping is the hands-down winner of the best solar project because you get so much in return.

Planting hearty, healthy, happy deciduous trees in the right location around your house gives you cooler summers and warmer winters, but most of all, you can look out your windows and be reminded of why we care so much about our planet earth.

Planting bushes, shrubs, and trees as windbreaks allows you to enjoy natural breezes in your home, without the sound of whirring fan blades to remind you of technology.

Plants create oxygen out of carbon dioxide, the modern bugaboo of environmentalism. If the world had enough trees, global warming wouldn't be such an imposing issue.

Book VII

Solar Power

And finally, you get yourself outdoors, and you get exercise when you do your own landscaping. There's a certain simplicity to digging a hole. It's about as close to nature as you can possibly get, and that in itself is justification.

Installing PV systems to offset the most carbon pollution

Photovoltaic (PV) is the grand dame of solar investments and is going to experience hyper growth over the coming years. In Chapter 1 of Book I, you find out how to calculate your carbon footprint, and the results generally shock people. You can get a feel for just how much humans affect the environment when you realize that, on average, economically active Americans are responsible for nearly 40,000 pounds of carbon dioxide per capita.

When you install a large PV solar system, you cut out a tremendous amount of pollution because our electrical power grids are extremely inefficient. For each kWh of energy you create with a PV system, you save five or six times that much utility-generated power, most of which comes from coal-fired plants in North America. PV systems allow for tremendous environmental leverage, and that will never change.

Strictly from a monetary standpoint, PV systems are becoming more competitive, and as energy rates rise, they will become good investments. In addition, when you install a PV system, you lock in your energy rates for a long time, namely at zero. If you think energy rates are going to rise precipitously, PV is almost always a great investment. And really — what else is going to force America off its oil addiction than high energy rates?

Harnessing the sun to heat your water

Solar water heaters, when properly designed and installed, are great investments because they're much cheaper than PV systems, which are often out of the average person's financial range. Most homeowners can afford a few thousand dollars for a solar water heater system without taking out loans.

From a pollution standpoint, heating water typically makes up around 18 percent of your power bill, so you can save exactly that much from your carbon footprint.

As far as utility costs, if you're on a tiered rate structure, a solar water heater cuts into the most expensive part of your power bill first. For example, if you save 18 percent of the electrical energy you use, you may be able to save about 30 percent of your total power bill.

Lighting your yard all night long

For little cost, you can put a range of fun and interesting lights around your yard. They charge during the daylight hours and come on at night. They need little sunlight, given the amount of light they put out.

The alternatives are awkward, clumsy, and demanding. Low-voltage systems have thick-gauge wires that you need to run around your yard, tripping people and getting chewed up by the dog. And the lengths of runs you can get away with are limited because the wire is so expensive.

Putting in solar lighting is as simple as one, two, three. And if you don't like the way things look, changing the layout is as simple as four, five, six. Try the static lights and the changing-color decorative lights. You can get a whole range of different mounting schemes, so you can place the lights anywhere.

The lights don't even need to be in direct sunlight. Put them under a tree, and they work. You also can get ones that have the PV panels connected to the light by a wire, so you can put the PV panel in direct sunlight and the light under your porch roof.

Redecorating for functionality and appearance

Window blinds make a big difference in the overall look and comfort level of your home. Windows attract a lot of attention (they break up walls, which are monotonous), and they're a source of natural sunlight. The eye is naturally drawn to a window, particularly a big one in your family room or living room.

However (and this is a pretty big *however*), windows are a major source of heat transfer. In the summer, windows let in too much heat energy by both radiative sunlight and conductive movement. In the winter, windows allow a lot of heat to escape by conduction. Your house would be much more energy efficient if it didn't have any windows at all, but this setup is absurd. The solution? Put in window blinds that have good insulation and reflective properties.

With the right blinds, you can significantly reduce heat transfer as well as reflect most incident sunlight. The functional effect is dramatic. The aesthetic is even more so, if you choose the right ones. Large windows in family rooms and living rooms are the best candidates for installing blinds. You get the most bang for the buck when you cover these large areas of glass.

Putting up overhangs to make your home more comfortable

By using overhangs to shade your southern windows appropriately, you can increase natural warming in the winter and prevent overheating in the summer. You also can improve the natural light in your home by increasing the amount of sunshine you let in during the winter, when you want as much light as possible (it makes you feel warmer, and perception is half the game), and by decreasing it in the summer, when a lot of light makes you feel hot.

Controlling the sun as it shines into your house lets you regulate the temperature variations. Nobody likes a home where the temperature swings wildly over the course of a day. And temperature variations tend to make materials swell and shrink, which causes cracking and premature wear. When you install a well-designed overhang over a porch or sunroom, you minimize temperature variations.

Overhangs are very reasonable do-it-yourself projects. You don't need electrical experience or plumbing know-how. There are usually no extraordinary weight requirements that entail consulting a professional engineer. And if you keep things modest, you don't need to get a county building permit or permission from an association design committee.

Increasing your living space

You can add a solar room onto your home for far less cost than a conventional room. You can put in nearly any size you want, and do-it-yourself kits are straightforward and well designed. You can build a solar room out of aluminum or wood, and you can put in however many and whatever size windows you want. You can incorporate a concrete floor (for maximum thermal mass), or you can use an existing wooden or synthetic deck.

If you do it right, you can build a solar room without getting a building permit. (Forego electric power and don't connect it permanently to your house.) You can build a solar room out of plastic corrugated materials that cost very little. You can grow plants in a greenhouse year-round, or if you want to get really exotic, you can grow fruits, flowers, or vegetables. If you choose to build a sunroom, you can use it as extra living space when it's not too hot.

Banishing hot air with a solar attic fan

If you've ever gone into your attic on a hot summer day, you know what real heat is all about. It can get so hot that it's dangerous. Temperatures over 160°F are not uncommon. All that heat stays up there all night, and it tries to sink into your house through the insulation in your ceiling. Most homes have passive, natural venting schemes in the attic, but that doesn't do much to get the hot air out of your house.

A properly designed solar attic vent fan can move a lot of air over the course of a day. The system works hardest when there's a lot of sunshine. You don't need to run expensive electrical power up to the fan, which means you can install one just about anywhere you want.

As a do-it-yourself solar project, a solar attic vent fan is ideal because you get to use some PV panels, which is fun (if your definition of fun is cool hardware). You won't get any electrical shocks from the low voltages, and the tools required are minimal. You can complete the project in one day, and you'll discover a lot about your house by studying the layout and functionality of your attic.

Using a solar swimming pool heater or cover

Swimming pool covers basically accomplish the same thing as solar pool heaters but cost about 3 percent as much (they're about $150). They keep a pool cleaner, so you save on chemicals as well.

You can attach the cover to a retracting mechanism so that you won't hate your cover like you would if you had to fold it by hand every time you swim. The cheapest manual retractors cost around $300. You also can install an electric retractor, but now you're talking about the kind of money you'd spend on a solar water heater, so you might as well put in one of those instead.

Index